EARLY ENGLISH CHURCH HISTORY

BRIGHT

London

HENRY FROWDE

OXFORD UNIVERSITY PRESS WAREHOUSE

AMEN CORNER, E.C.

CHAPTERS

OF

EARLY ENGLISH CHURCH HISTORY

BY

WILLIAM BRIGHT, D.D.

REGIUS PROFESSOR OF ECCLESIASTICAL HISTORY
AND CANON OF CHRIST CHURCH, OXFORD

SECOND EDITION, REVISED AND ENLARGED

Oxford

AT THE CLARENDON PRESS

M DCCC LXXXVIII

PREFACE TO THE FIRST EDITION.

THE following Chapters are an expansion of Lectures which have been delivered to my Class, while we had Bede's 'History' before us with a view to the Theological Final School. Wishing to connect them, in their present form, with their original purpose, I have retained a few colloquial phrases, and a few local allusions, which seemed natural in addressing a number of Oxford students, of whom several were personally well known to me.

The first or introductory Chapter is devoted to the history of the ancient British Church. The general subject of the rest of the volume is the Age of the Conversion of the Old-English people to Christianity: a great, though comparatively a brief period, extending but little beyond a century, and closing naturally with the death, in 709, of their greatest native Bishop, himself the evangeliser of those among them who, from a peculiar isolation, were the last to receive the Faith.

My obligations to the 'Councils and Ecclesiastical Documents,' edited by the late Mr. Haddan and by Professor Stubbs, will be apparent throughout these pages. But I have enjoyed the special advantage of repeatedly consulting the Professor himself, who, with characteristic kindness, found time to read through the larger portion of what follows before it was offered to the Delegates of the Clarendon Press; to whom also my thanks are due for their ready acceptance of it in order to publication.

It is a pleasure to associate this book with the remembrance of those many attendants at my Lectures, on this and other subjects, who, by their intelligent and sympathetic interest, have again and again rendered me assistance at once more welcome and more effective than at the time they could understand.

CHRIST CHURCH,
    Dec. 20, 1877.

CONTENTS.

———— ♦♦ ————

CHAPTER I. (INTRODUCTORY).

CHAPTER II.

CHAPTER III.

CHAPTER IV.

CHAPTER V.

CHAPTER VI.

CHAPTER VII.

CHAPTER VIII.

CHAPTER IX.

CHAPTER X.

CHAPTER XI.

CHAPTER XII.

CHAPTER XIII.

CHAPTER XIV.

ADDITIONAL NOTES.

ERRATA.

P. 36, l. 2, *for* momentary *read* momentous

P. 78, l. 16, *for* Llandadarn *read* Llanbadarn

P. 139, note 2, *for* Northumbria *read* Northumbrian

P. 222, l. 22, *for* dated *read* placed

P. 312, l. 21, and p. 317, l. 13, *for* Ebba *read* Eaba

P. 322, note 7, *for* xix. c. 30 *read* iii. 2, p. 6

P. 460, l. 31, *for* mostly *read* closely

shadowy as the Greek fiction about Aristobulus, ordained CHAP. I
by St. Paul as a bishop for Britain[1],—or the Welsh story
of Bran the Blessed, father of Caractacus, who brought
to Britian the faith he had learned in Rome[2],—or that
beautiful mediæval romance which brought St. Joseph of
Arimathæa with twelve companions to Avalon or Glastonbury,
and made his staff take root in the earth, and grow into the
famous ' Holy Thorn[3].'

But what are we to say of the narrative which Bede inserts Story of
into his Church History[4], and which tells how Lucius, a British Lucius.
king, sent to Eleutherus, Bishop of Rome, a letter, entreating
' that by his commission he might be made a Christian, and
presently obtained the fulfilment of his pious request ; after
which the Britons retained the faith, thus received, inviolate
and in tranquil peace, until the times of the Emperor Diocletian ?' This is Bede's statement : looking at it as it stands,
and ignoring the pretended reply of Eleutherus to Lucius[5], and
the later embellishments as to the employment of Fagan and
Dyvan[6], and Elvan and Medwin[7], and still more, as to the substitution of twenty-eight bishops for twenty-eight flamens[8],
and the association of Winchester, Gloucester, and St. Peter's
Cornhill, with the name of Lucius or ' Lleuer Mawr[9],' and

---

[1] Whom the Welsh legends called Arwystli Hen.

[2] See Williams, Eccl. Antiq. of the Cymry, p. 54 ff.

[3] Malmesbury gives the story of Joseph of Arimathea with an ' ut ferunt :'
as he knew it, we find that it presupposed an apostolic visit of St. Philip to the
' regio Francorum ' (Prol. de Antiq. Glaston. Eccl.). The legend has been
gracefully versified by Dean Alford in his Ballad of Glastonbury (Poems, i. 16).
But, although Glastonbury was a Christian sanctuary before ' Saxon ' times, the
tale about St. Joseph is first heard of in ' Norman times ' (Soames, p. 23).

[4] Bede, i. 4.

[5] Not cited by Geoffrey of Monmouth : first printed in the twelfth year of
Henry VIII. See Collier (who believes the general statement), i. 35.

[6] See Geoffrey of Monmouth, ii. 1. So Malmesbury : see Gale, i. 293.

[7] Named by other Welsh authorities. See the Llandaff account in Monast.
Anglic. vi. part 3, p. 1218, and Chronicles of the Ancient British Church,
p. 45. Williams (p. 67) tells us that the king sent his request by these two,
and the Pope sent his answer by Dyvan and Fagan, who were probably sprung
from ' royal captives taken to Rome with Caradog.'

[8] Geoffrey, l. c. Elmham, in Hist. Monast. S. Aug. Cant. p. 134, speaks of
the ' abrogation ' of three flamens and the substitution of three archbishops.

[9] That is, ' Great Light :' Nennius, 18. (The book ascribed to ' Nennius ' is
of the ninth century.) Williams names him Lleirwg.

the varieties of statement as to the king's latter days, which,
by one story, were spent in a missionary episcopate, and
closed by martyrdom, in Switzerland[1],—setting aside all this,
as manifestly unhistoric[2], are we to give any credence to as
much as we find in Bede? The answer seems to be, that
Bede derived the account of Lucius' message to Eleutherus,
but not the statement as to its success, from the second of
the two Catalogues, so called, of Roman Bishops, in which
'Eleutherius' is said to have received a letter from Lucius,
'ut Christianus efficeretur per ejus mandatum[3].' The words
'were written in the time and tone[4]' of Prosper, although
the Catalogue containing them was not framed till about a
century later, in 530. The statement, then, about Lucius'
request is traceable to Rome, and to Rome in the fifth
century : the request, if made, was made in the latter part
of the second,—the accession of Eleutherus being commonly
dated A.D. 177. There would be no intrinsic improbability
in the supposition that a native prince in 'the Roman island'
had requested instruction from the Roman Church in Christian
belief ; but the lack of earlier authority has induced most
modern writers to reject the whole story : even Burton,
though habitually moderate in his language, denounces it
as a 'fable'[5], although he adds that 'perhaps there was
some circumstance about that time, which was favourable

Statement
of Tertul-
lian.

to the spreading of the Gospel in Britain :' and it is certain
that not many years after the accession of Eleutherus,—
probably, indeed, between A.D. 196 and 201,—Tertullian[6]

---

[1] Usher, Ant. 71. Geoffrey says that Lucius died at Gloucester.

[2] Of course there may have been actual persons bearing the names of Fagan
and the rest, who were afterwards mixed up with the Lucius story. A village
near Llandaff is called St. Fagan's; and four churches within the jurisdiction
of Llandaff are called after him, Lucius, Dyvan, and Medwin (Williams, p. 72 ;
Chron. Brit. Ch. p. 49).

[3] Anastas. Bibl. tom. i. p. 15, iv. p. ii.

[4] Haddan and Stubbs, Councils, i. 25 ; Haddan's Remains, p. 227.

[5] Burton, Eccl. Hist. ii. 206. Milman says briefly, 'The conversion of King
Lucius is a legend;' but he adds that 'Britain gradually received the faith
during the *second* and third centuries :' Lat. Chr. ii. 226.

[6] Tertull. adv. Jud. 7. According to Bishop Kaye (On Tertullian, p. 61),
the tract 'Against the Jews' was probably written before Tertullian became
a Montanist. That event is dated by Dr. Pusey not later than A.D. 201.

exultingly declares 'that places in Britain not yet reached by Romans were subjected to Christ.' We must allow for his fervid readiness to believe any story or rumour which enhanced the success of Christianity; and a high authority would explain the word 'inaccessa' as referring simply to Roman movements at that time against a British revolt[1],— but this is rather like explaining it away[2]. At any rate, there is Tertullian's statement, and he must have had some reason for making it. Indeed, although we are informed by Sulpicius Severus[3] that Christianity was 'somewhat late in crossing the Alps,' and Irenæus seems to have known of no Church in Britain, nor indeed in Northern Gaul[4], we cannot reasonably doubt that some Christians did cross the Channel to our shore during the second century, if not earlier, and planted here and there some settlements of the Church. It was 'almost certainly from Gaul[5]'—certainly not, as far as we can judge, directly from the East[6]—that these outposts, so to speak, of the advancing spiritual kingdom were sent forth among the Roman provincials of Britain. Their arrival may with much probability be dated either shortly before[7], or shortly after[8] the

Britain probably evangel- ised from Gaul.

Haddan dates the tract A.D. 208, the year in which Severus visited Britain (Remains, p. 223); yet see Bishop Kaye, p. 50.

[1] Haddan, l. c., and Councils, i. 2.

[2] Bishop Kaye, on Tertullian, p. 94, understands the passage as referring to the farthest extremities of Britain. So Burton, ii. 207, 'parts of the island which had not been visited by the Romans.' So Alb. Butler, for Sept. 16; Robertson, Hist. Ch. i. 218; Bishop Forbes, Pref. to Arbuthnott Missal, p. iii.

[3] Sulp. Sev. ii. 32. He thus explains the fact that the first martyrdoms in Gaul were those under M. Aurelius (Euseb. v. 1).

[4] S. Iren. i. 3 (circ. A.D. 180).

[5] Haddan's Remains, p. 216. See Folcard's Life of St. John of Beverley, i. (Raine's Historians of the Church of York, i. 242), 'Ut enim fideli patrum traditum est relatione, iamdudum fide illuminatis finibus totius Galliæ, serius perlatum est verbum Dei in hanc insulam Britanniæ.'

[6] The popular notion that the British Easter-rule points to such a directly Eastern origin of the British Church is based on a mistake as to that rule. For instances of Eastern influence, through the Gallic Church, on the British and Irish Churches, see Warren, Liturgy and Ritual of Celtic Church, pp. 47–57.

[7] Pryce's Ancient British Church, pp. 61 ff. He meets the difficulty of Irenæus' silence by observing that his argument was concerned with settled churches, whose tradition could be of weight.

[8] Warren, Liturgy and Ritual of the Celtic Church, p. 58. Comp. Acts xi. 19.

CHAP. I. persecution at Lyons and Vienne; and the Church thus formed was 'confined mainly' (in the face of Tertullian's words, we can hardly say 'exclusively') to 'Romanised natives[1]' and to the Roman residents, and 'struck, in consequence, but feeble roots in the land[2].' More of this hereafter : at present we pass on, in all but total dearth of information about the British Church in the third century[3], to the grand and touching scene which meets us at the opening of the fourth, and in which the heroism of generous self-devotedness is so beautifully blended with that early-ripened faith, which transfigured a neophyte into a martyr :—

> 'Self-offered victim, for his friend he died,
> And for the Faith[4]!'

St. Alban. The story of St. Alban, as given by Bede[5], is briefly this. During the persecution of Diocletian and Maximian, Alban, being then a Pagan, gave shelter to a Christian cleric flying from persecution. He watched his guest's habits, was struck with his perseverance in prayer 'by day and night,' gradually accepted his instructions, embraced the faith, and doubtless was baptized. Some days were spent in this companionship : then the 'wicked prince' heard that the fugitive was in Alban's cottage, and sent soldiers to arrest him. Alban put on his teacher's cassock[6], met the soldiers, gave himself

---

[1] Haddan, l. c.

[2] Origen speaks of converted Britons in Hom. 6 in Luc. 'The power of our Lord and Saviour is both with those who in Britain are divided from our world,' &c. (ed. Lommatzsch, t. v. p. 106); and more rhetorically of a conversion of *Britain,* in Ezech. Hom. 4 (xiv. 59). Yet, in Matt. Comment. s. 39, he says that of the Britons, or the Germans who are near the ocean, &c., 'plurimi' have *not yet* heard the word of the Gospel (iv. 271). These passages were written towards the middle of the third century.

[3] The story of the British-born St. Mellon, first bishop of Rouen in 256, represents him as converted from Paganism at Rome. See Usher, Ant. p. 75; Tillemont, Mem. iv. 487.

[4] Wordsworth, Eccl. Sonnets, No. 6.

[5] Bede, i. 7, and his Martyrology. See Alb. Butler, Lives of Saints, June 22. In the later middle ages the nationality of Alban was forgotten : he was hailed in a rude hymn as 'pro*th*omartyr Anglorum, miles Regis Angelorum.'

[6] 'Caracalla;' the name of that hooded coat stretching to the feet which the son and successor of Severus brought into fashion, and from which he took his nickname (Spart. Vit. Carac. 9), and which afterwards became a dress of clerics or monks. Jerome says that the high-priestly ephod was like a caracalla without a hood (Ep. 64. 15); but the ephod was a sort of amice,

into their hands, declaring himself to be a Christian, and was
at once carried before a magistrate, who was then engaged
in sacrificing, and who, indignant at his having thus shielded
a 'sacrilegious rebel,' ordered him to be dragged up to the
images of the gods, and gave him the choice between sacrificing and suffering the doom which the fugitive would have
incurred. Alban replied that he would not sacrifice. Being
asked of what family he was, he answered, 'What does that
matter? As for my religion, I am now a Christian, and
bound to act as a Christian.' He was asked his name, and
gave it; was again ordered to sacrifice; answered, in the usual
tone of Christian confessors, that the worship of 'demons'
would lead to eternal perdition; was scourged by torturers,
and, being still steadfast, was led to execution, across the river[1]
which ran by the great city of Verulamium[2], where his trial
had taken place. A vast crowd followed the prisoner and his
guards, so that the magistrate was left with none to wait on
him. The bridge being thus thronged,—so the story proceeds,
—Alban by prayer obtained a dry passage over the river-
bed: the executioner himself, astounded, and inwardly stirred
by grace, threw away his sword, and flung himself at Alban's
feet, desiring to suffer with, or, if possible, instead of him:
meantime Alban and the crowd ascended a beautiful flower-
clad eminence[3], where at his prayer a spring of water burst
forth to satisfy his thirst. Here he was beheaded: the man
who gave the stroke miraculously lost his eyes, and he whose

while the caracalla was akin to a 'cappa;' Ducange in v. Geoffrey names
the cleric 'Amphibalus' (de Gest. Reg. Brit. ii. 3). This is probably a confusion between the man and his garment; we find an 'amphibalus' worn by
St. Columba in Adamn. Vit. Col. i. 5; and see Gildas, Epist. 2. Later stories
made 'Amphibalus' himself suffer martyrdom near Verulam, after baptizing
many converts. See Usher, Antiq. pp. 78, 84, on this name, and the legend of
the death, as to which, he says, the martyrologists observe 'altum silentium.'

[1] The Ver. See Clutterbuck's Hertfordshire, i. 5.

[2] Verulamium is mentioned as a municipium by Tacitus, Ann. xiv. 33.
Cunobelin had transferred the Trinobantian capital from Verulamium to
Camulodunum (Merivale, vi. 225). Under the Romans it became 'a grand
municipal city, the fashionable town of the south-east' (Wright's Celt, Roman,
and Saxon, p. 123), where 'the chief lines of communication intersected one
another' (Merivale, vi. 248). See Turner, Angl. Sax. i. 197. Its site is S.W.
of St. Albans.

[3] Here stands the vast minster, now the cathedral.

substitute he was received in his turn the death-blow, being thus, in the ancient Church language[1], 'baptized in his own blood.' The day was the 22nd of June; the magistrate, overawed by what had happened, ordered the persecution to cease; but about the same time there were martyred Aaron and Julius, two citizens of 'the City of Legions[2],'—and many others, men and women, in divers places, after they had been 'lacerated' by hideous torments. This is the tale as it stands: if we put aside the three marvellous incidents, as probably an after-growth, and also allow for the inventiveness which, in default of official records, has described the dialogue between Alban and his judge,—is the rest to be accepted, or treated as mythical? There is no evidence that it was known earlier than the first part of the fifth century; but in 429 it was fully believed at Verulamium. In the sixth century it is narrated by Gildas[3], and alluded to in a line of Venantius Fortunatus[4], quoted by Bede. The time is disputed: Gildas and Bede refer it to the last great persecution which began in 303, while the Saxon Chronicle dates it in 283: if the former date is correct, the difficulty arises as to the possibility of a persecution in Britain while Constantius, whom Eusebius eulogises as most kindly disposed towards Christianity[5] and markedly tolerant of Christians, held authority as Cæsar over the island. But, previous to the abdication of Maximian in

---

[1] Tertull. de Bapt. 16; St. Cyprian, Ep. 73. 18, 19, &c. Comp. Euseb. vi. 4.

[2] Although Chester, the seat of the twentieth legion, was so named, as in Bede, ii. 2, yet in this passage Caerleon-on-Usk, or Isca Silurum, the head-quarters of the second legion, is meant (see Merivale, Hist. Rom. vi. 248). So in Liber Landavensis, ed. Rees, p. 27, as to these martyrdoms at 'civitatem Legionum super Huisc dictam;' and Geoffrey says (vii. 4) that churches of SS. Aaron and Julius existed there. Bede says that when persecution ceased, a church was built on the spot of Alban's martyrdom.

[3] Gild. Hist. 8.

[4] In his poem on Virginity, Miscell. viii. c. 6. He puts Alban after Vincent.

[5] Euseb. H. E. viii. 13; Vit. C. i. 16. Sozomen, i. 6, says that under him 'it was not thought unlawful for ... Britons ... to profess Christianity.' Lactantius says that he permitted Christian churches 'to be pulled down, but preserved unhurt that true temple of God which exists in men;' Mort. Pers. 15. This corrects Eusebius' assertion that under him churches were safe, but appears to need some modification as to men.

the May of 305, the benevolent prince who owned the superior
authority of a coarse and merciless tyrant, 'implacably'
hostile 'to the name and religion of the Christians[1],' might
be unable to restrain subordinate local persecutors: and on
the whole we may say with Milman, that 'there seems no
reason to doubt' the historic reality of the British Protomartyr[2], nor, we may add, of those other Christian sufferers
whose names are associated with his, and for whom Gildas
is the earliest authority[3].

The restoration of peace to the Christian body was too soon
followed by the troubles of the Donatist schism, which led to the
meeting of the great Council of Arles, in A.D. 314. Its records
show, among the bishops present, the names of three from
Britain; Eborius of York, Restitutus of London, and Adelphius
'de civitate Colonia Londinensium[4],' together with Sacerdos,
a presbyter, and Arminius, a deacon. 'Eborius of Eboracum'
is rather suspicious, but the name may be some British name
misread[5]. But what was the word which has been corrupted
into 'Londinensium'? It was once proposed to read 'Camu-
lodunensium,'—the men of that typical Roman colony which
has given its name to Colchester. But two other opinions are
now more popular: one is, that the original reading was
'Lindensium[6],' and then Adelfius would appear as bishop of

Council of
Arles.

[1] Gibbon, ii. 267. Compare Smith, App. 4. to Bede, that Constantius could
not, and did not, prevent all persecution in Gaul and Spain: 'he dared not
refuse to publish the edicts.'

[2] Lat. Chr. ii. 226. That the number of the martyrs of Britain at this
time has been exaggerated (e. g. Bede's Martyrology gives 888) is obvious.

[3] Martyrologists also name a St. Augulus, bishop, in Augusta, i. e. London
(in Bede's Martyrology, Augustus): see Haddan and Stubbs, i. 29. Nothing
is known of him. Alb. Butler (Feb. 7) thinks that he suffered soon after
Alban.

[4] Mansi, Conc. ii. 476.

[5] Haddan and Stubbs, i. 7. *Ivor* is an old British name; see Annal.
Camb. a. 501, 'Ebur (al. Ywor) episcopus pausat.' Geoffrey mentions an
Ivor in his 'History,' ix. 6; see too Giraldus on 'Ivor the Little' (Itin.
Camb. i. 6). Pryce gives Efrog as the Welsh equivalent to Eburius (Brit.
Ch. p. 88). But see also Raine, Fast. Ebor. i. 9. Adelfius and 'Hibernius'
are among the signataries of the synodal letter to Pope Silvester. Is Hibernius
another form of Eborius?

[6] Bingham, b. ix. c. 6. s. 20; Lingard, A.-S. Ch. i. 6; Routh, Rell. Sac. iv.
296; Lappenberg, Hist. Eng. (E. Tr.), i. 50; Robertson, i. 218. Compare
'Lindocolina' in Bede, ii. 16. See Freeman, Engl. Towns, &c. p. 192.

the 'Colony of Lindum' or Lincoln. Another would read 'Legionensium[1],' and place his see in 'the famous city of Caerleon, the camp of the Legion[2],' the great stronghold of Roman power in 'Britannia Secunda,' where even now the amphitheatre and the collection of Roman remains render the little village on the bank of the Usk one of the most impressive scenes in South Wales. For the former theory it is urged that Lindum was a colony, and that, as far as we know, Caerleon was not[3], and that the secretary of the Council would be more likely to misunderstand 'Lindensium' than 'Legionensium.' For the latter theory it may be said that Caerleon, the traditional home of the martyrs Aaron and Julius, and the traditional seat of an ancient British bishopric, appears more naturally to associate itself with the third delegate to Arles than a town within a short distance of York, and in the province[4] whose capital was London. On the whole, the reasons for the Lincoln claim would appear to preponderate.

Roman-British Church; little known of it.

During the rest of the 'Roman period,' the Church of Britain shows like a valley wrapt in mists, across which some fitful lights irregularly gleam. We know nothing of its episcopal succession, very little of its internal life, or of its efforts at self-extension. We read of some of its buildings as having been known to exist at Canterbury, Caerleon, Verulam, and, we may add, on one most interesting spot, then girdled in by waters and known as Ynys-vitrin, usually rendered 'the Glassy Isle,' or Avalon, 'the Isle of Apples;' our present

[1] Stillingfleet, Orig. Brit. p. 78; Haddan and Stubbs, i. 7. There is no good evidence for any Archbishopric in Wales; Pryce, p. 89.

[2] Merivale, vi. 248. Geoffrey's imagination endows it, in Arthurian days, with royal palaces, 'ita ut aureis tectorum fastigiis Romam imitaretur,' vii. 4. Somewhat later, Giraldus wrote, 'Videas hic multa pristinae nobilitatis adhuc vestigia et palatia immensa, ... thermas insignes, templorum reliquias, et loca theatralia ... egregiis muris partim adhuc exstantibus' (fragments of them are still extant) 'omnia clausa,' &c. Itin. Camb. i. c. 5 (vol. vi. p. 55). See Palgrave, Engl. Comm. p. 323; Lappenberg, i. 52.

[3] Hübner, Inscr. Brit. Chr., præf. p. vii.

[4] I.e. Flavia Cæsariensis. Maxima Cæsariensis stretched from the Humber to the southern wall, that of Hadrian; Valentia, from thence to the wall of Antoninus. Britannia Prima included all south of Thames and Severn. Britannia Secunda was our Wales.

Glastonbury, where the tall green peak of the Tor of St.
Michael looks down on the stately ruins of the great abbey
which succeeded to 'the old church' made originally of
twisted wands, the earliest sanctuary on that venerable
ground, of which Christianity has held uninterrupted possession [1]. Traces of some ecclesiastical Roman work have
been discerned here and there, as at Lyminge and Brix-
worth; but amid the crowd of monuments, and other relics of
Roman dominion [2],—among which occur not only altars to
Roman gods, properly so called, including Rome herself, the
manes of the dead, and the Genius of Fortune, but also names
of barbaric deities, and tokens of the wide diffusion of the
strangely fascinating worship of Mithras [3],—antiquarians
have found but very few memorials of Roman-British
Christianity,—the cross, or Christian monogram, here and
there, on a stone, a piece of pottery, or a tesselated pavement,
a grave-stone, alluding to 'peace' or 'rest,' or recording that
a 'Christian man' slept below [4]. To some extent, this disappointing lack of evidence may be accounted for by the
devastating fury of Saxon heathenism: but it seems impossible to doubt that the Church which has left so few visible
marks of its presence and activity was not strong in numbers,
or influence, or wealth [5], and that it had not, in fact, 'in-

[1] Haddan and Stubbs, i. 37. For Glastonbury in particular see Freeman,
Norm. Conq. i. 439, English Towns and Districts, p. 76 ff. He derives its
English name from 'the family of Glæsting,' and suggests that the interpretation, 'glassy isle,' put upon 'Ynysvitrin,' may have been a mere play on
words; see below, p. 313. Setting aside mere fables, it may be what
Malmesbury calls it (de Antiq. Glaston Eccl.), 'the oldest church, as far
as he knew, in England.' But its 'great temporal position' may probably
date from 601, when a Devonian king (Gwrgan?) 'granted the land called
Ynysvitrin to the old church which was situated there, at the request of Worgret
the abbot' (Malmesb. de Antiq. Glast.; Freeman, p. 86).

[2] See the 'Collection of Roman Inscriptions and Sculptures' in Horsley's
Britannia Romana, p. 192 ff.

[3] E. g. a large altar 'Sancto Mithræ' at Caerleon; and another to 'Mithras
the Sun-God,' given by Horsley, Cumb. No. 29. Horsley gives two inscriptions 'Deo Belatucadro.' There is a Mithraic sculpture in the museum at
York.

[4] See Haddan and Stubbs, i. 39, 162; Hübner, nos. 1, 7, 31, 131. Perhaps some of the Roman-British remains here alluded to belong to a somewhat
later period.

[5] Haddan, Remains, p. 332.

CHAP. I.

herited the land [1].' In regard to its relations with the Churches of Europe, we find it adhering to the orthodox side in the great Arian struggle : not only does Constantine, in his extant letter, include the Britons among those who accepted the ruling of the Nicene Council as to the calculation of Easter [2], but St. Athanasius ranks the British bishops with prelates of various provinces [3] who adhered to the decision of the Sardican Council, against those who had libelled his character by way of striking at the faith which he upheld. Hilary of Poitiers, in 358–9, congratulated his British brethren on their 'freedom from all contagion of the detestable heresy [4]:'

Council of Ariminum.

and in the next summer some British bishops took part in the Council of Ariminum. Sulpicius Severus [5] expressly tells us that three of them, being unable to pay their own expenses, would not receive contributions from other prelates, but accepted an allowance from Constantius, 'thinking it more consistent with duty to burden the treasury than individuals [6].' No doubt, the British delegates compromised their brethren at home by being cajoled or harassed into accepting the uncatholic formulary which made the name of Ariminum a by-word : but, like the great mass of those who then showed weakness, they appear to have returned to the

British orthodoxy.

Nicene position ; for in 363 Athanasius could reckon the Britons among those who were loyal to the Catholic faith [7].

[1] See Palgrave, Engl. Commonwealth, p. 154.

[2] Eus. Vit. Con. iii. 19. There is no evidence that any British bishops went to Nicæa.

[3] Ath. Apol. c. Ari. 1, Hist. Ari. 28 (yet see Apol. 50). It has often been said that British bishops actually sat in the Sardican Council. But that Council's letter, Apol. c. Ari. 36, reciting the countries there and then represented, names Spain and Gaul, and omits Britain : and Athanasius himself in the first passage speaks of 'more than 300' bishops, whereas he reckons the bishops present at Sardica as 170 ; Hist. Ari. 15.

[4] 'Dilectissimis et beatissimis patribus et coepiscopis' of Germany and of Gaul, 'et provinciarum Britanniarum episcopis.' De Synodis.

[5] Sulp. ii. 41. See Gibbon, iv. 134. He thinks that the British Church might have thirty or forty bishops.

[6] Sulpicius adds, 'I have often heard Gavidius our bishop mention this in a tone of censure. But I should regard it quite otherwise ; and I praise the bishops for having been so poor as to have nothing of their own, and for accepting supplies from no others, but only from the treasury, ubi neminem gravabant ; ... ita in utrisque egregium exemplum.'

[7] Ath. Ep. ad Jovian. 2.

It is evident, therefore, that Gildas, and Bede following him, have greatly exaggerated the influence of Arianism in Britain[1]. Eminent doctors of unquestioned orthodoxy, in the period following the Athanasian, speak as if the distant islanders were one in faith with themselves. Chrysostom says that 'even the British isles'—(observe the plural)—'have felt the power of the Word, for there too churches and altars have been erected:' there too, as in the extreme East, or beside the Euxine, or in the South, 'men may be heard discussing points in Scripture, with differing voices, but not with differing belief[2].' Jerome is not less emphatic: Britain, he affirms, 'worships the same Christ, observes the same rule of truth,' with other Christian countries: more than this, the enthusiasm for pilgrimages to Palestine had touched even Britons, as well as 'the swarms of the East,' and it seemed opportune to remark that 'the road to the heavenly hall stood open from Britain as well as from Jerusalem[3].' On one occasion we find that a discord had arisen among British Christians, the exact nature of which cannot be learned from the rhetorical generalities in which Victricius, bishop of Rouen, tells how, at the request of his 'fellow-bishops' in Britain, he had gone over thither to restore religious peace[4]. Our subject does not include the history of Christianity in North Britain: but we hear of Calpurnius, a deacon as well as a 'decurio,' resident probably at or near Dunbarton, whose father Potitus was a presbyter, and whose son Succat became the great St. Patrick[5]: nor can we forget how the northern extremity of England must have profited by the homeward journey of Ninian, a native of the Cumbrian dis- St. Ninian. trict[6], who, having studied at Rome, and received episcopal

---

[1] Gild. Hist. 9; Bede, i. 8.

[2] Chrys. Quod Chr. sit Deus, 12; Hom. in Princip. Act. 3. 1.

[3] Jerome, Ep. 146. 1; Ep. 46. 10; Ep. 58. 3. The last of these three sentences was written about 395. Cp. Prudentius, Peristeph. xiii. 103.

[4] Victric. de Laude Sanctorum, 1 (Galland. Bibl. Patr. viii. 228). This journey would be after A.D. 390.

[5] See Dict. Chr. Biogr. iv. 203. For the ascertained facts about Patrick see Whitley Stokes, Tripartite Life of St. Patrick, Introduct. p. cxxxiii.

[6] See Bede, iii. 4: A.-S. Chron. a. 565; Bp. Forbes, Kalendars of Scottish Saints, p. 422, and Lives of SS. Ninian and Kentigern, p. 257.

consecration from Pope Siricius, returned to Britain[1], established a missionary bishopric on a promontory of Wigtownshire, and built a church, not, as was usual among Britons, of wood, but, in the Roman fashion, of stone,—on account of which, as Bede tells us, the place was called the White House, 'Candida Casa[2],' otherwise Whithern,— where now a ruined cathedral, crowning a wooded mound, represents what was once emphatically named 'the Great Monastery[3],' and known as a centre of religious light and strength for all who dwelt along the Solway and between the two Roman 'walls,' and even for those 'Southern Picts[4]' whose proper district extended from the Forth to the great range of hills which divides our present Scotland. So it was that in after-ages St. Ninian was commemorated as the instrument by whom the 'Picts and Britons' had been 'converted to the knowledge of the faith.'

Those early years of the fifth century, during which Ninian was in his prime of work[5], witnessed the origin of a momentous controversy which went far to impair, in the eyes of zealous continental theologians, the reputation of the Pelagianism. British Church for simple-hearted orthodoxy. When Pelagius became obnoxious by speculations offensive to Christian piety, he was generally known as 'the Briton[6],' and was, indeed,

[1] On his way home he became acquainted with, and was profoundly impressed by, the great missionary bishop of Gaul, St. Martin of Tours,—and in his memory the 'white' church was hallowed ; Bede, l. c.

[2] Bede, iii. 4. Comp. v. 21 ; Hist. Abb. 5. Whithern was also called Rosnat. On the sculptures at Kirkmadrine in Wigtownshire—two stones with the Christian monogram, one having also the names of ' the priests Viventius and Majorius' (or ' Mavorius'), the other of ' Florentius '—see Haddan and Stubbs, ii. 51 ; Hübner, no. 205.

[3] Bp. Forbes, Lives, &c. pp. xlii. 292 ; Haddan and Stubbs, i. 120.

[4] Bede, iii. 4. See Skene, Celtic Scotl. i. 230. Haddan and Stubbs, ii. 105 ; Arbuthnott Missal, p. 369.

[5] He is said to have died on Sept. 16, 432. ' Many saints ' were believed to rest beside him : Bede, iii. 4.

[6] Augustine, Ep. 186. 1. So Bede here calls him, i. 10, and cites Prosper's lines, alluding to him as nourished by ' æquorei Britanni ' (in one of Prosper's Epigrams). Compare his De Ingratis, i. 13 :—
 ' Dogma quod antiqui satiatum felle draconis
  Pestifero vomuit coluber sermone Britannus.'
Comp. Prosper, Chron. A.D. 416, ' Pelagius Brito ;' Orosius, Apol. 12, ' Britan-

characterised by Jerome, in his coarse way, as 'that big dog of Albion [1].' It is right to remember that he had, in his own way, 'a zeal for God,' a grave indignation against the inertness of many professing Christians, who pleaded their weakness as an excuse for not striving after sanctity [2]. But he went astray through an exaggeration of human capacities for moral attainment [3]; he over-rated the power of the will, and denied the necessity of internal grace; and he grounded this denial on the rejection of that view of the Fall, as a source of inherited corruption and debasement, which is technically called the doctrine of 'original sin [4].' He had left Britain in early life, and does not seem to have returned; but a bishop, Severianus, who adopted his opinions, had a son named Agricola [5], who devoted himself with passionate ardour to the work of spreading the proscribed theory in the country of its author, so that, in Prosper's words, 'enemies of grace took possession of the heresiarch's native soil [6].' The British clergy were generally faithful to the received doctrines, although a severe interpretation might find a Pelagian leaven in a practical treatise written by a British prelate of this period, named Fastidius [7]. But some laymen of wealth and import-

---

nicus noster;' and Marius Mercator, p. 2, 'a Briton.' It is a mere guess that Pelagius is 'Morgan' Grecised.

[1] In Jerem. l. 3. præf. The devil, he says, 'latrat per Albinum canem grandem et corpulentum, et qui calcibus magis possit sævire quam dentibus.' The next sentence, 'Habet enim progeniem Scoticæ gentis, de Britannorum vicinia,' probably means, 'He is said to be of "the Roman island:"' one might rather suppose him to be of the adjacent "*barbarous* island."' Comp. Jerome, prolog. in Jerem.: 'stolidissimus, *et Scotorum pultibus prægravatus.*' And see Tillemont, xiii. 562. Others suppose Jerome to refer to Cœlestius as Irish, e. g. Haddan and Stubbs, Councils, ii. 290.

[2] See St. Augustine, de Dono Persev. s. 53.

[3] See Guizot, Civil. in France, lect. 5; Mozley on Doctrine of Predestination, pp. 58–64, 102; Dict. Chr. Biogr. iv. 283.

[4] See the writer's Introd. pp. vii.–xii. to 'Select Anti-Pelagian Treatises of St. Augustine.'

[5] Bede, i. 17.

[6] C. Collatorem, s. 58.

[7] 'Fastidius, Britannorum episcopus;' Gennadius de Vir. Illustr. 56. See Galland. Bibl. Patr. ix. p. xxx. In the 11th chapter of his 'De Vita Christiana' Fastidius approves of such a prayer as was made a matter of complaint against Pelagius ('Thou knowest, Lord, that these hands which I lift up are holy,' &c.; comp. Jerome, Dial. c. Pelag. iii. 14). See Tillemont,

ance were attracted by a system which tended to resolve
Christianity into a philosophy[1], and to explain away those
mysterious announcements, as to transmitted sinfulness and
the absolute need of grace, which demanded the humiliation
of the soul. Britain, it seems, had no divines competent to
resist it; and an appeal was therefore made to the Church,
one might say the mother-Church, in Gaul,—the Church of
Hilary and of Martin,—which was both able and ready to
assist out of its abundance the theological poverty of Britain.

Visit of
St. German
and Lupus.

Two Gallic bishops were commissioned to visit the island:
but there is a discrepancy between our authorities as to the
circumstances of their appointment. According to Constantius of Lyons[2], who wrote some sixty years later, with full
access to local information, and whose account is copied
by Bede, the prelates, Germanus of Auxerre and Lupus of
Troyes, were sent over by 'a numerous synod[3]' to 'uphold in
Britain the belief in Divine grace.' According to Prosper of
Aquitaine, the admiring defender of St. Augustine, Celestine
bishop of Rome is said to have sent German 'as his representative[4],' by which means Celestine 'took pains to keep the
Roman island Catholic[5].' Prosper has the advantage over

Mem. xv. 17, who adds that his language on the effect of the Fall is inadequate:
it is, 'omnes suo damnantur exemplo;' c. 13. Stillingfleet defends him, Orig.
Brit. p. 200.

[1] Michelet, Hist. Fr. bk. i. c. 3. That, at the same time, Pelagianism was
'raised on a basis philosophically' as well as 'religiously false,' see Mozley,
pp. 102–104.

[2] See Constantius' Vit. S. Germ., c. 19, in Surius, de Probatis Sanctorum
Historiis, vol. iv. p. 416; Life of St. German (in Lives of English Saints),
p. 122. Constantius dedicates this 'Life' to Patiens, bishop of Lyons, who had
often urged him to write it. Bede copies largely from this part of it, making
some verbal alterations, as 'magna' for 'numerosa synodus,' occasionally adding,
but usually abbreviating by the omission of some mere verbiage, and frequently
smoothing out the Latin.

[3] That the Council was held at Troyes, see Life of St. German, p. 122.

[4] Prosp. Chron. Integr. par. 2, 'Florentio et Dionysio Coss. (i. e. 429): Ad
actionem Palladii diaconi, papa Cœlestinus Germanum . . . . . vice sua mittit.'
(Migne, Patr. Lat. ii. 594.)

[5] Prosp. c. Collat. c. 21, s. 58: 'Nec vero segniore cura ab hoc eodem
morbo Britannias liberavit, quando quosdam inimicos gratiæ solum suæ originis
occupantes etiam ab illo secreto exclusit Oceani, et ordinato Scotis episcopo
(i. e. Palladius), dum Romanam insulam studet servare catholicam, fecit etiam
barbaram Christianam.' Palladius was sent in 431 as bishop to the 'Scots
(Irish) who believed in Christ' (Prosp. Chron.); the scattered believers among

Constantius in being a contemporary writer [1]; and he actually visited Rome to lodge a complaint before this Pope [2]. The two statements have been harmonised by supposing that Celestine recommended German to the Council [3]; or that after the Council had chosen its two envoys, German also 'received the Pope's sanction' for his journey [4]; or else, that Constantius' statement is true only of Lupus, and that German's commission was simply from Rome [5]. But who were German and Lupus? The former was by much the greater personage of the two. If, as is now admitted, the date of this mission is wrongly placed by Bede at A.D. 446, and should rather be 429, German had then been eleven years bishop of his native city. He had seen much of the world [6]; had studied at Rome, not for the priesthood, but for the bar; had held the high place of 'duke' of a wide district [7]; and had been suddenly, and as it were forcibly, ordained a cleric by Amator bishop of Auxerre [8], and soon afterwards succeeded him at his death, A.D. 418. He had forthwith adopted, with all his heart and without reserve, the strictest standard of episcopal conduct [9]. Lupus was a few years younger,—a

the Irish; see Todd's St. Patrick, p. 284. Whether he afterwards visited North Britain is at least very doubtful; Skene takes the negative view, Celtic Scotl. ii. 27.

[1] He wrote in support of St. Augustine about 428. The Carmen de Ingratis is dated about 429–430, the Contra Collatorem after 432; the Chronicle comes down to 455.

[2] His complaint was against Gallic 'Semi-Pelagians.' See Tillemont, xvi. 14, and Introd. to Anti-Pelagian Treat. p. lv.

[3] Life of St. German, p. 122: cp. Fleury, b. 25. c. 15.

[4] Todd's St. Patrick, p. 271 ff.; Tillemont, xv. 15.

[5] Lingard, Anglo-Sax. Ch. i. 8. Haddan and Stubbs, i. 17, practically set aside Prosper's statement, except as to the date of 429. But Prosper, a contemporary, must have known whether or no Celestine took action in the matter; although, from his point of view, he may have over-estimated such action. The Benedictine Life of Gregory the Great simply follows Constantius, bk. iii. 4. 2.

[6] Constantius, i. 1. He attended the Gallic schools before he went to Rome. On those schools cp. Bede, iii. 18.

[7] Armorica and Nervia, i. e. the first and second Aquitania, the Senonensis, the first and second Lugdunensis. He retained to the last his 'dignity of countenance;' Constant. ii. 10.

[8] See the scene described in the English Life of St. German, p. 37, from Constantius, i. 4.

[9] Tillemont, xv. 13, from Constant. i. 8–10. Austerities did not make

CHAP. I.

Discomfiture of Pelagians.

friend of Sidonius Apollinaris, who addresses him in a letter [1] as 'bishop of bishops :' two letters of his are preserved [2].

The Gallic prelates landed in Britain after a stormy voyage, the perils of which, says Constantius, were averted by the prayers of German [3]. 'They preached in churches, and even in streets and fields and in the open country [4],' to the great encouragement of the faithful: their teaching was generally accepted [5]: at last, however, the Pelagians, who had previously avoided a debate, took the resolution to confront the foreign bishops [6], apparently at Verulam. 'They came forward in all the pride of wealth, and richly attired,' amid a circle of dependants or disciples : a multitude of men, with women and children, assembled to hear the discussion. 'On one side,' says Constantius, 'was Divine authority, on the other was human assurance.' 'On one side,' Bede adds, 'was piety, on the other pride [7].' The Pelagians spoke first, with that fluency [8] which seems often to have distinguished the advocates of their system. Then the bishops replied, with arguments from 'the Apostles and Evangelists [9],' adding their own comments, adducing authorities in support of

German hard : see the beautiful anecdote in Constantius, ii. 9, that when he was seventy, on his journey across the Alps, he fell in with an old lame labourer, on the edge of a torrent crossed by slippery stones, and carried over first the man's burden, and then the man himself.

[1] Sidon. Ep. vi. 1. The letter accumulates expressions of reverence. In another, Ep. vi. 4, he speaks to Lupus as 'apostolatui tuo.'

[2] Sirmond. i. 573; Galland. Bibl. ix. 516; Migne, Patr. Lat. lviii. 63. In one of these letters he says to Sidonius, 'Gaudeo exui, postquam ecclesiam induisti.' He lived till 479.

[3] Constantius, i. 22 ; Bede, i. 17. The incident is also referred to by Adamnan, Vit. Col. ii. 34. Constantius, however, makes German pour oil on the waves : Bede omits 'oleo,' and turns 'levi aspergine' into 'levi aquæ spargine.' Dr. Todd thinks it not unlikely that German took with him Palladius as his archdeacon (St. Patrick, p. 318).

[4] 'Per trivia, per rura, per devia ;' Constant. i. 23. Bede omits 'per devia.'

[5] 'Itaque regionis universitas in eorum sententiam prompta transierat ;' Const., Bede. This implies that many had, till then, inclined to Pelagianism.

[6] 'Diuturna meditatione concepta ;' Const., Bede.

[7] Bede's antithesis, 'inde Pelagius auctor, hinc Christus,' is adopted from Constantius.

[8] 'Sola nuditate verborum diu inaniter ;' Bede. Comp. S. Aug. Op. imp. c. Julianum, præf., 'nimia loquacitate.'

[9] Probably Ps. li. 5 ; Rom. v. 12 ff. ; 1 Cor. iv. 7. xv. 21 ; Eph. ii. 3, 8 ; Phil. ii. 13 ; 1 John i. 8, &c.

'weighty propositions,' and urging objections against the whole Pelagian theory. The adversaries, we are told, were reduced to silence : the people exulted in their defeat [1]. Then follows an account of a blind girl who recovered her sight by aid of German's prayers [2], and after the application of a casket of relics which he always wore suspended from his neck [3] : after which Bede tells us, still following his Gallic authority, that the bishops visited the tomb of St. Alban, over which, as he had already said, 'a church of admirable workmanship had been reared' after the close of the persecution. German took away with him a mass of earth, which was imagined still to bear traces of the blood of the martyr [4]. Passing by another story of German's preservation from fire when lame through an accident, we come to the grand tale of the Alleluia Victory [5]. A combination of Picts and Saxons menaced the British : German and Lupus encouraged them to resistance, joined them in their march, and in the Lent of 430 induced the majority, who were still heathens,—the British clergy having made no impression upon them [6],— to accept daily instructions, and to ask for baptism. On Easter Eve the baptisms were administered [7], the great festival was

The Alleluia Victory.

---

[1] It is added that the people could hardly keep their hands off them.

[2] At first the bishops challenged the Pelagians to 'cure her ;' but they 'joined the parents in praying that the bishops would do so.'

[3] Constant. i. 24, comp. ib. 10. See Greg. Turon. H. Fr. viii. 15,—dust from St. Martin's grave, in a casket, hung round the neck of Wulfilac. Gregory the Great sent to a Gallic 'patrician' a small cross made from 'St. Peter's chains,' to be worn round the neck ; Ep. iii. 33.

[4] This is from Constant. i. 25, and it is the first known instance of any acquaintance with the story of St. Alban. Compare, as to the virtue ascribed to such 'dust,' Bede, iii. 10. German built a church at Auxerre, and there deposited the dust. Observe the strange 'conceit,' that 'a martyr's slaughter still keeps red when the persecutor is pale' (in death).

[5] Constant. i. 28 ; Bede, i. 20 ; and see Chron. a. 459. The story is not given in the original text of Nennius. Bede's silence about Patrick is less strange than that of Gildas about German, on which see Life of St. German, p. 159. Possibly he alludes to the 'Victory' in Hist. 18, on a British victory obtained by trusting in God ; but this he dates after A.D. 446.

[6] Pearson, in his Early and Middle Ages of Engl., p. 46, adds that there is some evidence for a revival of British Paganism in the fifth century.

[7] See the form in Forbes's Gallican Liturgies, p. 191. The words at the administration were, 'Baptizo te credentem in nomine Patris, &c., ut habeas vitam æternam in sæcula sæculorum.'

celebrated, in a 'church' formed out of boughs of trees : the British 'host' then advanced, the greater part of it fresh 'from the laver,' and under the generalship of the sometime 'duke of Armorica,' who showed his ability in the disposal of his inferior forces.   He drew them up, as if in ambush, under the rocks of a narrow glen, which he had ascertained to lie full in the path of the enemy : as the first ranks of the heathen drew near, expecting an easy triumph, German bade the Britons repeat after him the one sacred, joyous word which they had so lately uttered in their Paschal solemnities [1].   Three times he and Lupus intoned it, 'Alleluia, Alleluia, Alleluia ! ' Their followers, with ' one voice,' made the sound echo through the valley : it rang from cliff to cliff, it struck the invaders with panic,—they fled as if the very skies were crashing over them, and many leapt headlong into the river which intercepted their retreat : the Britons, successful without 'striking a blow,' exulted in a ' victory won by faith and clear of blood-shed [2].'   The scene of this flight is laid by Welsh tradition at Maes-Garmon, ' German's Field,' a mile from Mold, in Flint-shire [3].   He and Lupus returned home, after the island, as Constantius expresses it, had thus been freed from ' foes spiritual and corporeal.'   A second journey of German to Britain, in order to complete the overthrow of heresy, is referred to A.D. 447 : he was attended, this time, by a disciple of Lupus, Severus bishop of Treves [4].   A few, it was found, had

---

[1] See St. Augustine's Easter sermons 'on Alleluia,' 255, 256. 'Et ipsum Alleluia quotidie dicimus, et quotidie delectamur . . . Si rorem sic amatis, fontem ipsum quomodo amabitis ! . . . O felix Alleluia in cœlo !' See Neale, Essays on Liturgiology, p. 65.

[2] It has been thought that the words of Gregory the Great, ' Behold, the tongue of Britain . . . has long ago begun to resound the Hebrew Alleluia in the praises of God,' Moral. in Job xxvii. 21, may refer to this event : so Usher, Antiq. p. 179, who remarks that this work was finished before the mission of Augustine. Bede, ii. 2, and Paul. Diac. refer them to the conversion of Kent ; and they may have been added by Gregory in a revision of the 'Morals.' But would he have said 'jamdudum ?'

[3] Lingard, Anglo-Sax. Ch. i. 11, objects that Saxons would not be likely to penetrate into North Wales. But the description of the scenery points to some such scenery as that of Wales or Derbyshire. The river near Maesgarmon is the Alyn. The next parish to Mold is Llan-*armon;* Rees, Welsh Saints, p. 125.

[4] Constantius, ii. 2 ; Bede, i. 21 ; 'Severo, totius sanctitatis viro.'

relapsed into Pelagianism : they were reclaimed, and the false
teachers expelled from Britain, but settled in places on the
continent where they might unlearn their misbelief[1]. A
miracle, as usual, is recorded in connection with this visit;
from that time forth, says a later writer, the Britons never
harboured any heresy[2]; and German's name continued to be
held in honour among the people whom he had instructed[3],
and was attached to various places in Wales and Cornwall[4].
It is well to repeat the summary of his character, as contained
in the Liturgy of his native Church : the ' Missa Sancti
Germani' for July 31,—the day on which, as Bede expresses
it, he 'migrated to Christ' in 448,—after mentioning his
apostolic activity as extending to Britain, affirmed that 'he
so began as to increase, and so contended as to conquer[5].'

[1] 'That the country might get quit of them, and they of their errors,'—so we
might render the words of Constantius.

[2] Giraldus Cambrensis, Descr. Camb. i. 18.

[3] See Bp. Jones and Freeman, Hist. of St. David's, p. 257. Nennius'
History has various stories about German's proceedings, e. g. his attempt to
convert a wicked king of Powys, 31; his intercessions for the guilty Vortigern,
50, &c. Of his anti-Pelagian activities it only says that he came to preach,
and 'multi per eum salvi facti sunt: increduli perierunt;' c. 30. Some eminent
Welsh bishops are erroneously described as his disciples.

[4] Life of St. German, p. 1. Several ecclesiastical colleges in Wales were
said to have been founded by him; and although this may be legendary (Haddan
and Stubbs, i. 21), he was not unlikely to 'advise the establishment of such
institutions' as might guard the British Church against heresy in the future;
Pryce, Anc. Br. Ch. p. 124. A 'Missa S. Germani,' cited in Bp. Forbes's
Pref. to the Arbuthnott Missal, p. lii, and Haddan and Stubbs, i. 696, affirms
in its Præfatio that German, 'sent by Saint Gregory, shone forth as a lantern
and pillar to Cornwall, and bloomed like roses and lilies in the meadow of the
church of Aledh' (= St. German's). It is probable that in one or other of his
visits he did more for the British Church than had any interest for his Gallic
biographer. Giraldus traces to his influence several Welsh customs, e. g.
giving to the poor the first corner of every loaf, sitting by threes at dinner,
asking the blessing of any religious man; Descr. a b. i. 18. The legend of
a Germanus, bishop of Man, has grown out of the dedication of its cathedral to
St. German; Lanigan, Eccl. Hist. Irel. i. 306. Coindrus, Romulus, and
Maghould are otherwise named as its first bishops; ib.

[5] Forbes and Neale, Anc. Gall. Liturgies, p. 152. Among his last words
were, ' Well know I what country that is which God promises to His servants.'
This was in reference to a dream in which he seemed to see the Lord giving
him provision for a journey to his own country; Constant. ii. 19. He died at
Ravenna, whither he had gone as an envoy from the Armorican insurgents to
Valentinian III. See Life of St. German, p. 258.

We have heard of his confronting a combination of Picts with *Saxons*. That name, for ages so hateful to the representatives of the British race, had been a sound of terror along the island coast even in the third century[1]. Part of that coast, from the Wash to Southampton, had been known as 'the Saxon Shore[2]:' Claudian had depicted 'the Saxon' as wafted by winds towards Britain, and sung of a defeat of Saxons in distant Orkney[3]: but after many raids on their part had harassed Southern Britain and given them a foothold on its soil, they appear about the middle of the fifth century as entering on a more regular plan of conquest. It is one thing to form settlements, another to found kingdoms. And this 'series of constant, systematic, successful' occupations of British soil was, in the words of the historian of the 'Norman Conquest,' one of the most 'fearful blows' that ever fell on any nation[4]. In order to appreciate it, we must remember that it descended on a people whom the indignant rhetoric of Gildas depicts as divided against themselves[5], incapable of any noble national life[6], abandoned, within memory, by their Roman protectors to their Pictish tormentors[7], and rather weakened than disciplined by their experience of Roman civilisation[8]: a people, too, described by

[1] The Saxons are first mentioned in the second century. For their early connection with Britain, see Gibbon, iv. 388, note; ii. 70, note; iii. 262.

[2] I.e. the shore most exposed to Saxon invasion; Freeman, Norm. Conq. i. 11; Stubbs, Const. Hist. i. 67 (59, ed. 1); Green, Making of England, p. 20.

[3] De 4° cons. Honor. 31 : 'Maduerunt Saxone fuso Orcades.' Gibbon admits 'some degree of truth' in this poetical tribute to the elder Theodosius; iii. 271. For Stilicho's like achievements, see Claudian, de laud. Stil. ii. 253 :—

'Illius effectum curis . . . ne littore tuto
Prospicerem dubiis venturum Saxona ventis.'

(This is put into the mouth of Britain.) See Gibbon, iv. 53. For the Saxon inroads under Valentinian I, when Theodosius was employed, see also Ammianus, xxvi. 4, 5, 'Picti Saxonesque . . . . . Britannos ærumnis vexavere continuis.'

[4] Freeman, i. 13, 20.

[5] Gildas, de Exc. 19. The Welsh explained these denunciations by saying that Gildas had a grudge against Arthur for killing his brother; Giraldus, Descr. i. 2.

[6] Gild. freq. ; Gibbon, iv. 390.

[7] Bede, i. 12; Gibbon, iv. 131, A.D. 409. See too the Saxon Chron. for 418.

[8] 'Desidiosorum,' Gild. præf.; Stubbs, Const. Hist. i. 68.

the same authority as so prone to cruelty and falsehood that any one who showed any gentleness or any love of truth was denounced as an enemy of the country, and became a mark for his neighbours' darts[1]. And the blow was struck, at intervals throughout a century, by invaders as ferocious as they were energetic, of whom a contemporary Gallic bishop says that the Saxon pirates were 'the most truculent of all enemies,' and that they made it a point of religion 'to torture their captives rather than to put them to ransom,' and to sacrifice the tenth part of them to their gods[2]. An idolatry which had its centre in the worship of Woden and of Thunor[3] was sure to render its votaries doubly terrible to a Christian population. Hence it is that we have to read of devastations which Gildas[4] cannot narrate without being reminded of the Psalms of the Captivity. In his declamatory verbiage we see, clearly enough, a grim picture of 'flashing swords and crackling flame,' of ruined walls, fallen towers, altars shattered, priests and bishops and people slain 'in the midst of the streets,' and corpses clotted with blood and left without burial[5]: of the 'miserable remnant,' slaughtered in the mountains, or selling themselves as slaves to the invader, or flying beyond sea, or finding a precarious shelter in the forests[6]. He wrote about the middle of the next century, and at a time when the 'foreign wars' appeared to have ceased[7]: but must have conversed in his youth with those who had witnessed the devastation in the south-east of what we now call England: and Bede almost transcribes him, although

[1] Gild. 21; followed by Bede, i. 14: 'Crudelitas præcipuc, et odium veritatis,' &c.

[2] Sidonius Apollinaris, Ep. viii. 6. See Turner, i. 206; Milman, Lat. Chr. i. 332; Lingard, Angl.-Sax. Ch. i. 45. Yet they were not cruel in cold blood.

[3] See Green's Making of England, p. 164; Taylor's Words and Places, p. 321, for these gods, and for 'Tiw' (whence 'Tuesday').

[4] Gild. 24 (Galland. Bibl. xii. 198). He quotes 'Incenderunt igni sanctuarium tuum,' and 'Deus, venerunt,' &c.

[5] Welsh legends speak of members of the pious 'family of Brychan' who were 'martyred' by the Heathen, as Cynog at Merthyr Cynog, and Tydvyl, a woman, at the better-known Merthyr Tydvil. See Williams, Eccl. Ant. Cymry, p. 115; Rees, Welsh Saints, p. 151.

[6] Gild. 25. Cp. Green, p. 67.

[7] He speaks of the present tranquillity, the unexpected help given to Britons, &c., 26.

CHAP. I. simplifying his turgid phraseology [1]. Thus we are enabled to feel, as it were, with the British Christians of the age of the conquest, while their brethren in Kent, after the defeat at Crayford, 'fled in terror to London [2],' and the native forces, sixteen years later, 'fled from the Angles like fire [3];' while, about the time of the fall of Augustulus, Ella was taking possession of Sussex; while Anderida—now Pevensey—was being taken, and not a Briton left alive [4]; while the kingdom which was to absorb all the rest was being formed by the victories of Cerdic the West-Saxon, in 508 and 519 [5]. Then came something like a definite rally of the natives: the name of Arthur, shining through a golden mist of fable, may represent a historic West-British prince, who did much, though in a limited area, 'to break the heathen and uphold the Christ [6].' That fight on Badon Hill, in which, according to a vivid Welsh legend, 'Arthur bore the cross of our Lord Jesus Christ three days and three nights on his shoulders, and the Britons were conquerors [7],' and which the wild ex-

---

[1] Bede, i. 15. Wendover adds details about the burning of the Scriptures, and heaping earth up to conceal the tombs of martyrs; Flor. Hist. 19.

[2] Chron. a. 457; Green, Making of England, p. 37.

[3] Chron. a. 473.

[4] Ib. a. 491. See Gibbon, iv. 394. Henry of Huntingdon says, 'Locus tantum, quasi nobilissimæ urbis, transeuntibus ostenditur *desolatus.*' The Roman walls and towers enclose the ruins of a mediæval castle, and form a parallelogram of three sides. See Freeman, iii. 401; Green, p. 43.

[5] Chron. a. 491. In 508 Cerdic slew the British king Natanleod. The second battle was at Cerdicsford or Charford in 519. Cerdic appears in the Chronicle as an ealdorman from 495 to 519, when he is described as having won the kingdom.

[6] Tennyson, Idylls of the King, p. 249. 'A *genuine* record of Arthur would be precious beyond words. . . . Arthur is a real man; but, whatever were his acts, they could not have been the acts attributed to him in the legends;' Freeman, v. 584. 'In our Chronicle there is nothing about Arthur;' Freeman, Old-Eng. Hist. p. 34. Yet the Chron. names Natanleod. We may observe Giraldus Cambrensis' phrase, 'Arturi nostri famosi, ne dicam fabulosi,' Descr. Camb. ii. 2. 'History only knows him as the petty prince of a Devonian principality. . . . The modern conception of him appears first in Nennius;' Pearson, Early and Middle Ages of England, p. 57.

[7] Annales Cambriæ, a. 516. A clause of dubious genuineness in Gildas, 26, 'qui prope Sabrinum ostium habetur,' has led to the identification of Mons Badonicus with a hill above Bath. But Freeman (l. c.) and Green (Making of England, p. 89), following Guest (Orig. Celt. ii. 189), place it at Badbury in Dorset. 'Nennius' connects the 'cross' with another battle.

aggerations of the History ascribed to Nennius rank as the
twelfth of his victories[1], may be assigned to some such date
as 516, or rather in 520[2]; and appears to have been 'followed
by a general pause in the English advance[3].' But while the
tide of Teuton triumph was thus far stayed in the south, a
new body of Saxons was beginning the foundation of the
little realm of Essex, destined to include London[4], and
other invaders of properly *Anglian* race were taking hold of
the eastern district which was to be divided between them
as Northfolk and Southfolk[5], extending their grasp over
Lindsey or North Lincolnshire, and so completing the
conquest of the long coast-line of 'the Saxon Shore.' Other
Anglians next invaded Yorkshire; and the 'imperial city'
on the Ouse, which had seen the deaths of Severus and
Constantius, became the prey of the barbarian, probably
about the beginning of the seventh century[6]. Still the
destroying storm rolled northward; and at length, in 547,
as the Chronicler tells us with emphatic simplicity, 'Ida began
to reign, from whom arose the royal race of Northumbria.'
The base of his operations was grandly chosen. High on the
coast of our present Northumberland, towers up a rock which
might seem marked out by nature for the stronghold and
palace of a conqueror: it had been called Dingueirin, and
took the name of Bamborough, or Bebba's burgh, from the

---

[1] 'Nennius' says that 840 men, in that one day, fell by the king's single
hand. The Historia Britonum is ascribed to 'Nennius,' a disciple of Elbod
(bishop of Bangor, who died in 809), and is dated in A.D. 858. But this date
is only in one MS., and the shorter prologue which names the author without
giving the date is only in five out of thirty. See Mon. Hist. Brit. i. 63. The
work is a compilation, of various dates; see Stevenson's Nennius, p. xv; Dict.
Chr. Biogr. iv. 17; Stokes on Life of St. Patrick, i. p. cxvii.

[2] The Annales Cambriæ say 516. Gildas, c. 26, seems to say that he
is writing in the 44th year from this battle: Bede misunderstood him to
reckon it as the 44th year from the first invasion; i. 16. For the date 520, see
Annals of Engl. p. 29; Green, Making of England, p. 89; Palgrave, Engl.
Commonwealth, p. 397.

[3] Green, l. c. See Gildas, l. c.

[4] Erkenwin, the first East-Saxon king, is dated in 526 or 530. Essex was
never an independent kingdom; Palgrave, Anglo-Sax. p. 40.

[5] Green, p. 51. It was then that the great Roman fort of Garianonum or
Burghcastle, near Yarmouth, became a ruin, which afterwards sheltered an
Irish missionary saint, Fursey.

[6] See Raine, Historians of Church of York, i. p. xviii; Green, p. 63.

wife of a later Anglian prince[1], some thirty years after it had been roughly fortified[2] by King Ida. The Britons, who trembled[3] as they heard of his progress through Bryneich, Berneth, or Bernicia, the region between the Tees[4] and the Firth of Forth,—lying north of that district of Deifyr, Deur, or Deira, which after his death obeyed the strong rule of another Anglian, Ælla or Ella,—would hardly have believed a prophet who should have told them that within about eighty years from Ida's arrival, his royal seat would be occupied by a far mightier prince, devoted heart and soul to Christianity. A fresh impulse now stirred among the West-Saxons, and Cynric, son of Cerdic, defeated the Britons at Sarum and Barbury[5]: his successor Ceawlin, after defeating at Wimbledon a young Kentish king named Ethelbert[6], acquired our own Oxfordshire country through his brother's victory at Bedford in 571[7]; and after slaying three British kings at the battle of Deorham in 577, became master of their three cities, Gloucester, Cirencester, and Bath[8]. Six years later he penetrated to the borders of Cheshire, and took two towns

---

[1] Ethelfrid, according to the 'appendix' to Nennius. See Mon. Hist. Brit. pp. 74, 76. Bede says, 'a regina quondam vocabulo Bebba,' iii. 6; cp. 16. Alcuin calls the city Bebba, De Pontif. Ebor. 305. See Freeman, Engl. Towns and Districts, p. 273.

[2] A.-S. Chr. a. 547: 'At first enclosed by a hedge, afterwards by a wall.' For the later castle see Marmion, ii. 8.

[3] Palgrave, Anglo-Sax. p. 43; Green, Making of England, p. 72. Burton says that he seems to have ruled northwards to the Tay; Hist. Scotl. i. 278. It is commonly said that the Britons called him the 'Flamebearer.' But Skene says that it was Theodric, the sixth Bernician king, for whose name they substituted that epithet; Celtic Scotland, i. 159.

[4] Lingard makes the Tees the northern limit of Deira, i. 69. So Freeman, Old-Engl. Hist. p. 38; Raine, Historians of Ch. of York, i. p. xvii. Palgrave says that the land between Tees and Tyne, at first neutral, was ultimately included in Deira; Anglo-Sax. p. 43. It must be observed that Reged, a district placed by Palgrave and Freeman on the north of the Solway, offered fierce resistance to the Angles; and Elmete, a part of the West Riding, was not conquered until the reign of Edwin; Nennius, 63, (66).

[5] Sax. Chron. a. 552, 556; see Gibbon, iv. 391; Green, p. 94. Barbury Camp is near Swindon.

[6] 'Æthelbriht,' Chron. 568.

[7] Chron. 571. Cuthwulf took Bensington, Aylesbury, Eynsham, and Leighton Buzzard; Green, p. 123.

[8] Chron. 577. This victory cut off British communication between Wales and the south-west; Green, p. 128.

belonging to the Welsh kingdom of Powys[1]: and though
sustained a severe check, which forced him to retire southwards, his name must have represented to the Britons that
force and fury of 'Heathen' aggression which they might
now have come to regard as irresistible. Large masses of
their race had been simply slaughtered[2]: many had become
slaves, or passed into a 'half-servile condition:' it seemed to
be only a question of time when the work of conquest should
be perfected: but there was still a large tract, the whole
west, independent of the invader. The kingdom of Cumbria,
or, in the broadest sense, Strathclyde[3], extending from the
Firth of Clyde to the Derwent, and the district between the
Derwent and the Dee, were purely British: the region which
the English gradually came to look upon as 'Wales,' the land
of the 'foreigners[4],' and 'West Wales,' or Devon and Cornwall and part of Somerset, including the sacred 'Avalon[5],'
were still, in British eyes, unpolluted by the barbarian's
tread. Cornwall had been for many years receiving and
honouring a succession of missionaries from Ireland, including
some women, whose pious toil has dotted the county with

CHAP. I.
The

. Celt. ii. 288 ff., for the destruction of Pengwern (Shrews-
...m at the base of the Wrekin, by the West Saxons, and their
...t at Fethanleagh (Faddiley). The Welsh elegy on 'Kyndylan'
as slain in fight, and buried at 'Bassa's churches' = Baschurch.
Making of England, p. 206.

...ubbs, Const. Hist. i. 69; Freeman, i. 18, and Four Oxford
. p. 75. The 'extermination,' where it took place, was such as to be
..ble with the continuance of many Britons as slaves or as 'impoverished
..nts' (Gneist, Hist. Engl. Constit. i. 2), while one race, as such, 'dis-
..ced' another in possession of the territory. Late in the seventh century,
..ne's laws recognise a number of free as well as of enthralled 'Welsh.'

[3] Freeman, i. 14. The close connection of Strathclyde with 'Wales' appears
in the Life of St. Kentigern. Persecuted at Glasgow in 540, he retires into
Wales, until recalled in 573 by a truly Christian king of Strathclyde,
Rederech or Rhydderc, 'the Generous;' Bishop Forbes, Kal. p. 369. Palgrave
divides the Regnum Cumbrense into Strathclyde proper, Reged, and Cumberland with Westmoreland and Lancashire. The capital of the kingdom was
Alcluid, or Dunbritton, now Dunbarton. The name of 'Cumbri' was not used
for its inhabitants until the eleventh century; Skene, ap. Bp. Forbes, Lives
of Ninian and Kentigern, p. 331. The country was called both 'Cumbria' and
'Cambria.'

[4] Compare 'Walling-ford' and 'Corn-wall.'

[5] The land between the Mendips and the Parret became Saxon in 658.

...ces bearing a saintly name[1].   But what of the Cymrians generally?   If we take the date of Gildas' work, the 'History,' so called, and the Epistle, or Admonition, to be about 564[2], we find the condition of the Britons or Cymry, in the middle of the century, to be morally, as well as politically, deplorable. The vague charges against the Britons of the fifth century reappear as detailed indictments against those of the sixth. The first shock of invasion had awed the nation into repentance ; but with quieter times the old sins came back[3].   The 'kings' or princes of the purely British districts were 'tyrants' who acted as if almsgiving would compensate for any sin.   One of them, in contempt of his solemn oath, had slain two royal youths close to an altar[4]: another 'thirsted for civil war and spoil[5]:' a third[6] and a fourth[7] were the slaves of sensuality: a fifth, Maelgwyn, chief among British kings, after overthrowing his predecessor had in compunction taken the vows of a monk, and then relapsed into worse than his former excesses[8].   The clergy were debased by secular and even vicious habits[9], and neglectful of sacred duties, and

[1] E. g. SS. Piran, Sennen, Feock, Germoc, Rumon or Ruan, and the virgin saints Breaca, Burian, and Ia, the last of whom is said to have been martyred, with her brother Uni and with Gwythian, near St. Ives Bay.   Yet as to Piran see Haddan and Stubbs, i. 164.

[2] For Gildas see Lingard, A.-S. Ch. i. 356; Lappenberg, i. 123; Haddan and Stubbs, i. 156; Pearson, Vindic. Ignat. i. 79.   He seems to have written in 564, if we interpret a confusedly written sentence in c. 26 as meaning that he wrote in the 44th year after the battle of Badon Hill (p. 25), which was fought in the year of his own birth.   He is called Gildas the Wise, or Gildas Badonicus; see Alb. Butler, Jan. 29.

[3] Gild. 26; Bede, i. 22.   'Attamen recente adhuc memoria,' &c.   Compare St. Patrick's denunciation of Coroticus (Ceredig, who gave his name to Cardigan), who, professing Christianity, had committed unchristian cruelties in Ireland, and might be supposed to despise Irish Christianity (Ep. ad Christianos Coroti [tyranni subditos).

[4] Constantine of Devon and Cornwall. Gild. 28.   Yet he became 'St. Constantine,' having 'turned to the Lord in 589;' Ann. Camb., and see Bp. Forbes, Kalendars, p. 312, and Bp. Jones and Freeman, p. 244.

[5] Aurelius Conanus, of Powys; Gild. 30.

[6] Vortipor of Demetia, the west part of South Wales; Gild. 31.

[7] Cuneglas; Gild. 32.

[8] King of Gywnedd or North Wales; a man of great force, mostly for evil. Gildas reproaches him for his backsliding; 35.   He endured patiently a curse from Taliessin; Williams, Eccl. Ant. Cym. p. 128.   He combined sensuality and tyranny with moods of fervid devotion.

[9] Gildas begins this ' increpatio,' ' Britain has priests, but they are foolish.'

of pastoral exhortation, and even of the decencies of priestly
life ; simony was rife among priests and bishops[1] (it is evident
that a bishopric was still a well-endowed office[2]); and even
those who lived respectably were careless or cowardly in
regard to rebuking sin[3]. Gildas may have carried the
vehement ' reproaches,' which characterise his ' book of
Complaints[4],' to a point beyond equitable and discriminating
rebuke ; they provoke some incredulity by their very violence ;
but they cannot be without some serious foundation. We
learn from him incidentally, not only that the hierarchy was
regularly organised, that the ' priests' claimed power to bind
and to loose, and that bishops were believed to succeed the
Apostles[5], and indeed to sit in the chair of Peter[6] (a significant phrase when used for *any* bishop's office), but that
the hands of priests and inferior ministers were anointed[7],
and certain lessons, from the Epistles and from the Acts, were
read at ordination[8]. That the British ritual had a special
character, distinct not only from the Roman, but also from
the Gallican, has been inferred from a curious document of

See Lingard, A.-S. Ch. i. 13, 359. Gildas owns that there are a few good
pastors, 110, and that he prefers their lives ' cunctis mundi opibus ;' 65.

[1] He speaks of bad men attempting to cover their evil reputation by thus
purchasing ecclesiastical dignity. Some, if public opinion condemned them,
would travel abroad, and return in stately array ; 67. Columban refers to this
language of ' Giltas,' ap. Greg. Ep. ix. 127.

[2] ' Vos episcopatum . . . . avaritiæ gratia . . . cupitis ;' Gild. 108 ; see
ib. 67, ' tam pretiosum quæstum.'

[3] He cites Eli ; ' Quid profuit Heli sacerdoti,' &c., 69.

[4] De excidio Britanniæ Liber Querulus. Comp. Bede, i. 22, ' flebilis sermo.'
He says that he had refrained for ten years from writing, but his indignation
at the sins of his countrymen could no longer be suppressed. It is divided
into the ' Historia ' and the ' Epistola' (Mon. H. Brit.), which is subdivided
into the ' increpatio in reges' (described by Gallandius, Bibl. Patr. xii. 200, as
the ' Epistola' proper) and that ' in clerum.'

[5] Increp. in Cler. 66, 92, 108, 109.

[6] ' Sedem Petri Apostoli immundis pedibus usurpantes ;' 66. Compare
Lib. Landav. p. 18. This way of speaking carries out the old idea that St.
Peter was (not the ruler, but) the representative, of the other Apostles, and
in them of their successors the bishops. See Transl. of St. Cypr. in Lib.
Fath. vol. i. p. 150. Gildas also takes Matt. xvi. 18 as ' said to the true
priest.'

[7] Gild., 106, ' initiantur sacerdotum vel ministrorum manus.' See Haddan
and Stubbs, Councils, i. 141.

[8] 1 Peter i. 3-5, 13-16, 22, 23, ii. 1-3, 9 ; Acts i. 15 ff. ; 1 Tim. iii. 1 ff.

the eighth century, which traces the 'Scotic' Liturgy through German and Lupus to St. Mark, the Gallic through St. Irenæus to St. John[1]. But the statement, which has some wild errors of detail, really says nothing about the original British use, which was apparently identical with the Gallican; nor is it probable that German materially altered the use which he found in Britain. The peculiarities of the British and Irish—then called Scottish—Churches, in regard to the calculation of Easter and one or two points of ceremonial, will come before us hereafter.

One is almost led to think that Gildas' bitter complaints were effective; for there was certainly a burst of religious activity in the Welsh Church during a large part of the sixth century, although that activity did not involve any attempt to evangelise the detested and dreaded Saxons[2]. Colleges or monasteries did much for study and devotion,— usually bearing the name of *Bangor*[3], that is 'high choir' or 'circle,' or eminent community. One of these was the famous

[1] This document affirms that (1) John the Evangelist first sang the 'Cursus Gallorum:' from him it came to Lyons: in time it was enlarged and widely diffused: (2) according to St. Jerome, St. Mark first sang the 'cursus' now called Scotic,—and after him Gregory Nazianzen (!), then Cassian, and Honoratus of Lerins, and German and Lupus, who preached in Britain and appointed Patrick archbishop in Britain and Ireland, who sang the same course,—as did Comgall and Columban; 'and if you do not believe us, search in the life of blessed Columban.' See Haddan and Stubbs, i. 139. Palmer thinks that the writer is not referring to the *British* Liturgy as such; that this Liturgy was essentially Gallican; that, before Patrick's time, Irish Christians had a similar use; that for some time after Patrick, the Roman use prevailed in Ireland, but that a different use was introduced by means of David, Gildas, and Cadoc; Orig. Lit. i. 178 ff. Bp. Forbes infers from early Irish liturgical remains that, so far as we can learn, the earliest Liturgy 'used in these islands was Ephesine,' i. e. Gallican; Preface to Arbuthnott Missal, p. x. Cp. Warren, Liturgy and Ritual of Celtic Church, p. 61.

[2] Bede, i. 22; 'addebant ... ut nunquam genti Saxonum ... verbum fidei prædicando committerent.' See Stubbs, Const. Hist. i. 252. Archdeacon Pryce pleads that 'the merciless policy of the invaders' would have made such an enterprise hopeless; Anc. Brit. Ch. p. 113. Yet see Green, Making of England, p. 90, on the long 'inaction' of the West Saxons after their defeat at Badbury, A.D. 520–552. The point is, not that much was not done, but that nothing was attempted.

[3] For the great Irish 'Bangor,' near Carrickfergus, founded by St. Comgall about 559, see Lanigan, Eccl. Hist. Irel. ii. 62. Glastonbury was sometimes called Bangor Wydrin; Williams, Eccl. Ant. Cym. p. 212.

Bangor 'Iscoed,' founded by Dunawd, or Dunod, and his three
sons, in the south-east corner of Flintshire, for a community
which was said to contain more than two thousand monks at
the time of its sudden and total destruction [1]. Another was
the Bangor still known as such, of which Daniel was the first
head [2], at once abbot and bishop, a combination not unfrequent
in Celtic churches [3]. Another Bangor was our St. Asaph, or
Llan Elwy, said to have been founded under the direction of
Kentigern [4], the famous bishop of Glasgow, surnamed Munghu
(kind and dear), the teacher and friend of Asaph [5]. Another
celebrated house, to which a fabulous antiquity was ascribed [6],
flourished at Caer Worgorn, and had for its president Illtyd,
who is said to have taught his scholars 'all the arts' then
current, and from whom the place takes its present name of
Llantwit Major. Besides these there were St. Cadoc's [7]
college at Llancarfan ;—the White House, or Whitland, in
Carmarthenshire, founded by Paulinus or Paul Hên [8];—and

[1] Bede, ii. 2. Iscoed = underwood. This house was called also 'the great
Bangor in' (the district of) 'Maclor.' See Chron. Anc. Brit. Ch. p. 162 ;
Rees, Welsh Saints, pp. 206, 259. It was said to be occupied by seven classes
of monks, each containing 300 men. See Raine, Fast. Ebor. i. 13 ; Pryce,
Anc. Brit. Ch. pp. 176, 184.

[2] He is said to have died in 584 (Annal. Camb.). His house was called
'the great Bangor over Conway ;' Chron. Anc. Brit. Ch. p. 81 ; Pryce, p. 146.
He ranks as 'one of the three blessed youth-trainers of Britain.'

[3] Haddan and Stubbs, i. 142 ; Chron. of Brit. Ch. pp. 83, 127 ; Todd, St.
Patrick, p. 27.

[4] According to the legend, a North Welsh king, probably Maelgwyn, gave
Kentigern the ground by the Elwy. 'Men of all ages and ranks pressed into
"the monastery," to the number of 965 ;' Bp. Forbes, Kalendars of Scottish
Saints, p. 368. Kentigern, on his way into Wales, appears to have 'turned
aside' to evangelize parts of Cumberland where heathenism still lingered, and
to have erected a cross at 'Crosfeld' or Crosthwaite. Bp. Forbes, Lives of
SS. Ninian and Kentigern, p. lxxxiii, names eight Cumbrian churches as dedicated to him.

[5] 'They who withstand God's word,' said Asaph, 'envy man's salvation.'

[6] It was called Cor Tewdws, as founded by Theodosius I. or II (!). See
Rees, p. 128. On Iltutus, 'the knight,' 'the excellent master,' see Alb.
Butler, Nov. 6 ; Smith's Bede, p. 724 ; Rees, p. 180 ; Williams, p. 132 ; Pryce,
Anc. Brit. Ch. p. 182.

[7] Rees, p. 142 ; Chron. Anc. Brit. Ch. p. 81 ; Williams, p. 219 ; Pryce, p.
182. Cadoc, or Cattwg, called the Wise, is said to have resigned a princely
heritage for the sake of a religious life.

[8] Bangor y Ty-Gwyn. 'Alba Domus,' Girald. Itin. Camb. i. 10 ; Pryce,

the great college of Llanbadarn-faur, founded by a Breton named Padarn, the first of a line of bishops that sat within its precinct[1], where one of the most venerable churches in the Principality still attracts English visitors from the neighbouring Aberystwyth. We also read of Welsh synods; one at Llanddewi-Brefi, in Cardiganshire, which has been erroneously supposed to have renewed the defeat of Pelagianism[2]; another, which from a similar error was called 'the Synod of Victory[3],' and is dated by the Cambrian Annals in 569; it was properly the Synod of the *Wood* of Victory, being held on the site of a defeat of Romans. Canons 'preserved in the north of France, obviously through Brittany,'—the old Armorica now acquiring that name as the refuge of Britons[4],—are probably to be assigned to these assemblies: one of these enactments is suggestive, for it fixes the penance of 'a Christian who has acted as guide to the barbarians[5].' We find the Welsh Church receiving Irish disciples, such as Finnian of Clonard, and thus promoting a revival of religious devotion in their country.

p. 181. David, and Teilo the second bishop of Llandaff, are said to have studied under Paulinus. The latter's epitaph exists in Carmarthenshire; Haddan and Stubbs, i. 164; Hübner, No. 82 ('Servator fidei . . cultor pientissimus æqui,' &c.).

[1] He sat there for twenty-one years, and afterwards returned to Armorica; thence went to the Franks, among whom he died. He is said to have twice excommunicated the king of Gwent; Pryce, p. 165. See Haddan and Stubbs, i. 145. One of his disciples was Avan, who was bishop of Llanafanfaur; ib. 146, 166. On that church see Girald. Itin. Camb. i. 1. The last bishop of Llanbadarnfaur, Idnerth, was slain by his people (Bp. Jones and Freeman, p. 266) in the eighth century.

[2] This is obviously a 'reverberation' of the proceedings of German. (I owe this expression to the present Bishop of St. David's, formerly its historian.) The date sometimes given, 519, is much too early: see it in Mansi, viii. 583, where Giraldus' account is cited—how Daniel and Dubricius induced David to attend the synod, when attempts to convert the Pelagians had failed; how David, though standing on level ground, made himself heard by the whole assembly; how the ground beneath him rose into a hill, on which afterwards a church was built in his honour; how the heresy utterly vanished; how David succeeds Dubricius as archbishop of all Cambria (having been previously consecrated at Jerusalem), and removes the archbishopric to Menevia. Giraldus (Rolls Series), iii. 399, &c.

[3] Giraldus, De Vit. Dav. 9 (iii. 401), and Itin. Camb. ii. 4 (vi. 120). He calls it a synod of bishops, abbots, and all the clergy, 'una cum populo.'

[4] Among the Britons who became saints of Armorica were Maclovius or 'St. Malo,' the Machutus of our calendar, and Sampson of Dol.

[5] Haddan and Stubbs, i. 116-118.

Gildas himself crossed the Irish sea in order to aid in this
work, and died in Ireland in 570[1]: and the great Irish-born
missionary St. Columba directed a criminal who professed
contrition to spend twelve years in penance among the
Britons[2]. Finally, among the eminent Cymric bishops[3] of
this period, beside those who have been mentioned, two stand
out as typical, Dubricius or Dyfrig, whom the church of
Llandaff, in its renovated beauty, owns as its first bishop[4],—
who lived on through twelve years of the seventh century
and died in retirement in the sacred isle of Bardsey[5]: and he
whose late and extravagant legend[6] is in such strange contrast
to the little that can be ascertained about his life,—the
national saint of Wales, Dewi or David. His time, like that St. David
of Dubricius and others, has been antedated, for the sake of
connecting him with the days of King Arthur[7]: he seems

[1] The Irish saints who had come under the influence of David, Cadoc, and
Gildas, were called those of ' the second order.'

[2] Adamnan, Vit. S. Columb. i. 22.

[3] The reverence of the Welsh for their sainted bishops appeared, as otherwise, so in their regarding an oath on a saint's handbell, or pastoral staff, as
more sacred than on the Gospels ; Girald. Itin. Camb. i. 2.

[4] See Monast. Angl. vi. p. 1217 ff.; Haddan and Stubbs, i. 158; Pryce,
Anc. Brit. Ch. p. 160. The second bishop, after his resignation, was Teliau or
Teilo, who, according to the legend, was the pupil of Dyfrig and the friend of
David, and, after sitting as bishop at Llandaff, spent some years in Armorica,
and then returning, held Menevia with Llandaff (see Lib. Landav. p. 92).
The third was Oudoceus, said to have excommunicated King Mouric for
perjury and murder, in a synod of all his clergy, including three abbots ; Mon.
Angl. vi. 1223. Such synods are repeatedly mentioned in these documents.
St. Teilo's shrine remains near the sedilia at Llandaff.

[5] Annal. Camb. a. 612. Benedict of Gloucester, his biographer, dates his
death Nov. 14, 612 ; Wharton, Angl. Sac. ii. 661. But the Llandaff story
was that his body was removed to Llandaff in 1120. In Bardsey, or Ynys
Enlli, says Giraldus, ' ut fertur, infinita sanctorum sepulta sunt corpora ; ' Itin.
Camb. ii. c. 6. Legend reckoned them as 20,000 ; Liber Landav. p. 2. It
was called the Rome of Wales ; ib. p. 1 ; cp. Pryce, p. 181.

[6] See it in Bp. Jones and Freeman, p. 241 ; Rees, Welsh Saints, p. 194 ;
Pryce, p. 129.

[7] In Geoffrey's romance Dubricius addresses Arthur's army, crowns him,
resigns the archbishopric of Caerleon. The author of ' Chronicles of Anc.
Brit. Church' makes Dyfrig, first, bishop of Llandaff, and secondly, in 490,
archbishop of Caerleon ; p. 115. See too the uncritical account in Williams,
Antiq. of Cymry, p. 130. The Liber Landavensis extends his life beyond
a century and a half. Geoffrey tells how David succeeded Dubricius at
Caerleon, and died at Menevia, viii. 1 ; the early and fictitious date for his

to have taken part in the synod of Llanddewi, and certainly
established an episcopal seat at Kilmuine or Mynyw, better
known as Menevia, that remotest extremity of South Wales
where now the cathedral that bears his name presents so
unique and pathetic a combination of indefeasible majesty and
irreversible decay.   He appears to have died in 601 [1].   The
stories about a regular Welsh archbishopric, held at first by
Dubricius, and then transferred by David to Menevia, are
without foundation: the Welsh Church of that age had no
metropolitans [2], and the tale about St. Sampson of Dol in
Brittany, which represented him as having been archbishop at
York [3], and then at Menevia, is a myth of yet later date: the
fact being simply that he was consecrated in Wales, and
thence proceeded to Armorica, and sat in a Council of Paris in
557 [4].   Setting aside such fancies, it is worth while to observe
how the situation of St. David's illustrates the fact that these
old Celtic bishops valued monastic seclusion even more than
facilities for episcopal administration [5].

One of Geoffrey's statements as to the prelates of Teuton-

---

death is 544.   Montalembert in both cases follows the legend; see his 'Monks
of the West.'   The most picturesque story about him is that of the 'Evan-
gelium Imperfectum;' that he was copying St. John's Gospel, left his
work on hearing the church bell, at his return found the page completed in
gold letters, and out of reverence added nothing to the copy; Girald. Op.
iii. 393.

[1] Annal. Camb. (written some 200 years later).   In Giraldus Cambrensis'
Life of him (Works, iii. 403), he is said to have had, when dying, a vision of
Christ, and to have expired saying, 'Lord, take me up after Thee!'   A yet
later date for his death is 642.   He is said to have been succeeded by Teilo
(Girald. Itin. Camb. ii. 1), or by Cynog, or by Ismael (Lib. Landav. p. 109).

[2] Haddan and Stubbs, i. 148; Bp. Jones and Freeman, p. 253.   The story
was that Teilo, on becoming archbishop of Menevia, transferred the primacy to
Llandaff; see Rees, p. 243.   See, however, his remarks on p. 291.

[3] Geoffrey, vii. 3 (ix. 8), makes Arthur see with grief the ruin of religion at
York, after the Saxons had driven out 'blessed Sampson the archbishop.'   This
fictitious connection of Sampson with York is ignored by Alb. Butler (July 28);
nor does it appear in the Liber Landavensis.   Giraldus makes him twenty-fifth
archbishop of St. David's, and tells the story about his removal of the pall to
Dol; Itin. Camb. ii. 1.   (Op. vi. 102.)

[4] Mansi, ix. 747.   See Haddan and Stubbs, i. 149, 159.

[5] Bp. Jones and Freeman, p. 251.   Caerleon, says Giraldus, was 'far more
fitted for a metropolitan see than this angulus remotissimus, terra saxosa,
sterilis, infecunda: it was of set purpose that saints chose such abodes,—much
preferring the eremitic to the pastoral life;' Itin. Camb. ii. 1.

ised Britain may represent a modicum of fact. He says[1] that CHAP. I.
when the Saxons drove the British fugitives into Wales and
Cornwall, Theon bishop of London, and Thadioc of York, fled
into Wales with the 'archbishop' of Caerleon and their surviving clergy. This he dates in the latter part of the sixth
century. But if London fell soon after the middle of the
century, while Deira had been conquered soon after its commencement, these prelates can hardly have been companions
in flight. However, we know that in the latter part of
the seventh century there was a clear tradition as to the
names of 'sacred places abandoned by the British clergy'
of the North country (except in 'Elmete') when they
'fled from the sword' of the conquering race[2]. If this
was so, when we think of what the Divine mercy was preparing at this time for a country bereft of pastors and even
of flocks, we may observe a new verification of the devout
proverb, that man's necessity is God's opportunity. It did, Christi-anity ruined in most of South Britain.
indeed, seem as if Heathenism had fairly beaten down Chris-
tianity in the largest portion of South Britain: the East-
Anglians, and the settlers in the Lichfield and Repton district
who were called Mercians, as dwelling near the Welsh border
or march[3], had been forming themselves into regular kingdoms: the West Saxon Ceawlin's defeat at Wodensburg, or
Wanborough, in 591, soon followed by his death, was indeed
the aggrandisement of his revolted nephew[4]. But it was
more. It opened the way to supremacy for a prince who,
twenty three years earlier, had been checked by Ceawlin in

---

[1] Geoffrey, viii. 2. See Stubbs, Registrum Sac. Angl. p. 152. The traditional date is 586. For the fall of London, see Green, Making of England,
p. 110.

[2] Eddius, Vit. S. Wilfridi, 17. See Chaucer, 'Tale of the Man of
Lawe':—
> 'To Walys fled the cristianitee
> Of olde Britons, dwelling in this ile.'

[3] Green, p. 15 : see Palgrave, Anglo-Sax. p. 45 ; Freeman, i. 26 ; Pearson, i.
106. The Mid-Anglians, as far as they are distinct from the Mercians, dwelt
eastwards towards Leicester.

[4] Sax. Chr. and Florence. Hen. Huntingdon's account of the battle of
Wodensburgh, 'God gave the victory to the Britons,' is explained by the fact
that Britons, and even Scots, were allied with Ceolric the 'Hwiccian,' against
his uncle Ceawlin. See Palgrave, p. 404 ; Guest's Orig. Celt. ii 243 ; Green,
Making of England, p. 207.

CHAP. I. his attempt to extend his realm. That victory on the Berkshire downs was momentous, for it helped Ethelbert of Kent, who had recently espoused a Frankish princess, to become the overlord of East Saxony and East Angles. North of Humber, indeed, he had no ascendency; Edwin, the child of Ella, had been dispossessed, after his father's death, by the king of Bernicia[1], Ethelric, who was succeeded within five years by his son, a prince of equal energy, and known by the appellations of 'the Fierce[2]' and 'the Devastator[3],' that Ethelfrid, properly Æthelfrith, whom Bede describes as, like Benjamin, a ravening wolf, and of whom he says that no other Anglian chief wrought such havoc among the race of Britons[4]. Every one of these rulers and nations was bound by habit and tradition to the old Teutonic Paganism; it might even seem that their very successes had hardened them in antipathy to the religion of the Cross: was it to be expected, under these conditions, that ministers of that religion, foreign to conquerors and conquered alike, could appeal to such a people and be heard? Yes, it was the hope and the faith of the greatest Christian of that time: and to his action, in the strength of such hope and faith, we owe the beginnings of our English Christianity.

[1] Florence, Chron.
[2] Hen. Hunt. a. 593.
[3] 'Flesaur,' in Nennius, = Devastator.
[4] Bede, i. 34; Palgrave, Engl. Comm. p. 428.

CHAPTER II.

'GREGORY our father[1],' who 'sent us baptism[2];' such were Gregory the Great. the terms of simple and grateful affection in which the early English Christians spoke of that greatest and most loveable[3] of Roman bishops, whose pontificate extended from 590 to 604. The fatherly title was signally appropriate to a character so rich in tenderness and so profuse in energetic charity. He who, unlike 'other pontiffs,' spent yet more on the poor than on the building of churches[4]; he who once debarred himself from celebrating the Eucharist, because a poor man had been starved to death in a great scarcity[5]; he whose correspondence with distant friends overflows with such vivid consciousness of a oneness which no distance could affect[6]; he whose thoughtful and discriminating sympathy gave directions that a sick cleric was not to lose his stipend[7], forbade a prelate in bad health to keep fast or vigil[8], remitted the Church's claim on the property of three orphans[9], and provided bedding for the pilgrims of Mount Sinai[10], and a yearly allowance of wheat and beans for a man with bad eyesight[11], was just the man to unite this natural and genial

---

[1] Council of Clovesho, A. D. 747; Haddan and Stubbs, iii. 368.

[2] A.-S. Chr. a. 565. Compare Aldhelm, de Laude Virginitatis, 55: 'Gregorius . . . pædagogus noster, noster, inquam, qui nostris parentibus . . . regenerantis gratiæ normam tradidit.'

[3] See Robertson's Growth of the Papal Power, p. 115: 'Gregory stands in the foremost rank of Popes who have contributed to the exaltation of their see . . . He is the only one of those Popes whose memory we can regard with much affection.'

[4] Paul the Deacon's Life of Greg. c. 16.

[5] John the Deacon's Life of Greg. ii. 29. See Gibbon, v. 362.

[6] Greg. Ep. i. 66; iii. 48, 54; vi. 60; viii. 2; xii. 1.   [7] Ep. ii. 8.

[8] Ep. xi. 33. Gregory offered to tend him personally.

[9] Ep. iii. 21. Compare a remission of money due from an old man, if found to be poor, Ep. xii. 9.

[10] Ep. xi. 1.   [11] Ep. i. 67.

CHAP. II. kindness with that Christian love for souls, so fervent as an emotion and so vigorous as a motive, which betokens and crowns the genuine pastor.

Story of the English boys.   We all know the immortal story of the origin of his interest in our heathen ancestors, and therefore of that work which he did for England, and which made Bede say with such loving emphasis, 'Though he be not an apostle to others, yet he is to us, for the seal of his apostleship are we in the Lord[1].' It was either shortly before 578, when he went as the Pope's confidential agent[2] to Constantinople, or soon after his return in 585[3], that Gregory, then a deacon, passing through the Roman market, saw some[4] boys exposed for sale. The traffic in slaves was rife at this time, and indeed long afterwards: the spirit of that creed which acknowledged all to be one in God and in Christ had not yet undermined the inveterate usage which treated human beings as capable, under certain circumstances, of becoming lawful property: canons of councils had freely owned the right of Christian laymen, even of clergy or monks, to possess bondsmen[5]: to emancipate one's slave was an act of benefice, but beyond that point Church teaching did not go. Gregory was among those Church teachers who did much to abate the evils of slavery, and in that sense to prepare for its extinction[6]: he, as Pope, sold sacred vessels to

---

[1] Bede, ii. 1. So in the coronation office of king Ethelred: 'Sanctæ Mariæ ac beati Petri Sanctique Gregorii Anglorum Apostoli ... meritis.' Maskell, Mon. Rit. ii. 36.

[2] 'Apocrisiarius.' Benedict I. was Pope 574–578, Pelagius II. 578–590. Gregory was at Constantinople from 578 to 585, under Pelagius.

[3] Paul, c. 19, gives the later date; 'apostolico Pelagio.' John, i. 22, gives the earlier; 'ad Benedictum.' So does the earlier 'Life' edited by Ewald from a MS. at St. Gallen, Eng. Hist. Review, iii. 301. So the Benedictine biographers, b. i. 4. 5. Gregory became a monk cir. 575, deacon in 577, abbot in 585, pope on Sept. 3, 590, *not* 591, as Bede implies (i. 23). Gregory's predecessor, Pelagius II., died Feb. 8, 590, and the day of his own accession was Sept. 3, which fell on a Sunday in 590. For the year 590 see the Benedictine Life, L'Art de Vérifier, iii. 277, &c. It is adopted by modern writers.

[4] Thorn says *three*.

[5] E. g. Council of Agde, c. 7, 56; first of Orleans, c. 3. Comp. Greg. Ep. iii. 1; v. 34.

[6] See Milman, Lat. Chr. ii. 47, 52; Hist. Jews, iii. 48. On the three ways in which Christianity acted in this direction, see Lecky, Europ. Morals, ii. 70.

ransom captives[1], and in an act of manumission declared that,
'since the Redeemer had become incarnate to set men free, it
was a good thing to restore to their natural freedom those
whom the law of nations had deprived of it[2].' Let us try to
picture him, with his ruddy face, scanty darkish hair, kindly
look, and beautiful hands[3], as he stands still, attracted by the
sad sight of those helpless lads, whose white skin[4] and golden
hair were proof enough of their Northern parentage, and were
associated with a beauty of face which their unhappy condition would make all the more touching. He who, in after
years, used to take pains with the teaching of his young
choristers[5], was moved to the very soul with pity for the
slave boys, and asked from what country they came. The
slave-owner—probably a Jew[6]—answered, 'From Britain :
the people there have these fair complexions.' Then came
the question, as from Gregory's full heart, 'Are they heathens
or Christians[7]?' 'Heathens.' He sighed, as a servant of Christ
might well sigh : 'Alas! that such bright faces should be in
the power of the prince of darkness—that with outward forms
so lovely, the mind within should be sick[8] and empty of
grace! How do you call their nation?' 'Angles.' Then,

[1] See Ep. vii. 13, 38. Compare St. Ambrose, de Offic. Ministr. ii. 28, and
Acacius in Soc. vii. 21. See Bingham, v. 6. 6.

[2] Ep. vi. 12. Comp. Greg. Reg. Pastoral. iii. 5 : masters are to be admonished ' ut naturæ suæ, qua æqualiter sunt cum servis conditi, memoriam non
amittant.' See the expressions of Old-English feeling on this point in Pref. to
Chron. of Abingdon, vol. ii. p. lii.

[3] John the Deacon's Life of Greg. iv. 84. From Ep. xi. 44 he would seem
to have been stout, until the gout brought him low. See Barmby's Gregory
the Great, p. 142.

[4] Paul, 17 : 'Lactei corporis, ac venusti vultus, capillos præcipui candoris,'—
shining sunny hair. John, i. 21 : ' corpore candidos, forma pulcherrimos,
vultu venustos, capillorum quoque nitore perspicuos.' Bede, earlier than both,
has, ' candidi corporis et venusti vultus, capillorum quoque forma egregia ;' ii. 1.
The St. Gallen Life, ' forma et crinibus candidati.'

[5] Joan. Diac. ii. 6.

[6] Milman, Hist. Jews, iii. 48. Cp. Greg. Ep. ix. 36, that Jews bought
Christian slaves from Gaul, and a Jew explained to him that the magistrates
ordered them to buy slaves. In Ep. iii. 38 he exhorts a prefect to set free
slaves bought by a Jew.

[7] Ethelwerd, in his Chronicle, ii. 1, gives a corrupt version of this colloquy,
making Gregory address the young Angles, who answer that no one has opened
their ears to Christianity.

[8] Paul. Diac. Bede omits ' ægram.'

with that fondness for playing on the sound of a name, with a serious thought under the playfulness[1], which we see in Eusebius[2], and also in Bede himself[3], he replied, ''Tis well,—they have Angels' faces; it were meet they should be fellow-heirs with Angels in heaven. What is their native province?' 'Deira;' we might translate, Yorkshire,—for the southern of the two Northumbrian realms may for practical purposes be identified with the land between the Tees and Humber: and Gregory's ear, catching its name, suggested the comment, 'They must be rescued *de ira Dei.*' One more question: who was their king? 'Aella[4].' 'Alleluia, praise to God the Maker, ought to be sung in those parts.' He passed on, and saw the boys no more; but the thought of their nation's spiritual need impelled him to wring from the Pope—either Benedict I. or Pelagius II.—a permission to go and preach to the Angles. But this was not to be: the Romans beset the Pope with outcries, demanding the recall of Gregory[5]; and Gregory was recalled, and obeyed. A few years—perhaps only two or three—elapsed, and he himself occupied the see, being then just fifty years old[6]. He was at once immersed in business of all kinds; troubles caused by Donatism in Africa, a schism in Istria on the question of the 'Three Articles,' heresy vexing Eastern Christendom, practical corruptions tainting the Gallic Church, pestilence in Rome, Lombards even encamping before its walls, vexations connected with the see of Ravenna and other churches, a dispute with the Emperor Maurice, a more famous controversy with John bishop of Constantinople as to the title of Œcumenical

---

[1] 'Rhetorice ethimologizans,' Thorn, in X Script. 1757.

[2] Euseb. v. 24, *Irenæus*; vi. 41, *Macar*; vii. 10, *Macrianus*; vii. 31, *Manes.* Two of these passages are quotations.

[3] Bede, ii. 15, *Felix.* So in his Life of St. Felix of Nola, c. 1: 'nominis sui mysterium factis exsequens.' So Columban in his letter to Gregory, 'Tua Vigilantia;' Greg. Ep. ix. 127. So Columba on Libranus, Adamnan, ii. 39; and St. Augustine on Pelagius in De Orat. Chr. 45; and St. Athanasius on Hosius in Hist. Ari. 49.

[4] Ella died in 588. He appears as 'Alla' in Chaucer's 'Man of Law's Tale.'

[5] John puts their outcry into a jingle: 'Petrum offendisti, Romam destruxisti, quia Gregorium dimisisti;' i. 23, abridged from Paul.

[6] He was probably born in 540; Bened. Life, i. 1. 6; Barmby, p. 29.

Patriarch[1] : he had also literary work, the composition of his CHAP. II. Pastoral Care, the compilation of his Sacramentary, and other such designs to be carried out, beside his preaching and other pastoral duties. Yet we may well believe that he never lost the remembrance of those 'bright faces' of the Yorkshire lads in the slave-market : and at last, in 596, he took some steps towards an English mission by ordering the steward of his church's estates in Gaul to spend some of their proceeds in purchasing boys of seventeen or eighteen, of English birth, that they might receive a Christian education[2]. But immediately afterwards he resolved on more direct action. He had founded in 575 a monastery, dedicated to St. Andrew, on his own estate on the Coelian hill, and had lived there as monk and as abbot[3]. He still retained the abbatial care for this long-loved home, within whose precincts he had been so happy, but had also, we must confess it, on one occasion shown towards a monk who had broken the rule a relentless severity, the effect of monastic rigorism prevailing over his natural kindness of heart[4]. In the monastery the officer next to the abbot was called the 'præpositus' or provost[5]. Gregory in one passage says that an abbot's negligence must be remedied by means of a vigilant 'præpositus[6] :' we hear of one Pretiosus as his 'præpositus' at the time just referred to[7] : and at the period which we have reached the office was held by Augustine, who had once been a pupil of

---

[1] See below, p. 65.

[2] Ep. vi. 7, to Candidus. Cp. Hardwick, Ch. Hist., M. Ages, p. 111, on a similar scheme as carried out by St. Anskar.

[3] John the Deacon, i. 6: cp. Paul, c. 4. The site of the monastery was 'ad clivum Scauri.' 'There exist no documents from which we may learn what were the peculiar enactments' of the rule established in Gregory's monastery, nor 'the points wherein it differed from other rules;' Lingard, A.-S. Ch. i. 199.

[4] Dial. iv. 55. Milman, Lat. Chr. ii. 104, gives the story as the most signal case of such austerity, or rather pitiless harshness, on the part of Gregory. Yet see Barmby, p. 38.

[5] So in Benedict. Reg. 65. 'Præpositi' appear in the Life of St. Columba, Adamn. i. 30, 31. In Columban's Rule, c. 10, penance is assigned to a monk who says to the præpositus, 'Tu non judicabis causam meam, sed noster abbas,' &c. Boisil was 'præpositus' of Melrose under Eata as abbot; Bede, iv. 27, v. 9. The word 'prior' would best express 'præpositus.'

[6] Ep. v. 6. Cp. Dial. i. 2, 7.

[7] John, l. c.

CHAP. II.
Mission of
Augustine
and his
compan-
ions.
Felix bishop of Messana[1]. Gregory selected him[2], and several others of the house, to undertake a mission to the English. Probably, with his 'wonderful capacity for business, his wide, various, and minute supervision[3],' which seemed to sweep the whole area of Christendom, from the internal troubles of African Churches to a local feud in Jerusalem and the griev-ances of a priest of Lycaonia[4], and which caused one of his biographers to call him an 'Argus full of eyes[5],' he had pro-cured information as to the state of the English which showed that the native district of the 'angel-faced' boys was no

promising mission-field while Ethelfrid ruled over it, and on the other hand that the part of Britain most accessible from the continent was precisely that which seemed to offer an 'open door.' For Ethelbert, properly Æthelberht[6], king of the Jutish realm of Kent, who now, after thirty years of royalty, stood preeminent[7] among the South-Humbrian princes, might be supposed likely to give a favourable hearing to preachers of the religion professed by his wife. Bertha, daughter of a former Frankish king, Charibert of Paris, had been long before espoused by Ethelbert on the express condition that she should be free to worship as a Christian, under the guidance of a Frankish bishop, Liudhard[8]. This condition had been observed: Liudhard resided in Kent, and while 'Bertha had made no attempt to convert' her Pagan husband[9], he had never disturbed his wife

[1] See Greg. Ep. xiv. 17, 'alumno tuo.' Felix calls him 'consodalis.'

[2] Augustine was afterwards (by Leo III.) described as holding the office of *syncellus*, or companion in the cell or private room, to Gregory; Haddan and Stubbs, iii. 539; and cp. can. 22 and 23 of fourth Council of Toledo, Mansi, x. 626. See Fleury, b. 25 c. 5 (Oxford ed. vol. iii. p. 13).

[3] Robertson, ii. 371; cp. Milman, Lat. Chr. ii. 112.

[4] Ep. i. 77; vii. 32; vi. 66.

[5] John, ii. 55.

[6] Albert, as Dean Stanley observes (Mem. Cant. p. 31), is but this name abbreviated (Ethelbert = Adalbert).

[7] Bede, ii. 5. On the leadership or primacy which has been associated with the title of Bretwalda, cp. the somewhat differing views in Kemble, Sax. in Engl. ii. 11, Freeman, i. 548, and Green, Making of England, p. 307; and see Stubbs, Constit. Hist. i. 190 (or 162, ed. 1).

[8] 'Quam ea conditione a parentibus acceperat,' &c.; Bede, i. 25. See Greg. Turon. Hist. Fr. iv. 26, 'filiam quæ postea in Cantiam, virum accipiens, est deducta.' Charibert (Haribert) died in 567.

[9] Lingard, A.-S. Ch. i. 23.

in regard to her Christian duties. This, probably, the Pope had learned; and he himself declares that he had been informed of a desire on the part of the English for Christian instruction, and reprobates the neglect of the Gallic bishops to impart it[1]. He could, indeed, have had but an imperfect idea of the complexities of the political condition of Britain, or of the difficulties which it would offer to a missionary: yet had he known more, he would still have acted in faith, and sent forth his agents in the all-sustaining Name.

And so, apparently in the spring of 596, they went forth, obedient and hopeful, and 'got through some small part of their journey.' So Bede tells us[2]; in fact, they had reached Provence, and probably rested in that illustrious monastery which for nearly two centuries had made the name of the isle of Lerins[3] sacred and venerable to all who had heard of its discipline and its devotion, and of the light of sacred learning there kept alive in a country dark with spreading ignorance, and darker yet with stormy crime. Stephen abbot of Lerins, as well as Protasius bishop of Aix and the 'patrician' or provincial governor[4] Arigius, welcomed the strangers heartily. But they also heard more than they had dreamt of as to the hard fierce nature of the Saxons, and began to realise the obstacle involved in their ignorance of the Saxon tongue[5]. With somewhat of the weakness shown by St. Mark after he landed in Pamphylia[6],

---

[1] Greg. Ep. vi. 58, 59.

[2] Bede, i. 23. He dates their journey in the fourteenth year of Maurice, which began August 13, 595. Haddan and Stubbs, iii. 3, Robertson, ii. 387, and Moberly (on Bede, l. c.) think that they set out in 595. But Gregory's letter sent back with Augustine is dated on July 23 in that fourteenth year; i.e. in 596. It is not likely that the voyage to Provence, a short sojourn there, and Augustine's return voyage, would occupy more time than between the early spring and the middle of July of that year. The Benedictines date the first journey in 596: so does Smith, on Bede, l. c.: so Lingard, A.-S. Ch. i. 21.

[3] See Tillemont, xii. 473; Fleury, b. 24. c. 58; Sirmond. Op. i. 1029. 'From the isle of Lerins came forth the greatest saints and scholars of the time;' Kitchin, Hist. France, i. 65.

[4] See Greg. Op. ii. 493, and Kitchin, i. 85. On the Constantinian use of the word, see Gibbon, ii. 309. Gregory thanks Arigius for his kindness, Ep. vi. 57.

[5] Life of St. Augustine (Lives of Engl. Saints), p. 74.

[6] Acts xiii. 13.

CHAP. II. they began to think they had undertaken more than they could compass, and, doubtless, to long for the hallowed quiet of their old home on the Cœlian. ' Struck with a sluggish timorousness,' so Bede phrases it, ' they thought of returning home, and after taking counsel together, determined that this was the safer course [1].' But as Fuller fairly remarks, their shrinking was not unnatural, although it were easy to call them cowards [2]; and a modern historian of the Saxons fully recognises the extreme onerousness of their task [3]. ' No sooner said than done,' Bede continues: ' they send back Augustine, who according to Gregory's plan was to be ordained their bishop if they should be welcomed by the English, and commission him to induce Gregory by humble supplication to excuse them from a journey so full of perils, of toils, of uncertainties.'

Gregory urges them to proceed.

They might, one would think, have known Gregory better. When Augustine reached Rome, and presented their request to the Pope, it was refused: Gregory, on July 23, 596, sent a letter to them by Augustine [4], to this purpose:—It were better not to begin a good work than to begin it and turn back from it [5]: you have undertaken this work by the Lord's help,—carry it out with activity and fervour, knowing that much labour wins all the greater reward. It is beautiful to see the wise gentleness [6] with which he treats his ' dearest

[1] Bede, i. 23.

[2] Fuller, Ch. Hist. p. 52.

[3] Kemble, ii. 357. He calls the mission-journey of Augustine and his companions ' heroic.' If this phrase is too strong, Haddan's representation of their fears as groundless is far from fair (Remains, p. 305). Gocelin, in order to save St. Augustine's honour, assumes that he ' was not able to resist' their urgency; Vit. Maj. Aug. c. i. s. 6 (cir. 1080).

[4] Ep. vi. 51 ; Bede, l. c. Here we may remark on the reckoning by 'indictions,' which appears in this and other papal letters given by Bede. Early in the fourth century arose the custom of arranging years in periods of fifteen, in accordance with the rule that property should be revalued after such periods : each year in such a series was reckoned as ' indiction 1, 2,' &c. The oldest or ' Constantinopolitan' scheme took Sept. 1 for its starting-point. Gregory was the first pope who reckoned by indictions, and he employed the Constantinopolitan (Bened. Edd. in Ep. i. 1). Cf. Nicolas, Chron. Hist. p. 6 ; Dict. Chr. Ant. i. 832.

[5] See Greg. Reg. Past. iii. 34 ; it were more tolerable ' recti viam non arripere, quam arrepta post tergum redire.'

[6] Yet Pearson says that he wrote ' sternly,' Hist. Engl. i. 122 ; and Hook,

sons:' an inferior man would have vented his annoyance in harsh rebukes, which would have by no means upheld 'the feeble knees,'—but Gregory knew better. There is something Pauline in the delicacy with which he hopes that 'in the eternal Country he may see the fruit of their labour and share in the reward, as he had wished to share the work.' Other evidence of his tact is given by his appointment of Augustine to be their abbot ; no longer a mere prior, but the father and director, who would be able in future, authoritatively and on the spot, to repress any deliberation or common action such as had 'sent him back' to Rome. Gregory also wrote, at the same time, letters in behalf of the missionaries to the bishops of Lyons, Tours [1], Marseilles, Arles, Vienne, Autun, Aix, and to abbot Stephen, who had sent to him, by Augustine, certain 'spoons and round dishes [2]' for the use of poor folks in Rome. The letter to Etherius of Lyons is given by Bede, but with a mistaken address, Arles being put for Lyons. The Pope also State of commended the monks to Theodoric II. and Theodebert II., Gaul. the boy-kings of Burgundy and Austrasia [3], and to their grandmother, the widow of the Austrasian Sigebert I., famous in early French history alike for royal energy and tyrannous vindictiveness under the name of Queen Brunehaut, properly Brunhild [4]. We must pause here a moment ; for Gregory's confidential letters to this princess, whom he once praises for bringing up her son well, and in other letters

while blaming Augustine, says that Gregory 'was unable even to understand his feelings,' Archbishops, i. 51. Gocelin remarks beautifully that the timorous request 'might have troubled the high-souled Gregory's charity, as if his undertaking were frustrated—nisi speraret in nomine Domini, in quo sua cœpta credebat feliciter perfici.'

[1] See Ep. vi. 52–56.

[2] 'Cochleares et circulos,' Ep. vi. 56. This reminds us of the old charities of the Roman Church administered by St. Laurence.

[3] Ep. vi. 58. They were the sons of Childebert, under whom the two realms had been united. For Burgundy see Kitchin, Hist. Fr. i. 59, 71, 84. For Austrasia, Oster-rik, the Eastern realm, see ib. 72, 81, 84 ; Guizot, Hist. Fr. c. 8.

[4] Ep. vi. 59. Fredegarius speaks of the evils and bloodshed ' a Brunichildis consilio in Francia facta,' Hist. Fr. Epit. 59. He calls her a second Jezebel, Chron. 36. But see Ruinart's note to his Chron. 42. On Brunhild see Kitchin, i. 89 ; and on Gregory's complimentary language to her, Barmby's Gregory the Great, p. 109.

CHAP. II. exhorts to suppress ecclesiastical abuses [1], have formed a difficulty somewhat analogous to his repulsive laudation of the odious tyrant Phocas [2]. But Brunhild's worst deeds, the result of pride and power, were done at a later time [3]: and her vigorous zeal for Roman organisation [4] as against barbaric licence, the capacity which she had shown for wise and beneficent government, and also her munificence to the Church, might well win the esteem of the great pontiff who had once himself been Prætor of Rome.

'Strengthened [5]' by these and similar letters, Augustine resumed his undertaking, and helped his companions to nerve their wills to their great task. They travelled by Marseilles to Aix, Arles, Vienne, Lyons, to the Burgundian court at Chalons [6], and thence to Autun. The journey would be rich in elevating and inspiriting remembrances, especially when it brought them to the scene of the martyrdom of Pothinus and of the labours of Irenæus. Thence, in the advancing autumn, they proceeded to Reims, the capital of Austrasia; visited Tours, where its historian bishop had died in the year preceding; and, as we infer from a later letter of Gregory [7], were well received at Paris by the ruler of Neustria. That ruler was no other than the atrocious Fredegond, then acting as regent for her son Chlotair II. and drawing near to the outwardly tranquil conclusion of a life which had been 'a calendar of crimes [8].' The missionaries wintered in Gaul [9]; and soon

---

[1] Ep. vi. 5; ix. 11, 109; xi. 63; xiii. 6.   [2] Ep. xiii. 31.

[3] The murder of Chilperic in 584 is ascribed to her by Fredegarius, Hist. Fr. Epit. 93, but by others to Fredegond. It was in 606 that she procured the murder of St. Desiderius of Vienne; in 612 she put to death Theodebert. Her own terrible death took place in 613.

[4] Guizot, Hist. France, c. 8; Kitchin, i. 89.

[5] 'Roboratus,' Bede, i. 25.

[6] The residence of Theodoric of Burgundy. See Smith's Bede, p. 680.

[7] Ep. xi. 61.

[8] Kitchin, i. 88. Chlotair became king in his infancy, A. D. 584; Fredegond died in 597.

[9] A story current in the eleventh century described them as encountering, in a town of Anjou, rude insults such as men like them in those days might easily provoke by their grave aspect and strange attire. Women, says Gocelin, were foremost in this barbarous inhospitality, driving them away like so many 'wolves,' with wild outcries, and not allowing them even to sleep under an elm. Vit. Maj. Aug. c. i. s. 10.

after Easter—which fell in 597 on April 14—they crossed
the Channel; and thus, after all these preliminary experiences,
came face to face with their real work.

Where did they land? we ask. The answer is ready. Landing of
About four miles westward from Ramsgate, towards the Augustine.
corner of Pegwell Bay, a white corner-house on the road,
standing far within the old line of the coast, retains the
name of Ebbsfleet[1], the traditional landing-place of Hengest[2],
the actual landing-place of Augustine. The river Stour
then expanded into an estuary; so that the 'Isle of Thanet'
was really an island[3], the stream forming a strait[4] from
Richborough, the venerable Roman town of Rutupiæ, to
the south, and Reculver, the Roman Regulbium, to the
north, on the mouth of the Thames. After thus touching
British ground, Augustine sent a message to King Ethelbert to this effect, 'that they were come from Rome with
the best of all messages, and that if he would accept it, he
would undoubtedly ensure himself an everlasting kingdom.'
Ethelbert answered at once kindly and cautiously; he would
not hastily commit himself. Let the strangers abide in the
isle of Thanet until he could see what to do with them:
their wants should be well supplied. 'Some days after, he Meeting
came into the isle,' prepared to give them an audience: but, with
as a Teuton, he believed in witch-lore[5], and, after 'using Ethelbert.
augury,' concluded that the foreign priests might employ
spells[6] to mislead him, if he received them under a roof. He
stipulated, therefore, that they should address him in the open
air, and the meeting was thus arranged[7]. Ethelbert and his

[1] See Stanley's Memorials of Canterbury, p. 29. Thorn calls the landing-
place Retesborough, X Script. 1759.

[2] 'Heopwines fleot,' Sax. Chr. a. 449. 'Fleet' = harbour.

[3] See Pearson's Hist. Maps of Engl. p. 2.

[4] Called 'the river Wantsum;' Bede, i. 25. See the maps in Hasted's Hist.
of Kent, iv. 288.

[5] Kemble, i. 428; Turner, iii. 135.

[6] Bede, i. 25. Cp. iv. 27, 'per incantationes;' Theodore's Penitential, i. 15;
Egbert's, i. 6; Council of Clovesho, c. 3; of Celchyth, c. 3.

[7] 'According to tradition, at Richborough;' English Life of St. Augustine,
p. 93. A cruciform ridge there was long called 'St. Augustine's Cross.'
Another traditional site is the high ground above Minster.

attendant thanes [1] took their seats, and saw some forty men
advancing, with a lofty silver cross [2] borne up in front, and
beside this a board, on which was painted the figure of the
Crucified [3]. He must have seen some such emblems of
Christianity belonging to his wife or to her chaplain, but he
had never perhaps beheld their faith represented with such
ritual solemnity ; and Gregory's well-known opinion of the
value of sacred paintings [4], as impressing religious truths on
the mind, was probably Augustine's reason for displaying one
in this momentous conference. A procession, too, was associated with choral supplications, and Gregory had instituted
a 'sevenfold litany,' or procession, to implore the Divine
succour during a pestilence [5] ; on this occasion, therefore, his
emissaries, as they approached, 'sang litanies, entreating the
Lord for their own salvation and that of those to whom they
came.' The chant, although in a strange tongue, must have
brought to the rude listeners a sense of spiritual power : and
Augustine's majestic person, towering up above all his companions [6], was certain to contribute to the imposing effect of

[1] 'Comitibus,' his personal companions, 'gesiths' (properly, 'fellow-
travellers'), who acted as his 'thanes,' ministri. See Kemble, i. 168 ; Stubbs,
Const. Hist. i. 149 ; Lappenberg, ii. 317 ; Freeman, Growth of Engl. Constit.
p. 50. Compare Bede, iii. 22 ; iv. 22 ; v. 5.

[2] In later times, 'on donna le nom de *Croix* à toutes les processions ;' L'Art
de vérifier, ii. 5.

[3] Gocelin, Vit. Maj. S. Aug. s. 16 : 'imaginem Domini Salvatoris, formose
atque *aurose* in tabula depictam.' 'Wise pomp,' remarks Haddan, Remains, p.
305. Compare Wordsworth, Eccl. Sonnets, No. 14 :—

'The Cross preceding Him who floats in air,
The pictured Saviour.'

[4] Greg. Ep. ix. 52, that paintings of Christ are not to be worshipped, but to
be used as stimulants to devout affection. '*Illum* adoramus quem per
imaginem aut natum, aut passum, sed et in throno sedentem recordamur.'
So in Ep. ix. 105, to a bishop who had broken some pictures which had been
'adored :' 'Your duty was et illas servare, et ab earum adoratu populum
prohibere.' And similarly Ep. xi. 13, dwelling on the usefulness of sacred
paintings to those who cannot read, but absolutely forbidding them to be
'adored.'

[5] Joan. Diac. i. 42. 'Litany' is here used as = procession. 'Let the litany
of clergy start from St. John Baptist's,' &c. See Palmer, Orig. Lit. i. 271, and
the note to Greg. Op. iv. 1284. In Ep. xi. 51 Gregory exhorts the Sicilian
bishops to have litanies on Wednesdays and Fridays, in order to obtain protection against barbarian invaders.

[6] If we can at all rely on the traditional account in Gocelin, Vit. Aug. 49,

the scene. The king bade his visitors sit down, and Augustine
spoke, assisted by a Gallic interpreter [1]. He told, said a
Saxon homilist long after, ' how the tender-hearted Jesus by
His own throes,'—and here, doubtless, he pointed to the cross
and the painting,—'had redeemed the sinful world, and opened
the kingdom of heaven to all believers [2].' Bede says simply,
that ' he preached to them the word of life ;' and Ethelbert's
answer was ' exactly what a king should have said on such an
occasion [3].' ' Fair words and promises are these ; but seeing
they are new and doubtful, I cannot give in to them, and
give up what I, with all the English race, have so long
observed. But since you have come a long way from a
strange country, in order—as I think I clearly see—to make
known to us what you believe to be best and truest, we [4] do
not mean to do you any harm, but rather will treat you
kindly, and take care that you have all that you need ; and
we shall not hinder you from bringing over any of our people
to your own belief.' One thing this royal answer lacked,—a
promise to hear their preaching again : but they had got as
much as at first they could hope for in what Montalembert [5]
calls the ' sincere and truly liberal' speech of a king evidently
desirous to do justice, and to weigh his words in order fully to
make them good. Such a typical Teuton prince might well
represent that kind of preparedness for Christianity [6] which
consisted in a sense of the spiritual world, of the gravity and
solemnity of life, of rights as involving obligations, in a regard
for truth and noble manliness, for liberty in combination with

professing to come from an old man whose grandfather Augustine had converted and baptized. 'Staturam proceram et arduam, adeo ut a scapulis populo
superemineret.' In this he resembled St. Columba : see Adamnan, Vit. Col.
i. 1.

[1] He was to procure some such, Greg. Ep. vi. 58.

[2] Haddan and Stubbs, iii. 11 ; Churton's Early Eng. Ch. p. 39.

[3] Stanley, p. 34. See the rendering in Freeman's Old-Engl. Hist. p. 47.
Malmesbury remarks on the kindness and fairness of the speech ; Gest. Reg.
i. s. 10.

[4] Observe the plural, ' Nolumus molesti esse vobis.' The king unites his
thanes with him in this announcement.

[5] In his ' Monks of the West.'

[6] Cp. Church's Gifts of Civilisation, &c. p. 320 ff., and Merivale's Conversion
of Northern Nations, p. 88 ff.

CHAP. II. authority, for the purity which could dignify the home. It was natural for him to be fair and serious at a crisis of such magnitude. He could discern the presence of something great in these representatives of an unseen Kingdom: and so he might be trusted to give them another opportunity of stating their case [1]. Meantime, he promised them a house in the 'metropolis,' as Bede loftily calls it, of his empire, the old Roman town of Durovernum, which had become 'the Burgh of the men of Kent,' and from which, in the words of an old English rhythm, were now to come 'to *Angle-kin* Christianity and bliss, for God and for the world [2].'

Entrance into Canterbury.

Thither let us follow them, as they take the Roman road across the downs to the top of the present St. Martin's hill, and look forth, first on a little Roman-British chapel on the slopes below them, and then on the wood-built city further down, the Canterbury of Ethelbert. That little oratory was St. Martin's, where Bertha and Liudhard had for many years worshipped, and probably prayed for such a day as was now dawning. We, as we look back to its sunrise, may well enter into Dean Stanley's remark, that the view from the present church of St. Martin is in this sense 'one of the most inspiriting that can be found in all the world [3].' Let any one visit that venerable building, where the lines of Roman brick seem to assert its continuity with Bertha's place of prayer, and then ascend to the brow of the hill, and recall that day in the Ascension week of 597 when Augustine first beheld the future seat of his archbishopric. He would take possession of Canterbury for Christ. The cross was again uplifted by the cross-bearer, and with it 'the likeness of the great King, our Lord [4]:' and the brethren accompanied their abbot in solemn order down the hill, chanting a pathetic antiphon belonging to the Rogation days, which they had perhaps heard in the previous spring on their arrival in Provence [5],

---

[1] Elmham ascribes it to Bertha's influence that her husband's mind was favourably disposed towards Augustine's preaching; Hist. Mon. S. Aug. p. 209. So Malmesbury as to Liudhard, Gest. Reg. i. s. 9.

[2] Chronicle, a. 1011.

[3] Stanley, p. 54.

[4] Bede, i. 25.

[5] The institution of Rogations, or processional supplications in time of

and which long remained in the Rogation services of the
Church of Lyons [1], uniting the urgent intercession of 'the
man of desires' for the ruined sanctuary of Judah [2] with that
characteristic watchword of Paschal joy to which Gregory had
hoped that 'Angles' might yet listen. 'We beseech Thee,
O Lord, in Thy great mercy, let Thine anger and wrath
be turned away from this city, and from Thy holy house, for
we have sinned. Alleluia!' With such a combination of
humility [3] and thankfulness was inaugurated the foundation
of the English Church properly so called.

If we follow the missionaries, in imagination, into Canterbury, and over the ground now called St. Alphage Lane,
almost under the shadow of the vast metropolitan church,
we are near the 'Stable-gate,' where, in close vicinity to a
heathen temple, they were to make their temporary home [4].
There they dwelt, as Bede says [5], 'after the primitive Church Life of the
model, giving themselves to frequent prayers, watchings, Missionaries in
and fastings; preaching to all who were within their reach, Canter-
disregarding all worldly things as matters with which they bury.
had nothing to do, accepting from those whom they taught
just what seemed necessary for livelihood, living themselves
altogether in accordance with what they taught, and with
hearts prepared to suffer every adversity, or even to die, for
that truth which they preached. What need to say more?'
he proceeds significantly : 'some believed and were bap-

distress, had been invested with new solemnity by Mamertus of Vienne
before the Ascension-day of 468; see Greg. Turon. H. Fr. ii. 34. Thence
the observance spread. Augustine would have heard how St. Cæsarius
had recommended it : and although it had not as yet been adopted at
Rome, he made it an institution in the English Church (Council of Clovesho,
a. 747). Bede himself died on the Rogation Wednesday of 735. In 597
Ascension Day was on May 23.

[1] Martene, de Ant. Eccl. Rit. iii. 529.

[2] Based on an old Latin version of Daniel ix. 16.

[3] The verse is also in a hymn composed by a teacher, himself a penitent,
at Whithern; Bp. Forbes, Lives of Ninian and Kentigern, p. 292.

[4] Elmham, Hist. Mon. S. Aug. p. 91 :—

'Mansio signatur, quæ Stabelgate notatur.'

Thorn (X Script. 1759) describes the place as 'in the parish of St. Alphege,
over against the King's Street, on the north.'

[5] Bede, i. 26.

tized[1], admiring the simplicity of their blameless life, and the sweetness of their heavenly teaching.' It is the first of several beautiful summaries, given by the single-hearted and thoroughly pious historian[2], of the results produced by 'the argument of a pious life,' the evidence derived from self-devotion and consistency. Doubtless there were among their hearers not a few who were 'feeling after God:' the serene brightness, the mysterious majesty, the unimaginable tenderness of the new faith had a fascinating power, which became irresistible in connection with such signal purity and single-heartedness as the lives of its preachers displayed. They were daily to be seen moving to and fro between the Stable-gate and St. Martin's[3], where they 'sang the Psalms, prayed, celebrated

Baptism of Ethelbert.

mass[4], preached, baptized.' According to the usual story[4], which was a part of the Canterbury tradition, the Whitsuneve which followed on their entrance into Canterbury, that is, the 1st of June, beheld the most signal of their successes in the baptism of Ethelbert[5]. Whenever it took place[6],—and it must have taken place during this summer, or at least in

---

[1] 'You,' wrote Alcuin to the Kentish people, 'are the origin of the salvation of the English, the beginning of prosperity,' &c.; Ep. 59. (Op. i. 78.)

[2] See Bede, iii. 5, on Aidan: 'Quod non aliter quam vivebat cum suis, ipse docebat.' Ib. iii. 17: 'Industriam faciendi simul et docendi mandata cælestia.' Again, Fursey wrought on many souls 'et exemplo virtutis et incitamento sermonis,' iii. 19: Tuda 'et verbo cunctos docebat et opere,' iii. 26: and so of Cuthbert in iv. 27, 'verbo prædicationis simul et opere virtutis.' Cp. Ep. ad Egbert, 2, 'et operatione et doctrina . . . Neutra enim hæc virtus sine altera rite potest impleri,' &c. Compare Eusebius vi. 3, on Origen.

[3] Gocelin makes 'the blessed prelate Letard' attend at St. Martin's when the Roman teachers, superior to him as gold to silver, 'ibidem quæ Dei sunt agebant;' Vit. Maj. i. s. 20. In 1035 St. Martin's appears as the see of a bishop-suffragan for the diocese of Canterbury.

[4] 'Missas facere,' a phrase which appears first in St. Ambrose, Ep. xx. 4, 'Missam facere cœpi; dum offero,' &c.; but here it *might* have its original meaning of performing the dismissal of catechumens before the oblation. In the 84th canon of the so-called 4th Council of Carthage, heathens are permitted to remain in church 'usque ad missam catechumenorum.' From this dismissal, as the dividing line between the two parts of the Liturgy, the whole derived a name convenient from its brevity, but possessing no other merit. See Hammond, Liturgies E. and W., p. xxxi. (Missa = missio.)

[5] Elmham, Hist. Monast. S. Aug. p. 137: 'In die Pentecostes . . . Ethelbertus baptizatus est.' So Thorn. X Script. 1759.

[6] The forms used would be those of the Gregorian Sacramentary, Muratori, Lit. Rom. ii. 62. See especially the Benedictio Fontis.

the next autumn,—it was an event standing by itself[1]; for
no royal conversion that we read of[2] could in all its circumstances, and with regard both to moral reality or to
grandeur of result, come up to that which led the Kentish
monarch to profess the Christian faith with a triple 'I
believe,' and descend as a proselyte into 'the salutary laver,'
that, in the words actually used, 'he might be born again
into the new infancy of true innocence,' and be 'strengthened
by the clear shining of the Holy Spirit[3].' His example
told naturally upon his subjects : 'day after day more people
came together[4] to hear the Word, and, forsaking heathen
rites, to embrace the faith, and so attach themselves to the
unity of Christ's holy Church. It is said that the king
so far encouraged their conversion as on the one hand to
compel no man to become a Christian[5], and on the other
to show a closer affection to those who believed, as being
heirs with him of the heavenly kingdom. For he had
learned from his teachers that the service of Christ ought
to be voluntary, not compulsory.' They had learned this
lesson from their teacher : Gregory had written, some years
before, ' He who is brought to the font by coercion, instead
of persuasion, is but too likely to relapse[6].'

---

[1] 'Illuxit dies,' exclaims Gocelin, ' Anglis et Angelis solemnissimus ;' s. 22.
From the verses in Elmham, p. 91, it might be inferred that the King's
baptism was only a month before Augustine's consecration.

[2] Contrast it, e.g. with that of Chlodwig.

[3] Muratori, Lit. Rom. ii. 157, 65, 89.

[4] One would like to think that there is some truth in the story which
Gocelin professes to have gained from tradition (see above, p. 48). A youth
mingles in the throng in order to gratify a scornful curiosity. Augustine
gazes fixedly at him, and says to his attendant, ' Bring that young man to me.'
The youth, overawed, clasps the Saint's feet ; all his pride and levity give
place to faith : Augustine embraces, instructs, baptizes, solemnly blesses him.
Vit. Maj. 49.

[5] See Freeman, Norm. Conq. i. 29. In this Ethelbert towers above various
royal promoters of Christianity, such as Harold Blaatand of Denmark, and the
two Olafs, and Eric IX. of Sweden among the Finns. Even Stephen of Hun-
gary, who began like him, was provoked by Pagan rebellion to banish or
enslave those who clung to the old worship. The result, says Hardwick,
Ch. Hist., M. Ages, p. 139, was ' a terrible revulsion at his death in favour of
the Pagan creed.' Cp. Maclear, Conversion of Slavs, p. 58.

[6] Greg. Ep. i. 47. Cp. i. 10, 35, viii. 25, ix. 6, xiii. 12, against coercion of
Jews, or interference with their worship. Yet Gregory was not thoroughly
consistent : in Ep. iv. 26 he suggests that Sardinian rustics obstinate in

So ends the first scene of this great drama: nor can
we fail to be interested in the coincidence, that on the
Sunday morning next after that Pentecost, i. e. on June 9,
597[1], the noblest missionary career ever accomplished in
Britain came to its end in the distant monastery of Icolmkill[2]. While Augustine was building up the first Church
of Englishmen, Columba was, in his own words, 'entering
on the way of his fathers[3],' and leaving to his disciples the
glory of an apostolic example, and the impulse which was
destined to take up the work of the Augustinian mission
itself in the northern English realms, and to succeed where
that mission had seemed to fail, or at any rate where its
energy had been arrested. One can hardly read the history
of the Christianising of our forefathers, with its unexpected
disappointments and its unexpected triumphs,—its tale of
lights kindled and then quenched, and again 'relumed' *quo
minime reris,* of instruments changed with startling sudden-
ness, and hopes realised in forms far out of calculation,—and
not remember how St. Paul was at one time forbidden to preach
in 'Asia[4],' and how baffling to sanguine hearts must have
been his detention under Felix. These mysterious 'chains
and sequences,' to use Origen's phrase[5], in the Divine
action upon men or nations, ought assuredly to teach us
two things—an awe of the plan that so far transcends its
agents, and a patient assurance that it will fulfil itself in
its time[6].

Paganism should be heavily taxed. See Dean Church, Miscell. Essays,
p. 245.

[1] See Reeves's Adamnan, p. 310.

[2] Bp. Reeves (p. 259) supposes Iona to be a corruption of Io*u*a, the adjectival
form of Iou, Ia, Hy, 'Hii' (Bede) or Y, i.e. 'The island,' lengthened into
I-colum-kill, the Island of 'Columba of the Church,' a name given him for
his early piety (p. lxx).

[3] Adamnan, Vit. Col. iii. 23. Columba was born in Donegal, A.D. 521;
founded a monastery at Derry in 546, another at Durrow, cir. 553; came over
to Hy in 563 (not, as Bede says, 565; Lanigan, ii. 158; Reeves, p. lxxv).
He is said to have studied under Finnian of Clonard. (See p. 32).

[4] Acts xvi. 6; cp. xix. 10.   [5] Orig. c, Cels. iv. 8.

[6] 'Lord! who Thy thousand years dost wait
            To work the thousandth part
        Of Thy vast plan, for us create
            With zeal a patient heart.'

Newman's Verses, p. 156.

The next step, for Augustine, was to obtain episcopal consecration. For this, 'according to Gregory's directions,' he
was to apply to that Gallic hierarchy which the Pope could
not but regard as having been apathetic and inert with reference to the evangelisation of the heathens of Britain[1]. To
Gaul, and to the principal church in South Gaul, that of
Arles,—which had made good its precedence among Gallic
bishoprics[2], and could boast of such prelates as the younger
Hilary and as Cæsarius,—Augustine repaired in the autumn.
He was consecrated by the archbishop Virgilius[3], and by other
Frankish prelates, on the 16th of November, to be himself
'Archbishop of the English.' Hastening home, he found, to
his joy, a multitude of new proselytes : and on Christmas Day,
as Gregory, in a letter glowing with thankfulness, informed
his brother patriarch Eulogius of Alexandria[4], more than ten
thousand Kentish men were baptized,—many of whom, no
doubt, may be reckoned as rather conformists to their king's
new religion than genuine believers in its truth[5]. Established
as bishop in Canterbury, Augustine received from Ethelbert
the gift of his own palace[6] : and the king, according to tra-

[1] See above, p. 43.

[2] See Fleury, b. 23. c. 45, compared with Gregory's words, referred to below.
Zosimus favoured Arles ; other popes, as Leo, did not, until Symmachus made
its bishop his vicar ; Bened. Edd. note on Greg. Ep. v. 53, where Gregory,
following ancient custom, grants a pall to the bishop of Arles. On the civil
grandeur of Arles as the residence of the Gallic Prefect, see Life of St. German,
p. 187. The Benedictine biographers of Gregory (Vit. Greg. iii. 3. 3), after
observing that the city of Arles had been made the civil capital of Gaul, add,
'Ab ea dignitate politica primatus ecclesiasticus initium duxisse videtur :'
yet the bishops of the province in 450 had asserted the primacy of the see on
the ground that it was founded by the apostolic Trophimus ; Leo, Ep. 65.

[3] Bede mistakenly says, by Etherius, whom, further on, he treats as
predecessor of Virgilius at Arles, i. 27, 28. Etherius was archbishop of Lyons,
contemporary of Virgilius of Arles. Virgilius had been abbot of Autun ;
Greg. Tur. H. Fr. ix. 23. He died an old man, while reclining on his couch
and saying his office ; Mabillon, Ann. Bened. i. 312. Bede's mistake is ingeniously accounted for by Lingard, A.-S. Ch. i. 369 : Nothelm, who copied
Roman documents for Bede, copied one letter (out of a series of commendatory
letters) to Etherius, of 596, another to Virgilius, of 601, and Bede supposed
both to have been written to the bishop of Arles.

[4] Greg. Ep. viii. 30. Gocelin says they were baptized in the Swale : if so,
it was the passage so called between Sheppey and the mainland.

[5] See Bede, ii. 5 : 'vel favore vel timore regio,' &c.

[6] See Palgrave, Engl. Comm. p. 156 ; Stanley, p. 39.

dition, actually withdrew from his capital to Reculver[1]. Near the palace stood a desecrated church, built 'by the old handiwork of Roman Christians[2]:' Augustine, with the royal sanction, reclaimed it, and re-dedicated it, in imitation of the Lateran basilica at Rome, 'in the name of the Holy Saviour, Jesus Christ our God and Lord[3].' This was the beginning of our original and metropolitan 'Christ Church,' the mother-church of English Christianity. In restoring the old fabric, Augustine enlarged it into stately proportions, and modelled its arrangements from the Vatican basilica of St. Peter. The nave had aisles[4], and towers on the north and south : eastward of the 'choir of the singers' there was, as in the present church, a lofty ascent, required by the construction of a crypt 'such as the Romans call a Confession.' The account extant speaks of two apses, at the eastern and western ends, each with its altar : in the western, against the wall, stood the episcopal throne, and some way to the east of it was an altar which is distinguished from 'the great altar' at the east end, but which, from its nearness to the 'cathedra,' is thought to have been the original altar, as was the case in St. Peter's[5]. Augustine had a general license from Ethelbert to restore for Christian use any old British churches : and one such, which had long been Paganised, and which stood between the wall of Canterbury and St. Martin's, was hallowed by him in memory of the Roman boy-martyr St.

---

[1] See Stanley, p. 45.

[2] Bede, i. 33 : 'antiquo Romanorum fidelium opere factam fuisse didicerat.' Cp. his reference to the Roman fountain at Carlisle, Vit. Cuthb. 27.

[3] Ælfric, on coming to the archbishopric in 995, was told by the oldest men whom he could consult that Augustine hallowed the minster in Christ's name and St. Mary's, on the mass-day of SS. Primus and Felicianus, i.e. June 9 ; Chronicle, a. 995. King Wihtred's 'Privilege to Churches' describes it as 'the Church of the Saviour;' Haddan and Stubbs, iii. 240. For the service of dedication see Muratori, Lit. Rom. i. 613.

[4] See the description cited and commented on in Willis's Hist. of Cant. Cath. p. 9 ff. On the ancient St. Peter's see Fergusson, Hist. Architect. i. 365 : it had two aisles on each side of the nave ; the walls rose to a great height above the pillars ; the sanctuary was 'small and contracted,' but projected like a transept either way on each side of the apse.

[5] Willis, p. 29. At this altar in the western apse the priest when celebrating in the 'basilican' manner, 'having his face turned towards the people,' would look eastward, while they stood below him looking westward.

Pancras, whose family had once owned the ground on the CHAP. II.
Cœlian, where St. Andrew's monastery stood[1]. Those who
visit St. Augustine's College may see, somewhat eastward of
its precinct, an old brick arch, which has been supposed to be
a relic of this building. While establishing the conventual
life in connection with 'Christ Church,' Augustine planned
the erection of another monastery[2], chiefly in order to secure
holy ground for his own grave[3], which must necessarily lie
outside the city wall. The site chosen was that on which
stands the present 'St. Augustine's.'

But now the archbishop found reason to send to Gregory Messengers
an account of his proceedings, with a statement of some points sent to
on which he desired instructions from Rome. We had better Gregory.
consider these matters in connection with Gregory's replies
to Augustine. The bearers of the letter were Laurence, a
priest, and Peter, a monk[4]. They set forth, it would seem,
in the spring of 598: but here comes one of the difficulties of
the narrative. Bede says that the Pope replied 'without
delay:' but the replies are expressly dated June 22 in
601. If the date is correct, how are we to explain the
delay? Partly, perhaps, by the necessity of finding recruits
for the English mission, partly by the press of anxiety
and business which, coupled with long and painful illness[5],
weighed heavily even on such a spirit as the great Pope's,
and made his office a daily burden. If the 'swords of

[1] For St. Pancras, see Alb. Butler for May 12. Elmham associates the
memory of the boy-martyr with the impression produced by the English boys
in the forum on Gregory, then abbot of the monastery which he had founded
'ad clivum Scauri de patrimonio S. Pancratii;' Hist. Mon. Aug. p. 80.

[2] Bede, i. 33 : 'in qua et ipsius . . . et omnium episcoporum Doruvernensium,
simul et regum Cantiæ, poni corpora possent.'

[3] See Stanley, p. 41, and Hardwick's Preface to Elmham, p. iv. The
planning or 'fundatio' of the monastery was in 598, the 'dotatio' in 605, says
Elmham, p. 81, but on the authority of untrustworthy 'charters.' Elmham
says that Augustine chose there 'locum sepulturæ, removed from the noise of
the world, ut sic exiret cum passo Domino extra portam;' p. 82.

[4] Bede, i. 27. 'Reversusque Britanniam, misit continuo Romam Laurentium.
. . . . Nec mora . . . responsa recepit.'

[5] See Greg. Ep. x. 35. 'For nearly two years I have had to keep my bed,
suffering such pain from gout that I could hardly get up even for three hours,
on festivals, to celebrate the solemnity of the mass. . . . I am compelled to
exclaim, "Bring my soul out of prison!"' Cp. xi. 30, 44; xiii. 22.

CHAP. II. the Lombards[1]' were sheathed in a truce, there were urgent
Church affairs in Gaul[2] to be dealt with, and Gregory was
interested, now in a theological controversy which grew out
of the Eutychian[3], now in the proceedings of a high judicial
officer sent to Rome from Constantinople[4]. These are but
specimens of his cares: yet still it remains somewhat surprising that he did not find the men he wanted and answer the
questions proposed until three years had passed.

Mission of
Mellitus
and three
others.

The men selected were four[5], Mellitus, Justus, Paulinus,
and Rufinianus. Of these, the first three became eminent in
our Church history; the third being the most eminent of all.
Several letters were entrusted to them.

Letters of
Gregory.

The longest was the reply to Augustine's various queries[6].
Of these, the first had referred to the division of the contributions of the faithful for Church purposes, and to the
arrangement of Augustine's own life in relation to his clergy.

Reply to
Augus-
tine's ques-
tions.

Gregory answers: The best scheme of distribution is that
which the Roman see is wont to recommend, a fourfold[7] partition between the bishop, the clergy, the poor, and the needful
repair of churches. But this will not apply to the present
case: Augustine, as a monk, will continue to live in community with his clergy[8], and thus far perpetuate the life
of those early Christians, of whom none said that what

---

[1] Ep. vii. 26. In ix. 43 he thanks the Lombard Queen for promoting this
truce. In 599 the Lombards became orthodox; Milman, ii. 137.

[2] Ep. ix. 106–116.

[3] Ep. x. 39, on the Agnoetæ; Liddon, Bamp. Lect. p. 470.

[4] Ep. x. 51.

[5] Thorn says that Nathanael, afterwards abbot of SS. Peter and Paul, came
with them; X Script. 1769.

[6] Ep. xi. 64; Bede, i. 27. St. Boniface (Ep. 40) asked Archbishop Nothelm,
in 736, to send him a copy of this letter, because the registrars of the Roman
Church said that it was not to be found in their 'scrinium.' On Gregory's
'large-minded sagacity' shown in it, see Pearson, Hist. Engl. i. 123.

[7] Cp. Greg. Ep. v. 44. So Gelasius I. had ordered; Ep. 9. 27, in Mansi, viii.
45. A Council of Braga, in 563, had made a triple division, not mentioning
the poor, Mansi, ix. 778; yet the next Council of Braga forbade the bishop
to receive the third part of the offerings, ib. ix. 839. But this prohibition
is cancelled in 4th Toledo, c. 33. See on the old division, Bingham, b. v. c. 6. s. 3.
That the fourfold division was not imposed by Gregory on the new English
Church, see Lord Selborne's Anc. Facts and Fictions concerning Churches and
Tithes, p. 104.

[8] Compare Bede, iv. 27; S. Aug. Serm. 353.

he possessed was his own[1]. Clerks in minor orders[2] might CHAP. II.
marry and live outside the bishop's household, receiving their
due stipends ; but care must be taken that their lives be spent
under ecclesiastical rule, consecrated by devotional offices,
and kept pure from all things unlawful. The second question
grew out of Augustine's observation of peculiarities in the
Gallic ritual. 'Why, seeing that the faith is one, are
there different customs in different Churches, and one custom
of masses in the holy Roman Church, another in that of
Gaul?' In Gaul he had evidently noticed the number of
collects in the Mass, the frequent variations of the Preface,
the invocation of the Holy Spirit on the elements, the solemn
episcopal blessing pronounced after the breaking of the Bread,
and before 'the Peace' and the Communion[3]. Gregory, who
was deeply interested in liturgical questions, and had revised
and re-edited the 'Sacramentary' of his predecessor Gelasius[4],
and brought the Eucharistic ceremonial to what he considered
an elaborate perfection, was at the same time far from being
a pedant or a bigot on such points : he advised, on the contrary, a wise eclecticism. Let Augustine 'collect into a sort of

Liturgical differences.

---

[1] Comp. Sozomen, vi. 31, on the clergy of the church of Rhinocurura.

[2] He calls them 'extra sacros ordines,' meaning the ostiary, lector, exorcist,
acolyth, those below the subdiaconate (cf. Muratori, Lit. Rom. ii. 408) ; for
this order, although confessedly not of apostolic institution, had come to be
regarded as sacred in a sense in which those of readers or acolyths were not.
In imposing celibacy on subdeacons, Ep. i. 44, Gregory was following Leo the
Great ; see his Ep. 14. 4. The 10th canon of Ancyra had allowed deacons to
marry, if at their ordination they had stipulated for it ; but not otherwise.
See Routh, Rell. Sac. iv. 189, that there are no cases in antiquity of bishops,
presbyters, or deacons who married *after their ordination*, 'nisi diaconi de hac
re prius cavissent.' But at the time of the Council of Chalcedon (can. 14)
the limited permission as to deacons was obsolete, and subdeacons also were
bound to celibacy. The 27th 'Apostolic' canon must be later than that of
Ancyra.

[3] See Muratori, Lit. Rom. Vet. ii. 517 ff. ; Neale and Forbes, Gallican
Liturgies, p. 32 ff. The 'Gothic' (rather, Celtic) Liturgy is that which was
used in Southern Gaul, the 'Gallic,' distinctively so called, in Central. See
Wilberforce on H. Eucharist, p. 48. On the episcopal benedictions in question
see Maskell's 'Ancient Liturgy,' p. 160 ; Warren's Lit. and Ritual of Celtic
Ch. p. 101. They are referred to by Cæsarius, Serm. 281, in app. to Aug.
Serm. See a long series of them in Egbert's Pontifical, ed. Surtees Soc. p. 58 ff.
That they were not originally in the Gregorian Sacramentary, see Muratori,
Lit. Rom. i. 80.

[4] John the Deacon, ii. 17. See Palmer, Orig. Lit. i. 113 ; Muratori, i. 63.

bundle' the best usages of Rome, of Gaul, or of other Churches, whatever he had found to be most pious, religious, righteous, and most likely to be pleasing to God, and so form a ritual for the English Christians, who were as yet young in faith, and could become accustomed to whatever was given them. There was no need to stick blindly to the Roman observances as such. 'For we ought not to love things for the sake of persons, but persons for the sake of things[1].' Again, Augustine had asked how theft from a church was to be punished. Distinguish the motives, says Gregory: make allowance for the temptations of poverty; let there be a scale of penalties fairly adjusted; let charity be the motive and the regulating principle of your discipline[2]; when you punish, still regard the offender as a son. What is thus stolen must be replaced; but (observe his indomitable fair-mindedness) never let a church receive more compensation than the amount of the robbery.

The fourth and fifth questions related to marriage. Might two men marry two sisters not near akin to them? It was strange that such a question should have been put. Gregory despatched it by a brief affirmative. But it was stranger yet that Augustine should have asked whether a man might marry his stepmother or his sister-in-law: Gregory's negative answer alluded to Herod and the Baptist. Converts must know that for a Christian to contract such unions is a deadly sin: those who had contracted them while heathens[3] are to treat them as null, and may then be admitted to the Eucharist. As to the matrimonial degrees, the Roman secular law allowed the

[1] See Ep. i. 43: 'Where the faith is one, differences of custom do no harm to Holy Church.' In ix. 12 he defends himself for having introduced Alleluia out of the Paschal season, and the Kyrie and the Lord's Prayer 'soon after the Canon.' He says he is willing to imitate his inferiors (the church of Constantinople) in what is good. See Stanley, Mem. p. 49.

[2] He mentions fines and beatings as penalties. An old Irish canon wrongly ascribed to St. Patrick had specified, as one among three penalties, the amputation of hand or foot; Mansi, vi. 519.

[3] As Eadbald did afterwards; see p. 104. It was regarded by heathen Teutons as more than permissible: see Kemble, ii. 407; Haddan's Remains, p. 311. It had been forbidden, together with the marriage of a widower with his wife's sister, &c., by the third Council of Paris in 557; Mansi, ix. 745. See also Council of Auxerre, ib. ix. 914; Council of Epaon, c. 30, ib. viii. 563.

marriage of first cousins; but on natural and on religious grounds, Gregory declared against it[1]. Persons nearer akin than the third degree (i. e. that beyond first cousins) ought not to marry[2].

The sixth and seventh questions recurred to the subject of Church order. Might one bishop consecrate a bishop-elect if other prelates were not within reach? Gregory's answer shows that he thought such consecrations spiritually valid[3]. 'In the English Church, while you are its only bishop, you cannot consecrate save in the absence of other bishops. For when bishops shall come over from Gaul, they will attend the consecration as witnesses[4].' (It is observable that Gregory here

[1] It was disapproved, says St. Augustine, by Christian public opinion, although not forbidden by God's law, and before it was forbidden by man's; Civ. Dei, xv. 16. See Council of Epaon, in 517, can. 30, Mansi, viii. 563, forbidding union with a '*consobrina*,' as incestuous; and of Auxerre, c. 31. Compare Gibbon, v. 299; Bingham, b. xvi. c. 11. s. 4.

[2] In the last year of Gregory's life, a bishop asked him to explain the rumour that he had thus sanctioned, for the English converts, marriages within the fourth degree. Were not marriages up to the seventh degree unlawful? Gregory answered in effect, It is well known in Rome that my permission referred only to the early days of the English mission: when its converts are ripened in faith, I intend that they shall not be allowed to marry within the sixth degree; Ep. xiv. 17. Giraldus denounces the Welsh for marrying within it; Descr. Camb. ii. 6.

[3] If we compare (1) the varying language of the canons ordering a plurality of consecrators, e.g. Apostolic can. 1, two or three; 1st Arles, 20 seven, or at least three, besides the metropolitan; Nicene 4, all comprovincials, if possible,—if not, three at least, having the written consent of the others; 2nd Arles, 5, the metropolitan or three comprovincials; with (2) the cases in which a consecration by two bishops, or even by one only, was held valid, although irregular,— e.g. the case of Siderius of Palæbisca, recognised as a bishop by St. Athanasius, and of Evagrius, recognised by Rome and Alexandria—see Bingham, b. ii. c. 11. s. 5—we must infer that though the rule in question was very ancient, and even Novatian, in the third century, took care to observe it (Eus. vi. 43), yet it was intended to guard against disorderly and clandestine consecrations, and its observance was not deemed a 'sine qua non' for the conferring of the episcopal character. Gregory's illustration from a wedding-party is significant on this point. Cp. Bp. Forbes SS. Ninian and Kentigern, p. 336. In the Scotic Churches consecration by one bishop was not unfrequent: see Lanigan, ii. 128. Palmer, who denies the validity of such consecrations save in absolute necessity, cites Habertus that in 'ancient MSS.' the reading is, 'Nisi cum episcopis,' instead of 'nisi sine episcopis;' On the Church, ii. 321. But this would make no sense.

[4] So in the Benedictine Gregory, 'illi . . . adsistent.' In Bede's text the sense is, 'For when do bishops come from Gaul to be present at a bishop's consecration?' ('qui . . . adsistant?').

CHAP. II. ignores the British Celtic bishops, to whom the next question
in part refers.) But it would be well to station new bishops
in such places as would allow of their assembling for a consecration, so that ultimately three or four bishops might
attend in every such case; or, as the true text probably runs,
so that there may be nothing to prevent the assembling of
other pastors, whose presence is very useful, for the consecration of a new bishop[1]. He alludes to the ordinary social
custom whereby married persons were invited to a wedding,
to sympathise with the parties concerned : similarly, he says,
at a consecration, such persons should meet as might rejoice
in the elevation of the new bishop, or pray to God for his
preservation.   Again, Augustine had asked, ' How ought I to
deal with the bishops of Gaul and Britain?'   The question
as to the former may seem to show some ignorance, possibly a
touch of self-importance.   Gregory answered decisively, that,
as bishop of the English, Augustine could have no manner of
jurisdiction in Gaul.   Should he visit that country, he might
give brotherly counsel to the bishop of Arles, who had received the 'pall' from Gregory's predecessor, and must not be
interfered with in his (metropolitan) authority : the Pope had
directed him to confer with Augustine[2], and Augustine
might do a good work by 'persuading' the Gallic bishops to
correct abuses, and setting them a good example; but more
than this he could not have a right to do.   Here we must
ask, What was the pall, and what did it indicate?   The
ancient garment called *himation*, square-shaped and blanket-
like, which was worn over the tunic in ancient Greece, may
be identified with the 'pallium,' or cloak, which Tertullian
commends as more convenient than the toga[3].   Such a garb

---

[1] ' Quatenus nulla sit necessitas ut in ordinatione . . . convenire non possint,'
&c., as in Bened. Greg. Bede's text seems partially corrupt, 'quatenus . . . .
ut . . . facile debeant convenire.'

[2] Ep. xi. 68 ; Bede, i. 28. It is dated on the same day as the rest.
It directs Virgilius to avail himself of the help of ' our common brother
Augustine,' if he should visit Arles, for the correction of ' offences of priests or
others.' For, says Gregory significantly, ' it often happens that those who are
at a distance are the first to understand what has to be set right.'

[3] Tertull. de Pallio, 5. It was a loose garment, which might be so worn as to
leave the breast or arm bare, or to conceal the whole person (hence ' palliate ').
See the catacomb painting found in the cemetery of St. Callistus, in which a

might be of plain or of rich materials : the coarse 'pallium[1]' of
philosophers was retained by scholars who became Christians,
and adopted by Christian ascetics : Alexandrian bishops in the
fifth century wore a white woollen scarf round the neck,
called an 'omophorion'[2], apparently a diminished pallium : the
original shape, that of a cloak, is thought to have been used
in the West in the fifth century[3]. But a rich form of this
garment became part of the Imperial attire, and was granted
by emperors, as a mark of honour, to patriarchs[4] : then the
popes began, originally in the emperor's name[5] or by his
desire, to 'allow the use of the pall' to certain bishops,—to
those who represented the 'Apostolic see,' or to some metropolitans, or to other prelates of influence and distinction[6]. In
Gregory's time it was thus variously granted : his language
shows that it was splendid, and somewhat cumbrous[7] : the
wearer was to guard against self-complacency[8]; it was not
to be worn except at mass[9]. Although in several cases it

man clad in the pallium, but with shoulder and breast bare, extends his hands
towards bread and fish on a tripod ; Northcote and Brownlow, Roma Sotter-
ranea, p. 267, Plate 14.

[1] Also called τρίβων, Soc. iii. 1. It was worn by Justin (Euseb. iv. 11) and
Heraclas (Euseb. vi. 19). Nepotian, a presbyter, wore it until his last moments ;
Jerome, Ep. 60. 13. Salvian describes a monk's usual appearance by 'palliatum;'
Gub. Dei, viii. 4. The first Council of Orleans uses 'pallium accepisse' as
equivalent to monastic profession, c. 21 ; Mansi, viii. 355,

[2] See the story of Theophilus of Alexandria in Fleury, b. 21. c. 3. Symeon
of Thessalonica describes the omophorion as encircling the shoulders before
and behind ; De Templo et Missa, ap. Goar, Euchol. p. 220. That it was
worn about the neck appears from Liberatus' account of the 'pall of St. Mark,'
Breviar. 20. All Eastern bishops now wear it : they lay it aside at the Gospel,
and resume it before communion ; see Goar, 147, 305. Cp. Neale, Introd.
East. Ch. i. 312.

[3] Life of St. German, p. 244. The word is also used for a woman's cloak,
Greg. Tur. H. Fr. iii. 29, and for a silk cloak for men, Bede, Hist. Abb. 8,
and in Adamn. Vit. Col. iii. 1 as an equivalent 'for peplum' and 'sagum.'

[4] Collier, i. 160 ; Robertson, Hist. Ch. iv. 133, and Growth of Papal Power,
p. 121. Valentinian III. gave a pallium of white wool to the bishop of Ravenna ;
Hodgkin, Italy and her Invaders, i. 485.

[5] See Greg. Ep. i. 28, ix. 11. Pope Vigilius would not grant the pall to the
archbishop of Arles until he gained the emperor's consent.

[6] Note of Bened. Edit. on Ep. i . 11. Gregory sends it to the bishop of
Corinth ; Ep. v. 57.

[7] Ep. iii. 56 ; v. 53 ; vi. 9. His own pall was *mediocre* ; John Deac. iv. 84.

[8] Ep. iv. 1 ; v. 11 ; ix. 125.

[9] Ep. iii. 56 ; v. 56. Gregory objected to its being worn in penitential

was an accompaniment of metropolitan dignity, it did not become a necessary badge of that dignity until a later stage in the development of Papalism[1]. Now to return to the letter; Gregory says of the British bishops, in contrast to the Gallic, that they are all committed to the care and authority of Augustine. Herein he was asserting a claim which those bishops, as we shall see ere long, would not admit. They recognised the primacy or precedency of Rome, but did not deem themselves under subjection to its supremacy[2]. Gregory relied on the 'apostolic' prerogatives of the 'see of Peter' throughout the West, not to speak of Eastern Christendom. Had he been reminded that the eighth canon of the Council of Ephesus had forbidden any bishop to assume power over any province that had not originally been under his jurisdiction[3], and that Britain was properly outside the Roman patriarchate[4], he would doubtless have fallen back on the

processions. Alcuin exhorts the archbishop of York not to wear his pall save when attended by deacons; Haddan and Stubbs, iii. 503.

[1] See Robertson, Hist. Ch. iv. 133.

[2] Lingard contests this, and says that Gregory had evidently no expectation that the British bishops would assert independence; A.-S. Ch. i. 380. But Gregory, after the manner of Popes, would take for granted that a claim made in the name of St. Peter would succeed. Lingard puts a manifest force on some words of Gildas' 'Increpatio' to clergy; and argues, as to earlier times, as if the burden of proof did not lie with those who hold that the British Church was from the first subject to Rome. He assumes also that the influence of the Roman see over Gaul would imply a parallel influence over Britain; p. 375. (He misinterprets the famous passage in St. Irenæus, iii. 3.) He does not dwell on the synodal letter of the Council of Arles: which, however, is open to some doubt.

[3] 'That none of the bishops shall take possession of a province that was not from the first and originally under his hand or that of his predecessors; and that if any one has taken possession of such, or has subjected it to himself by force, he shall restore it, in order that the rules of the fathers may not be transgressed, and the arrogance of (secular) authority may not come in unawares under the pretence of priestly action, and we may not by degrees and unconsciously lose the liberty which our Lord Jesus Christ, the liberator of all men, gave us by His own blood. Therefore it is the pleasure of the Holy Œcumenical Synod that to each province be preserved pure and inviolate the rights belonging to it from the beginning,' &c. Mansi, iii. 1469.

[4] The Roman patriarchate, properly speaking, included the ten provinces which were civilly under the Vicarius Urbis, i.e. Italy south of the 'Italic diœcese,' with the three adjacent islands; the churches of this region being called 'suburbicary.' Thus Africa, Spain, Gaul, and Britain were not originally within the Roman 'patriarchate.' See Bingham, b. ix, c. 1.

inherent supremacy of his see. Vehement as were his protests against the adoption by another patriarch, or the application to himself, of the title of ' Universal Bishop[1],' he always acted on that theory respecting his own office which had been gradually developing itself from the early part of the fifth century, and was to develope itself yet more in after-times, Pope after Pope 'never retracting, but adopting and uniformly improving upon the pretensions of their predecessors[2].' This system Gregory inherited, believed in it firmly, acted on it persistently[3] : his virtues, in fact, recommended and fortified what was in itself, and as judged by the light of genuine Catholic tradition, nothing better than a gradual corruption, by excess, of the ecclesiastical polity of the first ages. It would be most unjust to compare him to a Gregory VII. or Innocent III., to Martin V. or to Pius IX.; yet the line which he took was preparing the way for such successors, and formed an element in the process by which an indefinite precedency and a limited patriarchate were, in effect, to be superseded by a claim to dominion at once œcumenic in its scope and autocratic in its character. The result to the English Church was, that it became more and more dependent on Rome. While Gregory was perfectly in his rights in occupying the ground which British bishops had abandoned; while gratitude for the sending of Augustine, and again afterwards for the appointment of Theodore,—the results of which tended to obscure the amount of non-Roman mission-work done among the English,—naturally led the English Church, when organised, to lean to Rome as colonists look to a mother-country, without raising questions as to

---

s. 9 ff.; Bp. Wordsworth, Theoph. Anglic. p. 134; and the writer's 'Notes on Canons of First Four Councils,' p. 122.

[1] Greg. Ep. v. 18, 19, 20, 43; vii. 31, 33; viii. 30; ix. 68. He calls the title new, foolish, frivolous, proud, perverse, wicked, blasphemous, anti-christian. His indignation is sharpened by jealousy of the see of Constantinople; and he strains the title beyond what its use in the East implied, e.g. 'Si unus, ut putat, universalis est, restat ut vos episcopi non sitis;' ix. 68.

[2] Hussey's Rise of the Papal Power, p. 149.

[3] See e.g. the celebrated letter to Desiderius of Vienne about his lecturing on 'grammar,' Ep. xi. 54. In ix. 59 he says broadly that he knows not what bishop, in case of misconduct, is *not* subject to the apostolic see. See Church, Misc. Essays, p. 256.

what the Roman Church might in strictness claim on account of these great services[1]; a yet stronger tie to Rome was formed by that current and growingly dominant exaggeration of a primacy into supremacy, under the influence of which it seemed a religious duty to regard the chair of St. Peter as the one centre of unity, and, more than that, as the permanent seat of decisive authority, for the universal Church of Christ.

We may say of Augustine's questions, taken altogether, and including some which referred to matters of ceremonial purity, that they illustrate his monastic inexperience of pastoral administration, and also, perhaps, indicate a certain want of elevation of character. They are hardly, at any rate, the questions which a great mind would have found it necessary to refer to a distant superior; in fact, some of them give the notion of a mind cramped by long seclusion, and somewhat helpless when set to act in a wide sphere. Other questions may occur to us, as naturally arising in presence of spiritual interests and requirements so vast and so absorbing: but Augustine does not propound them. One feels a sort of chill, a sensation akin to disappointment, in reading of his 'difficulties[2].'

Stories of miracles.

A letter of which Bede[3] gives a fragment, and which was probably sent at this time, although the original date is lost[4], was intended, in great part, as a warning against spiritual elation. It brings us in front of a question which mediæval narratives perforce suggest. Gregory had heard from Augustine's messengers that miracles had been wrought by his means among the English. Now, of the mediæval stories of miracles the great bulk may be summarily dismissed,—not

[1] See Bp. Wordsworth, Theoph. Anglic. p. 140.

[2] In the Benedictine text of Gregory, the questions are broken up into eleven; and there is also a request for relics of St. Sixtus, which is probably an after addition.

[3] Bede, i. 31. The entire letter is in Ep. xi. 28. It begins, 'Gloria in excelsis . . . . quia granum frumenti mortuum est cadens in terram, ne *solum* regnaret in cœlo. . . . . Who can describe the joy that has arisen in the hearts of all the faithful here, quod gens Anglorum . . . . sanctæ fidei luce perfusa est?'

[4] Both this letter and the 'Replies' were probably written, though not sent, before 601; Haddan and Stubbs, iii. 32.

merely, nor indeed mainly, because of the contrast which so
many of them present, by their grotesqueness, or puerility,
or matter-of-course profusion, to the 'signs' recorded in
Scripture[1], but because the interval between the alleged
occurrence and the account of it is usually long enough to
allow of a rank upgrowth of legend, encouraged by the fixed
preconception of the age, that miracles must always attend
upon, and attest, high sanctity. Such an interval, for instance,
is found in the case of the marvels connected with St. Alban.
But in other cases we have something like contemporary
evidence; yet, even here, deductions must be made for that
craving after wonders[2] which would not think of sifting
testimony[3], if not also for that strange mixture of belief
and untruthfulness which tempted men,—especially if any
selfish end could be served,—to promote a cause by inventing
fresh samples of that supernatural vindication, which they
never doubted it to have received in times and circumstances
parallel to their own. To these considerations must be added
the obvious intrinsic difference between the miraculous
elements in the New Testament narrative, professedly connected, as they are, with the inauguration of a revelation, and
the luxuriant and often fantastic thaumaturgy which confronts

[1] Take, for instance, the legends of St. Teilo and St. Oudoceus, as given in
the Liber Landavensis; and see Trench on Miracles, p. 47.

[2] See the judicious remarks of Lingard, A.-S. Ch. ii. 101 ff. Sometimes an
ordinary, or at least a clearly natural occurrence, is not embellished by
miraculous adjuncts, but simply assumed to be supernatural : as when
Cuthbert, suffering from a swollen knee, and lying in the open air, is advised
by a horseman in white to apply a poultice of wheaten flour boiled in milk,
which proves efficacious, whereupon 'agnovit angelum fuisse.' Bede, Vit.
Cuthb. 2. See too the stories about animals, as the two otters in Vit.
Cuthb. 10. Comp. Chr. Remembr. Jan. 1852, p. 83: 'Bede regarded as
miraculous, and called a miracle, what we neither regard nor call so.' Comp.
Hardwick, Ch. Hist., M. Ages, p. 113. See Barmby, Gregory the Great,
p. 117 : 'Most of the incidents on record, supposed to be miraculous, may now
be accounted for by the' then 'prevalent state of feeling and expectancy,' &c.
Gregory himself, as his 'Dialogues' show, 'was predisposed to interpret every
marvellous incident as a special harbinger of the Second Advent;' Owen on
Dogm. Theol. p. 312.

[3] It must, however, be remembered that Bede is often careful to mention
his informant and attest his credibility; see Vit. Cuthb. 5, 36; H. E. iii. 13,
19; iv. 25, 31, 32; v. 2, 3, 4, 5, 6, 13. Lingard says, 'Bede relates several
wonderful events, but not one on *his own* knowledge ;' A.-S. Ch. ii. 103.

CHAP. II. us in mediæval books. At the same time, no serious believer in Christianity will fail to disentangle the question of mediæval miracles from the so-called scientific presupposition, which would put the 'signs' or 'mighty works' of the Gospel itself out of court as *ipso facto* impossible. It is a question of evidence: a very acute writer on Christian evidences has said that 'we reject the mass of later miracles because they want evidence, not because our argument obliges us to reject all later miracles, whether they have evidence or not[1]:' and a great Christian historian has not hesitated to avow his belief that 'with regard to some miracles, there is no strong *a priori* improbability in their occurrence, but rather the contrary; as, for instance, where the first missionaries of the Gospel in a barbarous country are said to have been assisted by a manifestation of the Spirit of power; and *if* the evidence appears to warrant' our 'belief,' we may 'readily and gladly yield it, . . . most thankful to find sufficient grounds for believing that not only at the beginning of the Gospel, but in ages long afterwards, believing prayer has received extraordinary answers[2].' Augustine was not the man, we may well think, to impose on Gregory by an account which was a fraud. Some things evidently *did* happen, in relation to his converts, which he took to be miraculous: what they were, we know not: but if, at such a time, and amid such a work, he received some signal answers to prayer, that can be no difficulty to believers in the Gospel[3]. Gregory's warning, at once tender and thoughtful, has the true Gospel mark upon it. He reminds his 'dearest brother' that Christ bade the Seventy rejoice, not in their power over the spirits, but rather that their names were written in heaven; that the grace which is open to all is better than the gifts entrusted to a few, and ought to be the subject of a deeper joy than could be caused by any individual endowment[4]; that such gifts

---

[1] Mozley, Bamp. Lect. p. 229.

[2] Arnold's Lectures on Mod. Hist. p. 133. He adds, 'If we think that, supposing the miracle to be true, it gives the seal of God's approbation to *all* the belief of him who performed it, this is manifestly a most hasty and untenable inference.'

[3] See Christlieb, Mod. Doubt and Christian Belief, E. Tr. p. 332.

[4] Comp. Greg. Dial. i. 2, 'Ego virtutem patientiæ signis et miraculis

carried with them a special temptation to spiritual self-
confidence, and that their possessor should make them an
occasion for self-scrutiny and deepened penitence, and regard
them as, in effect, bestowed not on himself, but on those
for whose benefit they had been given. 'I have a sure
hope,' he proceeds, in a part of the letter which Bede omits,
'that your sins are already forgiven, and that you are a
chosen instrument for bringing others to the same mercy[1].'

A third letter, sent with the others[2], informed Augus-Scheme for
tine that he would receive with it a pall, to be used only Bishoprics.
in the celebration of mass. This was, for him, a token
of archiepiscopal jurisdiction; but in the exercise of that
jurisdiction, Gregory seems to have thought of him as
seated permanently in London[3]. For he contemplates, with Plan for
a sanguine hopefulness as to the probable extent of the organisation of
missionary successes, the formation of twelve dioceses to be English
subject to Augustine as metropolitan, 'so that the bishop of Church.
London'—meaning evidently the successor of Augustine—
'might in future be always consecrated by his own synod' of
suffragans, over whom he was to preside as archbishop.
Further, Augustine was to consecrate a bishop for York,—
here Gregory's thoughts went back to Deira,—and if that
city and the parts near it should receive the word of God,
that bishop should also consecrate twelve suffragans[4], and act
as their metropolitan; for Gregory intended, if he lived (he
did not then think he should live much longer[5]), to send him
also a pall. Augustine, for his life, was in this case to be
supreme over the northern metropolitan; 'we will that he
should be subject to your control:' but after Augustine's

majorem credo;' ib. i. 12, 'Vitæ vera æstimatio in virtute est operum, non
in ostensione signorum;' and ib. iii. 17, that spiritual miracles transcend
physical.

[1] 'If,' he concludes, 'there is joy in heaven over one penitent, what must
there be over a penitent nation! .... Let us then say, let us all say, Gloria
in excelsis!'

[2] Bede, i. 29; Greg. Ep. xi. 65.

[3] Thus it was not Gregory, but the ecclesiastical and civil authorities of
England, who established the southern archbishopric at Canterbury.

[4] See Bede, Ep. to Egb. 5. 'The parts near York' would, in Gregory's mind,
include a large part of Scotland. See Freeman, Norm. Conq. iv. 349.

[5] See Ep. xi. 33, 'Me proximum morti video.'

death the metropolitans of London and York were to be independent of each other, acting in concert [1], and taking precedence according to seniority. Gregory reiterated his intention to place *all* the bishops in Britain under Augustine's personal supervision; 'that from the tongue and life of your Holiness they may receive the rule of believing rightly and living well.' The scheme drawn out, symmetrical and theoretically satisfactory as it was, remained a paper-scheme only: the fair vision of twelve bishops under Augustine, and twelve more under a bishop sent by him to York, was not realised. Canterbury, of which Gregory took no account, remained the seat of the archbishopric, for the sufficient reason that London, as we shall see presently, could not for long years be regarded as, in any real sense, Christian. Augustine himself did not succeed in settling more than *two* bishoprics; and it was in the time of his third successor that York became an English see.

Gregory's gifts.

Beside the pall, Gregory sent a supply of sacred 'vessels[2],' altar-cloths[3], and church-furniture, with vestments[4] for priests and clerics, relics of the Apostles and martyrs[5], and also a great number of manuscripts. The monastic chronicler[6] recites a long list of these 'first-fruits of the books of the whole Church of England,' including a 'Gregorian Bible' in two volumes, two copies of the Gospels[7],

---

[1] 'Communi consilio et concordi actione quæque sunt pro Christi zelo agenda,' &c.

[2] See Greg. Ep. i. 68, 'in argento calices duos.'

[3] See Ep. i. 68, 'where 'pallia' is thus used, and Dial. i. 10 for the 'sindon' on the altar. Gregory of Tours speaks of the altar and the oblations being covered 'pallio serico;' H. Fr. vii. 22. Cp. Dict. Chr. Antiq. i. 469.

[4] See Ep. vii. 40, 'duo oraria:' Dial. i. 9, 'episcopus ... elevatis manibus extenso vestimento:' ib. iv. 40 on a deacon's dalmatic. See Elmham, p. 99, on six ancient copes at St. Augustine's.

[5] See Ep. iii. 19; iv. 30; ix. 122; and above, p. 66. The monks of St. Augustine's believed that this gift of relics included a part of 'Aaron's rod;' Elmham, p. 102.

[6] Elmham, Hist. Monast. S. Aug. pp. 96-99 (see Introd. p. xxv).

[7] Two MSS. still extant have been supposed to be these 'Textus Evangeliorum.' One is in the Bodleian; the beginning and end are lost. It lies open at Mark xv. 28, ET ADIMPLETA EST SCRIPTURA QUAE DICIT .. But, on the authority of the late Bodleian Librarian, H. O. Coxe, it may be confidently dated some fifty years later, i. e. 'circ. 650-700.' Another, in the library of

two Psalters, a book on the Apostles' lives and deaths, a
Passionary or Martyrology, an exposition of the Epistles
and Gospels for several Sundays, all adorned with silver
or jewels, and carefully preserved in St. Augustine's abbey.
But we cannot be sure that all these treasured volumes,
four of which were kept above the high altar itself, were
veritable 'libri Gregoriani.'

To the same date belong two letters which Gregory addressed to Ethelbert and Bertha. He exhorts the former[1],
as 'set over the English race,' with 'kings and peoples subject
to him,' to follow the example of the first Christian Emperor:
and he particularly advises him to put down idolatry, and to
destroy its temples[2]. In the letter to Bertha[3], some gentle
rebuke for her apparent tardiness[4] in the good work is blended
with the assurance that what she had at last done has made
the Romans pray for her long life, and excited interest even
in Constantinople. Let her take Helena, the mother of Constantine, for a model, and make up for past neglect by greater
zeal in support of the mission. Commendatory letters were
also addressed to eleven Gallic prelates[5], and to Theodoric,
Theodebert, Chlotair, and Brunhild. One of these letters
requested the archbishop of Lyons to see that nothing should
delay the journey of the four monks through that part of
Gaul[6].

Some weeks passed away: Gregory received no tidings
from them, and became anxious about their safety. He had
also time to reconsider his advice given to Ethelbert in

Corpus Christi College, Cambridge, is thought by Hardwick to be probably a
'veritable relic of St. Gregory's benefaction;' Pref. to Elmham, p. xxvi.

[1] Bede, i. 32; Ep. xi. 66. The letter contains an expression of his belief
that 'the end of the world was approaching.' If the troubles that are to
herald it should occur in Ethelbert's country, let him not be disturbed by them.

[2] 'Fanorum ædificia.' Comp. Bede, i. 30; ii. 13, 15; iii. 30.

[3] Ep. xi. 29: not in Bede. This letter is not dated, but is evidently a companion letter to the former.

[4] 'Jamdudum . . . debuistis . . . Nec tardum . . . debuit esse nec difficile . . .
Agite ut . . . possitis quod neglectum est reparare.'

[5] Ep. xi. 54–58.

[6] Ep. xi. 56. This letter has a special interest. Gregory tells the archbishop
that as yet he has searched in vain for the writings of St. Irenæus (i. e. the
Greek original), or for the record of his death.

favour of the destruction of Pagan temples. On this subject two views were open: in the fourth century many temples were overthrown by the zeal of individual Christians, and some acts of this sort in the reign of Constantius provoked unsparing reprisals in that of Julian [1]. As Paganism grew weaker in the latter years of that century, these attacks were renewed by St. Martin in Gaul [2], by Marcellus of Apamea in Syria [3], by Theophilus at Alexandria [4]. Bishops in Africa petitioned the Emperor that such temples as were not among the ornamental buildings of cities might be utterly destroyed [5]: those in Rome itself, according to Jerome, were 'covered with dust and cobwebs' in 403 [6]; but we may allow for his characteristic exaggeration, and his own words show that these old fortresses of idolatry had not been levelled to the ground when the whole system of Pagan worship was put under the ban of imperial law in 392, several years after the closing of temples had been enforced in parts of the empire [7]. Gradually the temples fell into ruin, or were pulled down under authority, or converted into Christian churches, as was sometimes the case, St. Augustine tells us, in Africa [8]. And to this latter treatment of them Gregory, on reflection, now decidedly inclined [9]. 'They ought by

---

[1] See the case of Mark of Arethusa, Soz. v. 10 ; Theodoret, iii. 7.

[2] Sulp. Sev., Vit. Mart. 13,—the story of the ancient temple and its adjacent pine-tree.

[3] Theodoret, v. 21. Marcellus had the support of the prefect.

[4] Soc. v. 16. Theophilus acted under special orders from Theodosius.

[5] Cod. Afric. 58 ; Mansi, iii. 766.

[6] Jerome, Ep. 107. 1. He says that the destruction of the great temple at Gaza was continually expected ; ib. 2.

[7] See Robertson, Hist. Ch. i. 393 ff.

[8] Aug. Ep. 47. 3 : ' Vel in honorem Dei veri convertuntur.' See Add. Notes, A. But in Bede iii. 30 we find, ' Ut relictis sive destructis fanis . . . . aperirent ecclesias.'

[9] It had been already carried out as to a temple at Novara in the early part of the sixth century : see Ennodius, Dictio 2, and Carm. ii. 11 :—

'Perdidit antiquum quis relligione sacellum,
 Numinibus pulsis quod bene numen habet?'

So also in the case of the Roman temple of Romulus or Remus, dedicated in 527 by Felix IV. to SS. Cosmas and Damian. And a few years after Gregory's death it was carried out in regard to the Pantheon, which became a church of St. Mary *ad Martyres,* or, as Bede, who refers to this act of Boniface IV., describes it, ' Sanctæ Dei genetricis et omnium martyrum Christi ;' ii. 4.

no means,' so he wrote in a letter to Mellitus[1], 'to be destroyed:' Mellitus was to tell Augustine, when he saw him,
that Gregory desired them, if solidly built, to be cleansed
and hallowed for Christian worship. The people might be
the more ready to attend that worship if it were solemnised
in places which they had formerly frequented; and as they
had also been wont to hold sacrificial feasts[2], it would be
wise to provide them with some other enjoyments by way of
compensation. On the day of the dedication, or on the festivals
of those saints whose relics are there deposited, let the converts
make themselves 'tabernacles' with boughs of trees[3] around
the temples now turned into churches, and there kill oxen, no
longer in 'sacrifice to devils,' but as the materials of their meal,
and with thanks to the Giver of all things[4]. For, he proceeds, with a true insight into the need of patient training
and much tolerance for such rude proselytes, 'you cannot cut
off everything at once from rough natures: he who would
climb to a height must ascend step by step, he cannot
jump the whole way[5].' Some pleasures permitted to the
English country folk, in connection with places familiar from
their earliest remembrances, and now associated with their
new belief, might be really helpful: the 'outward enjoyment' might open their hearts to a deeper and a spiritual
joy. A wise and a hopeful policy, if the old scenes and the
old usages could be thus effectually cleared of heathen taint.
Probably St. Martin, and others who felt and acted like

[1] Bede, i. 30.

[2] Comp. Greg. Turon. Vit. Patr. 6. 2.

[3] Trees were often directly associated with idolatry. See the passage in
Sulpicius, above referred to; and the custom of hanging up skulls of slain
animals on a pear-tree in Auxerre, Constantius' Vit. S. Germ. i. 2. Cp.
Greg. Ep. ix. 11.

[4] Gregory's kind heart took pleasure in helping the poor to enjoy themselves.
See his Ep. i. 56: he bids a subdeacon furnish to some poor people, on the
occasion of dedicating a monastic oratory, 200 lambs, 100 hens, 30 amphoræ of
wine, &c.,—' and charge it in your accounts.'

[5] 'Quia et is qui summum locum ascendere nititur, gradibus vel passibus,
non autem saltibus, elevatur.' Memorable words, which might be used in a
deeper sense, to represent the momentous principle of a gradual Divine education of humanity, adapting itself to the fact that ' the natural motion of the
human understanding is by steps and stages,' (Mozley, Ruling Ideas in Early
Ages, p. 244.)

him[1], would have demurred to the possibility of such a clearing: and the intense tenacity of Heathen customs in mediæval Europe might be urged in support of their severer view[2]. If the old idol-fanes were left, if any likeness of the old Pagan feastings were tolerated or encouraged, would any Christian benediction prevent a revival of the heathenish spirit? would not 'the cask retain its odour,'—would not the ejected fiend return to his old house? Experience had proved this to be too possible in regard to the 'merry-makings[3]' which African bishops had endeavoured to Christianise, but which St. Augustine had found it necessary, in the interests of Christian morality, to condemn. Yet the 'condescension,' the 'economy,' which Gregory here recommended, and which his namesake of Neocæsarea in the third century had carried out exactly in the same method[4], and apparently with great

[1] See Willibald, Vit. S. Bonifac., 8, on the destruction of the oak of Thunor; and Maclear, Conv. of Slavs, p. 134, on St. Otho of Bamberg.

[2] To take sixth-century documents only,—Councils of that age had forbidden the eating of idol-meats, and the swearing by the heads of animals (Orleans, in 533 and 541); the worshipping or making vows at rocks or under trees (Tours, Auxerre); the Pagan revelries on New Year's Day, the use of lots made of wood or bread (Auxerre): see Mansi, viii. 838; ix. 116, 803, 911; and sermons 265, 277, 278, apparently by St. Cæsarius, in appendix to S. Aug. Serm. For Gregory's own vigilance on this subject, see his Ep. viii. 18, 'Pervenit ad nos quosdam illic' (at Terracina) 'arbores colere;' and his Dial. ii. 8, for the story of St. Benedict destroying the altar of Apollo and erecting an oratory on its site. Heathen usages as to idol-sacrifices, eating of such sacrifices, divinations, auspices, auguries, lots, amulets, spells, eating horse-flesh, cutting of the body (like Baal-priests), vows or worship at fountains or trees or stones, heathenish observation of dreams, heathen rites on Thursday or on January 1, shouting in order 'to defend oneself' during an eclipse, 'placing a daughter on a roof or above a furnace to cure fever,' had to be denounced by various English penitentials and canons. See Haddan and Stubbs, iii. 190, 364, 424, 458; Johnson's E. Can. i. 378, 415, 513: compare Bede's own statement in iv. 27. The most compendious account of such customs as existing in Germany in the eighth century is the 'indiculus . . . paganiarum' in the 'Concilium Liptinense' of St. Boniface: 'De sacrilegio,' &c.

[3] 'Lætitiæ.' S. Aug. Ep. 29.

[4] Gregory of Neocæsarea allowed the common people after their conversion 'to enjoy themselves at the memorials of the holy martyrs, hoping that they would in time advance to a graver and more regular life, while even the faith was guiding them to that result; which has, in fact, been already accomplished in the case of the majority, all their enjoyment having been transferred from bodily pleasure to the spiritual kind of joy.' Greg. Nyss. Vit. Greg. Thaumat. 27 (Op. iii. 574; Galland. Biblioth. Patr. iii. 466).

success, might seem, to bold and ardent minds, a natural
result of that Christian considerateness and hopefulness which
were inseparable from the true missionary character. Such
persons would say that children must be fed with milk, that
spiritual education must be gradual, that the 'spoils of the
strong man' might in a true sense be 'divided,' that the
Faith might be trusted to transform whatever it touched[1].
And if in some cases this policy of adaptation failed, if much
of what made up European life was only superficially Christianised, and religion suffered from the unguarded borrowing
of notions or customs really foreign to its spirit[2], in other
cases the 'deadly pottage' was made harmless, the leaven
pervaded and assimilated the lump: forms of beauty, once
bound up, inextricably as it might seem, with idolatry and
its attendant sensuality, were gradually detached, and, so to
speak, baptized[3]: words once suggestive of Paganism lost
by degrees their evil significance, as we, for instance, may
remember whenever we name the days of the week[4]: and in
ways which Tertullian, for instance, would never have dreamed

[1] So the Irish believed that St. Patrick, finding three pillar-stones which
were connected with Irish paganism, did not overthrow them, but inscribed on
them the names, Jesus, Soter, Salvator; Stokes, Tripartite Life, i. 107. A
Pictish well, said to have baleful powers, was said to have been made holy by
Columba's blessing and touch; Adamnan, Vit. Col. ii. 11. One of the boldest
acts ever done on this principle is recorded of St. Barbatus of Benevento, who
melted down a golden image of a viper which the half-heathen inhabitants had
venerated, and made a paten and chalice out of it; see Baring Gould, Lives
of Saints, Feb. 19.

[2] E. g. the traces of polytheism in the 'worship' of saints; the tendency to
an idolatrous use of images; old heathen spells retained with Christ's name
inserted into them (Kemble, i. 365); the old divination by lots disguised as
'sortes sanctorum' (Council of Agde, c. 42); Pagan superstitions linked to
Christian holy-tides, as the eves of St. John Baptist and All Saints. See
Todd's St. Patrick, pp. 128, 500. There was sometimes a temptation to make
compromises with Heathenism, as in Norway and Iceland in the tenth century;
see Maclear's Conversion of Northmen, pp. 57, 185.

[3] See the noble passage in Abp. Trench's Huls. Lect. p. 121, ed. 3.

[4] See Taylor's Words and Places, p. 320; Trench, Study of Words, p. 93.
Bede says, De Temporum Ratione, 15, 'people now call the Paschal time after
the goddess Eostre, consueto antiquæ observationis vocabulo gaudia novæ
solemnitatis vocantes.' So Kemble, i. 376; Neale, Essays on Liturgiology,
p. 521; Skeat, Etymol. Dict. Compare Yule, the midwinter feast, turned
into a synonym for Christmas; and on the change of the midsummer festival
of Balder into the holyday of St. John Baptist, see Thorpe's Glossary,
letter W.

CHAP. II.　of, Christianity 'inherited the earth' by the boldness with which it claimed and took possession [1].

This letter of Gregory to Mellitus was the last of his gifts to the English mission [2]: and the arrival of Mellitus and his companions in Britain, which probably took place about the end of 601, seems to open a new chapter in the history of the newly-founded Church. The staff of the mission was now complete: the next few years would show what it could effect in the region subject to the immediate rule, or to the less definite supremacy, of the king who, after cautious deliberation, had so heartily adopted at once the hopes and the obligations which were involved in the reception of its creed.

---

[1] 'Christianity, always ready *to apply and hallow every legacy of the past.*' Lappenberg, i. 53.

[2] Bede says, ii. 1, that Gregory died in 605, having held 'the see of the Roman and apostolic church thirteen years, six months, ten days.' According to this, he came to the see in 591 ; but the true year seems to be 590 (see p. 38), and, adopting the same reckoning of the years of his pontificate, we gain 604 as that of his death. So L'Art de vérifier, iii. 278, and the Benedictine Life, Greg. Op. iv. 304, and Barmby, p. 141. John the Deacon says that a story was current in the English Churches to the effect that Gregory, remembering an instance of Trajan's justice and kindness, prayed for the deliverance of his soul from hell; ii. 44. He asserts that Gregory did not pray, but only wept; and that the result was that Trajan's soul was—not translated to paradise, but—simply 'ab inferni solummodo cruciatibus liberata.' The Benedictine 'Life' sets aside the story, including John's modification of it, as a fable; b. 3. c. 10.

CHAPTER III.

ONE of Augustine's first acts, if not the very first, after the arrival of the four new missionaries, was to act upon that sentence in Gregory's answers to his questions, which encouraged him to form relations with the British bishops and their Church. Ethelbert could in some ways promote his wish to confer with them personally, and to request their co-operation for the mission. Bitter as was their animosity against the Saxon name and race, they would at all events distinguish between heathen Saxons close to their border and the distant 'Bretwalda' who had so recently become a convert to the faith[1]. By some means or other, they were induced to agree to meet Augustine, in 602, or perhaps 603, 'at a place still called Augustine's Oak, on the confines of the Hwiccians and the West-Saxons[2].' The Hwiccians dwelt along the south bank of the Severn, so as to include Gloucester, Malmesbury, Bath, and Cirencester, in their district, as Bede knew it in his time[3]: so that a border line between this district and

First conference with British Bishops.

---

[1] Bede's account of the great kings in ii. 5 implies that Edwin was the first who gained a regular supremacy over the Britons; but Ethelbert was overlord to West-Saxons and Hwiccians; Freeman, i. 551.

[2] Bede, ii. 2. To hold a meeting under an oak was in conformity with old Gothic usage. 'Very many of the trysting-places of the English courts were marked in like manner by the oak, the beech, or the elm;' Palgrave, Eng. Comm. pp. 139, clviii. Oaks were taken as boundary-marks; see Shireoaks near Worksop, and Sevenoaks in Kent. See also Stevenson's Chron. Abingd. ii. p. xlii. In one list of boundaries, Chr. Ab. i. 26, the 'Foul Oak' occurs, so called from the Pagan worship once connected with it. See above, p. 73.

[3] For the province of the Hwiccas see Bede, iv. 13, 23. It included the counties of 'Gloucester, Worcester, and part of Warwick;' Freeman, Old-Engl. Hist. pp. 39, 82. See Green, Making of England, pp. 129, 147, 224.

CHAP. III. Wessex proper would run too far to the east to allow of our placing 'Augustine's Oak' at Aust or Austcliff, near the Bristol Channel. It was probably well within the territory of the Hwiccians, with whom, eleven years before, Britons had joined in the rising against Ceawlin[1]. And so we may imagine the feelings with which the Welsh prelates, doubtless provided with assurances of safety, left their own country to confer with a 'bishop of the Saxons' who derived his authority from Rome. We cannot identify these bishops. David, apparently, had died a year or two before ; Dubricius seems to have been already a recluse in Bardsey; Teilo was now bishop of Llandaff, if he had not been succeeded by Oudoceus[2]. If there was a successor of David at Menevia[3], he would probably accompany the successor of Dubricius. Caerleon was evidently merged in Llandaff: but there were bishoprics at Bangor, St. Asaph, and Llanbadarn, and also, there is some reason to think, at Llanafanfaur, at Margam, and perhaps at Weeg in Herefordshire[4]. The fresh recollection of a national synod, holden at Caerleon in the year of David's death[5], would render the prelates specially indisposed to any compromise of their independence, or any surrender of their usages. It was probably with some amount of jealous suspicion that they met the Roman strangers at 'the Oak.' Augustine, says Bede, 'began to try to persuade them by brotherly

[1] Malmesb. G. R. i. 17 ; Green, p. 209.

[2] Llandaff was the bishopric for Gwent, which is identified with Monmouthshire. Dyfed or Demetia is Pembrokeshire with part of Caermarthenshire, and was under St. David's. In the eighth century, according to Giraldus, Wales was divided into Venedotia, Deheubarth including Demetia, and Powys ; Descr. Camb. i. 2. Of these, Venedotia or Gwynedd comprised Carnarvonshire, Anglesey, most part of Merionethshire, part of Denbigh and Flint : its bishopric was at Bangor. Powys, under St. Asaph, included parts of Flint and Denbigh, part of Merioneth, and also of Shropshire, all Montgomery, part of Radnor and Brecknock. Deheubarth comprised the six southern counties.

[3] See above, p. 34. The Annal. Camb. date the death of Bishop Cynog or Cynauc, who by one account succeeded David, in 606.

[4] Bp. Jones and Freeman, Hist. St. David's, p. 266 ; Haddan and Stubbs, i. 148, iii. 41 ; Pryce, p. 145. If these latter bishoprics existed, they would be for Glamorganshire and Herefordshire. Llanafanfaur was in Brecknock.

[5] Annal. Camb. a. 601.

admonitions to hold Catholic peace with himself, and to CHAP. III.
undertake in conjunction with him the work of preaching the
gospel to the heathen, for the Lord's sake.' This was very
well, the Britons might remark; but what was meant by
Catholic peace? It appeared that there were some matters in
which the Britons were not at one with the rest of the Church.
What were they?

The first and chief point of difference was as to the mode of Paschal
reckoning Easter. The Paschal question is not attractive to question.
the reader of Eusebius; it is profoundly wearisome to the
reader of Bede[1]. The original form of it was simple. It
being agreed on all hands that there must be a yearly festival
in memorial of the Redemption, as effected by the Passion
and Resurrection of Christ; that a fast of some undefined
duration should precede it; and that this Christian Passover,
thus preceded by a fast, should to some extent be regulated by
the season of the Jewish Passover;—the question arose[2], 'To
what extent? Shall we conclude the fast, and begin the
festival, on that fourteenth day of the moon on which the
Jews were to kill their Passover, on whatever day of the
week it may fall? or shall we take as our fixed point
that first day of the week on which the Lord rose again?'
The majority of Churches took the latter alternative:
the Church of Ephesus, and those dependent on it in the
province of 'Asia,' took the former, and were therefore afterwards called Quartodecimans. Fresh complications arose

[1] Especially when one is forced to see the absence of a due sense of proportion
in his treatment of the subject; when he associates with these disputes such
a phrase as 'spiritalis gratiam lucis,' ii. 2; and again, 'Movit hæc quæstio
sensus et corda multorum, timentium ne forte accepto Christianitatis vocabulo,
in vacuum currerent aut cucurrissent,' iii. 25; and Egbert's success in winning
over the monks of Hy to 'the true Easter' just before his own death is
described as his 'seeing the day of the Lord,' &c., v. 22. Contrast Socrates,
v. 22.

[2] See Eus. v. 23, 24. He uses the phrases, 'the closing of the fast,'
'the festival of the Saviour's Passover,' 'the celebration of the mystery
of the Lord's Resurrection,' to describe one and the same thing. Polycrates,
the representative of the Quartodecimans, insists repeatedly on the duty
of adhering to (τηρεῖν) 'the fourteenth.' See Eus. v. 24. Our English
use of 'Easter' instead of 'Pasch,'—which was the usual term in
Scotland, as in Wales,—obscures to some extent the bearings of the
question.

in the third century, in connection with a question whether the festival should be always kept *after* the vernal equinox[1] : and different canons or 'cycles' were proposed, in order to ascertain for a number of years the true beginning of the 'first lunar' or the 'Paschal' month[2]. Thus Hippolytus made such a cycle, or table, for sixteen years[3] : Dionysius of Alexandria for eight[4] : Anatolius of Laodicea for nineteen[5]. The Nicene Council reaffirmed the maxim upheld against the Quartodecimans,—that the festival should always be on a Sunday ; and further directed, that if the fourteenth should fall on a Sunday, then Easter should be deferred to the Sunday after ; and that Easter Sunday should always follow the equinox,—in the calculation of which they virtually gave preference to the Alexandrian reckoning, which placed it on March 21, over the Roman, which placed it on March 18[6]. However, the Roman Church adhered to its own way in this matter ; and the result was that between A. D. 325 and 343 the Roman Easter fell six times on a different day from the Alexandrian[7]. In 344 the Sardican

---

[1] Hefele, Councils, i. 316 ff., E. Tr. 'The Jews had always determined the 14th' as falling after the equinox 'until the fall of Jerusalem;' afterwards they sometimes kept it before the equinox.

[2] Hefele, Councils, i. 318, E. Tr. Dict. Chr. Antiq. i. 591 : 'The use of cycles arose out of the necessity, when lunar months were in use, of linking together in some manner the changes of the moon and the sun.' King, Ch. Hist. Irel. i. 195 : 'In order to determine on what days the full moons will occur in coming years, different cycles or periods of so many years have been invented after the expiration of which the new and full moons were found to fall again on the same days as before.'

[3] Euseb. vi. 22. See it in Galland. Bibl. Patr. ii. 516 ff. It was inscribed on the marble chair of the statue of Hippolytus, on the right side of which was a table of Paschal full moons, on the left, of Easter Sundays, calculated according to a cycle of sixteen years. It began from the first year of Alexander Severus. Hippolytus would defer the Paschal festival for a week not only if the fourteenth, but 'also if the fifteenth moon fell on a Sunday' (Bucher. in Gall. p. 520). See his canon reduced to the form of that of Victorius, ib. p. 522 ; and see Hefele, i. 318 ; Dict. Chr. Antiq. i. 592 ff.

[4] Euseb. vii. 20.

[5] Euseb. vii. 32 ; Hefele, i. 320, 'the completion of this cycle of nineteen years is attributed to Eusebius of Cæsarea.' But see Bp. Lightfoot in Dict. Chr. Biogr. iii. 314.

[6] See Hefele, i. 325–327. Cp. Leo the Great, Ep. 121.

[7] Hefele, i. 328. See Smith's Bede, p. 697.

Council attempted a settlement, which was not in effect observed. Two successive archbishops of Alexandria, Theophilus and Cyril, framed Paschal tables based on the nineteen years' cycle: and although Rome for some time used the cycle of eighty-four years[1] which had superseded that of sixteen, and was 'a little improved by Sulpicius Severus,' 'it has been conjectured,' says Hefele, that Pope Hilary adopted the better scheme which had been framed by Victorius of Aquitaine[2], an abbot at Rome, in 456–7; and finally, in 527, one still more accurate, and completely in accordance with Alexandrian calculations, was proposed by Dionysius Exiguus, and accepted by Rome and Italy[3], while the Victorian cycle 'long held its ground in Gaul,' and the old cycle of eighty-four years was retained by the British and Irish Churches[4]. But the mere retention of an old-fashioned cycle was not the main ground of offence, which consisted in the circumstance that the insular Celts departed in fact from a Nicene rule[5], by allowing the fourteenth of the moon to be Easter Day, *if* it fell on a Sunday[6]; whereas in that case they ought to have

---

[1] Hefele, l.c.; Dict. Chr. Ant. i. 592. See Lanigan, Eccl. Hist. Ireland, ii. 374. Owing to these differences the Roman Easter in 387 was on March 21, the Alexandrian on April 25; in 444 the Roman rule would place Easter on March 26, the Alexandrian on April 23, and Leo adopted for the time the Alexandrian calculation: so in A.D. 455.

[2] For Victorius of Aquitaine's cycle of 532 years, found by multiplying the lunar cycle of 19 years by the solar of 28, see Prideaux, Connection, ii. 255; Smith's Bede, p. 700; Lanigan, ii. 377; Hefele, i. 330; Dict. Chr. Biogr. iv. 1139. The cycle began with A.D. 28.

[3] Hefele, i. 330; Prideaux, ii. 257; Smith's Bede, p. 701; Haddan and Stubbs, i. 152. The revision of the Victorian table by Dionysius 'transferred to him most of the merit which belonged to Victorius;' Dict. Chr. Ant. i. 594.

[4] Dict. Chr. Antiq. l. c.; Hefele, i. 330; Lanigan, ii. 384. For Gaul see fourth Council of Orleans, A.D. 541, can. 1, Mansi, ix. 113; Greg. Turon. Hist. Fr. v. 17, implies that most of the Gauls kept Easter in 577 according to Victorius: cp. ib. x. 23; and see Columban in Greg. Ep. ix. 127.

[5] Haddan and Stubbs, i. 153. See Bede, ii. 19, 'quod in Nicæna synodo,' &c.

[6] As Bede says, they observed Easter 'a quarta decima usque ad vicesimam lunam,' i. e. would include the fourteenth moon among those which might belong to Easter Sunday, and from it onwards to the twentieth. Cp. Bede, ii. 4, iii. 3, 17, 25, 28. Lanigan says that Sulpicius found that by a mistake in the Roman reckoning of the days of the moon, the fourteenth moon was called the sixteenth: he restored to it the name of fourteenth, and directed that as it was really the same day as the sixteenth of the unrevised cycle, Easter

G

CHAP. iii. deferred Easter till the twenty-first. According to the orthodox reckoning[1], the fifteenth was the first day of the moon which could be Easter Sunday; this method, starting at the fifteenth, and going on to the twenty-first, kept clear of the Jewish day ; whereas the Celtic did *not* keep clear of it[2]. That is, the Celtic calculation was objectionable as adhering to a discredited cycle for the Paschal moons, but distinctly offensive as including the fourteenth within the days on which Easter Sunday might fall. But, as we see at once, the Britons were not really Quartodecimans, inasmuch as they made a point of keeping Easter on a *Sunday*[3]; and their own claim to derive their traditional method from the Churches of Asia, and so from St. John himself, was without foundation. This, it may be added, annihilates an argument which has been often advanced in favour of a directly Oriental origin for the ancient British Church[4]. It appears also that the Britons relied on the authority of a Paschal canon ascribed to Anatolius, but now admitted to be a forgery, and 'perhaps designed to support' the Celtic rule[5].

Baptismal
Rites.

Another difference, but vaguely alluded to in Bede's account of the conference, consisted in this, that the Britons did not 'perform the ministry of baptizing fully according to the Roman manner[6].' If we ask in what respect they fell short, we are left without any certain answer. If they did not use

Sunday might fall on it. This rule was adopted by the Irish and British (ii. 384).

[1] In the fifth century, the Latins would not allow even the fifteenth to be kept as Easter Sunday : their Paschal limits began with the sixteenth; Lanigan, ii. 375, 378 ; Dict. Chr. Ant. i. 594. By one reading, the account of the 'third order of Irish saints' says that some of them kept Easter on the fourteenth moon (as did those of the first and second order), others on the sixteenth. See Todd's St. Patrick, p. 89.

[2] Prideaux, ii. 258. See Bede, v. 21.

[3] So says Bede of the Irish, who agreed with the Britons: iii. 4, 'Quem tamen et antea non semper in luna quarta decima, cum Judæis, ut quidam rebantur,' &c. Ib. iii. 17, 25. Nor had the earlier British Christians been Quartodecimans. See Euseb. V. C. iii. 9 ; Soc. v. 22 ; and the subscriptions of the three British bishops to the Council of Arles ; cp. Hefele, i. 321.

[4] Lingard, A.-S. Ch. i. 51 ; Lanigan, ii. 385 ; Haddan's Remains, p. 215.

[5] Dict. Chr. Ant. i. 594. See this 'canon' in Galland. Bibl. Patr. iii. 545. According to it, in nineteen years Easter Sunday fell three times on the fourteenth moon.

[6] 'Compleatis,' Bede, ii. 2.

trine immersion [1], this need not have been a serious difficulty
to the 'disciples' of a Pope who not only admitted that either
trine or single immersion might have an orthodox significance,
but advised the Spanish Church, under the circumstances of
its own position in regard to Arianism, to retain the latter
use [2]. Possibly the Britons did not practise that unction of
the crown of the head which usually came between the baptism
and the confirmation [3]; or they may have omitted some other
ceremonies which formed part of the Roman rite [4].

A third peculiarity, not mentioned here by Bede, although
he has enough to tell us about it in other passages [5], related to
the visible appearance of the Celtic clergy. To cut the hair
short was an ascetic fashion, which gradually extended itself
to all ecclesiastics [6]; it was supposed to carry out St. Paul's
hint in 1 Cor. xi. 14, to serve as a protest against effeminate
luxuriousness, and to represent 'seclusion from worldly pleasure [7],' and a special dedication to the service of God. By
degrees, an actual 'tonsure' came into use; and late in the
fifth century [8] it took the 'coronal' form, the top of the head

[1] Haddan and Stubbs, i. 153; Haddan's Remains, p. 320. Trine immersion was, however, the Irish practice; Stokes, Tripartite Life of St. Patrick,
i. p. clxxxiii.

[2] Greg. Ep. i. 43.

[3] Muratori, Lit. Rom. ii. 157. The unction of Confirmation was on the
forehead; ib. i. 571; Innocent I. Ep. 1. 3. The Irish certainly used chrism
in connection with baptism; Warren, Lit. and Ritual, p. 65.

[4] Hussey's Bede, p. 78. If the British clergy were careless as to naming each
Person of the Holy Trinity at the time of the 'immersion,' Augustine would surely
have insisted distinctly on a point so essential to the Sacrament. It is observable that St. Boniface asked for, and obtained, the Papal approval of an
English canon, to the effect that 'quicunque sine invocatione Trinitatis lotus
fuisset, sacramentum regenerationis non haberet;' Zach. Ep. ii. But the
Pope's words do not show that this canon was framed under Augustine (Warren,
Lit. and Rit. of Celtic Church, p. 66); on the contrary, he calls it a 'capitulum
pro *synodo* provinciæ.' See below, p. 94.

[5] Bede, iii. 26; iv. 1; v. 21, 22.

[6] See Bingham, b. vi. 4. 16; vii. 3. 6, that anciently the crown of the head
was not shaved, but the hair was kept short. He cites Jerome in Ezech. l. 13
to this effect, and Salvian de Gub. Dei, viii. 4, 'recisis comarum fluentium
jubis.' See also Greg. Turon. de Mirac. S. Mart. iii. 15, 'humiliatis capillis.'
Mabillon owns that in Benedict's time 'monachi ad cutem resecti *non* erant;'
Ann. Bened. i. 53. Yet some ancient ascetics shaved the head bare; Soc. iii. 1.

[7] Lingard, A.-S. Ch. i. 54.

[8] Smith's Bede, p. 712; Lanigan, iii. 68 ff. In 633, the fourth Council of

being shaved close, and a circle or crown of hair left to grow
around it. This fashion obtained in Gaul and in Italy.
But the Celtic clergy exhibited a semicircle of hair on the
front of the head [1], so that their continental brethren,
on inspecting them from behind, were scandalised by
finding 'the seeming crown lopped off [2].' The Roman tonsure was, of course, traced up to St. Peter [3]; and its wearers,
or at any rate the more zealous among them, were pleased
to attribute the rival fashion to Simon Magus [4]. If these
various disputes seem more or less trivial, let us remember
that when the Church was still fighting against masses of
heathenism, such points of external uniformity might 'well
have appeared, even to the strongest and most spiritual
minds, far graver than charity can allow them to be in our
time [5].'

To return to the conference. Bede tells us [6] that 'after a
long discussion,' in which the British delegates 'refused to
comply with the prayers, or the exhortations, or the reproaches of Augustine and his companions, but preferred their
own traditions to all the Churches which throughout the

Toledo, c. 41, ordered all clerics to shave the whole of the top of the head,
and leave below 'solam circuli coronam,'—not like the 'lectors' in Gallicia, who
wore long hair like laics, and shaved a small circle on the top of the head only.
The portrait of Gregory the Great shows the coronal tonsure.

[1] As the Irish themselves expressed it, 'one tonsure from ear to ear;'
Todd's Life of St. Patrick, p. 487. Patrick was called the Tailcend, or 'Shaven-
head;' ib. p. 411; Stokes, Tripartite Life, i. p. clxxxiv.

[2] 'Decurtatam;' Bede, v. 21. See this represented as on the head of St.
Mummolinus of Noyon, who had been a monk of Luxeuil; Mabillon, Ann.
Bened. i. 529.

[3] Aldhelm supposes St. Peter to have had three reasons for instituting it;
Ep. to King Geraint. Gregory of Tours says that Peter 'caput desuper tonderi
instituit' in order to teach humility; De Glor. Mart. i. 28; but see Maskell,
Mon. Rit ii. p. xcvi.

[4] Bede, v. 21: 'Tonsuram eam quam magum *ferunt* habuisse Simonem,'
&c. Aldhelm gives this as 'the opinion of very many.' See Stokes, Tripartite
Life, ii. 509. But it was also traced up to 'the swineherd of Laeghaire,
the Pagan king who resisted Patrick;' Reeves's Adamn. p. 350; Lanigan,
iii. 71.

[5] Goldwin Smith, Irish Hist. and Irish Character, p. 29. See Prof. Stokes,
Ireland and the Celtic Church, p. 155, that any approach to Judaising was
'still a real terror.'

[6] Bede, ii. 2: 'Qui cum longa disputatione habita,' &c.

world were at unity with each other in Christ,' Augustine
proposed to appeal to God for a sign that might 'declare
which tradition was to be followed, and by what path men
were to hasten to enter His kingdom.' The criterion which
he proposed was, 'Let a sick man be brought forward, and
let the party whose prayers shall avail for his cure be accepted as having the right faith and practice.' The Britons,
though reluctantly, agreed : a blind man of English race
was brought forward : 'the British priests' failed to cure him,
but Augustine prayed, the blind man received his sight, and
the Britons owned that it *was* the true way of righteousness
which Augustine taught, but added that they could not give
up their old customs without the consent of their brethren :
they therefore requested that a second synod might be held,
in which a larger number would be present. This part of the
story reads very like an 'interpolation[1]' into the original
narrative. Bede, no doubt, reported faithfully what was in his
time the Canterbury tradition[2] : but the incident of the
miracle might have become embodied in that tradition in the
course of a century or more ; and the Britons are represented
as acting with such inconsistency as they would hardly have
shown, especially when we read what follows. The second Second
meeting was held : seven British bishops, 'as is related[3],'— Conference.
so Bede with his usual caution tells us,—resolved on attending. This implies that the former gathering had not included
all the prelates[4]. They were accompanied by 'many most
learned men, especially' from the great monastery of Bangor
Iscoed, then under the rule of Abbot Dunod, whom Bede

---

[1] Hook, i. 68, treats it as a mere 'Canterbury tale.' It appears that the
delegates to the second conference knew nothing, or else thought nothing, of
the story of the blind man.

[2] Lingard observes that the abbot Albinus of Canterbury, who was Bede's
informant about Kentish Church affairs, derived his account partly from
documents, partly from 'seniorum traditione' (Bede, Præf.), and that this
'traditio,' at the distance of more than a hundred years, 'must have received
embellishments;' A.-S. Ch. i. 68.

[3] 'Ut perhibent.' Cp. i. 25, 'fertur;' ii. 1, 'dicunt;' ii. 5, 'ut vulgo
fertur;' ii. 12, 'ut ferunt;' ii. 16, 'perhibetur;' iii. 2, 'fertur ;' iii. 5, 12, 16,
'ferunt;' iii. 14, 16, 'fertur;' iv. 13, 'ferunt;' iv. 14, 'perhibentur;' iv. 19,
'ferunt,' 'sunt qui dicant;' iv. 23, 30, 'ferunt,' &c.

[4] See above, p. 31.

calls Dinoot. The deputies repaired beforehand to a hermit [1] famed for prudence and holiness, and asked whether he would advise them to give up their own traditions at Augustine's request, or not. The response was, 'If he be a man of God, follow him.' 'But how shall we ascertain that?' 'Our Lord,' replied the hermit, 'spoke of Himself as meek and lowly in heart. If Augustine shows that temper, you may believe that he has learned of Christ, and taken up His yoke, and is offering it to you. But if he is harsh and proud, it is clear that he is not from God: we are not to care for his words.' 'But how is *this* to be discerned?' The oracle gave a precise answer: 'Manage [2] so that he shall come to the meeting-place before you. If, when you approach, he rises to meet you, be sure that he is a servant of Christ, and listen to him obediently. If he does not rise up, but treats you contemptuously,—you are the more numerous body, and can show contempt in your turn [3]!' Some grains of fact may lie in this anecdote; yet the Britons would hardly have made so much depend on so little. But, if they consulted any such adviser, or agreed to apply so purely personal a test, it is clear, on Bede's own showing, as, indeed, it would be clear apart from this incident in the story, that they did not deem themselves bound to accept the exhortations of a bishop sent from Rome, and thus far a representative of Rome [4], as such. They treated the question as open: Shall we adopt his ways, or shall we not? They came, as they had resolved, to the

---

[1] The hermit-life was much honoured in Wales; compare the retirement of Dubricius to Bardsey. King Tewdric (see below) gave up his realm to his son Mouric, 'et vitam heremitalem in rupibus *Dindyrn* cœpit discere;' Monast. Angl. vi. 1222. See Girald. Descr. Camb. i. 18: 'Heremitas . . . . abstinentiae majoris, magisque spirituales, alibi non videas.' See Williams, Eccl. Ant. Cym. p. 232.

[2] 'Procurate ut ipse prior,' &c.

[3] 'Et ipse spernatur a vobis.'

[4] Lingard argues that the subjects of Papal authority and British independence did not come into consideration; Angl.-S. Ch. i. 380. This is futile. The British delegates could not fail to know that Augustine did come to them as specially empowered from Rome. And their reverence for Rome did not, in their view, commit them to obedience to its emissary. But it *must* have done so, had it included a belief in Papal supremacy. And the relation of the Celtic Churches to Rome was one of veneration without subjection, as is manifest from the language of such a typical Celtic saint as Columban.

meeting, after Augustine had taken his seat.   He continued
sitting [1] : he probably thought that he must assert his
dignity as archbishop, and did so in a manner as deficient in
tact as in courtesy.   According to Bede, the Britons at once
showed temper, 'charged him with pride, and made a point
of contradicting all that he said.'   He intended, no doubt,
to speak with calmness and moderation : 'You go against
our custom, or rather that of the Universal Church, on many
points : but if you are willing to yield on these three [2], to
keep Easter at its right time, to perform baptism according
to the manner of the holy Roman and apostolic [3] Church, and
to join with us in preaching the word of the Lord to the
English,—we will quietly bear with your other practices,
however contrary to our own.'   A speech so worded would Failure of
seem magisterial to the sensitive and suspicious auditors.   We the Conference.
are told that they said to each other, 'If just now he would
not rise to greet us, he will be yet more overbearing if we
begin to obey him ;' and that thereupon they gave their
decisive answer, 'We will do none of these things which
you require, nor will we have you as our archbishop [4].'   Not

[1] 'Sederet in sella,' Bede.   'Romano more in sella residens,' Bromton.
Various explanations of 'this apparent discourtesy' are offered in the English
'Life of St. Augustine,' p. 229.   After all, the writer pleads that at worst it
was but 'an excusable negligence,' and blames the British bishops for 'taking
such a trifle so much to heart.'   Elmham boldly contends that it would not
have been 'decens ut tam feros et erroneos . . . assurgendo inflaret,' after
having granted them a second conference; p. 105.   A reference to 'sellæ
plectiles' is in Greg. Ep. xii. 19.

[2] Pearson goes so far as to say that 'fresh from the large-minded concessions
of Gregory, Augustine made up his mind to great concessions, but he felt that
three points were too important to be sacrificed;' Hist. Engl. i. 125.   One of
the points waived was evidently the tonsure.   Another, as evidently, was the
use of a peculiar Liturgy; Warren, Lit. and Rit. of Celtic Ch. p. 76.   This
concession is ignored by those who exaggerate Augustine's stiffness.

[3] This phrase (cp. Bede, ii. 1, 7, iii. 29) has not the sense of 'the one Catholic
and Apostolic Church' of the Creed, but refers to the distinctive claim of Rome
among Western Churches to be of apostolic foundation.   Cp. the phrase
'apostolicus papa,' Bede, iv. 1, v. 19, or simply 'apostolicus.'

[4] The speech ascribed to Dunod, disowning the supremacy of the Pope, or, as
it is expressed, of 'him whom ye call Pope and Father (Daad) of fathers,' and
describing the British Church as under the government of the 'Esgob Kaerllion,'
is spurious, 'drawn up by some mediæval Welsh antiquary, and probably
enough suggested by Bede's account of the matter,' as 'it truly represents the
feeling of the then British Church towards Rome;' Haddan and Stubbs, i. 149.

CHAP. III. till this moment, as far as Bede's tale goes, had the archiepiscopal pretensions of Augustine been mooted; but the Britons must at any rate have been aware from the first that he claimed that rank among the English, and must have presumed that his proposals would involve their recognition of it, in case they agreed to work with him. He had not been faultless in his conduct of the matter: but even in the vehement words which at last broke from him [1], one sees that, what stirred him to grief and anger was not so much their defiance of his authority, as their refusal to aid in his missionary enterprise. 'If you will not accept peace with brethren, you will have to accept war from enemies: if you will not preach the way of life to the English, you will be punished with death by English hands.' These words have met with very opposite treatment, in consequence of a tragedy which happened some years after Augustine's death, probably in A.D. 613 [2]. Ethelfrid the 'Fierce' or the 'Destroyer,' who, ten years earlier, had utterly broken the aggressive power of the Argyllshire Scots at Degsastone [3], turned his arms against the Britons, and besieged the northern 'City of Le-

It was first edited by Spelman, and accepted by Stillingfleet; ii. 536, and Bramhall, i. 162, &c. See it in Migne, Patrol. Lat. lxxx. 22, and, in Welsh and Latin, in Smith's Bede, p. 716. Geoffrey makes Dunod say that they owed no subjection to Augustine, for they had an 'archipræsul' of their own,—and that they 'would not bestow their preaching on their enemies;' viii. 4 (xi. 12). The Llandaff story (see Usher, Antiq. p. 46), that Oudoceus of Llandaff submitted to the authority of Augustine, is a gross fiction; see Rees, Welsh Saints, p. 274. He observes that at the conference there was no question between the archbishop of the English and a British metropolitan; which would show that the archbishopric of Caerleon was extinct, '*if* indeed it had ever been firmly established;' ib. p. 291. See above p. 10.

[1] '*Fertur* minitans prædixisse,' Bede. 'In the anguish of disappointment,' Lingard, A.-S. C. i. 71. Milner (Hist. Ch. cent. 6. c. 1) charges him with 'ambitious encroachment,' but believes also that he was acting 'from charitable views.'

[2] Annal. Camb. a. 613. This date, rather than 605, or 607 (the two readings of Sax. Chron.), is adopted in Annals of Engl. p. 30; Haddan and Stubbs, iii. 41; Guest, Orig. Celt. ii. 309; Green, Making of England, p. 240.

[3] Bede, i. 34; S. Chron. a. 603. The kingdom of the Scots of Dalriada, then held by Aidan, seventh of the line, had been founded 100 years before, by Fergus Mor, son of Erc; but their original immigration into North Britain cannot be dated. See Skene, Celtic Scotland, i. 140; Haddan and Stubbs, ii. 105. 'Degsastan' seems to be Dawston near Jedburgh; Skene, i. 162; Green, p. 233.

gions,' i. e. Chester. The inhabitants risked a battle: just
before it began, Ethelfrid saw, 'standing apart in a place of
comparative security,' a large body of British priests, including a number of monks from the neighbouring monastery
of Bangor Iscoed, who, after a three days' fast, had come
under the escort of Brocmail[1], king of Powys, to pray for the
success of their countrymen. 'If,' said the stern Northumbrian,
' they are crying to their God against us, then are they fighting against us by curses, though not with arms. Attack them
first!' It was done, and only fifty escaped; Brocmail having
fled without striking a blow for those who had been entrusted
to his protection. Such was ' the battle of Cair Legion, wherein
the holy men were slain,' as it was described in Irish records [2];
' the battle of the orchard of Bangor [3],' as the Welsh sometimes
called it, from the subsequent destruction of that great house
with all its literary treasures: the remains of Bangor Iscoed exhibited, centuries later, a mass of ruined walls and
cloisters, and the rubbish of two gates of the town, called
Porth Kleis and Porth Wgan, a mile apart [4]. Chester was
taken [5], and apparently destroyed: but the slaughter of the
ecclesiastics was regarded by their countrymen as the most
tragic feature of the event [6], by Bede and the Saxon Chronicler

[1] Or Brochwel; Rees, Welsh Saints, p. 208. According to the Ann. Cambr.,
he survived till 662. But of the three British chiefs who fell in the battle,
Guest considers one to have been his grandson; l. c.

[2] Tighernach; O'Connor, Rer. Hib. Scr. ii. 182. On this battle see Freeman,
Engl. Towns and Districts, p. 278. Chester remained desolate until it was
restored by Æthelfled, Alfred's daughter, in 907.

[3] Rees, Welsh Saints, p. 293.

[4] Malmesb. Gest. Reg. i. 47; and Vaughan, ap. Camden, i. 666.

[5] See Palgrave, p. 455: 'The capture of the City of Legions was long
lamented by the Britons.' But about the same time, they had a triumph over
Ceolwulf of Wessex in the battle of Tintern, when the royal hermit Tewdric,
once king of Morganwg and ever victorious in war, left his cell at ' the cry of
his people,' and secured their victory at the cost of his own life, for one of the
foemen turned round in his flight and wounded him with a spear. According
to the legend, the dying hermit-king was borne in a wain to a place near the
Severn, where he bade his attendants depart, and expired alone; Mon. Anglic.
vi. 1223; Turner, i. 334.

[6] See Scott's lines, written for an old Welsh air, 'The Monks' March:'—
  'Woe to Brocmail's feeble hand,
  Woe to Olfrid's bloody brand,
  Woe to Saxon cruelty,
  O miserere, Domine!'

as a fulfilment of Augustine's 'prophecy:' and Bede so far forgets his better nature as to apply the word *nefandæ* to the patriotic British host [1]. On the other hand, some moderns, hostile to Augustine's memory, have imagined [2] that he himself, in revenge for the obstinacy of Welsh bishops, had induced the Northumbrian 'Destroyer' to slaughter the Welsh priests : whereas the battle took place, according to Bede, 'long' after his own death, which was not later than 605 ;— and even if it had been fought in his lifetime, he had as little interest with the heathen Ethelfrid [3] as he had heart for so atrocious a suggestion.

He returned home in bitter disappointment. Whether he visited any other parts of Saxon Britain, endeavouring to do what he could for their heathen inhabitants, we cannot tell: the stories which ascribe to him some such journeys have no sufficient authority [4]. But he found a prospect opening before

---

[1] So 'gentis perfidæ,' 'perfidi.' He reflects bitterly on the Britons in other passages, ii. 20, v. 22. For this he has been severely blamed: but he was thinking of the repulse of Augustine's overtures, of the cruelties of a British invader of Northumbria, and of the Britons' contempt for English Christianity. That his feeling was not simply anti-Celtic, is proved by his cordial language respecting the Irish as a nation; iii. 27; iv. 26.

[2] A 'charge too absurd to merit any serious notice;' Milner, cent. 6. c. 1. 'An abominable calumny of some writers;' Lanigan, ii. 379. 'A crowd of modern writers have re-echoed the calumny;' Lingard, A.-S. Ch. i. 72. 'A preposterous libel;' Haddan's Remains, p. 316. To deny it was, in 1673, and at Oxford, to incur suspicion of Popery! (see Ant. Wood's Life, p. 191). Writing thirty years later, Inett says, 'I willingly yield to the side of charity;' Orig. Angl. i. 35. Geoffrey of Monmouth had suggested it, by the absurd fiction that 'Edelbertus Edelfridum instimulavit' (viii. 4).

[3] How could such a 'prophecy hardly fail to hasten its own fulfilment'? Milman, Lat. Chr. ii. 234. See Hook's good remarks, Archbishops, i. 73.

[4] E.g. Thorn says, X Script. 1760, that he 'sowed the seed of God's word everywhere throughout the whole land of the English,' always 'pedes sine vehiculo :' and Gocelin, in his longer Life of Augustine, 37 ff., makes him work miracles at *York*, e.g. on a leper,—inflict a grotesque punishment on some Dorsetshire rustics who had fastened fishes' tails to his and his brethren's garments (s. 41),—and even visit Colman 'king of Ireland,' and baptize the future Irish saint Livinus (s. 48; cp. Vit. S. Livini, Migne, Patr. Lat. lxxxix. 871, 873). These stories grew up out of a desire to make Augustine apostle of all England, not merely of a small part of it. Cp. the legend in Thomas of Ely (Angl. Sac. i. 594), that he founded a church in Cratunden, 'a mile from the present city' of Ely; and the weird story of the 'dead-alive' excommunicate and excommunicator, told by Bromton with a prefatory reference to Augustine's preaching in Oxfordshire; X Script. 736.

him among the East-Saxons, whose king, Sigebert I., or
Sabert, was Ethelbert's nephew as well as vassal, being the
son of his sister Ricula. Mellitus was sent to London, and
converted Sabert : in consequence, he was made bishop of
London in the beginning of 604 [1], and Ethelbert and Sabert
were both concerned in the erection of a cathedral church on
the site of the present St. Paul's, which had been formerly
occupied by a Roman camp. The story that a temple of
Diana had stood there [2] is at least doubtful : but an altar
of Diana, discovered near the spot not very many years since,
may have belonged to the prætorium [3]. It was afterwards
believed that Sabert had also been the founder of a monastery
of St. Peter which was called ' the West Minster,' on ' Thorney '
Island, a place then ' terrible ' from its desolate aspect as
a mass of marsh and brushwood [4]. Augustine, when he consecrated Mellitus, may have indulged in expectations of successful mission-work in the great city and its neighbourhood :
but his hopes were not to be speedily realised. In no part of
England was there so much tenacity of heathenism, so much
resistance to the new faith, as in the ' emporium of many
nations [5],' and generally in the East-Saxon realm. More than
one effort [6] was necessary before the church of London or the
parts adjacent could be considered as firmly restored upon its

[1] Bede, ii. 3.

[2] In the later Middle Ages the 'festum Sancti Adelberti' was a festival
of the first class at St. Paul's ; Statutes of St. Paul's, ii. 52.

[3] See Dugdale's Hist. of St. Paul's, p. 2, on the structure 'called Diana's
Chambers, and the ox-heads digged up' in the time of Edward I. ; and Milman,
Annals of St. Paul's, p. 5.

[4] See Stanley's Memorials of Westminster Abbey, p. 9; Freeman, Norm.
Conq. ii. 511. Thorn ascribes the foundation to ' a citizen of London at the
suggestion of Ethelbert ;' X Script. 1768. This was a tradition which in
Malmesbury became mixed up with a wild story about a dedication of the
church by St. Peter himself ; Gest. Pont. p. 141. So Ailred of Rievaulx, in
X Script. 385. A 'West Minster' did exist, as a church of some importance,
long before the Confessor's great foundation; Freeman, l. c. Bede's silence
would not disprove the tradition, for he might not think it necessary to mention
a foundation which was not connected with the bishopric. The traditional
tomb of Sabert is to the south of the altar in the present church.

[5] Bede, ii. 3. Cp. Tacitus, Ann. xiv. 33, 'Londinium . . . copia negotiatorum
. . . maxime celebre.' ' The commercial fame of London dates from the early
days of Roman dominion ;' Freeman, i. 281.

[6] See Bede, iii. 22, 30; cp. ib. 7.

Saxon basis: and it might seem that Augustine soon became conscious of some of the difficulties that lay in the path of the new bishop.

Bishopric
of Roches-
ter.

Matters were easier in regard to that district of Kent [1] which was dependent on the little city of Rochester, or Hrof's Castle, which in British times had been called Durobrivæ, from 'the swift stream' of the Medway. There Ethelbert built a church, which, in fond remembrance of his Roman monastery, Augustine dedicated in honour of St. Andrew. The 'Bretwalda' was bounteous in his gifts to this church [2], as to that of London; and Justus was consecrated as bishop of the new diocese, which for ages held a specially close relation of dependence on the arch-diocese of Canterbury,—the successors of Justus being, beyond all other suffragans, under the control of, and expected to do episcopal work for, the successors of Augustine [3].

The grants made by Ethelbert to churches, and his recognition of the status of bishops and clergy within his dominions, led naturally to the promulgation of certain enactments under the sanction of his Witan; that is, the assembly of the freemen of his kingdom,—which was practically the assembly of the great officers and the 'king's thegns,'—bearing the title of the Assembly of the Wise, or
Church re-
cognised by
Witan.
Witenagemôt [4]. Thus Bede tells us that Ethelbert introduced among the English, 'with the counsel of the Wise Men,

---

[1] It has been thought that there was then a sub-king of West Kent. Yet see Stubbs, Const. Hist. i. 198. Malmesbury describes Rochester as a town of narrow area, but, from its high position above a very swift river, not easily accessible to foes; Gest. Pontif. p. 133.

[2] See the 'Charter of Ethelbert to the church of Rochester,' Kemble, Cod. Diplom. A. S, i. 1. It is subsequent to the death of Augustine. The King addresses the Apostle: 'To thee, Saint Andrew, and to thy church which is established in the city *Hrofibrevi*, where Justus, bishop, is seen to preside, I deliver a small portion of my land.' The exact limits are stated in Saxon. Kemble does not doubt its authenticity: but there is a difficulty as to the date; see below. The Rochester tradition said that Ethelbert gave to the church some land thence called Priestfield, south of the city, and other land towards the north: Angl. Sacra, i. 333.

[3] The archbishop had the appointment to this bishopric until A.D. 1148. On this 'dependent' position of Rochester, see Freeman, iv. 365. The bishop of Rochester is the 'cross-bearer' of the province.

[4] See Freeman, i. 100; Kemble, ii. 194; Stubbs, Const. Hist. i. 140 (or 119).

judicial decrees after the Roman model, which, written out in
the English tongue, are extant and are observed to this day.
... Among which he first laid down the mode of satisfaction
to be made by any one who should take away by theft
anything belonging to the church, or the bishop, or the
other orders; inasmuch as his intention was to afford protection to those whose persons and whose teaching he had
accepted[1].'   Accordingly, among the extant Laws of Ethelbert[2], and indeed first among them, stands a brief ordinance
fixing a scale of payments—such as the Saxon law called *bóts*[3]
—for wrong done to ecclesiastical property as such; in case of
property, or *feoh*, of God and the Church, the satisfaction to
be thus made was twelve-fold; for a bishop's property, eleven-
fold; for a priest's, nine; for a deacon's, six; for an inferior
cleric's, three.   For violation of the *frith*, i. e. the peace or
privileges, of a church or of a monastery[4], a two-fold 'bôt'
was exacted.   Here, then, we have definite proof of the
recognition of Christianity and the Church by the 'Parlia-
ment,' so to speak, of the first English Christian king.

Augustine's life was now drawing to a close.   In regard to Liturgical
his general arrangements for the new English Church, he arrangements.

---

[1] Bede, ii. 5 : 'Qui inter cætera bona,' &c.   See Palgrave, Engl. Commonwealth, p. 44; Haddan's Remains, p. 306.

[2] Thorpe, Anc. Laws, p. 1 ; Haddan and Stubbs, iii. 42.   Palgrave, Engl.
Comm. p. 45, doubts the integrity of the text of the compilation made by
Bishop Ernulf in the twelfth century.

[3] The word means compensation or atonement (*bettering*) due to an injured
party.   See Thorpe's Glossary, and his Ancient Laws, pp. 17, 28, 45 (Ine's
laws), 71, &c. ; Stubbs, Const. Hist. i. 208.

[4] Compare Thorpe, Anc. Laws, p. 9 (Alfred), and his Glossary, 'frith' and
'grith.'   At Beverley and at Hexham the seat of him who claimed the 'peace'
or privilege of sanctuary was called the Frith-stool.   Compare the 'Peace of
St. Oswin' at Tynemouth.   See also Bede, Vit. Cuthb. 37 ; Stevenson, Pref. to
Chron. of Abingdon, p. xlviii ; and Lingard, A.-S. Ch. i. 273 ff.   As to British
churches, Giraldus says (Descr. Camb. i. 18) that the chief of them offered
'peace' (often abused) 'quantum armenta mane ad pascua exire, et vespere
redire possunt :' see too Haddan and Stubbs, i. 225.   For Gaul, compare first
Council of Orange in 449, c. 5, Mansi, vi. 437, and first of Orleans, in 511, c. 1,
ib. viii. 350; and Gregory of Tours, Hist. Fr. v. 14, on his own refusal to give
up Meroveus: also ib. ix. 3, 38.   See also Gregory the Great, Ep. x. 50; and
generally, Bingham, b. viii. c. 11 (vol. ii. p. 565), and Gothofred, Codex Theodos.
t. iii. p. 400, on Theodosius II.'s law of A.D. 431, 'Pateant summi Dei templa
timentibus,' &c.

CHAP. III. seems to have made but little use of Gregory's suggestion
to be eclectic as to liturgical practices. He established the
Roman Liturgy on the whole as a matter of course, but
apparently inserted in it the Gallic 'benedictio populi' already
mentioned[1]; and also introduced the Gallic 'Rogations' before
the Ascension[2], and possibly some other matters[3]. We learn
from a letter of Alcuin to Eanbald archbishop of York, in the
end of the eighth century, that there were then in use some
large sacramentaries representing an old Use, which did not
entirely agree with the Roman[4]. That Augustine never
thought of a vernacular Liturgy for the English was indeed
an error, but under the circumstances 'natural and pardonable[5].'
We must reject the notion that some words of St. Boniface,
and some other words of his contemporary Pope Zacharias[6],
refer to definite synodical resolutions arrived at by the first
archbishop and his two suffragans on questions of matrimonial
degrees and the form of administering baptism: the passages
in question refer to the 'synod' of London or the synod of the
province, i. e. the provincial episcopate of southern England,
which was 'founded' by Augustine, or 'governed' by Augustine, and his successors, as the authority for the regulations
in question. Augustine would of course take counsel on many
points of ecclesiastical administration with his two suffragans
of London and Rochester; but no formulated results of such
Monastery conferences are now extant. His interest in the last year of
of SS.
Peter and his episcopate was much taken up, we may assume, by the
Paul.

---

[1] Lingard, A.-S. Ch. i. 295 : comp. Egbert's Pontifical, p. 58 ff. Some
variations remained up to the Council of Clovesho, in 747, can. 13.

[2] Council of Clovesho, c. 16, 'secundum morem priorum nostrorum.' The
Roman Litany on St. Mark's day was adopted by that Council.

[3] Archd. Freeman (Princ. of Div. Serv. i. 246) conjectures that certain peculiarities in the Old-English daily offices as compared with the Roman were
originally brought in by Augustine from the South Gallic rites, as probably
constructed by Cassian on an Eastern model. But it is not on the whole
a likely conjecture. The Council of Clovesho, c. 15, prescribes adherence to
the Roman use for the canonical hours. Some peculiarities of the Old-
English Ordinal are traced by Maskell to the Celtic Church; Mon. Ritual.
ii. pp. 209, 211.

[4] Alcuin, Op. i. 231.

[5] Freeman, Norm. Conq. i. 32. Lappenberg strangely imagines that the
converts heard the Liturgy in their Germanic dialect; i. 168.

[6] See above, p. 83.

progress of his new monastery outside the walls of Canterbury[1].
He saw the walls of the church rise higher and higher, but
was not permitted to witness its completion. He could, however, make all the essential arrangements for the foundation
and constitution of the house : by his exhortation, says Bede[2],
Ethelbert built the church, and enriched it with divers gifts ;
and he selected his old companion Peter to be the first abbot[3]
of this house of SS. Peter and Paul, a choice which, according
to the monastic documents, was confirmed by the royal
nomination[4]. The last year of Augustine's life must have
been either 604 or 605. For the earlier date,—in the absence
of any help from Bede or the Saxon Chronicle,—is cited the
alleged charter of Ethelbert to the Church of Rochester,
which is dated April 28, 604, and ignores Augustine,
referring to his successor as the bishop of Canterbury : but
this would place Augustine's death earlier than the May
of that year, whereas he died on the 26th of *a* May[5]. Later
authorities differ : the chronicles of St. Augustine's Abbey
(i. e. SS. Peter and Paul's) give 605, an earlier annalist[6] 604 :

[1] Elmham, p. 111, says that at Christmas, 605, Ethelbert, in a council of
clergy and laity, confirmed and enlarged the grants to this monastery. He
then gives the so-called second charter, reciting the boundaries of the property.
See Haddan and Stubbs, iii. 55. Elmham becomes rhapsodical : ' Eja, vere
nostra Augustea regia !'

[2] Bede, i. 33 : ' Fecit autem . . . in quo, ejus hortatu,' &c.

[3] A document called a 'bulla,' or 'privilegium sub bulla plumbea,' professing
to come from Augustine, and exhorting his successors to ' ordain ' the abbots of
this monastery, but not to claim authority over them,—to treat them as
colleagues in the Lord's work,—is clearly an ' Augustinian' invention ; see it
in Kemble, Cod. Dipl. i. 6 ; Elmham, p. 119. Such ' privilegia ' were, at this
period and later, often granted by bishops, e.g. St. Landry's, or Landeric's, to
St. Denis (Mansi, xi. 61) : but the language of the Augustinian charter betrays
it. Comp. a privilegium of Bertfrid of Amiens to Corbey (ib. 107), and one
of Marculf (ib. 113). On such privilegia see Guizot, Civil. in Fr., lect. 15.
He gives the usual formula. See a curious letter of Archbishop Peckham
to the convent of St. Augustine's, ' Licet in ipso vestro sancto monasterio, et
quibusdam locis aliis et ecclesiis, a jurisdictione nostra exempti esse credamini,'
&c. : Peckham's Registr. No. 64 (vol. i. p. 74).

[4] The (spurious) charter of Ethelbert, ranked as ' third,' uses remarkable
language : ' Cum consilio . . . Augustini . . . Petrum elegi, eisque . . . abbatem
præposui.' Elmham, p. 114.

[5] See the epitaph in Bede, ii. 3 : ' Septimo Kal. Junii ' (May 26).

[6] Florence of Worcester. Thorn says, c. i. 11 (X Script. 1765), that Augustine's
death has been erroneously placed by many in 613, and that he died 605.

and there is a difference as to whether the day of his death was a Tuesday or a Wednesday, May 26 being a Tuesday in 604, a Wednesday in 605. Probability would point to 605 as allowing more time for the arrangements of Augustine and Ethelbert in regard to London and Rochester, after the return of the former from his conferences at Augustine's Oak[1]. One act which the archbishop performed 'while yet in health,' but shortly before his end,—his last public act,—was the consecration of Laurence to be his future successor[2]. It was an act, strictly speaking, which the ancient canons forbade : his own great namesake[3] had been ill at ease on observing that the text of a Nicene canon[4] seemed to tell against the consecration of a bishop as coadjutor and future successor by the actual bishop of the see ;—but, fairly interpreted, the words did not condemn such a proceeding, which had been resorted to in several cases before Augustine of Hippo was thus raised to the episcopate[5]. However, exceptions were recognised in regard to such rules as were embodied in a canon of the Council of Antioch in 341, prohibiting the consecration of a future successor by a living bishop[6]. St. Athanasius (who, indeed, did not recognise that council) had thus consecrated his friend Peter[7]; and, what seemed more to the purpose, the majority of the 'Latins' in Jerome's time[8] held that St. Peter, as bishop of Rome, had consecrated Clement to succeed him ;—so that Bede expressly describes Augustine as having followed the example of the chief of the Apostles. But why did he not

Smith adopts 605, and says that the chronology from which Thorn took his computation clearly points to a Wednesday as the day of the week, and to 605 as the year (p. 81). See the 'Chronologia' in X Script. 2229.

[1] Hussey decides for 605, Haddan and Stubbs for 604.

[2] Bede, ii. 4 : 'Successit Augustino . . . quem ipse idcirco adhuc vivens ordinaverat.'

[3] St. Augustine, Ep. 213.

[4] Nic. Can. 8: ἵνα μὴ ἐν τῇ πόλει δύο ἐπίσκοποι ὦσιν.

[5] Bingham, b. ii. c. 13. s. 4 (vol. i. p. 180).

[6] Mansi, ii. 1317. A later canon, called the 76th Apostolic, had forbidden a bishop to consecrate a relative to succeed him

[7] Chronicon Acephalum : 'Five days before his death he ordained (consecrated) Peter.'

[8] Jerome, de Vir. Illustr. 15: comp. Comm. in Isai. b. 14. Ruffinus suggested a modified view, that Linus and Clement were both bishops at Rome before Peter's death. To this Bede refers in Hist. Abb. 6.

pass on the archiepiscopate to Mellitus? The question is

twofold. Why did he ignore Gregory's evident intention
that the metropolitan see should be fixed in London? Clearly
because, being better acquainted than the Pope could be with
the local circumstances, among which, probably, the difficulties
of mission work among the inhabitants of London would hold
a chief place, he deemed himself free to act on his own
judgment, which, no doubt, coincided with his personal
feeling; for his affections had become closely entwined
with the church and the monasteries of Canterbury, and he
naturally wished the archiepiscopate to be permanent in that
beloved home[1]. His resolution has determined the history of
the Church of England as depending on the see of Canterbury.
' But why not transfer Mellitus to Canterbury, or else, leaving
him to his London work, summon Justus to the greater
Kentish see?' If the question presented itself to Augustine,
he probably answered it by considering that episcopal
translations were technically, at any rate, discouraged by
Church law[2]; and that he saw a man well qualified for the
archbishopric among those who had been his original companions,—whose hearts he had comforted and inspirited by
the letter brought from Gregory, who had travelled with him
through Frankish districts, had stood by his side when he
first confronted Ethelbert, and had raised their voices in
the litany along the slope of St. Martin's hill. This friend
was Laurence. On his head the feeble hands of Augustine
were laid, and Augustine's voice uttered the solemn prayers
of benediction with which the prelates of Latin Christendom
were set apart for their work[3]. Laurence was now qualified
to preside over the ' Church of the English;' and although

---

[1] See the letter of Kenulf king of Mercia to Leo III., stating that Gregory
had intended London to be metropolitical, but that because Augustine died and
was buried in Canterbury, it seemed good to the Witan (nostræ gentis
sapientibus) that the 'metropolitanus honor' should abide there. Haddan and
Stubbs, iii. 522. See above, p. 69.

[2] See Bingham, b. vi. c. 4. s. 6.

[3] See Muratori, Lit. Rom. ii. 357, for the long ' consecratio' beginning, ' Deus
honorum omnium.' . . 'Comple in sacerdote tuo ministerii tui summam . . . .
Abundet in eo constantia fidei, puritas dilectionis, sinceritas pacis. Tribuas
ei cathedram episcopalem,' &c. Cp. Egbert's Pontif. p. 2.

CHAP. III. Augustine's last days may have been partly saddened by the thought that this Church had not 'broken forth on the right hand and the left,' with anything like the amplitude and vigour of self-extension which the joyful Christmastide of 597 had seemed to promise, he would take comfort in hoping that those who came after him would 'see the glory of the Lord' revealed in some richer spiritual conquests, and some stronger and broader consolidation of the Church's organic unity. It was in fact the latter work, rather than the former, which was reserved for the see of Canterbury,—and that after some sixty years had passed.

The work of Augustine.

Augustine died, as we have seen, in the last week of May, and probably in 605; and his body was temporarily laid 'outside, but close to[1],' the yet unfinished church of his new monastery. The brief period allotted to him for work as a missionary bishop should modify any unkindly estimate of the amount of work that was done. He had at any rate laid the foundation 'nobly[2]:' he had converted a typical English monarch; he had baptized multitudes of Kentish proselytes; he had secured a formal and public acceptance, by a national assembly, of Christian obligations, and of the Church as an organised institution; he had planted an offshoot of the Kentish Church in London; he had rooted in Canterbury a future centre for any amount of Church extension; he had definitely connected the reviving Christianity in Britain with the theological culture and ecclesiastical discipline of the continental Western Church. Briefly, he had made the beginning, opened the door, formed the precedents: later missionaries in England, who had other opportunities, whose successes covered a wider area, were, consciously or not, carrying on the impulse first given by the Gregorian mission, and therefore, in some effective sense, by him whom an ancient English Council[3], when appointing a festival in his honour, described as having brought to the English people 'the

---

[1] Bede, ii. 3. See Gocelin's Hist. Minor, 39: 'Regnas, Augustine, Augustis sæculi nomine et dignitate sublimior. . . . In monasterio . . . reconditur pretiosissimum corpus ejus festivo cum jubilo.' (Angl. Sax. ii. 70.)

[2] Bede, ii. 4. 'nobiliter jacta.'

[3] Council of Clovesho, c. 17; Haddan and Stubbs, iii. 368.

knowledge of their heavenly country.' So much as to what he did. As to what he was in himself, it cannot be said that he was a man of genius, or of signal insight into human nature, or of any such qualities as exercise a commanding power over men's admiration, or an attractive influence on generations of human hearts. He was not a Boniface, not an Anskar, not a Xavier, not a Martyn. His monastic training, carried on probably until he was past middle life, had tended to stiffen his mind and narrow his range of thought; something of smallness, something of self-consciousness, some want of consideration for unfamiliar points of view and different forms of experience, may be discerned in him without injustice, and thus explained without any ungenerous forgetfulness of the better side of the monastic character. Whatever were his shortcomings, Augustine of Canterbury was a good man, a devout and laborious Christian worker, who could, and did, face threatening difficulties and accept serious risks in loyalty to a sacred call; a missionary whose daily conduct was a recommendation of his preaching, who could impress and convince men of various classes in a Teutonic people that had little in common with his Italian antecedents; who, as archbishop, did his duty, as he read it, with all his might, if not without mistakes or failures, such as we may be tempted to judge more harshly than they merit; who, acting thus, accomplished more than appears at first sight, in that he originated so much of the work which was to make England Christian.

'Laurence began his archiepiscopate with strenuous efforts Laurence to extend the foundations of the Church, and took pains to Archbishop. carry up its fabric to the due height, by the frequent utterance of holy exhortation, and the continual example of pious conduct.' Such is Bede's eulogy [1]. It was part of Laurence's Overtures plan to make a fresh attempt in the direction of co-operation to Irish and union with the Celtic bishops and Churches. He had, at Church. first, some hope that the Irish might be more amenable than the Britons. But he became in some way aware of the resolute Celticism, in regard to Paschal observance, of the great Irish-

[1] Bede, ii. 4 : 'Laurentius ... strenuissime fundamenta ecclesiæ,' &c.

born abbot and missionary Columban, who had now for about fifteen years[1] been presiding over three monasteries in the wild country of the Vosges, and in spite of the exacting severities of a rule far more onerous than Benedict's[2], had exercised a strong moral and spiritual fascination over many earnest souls that recognised in him a true zealot for Christian strictness, whose passion it was, as the historian of French civilisation expresses it, to cast the Divine fire abroad on every side, 'without troubling himself about the conflagration[3].' With all his intense Christian devotion[4], the Irishman's 'perfervidum ingenium' made itself apparent in his conduct. He had denounced the Gallican Easter cycle, that of Victorius, as ridiculous in the eyes of scholarly Irishmen[5], and had upheld the reckoning which included 'the fourteenth of the moon' among the days on which Easter Sunday could be kept[6]. This he did in a letter to Pope Gregory; and about the time when Mellitus and his companions were passing through Gaul, he excused himself from attending a

[1] Columban came into Gaul, in order to preach the Gospel to heathen tribes on the continent, about 590. He settled at first among the pine-forests of Burgundy; disciples gathered round him; he founded four monasteries in succession, at Anegray, Luxeuil, Fontenay, and (after his removal into Italy) at Bobbio. See Lanigan, ii. 261; Milman, Lat. Chr. ii. 285; Maclear, Apostles of Med. Eur. p. 58; King, Ch. Irel. i. 249. He died in 615. For his writings, see Galland. Bibl. xii. 321 ff.

[2] See the Rule (in Galland. p. 324), c. 10. The elaborate rules of penance embodied in 'Penitentials' originated in 'the overstrained and indiscreet zeal of Cummian and Columbanus;' Haddan's Remains, p. 267; see ib. 278, and Dict. Chr. Biogr. i. 607.

[3] Guizot, Civil. in Fr., lect. 16.

[4] See his tenth 'Instruction' and second 'Carmen.'

[5] Columb. Ep. i. He says that Victorius transgressed the rule that Easter could not precede the equinox, and that by admitting the twenty-first moon within the limits, a *Pascha tenebrosum* was introduced, *because* the twenty-first moon rises after midnight. He opposes to Victorius the authority of Anatolius and Jerome. This Ep. ranks as Greg. Ep. ix. 127. Compare Greg. Turon., H. Fr. x. 23: 'In cyclo Victor luna decima-quinta Pascha scripsit fieri; sed ne Christiani, ut Judæi, sub hac luna hæc solemnia celebrarent, addidit, Latini autem luna vigesima-secunda,' &c.

[6] He says that the plea for excluding the fourteenth, 'cum Judæis Pascha facere non debemus,' was 'once urged by Bishop Victor, but no one of the Easterns (!) *suum recepit* commentum.' We must, he insists, keep Easter from the fourteenth to the twentieth inclusive, not from the fifteenth to the twenty-first. See above, p. 82.

Gallic synod by a letter [1] in which he claimed the authority
of all the Western Churches for not extending the Paschal
limits beyond the twentieth of the moon, and upheld the
cycle of eighty-four years as representing the mind of
venerated writers, and contrasting with the 'doubtful and
indefinite language of Victorius [2];' while at the same time
he was content to deprecate intolerance, to ask 'leave to
dwell silently in these woods beside the bones of his seventeen
departed brethren,' and to 'pray that Gaul might find room
for all,' of whatever race, who were on their road to the
heavenly kingdom [3]. But it was obvious that Columban
would not depart in any particular from the Irish usages on
this point. Laurence may have learned from some Gallic
bishops, or from a personal visit to the abbot of Luxeuil, how
strong was his resolve against any conformity to their practice : and the tenacity of the Irish Churchmen's adherence to
Celtic rules was painfully brought home to the archbishop
when an Irish bishop, named Dagan [4], having come to
Britain [5], for the purpose, as we may suppose, of conferring
with the three bishops [6], was apparently so much irritated by
what passed in the discussion that he flatly refused to eat
with them, or even to eat in the same place in which they
were taking their meal. Laurence wrote, in his own name
and in those of his two suffragans, to their 'most dear lords
and brothers, the bishops and abbots throughout all Scotia,'
i. e. Ireland. Only part of the letter is given by Bede : but

[1] Columb. Ep. 2 : 'Patribus vel fratribus episcopis, presbyteris . . . Columba
peccator.'

[2] 'Victorium nuper dubie scribentem, et ubi necesse erat, nihil definientem
. . . who wrote under Hilarus, 103 years after the times of . . . Pope Damasus.'
His chronology is inaccurate.

[3] 'Ut mihi liceat . . . in his silvis silere et vivere juxta ossa . . . as up
to this time we have been free to live among you twelve years. . . Capiat
nos simul, oro, Gallia,' &c. See Milman, ii. 288 ; Maclear, p. 64; King, i.
294.

[4] Probably the bishop of Inverdaoile of that name.

[5] Bede, ii. 4. 'Ad nos veniens' might imply a visit to Canterbury, although
the words 'in eodem hospitio quo vescebamur' have been understood otherwise.
See Lingard, A.-S. Ch. i. 59.

[6] See Lanigan, ii. 367. He adds that on this supposition, Dagan could not
have intended all along 'to keep up no sort of communion with them.' He also
quotes the appellation *præplacidum*, given to this prelate.

CHAP. III. he tells us that in the rest Laurence entreated them to be at one in ' Catholic observance ' with the Church throughout the world. Another letter to the like effect was sent to the British bishops [1], evidently in order that Laurence might discharge his conscience, and be able to feel that he had done all he could to promote unity. ' How much good he got from it,' says Bede with something of condensed bitterness, ' even our present times can show,'—for he well knew how, in the days of his own elder contemporary, Aldhelm bishop of Sherborne, the British priests beyond the Severn used to cleanse elaborately the plates or cups from which Saxons had fed, after throwing the remnants of their food to dogs and swine [2]; how, at the time at which his History was written, the Britons ' regarded the Christianity of the English as a thing of nought [3].' In effect, the Southern Irish gave up their Paschal reckonings in deference to Papal exhortations, to the opinion of some of their own leading men, e. g. St. Cummian, and to evidence obtained as to the prevalence of the ' Catholic Easter,' not only at Rome, but in other leading Churches,— about A.D. 634 [4]: the influence of the monastery of Hy upheld those reckonings longer in the north of Ireland until 704: and Hy itself, in 716, adopted the ' Catholic Easter[5].' The Strathclyde clergy yielded about 704; the North Welsh, under the influence of Elbod bishop of Bangor, in 755 or 768 ; the South Welsh, under strong pressure, in 777 [6]. It was then, and not until then, that the English Church, which had been founded and organised without the aid of the British, absorbed the latter into its own body. It was thus, and only thus, that it acquired continuity with the Church which had been represented at Arles and at Ariminum, which could look back to Alban as its protomartyr, and to

---

[1] Bede, ii. 4: ' Misit idem Laurentius . . . etiam Brettonum sacerdotibus.'

[2] Aldhelm, Ep. 1.   See above, p. 90.

[3] Bede, ii. 20; cp. v. 22.

[4] Lanigan, ii. 389.   King dates the Synod of the Field of Lene in 630, and distinguishes it from the Synod of the White Field in 634 ; Ch. Irel. i. 171. He gives the substance of Cummian's letter in defence of his adoption of the Roman Easter; ib. 154.   See the original in Usher's ' Sylloge,' Ep. 11.

[5] Bede, v. 22 ; Haddan and Stubbs, ii. 114.

[6] Haddan and Stubbs, ii. 6 ; i. 203.

German as its deliverer from the heresy invented by one of CHAP. III. its own sons.

The ecclesiastical society at Canterbury sustained a loss at the close of 607, when the abbot Peter, sent by Ethelbert as an envoy to Gaul, was drowned in the bay of Ambleteuse; his body was recovered, and buried in St. Mary's church at Boulogne[1]. John, one of 'the Forty,' succeeded him: and in the same year, 608, bishop Mellitus went to Rome to consult Mellitus at
Rome. Pope Boniface IV. on the affairs of the English mission, and was honourably received in a Roman synod held on Feb. 27, 610, the decrees of which he subscribed[2]. The Pope sent back with him a letter to Ethelbert, and others to Laurence and his clergy[3]: and after his return he was probably present at the long-delayed dedication of the monastery church of Dedication
of SS.
Peter and
Paul's. SS. Peter and Paul, outside the east wall of Canterbury. Laurence performed the ceremony, and then transferred the remains of Augustine, with all honour, to a grave in the northern 'porch' of the church[4]. The monastery, as it grew in resources, became a conspicuous specimen of monastic exemption from diocesan rule; it was called 'the Roman Chapel in England,' as being immediately subject to the Pope[5]. Its community carried on a tradition of jealous independence as regards the archbishop[6], and a sort of standing feud with their neighbours of the metropolitan cathedral.

---

[1] Bede, i. 33; Elmham, Hist. Mon. S. Aug. p. 126.

[2] 'Confirmaret,' 'assent to.' Bede, ii. 4; cp. Haddan and Stubbs, iii. 459.

[3] Bede, l. c. : 'Una cum epistolis,' &c. But the letter beginning 'Dum Christianitatis vestræ,' Malmesb. G. P. i. 30, Haddan and Stubbs, iii. 65, professing to grant the king's request that a regular community of monks might be established in the cathedral monastery, looks like an 'Augustinian' invention, meant to establish the seniority of that community over the former. Cf. Elmham, p. 85. Elmham says that Mellitus brought home this letter after a second journey in 615; p. 134. A letter or bull ascribed to Boniface, in Elmham, p. 129, is spurious. See Hardwick's Introduction to Elmham, p. xxviii.

[4] Bede, ii. 3 : 'Mox vero,' &c.

[5] 'Life of St. Augustine,' p. 133. See Elmham, pp. 386, 392, 404 (Eugenius III. said that the monastery was 'beati Petri juris,' &c.). An earlier Pope, Agatho, forbade any 'sacerdos' (bishop) to exercise authority in the monastery, 'præter sedem apostolicam,' it being specially under the jurisdiction of Rome; p. 247. Guizot says of the Frankish monasteries that Fulda was the first to be placed under the direct jurisdiction of Rome; Civil. in Fr. lect. 15.

[6] See Hardwick's remarks in Introduction to Elmham, p. viii. For the

King Ethelbert, when he witnessed the removal of Bertha's corpse, as well as Augustine's, to the minster newly dedicated, may well have felt that his life's work was done. Yet he lived three years longer, probably saddened in his last days by apprehensions as to the fortunes of the Church under his son Eadbald, who, according to the Chronicle, had been baptized, but, according to the higher authority of Bede, 'had refused to receive the faith of Christ [1] : '—if this phrase is to be taken literally, it implies that Eadbald had resisted the exhortations of his father's religious guides. Ethelbert's reign of fifty-six years came to a close on the 24th of February, in 616 : but in assigning to him twenty-one years of Christian life, the historian [2] is inconsistent with his own date of 597 for the arrival of Augustine. Ethelbert was buried in St. Martin's 'porch' within the church of SS. Peter and Paul [3]. 'Eadbald, on assuming the government, did much harm to the Church, which was still in its tender growth.' He would have none of the new lore : he would cleave to the old worship : and he followed an old Teutonic rule [4] by uniting himself to his father's widow, the successor of Bertha. We can well understand how, as Bede tells us, those who under Ethelbert had acquiesced, without conviction, in the creed which he adopted, —had 'accepted the laws of faith and chastity [5] either for fear

---

story of the monk of St. Medard, who on his death-bed confessed that he had forged bulls of exemption in favour of St. Augustine's and other monasteries, see Palgrave, Eng. Comm. p. ccxi. See the spurious deeds in Haddan and Stubbs, iii. 67–70 ; and cp. Freeman, iv. 408.

[1] See Elmham, p. 87, for a sample of animosity on the side of the cathedral monks ; and cf. ib. 317 for archbishop Cuthbert's successful scheme for ensuring his own burial in the cathedral. After Bregwin's similar burial the Augustinians were on the point of having recourse to arms ; ib. 328.

[2] Bede, ii. 5. Elmham corrects this to 'nineteen.'

[3] In the south part of the church, Elmham, p. 137, where Bertha and Liudhard were buried. Against the story of his having been buried at Reculver, see Stanley, Mem. Cant. p. 46.

[4] See above, p. 60, on this custom, and Robertson's Hist. Essays, p. lxvii. The Council of Agde, in 506, had included those who married their step-mothers among the incestuous who were never to be absolved, 'nisi cum adulterium separatione sanaverint ;' c. 61 ; Mansi, viii. 335.

[5] Compare St. Boniface's bitter complaints about those whom he had taken for sheep and who proved to be goats ; Ep. 22 ; and Ep. 27, on 'false Christians.'

or for the sake of favour' (although indeed Ethelbert had
never imposed Christianity on any of his subjects), took occasion to resume their heathenism under a king who, as they
would express it, was not the dupe of the shavelings from
Rome. 'Eadbald was troubled with fits of madness, and by
the attacks of an unclean spirit:' such is Bede's statement,
and in these moods, as they probably were, of wild excitement
the Christian subjects of Eadbald would deem that they
beheld a corrective visitation. But Eadbald appeared obstinate; and to add to the anxieties of Laurence, Mellitus was
just now exposed to an equally trying reverse of his former
prosperity. Sabert was just dead: the East-Saxon realm was
left to his three sons, named Sæward, Sexred, and Sigebert.
Although 'in their father's lifetime they had seemed to give
up a little of their idolatry [1],' they now openly resumed it.
One day they came into St. Paul's church, while the bishop
was administering the Holy Communion [2]. 'Why do you
not,' they rudely asked him, 'give us also a share in the white
bread [3], which you used to give to our father Saba [4], and
which you still continue to give to the people in the church?'
'If,' answered Mellitus with calm dignity, 'you are willing to
be washed in that font of salvation [5] in which your father

---

[1] 'Aliquantulum intermisisse;' Bede, ii. 5.

[2] Bede says, 'celebratis missarum sollemniis,' meaning, the mass which
was being celebrated, and which was then considered to be in one sense
finished by the celebrant's communion. 'Censebantur sollemnia missarum
consummata priusquam communio, saltem laicis, distribueretur;' Ruinart,
Præf. ad Greg. Turon. s. 46. Cp. first Council of Orleans, c. 26, (Mansi,
viii. 355,) and Cæsarius in App. to Aug. Serm., no. 281, that the 'missæ
solennitas' was 'completed' when the bishop gave his benediction (see above,
p. 59). Mellitus might have done this before the princes came in. See also
Cyprian de Lapsis, 25. The use of 'missæ' for a single celebration occurs in
the wild tale of Mamertinus' dream in Greg. Turon. Hist. Tr. v. 14, in Bede,
iv. 14, and in Adamn. Vit. Col. i. 40, iii. 17, 23, &c. It refers to the double
dismissal of (1) catechumens, (2) the faithful.

[3] Hook, i. 97, 'slips in' (see Haddan's Remains, p. 301) a mention of 'wine.'
Of course, 'both kinds' were administered; but 'something in the bread . .
attracted the eye of the heathen princes.' And they would naturally look at
Mellitus, not at his deacon who would be administering the chalice.

[4] A familiar abbreviation of Sebert. Comp. Elmham, p. 338: 'It is a Saxon
fashion nomina transformare . . . . syncopando, ut pro Thoma *Tomme* . . . . pro
Johanne . . . *Jacke.*'

[5] Comp. Bede, ii. 14, 'lavacrum sanctæ regenerationis;' iii. 21, 'fidei fonte;'

was washed, then you may also partake of the holy bread of which he used to partake : but if you despise the laver of life, you cannot possibly receive the bread of life.' They answered, ' We will not go into that font, for we know not what need we have of it : but for all that, we choose to eat of that bread.' It was sheer barbaric curiosity, combined with the self-will of young princes suddenly left to their own guidance. They could not brook any curb on their caprices : and when Mellitus ' repeatedly and earnestly' set before them the necessity of baptism as a pre-requisite for ' communion in the most holy oblation [1],' they cut him short in senseless wrath, saying, ' If you will not give us our way in so small a matter, you shall not remain in our province : ' and ' they commanded him, and all who belonged to him, to leave their kingdom.' Thus it was that for adhering to the principle that religious privileges implied religious obligations, and were not to be had without them,— for refusing to degrade his religion by imparting its holiest treasures to outsiders who would not qualify themselves for such reception by the one indispensable initiatory rite,— Mellitus lost his church and bishopric, and had perforce to see his work abruptly arrested : and from that day, for nearly forty years, London and Essex were lost to Christianity.

The expelled bishop hastened to Canterbury, whither Laurence had summoned Justus from Rochester ; and the three prelates held a sorrowful consultation, and resolved unanimously to abandon the mission. It was an access of such faint-heartedness as was only too natural, when all around seemed hopelessly dark : but the resolution was couched in religious language, and reference perhaps was made to cases in which primitive bishops had fled during persecution,—although, as yet, persecution, properly so called,

---

iii. 23, ' lavacri salutaris ; ' iv. 16, v. 19, ' fonte Salvatoris ; ' v. 6, ' salutari fonte . . . vitali unda.'

[1] Comp. Bede, iii. 2, ' victimam sacræ oblationis ; ' iv. 14, ' sacrificiis cœlestibus . . . de sacrificio Dominicæ oblationis particulam ; ' iv. 22, ' oblationem hostiæ salutaris . . . victimas sacræ oblationis ; ' iv. 28, v. 10, ' sacrificium victimæ salutaris.' Compare Gildas, 28, ' sacrificii cœlestis sedem,' and 67, ' manus . . . sacrosanctis Christi sacrificiis extensuri ; ' and Adamn. iii. 17, ' sacram oblationem consecrantis.'

had not begun. 'Better,' they said, 'return to Italy, and there
serve God in freedom, than stay here where no good is to be
done, among barbarians who have revolted from the faith.'
Accordingly, Mellitus and Justus crossed the Channel, and
took up their abode in Gaul, intending to await events.
Laurence was to follow : on the night before his intended
departure, he caused his bed to be prepared within the church
of SS. Peter and Paul. After praying long, with tears, for
his people, he lay down, and slept. Bede then reports what
he had received from his informants[1], that St. Peter appeared
to Laurence, scourged him, and demanded 'why he was forsaking the flock whom he himself had entrusted to his care'
(a phrase which obviously refers to the origination of the
mission from a successor of St. Peter); and that this
rebuke was enforced by a reference to the apostle's own
endurance of suffering and even martyrdom 'for the little
ones of Christ.' Next morning Laurence hastened to
Eadbald, 'drew aside his garment,' and showed the actual
marks of nocturnal castigation. 'Who has dared,' asked
the king, 'to inflict such blows on a man of your rank?'
Laurence told what had happened : Eadbald was deeply
awed, cast away his idols, 'renounced his unlawful marriage, embraced the faith of Christ, and after receiving
baptism, took pains to promote in all things, to the utmost
of his power, the interests of the Church.' It has been
suggested that this story of the appearance of St. Peter
and the scourging is probably the legendary exaggeration of
a dream, in which Laurence imagined himself to receive such
discipline from his heavenly visitor[2], and after which in
compunction he perhaps inflicted it on himself[3] ; that he may
have succeeded in producing a salutary effect on Eadbald by
the mere recital of his dream,—possibly also by the visible
tokens of his penance ; and that there is therefore no necessity

---

[1] The story is referred to by Alcuin in his letter of remonstrance to archbishop Ethelheard; see Haddan and Stubbs, iii. 519; and in Laurence's
epitaph, Elmham, p. 149,—

'Pro populo Christi scapulas dorsumque dedisti.'

[2] Hook, i. 89 ; Green, Making of Engl. p. 247.

[3] This suggestion is Churton's ; Early Engl. Church, pp. 53, 54.

CHAP. III. for imputing to him a fraud[1], such as, doubtless, a lax casuistry has often miscalled 'pious,' in forgetfulness of the condemnation of 'lying for God.' As it stands, the story reads like an imitation of what a writer of the third century affirms to have happened to Natalius, who had been a confessor, and having become a 'bishop' among heretics, was scourged all night long by angels, and showed his bruises next day to the orthodox Roman bishop and church[2]. There is, at any rate, no doubt that an impression was made on Eadbald, which produced a conversion of the most genuine and practical kind, such as Bede has described in words already quoted, and in a sentence a little further on: 'He gave himself up in good earnest to the Divine precepts[3].' He sent into Gaul to summon home the two fugitive bishops; they however, somewhat unaccountably, delayed their return for about a year. Eadbald could uphold Justus, as his father had done, at Rochester: but he was not, like his father, supreme over Essex. The young kings who had expelled Mellitus were soon afterwards[4] slain in battle by the West-Saxons: and whatever Sigebert the Little, their successor[5], may have done or wished to do in the matter, we are expressly told that 'the Londoners would not receive Mellitus back as their bishop, preferring to be under their own idolatrous high priests,'—that 'the common people, after having been stirred up to the crime' of apostasy, 'could not be corrected and reclaimed to the faith,'—and that 'Eadbald had not power

---

[1] This is, however, the view of Lappenberg, i. 143, of Haddan (Remains, p. 309), and apparently of Milman, ii. 235; and Hardwick thinks it 'difficult entirely to acquit' Laurence; Ch. H. Mid. Ages, p. 9.

[2] The author of the Little Labyrinth (Caius?) in Euseb. v. 28. Compare Tertullian de Idololatria, 15, 'Scio fratrem per visionem . . . castigatum,' &c.; and Jerome's strange story of his having been rapt 'in spirit' before the Divine Judge (while his body seemed stiffened in death from the effects of fever), and scourged for his love of heathen literature. 'Liventes fateor me habuisse scapulas;' Ep. 22. 30. And the story in Adamn. Vit. S. Columb. iii. 5, that 'quadam nocte in ecstasi mentis' Columba was 'struck with a whip' by an angel, and retained the mark through life.

[3] Bede, ii. 6. He built a church of St. Mary to the east of SS. Peter and Paul's beyond the cemetery of the monks. See Elmham, p. 144.

[4] Bede, ii. 5: 'Sed non multo tempore,' &c.

[5] Bede, iii. 22. He was son of Sæward, and had a long reign.

enough to restore the prelate to his church in the teeth of
heathens saying him nay [1].'

The year after Eadbald's accession,—the year of this obstinate rejection of the faith by the greatest of English cities,—
was marked by an event which, in its ultimate results, was
a momentous gain to English Christianity. The East- Redwald
Anglians of Norfolk and Suffolk were now ruled by a king of East-Anglia.
named Redwald, grandson of that Uffa from whom the
dynasty took the name of Uffingas. He is reckoned as
fourth of the 'Bretwaldas [2].' He had visited Kent in
Ethelbert's time, and had even accepted baptism; but on his
return home, his Pagan wife 'and certain perverse teachers,'
appealing to his lingering superstitions or to his political self-
interest, drew him into a compromise which Bede likens to
the mixed worship of the old Samaritans, who 'feared the
Lord and served their own gods [3].' He had 'in the same
(heathen) fane an altar for Christ's sacrifice,' and a smaller
one for the worship of idols [4] :—it was a combination essentially resembling the attempt of many in that age to keep
terms with both religions by attending indiscriminately the
churches and the old heathen temples [5], or the subsequent
expedient of a Norwegian king who, while signing the cross
over his cup, told his people that it meant 'the hammer of
Thor [6].' Redwald had a consciousness of the claims of Christianity, but he durst not admit them without reserve, and in

[1] Bede, ii. 6: 'Mellitum vero Lundonienses episcopum recipere noluerunt
... Non enim tanta erat ei, quanta patri ipsius, regni potestas,' &c. And ib.
ii. 5, fin.: ' Nec, licet auctoribus perditis . . .' &c.

[2] He acquired this ascendency when Ethelbert's energies had begun to fail;
Bede, ii. 5.

[3] 2 Kings xvii. 33.

[4] 'In eodem fano et altare ad sacrificium Christi, et arulam ad victimas
dæmoniorum.' King Aldwulf of East-Anglia, when a boy, saw this 'fane.'
Bede, ii. 15. Compare Maclear, Conv. of Slavs, p. 136.

[5] Gregory, Ep. ix. 11: see too ib. viii. 18. Compare Willibald's Vit. S.
Bonifacii, c. 8, that some of the Hessian converts would not receive Christian
teachers 'integre,' but sacrificed to trees or fountains, some 'clanculo,' some
openly (Migne, Patr. Lat. lxxxix. 619). So the Magyars, who had conformed
to Christianity, often kept up the worship of their god Isten within the forests
or beside the fountains. See above, p. 75.

[6] Hacon, son of Harold Haarfager. See the story in Maclear's Conversion
of Northmen, p. 57.

their exclusive absoluteness;—he fancied that he could treat his baptismal creed as one form of religion with which older forms might be associated [1] : or perhaps he persuaded himself that, in exceptional circumstances, the baptized king of heathen subjects might reasonably accommodate himself, to a certain extent, to the religious prejudices of his people. Be this as it may, Redwald, in the beginning of 617, was still harbouring at his court an exiled Northumbrian prince, whose name of Edwin should not be uttered by any Englishman without grateful respect, although his early life gave little promise of such a career as in fact awaited him. A son of the Northumbrian Ella whose name had been played with by Gregory as suggestive of Alleluia, Edwin, as a child [2], had been despoiled of his royal inheritance by Ethelric, the father of Ethelfrid,—had been sheltered, according to a Welsh tradition, by king Cadvan of North Wales [3],—had certainly at some time fled into Mercia [4], and thence into the more remote East Anglia. Thither, however, Ethelfrid's hate pursued him : Redwald received message after message, offering 'a large sum of money for the slaughter of Edwin :' at last, threats of war were combined with the promises, and Redwald, allured or alarmed, gave consent. It was then, according to the famous and impressive story [5], that a friend of Edwin entered the exile's bedchamber, called him out, told him what the king had promised to do with him, and offered to conduct him, that very night, out of the province, and out of the reach of Ethelfrid or Redwald [6]. Edwin declined the offer, not thank-

Early life of Edwin.

---

[1] Pearson calls this 'the first authentic mention of a process of development which purified and rationalised Odinism during several centuries,' and 'irradiated it with gleams of love and hopefulness from Christianity' (Hist. Engl. i. 127, 155), as the bright and beloved Balder was invested with some attributes of 'the White Christ;' see Kemble, i. 369.

[2] Edwin was born in 585, three years before his father's death. Then Ethelric, the Bernician, seized Deira, and Edwin's troubles began, in 588.

[3] So Lappenberg, i. 145. But would he not, in that case, have been bred up a Christian? See Haddan and Stubbs, iii. 75. The Welsh story was that Cadvan, who became king in 603, 'hazarded a war with the persecutor of Edwin, which ended in the battle of Chester;' Lappenberg, i. 145.

[4] He married a Mercian princess; see below, p. 117.

[5] See it exquisitely told by Bede, ii. 12, 'Quod ubi fidissimus quidam,' &c.; and the rendering in Freeman's Old-Engl. Hist. p. 52.

[6] 'Si ergo vis, hac ipsa nocte,' &c.

lessly, but, according to Bede's representation, partly from a
scruple of honour, partly from moody hopelessness. He would
not be the first to break friendship with Redwald, who as yet
had never wronged him ; if he was to die, let his death come
by Redwald's hand rather than by any less noble. What
new refuge could he find after nearly thirty years of wandering ? His friend retired, leaving him seated on a stone outside the palace, and distracted by 'many a tide of thought'
as to what he should do, or whither he should go. When he
had spent a long time in silent distress, he seemed to see,
in the dead stillness of night, a man approaching him
whose face and garb were alike strange, and who, after
greeting him, asked why he was sitting there, alone and
sorrowful, while every one else was taking repose. 'What
matters it to you,' asked Edwin impatiently, recovering
from a momentary dread, 'whether I pass the night within
doors or here ? ' 'Do not think,' rejoined the stranger, 'that
I am unaware of the reason of your sleeplessness and
anxiety. I know who you are, and what you are now afraid
of. But tell me what you would give as a reward to
any one who could deliver you from your peril.' 'I would
give all I could.' 'What if he could also assure you that
you should crush your foes and become a king, and a mightier
king than your forefathers, or even than all who have been
beforetime kings of the Angles ? ' Again Edwin promised
to requite such service as it merited. 'But,' said the stranger,
'what if he whose predictions should have been thus made
good were able to give you better counsel for your life and
safety than any of your kindred ever heard of ? would you then
follow his guidance ? ' Edwin promised that he would do so
absolutely. The stranger laid his hand on Edwin's head, saying,
'When this token is given you, remember our conversation,
and fulfil your promise : ' and instantly, as Bede heard the
story, he disappeared. Edwin was still sitting on the stone
seat, gladdened by the encouraging words, but much perplexed
as to their mysterious speaker [1], when his friend returned with

---

[1] Bede says he knew him to be a spirit. The St. Gallen 'Life of Gregory'
says, 'Quidam cum cruce Christi coronatus,' a supposed 'apparition of
Paulinus ; ' who, in fact, may have been visiting Redwald.

a glad countenance. 'Rise up, and go to rest without fear. The king told his wife of his resolution against you, and she told him that it was nowise meet for a great king to sell for gold a good friend in distress, or rather for love of gain to ruin that which was more precious than all ornaments, his honour. This has changed his mind again.' It was true: Redwald had determined not only to protect Edwin, but to anticipate the threatened attack of Ethelfrid. He gathered all his forces, marched rapidly northward, and giving the 'Destroyer' no time to make full preparations, met him on the borders of Mercia, on the east bank of the Idle, probably at Idleton near Retford [1], and, as we infer from a calculation of Bede, before the 11th of April in 617 [2]. Here Ethelfrid was defeated and slain: a popular saying commemorated the day when 'Angles' blood stained Idle-flood [3]:' and Edwin, the hunted and all but betrayed fugitive, became at once the sovereign of the whole Northumbrian region, uniting his hereditary Deira to Bernicia. 'He drove out the Ethelings, sons of Ethelfrid [4],' says the Saxon Chronicle; and we must mark three names,—Eanfrid, Oswald, and Oswy,—one destined to a brief and shameful elevation, the two others to a high rank among Old-English monarchs, and one of these to the purest form of royal glory—but all three at present cast aside into the gloom of a common ruin. To all appearance, Edwin was simply another mighty prince of the Northern Angles, with something of the terrible energy of Ethelfrid, as the Christian Britons of Loidis [5] would feel to their cost, when in

Battle of Retford.

Edwin King of Northumbria.

---

[1] See Pearson, Hist. Engl. i. 127.

[2] For Edwin was baptized on April 11, 627, in the eleventh year of his reign; Bede, ii. 14.

[3] Hen. Hunt. ii. 30. On this battle see Palgrave, English Commonwealth, p. 428; Green, p. 252.

[4] 'Eanfrid, Oswald, Oswy, Oslac, Oswudu, Oslaf, Offa,'—all Edwin's nephews, for Acha his sister had married Ethelfrid; Bede, iii. 6.

[5] See Bede, ii. 14, iii. 24, for Loidis; it was a district dependent on the Cumbrian British realm, and embracing the lowest portion of the valleys of the Calder, the Aire, and the Wharf; Whitaker, 'Loidis and Elmete,' p. 1; Palgrave, Engl. Comm. p. 435. The name of course survives in Leeds. Green, Making of England, pp. 64, 254, speaks of the whole territory as 'Elmet.' Others make Elmet the west part of Loidis; see Murray's Yorkshire, p. 345. Bede mentions it in ii. 14.

revenge for the poisoning of his nephew Hereric, the father of
the future St. Hilda, Edwin expelled their king Cerdic, and
annexed Loidis to Deira [1].

Two years after the battle of the Idle, Laurence died, on
the 2nd of February, 619, having added, as it would seem,
to the churches of Canterbury a 'martyrium' on the south
of the cathedral, in honour of 'the Four Crowned Brothers,'
Roman martyrs in the time of Diocletian [2]. He was succeeded by Mellitus, whose character, as we have already
seen, was that of a man faithful in his stewardship of
sacred ordinances, although in a great trial of patience he
despaired of the English mission. He exhibited, as archbishop, a truly pastoral zeal; which, as in Gregory's case,
overcame the painful infirmity of the gout from which
he suffered. As Bede expresses it [3], his *mind,* if not his
feet, 'could walk healthily, leaping over all earthly considerations, ever winging its way upward, to love and
follow after things heavenly: noble in birth, nobler still
in loftiness of spirit,—a true man of God, enkindled with
the fire of Divine love,' which, says Bede, was manifest
in him when he caused himself to be carried towards
a conflagration that was laying waste a large part of
Canterbury, and occupied himself in prayer while a number
of strong men were vainly struggling to quench it;
whereupon the wind shifted round to the north, and the
rest of the city—including the cathedral and the episcopal
house—was saved. This incident, and the dedication
of the church of St. Mary, built by Eadbald within the
precinct of SS. Peter and Paul, are all that we know of the
archiepiscopate of Mellitus. He died on the 24th of April,
624, and Justus of Rochester was removed to Canterbury,
the circumstances requiring this technical departure from old
canons. Boniface V. speedily sent him a pall, and authorised

---

[1] Compare the App. to Nennius, and Bede, iv. 23, with Hussey's note.
'Nepotis,' nephew, not (as Florence took it) grandson. Hereric was the
son of Edwin's elder brother, and probably but little younger than Edwin
himself (Green, p. 248). His other daughter was Hereswid.

[2] Bede, ii. 7. For these martyrs see Alb. Butler, Nov. 8.

[3] Ib.: 'Erat autem Mellitus corporis quidem infirmitate, id est, podagra
gravatus, sed mentis gressibus sanis' (qu. sanus?).

CHAP. III. him to consecrate, single-handed[1], a new bishop for Rochester,
—the person selected being Romanus. This letter contains
an allusion to the disappointment of those more brilliant
hopes which had been centred in the Gregorian mission.
The Pope consoled Justus by observing that what had been
done was a pledge that in due time all would be done. The
slow progress was a trial of 'patience and endurance[2]:' let it
be borne in faith, and with a humble confidence that the
actual consolidation of Christianity in Kent would promote
its extension among the neighbouring realms. Justus may
well have needed this encouragement at the end of those
twenty-three years of experience; the programme drawn out
by Gregory, in one of the letters brought by himself and
his companions, appeared still to be so far from fulfilment:
outside Kent, not a single kingdom had been secured for
Christianity, and one had been lost. If hopes had been
entertained as to East-Anglia, they had been blighted. The
Celtic bishops and clergy had repelled successive overtures.
One bright spot there was, which of itself suggested a coming
revival of prosperity; for Eadbald, who had once been such
a cause of despondency, was now, as it were, a second Ethelbert. He who had refused baptism, and emphasised his
opposition to Christianity by contracting a marriage which it
abhorred, was now, as Boniface had written after reading a
letter from him[3] on the occasion of the accession of Justus,
a signal example of 'a real conversion and of an unquestion-
able faith.' With him the archbishops and their clergy could
work cordially: at his bidding churches rose up;—one such
has already been mentioned, and another is still substantially
extant, and has lately, after long desecration, been restored to
its high purpose,—that most venerable church of St. Mary,

---

[1] The permission, indeed, was general: 'Exigente opportunitate.' Above,
p. 61. This Pope sat from 618 or 619 to 625.

[2] 'Laudabili patientia redemptionem gentis illius expectatis . . . Salvati ergo
estis spe patientiæ et tolerantiæ virtute . . . . quatenus . . . . consummati
operis vobis merces . . . tribuatur,' &c. He quotes Matt. x. 22, xxviii. 20.
Compare a despondent letter of St. Boniface, Ep. 22, asking some nuns to pray
for him that he might not die 'omnino sine fructu evangelii sterilis,' and
receive 'ultionem infructuosi laboris.'

[3] The pope, by some mistake, calls him *Adul*wald; Bede, ii. 8.

which, attached to a far older Roman lighthouse, crowns the southern cliff within the limits of the castle of Dover[1]. Eadbald also built a church at Folkestone, and his daughter Eanswith, who founded there a religious society, is still remembered as the local saint[2]. But it is with the King's sister Æthelburh or Ethelburga, whom her family called by the fond name of Tata, 'the darling,' that our history is now concerned.

It must have been very soon after the receipt of the Pope's letter that envoys from Edwin of Northumbria presented themselves to Eadbald. In the name of their master they asked for Ethelburga's hand[3]. Eadbald answered like a Christian, and more uncompromisingly than his own Frankish grandfather had replied to Ethelbert. 'I cannot give my sister to a heathen : my religion forbids it[4].' The answer thus returned produced a second request from Edwin : if only he might obtain the Kentish princess, he would give to her and her attendants full liberty of worship,—and, more than that, he would himself be willing to adopt her faith, if wise men, after examining it, should pronounce it better than his own. We can easily see how Justus would exhort Eadbald to accept this offer. What if this were the opening of a door, the first beginning of new successes which should verify the assurances of Boniface, the long-expected opportunity which might fulfil Gregory's aspirations by setting Deira free from 'the ire of God?' Eadbald took his resolution : Edwin's terms were accepted, and Paulinus, one of the three companions of Justus in 601, was consecrated by him to the

---

[1] Freeman, iii. 535 ; J. H. Parker, Introd. Goth. Archit. p. 10.

[2] See Dugdale, Mon. Anglic. i. 451, that Eanswith chose this place as 'a vulgi frequentatione remotum,' and her father built there a church of St. Peter, about A.D. 630. See also Alb. Butler, Sept. 12. This church was washed away by the sea in the tenth century. In 1885 some workmen employed in the present church found behind the altar a reliquary containing a skull and some bones, which had evidently been hidden there at the Reformation. These relics of the foundress are preserved in a closed recess, on the north side of the sanctuary.

[3] Bede, ii. 9. He writes her name ' Ædilbergæ.'

[4] Bede amplifies the refusal : ' Ne fides et sacramenta cælestis Regis consortio profanarentur regis, qui veri Dei cultus esset prorsus ignarus.' Cp. ii. 15, and 'fidei sacramenta' in ii. 9, 15 ; iii. 1, 30; iv. 14, 16, 27.

CHAP. III. episcopate, on the 21st of July, 625, in order that he might be to Ethelburga in her Northern home what Liudhard had been to her mother in the still heathen Kent. We have now reached another landmark : the mission of Paulinus was the first onward step that had been taken since Mellitus addressed the East-Saxons ; and it soon proved to be, what that attempt was not, a great event for Christianity.

CHAPTER IV.

IT was, then, in the late summer of 625 that Edwin of Northumbria received his bride from Kent. He had been previously married to Cwenburga, 'the daughter of Cearl king of the Mercians[1],' and she had left him two sons, Osfrid and Eadfrid. He himself was just forty years old[2]. He treated his new wife's chaplain with respect, and never interfered with their religious practices; but he showed no disposition to fulfil the second part of his promise by instituting an examination of their creed. Paulinus lived in the Northumbrian court, for some months, without any apparent prospect of doing anything as a missionary. His personal appearance must have given an impression of grave dignity: a few words of Bede have pictured it from the description transmitted by one who had reason to remember it well. He was 'tall, with a slight stoop, black hair, a thin face, an aquiline nose, an aspect at once venerable and awe-striking[3].' He had with him as his confidential attendant a deacon named James, who was alive in Bede's own childhood, and whom he justly describes as 'a man of great zeal and fame in Christ's Church[4].' Paulinus made some attempts to win over the heathens of Deira; but in all these he failed. As Fuller in his quaint way words it, 'Seeing he could not be happy to gain, he would be careful to save[5].' If 'the god

---

[1] Bede, ii. 14.

[2] For he was forty-eight when he died in 633; Bede, ii. 20.

[3] Bede, ii. 16. An old man whom Paulinus had baptized in the Trent gave this account to Deda abbot of Bardney, who related it to Bede. See Wordsworth's Eccl. Sonnets, No. 15 :—

> 'Mark him, of shoulders curved, and stature tall,
> Black hair, and vivid eye, and meagre cheek,' &c.

[4] See Bede, ii. 16, 20; iii. 25; iv. 2.

[5] Fuller, Ch. Hist. p. 72. Compare Bede, ii. 9, 'Laboravit multum,' &c. He cites 2 Cor. iv. 4. See archbishop Ebbo's consolatory words to St. Anskar, Vit. S. Ansk. 34 (Pertz, Mon. G. H. ii. 717).

CHAP. IV. of this world had blinded the eyes' of the Yorkshire folk, he could at least, by daily exhortations, do his best to guard the queen's attendants from the contagion of Yorkshire heathenism. So passed the winter: on the 19th of April, Easter-eve in 626, Edwin, then living at a royal country-house near Stamford-bridge, had a narrow escape from sudden death[1]: a West-Saxon named Eumer, sent as an envoy by the West-Saxon prince Cwichelm, who was then reigning under his father Kynegils[2], struck at Edwin with a two-edged and poisoned dagger; Lilla, the king's most trusted personal retainer[3], rushed forward to receive the blow, but Edwin himself was wounded through the body of this devoted servant. On that same 'most holy night of the Lord's Passover,' Ethelburga bore a daughter; Edwin thanked his gods in the hearing of Paulinus, who thereupon assured him

Baptism of Eanfled.

that *he* had been praying for this happy event. The king, well pleased, promised that if he should succeed in his meditated vengeance on Wessex, he would take Christ for his Lord: in earnest of which, he at once gave over the infant to Paulinus 'to be dedicated to Christ.' Accordingly, at Pentecost[4], she was brought to baptism, being the first of the

[1] Bede, ii. 9: 'juxta amnem Deruventionem' (Derwent, the white or clear water, a tributary of the Ouse). The 'villa regalis' was probably at Aldby. 'There stood a royal house of the Northumbrian kings, the apparent site of which . . . a mound surrounded by a fosse, still looks down on a picturesque point of the course of the river;' Freeman, iii. 355. For other 'villæ' see Bede, ii. 14; iii. 17, 22; v. 4.

[2] Kynegils began to reign in 611: he and his son Cwichelm fought against the Britons at Bampton in 614, and slew 2065: see the Chronicle.

[3] 'Minister,' here used as equivalent to 'miles:' 'alium de militibus.' We have 'ministri' in ii. 13: 'ministri' attend Edwin on his progresses, ii. 16. Oswald has a 'minister' charged to look after the poor, iii. 6. Oswin sits at the hearth 'cum ministris,' iii. 14. Benedict Biscop was a 'minister' of Oswy, Hist. Abb. 1, and Easterwin of Egfrid, ib. 7. Alfred and the Chronicle call Lilla a thane, a title variously explained as 'servant' and as 'warrior.' See Kemble, Saxons, i. 168; Freeman, i. 87; Bp. Stubbs, Const. Hist. i. 181 (or 155, ed. 1). In 'Cædmon's' paraphrase the angels are called thanes of God. Compare the offices of 'bower-thane' (cubicularius), dish-thane, rede-thane. 'Ministri' often subscribe royal charters; see Cod. Dipl. ii. 13, 29, 74, &c. One, by Egbert, is signed by eight 'ministri;' ib. i. 320.

[4] 'On the holy day of Pentecost,' Bede: but he means, of course, the eve, a solemn time for baptisms: so S. Chron. Whitsun-eve, that year, fell on June 7. Compare the Gregorian 'prayers at mass' after Whitsun-eve baptisms

Northumbrian race who received it, with eleven [1] others CHAP. IV.
of her household.   The little Eanfled was reserved for
a high place among the Christian princesses of England [2].
Her father, when his wound was cured, descended like a
'Destroyer' on Wessex, slew five of its sub-kings [3], and
returned triumphant: but he still deferred full performance
of his promise, although he absented himself from idolatrous
observances.   A man of thoughtful [4], cautious temperament,
trained by his early misfortunes in reticence and vigilance,
with nothing of the enthusiast about him,—a man of middle
life, whose impulsiveness, if he had ever had any, was extinct,—
hating the notion of taking a false step, determined not to be
hurried in any grave matter,—can we not easily imagine what
Edwin was in those eventful months, during which, no doubt,
Ethelburga felt the sore sickness of hope deferred?   She was
urged by a letter from the Pope [5] to use all her influence in
behalf of her husband's conversion: the letter had been
delayed, if we are to take Bede's words literally [6], on its
journey to Britain, for Boniface had died in the October of
625, and was therefore near the end of his life when he thus
wrote, reminding Ethelburga of the text about 'the un-
believing husband,' and in a companion letter exhorting

Muratori, ii. 88;   the collect prays 'ut . . . lux tuæ lucis corda eorum, qui
per gratiam tuam renati sunt, Sancti Spiritus illustratione confirmet.' See
above, p. 52.

[1] One form of the Chron., 'twelve,' includes Eanfled.

[2] See Bede, ii. 20; iii. 15, 24, 25; iv. 26; v. 19.

[3] On these five sub-kings, as indicating the lack of unity in Wessex, see
Freeman, i. 27.   Yet they were apparently 'princes of the line of Cerdic;'
ib. and 99.

[4] 'Thoughtful Edwin;' Wordsworth, Eccl. Sonnets, No. 15.

[5] Bede, ii. 11.   Boniface says in this letter that he has heard with grief that
Edwin 'up to that time has delayed to listen to the preachers:' and this
suggests a difficulty, in that Ethelburga could not have reached York until
the end of July, and the tidings of Edwin's 'delays' could hardly have reached
Rome before the end of October, when Boniface was dead.   Could 'Boniface,'
in the address of the letters, be a scribe's error for 'Honorius'?

[6] 'Quo tempore . . . accepit,' Bede, ii. 10.   The pope's reference to 'the
preachers' implies that Paulinus had some attendant clergy.   He sends
Ethelburga a silver mirror and a gilt ivory comb, and to Edwin a soldier's
shirt (so Jerome, Epist. 64. 11, uses 'camisia') ornamented with gold, and
a camp-cloak of Ancyran fashion,—all these as 'blessings (i. e. gifts) of their
protector St. Peter.'

Edwin to forsake the senseless worship of idols, the 'follies of Pagan temples, the deceitful flatteries of auguries,' and to secure eternal life by confessing the undivided Trinity. The latter epistle expressly suggests the breaking to pieces of idols as a demonstration of their impotence. 'You, who have received a living spirit from the Lord, are assuredly superior' to things 'framed by your own subjects.' These arguments were perhaps no longer apposite ; Edwin was in an untenable half-way position, neither an idolater nor a believer; his difficulty consisted in the humiliation demanded by Christianity; it was hard for the self-reliant Teuton 'to bow down and receive the mystery of the life-giving Cross[1].' Paulinus, whenever he had opportunity, argued, pleaded, exhorted : still the king was undetermined, and used 'often to sit for hours in silence[2],' pondering the great alternative. At last, during one of these moods, Paulinus drew near, laid his right hand on his head, and asked, 'Do you recognise this sign ?' The allusion to words and gestures which had either formed part of a dream, and had as such been communicated, in some way unexplained, to Paulinus[3], or had been really employed by an unknown visitant with whom Paulinus was acquainted[4], or who may have been Paulinus himself[5], struck home at once, and told on Edwin decisively. Trembling with awe, as if in the presence of one who could read his secret history, he was about to throw himself at the bishop's feet. Paulinus was master of the situation; he raised him up, and in a tone of friendly confidence referred to what had been done for him, and what he was pledged to do in return. 'See, you have escaped those perils;—see, you have been elevated to this kingship: delay no longer to embrace the faith and the precepts of Him who wrought that deliverance, and who granted that exaltation.' 'I will

Conversion of Edwin.

---

[1] Bede, ii. 12.

[2] Bede, ii. 9, 'sæpe diu solus residens :' and ib. 12, 'horis competentibus solitarius.'

[3] Lingard (Hist. E. i. 83) and Turner (Angl.-Sax. i. 356) suppose that Edwin had had a dream, and that Paulinus had heard of it.

[4] Churton thinks that the strange visitor was a Christian who had accompanied Redwald from Kent; E. E. Ch. p. 56.

[5] Haddan and Stubbs, iii. 75 ; Hook, i. 103 ; Raine, Fast. Ebor. i. 38.

do so,' said Edwin: 'but I will first confer with my chief
friends and counsellors, so that, if they are willing, they may
become Christians also.' Paulinus assented: Edwin assembled
his 'Witan[1]' near 'Godmundingaham,' now Goodmanham,
some twenty-three miles from York; it was probably about
the close of 626, or very early in 627.

At this memorable gathering he asked his 'wise men'
individually what they thought of the new faith, which now
for more than a year had been impersonated in Paulinus,
the bishop, there present. The chief Pagan priest, whom
Bede calls Coifi[2], answered with a frank avowal of self-
interest which showed a nature of coarse mould: 'The old
worship seems to me worth nothing: no man has practised
it more than I, and yet many fare better, and have more favour
at your hand. If the gods had any power, they would rather
help *me*, who have served them more than others. Let us
then see what this new lore is good for; if it is better than
the old, let us straightway follow it.' Far different, and
indescribably suggestive and pathetic, was the speech of
a thane[3], who expressed in a vivid simile that bewilderment
as to the mystery of life which weighed heaviest on the
worthiest of the heathen: 'I will tell you, O king, what
methinks man's life is like. Sometimes, when your hall is lit
up for supper on a wild winter's evening, and warmed by a

Witena-
gemot of
Goodman-
ham.

---

[1] See Stubbs, Constit. Hist. i. 148. Godmundingaham has been explained as
the place under the *mund* or protection of the gods; Taylor's Words and
Places, p. 335; but also (Murray's Yorkshire, p. 131) as the home of the sons
of Godmund. It is near Weighton, which means 'sacred enclosure.' This
Witan certainly did not include the people as such, see Bede, ii. 13.

[2] This has been called a *Celtic* name for a pontiff; and Palgrave infers that
Druidism had won its way in Deira; Engl. Commonw. p. 155. But it is
answered that Coifi is an equivalent to the Saxon Coefig, and means 'the
active one.' Collier's version of this speech is a curious specimen of his humour,
and also of his utter want of the sense of congruity; i. 196.

[3] The speech is well versified in Professor Palgrave's Visions of England,
p. 27; and compare Wordsworth's Eccl. Sonnets, No. 16 :—
'Man's life is like a sparrow, mighty king,' &c.
Cp. Lingard, A.-S. Ch. i. 29; Milman, ii. 238; Freeman's Old-Engl. History,
p. 57; Green, Making of Engl. p. 263. The speaker is called by Bede one of
the 'optimates:' Alfred renders, 'Ealdorman.' We find 'optimatibus' in iii. 30.
As to the winter banquets, see Bede's 'Cuculus ;'—Hiems says,
'Sunt mihi divitiæ, sunt et convivia læta,
Est requies dulcis, calidus est ignis in æde.'

CHAP. IV. fire in the midst [1], a sparrow [2] flies in by one door, takes shelter
for a moment in the warmth, and then flies out again by
another door, and is lost in the stormy darkness.   No one in
the hall sees the bird before it enters, nor after it has gone
forth ; it is only seen while it hovers near the fire.   So it is,
I ween, with this brief span of our life in this world [3] ; what
has gone before it, what will come after it,—of this we know
nothing.   If the strange teacher can tell us, by all means let
him be heard.'   The words struck home to the listeners' hearts,
as fraught with a solemn and urgent reality ; they felt, with
the speaker, that they must not miss such an opportunity
of learning more about the ' whence ' and the ' whither ' of
their existence, of obtaining some sure warrant for the hopes
which struggled with dark uncertainties as they thought of
death and of the Beyond ; and just then, at the right moment,
the chief priest proposed that Paulinus should set forth his doctrine.   Paulinus, of course, welcomed and used the opportunity ;
and Coifi, as if lifted up by the power of the discourse into a
higher strain of feeling, spoke out : ' Now I understand what
the truth is : I have long known that it was not with us ;
but now I see it shining out clearly in this teaching.   Let us
destroy those useless temples and altars, and give them up to
the curse and the flame ! '   Then, at last, Edwin, as king,
publicly accepted the Gospel, and asked Coifi who should
begin the work of desecrating the altars and temples of
idolatry.   ' That will I do,' was the prompt answer : ' who
could more fittingly destroy, as a lesson for all, what once
I reverenced in my folly ? '   It was unlawful for a high priest
to bear arms, or to ride except on a mare ; therefore Coifi
emphasised his resolution by calling for arms and a horse, and,
thus equipped, he rode straight at the venerated temple of

---

[1] ' While you are sitting at supper cum ducibus ac ministris tuis.'   The ' dux '
appears in Bede, iii. 24 (three Mercian duces), iv. 13, 15 (of Sussex), and iv. 26.
It seems to be here equivalent to Ealdorman.   So Alfred, ' with thine ealdormen
and thanes.'   See Kemble, ii. 125 ff.

[2] Cp. M. Aurelius' ' Ad Seipsum,' vi. 15.

[3] ' The Northern nations . . . demanded immortality,' and hence ' they took
Christianity to their hearts ; ' Merivale, Conversion of Northern Nations, p. 130.
He gives a free version of this speech, and proceeds to dwell on the ' intense
realisation of another life ' which characterised the converted Teutons.

Goodmanham, hurled his spear against it, and bade his companions set fire to the building together with its surrounding sacred precinct[1]. Thus did Northumbria, by a national act, accept Christianity. The king caused a little wooden chapel to be hastily reared at York, on part of the ground now covered by the glorious Minster; and within its walls he went through the training of a catechumen[2], and received baptism on Easter-eve[3], April 11, 627. His nobles were baptized with him; and among the neophytes was his grand-niece Hild, the future St. Hilda, abbess of Whitby[4]. Many of the people followed his example. It was the birth-day of the Northumbrian Church.

Baptism of Edwin.

The realm of Edwin, stretching from the Humber to the Forth, and including 'Edwin's burgh[5]' on its northern frontier,—the wide-spread over-lordship which he exercised throughout all the kingdoms save that of Kent, and even over the Britons of Strathclyde, the Isle of Man, and that of Mona[6], which after his conquest of it was called Anglesey, may represent to us the great political importance of the baptism of the fifth 'Bretwalda.' So effective was the 'peace[7]' established under his government that, according

---

[1] 'Cum omnibus septis suis'—the whole τέμενος or 'frith-geard;' Thorpe's Glossary; also called 'healh-tun,' Chron. Abingd. ii. 483. Here Bede shows his fondness for Virgilian quotation: 'Quas ipse sacraverat aras.' Cp. Æn. ii. 502. See too Bede, ii. 12; iv. 26.

[2] 'Cum catechizaretur.' Bede, ii. 14; see below, p. 125.

[3] 'Die sancto Paschæ' means here the eve. The Cambrian Annals say, 'Run filius Urbgen baptizavit eum.' So the 'Appendix' to 'Nennius,' 'Si quis scire voluerit, quis eos baptizaverit, Rum map Urbgen baptizavit eos, et per quadraginta dies non cessavit baptizare omne genus Ambronum.' This is plainly a Welsh fiction, possibly based on some confusion between Paulinus and Paul Hên, the Welsh founder of Whitland. Urbgen, or Urien, had fought against Theodoric some forty years before this event: even if his son were then alive and were a priest, Paulinus would never have yielded to him the privilege of baptizing Edwin. Two MSS. of 'Nennius,' appealing to the authority of two Welsh bishops, read 'Run . . . id est, Paulinus.' This identification is incredible. See Haddan and Stubbs, Councils, i. 213.

[4] Bede, iv. 23.

[5] Freeman, i. 35; Burton, Hist. Scot. i. 281; Green, p. 253. Its old name was (not Eiddin, but) Agned.

[6] 'Mevanias insulas,' Bede, ii. 5, 9. See Lappenberg, i. 149. Aberfraw in Anglesey was the capital of Gwynedd or North Wales.

[7] Bede, ii. 16; Malmesb. G. R. i. 48. See Stubbs, Const. Hist. i. 208 : 'The peace, as it was called, the primitive alliance for mutual good behaviour

CHAP. IV.   to a proverb still current in Bede's time, a woman with her
infant could walk unharmed from sea to sea.   At every clear
spring along the high roads, he set up posts with brazen
drinking cups; and no man durst use them for any other
purpose,—so greatly was he feared or loved.   He loved state
and kingly display: not only in battle, but in times of peace,
wherever Edwin was on a progress, a banner-staff with a tuft
of feathers—'the standard,' says Bede, 'called by the Romans
tufa[1]'—was borne before him and gave warning of his
approach.   Such was Edwin as a monarch and suzerain; as
a convert, he was thoroughly true to his tardily-formed con-
victions.   He established Paulinus as bishop of York, and
'began to build a larger and more august church of stone,
square in form, in a space enclosing' the wooden one[2] in which
he had kept his first Easter, and listened to the 'Alleluias'
then heard at last in the realm and royal city of 'Ella.'
This new church was to be dedicated to St. Peter; but Edwin
did not live to see its walls raised to their full height,—and
its non-completion during his reign was symbolic of much
that he saw begun and not finished in the work of Christianising his kingdom.

Paulinus
Bishop of
York.

There was, indeed, a great impulse given, a great ardour
excited: not only were royal baptisms solemnised, as when
Edwin's sons by his former wife entered the 'laver[3],' and
when children of Ethelburga followed,—of whom two died
while still clad in their white christening-garments[4],—but

. . . was from the beginning of monarchy under the protection of the king,'
and it was in later days that the 'national peace of which he was the guardian'
became, in a personal sense, *his* peace.   For Edwin's overlordship see Freeman,
i. 553, and Engl. Towns and Districts, p. 276.

[1] Cp. Ducange in v.; a standard 'ex consertis plumarum globis.'

[2] Bede, ii. 14: 'Mox autem ut baptisma,' &c.   See Chron. of Anc. Brit.
Church, p. 137.   This wooden sanctuary was carefully preserved, and enriched
with splendid altars and vessels, by archbishop Albert; Raine, i. 104.   See the
plan of the ancient Eboracum in Freeman, iv. 202.   Some stones of Edwin's
church may still exist in the crypt of York Minster; Freeman, Norm.
Conq. v. 610; Ornsby, Dioc. Hist. York, p. 19; Raine, Historians of Church
of York, i. p. xxiii.   Edwin now restored the temporal glory of the city
which had been imperial; Freeman, Engl. Towns and Districts, p. 272.

[3] Bede, ii. 14.   Osfrid and Eadfrid; also Osfrid's child Yffi, and Osric the
nephew of Ella and first-cousin of Edwin; cp. ib. iii. 1; Green, p. 248.

[4] 'Albati.'   Cp. Bede, v. 7, Cadwalla fell sick 'in albis adhuc positus.'   On

the people crowded eagerly to hear the bishop, and to present
themselves as candidates for reception into his fold.   In one
of his missionary journeys, he was occupied for thirty-six
days, from morning to night, at the royal 'vill' of Yevering
under the Cheviots, in the work of 'catechising[1], and
baptizing,' in other words, 'instructing the people, who
flocked to him from all the villages and places, in the word of
Christ's salvation, and washing them, when instructed[2], with
the laver of remission, in the river Glen[3] which flowed
close by.'   Another place in the same Bernician district, not
mentioned by Bede, preserves the tradition of a similar visit
in its name of Pallinsburn, where a lake, probably used for
baptism, lies some three miles off the Tweed.   But, as bishop
of York, Paulinus naturally spent most of his time in Deira :
the scenes of the Glen were reproduced, to some extent, at that
tranquil and beautiful spot where the Swale glides, soft and
shallow, beside the high wooded bank that represents the
Roman camp of Caractonium, just above the existing Catterick-
bridge.   In these general baptisms, as in other ministrations,
Paulinus would be 'served' by his deacon James[4], who afterwards laboured many years in the neighbourhood of Catterick.

the white garments or 'chrisoms' of the new-baptized, see Bingham, xii. 4.
1–3. Gregory alludes to a 'birrus albus' as put on just after baptism; Ep.
ix. 6. See too ib. viii. 1 and 23, on his supplying such garments for poor
converts. For the death, 'in albis,' of the infant son of Chlodwig, see Greg.
Tur. H. Fr. ii. 29 ; and cp. Vit. Anskar. c. 24 ; and St. Patrick's letter to the
men of Coroticus, mentioning ' neophyti in veste candida.' Compare the
Baptismal Office of 1549.

[1] See Bingham, b. x. c. 1. s. 5.

[2] In utter defiance of this expression Whitaker says, 'There were no
opportunities of previous instruction ;' Loidis and Elmete, p. 300. Compare,
on the combination of instruction and baptism, Bede, iii. 1, 'catechizati, et
baptismatis gratia recreati ;' iii. 7, 'rex ipse catechizatus;' iii. 22, 'in verbo
fidei et ministerio baptizandi ;' iii. 26, 'praedicandi, baptizandi ;' iv. 16,
'instructos . . . ac . . . ablutos.' See also v. 6.

[3] The Glen appears in the Arthurian legend, in connection with the first of
the 'twelve' battles ; Nennius, 64. But this transference of Arthur's activities
to the North is an addition to the genuine story; Freeman, Eng. Towns and
Districts, p. 438. See above, p. 24.

[4] Cp. Bede, iii. 20, Thomas, 'the deacon of' Felix. For the ancient close
relation of the deacon to his bishop see S. Athan. de Fuga, 24 ; and the story
of St. Laurence. So Const. Apost. ii. 44: ' Let the deacon be the ear, eye, and
mouth of the bishop.' Cp. Bingham, b. ii. c. 20. s. 16–18 (i. 302).

Yorkshire traditions bring Paulinus to Dewsbury and to Easingwold : but if we ask whether he raised any permanent memorials of these circuits, the answer might be that neither church nor altar, nor even a cross such as might mark a service-station, was erected during his episcopate in Bernicia [1]; while as to Deira, not only were there no baptisteries, but Bede mentions as exceptional a (wooden) 'basilica,' with a stone altar, near a royal 'vill' at Campodonum, a place which Alfred's version names Donafeld, and which may be probably identified with Doncaster [2], and in that case must be distinguished from the Roman station of Cambodunum, which has been variously placed at Slack near Huddersfield, and Tanfield near Ripon [3]. Paulinus had not time to consolidate his work in Bernicia ; and even in Deira he could only lay a foundation, on which another saint was destined to build.

Paulinus' work.

Such, for the six years of his Northumbrian episcopate, was the work of Paulinus,— a work of foundation, not properly of construction. He had, it seems, but few clergy: he could do little else than travel about, planting wherever he best could, in the hope that he might afterwards be enabled to water : and we may best judge of his capacity for organising a church by what he did in the way of preparing for its organisation. 'The labours of this great missionary must have been prodigious [4].' He has been blamed for appealing

---

[1] Bede, iii. 2 ; ii. 14. The cross which Camden heard of as having once existed at Dewsbury, with the inscription 'Hic Paulinus prædicavit et celebravit,' must have been of later date : an imitation of it, in form of a Saxon wheel-cross, was accidentally destroyed in 1812 ; Whitaker's Loidis and Elmete, p. 299. There was another cross near Easingwold in the reign of Edward I ; Raine, i. 42. Near Easingwold, too, is Brafferton, where local tradition says that Paulinus baptized ; Murray's Yorkshire, p. 230. The erection of crosses at preaching-stations is said to have been a practice of St. Kentigern : see above, p. 31.

[2] See Whitaker's Loidis, p. 152, and Hunter's Deanery of Doncaster, i. 5. One argument for Doncaster (the Roman Danum) is that this church was burned after Penda had slain Edwin at Hatfield, a few miles east of Doncaster. See also Ornsby's Dioc. Hist. York, p. 20.

[3] For these two views see Whitaker, Loidis and Elmete, p. 374, and Raine, Fast. Ebor. i. 43. Cambodunum is in the second 'Iter,' between Tadcaster and Manchester.

[4] Raine, Fast. Ebor. i. 42.

to temporal motives, by promising earthly prosperity as the
reward of conversion; but it is remarkable that in his recorded
words to Edwin, when he reminded him of 'the token,' his
assurances as to the future take a purely spiritual form[1].
Within certain limits, he might not unreasonably believe
that 'the promise of the life that now is' might be included
among the topics of a missionary sermon: but to say that his
converts were 'encouraged' by him to test 'the merits of a
religious scheme by the temporal advantages which followed
its reception[2]' is a grave unfairness to his memory, and to the
evidence furnished by Bede. That solemn setting forth of
'the way of salvation' through the Cross, that emphatic warning as to a choice made in time for all eternity, that assiduous
indefatigable 'catechising' and 'preaching of the word of
God,' came, we must needs think, from the heart of a man
'whose whole mind was set on bringing the Northumbrian
people to the recognition of the truth[3],' and characterised an
episcopate which, though short in itself, endeared his name for
ages to their memory.

But he was not content to work for them alone. Very soon Paulinus at Lincoln.
after the baptism of Edwin, he had not only thought, but
acted, in behalf of their neighbours in the district of Lindsey[4],
just south of the Humber. He preached in the old Roman
hill-town of Lincoln[5]; and its reeve, or 'prefect' as Bede
calls him[6], Blæcca by name, became a convert, and began to
build 'a stone church of noble workmanship,' the roofless
walls of which were standing in Bede's own day. In this
church, represented now by one that is corruptly named St.
Paul's, and stands at some distance to the north-west of the
cathedral on the platform of that 'sovereign hill[7],' an important

[1] Bede, ii. 12: 'A perpetuis malorum tormentis te liberabit, et æterni secum
regni in cælis faciet esse participem.'
[2] Hook, i. 107, 117. Correct by Raine, i. 44. Hook owns that, when he
went about Northumbria, 'the Spirit of God blessed the preached word;' p. 112.
[3] Bede, ii. 9: 'Ipse potius toto animo intendens.'
[4] Lindsey occurs in Bede, Præf.; ii. 16; iii. 11, 27; iv. 3, 12. Its name is
obviously derived from Lindum; see Green, Making of Engl. p. 58. It was
then subject to Northumbria but was soon annexed to Mercia.
[5] Bede, ii. 16. See Freeman, iv. 212; Engl. Towns and Districts, pp. 199–201.
[6] On the burgh-reeve see Stubbs, Const. Hist. i. 106 (or 93).
[7] Wordsworth, 'Urbs situ splendida,' Hen. Hunt.

ceremony took place, probably at some time in 628[1]. Justus had died in the preceding November[2], his last days cheered by the happy tidings from the North. His successor-elect was Honorius, whom Bede calls one of the 'disciples of Pope Gregory[3]'—a phrase which naturally means that he belonged in some sense to the same class as Augustine and his three successors, as having personally received instruction from the great Pope, so that he was, as Bede further tells us, 'a man who had received the highest training in things ecclesiastical[4].' But who was to consecrate Honorius? Romanus of Rochester, sent by Justus on Church business to Rome, had met with the same death by drowning, in the Mediterranean[5], as befell the abbot Peter of Canterbury in the British Channel. To Paulinus, therefore, as the only English bishop, Honorius repaired: they met at Lincoln, and here the fifth archbishop of Canterbury was consecrated by the sole ministry of the first of a new line of bishops of York. It may here be mentioned that at some time during his episcopate, Paulinus, accompanied by Edwin, visited Nottinghamshire, and baptized a multitude of people, at midday, in the Trent, near a town whose uncouth Saxon name of 'Tiovulfingacæstir[6],' or castle of the Tiovulfing family, has otherwise entirely perished, but which may be conjecturally identified with Littleborough, where the river was crossed by the Roman road from Lincoln northwards[7]. It seems also that he visited the southern Cumbria,

He consecrates Honorius.

Baptisms in the Trent.

---

[1] So Haddan and Stubbs, iii. 73, 82. We want twenty-two years for the episcopates of two East-Anglian bishops before the consecration of a third by Honorius, who himself died in 653 (Bede, iii. 20); and, so far, 631 might serve as the latest possible date of his own consecration.

[2] Nov. 10; Bede, ii. 18. For the date of 627, see Chronicle. It is interesting to find his name preserved in the remote Cornish village of St. Just-in-Penwith. See Gilbert's Paroch. Hist. of Cornwall, ii. 282.

[3] Bede, ii. 20; v. 19, 20: Hist. Abb. 3.

[4] Bede, v. 19. Probably he had been one of Gregory's choir-boys; Hook, i. 112.

[5] Bede, ii. 20.

[6] Bede, ii. 16. See above, p. 117.

[7] I am indebted for this suggestion to Mr. James Parker, who has pointed out that Littleborough is the Segelocum of Antoninus' fifth Iter, and was a station between Lindum and Danum, so that Paulinus, coming to, or returning from Lindum, would naturally cross the Trent there. Torksey, to the south, on the Lincolnshire side, has also been thought of, but it was not on that road. Southwell would hardly have been proposed but for the local tradition that its

and left a tradition of his having preached and officiated at CHAP. IV. Whalley[1].

His royal convert was also active in extending Christianity Conversion of East-Anglia. beyond the Northumbrian border. Edwin's old protector, Redwald of East-Anglia, had been succeeded by a son named Eorpwald ; and Edwin made the best return for old kindness by ' persuading Eorpwald, with his province, to embrace the faith[2].' But the Pagan antipathy of the East-Anglian nobles, which had contributed to produce the ' Samaritan ' policy of Redwald, was fiercely aroused against a new king who was far more resolute in his new religion. One of these men, named Ricbert, inflicted on him a death which was virtually a martyrdom, in the year of his conversion, 627 or 628[3]. For three years afterwards, East-Anglia was again heathen: and Edwin must have grieved over this failure of his efforts in behalf of the land where he had once found refuge. But again, unexpectedly, 'the day broke.' Eorpwald's half-brother[4], Sigebert the Learned. Sigebert, had formerly been driven by his step-father Redwald into Gaul. The family quarrel and the exile were overruled for good of the truest kind. During his sojourn among the Franks, Sigebert was ' instructed in the mysteries of the faith,' and moreover, in some of the Church schools of the country[5],

---

venerable church, now a cathedral, was originally founded by Paulinus,—a tradition which probably grew out of the fact that from Saxon times St. Mary's of Southwell was subject to St. Peter's of York.

[1] Raine, i. 42 ; Whitaker, Hist. of Whalley, p. 33.

[2] Bede, ii. 15. This, then, was a fruit of Paulinus' mission.

[3] There is a difficulty as to these dates. The Chronicle dates Eorpwald's baptism in 632, and the coming of Felix in 636. So Florence of Worcester. But (see above) by tracing back twenty-two years before the year 653, in which Honorius died, we reach 631 for the coming of Felix (and therefore for the accession of Sigebert) and must go back three years further for Eorpwald's baptism and death.

[4] Florence, Append. : ' Frater ex parte matris.' For him see Bede, ii. 15 ; iii. 18.

[5] The ancient fame of the Gallo-Roman schools, as of Lyons, Autun, Marseilles, had been to some extent revived by the Frankish ecclesiastical and monastic schools, in which the literature of the age was studied together with theology, as at Vienne, where Bishop Desiderius, to the disgust of Gregory the Great, gave lessons in ' grammar,' i.e. profane literature, and also at Treves, Troyes, and Poitiers, where youths were trained in 'liberal' and 'secular' studies of all kinds. See Smith's Bede, p. 723. Guizot, Civil. in Fr. lect. 16, mentions as the most flourishing cathedral schools in France, from the sixth

K

CHAP. IV. acquired whatever learning they could impart, and a genuine intelligent sense of its value. He now returned to be king of the East-Anglians: and as a man 'thoroughly Christian and very learned, a good man and religious,'—so Bede sketches his character [1],—he made it his first object to carry out the work which his brother had begun at the cost of his life : and just then, by one of these coincidences which betoken a far-reaching providential order, there arrived at Canterbury a bishop named Felix, from that Burgundian territory, bounded by the Rhone and Saone and the Alps [2], which had now for

Felix bishop of Dunwich.

nearly a century been subject to the Franks. Felix had been strongly moved to preach the Gospel to English heathens, and Honorius, after hearing his wish, recommended him to go into East-Anglia. Sigebert at once recognised him as the very man he needed for his object. King and bishop accepted each other: Felix, settled at Dunwich, then a city on the Suffolk coast, now annihilated by the ocean [3], began in 631 an episcopate of seventeen years, so full of 'happiness' for the cause of Christianity that Bede might well describe his work with an allusion to the good omen of his name [4]. 'He delivered all that province,' adds Bede, 'from longstanding

to the middle of the eighth century, those of Poitiers, Paris, Le Mans, Bourges, Clermont, Vienne, Chalons, Arles, Gap. These schools, he says, superseded the great civil schools. Monastic schools were also numerous. Sigebert was in Gaul during the brilliant opening of the reign of Dagobert I. as sole king of the Franks ; see Fredegar, Chr. 58.

[1] Bede, ii. 15 ; iii. 18.

[2] See Freeman, Hist. Essays, pp. 172, 201 ; Gibbon, iv. 356. The name was derived from the burgs or castles built by this race ; Fredegar, Fragm. 2. Chlodwig took his wife Clotilda from Burgundy ; his sons conquered it in 534 ; Greg. Tur. Hist. Fr. iii. 11. It accepted the Catholic faith, having been previously Arian, and became one of the Merwing kingdoms ; but in 628 it was united to the others under Dagobert I. See Kitchin, Hist. Fr. i. 59, 85 ; Guizot, Hist. Fr. i. c. 7.

[3] Under the Conqueror, Dunwich, though no longer an episcopal city, had 236 burgesses and 100 poor ; and it was prosperous under Henry II. Spelman heard that it was reported to have had fifty churches. When Camden published his 'Britannia' (vol. i. p. 448) in 1607, it lay 'in solitude and desolation,' the greater part being submerged. One local tradition places the first preaching of Felix at Saham.

[4] 'Sacramentum sui nominis.' So in Bede's Life of St. Felix of Nola, c. 1, 'Felix, nominis sui mysterium factis exsequens.' This most successful mission was in direct connexion with the (often disparaged) Augustinian mission at Canterbury. Bede says that Honorius 'misit eum,' ii. 15.

unrighteousness and unhappiness:' as 'a pious cultivator of the spiritual field,' he 'found abundant fruit in a believing people:' and an important feature of this mission, as it was of the Kentish, was the combination of education with religion by means of a school such as Sigebert had seen abroad, and as by this time existed at Canterbury in connection with the house of SS. Peter and Paul. This school, for which Felix provided teachers 'after the model of Kent,' was probably attached to the primitive East-Anglian cathedral[1]. It must have been about two years after the coming of Felix that Sigebert 'honourably received[2]' an Irish monk famous for learning and holiness, named Fursey, who had come over with two brothers of his, and two priests[3], into East-Anglia, and there taking up his accustomed work of preaching the Gospel, did much, by example and by exhortation, for the conversion of unbelievers, and the confirmation of Christians in faith and love. Receiving a piece of ground within a 'camp' called Cnobheresburg, previously Garianonum, now Burgh Castle, in Suffolk, which still exhibits huge masses of Roman fortress-work[4], he built what Bede calls a 'noble monastery,' where he used to tell how, years before, he had seemed, in a trance, to see visions of the other world[5], such as were afterwards related by Drythelm of Melrose[6], and by the monk of Wenlock who

---

[1] See Churton, p. 63, Smith, as against 'Oxonian' zealots, argues that this school *might* have been at Cambridge, but concludes that, if it was not, it was most probably at Dunwich, or else at Saham; App. to Bede, No. 14.

[2] Bede, iii. 19. For St. Fursey's life see Lanigan, ii. 449.

[3] His brothers Fullan and Ultan (of whom the latter lived as a hermit in East-Anglia), and two priests, Gobban and Dicul. For the other Dicul of Bosham, see Bede, iv. 13.

[4]   'Rock-rampart huge, work worthy Roman hands,
         Indurate flint and brick in ruddy tiers,' &c.
                              Palgrave, Visions of England, p. 20.

[5] When Bede wrote, an old monk was still living at Jarrow, who had heard from a 'very veracious' monk that he had heard Fursey, in East-Anglia, tell his marvellous tale, and that while he told it, though it was in a hard frost and he was sitting in a thin garment, 'quasi in media æstatis caumate sudaverit.' Mabillon, disbelieving many stories of visions, as imaginary or even invented to serve as apologues, does not deny that some, as Fursey's, were 'veras *aut* vere creditas;' Ann. Ben. i. 548. Fursey died in Gaul, in 654. On the severe asceticism of the Irish saints, see Whitley Stokes, Tripartite Life, Introd. p. cxcv.

[6] Bede, v. 12. See Card. Newman's Verses on Various Occasions, p. 201. Compare Gregory's Dialogues, iv. 36.

told his story to St. Boniface[1], and might be deemed anticipations of the sterner parts of the 'Divine Comedy.' It was probably under Fursey's influence that Sigebert ere long set the bad precedent of abandoning his royal duties while in full vigour of life, and retiring into a cell which he had made for himself on the site of Bury St. Edmunds[2].

But while the Church was being quietly built up in East-Anglia, it was on the verge of a terrible catastrophe in the North. Cadwallon, or Cadwalla, king of Gwynedd[3] or North Wales, had, some years before, invaded Northumbria, in requital of the 'devastating' fury of Ethelfrid. Edwin had defeated him near Morpeth, driven him into Wales, and besieged him in the isle of Priestholm[4] near Anglesey. He found refuge in Ireland, and thence returned, and in his thirst for vengeance allied himself, Briton and Christian as he was, with a Saxon prince who combined in his own person the fiercest energy of a Teuton warrior with the sternest resistance to the progress of the new creed: who, succeeding to power at fifty years old[5], was for thirty years the prop and the sword of Heathenism, and also came near to reducing the various kingdoms to a monarchy centred in the youngest of them all[6]. This was Penda 'the Strenuous[7],' king of the Mercians, whose name was long a terror to the inmates of cell and minster in every Christianised district. There is a sort of weird grandeur in the career of one who in his time slew five kings, and might seem as irresistible as destiny. He had begun to reign in 626, on the death of Edwin's father-in-law

---

[1] Bonif. Ep. 20.

[2] Bede, iii. 18. The example was followed by Kenred of Mercia and Offa of Essex, and others not in their prime, as Ceolwulf and Ethelred.

[3] 'Catgublaun, king of Guenedotia,' App. Nenn.; Catguollaaun, al. Catwallaun, Ann. Camb. p. 7, Rolls Series. He was son of Cadvan (Angl. Sac. ii. p. xxxii). See above, p. 110.

[4] Ann. Camb. a. 629, calling the island Glannauc. 'The British Triads characterise Edwin as one of the three plagues which befell the Isle of Anglesey;' Turner, i. 364. Reginald, Vit. S. Osw. c. 9, says that Edwin chased 'Cadwallon into Armorica:' this seems to be a confusion with the fictitious retirement of his son Cadwalader into Armorica; see Ann. Camb. p. 8.

[5] So the Chronicle, a. 626.

[6] Freeman, i. 36; Lappenberg, i. 164.

[7] So Hen. Hunt. calls him, from Bede's 'viro strenuissimo,' ii. 33, and adapts Lucan, Phars. ii. 439.

Ceorl: in 628 he had encountered at Cirencester the West-
Saxon king Kynegils with his son and sub-king Cwichelm
(the prince who had sought Edwin's life), and after a day of
exhausting but indecisive conflict, had made a treaty with
them, implying a cession of West-Saxon land [1]: and now, in
order to humble Northumbria, he joined forces with Cadwallon, and attacked Edwin at Heathfield or Hatfield [2], in
south-east Yorkshire, on the 12th of October, 633. Here
ended the glorious course of the great Edwin. After seeing
his son Osfrid fall [3], he was himself slain, and 'his whole
army destroyed or dispersed [4].' The victorious confederates
made 'a very great slaughter throughout the church and
nation of the Northumbrians,' one of them, as Bede remarks,
being a Pagan, and the other, because a barbarian (i. e. a
Briton), 'more cruel than a Pagan.' The Mercians burned
the royal mansion and church at 'Campodonum:' but its
altar, being of stone, escaped the fire, and was preserved in
Bede's time at a monastery in the wood of Elmet [5]. But it
is of the Welsh king that we read, 'He spared neither women
nor children, but put them to torturing deaths, raging for a
long time through all the country, and resolving that he
would be the man to exterminate the whole English race
within the bounds of Britain [6]: nor did he, though a Christian in profession, show any respect to the Christian religion
which had grown up among them [7].' However, two princes of

Battle of Hatfield.

Devastation of Northumbria.

---

[1] Chron. a. 628; Hen. Hunt. ii. 31; Green, Making of England, p. 267.
Wessex was just then weak, after Edwin's invasion.

[2] See Hunter's Deanery of Doncaster, i. 152. The scene of the battle was
probably west of Hatfield church. The country is flat for miles, and in those
days was a fen. The Welsh called the place Meiceren, or Meicen; Ann. Camb.
and Nennius. Alb. Butler places 'St. Edwin, king and martyr,' on Oct. 4.

[3] 'Juvenis bellicosus,' son of Cwenburga, and father of the child Yffi. His
brother Eadfrid threw himself on Penda's mercy, and was afterwards put to
death by him 'in spite of his oath.' But Bede, ii. 20, does not say that this
was done 'at the pressure of Oswald,' Green, p. 291.

[4] Bede, ii. 20.

[5] Bede, ii. 14. This monastery of abbot Thrydwulf was 'probably on the
site of the existing parish church of Leeds;' Murray's Yorkshire, p. 345.

[6] 'Erasurum se esse.' So iii. 1, 'tragica cæde dilaceraret,' &c. His idea was
to purge 'Lloegria,' our present England, of its foreign invaders.

[7] Bede adds that even in his own day the Britons were wont to regard
English Christianity as no better than Paganism. See above, p. 102.

the Northumbrian line secured for a while a precarious and shameful royalty: Edwin's cousin Osric [1] was regarded as king in Deira; and the sons of Ethelfrid returned from their exile, and the eldest, Eanfrid, became king in Bernicia. Both kings had been baptized, the former by Paulinus [2], the latter among the 'Scots [3]': but both, in order to gain Penda's favour, and the support of those Northumbrians who clung to Paganism, disowned their Christian belief [4]: and both were slain by the Christian Cadwalla. Osric, while 'rashly' besieging the Britons in York [5] during the summer of 634, was cut off by an unexpected sally: and in the autumn, Eanfrid, with still greater folly, came to Cadwallon 'to sue for peace, and met with a similar doom.' Flushed with these successes, Cadwallon vaunted himself as irresistible [6], and ravaged Northumbria 'not like a conquering king, but like a raging tyrant.' This year which followed the battle of Hatfield was even in Bede's time 'hateful to all good men [7].' It was the year of foreign tyranny, exercised by a fierce conqueror who deemed himself irresistible; it was also the year of two kings' apostasy, and, it must be added, the year in which the Northumbrian Church was abandoned by its chief pastor. Paulinus may well have been bowed down by the shock of seeing Edwin's head brought to York [8], and of knowing the misery which had come on the whole kingdom.

---

[1] Son of Elfric the brother of Ella, and father of St. Oswin.

[2] Bede, iii. 1.

[3] Eanfrid had become, during his exile, the father of Talorgan, afterwards king of the Picts; Robertson, Scotl. under Early Kings, i. 12; ii. 185. This, together with Bede's phrase, 'apud Scottos sive Pictos' (iii. 1), and with the legend of Columba's appearance to Oswald before his victory, would favour the current opinion that he had taken refuge in Dalriada, not, as Lanigan thinks, in Northern Ireland (i. 418). See also Haddan and Stubbs, ii. 106.

[4] 'Anathematizando prodidit' is Bede's phrase.

[5] 'In oppido municipio;' Bede means York. Roman York was a 'colonia.'

[6] Bede, iii. 1: 'Copiis quibus nihil resistere posse jactabat.'

[7] Bede, iii. 1: 'Infaustus ... exosus usque hodie permanet.' It was not reckoned by the reigns of the two apostates, but of their saintly successor. Cp. iii. 9, 'adnumerato etiam illo anno, quem feralis impietas ... et apostasia .... detestabilem fecerunt.'

[8] Bede, ii. 20: 'Adlatum est autem caput,' &c. The body was also recovered, and afterwards buried at Whitby; iii. 24.

He thought that it was a case for 'flying from persecution;' CHAP. IV.
and this, as it would seem, without any such sufficiency of
clergy in the bishop's absence, as, in St. Augustine's carefully
formed opinion, would alone justify a chief pastor's flight [1].
But he persuaded himself that he had a primary duty to the
widowed queen whom he had escorted to Northumbria,
although a brave thane [2] named Bass was at hand to guard
her return. He set sail with her, and with her younger son Flight of
and daughter, Wuscfrea and Eanfled, and Yffi, the infant Paulinus.
son of her stepson Osfrid [3]: 'he took with him a large golden
cross [4], and a golden chalice hallowed for the service of the
altar [5],' which were long shown in the church of Canterbury;
and the fugitive party, under the care of Bass, arrived safely
in Kent, where Paulinus accepted from Honorius and Eadbald the long vacant see of Rochester. It was not till the
following autumn that he received a pall, intended for him as
archbishop of York [6]; it came too late for him, but with a
similar one for archbishop Honorius from his namesake, the
first Pope of that name, whose letter to the archbishop of
Canterbury, evidently the duplicate of one addressed to
Paulinus, and dated on June 11, 634, empowered the surviving metropolitan in case of a vacancy to consecrate a
successor, 'so that their churches might suffer no loss [7].'
Another letter then received must have been read with

[1] S. Aug. Ep. 228. See Fleury, b. 25. c. 25; Newman, Ch. of the Fathers,
p. 238. Augustine also allowed a bishop to fly if his flock fled, or if he had no
flock left. Malmesbury describes Paulinus as expelled from his see by foes;
Gest. Pont. i. 72, p. 134 (Rolls Series).

[2] He is called 'miles.' See above, p. 118.

[3] He and Wuscfrea were afterwards, says Bede, sent by Ethelburga, for fear
of her brother Eadbald and of Oswald, to the court of her friend the Frankish
king, Dagobert, where they died in their childhood.

[4] St. Willibrord used to carry with him on his journeys a golden cross;
Vit. 30.

[5] See the prayer 'ad calicem benedicendum' in St. Gregory's Sacramentary;
Murat. Lit. Rom. ii. 186, and Egbert's Pontif. p. 48.

[6] So that he was never really archbishop. Egbert, who was bishop of York
in Bede's last days, became the first archbishop in 735. Wilfrid has often
been called 'archbishop,' but quite erroneously: so too Bede's epitaph in
Durham cathedral gives the title to St. John of Beverley.

[7] Bede, ii. 18. The Pope here quietly assumes that, but for this permission,
an archbishop elect would have to travel to Rome for consecration; as if he
could not, like Augustine, seek it in Gaul.

mournful interest : it exhorted the Pope's 'most excellent son, Edwin king of the English,' to persevere in the pious course which he had begun [1]. We may here observe that when Paulinus settled down to his tranquil work at Rochester, Ethelburga founded a convent at Lyminge, where to the west of the existing church, which contains much Roman brick-work, are the excavated remains of an original 'basilica of St. Mary,' belonging to the Roman period [2] ; where the place of her burial is marked by a modern tablet on the south wall of the church [3], and her name of endearment is still per-petuated in a neighbouring common called ' Tatta's Leas [4].'

The Northumbrian Christians were 'cast down, but not destroyed.' They had lost their bishop, but they had still with them one who, though not even a priest, did a true pastor's work among them, keeping the fire of faith alive in those dark days, and, as Bede expresses it [5], 'taking away great spoil from the old enemy by teaching and baptizing.' This

James the Deacon.

was James the Deacon, otherwise known as the Chanter, from his skill in Roman church music [6]; a really noble instance, in the third rank of the ministry, of courageous stedfastness under exceptional trial, and simple fidelity to a sacred trust. His name was attached in Bede's time to the 'township' near Catterick, which was his centre of opera-tions [7]. It was within Deira, but near the Bernician frontier : and after the renegade kings of Deira and Bernicia had fallen

[1] Bede, ii. 17. He advises Edwin to have the writings of Pope Gregory frequently read to him. Edwin, it seems, had asked for a pall for Paulinus as well as for Honorius : ' Ea quæ a nobis pro vestris sacerdotibus,' &c.

[2] Haddan and Stubbs, i. 38 ; Murray's Kent and Sussex, p. 154.

[3] ' The burial-place of St. Ethelburga the queen, foundress of this church and first abbess of Lyminge.'

[4] I owe this information to the kindness of the Rev. R. C. Jenkins, rector of Lyminge. ' St. Ethelburga's well ' is to the east of the church.

[5] Bede, ii. 20 : ' Reliquerat autem in ecclesia sua,' &c.

[6] On the ecclesiastical chant as brought from Rome, see Smith's Bede, p. 719. We must connect with James's name those of Stephen Eddi, John the arch-chanter (Bede, iv. 18), and Maban the chanter of Hexham (v. 20).

[7] Akeburgh, a farm not far from Catterick,—on the site of a village,—is supposed to be ' Jacobsburgh.' See Churton, p. 63 ; Raine, i. 44 (although the place is not mentioned in Domesday ; Murray's Yorkshire, p. 284). At the neighbouring church of Hauxwell is a cross, on which the inscription could once be read, ' Hæc est crux Sti Gacobi ;' Hübner, p. 68.

in the summer and autumn, James would hear with wonder
and thankfulness that a younger brother of Eanfrid was
preparing, in the character of a Christian prince, to make a
stand for the independence of Northumbria. This was he
who for ages was honoured throughout the North-country,
and far beyond it, as Saint Oswald. When the Christians
for whom he was to fight remembered that he was the heir
of the 'fierce' Pagan Ethelfrid[1], they would also hail him as
the nephew of Edwin, whose sister had been the wife of her
brother's early foe[2]. 'With an army small in number, but
fortified by faith in Christ,' he took up his position within a
few miles of Hagulstad or Hexham[3], on a rising ground[4] to
the north of the Roman wall[5], where now stands the humble
chapel of 'St. Oswald's,' commanding a wide view. The
time was apparently at the close of 634[6]. The winter
morning had just dawned[7] when Oswald caused a cross[8] of
wood to be hastily made, and a hole to be dug for it

[1] 'Ille ut rosa de spinis effloruit;' Simeon of Durham, de Dunelm. Eccl. i. 1
(Op. i. 18, Rolls Series). He came with twelve companions; Adamnan, Vit.
Col. i. 1.

[2] See p. 112.

[3] Also called Hestaldesige, Sim. Hist. Reg. c. 58; or Hestoldesham, from
the brook Hestild, Richard of Hexh. in X Script. p. 289.

[4] 'Ad locum ejusdem sanctæ crucis *ascendere*;' Bede, iii. 2.

[5] On the great Roman wall from the Tyne to the Solway, see Burton, Hist.
Scotl. i. 21; Freeman, Engl. Towns and Districts, p. 435. Near St. Oswald's
the track of the wall clearly exhibits the northern foss, the line of the stations
and forts, and the southern vallum-line. A fragment of the wall, some thirty
yards long, stands not far off.

[6] See Bede, iii. 1, 2. There is some difficulty about the date. Cadwallon,
according to Bede, tyrannised over Northumbria for an entire year from October,
633. 'After this,' Osric having been slain in the summer of 634, 'at length'
Eanfrid met a like fate. The year from Oct. 633, to Oct. 634, was 'the year
abhorred,' afterwards reckoned as a regnal year of Oswald. His victory cannot
well have taken place *before* December, 634: Bede does not say how soon it
followed on 'the slaughter of his brother Eanfrid;' iii. 1. He reigned eight
years, without counting the 'annus infaustus;' Bede, iii. 9; A.-S. Chr. a. 634;
and he was slain August 7, 642; therefore the eight years must begin within
A.D. 634. The Chron. dates his accession in that year, but modern writers
have usually dated it in 635 (e.g. Lingard, A.-S. Ch. i. 32).

[7] The day before, Oswald dreamed that Columba appeared to him and promised
him victory. This he afterwards told to abbot Seghine; Adamn. V. Col. i. 1.

[8] This was the only cross, as far as Bede could learn, that had been set up
in Bernicia. He tells us that splinters of it had a healing virtue on men and
cattle. See Alcuin's apostrophe to it, de Pontif. Ebor. 427.

in the earth, and held it up with his own hands while his men heaped the soil around it. Then, when the symbol of their faith stood firmly fixed, and pointing heaven-wards, he raised his voice, and bade his soldiers kneel with him, and 'entreat the true and living God, who knew how just was their cause, to defend them from the proud and fierce enemy.' They charged Cadwallon's greatly superior force; and their onset was overpowering. Far away he fled, down the slope into the valley, till he reached the Denisburn, as Bede calls it, probably a brook near Dilston [1], eastward of Hexham; and there he fell, amid carnage long-remembered,— 'That slaughter of Cadwalla's men that stayed the Denis' flow.'

This was the battle of 'Heavenfield [2],' for that significant name had already belonged to the place: the Welsh called it, in their accounts, 'Catisgual,' the battle below the wall [3]. Few fields of conflict should be more interesting to English-men than this which witnessed not only the death-blow to Welsh schemes of reconquest, but the definitive triumph of the Christian cause in Northumbria. Heavenfield had fully made up for Hatfield: for Oswald, now king of the reunited

Oswald,
King of
Northum-
bria.

---

[1] 'Caedes Cedwalensium Denisi cursus coercuit;' ap. Hen. Hunt. Smith, p. 720, supposes the Denisburn to be the Erringburn, north of St. Oswald's and of the Wall, and places the scene of the battle in that neighbourhood, e.g. near Hallington or Bingfield. But see Bruce's Hist. of the Wall, p. 142, that a charter of the thirteenth century describes twenty acres of land as between Denisburn and Divelin (Dilston). Oswald would cross the Wall-line.

[2] Not so called by 'after times' (Green, Making of Engl. p. 275). Bede expressly says that the name was earlier.

[3] Ann. Camb. (dating it wrongly in 631) 'Cantscaul;' App. Nenn. 'Catscaul, cum magna clade exercitus sui.' On the death of Cadwallon, see Lappenberg, i. 156. He had fought, it was said, in fourteen battles and sixty skirmishes: he was succeeded by his son Cadwalader, called 'the Blessed,' who died of 'the plague' in 664 (Catgualart, in App. to Nennius). See Rees, Welsh Saints, p. 301; Haddan and Stubbs, i. 165. Skene, on the authority of Welsh records, would prolong Cadwallon's life to 659, supposing his father Cadvan to have been the 'Catgublaun' who fell 'in bello Catscaul;' Four Ancient Books of Wales, i. 71; comp. Reginald, Vit. Osw. i. c. 9, in Sim. Op. i. 345. But the Ann. Camb. clearly identify the victor of 'Meiceren' (Hatfield) with him who 'fell' in 'Cantscaul:' and Bede's 'infandus Brettonum dux,' who fell at the Denisburn, is clearly his 'rex Brettonum Cadvalla.' 'Catguollaun,' in Nennius, seems to be only another form of 'Catgublaun.'

Bernicia and Deira, was to Christians all that Edwin had CHAP. IV.
been, and more: in reading of him, we think instinctively of
Alfred. Strength and sweetness were united in a character
which almost represents the ideal of Christian royalty. He
was now about thirty years old [1], in the prime and glow of a
pure and noble manhood; he was granted to his country in
her extreme need for some eight years, in which he signally
'fulfilled a long time.' On the one hand, so able a captain
and ruler that he extended the area of an overlord's supremacy until it even included the Picts and Scots [2],—on the
other hand, as devout as if he lived in a cloister, thinking
little of half a night spent in devotion [3], and accustomed
from such habits to keep his palms instinctively turned
upward, even while sitting on his throne; thus 'wont, while
guiding a temporal kingdom, to labour and pray rather for
an eternal one [4];' withal, as generous and affectionate as he
was pious, 'kind and beneficent to the poor and to strangers,'
humble of mind and tender of heart, amid all that might
have 'lifted him up to arrogance [5],' Oswald was altogether
a prince of men, one born to attract a general enthusiasm of
admiration, reverence, and love.

His first object was to restore the national Christianity;
and for this, he needed a bishop. He naturally applied to Icolmkill.
the 'elders' of that Northern Celtic Church which had been
for years his religious home. Of these elders the principal [6]
were the community of Hy or Icolmkill, where Seghine was

[1] Bede, iii. 9. Tradition describes him as tall, with a rather long face,
bright glancing eyes, yellow hair, and a very thin beard; Hist. Transl. S.
Cuthb. 6, in Bed. Op. vi. 409; Reginald, Vit. Osw. c. 50.

[2] Bede, iii. 6: 'Denique omnes nationes,' &c. So that Oswald anticipated
the over-lordship of such a 'Basileus' of Britain as Athelstan or Edgar. See
Freeman, i. 554. 'Totius Britanniæ imperator,' Adamnan, i. 1. Elsewhere
Bede attributes this extension of Northumbrian overlordship to Oswy; ii. 5.

[3] Bede, iii. 12: 'Denique ferunt quia a tempore matutinæ laudis sæpius ad
diem usque in orationibus perstiterit.' Comp. 'matutinæ laudis,' iv. 7.

[4] Bede, l. c.: 'Nec mirandum,' &c.

[5] Bede, iii. 6: 'Quo regni culmine sublimatus, nihilominus, quod mirum est
... semper humilis,' &c. See Alcuin de Pontif. Ebor. 269: 'parcus sibi,
dives in omnes, Excelsus meritis, submissus mente sed ipsa.' Reginald says,
'Neminem fidelem esse pauperem publice pertulit,' c. 10.

[6] Bede's phrase, 'majores natu Scottorum,' seems to include others besides
the monks of Hy.

CHAP. IV. then ruling, as fifth abbot [1], and, although only a presbyter, was exercising, by what Bede calls 'an unusual arrangement,' a supreme jurisdiction over all that province, the bishops not excepted [2]. The explanation of this anomaly lay in the extraordinary reverence [3] paid to the great Founder-Abbot and missionary saint, in whom the Church of 'Alban' felt herself, as it were, impersonated, and who was in some sense regarded as still living in his successors. There were in 'Alban' no diocesan limits [4]; the centre of unity was the monastery of Hy, and the idea of local authority was concentrated in its abbot, the 'coarb' or 'heir' of 'Columbcille [5].' From 'Iona,' then, we are told, a bishop [6], whom Scotch tradition has called Corman, was sent into Northumbria, but his first experience of its rude indocile heathens drove him home again in hopeless disgust [7]. 'It is of no use,' he told the assembled monks, 'to attempt to convert such people as they are.' A voice was raised in gentle remonstrance: 'Did you not, then, forget the Apostle's maxim about milk for babes? Did you not deal too rigidly with those untaught minds, and expect too much, and too soon, as the fruit of teaching too high for them to follow?' All eyes were fixed on the speaker, a monk named

[1] Baithen succeeded Columba; after him came Laisrean; then Virgnous or Fergna; then, in 623, Seghine. Bede warmly praises the successors of Columba for their strict, pure, and holy lives; iii. 4. For 'Segenus,' see also Bede, ii. 19. See a list of abbots of Hy in Reeves's Adamnan, p. 370 ff.

[2] Bede, iii. 4: 'Cujus juri et omnis provincia, et ipsi etiam *episcopi, ordine inusitato*, debeant esse subjecti, juxta exemplum primi doctoris illis, qui non episcopus, sed presbyter exstitit et monachus.' So A.-S. Chr. a. 565. See Skene, Celtic Scotl. ii. 44.

[3] See Lanigan, ii. 249 ff.; Grub, i. 69, 137; Todd, Life of St. Patrick, p. 10 ff. The primacy passed, in effect, from Hy to Dunkeld, and then to Abernethy, in the middle of the ninth century; Reeves's Adamnan, p. 297; Skene, ii. 307, 310.

[4] See The Book of Deer, ed. Stuart, pp. cii, cxxvi. The old British episcopate was diocesan, the old Irish might rather be called monastic.

[5] See Reeves's Adamnan, p. 364; Todd's St. Patrick, p. 156; Book of Deer, p. cvii; Skene, ii. 148; Grub, Eccl. Hist. Sc. i. 138; Haddan and Stubbs, ii. 106, 115.

[6] See Bede, iii. 5: 'Cum . . . rex . . . postulasset *antistitem* . . . missus fuerit primo alius,' &c.

[7] The community had had two 'Saxon' members, Genereus and Pilu, in Columba's time; Adamn. iii. 10, 22. On this see Grub, i. 60, that in them, as far as we know, 'Columba offered the first-fruits of the English nation to God;' and Lanigan, ii. 174.

Aidan[1] : all said at once that he was the right man[2]. 'And so,' says Bede, '*ordaining him*, they sent him forth to preach' to the Northumbrians ; a phrase which, taken in connection with the 'unusual arrangement,' has raised a question on which we must for a moment pause. These monks and their abbot were simple presbyters ; did they, then, profess to 'ordain' Aidan as bishop ? We may answer with certainty that they did not. First, the phrase 'ordaining' is used else-where for 'causing to be ordained[3].' Secondly, Bede's language about Aidan's ecclesiastical position shows that he, a Latin monk, accustomed to a strict system of episcopal ad-ministration, never doubted that Aidan had validly 'received the rank or degree of a bishop[4] :' he speaks of him just as he speaks of other prelates indisputably consecrated ; he tells us that Aidan was revered by archbishop Honorius and by bishop Felix[5]. Thirdly, the very point of the anomalous 'arrange-ment,' in Bede's view, is that 'even bishops' were subject to the abbot of Hy; and these bishops would of course perform the functions of their order, such as the consecration of new bishops[6]. Fourthly, Columba himself is recorded to have

[1] We find this name borne by a monk of Hy in Columba's time, Adamn. iii. 6, and by the Scottish king whom Ethelfrid defeated, Bede, i. 34. So too Adamnan speaks of Columba's 'ordaining' Aidan to be king, Vit. Col. iii. 5. This Aidan died in 606. The 'Chronicon Scotorum' mentions two abbots named 'Aedhan,' a. 663, 887.

[2] 'That he was worthy of the episcopate, because he had in an eminent degree the grace of discretion, which is the mother of virtues.'

[3] Compare Greg. Turon. H. F. viii. 22, where 'ordinaturum' is used of a king: and Rudborne, Hist. Maj. Winton. c. 3 (Wharton, Angl. Sac. i. 191), that Kenwalch, king of the West-Saxons, 'ordinavit in episcopum Agilbertum.' So Marcellinus and Faustinus, that the Catholic people of Oxyrinchos 'episcopum sibi per tunc temporis episcopos catholicos ordinavit,' Sirmond, Op. i. 152 : and Capit. Caroli M. a. 802, 'ut nullus ex laicis presbiterum . . . præsumat ad ecclesias suas ordinare absque licentia . . . episcopi sui,' Pertz, Monum. Hist. Germ. Leg. i. 106. Cp. Tillemont, Mem. iv. 95, as to Cyprian, Ep. 52 ; 'Novatus . . . diaconum constituit.' And Renaudot, Lit. Orient. i. 381, that Eutychius once uses 'ordained' for 'caused to be ordained.'

[4] 'Accepto gradu episcopatus,' Bede, iii. 5. Moreover, Bede calls him a 'pon-tifex' in iii. 3, 6, 17, an 'antistes' in iii. 14, 15, 16, 17. See too Bede's language about his successor Finan, iii. 17, 21, 25 ; and Cedd who was consecrated by Finan, 'accepto gradu episcopatus,' iii. 22 ; and Colman who 'succeeded Finan in the bishopric,' iii. 25, and 'held the pontificate,' iii. 26. See Bp. Russell, Hist. Ch. Scotl. i. 32. Bede has no doubt that those whom they ordained were really 'sacerdotes,' iii. 5, 26. See Skene, ii. 157.   [5] Bede, iii. 25.

[6] More than one bishop, then,—probably, according to Irish usage, many

CHAP. IV. honoured bishops as invested with peculiar prerogatives: on one occasion, when a bishop came to Hy, and attempted in his humility to pass himself off as a simple presbyter, Columba discovered his episcopal character when they were just about to join in consecrating the Eucharist, and desired him, for the honour of the episcopate, to 'break the bread alone in the manner of a bishop[1].' On the whole, therefore, if there was not at that time a resident bishop in Hy[2], as in St. Brigid's convent at Kildare, in St. Martin's at Tours, and in St. Denis' near Paris[3], we may be sure that the ministrations of one or more of the non-diocesan Scotic prelates would be employed by abbot Seghine when a 'bishop' was to be sent to king Oswald.

Arrival of St. Aidan.

So it was that in the summer of 635[4], just ten years after Paulinus came to Northumbria, his successor arrived from a quarter which he himself would have regarded with no friendly

more,—dwelt in the 'province' of Alban; Lanigan, ii. 253. Reeves says that there were at all times bishops resident at Hy *or* some dependent church, subject to the abbot's monastic jurisdiction (Adamnan, p. 340); and see Skene, ii. 133, on the bishops at Lismore and Kingarth.

[1] The stranger being asked by Columba 'Christi Corpus ex more conficere,' called Columba to him, 'ut simul, quasi duo presbyteri, Dominicum panem frangerent' (Maskell, Mon. Rit. iii. 215). Columba approached the altar, looked in his face, and said, 'Benedicat te Christus, frater; hunc solus *episcopali* ritu frange panem; nunc scimus quod sis episcopus. Quare hucusque te occultare conatus es, ut tibi a nobis debita non redderetur veneratio?' Adamn. Vit. Col. i. 44. The stranger's name was Cronan, from Munster. Lanigan, ii. 179, thinks that the 'episcopalis ritus' was the benediction given by bishops only, 'after the breaking of the Host,' in Gallican and other Churches. But it was clearly the prerogative of a Celtic bishop to consecrate alone, whereas priests used to 'concelebrate,' or repeat the words and acts of consecration together; Warren, Lit. and Rit. of Celt. Ch. p. 128, and Reeves, p. 86. See also the story of the ordination of Columba, indicating 'that the distinction between bishops and priests was well understood in Ireland;' Lanigan, ii. 130; and that of the ordination of Aedh the Black, see Todd's Life of St. Patrick, p. 8, and Reeves, p. 69. Cp. Tripart. Life, i. p. clxxx.

[2] Lanigan, ii. 253; Grub, i. 139.

[3] Lanigan, ii. 254; Russell, i. 26; Grant, Bamp. Lect. p. 330; Todd's Life of St. Patrick, pp. 12, 22. Todd also refers to the bishop of Aquino as under the abbot of Monte Cassino, and to the position of a bishop as resident in the monastery of Mount Sinai; p. 67. But these cases are not properly parallel to that of Hy; Grub, i. 137.

[4] Some time must be allowed for (1) Oswald's first request to the Scots, (2) the unsuccessful experiment, (3) the second request. Aidan could hardly arrive before the middle of 635. He died August 31, 651, after the seventeenth year of his episcopate had begun; see Bede, iii. 17. The statement in Bede, iii. 26, that the year of the Whitby conference, i. e. 664, was the thirtieth year of

feeling,—with something of mistrust, and even of resentment, CHAP. IV.
on account of the obstinacy, as he would call it, with which,
in his own experience, the Irish Church,—the mother Church
of Columba's monastery and its dependencies,—had rejected
the 'Catholic' Easter-rules, and adhered to their own 'erro-
neous observance [1].' Aidan, however, though a true son of his
national Church [2], was of very different temper from Dagan,
and even, on this point, from Columban: and we shall see
that, although he retained his own usages, he disarmed the
suspicion or the hostility which Celtic fashions too commonly
aroused. In another respect he indicated, at the very outset
of his Northumbrian work, a love for Celtic ways as distinct
from Roman. He did not establish himself in the capital of
the kingdom, although York had been the seat, not only of
Paulinus in Edwin's time, but of an ancient British episcopate [3]. It was not the mode of Celtic bishops to regard
practical and administrative convenience in the selection of
their seats: we have already observed how David chose the
remote and lonely Menevia, doubtless for the sake of ascetic
seclusion [4]. Aidan carried with him the perpetual remembrance Lindis-
of his old home in what was emphatically termed 'The farne.
Island:' and he found an irresistible attraction in the re-
semblance between Hy and Lindisfarne [5], a place which Bede
describes as 'twice a day contiguous to the mainland of
Northumbria, and twice a day like an island enclosed in the
sea, according to the ebb and flow of the tide [6]:' a description
which is now somewhat less accurate, for the path which can

the Scotic mission in Northumbria, may be a lax reckoning from the accession
of Oswald at the end of 634. Simeon of Durham gives the date 635; de Dun.
Eccl. i. 2 (Op. i. 19).

[1] See Bede, ii. 19, as to Pope Honorius' letter to the Irish: 'Quos in
observatione sancti Paschæ errare compererat.'

[2] 'He was son of Lugair, and of the same lineage as St. Brigid;' Reeves's
Adamnan, p. 374; see Bp. Forbes, Kalendars, p. 269.

[3] See Raine, Historians of Church of York, i. p. xxv, for the preference felt
by king and bishop alike for Bernicia.

[4] Bp. Jones and Freeman, Hist. St. David's, pp. 237, 251. And see Freeman,
Norm. Conq. i. 352: 'that remote bishopric whither Saint David had fled from
the face of man.' Above, p. 34.

[5] That is, the recess formed by the river Lindis. The Britons called it
Medcaut; the Irish, Metgoet. The App. to Nennius says that Urien of Reged
was treacherously slain while besieging some Anglian princes in the island.

[6] Bede, iii. 3. See Camden, Brit. ii. 1502, that the western point is joined

CHAP. IV. be traversed about low water from Beal is over sands 'at best very wet and plashy[1].' No sacred spot in Britain is worthier of a reverential visit than this 'Holy Island' of Aidan and his successors[2]. As you stand on its beach, or look around from the little eminence that seems to guard the ruins of its monastery[3], you see that beside its general likeness to Hy, and its facilities for devotional retirement, it had a more material advantage in its nearness to the royal fortress-rock of Bamborough, which rises up majestically to the south. Here, then, the new bishop established his head-quarters; here was all that he could call his own,—the ground on which he built his humble church, and a few adjacent fields[4]. In entering on his episcopate, he neither sought nor received any sanction from Rome or Canterbury; he was a missionary bishop sent from the neighbouring Scotic Church, at the request of the Northumbrian king : this was his position, and he would never have admitted the principle that all episcopal jurisdiction must be derived from Rome[5], or that a Pope had a right to make an English archbishop supreme over 'all the bishops of Britain[6].' Yet Rome acknowledges him as a canonised bishop[7].

Our next period, then, will be characterised by another great missionary effort, carried on in the north by St. Aidan of Lindisfarne.

to the main part 'by a very small strip of land; towards the south it has a small town, with a church and castle,' &c. Comp. Marmion, ii. 9 :—

'For, with the flow and ebb, its style
Varies from continent to isle.'

See Raine, i. 19 : 'Twice a day did a belt of living water encircle that little sanctuary; and when it was ungirt, there were the quicksand and the shoal.' The river Lindis, says Simeon, 'excurrit in mare,' and is visible at low tide; the isle is eight miles, or more, round; Hist. Reg. s. 56 (Op. i. 54).

[1] Murray's Durham and Northumberland, p. 226 ; Pearson, Hist. Maps, p. 2.

[2] 'Locus cunctis in Britannia venerabilior;' Alcuin to Ethelred, Ep. 12 ; Haddan and Stubbs, iii. 493.

[3] This little hill must have reminded Aidan of the eminences in Hy called 'the Great Fort' and 'the Angels' Mount,' favourite seats of Columba; Adamn. i. 30, ii. 4, iii. 16.

[4] Bede, iii. 17 : 'Utpote nil propriæ possessionis,' &c.

[5] Collier, i. 203.

[6] See above, p. 64.

[7] See Alb. Butler, Aug. 31.

CHAPTER V.

THE Scotic mission to King Oswald's people would engage historical interest by the wide area of its operation, affecting, as it did, not only the Northumbrian realm extending from Edinburgh to the Humber, but also, ultimately, the great midland district, and even the country of the East-Saxons. But it has also a yet stronger and more personal attractiveness in the wonderful beauty of character which made 'the path' of its chief 'a shining light,'—which acted like a spell on the rough Northcountry-men whose language he had to learn after his arrival,—which made him so effective a converter of souls, because so potent a winner of hearts,— which proved too much for anti-Scotic prejudices, national or ecclesiastical, and through various lines of testimony[1] impressed itself on the English-born Church-historian as virtually a model of Christian excellence. Let us put together what Bede takes such evident delight[2] in telling us as to what Aidan was, and how he lived and worked in Northumbria.

'A man,' he begins, 'of the utmost gentleness, piety, and moderation[3]:' and in subsequent passages he tells us that Aidan was earnest in promoting peace and charity, purity and humility, was superior to anger and avarice, despised pride and vainglory, and was a conspicuous example of entire unworldliness, strictly temperate in all his habits, sedulous in study and devotion, full of tenderness for all sufferers, and of righteous sternness towards powerful offenders[4]: that he

---

[1] 'Quantum ab eis qui illum novere didicimus;' Bede, iii. 17.

[2] 'His virtues,' says Dean Hook, 'were such as *compel* the *reluctant* admiration of the candid Bede,' (i. 120). This is not candid towards Bede, whose tribute of admiration for Aidan's character, recurring in several chapters, is unequivocally hearty: on its 'earnestness and eloquence,' as expressive of a 'thorough veneration,' see Burton, Hist. Scotl. i. 269.

[3] Bede, iii. 3.   [4] Comp. Bede, iii. 5, 17.

CHAP. V. 'took pains to fulfil diligently the works of faith, piety, and love, according to the usual manner of all holy men [1],' and, in a word, to 'omit not one of all the duties prescribed in the evangelical, apostolical, or prophetical Scriptures, but to perform them to the utmost of his power [2].' No wonder, then, that his doctrine was thus recommended by the absolute consistency of what he did with what he taught [3]. As for his daily life in Lindisfarne, it was that of a monk [4], governed by rules and habits which he brought with him from Hy. He obtained fellow-workers from his old country [5], whose spirit was as his spirit: he formed a school of English boys, twelve in number [6], who were trained up in holy ways under his own eye, that they might in due time preach to their own countrymen [7],—and among whom one was afterwards famous as St. Chad [8]. Occasionally Aidan would retire for devotional solitude to the chief islet of the Farne group, lying off Bamborough, on which, in Bede's time, 'it was usual to point out the spot where he was wont to sit alone [9].' We find also that he brought in the practice of fasting on all Wednesdays and Fridays until 3 p.m. except during 'the fifty days of Easter [10].' In his actual mission work, he travelled on foot, unless compelled by necessity to ride: we shall see ere long what he

---

[1] Bede, iii. 25: 'Opera tamen fidei . . . diligenter exsequi curavit.'

[2] Bede, iii. 17: 'Qui, ut breviter multa comprehendam,' &c.

[3] Bede, iii. 5: 'Cujus doctrinam,' &c. Compare i. 26, on Augustine and his companions; see above, p. 52.

[4] Bede, iii. 3; iv. 27. All the bishops of the line which began with him were monks, until 1072; Simeon of Durham, de Dunelm. Eccl. i. 2.

[5] Bede, iii. 3. Ireland is meant.

[6] Twelve was regarded as a sacred number. See instances in Reeves's Adamnan, pp. 299–303: and Tripart. Life, ii. 447. See above, p. 137, on Oswald's twelve attendants.

[7] Bede, iii. 26. So when St. Anskar began his work in Denmark, he began to form such a school of twelve or more Danish boys 'who might be educated for God's service;' Vit. S. Anskar. 8 (Pertz, Mon. Germ. H. ii. 696). It is needless to refer to the practice of Bishops Selwyn and Patteson.

[8] Bede, iii. 28. Another was Eata, iii. 26.

[9] Bede, iii. 16. This is called the 'House Island,' about a mile and a half from the shore. See it described in Bede, iv. 28; Vit. Cuthb. 17. Comp. Adamnan, iii. 8, that Columba one day, in Hy, 'remotiorem . . . locum aptumque ad orationem in saltibus quæsivit.' A similar practice was attributed to Ninian; Lives of Nin. and Kentig. ed. Forbes, p. 284.

[10] Bede, iii. 5. Cp. Adamn. i. 26; Warren, Lit. and Ritual, p. 146.

did with a horse, which was a royal gift intended to facilitate these journeys [1]. This habit of walking enabled him easily to turn aside and endeavour to enter into conversation with any one whom he met, rich or poor,—to win him over, if a heathen, to encourage and exhort him, if a believer. While he and his companions travelled, they used to 'meditate' on texts of Scripture, or recite psalms: 'this was' their 'daily work [2].' Aidan was happy indeed in having an Oswald for his king: and in the early days of his episcopate, Oswald was often to be seen employing that knowledge of the 'Scottish' or Irish tongue which he owed to his exile in interpreting the missionary addresses of the bishop,—a sight which Bede might well call 'truly beautiful [3].' In this, as in other matters, Oswald showed a depth and fervour of personal piety which we do not find in Edwin, and which reminds us of Alfred or St. Louis. He and Aidan worked together as Sigebert did with Felix. But knowing Aidan's ascetic habits, Oswald did not often invite him to the royal table: when the bishop appeared there, it was with one or two attendant clerics; 'and when he had taken a little refreshment, he would make haste to go out in order to read with his brethren, or to pray [4],' for he had 'a church and a bedchamber' near the 'royal city' of Bamborough [5]. We hear of his sharing the

[1] Bede, iii. 5, 14. While travelling, Aidan, as a monk, wore sandals; his garments consisted of a thick woollen 'cuculla' or 'cape,' or in winter an 'amphibalus,' and below it a shirt, 'tunica.' See Reeves's Adamnan, p. 356. The front of his head showed the Irish tonsure; behind, the long hair flowed down; see Reeves, p. 350, and Maclear, Apost. Mediæv. Eur. p. 57.

[2] Bede, iii. 5: 'In tantum autem,' &c. Bede contrasts this with 'the sluggishness of' his own 'time.' So Adamnan says, Columba 'never could pass a single hour without employing himself in prayer, or reading, or writing, or some other work;' Vit. Col. præf. 2.

[3] Bede, iii. 3: 'Ubi pulcherrimo,' &c. He implies that Aidan could speak English, though imperfectly. Comp. Rich. Hexham, X Script. 290: 'The race of the Bernicians was converted in 634 by the preaching of the saints Oswald . . . and Aidan.' So Simeon, Dun. Eccl. i. 1: 'Rex, utique Regis æterni minister devotus, adsistere, et fidus interpres fidei, ducibus suis et ministris ministrare solebat verba salutis.' As Churton says, E. E. Ch. p. 72, it is 'a striking instance of the care of Providence turning the misfortunes of his youth to a means of blessing.' A much later case of a king interpreting a missionary's sermons was that of Gottschalk, king of the Wends in the eleventh century; Hardwick, Ch. Hist. M. Ages, p. 128.

[4] Bede, iii. 5: 'Et si forte evenisset,' &c.

[5] Bede, iii. 17: 'In hac enim habens ecclesiam,' &c.

king's forenoon meal on a certain Easter Sunday, when 'a silver dish full of royal dainties was set before them on the board, and they were just about to stretch out their hands to bless the bread[1]:' then enters a thane, 'whose charge it was to relieve the poor, and informs Oswald that a great crowd of poor folk, assembled from all the country-side, were sitting in the streets begging some alms from the king: Oswald orders the contents of the dish to be carried to them, and the dish itself to be broken and divided for their benefit.' On this Aidan seizes the king's right hand, and says, 'May this hand never decay[2]!' In his dealings with the rich, Aidan showed his superiority to 'fear or favour:' he never withheld a rebuke deserved by misdoings of theirs, but always administered it with the authority befitting a bishop[3]. If a thane came to Lindisfarne, he was hospitably entertained, but got none of those money-presents which, in the Eastern Church, had been euphemistically called 'blessings[4],' and being professedly tokens of good-will from ecclesiastics, were often little else than bribes to secure the interest of a powerful layman, or even payments regarded as his due. On the other hand, if a rich man offered money to Aidan, it went promptly to the poor[5], whose sufferings were ever in the thought of this true 'cherisher of the needy and father of the wretched[6]:' or else it was disposed of, as Gregory himself might have disposed of such gifts, in ransoming those who had been unjustly sold into slavery, many of whom, when

---

[1] Literally, this implies that the king was to join with the prelate in this 'grace before meat.'

[2] The hand, Bede adds, was preserved in the royal city of Bamborough, and remained there, to his days, undecayed; iii. 6. Simeon of Durham (twelfth century) says that Swartebrand, a monk of that church, who had 'recently' died, declared that he had often seen this 'right hand,' undecayed; Dun. Ecc. i. 2. See Malmesbury's remarks on this marvel; Gest. Reg. i. 49. Oswald is called in Nennius 'Oswald Lamnguin,' the 'white hand.' See Green, Hist. Eng. People, p. 23; Lappenberg, i. 162, 'the fair or free of hand.'

[3] Bede, iii. 5, 17.

[4] 'Eulogiæ,' Fleury, b. 27. c. 12.

[5] Bede, iii. 5: 'Sed ea potius quæ sibi a divitibus,' &c. Comp. iii. 26: 'Si quid enim pecuniæ,' &c.

[6] Bede, iii. 14: 'Erat enim multum misericors,' &c.: ib. 5, 17. Compare Adamn. Vit. Col. i. 46.

thus delivered, became Aidan's pupils, and were ultimately promoted by him to the priesthood [1]. One thing alone Bede could not approve in Aidan,—the inevitable Celtic error about the Paschal reckoning. On this point Aidan's 'zeal was not fully according to knowledge [2] :' so Bede expresses himself, but takes off the edge of this gentle censure by suggesting in one passage that Aidan might be ignorant of the true reckoning [3], and by telling us in another that those in Northumbria who knew it were tolerant of his observance, because they understood ' that he was unable to deviate from the custom of those who had sent him ; so that he was deservedly loved by those who differed from him about the Pasch,' and respected even by such dignified representatives of 'Catholic observance' as archbishop Honorius and bishop Felix [4]. And after all, says Bede, ' he did *not*, as some have thought, keep the feast, in Jewish fashion, on the fourteenth moon on any week-day [5], but always on a Sunday, from the fourteenth to the twentieth;' that is, if the fourteenth were on a Sunday, he would make that his Easter Sunday, and so on until the twentieth [6] ; whereas, according to Catholic rules, he should in that case have deferred the festival until the next Sunday, the twenty-first. He would always, says Bede, ' celebrate' the ' Pasch' on a Sunday, ' because, with the Holy Church, he believed the Lord's resurrection to have taken place on the first day of the week, and hoped that our resurrection would in truth take place on the same day of the week [7], now

[1] Bede, iii. 5 : 'Denique multos,' &c.

[2] Bede, iii. 3 : ' Zelum Dei, quamvis non *plene* secundum scientiam,' for he kept Easter Sunday ' from the fourteenth to the twentieth moon.'

[3] Bede, iii. 17 : 'Quod autem Pascha,' &c. Cp. iii. 4, 'Sciebant enim,' &c.

[4] Bede, iii. 25 : 'Hæc autem dissonantia, &c. 'Pascha contra morem eorum qui ipsum miserant facere *non potuit*.' Cp. iii. 17, 'vel suæ gentis,' &c.

[5] ' In qualibet feria,' Bede, iii. 17. See above, p. 82.

[6] So that the seven days on one of which, if it were a Sunday, Easter might be celebrated, were, for Aidan and the Celtic churches, 'fourteenth moon—twentieth;' for the Roman and other churches, 'fifteenth moon—twenty-first.'

[7] Bede, iii. 17 : ' propter fidem videlicet,' &c. The British Christians thought that the Last Day would be a Sunday ; Williams, Eccl. Ant. Cym. p. 299. Some early Christians believed that the Lord would return in the night of the great Easter vigil. So Lactantius, Div. Instit. vii. 19 : ' Hæc est nox quæ nobis propter adventum Regis ac Dei nostri pervigilio celebratur ; cujus noctis duplex ratio est, quod in ea et vitam tum recepit cum passus est, et postea orbis terræ regnum recepturus est.'

called the Lord's day.' ' His keeping the Pasch out of its time
I do not approve of nor commend. But this I *do* approve
of, that what he kept in thought, reverenced, and preached,
in the celebration of his Paschal festival, was just what *we*
do, that is, the redemption of mankind through the Passion,
Resurrection, and Ascension into heaven of the Mediator
between God and men, the Man Christ Jesus.' In other
words, the root of the matter was found in him.

Such was he whom a recent historian with no ecclesiastical
prepossessions frankly calls the 'illustrious[1]' St. Aidan.
Being such as he was, he did great things for the good
cause in Northumbria, as a planter or a restorer of corporate Christian life. Churches, doubtless mostly of wood[2],
'were built in various places: the people flocked together
with gladness to hear the Word: possessions and pieces of
ground for founding monasteries were bestowed by the king's
gift: English children were taught, by Irish preceptors, the
rudiments of learning, together with more advanced studies
and the observance of regular discipline[3].' To some extent,
assuredly, Aidan was entering into another man's labours,
having found the soil prepared by Paulinus. But he left
behind him a stronger impression of spirituality and saint-
liness than we are led to associate with his predecessor: we

[1] Burton, Hist. Scotl. i. 269, 297.

[2] See below on the wooden church of bishop Finan at Lindisfarne. For
notices of primitive Irish churches built of wood or earth, see Reeves's
Adamnan, p. 177, and Whitley Stokes's Tripartite Life of St. Patrick, i. p. clvi.
When, in the twelfth century, Malachy archbishop of Armagh began to build
at Bangor a church of stone, the natives wondered, 'quod in terra illa necdum
ejusmodi ædificia invenirentur.' An opponent exclaimed against the innova-
tion: 'Scoti sumus, non Galli . . . Quid opus erat opere tam superfluo, tam
superbo?' S. Bernard. de Vit. Malach. 28. See Lanigan, Eccl. H. Irel. iv. 127,
392. But several primitive Irish churches were of stone (Petrie, Eccl. Arch.
p. 127 ff.), while most of the smaller ' Saxon' ones were of wood, such as the
wooden church of Dulting, where St. Aldhelm died; that at Wilton, superseded in 1065 by a stone church (Freeman, ii. 520); and the wooden chapel,
built before the Conquest, outside the east gate at Shrewsbury, in which, in
1080, Orderic Vitalis as a boy served mass, and instead of which his father
began to build a church of stone, the nucleus of a great abbey (Ord. Vit. v.
14, xiii. 45; Freeman, iv. 494). The little old wooden church of Greensted,
in Essex, is the sole representative of this class of churches. Its nave is composed of ' the trunks of large oak trees, split or sawn asunder.'

[3] Bede, iii. 3, 'Construebantur ergo,' &c.; Stubbs, Constitutional History,
i. 258 (or 225).

find that men believed his prayers to have special efficacy[1], CHAP. V.
and resorted to him, as to a second Columba, for such
intercessory help. And he was manifestly happier than
Paulinus, in that he was able to obtain a large supply of
'devoted[2]' clergy; and although he had his own heavy
sorrows and serious anxieties[3], his work, in an episcopate
of sixteen years[4], encountered no such shock as that which
followed the day of Hatfield. The religion which he taught
was essentially identical with that which prevailed at Canterbury or Dunwich, where his name was held in honour. Mass
was celebrated at Lindisfarne on Sundays and holy-days[5],
certainly with no splendour of visible surroundings, and
probably with rites differing in some measure (not, of course,
as to the essentials of the service) from those of the Gregorian
liturgy which Augustine had brought into Kent, and
cognate to the Gallican use which Felix, perhaps, had introduced into East-Anglia: but the usual language about 'the
mysteries of the sacred Eucharist[6]' was as familiar to a
disciple of Hy or of Lindisfarne as to the churchmen of Gaul
or Italy. Much importance was attached by Celtic monks
to acts of benediction[7]: and we find that Aidan was wont to
consecrate land designed for sacred purposes by an elaborate
process of fastings and prayers, performed for days beforehand
on the spot[8]. The Scotic conventual rule was severer than
that of Benedict[9]: and heinous offences were visited with

[1] Bede, iii. 15. Comp. Adamn. Vit. Col. ii. 13, 'sociis ut pro eis Dominum
Sanctus exoraret, inclamitantibus,' and ib. i. 50.

[2] 'Magna devotione,' Bede, iii. 3.   [3] Bede, iii. 9, 14, 16.

[4] Bede, iii. 17.

[5] In Columba's time there was not a daily celebration at Hy; Adamnan,
iii. 11, 12. It seems also that at Lindisfarne, at the close of the seventh
century, mass was only on Sundays; Bede, Vit. Cuthb. 44. So, according to
the Chronicle of Abingdon, it was on Sundays and chief festivals that the
monks of its first monastery assembled for mass; Chron. Ab. ii. 273.

[6] See the description of Columba ' standing before the altar, and consecrating
the sacred oblation,' Adamn. iii. 17; and ib. i. 40, 'the pure mysteries of the
sacred oblation.' Cp. iii. 12. See above, p. 106.

[7] See Adamnan, frequently, especially the simple and touching anecdotes in
i. 3, 9; ii. 31; and iii. 23. Cp. Tripart. Life, i. 37, 71, 163.

[8] This is implied in Bede, iii. 23, 'Dicebat enim,' &c.

[9] This may be inferred from the rule of Columban; Columba's was probably
milder, Reeves's Adamn. p. 355: but see Adamnan, i. 31, ii. 4, on the strict
obedience required by Columba, and Reeves's Adamnan, p. 343.

prolonged penances like those of antiquity[1]. The whole system had a rude and homely simplicity: it took no heed of sacred art, was untouched by the influence of the continental Church atmosphere, and kept its followers aloof from what might be called ecclesiastical civilisation.

Birinus in Wessex.

From a very different quarter, and in the year before Aidan's arrival[2], came another great awakening, with which we in Oxfordshire are specially concerned: for this district was then[3] West-Saxon, and the apostle of Wessex was Birinus. His origin is not ascertained[4]; the statement that he was a Roman may be only a conjecture[5]. He went to Pope Honorius, and solemnly promised before him[6] 'that he would scatter the seeds of the holy faith in those furthest inland territories of the English, which no teacher as yet had visited.' Honorius sent him for episcopal consecration to Asterius archbishop of Milan, who resided at Genoa[7]. Thus it was that, in 634, Birinus landed in Hampshire[8], and soon found that the West-Saxon districts contained heathenism so dark and intense[9] as to call for the immediate help of a missionary. These people were as truly sitting 'in the shadow of death' as any in parts more distant:

[1] See Adamnan, i. 22; ii. 39.

[2] The Chronicle dates it in 634.

[3] And on the whole, until the Mercian king Offa won the battle of Bensington in 777; A.-S. Chron. See Freeman, Old-Engl. Hist. p. 82.

[4] Malmesb. G. Pont. ii. 57; p. 157.

[5] Bromton says that 'fama suavissimæ opinionis sancti Birini presbyteri, de civitate Romana nati,' reached Pope Honorius; X Script. 755.

[6] 'Illo præsente,' Bede, iii. 7.

[7] He was not bishop of Genoa, as Bede says, but of Milan, A.D. 628–638. He died at Genoa on the 4th of June, and was buried 'in æde S. Syri;' Ughelli, Italia Sacra, iv. 92. Birinus was thus made a 'regionary' or missionary bishop, and left free to choose his own centre of operations,—as had been Ninian's case, and as was the case with Swidbert, Boniface (at first), Amandus, &c. (Maclear, Ap. Med. Eur. p. 77, &c.) Milner suggests that at Genoa Birinus could learn Saxon from 'Franks who frequented that mart;' Hist. Winch. i. 67.

[8] Bromton gives a story of a miracle connected with a pallula or corporal, 'Corpusque Dominicum in eadem involutum,' which, he says, Honorius had given to Birinus, and which he carried 'collo suspensum.' See Milner, l. c.

[9] 'Paganissimos.' See Chron. Abingd. vol. ii. p. v. On his landing, said the legend given by Bromton, he preached the faith for three days; among his audience were many who had been converted by Augustine.

why should he neglect them, and go further in search of others? Taking his discovery as a call to alter his original purpose, Birinus went about Wessex, preaching with such persuasive energy that he soon won a royal convert. Kyne- gils [1] had reigned for twenty-four years: he was probably weary of strife and bloodshed: he had, in his time, slain thousands of Britons, had seen his realm overrun by Edwin, had made terms, at some cost, with Penda. He listened to the foreign teacher [2]: Woden and Thunor and Tiu, the gods of war and storm and death, lost their hold upon him: he felt the strong 'drawing' of the Gospel, and asked to be prepared for admission into the Church. Birinus had suc-ceeded speedily in a work which had kept Paulinus under suspense: Kynegils was more prompt than Edwin, and seemingly not less sincere. And observe another coincidence. The successor of Edwin, now 'Bretwalda,' was desirous of being a friend to the West-Saxon princes; Kynegils was asked to give his daughter [3] in marriage as wife to Oswald. He consented: and, according to our chronology, it was at some time—probably late—in 635, towards the end of Oswald's first year of royalty, that he himself came into Wessex to take home his bride. Her father was just ready for baptism; and it was agreed that he should then become a Christian, before the Christian Oswald became his son-in-law. And now we are brought very near home; for the place selected [4] was that same Dorchester, so familiar to us at Oxford, where the venerable abbey church of SS. Peter and Paul now occupies the traditional spot that witnessed the Christianising of the dynasty which grew into the royal line of England. It is easy to realise the scene: the Saxon 'Dorcic [5],' retaining traces

---

[1] See Chron. a. 611. In 614 he had defeated the Britons at Bampton.

[2] Churn Knob, a hill near Chilton in Berkshire, is 'traditionally said to be the spot where Birinus' preached to Kynegils. See Murray's Handbook to Berks, &c., p. 74.

[3] Reginald calls her Kyneburg, Vit. Osw. c. 11.

[4] Bede does not say so, but the Chronicle does, a. 635.

[5] So Bede calls it, iii. 7. 'The old home of Birinus by the winding Thames;' Freeman, iv. 419: once 'Caer Dauri.' It must have been at that time within the West-Saxon border: Kynegils could not have thus dealt with a town actually Mercian. Oxfordshire, therefore, was not included in the territory

CHAP. V. of the Roman Dorocina, and guarded, southwards, by the embankment still called the Dykes, and beyond them by the twin clumps of 'the mighty hill fort of Sinodun[1],' whence Britons had in Roman days been dislodged by Aulus Plautius[2]. Briton and Roman have passed away from the Thames valley: there are kings here now, representing Ida the conqueror, and Cerdic the founder of a realm which is to absorb the rest: but the Kingdom here 'evidently set forth' is that which 'is not from this world.' There, in white pontificals, with attendant clergy on either side, stands its foreign representative, deriving his commission from the mighty Roman Church, and his episcopate from the great see of St. Ambrose : a font, large enough for immersion, is solemnly hallowed ; the war-worn royal convert steps into it, and is baptized : and 'as he comes forth from the laver,' he is 'lifted up,' according to the usual rite[3], by the future son-in-law who now acts as his sponsor[4], and who invests, for us, that river-side with the noble associations that attend the name of our truest royal saint.

It is natural, especially in Oxford, to dwell thus on an event only second in interest—when one considers the destinies of Wessex—to the baptism of Ethelbert himself. Its immediate consequence was the first organisation of a West-Saxon Church. Oswald and Kynegils, united in a triple relation, political, domestic, and religious, concurred in establishing Birinus as bishop of Dorchester. From this act may be said to have proceeded in different senses the three episcopates of Winchester, of Lincoln, and of Oxford. The village which we can so easily visit, and which has so long

Birinus at Dorchester.

gained by Mercia after the battle of Cirencester in 628 : see Green, Making of Engl. p. 267.

[1] Freeman, l. c.: comp. iii. 543.

[2] See Mr. James Parker's paper in the Proceedings of the Oxford Architect. and Hist. Soc. for Mich. Term, 1862.

[3] 'Eumque de lavacro exeuntem suscepisse;' comp. Bede, iii. 22, iv. 13; and Greg. Turon. H. Fr. vii. 22 : 'Eo quod filium ejus de sacro lavacro suscepissem.' So ib. v. 19 : 'Filio meo . . . quem de lavacro regenerationis excepi,' and x. 28. So in Gregorian Sacramentary, Muratori, Lit. Rom. ii. 157: 'Eo tenente infantem a quo suscipiendus est.' The phrase is as old as Tertullian : 'Ter mergitamur . . . Inde suscepti,' &c. ; De Cor. Mil. 3.

[4] 'Pulcherrimo prorsus et Deo digno consortio;' Bede, iii. 7. 'Satis perpulchro spectaculo;' Reginald, Vit. Osw. 3.

a history to redeem its present insignificance, thus holds a real CHAP. V. place in the annals of the Church of England. From 'Dorcic' Birinus went up and down among the West-Saxons, that is, from Dorset to Buckinghamshire, from Surrey to the Severn, preaching, catechising, baptizing, 'calling many people to the Lord by his pious labours,' and 'building and dedicating churches.' This is Bede's summary of a work as to which he could get no detailed information, but which must have had its own incidents and characteristics, its own experiences of hope and anxiety, of partial failure compensated by general advance, which, if preserved to us, might have made the conversion of Wessex as living a fact to us as that of Northumbria. As it is, we cannot recover a single feature in those missionary journeys of Birinus: but it is reasonable to think that although Oxford as yet was not, he would come up the valley to the junction of our two rivers, find there some few 'ceorls' ready to hear the name of Christ, and perhaps deposit 'seeds' which, a century later, produced in St. Frideswide's humble foundation the nucleus of the priory and the cathedral, and, in another sense, of the city and the university[1]. But one success Birinus had, which must have been specially welcome; Cwichelm, the son of Kynegils, followed his father's example within the year: it was just ten years since he had sent Eumer with the poisoned dagger to slay Edwin. He was baptized at Dorchester in 636; 'and that same year he died[2].' His name is perpetuated in 'Cwichelm's hlæw,' or 'hill,' now Cuckhamsley, a height crowned by trees at the summit of the Berkshire range, which we may see from the Wantage road, beyond the turn to Cumnor[3]. His son Cuthred, who like him was a sub-king under Kynegils, was baptized in 639 by Birinus, who took him for his godson[4].

---

[1] See Parker's Early Hist. of Oxford, pp. 106, 119.

[2] Chron. a. 636. Malmesbury says he was 'admonished by illness,' Gest. Reg. i. 22.

[3] Parker, p. 149. In 1006, says the Chronicle, the Danes made good their boast that they would reach Cwichelm's 'hlæw,' and get to their ships again. See Freeman, i. 332. A 'hlæw' (see Taylor's Words and Places, p. 212) frequently perpetuated the memory of celebrated personages; Chron. Abingd. ii. 483, and 'Oslafeshlau' in Kemble's Cod. Dipl. i. 283.

[4] Chron. a. 639. Another case in which the bishop who baptized acted also as godfather is Cadwalla's in 689; Bede, v. 7; and see Greg. Tur. H. Fr. v. 23.

We do not hear of any relations being as yet formed between the mission in Wessex and the see of Canterbury. The archbishop does not seem to have had any communication with Birinus, who was doing so effectively the work which Canterbury had never essayed. In Kent all was tranquil and

hopeful. Eadbald, whose genuine conversion had suffered no relapse, was succeeded in 640 by his son Erconbert, whose Christianity was more definitely aggressive upon Heathenism[1]. He was the first English king who used his royal authority for the utter destruction of idols, and the enforcement of the Lenten fast; and he appointed fitting penalties for disobedience to this law. He married Sexburga, the eldest daughter of Anna king of the East-Anglians[2], who had succeeded to that throne in 635 under strangely tragical circumstances[3]. Egric, who had become king on Sigebert's abdication, was menaced with invasion by Penda. His people, knowing themselves to be no match for the Mercians, and remembering the ex-king's former renown as a leader, besought him to come forth from his cell and aid them in the fight. He refused; whereupon, hoping that his mere presence might inspirit the national forces[4], they actually dragged him to the battle-field. There he stood, but, 'not unmindful of his profession[5],' or as we may think, in his overstrained scrupulosity, he would hold nothing but a wand. He and Egric were both slain, and the

East-Anglians utterly routed. Anna, now chosen king, was son of Eni and nephew of Redwald, and 'a very good man,' says Bede, 'and the parent of very good children,' and 'happy in a good and holy progeny;' 'a man,' as he elsewhere says, 'truly religious, and altogether excellent in mind and conduct[6].' In fact, he is chiefly remarkable on

---

[1] Bede, iii. 8: 'Hic primus regum Anglorum,' &c.

[2] Bede, l. c.: 'Cujus regis filia major,' &c. Properly, Sexburh.

[3] Bede, iii. 18.

[4] 'Sperantes minus animos militum trepidare;' Bede, l. c.

[5] Yet, in the preceding century, Irish ecclesiastics had occasionally taken part in warfare; Reeves's Adamnan, p. lxxvii. Gregory of Tours censures two Frankish bishops, Salonius and Sagittarius, for doing so; H. Fr. iv. 43: and ib. v. 21, 'tanquam unus ex laicis accincti arma,' &c. For two warrior bishops of Sherborne, see Chron. a. 845, 871 (in the Danish wars).

[6] Bede, iii. 18 and 7; iv. 19.

account of the zeal for monasticism shown personally by princesses of his house. 'At that time there were not many monasteries among the English; and therefore many used to go over from Britain to the monasteries of the Franks or Gaul[1], for the sake of monastic life,—and also to send their daughters to the same to be instructed and united to their Heavenly Bridegroom, especially at Brige,' or Brie, where a 'noble abbess' named Fara had built a convent, and at Cale, or Chelles, near Paris, and Andilegum, or Andely, near Rouen. Such is Bede's statement[2]. Anna's sister-in-law Hereswid[3] herself became a nun at Chelles: her sister, the famous St. Hilda, spent a year in East-Anglia with the hope of 'imitating her example.' Anna's step-daughter, Sæthryd[4], actually did so. Anna himself had four daughters: Sexburga, wife of Erconbert, who after surviving her husband, and even acting as regent, became abbess of a convent which she had founded in the Isle of Sheppey, and afterwards first a simple nun and then abbess at Ely[5]; Ethelberga, who became abbess of Brie[6]; a third whose enthusiasm for conventual life had important results in Northumbrian Church history, and whose name still stands in our calendar as St. Etheldred[7], the foundress of the famous church of Ely; and a fourth, Witberga, who lived as a recluse

[1] For monasteries founded in Gaul early in the sixth century, see Mabillon, Ann. Bened. i. 293, 295, 304, 310. Among those who resorted to them was St. Botulf.

[2] Bede, iii. 8: 'Nam eo tempore,' &c. Fara, or Burgundofara, had been 'dedicated' in her infancy by Columban, against her father's wish. She persisted in refusing to be married: she fled to a church, and said she would rather die on its floor than consent. Her father yielded: she founded a monastery (famous as Faremoustier) on some land of his in Brie, near Meaux. One of her nuns, Wilsinda, was a Saxon. She died about 655 (Mabillon, Ann. Bened. i. 304, 356).

[3] Compare Bede, iv. 23. Hereswid, says Bede, was mother of king Aldwulf; and in the appendix to Florence she accordingly appears as wife of Anna's brother and successor Ethelhere, father of Aldwulf (Flor. i. 249). She was grandniece of Edwin. Thomas of Ely is wrong in calling Aldwulf son of Anna; Hist. El. (Angl. Sac. i. 595).

[4] Bede, iii. 8. 'Sætrudis,' Ann. Bened. i. 434. She preceded Ethelberga as abbess.

[5] See Bede, iv. 19. 'Sancta Sexburga,' Florence, a. 640.

[6] See Bede's account of ' Ædilberg,' iii. 8.

[7] Bede, iv. 19. Tho. El. Hist. Eliens. (Angl. Sac. i. 597).

at Dereham[1]. Ercongota, daughter of Erconbert and Sexburga, became a nun at Brie, and is named in the Chronicle as a 'wondrous person,' because of a vision related by Bede, in which she was described as 'that golden coin which had come thither out of Kent[2].' Her sister Ermenild, after being queen of the Mercians, followed the family custom, received the veil under her mother at Sheppey, and succeeded her at Ely[3].

Erconbert had been reigning two years in Kent, and Anna six years in East-Anglia, when a dire calamity befell the Northumbrian realm and Church. Like that 'tender-hearted' and blameless king of Judah, of whom his life reminds us, Oswald fell in battle with the heathen. He was involved in a war with Penda and 'the South-humbrians[4]:' he had, it appears, reconquered the district of Lindsey from the Mercian: but on the 5th of August, 642, he was surprised by his enemy at a place named Maserfield[5], which the Cambrian Annals call Cocboy, and which may be Coedway, near the Shropshire town which still commemorates Oswald in its name of Oswestry[6]. It was, in a certain sense, another Hatfield. Bede tells us how the saintly successor of Edwin, seeing death inevitable, 'ended his life with prayer for the souls of his men; as they say in a proverb, "O God, have mercy on the souls, said Oswald falling to the ground[7]."' Another saying, probably

---

[1] Act. SS. Bened. ii. 740 ; Chron. a. 797.

[2] Bede, iii. 8: 'Aureum illud numisma quod eo de Cantia venerat.'

[3] Act. SS. Ben. ii. 756. It may be well to remember that Erconbert had a brother, Ermenred, as well as a sister, St. Eanswith. Ermenred, who was a sub-king, had two sons, Ethelred and Ethelbert (both cruelly murdered), and four daughters, Ermenburg or Domneva, wife of Merewald sub-king of the West-Mercians, another Ermenburg, Etheldrith, and Ermengith (Florence, App. Chron. i. 259).

[4] Chron. a. 642. Tighernach wrongly dates it in 639, just as he dates the defeat of Edwin in 631, and Oswald's victory over 'Cathlon' in 632.

[5] Bede, iii. 9. Reginald fixes it at half-a-mile from Offa's Dyke, and seven miles from Shrewsbury; and says that a church called 'White Church' was afterwards erected there. Vit. Osw. c. 14 (Sim. Op. i. 352).

[6] 'Id est, Oswaldi arborem;' Giraldus, Itin. Camb. ii. 12. In Welsh, Cross-Oswald. Reginald tells how a large bird carried off the slain king's right arm from the stake (see below) to an old ash-tree, which thereafter put forth fresh leaves, and was still revered as 'St. Oswald's tree;' Vit. Osw. c. 17.

[7] Bede, iii. 12 ; cp. iv. 14. See Churton, E. E. Ch. p. 75. Green mistakes this, as if he had been praying for his slayers ; Making of Engl. p. 294.

the fragment of a ballad, is preserved in a later chronicle :
'With the bones of holy men was Maserfield made white [1].'
Oswald was only in his thirty-eighth year. The ferocious
Mercian who had thus added his name to a growing list of
princely victims exposed the head and arms of the slain
monarch on wooden stakes [2]: but they were rescued the next
year, and carried into Northumbria. The hands were kept
in a silver box, at St. Peter's church on the summit of the
rock of Bamborough [3]: the head on which the death-blow had
descended was interred by Aidan—one can well imagine with
what an anguish of sorrow—at Lindisfarne,—and removed in
875 within the coffin of St. Cuthbert [4]: hence the common
representation of that saint,—visible, for instance, on the north
side of the steeple of St. Mary's in Oxford,—as holding the
head of St. Oswald in his hands. About thirty years after
the battle of Maserfield, his niece Osthryd [5], then wife to a
son and successor of Penda, removed 'the bones of her uncle'
to the great Lincolnshire monastery of Bardney; where the
Mercian monks afterwards told [6] how in their 'long-standing
animosity' against the Northumbrian who had 'gained the
dominion over them,' they refused to harbour his remains,
'although they knew him to be a saint,' and so left the
wain which had arrived with them in the evening to
stand outside their doors, with a covering spread over it:
how, all that night, they saw a pillar of light blazing

[1] Hen. Hunt. iii. 39.

[2] Bede, iii. 12: 'Porro caput et manus,' &c. Bede tells this as if by an
after-thought.

[3] Bede, iii. 6; Sim. Dunelm. Hist. Reg. c. 48 (Op. i. 45).

[4] Malmesb. Gest. Pontif. iii. 134, says that when (in 1104) the tomb of
Cuthbert was opened in Durham cathedral, 'the head of Oswald, king and
martyr, was found between his arms.' See Reginald's minute description of
the head, as it was preserved in a purple bag 'beside the head of Cuthbert,'
c. 51. He was told that it had for a time been taken away to Bamborough,
and thence, by a stratagem, brought back to Lindisfarne ; c. 49.

[5] She was killed by Mercian nobles, a. 697 ; Bede, v. 24.

[6] Bede, iii. 11. Florence says that Ethelred, king of the Mercians, Osthryd's husband, 'had himself built' this monastery, in which he afterwards
became monk and abbot (on a. 716). Tradition said that it contained 300
monks ; Mon. Anglic. i. 628. When the house, after long desolation, was
restored in the eleventh century, it was dedicated to SS. Peter and Paul, and
'St. Oswald, king and martyr;' ib.

heavenward above the wain, conspicuous to nearly all the province of Lindsey[1]: how in the morning they eagerly threw open the gate, carried in the bones with all reverence, washed them, placed them in a chest, and hung up over it the gold and purple banner which had waved in battle before the holy king[2]. We cannot wonder that, in such an age, the very spot where he had fallen seemed 'greener and fairer' than the ground adjacent, or that wondrous virtues were ascribed to its dust, to that of the floor on which had been poured out the water used in washing the relics, or to a splinter of the stake to which the head had been affixed[3]; that a little boy in Bardney monastery was said to have been cured of the fen-country ague by sitting close to the saint's tomb[4]; that a Northumbrian community of monks in Sussex believed an epidemic to have been stayed by the intercession of that 'king, beloved of God,' whose dying prayer might be available for men of his race, though dwelling far from home[5]; or that a great missionary, Willibrord archbishop of the Frisians, spoke of miracles wrought, even in that distant province, in presence of some relics of St. Oswald[6]. The collect prescribed, in the Sarum rite, for the 5th of August, referred to 'the joyous and blessed gladness' which had been associated with that day by his 'passion:' and when we remember the issues at stake in his contest with Penda, we may think it not too much to say with a foreign historian

---

[1] An abbess, Ethelhild, surviving when Bede wrote, told queen Osthryd that she had seen this light, 'ad cælum usque altam.' Alcuin de Pontif. Ebor. 364, 'ad fastigia cæli.' Malmesbury, 'lucernam de cælo.'

[2] In 909, says the Chronicle, St. Oswald's body was removed from Bardney into Mercia (properly so called). So Florence, a. 910. It was interred at Gloucester. See Alb. Butler, Aug. 5; Monast. Angl. vi. 82. Only three small bones remained at Bardney; Reginald, c. 43.

[3] Bede, iii. 10, 11, 13. The last anecdote was told by Willibrord, who had put the splinter into water which he gave to a plague-stricken Irish scholar.

[4] Bede, iii. 12. This was told to Bede by a monk, when the boy had grown up into a youth, and was still dwelling in the monastery.

[5] 'Pro suæ gentis advenis;' Bede, iv. 14. There is a vision of SS. Peter and Paul in this story, and an order to celebrate St. Oswald's anniversary by mass and communion. Acca, bishop of Hexham, is Bede's authority here. The monastery was Wilfrid's, at Selsey.

[6] Bede, iii. 13: 'Denique reverentissimus,' &c.

of ancient England [1], that as 'his life was distinguished' at
once by 'activity' and by a 'spirit of fervent Christian
beneficence,' so 'his Christian merits and his *martyrdom* made
him a hero of the Christian world.'

The history of the Church in Northumbria during the
larger part of the seventh century is conspicuously the back-
bone of the history of the Church in England. It is
striking to see how the region which was first to come before
St. Gregory's thoughts in regard to an English mission, and
yet, for just thirty years, was inaccessible to missionary
attempts, no sooner in any sense accepted Christianity than
it concentrated into itself the chief interest of the great
drama of national conversion; this being due, no doubt, in
part, to the relative scantiness of our information as to other
districts, but also largely to the force and impressiveness of
the characters that walk the Northumbrian stage. We
cannot help making Northumbria the main line of our
subject, towards which any record of Church life in Kent,
or Wessex, or elsewhere, may naturally radiate. And thus,
the tragedy of Maserfield must have sent a thrill of grief
and alarm through every Christian realm, whatever might
be its political bearing towards the kingdom which had
lost Oswald. We can imagine how the tidings would be
received in Kent; how Paulinus, safe in Rochester, and
Ethelburga in her minster at Lyminge [2], would think of
Hatfield, and pray for the soul of another Edwin; how in
East-Anglia, both king and bishop would feel renewed mis-
givings at a fresh victory of the arms that had struck down
Sigebert and Egric; how among our own Oxfordshire valleys,
as yet outside the Mercian limits, priests and converts would
tremble for new-built churches, and mourn for the generous
over-lord who had come among them as sponsor for their king.
Why was such a prop of the cause removed? Did it mean that,
after all, the work would be undone, that a heathen tempest
would spread from 'the Wall' to the Channel, and root out

---

[1] Lappenberg, i. 161. 'Sancti sanguinis effusionem,' Miss. Ebor. Aug. 5.

[2] It is interesting to observe that the little church of Paddlesworth, occupying
the highest ground in Kent, 642 feet above the sea, was of old a dependency of
Lyminge, and is dedicated to St. Oswald.

the worship of Christ wherever it had been planted? Such questions might be a trial to faith in many a South-country Church settlement: what must the blow have been to Christians in Bernicia and Deira?

Oswy
King of
Bernicia.

We may say, in Bernicia and *in* Deira; for, to add to the difficulties and perils of the crisis, the two realms, so thoroughly welded together by a hero who united the royal blood of both, were soon again to be shaken apart; Oswiu, or Oswy, the younger brother of Oswald, now about thirty years old, succeeding to the royalty of Bernicia, but failing to establish his hold on Deira, which had a strong leaning to the house of Ella, and in 643, according to Bede's reckoning[1], acknowledged the royal claims of Oswin, son of the unhappy Osric. Oswy was fain to agree to this partition: indeed, during his first year he had enough work in keeping the lands beyond the Tees, whither Penda, now more than sixty, but as energetic and as ruthless as after the battle of Hatfield, had penetrated as if he meant to destroy Northumbrian independence by the one stroke of taking Bamborough[2]. We seem to see the grim invader first trying to storm the city, then pulling down the wooden huts of neighbouring hamlets, piling the materials[3] in a huge mass close to the wall, and finally taking advantage of a south-west wind to set the

Aidan and
Penda.

timber on fire. And then Bede shows us the figure of Aidan in his place of 'retreat' on the Farne island, nearly two miles off: he looks up, and sees fire and smoke carried by the wind high above the city wall, which was evidently of timber: he lifts up his eyes and hands in supplication[4]: 'See, Lord, what harm Penda is doing!' Immediately the wind shifts, drives back the flames, scorching some of Penda's men and scaring all of them, 'so that they gave up attacking a city which they understood to be divinely protected.' In effect, Penda did suspend, soon afterwards, the attempt to conquer

---

[1] Bede says, iii. 14, that Oswin reigned between eight and nine years; and he died in August, 651. The date of 644, given by the Chronicler for his accession, is therefore a year too late.

[2] Bede, iii. 16: 'Pervenit ad urbem regiam, quæ ex Bebbæ quondam reginæ vocabulo cognominatur.'

[3] 'Trabium, tignorum, parietum virgeorum, et tecti fenei,' &c.

[4] 'Fertur,' says Bede, on this.

Northumbria : he re-annexed Lindsey to Mercia, and Church
history is concerned in his next attack on Wessex, where the
eldest of the three royal proselytes of Birinus survived his
sponsor and son-in-law about a year, dying in 643, the
thirty-second year of his reign[1]. Cwichelm, as we have
seen, had died before his father; and the crown passed, not
to his son Cuthred, but, as was often the case in Old-
English kingdoms, to his brother[2] Kenwalch or Coinwalch, Kenwalch.
the second son of Kynegils, probably a man of ripe years
and full strength, but firmly set against the creed of his
father and brother[3]. We can understand how he would
speak with bitter scorn of the new lore that the foreign priests
had brought in to turn the sons of Woden into weaklings :
he would have nought to do with Birinus, who had wrought
scathe enough to the house of Cerdic by womanish words
and outlandish rites. Those must have been anxious days at
Dorchester. But ere long Kenwalch, in the pride of newly-
acquired kingship, was bold enough to divorce the sister of
Penda, whom he had wedded, no doubt, for political considerations, and to take another wife[4]. Penda seized the
occasion, marched straight into Wessex, and drove out Kenwalch in 645. So it was, as Bede comments, that the prince
'who had refused to receive the faith and mysteries of the
heavenly kingdom, not long afterwards lost the power even
of the earthly kingdom[5];' but he was to furnish another
instance of the old rhyming Greek proverb, 'Tribulation,
education[6].' He found shelter in East-Anglia; and while
living 'for three years in exile, he acknowledged and
accepted the true belief[7].' He saw in Anna's household a
royal family simply and thoroughly Christian, believing absolutely in the new faith, and leading pure and worthy lives
under its influence. Felix, no doubt, found opportunities of

[1] A.-S. Chron. a. 643, cp. 611.
[2] See Freeman, i. 108, that minors were often passed by in favour of uncles.
[3] Bede, iii. 7 : ' Defuncto autem et rege,' &c.
[4] Seaxburg or Sexburga, who reigned after him; Chron. a. 672.
[5] ' Qui et fidem et sacramenta,' &c. ; Bede, iii. 7. See p. 115.
[6] Παθήματα, μαθήματα, Herod. i. 207. Cp. Malmesb. G. R. i. 19.
[7] Bede, iii. 7 : ' Apud quem triennio exsulans,' &c.

touching and opening the heart of the discrowned fugitive: and no episcopal work that he had done since he came to Sigebert would be more utterly 'happy' than the baptizing of Kenwalch in 646[1]. The convert may have been present, with Anna, at the deathbed of the bishop, whose labours as an evangelizer, an educator, and a Church ruler, were closed on the 8th of March, 647[2]. St. Felix, as he was fittingly called in after-ages, was buried in his own city of Dunwich[3]: and it is interesting to find the memory of the apostle of East-Anglia preserved in the name not only of Felixstowe to the south-east of Ipswich, but also of a Yorkshire village, far away in the north, Feliskirk, near Thirsk. His deacon Thomas, a native of the 'Gyrvian' or 'Fen' district, was chosen to fill his place, and was consecrated by Honorius, of Canterbury: he ranks second of native English bishops, the first being the Kentishman[4] Ithamar, whom Honorius had consecrated in 644 to succeed Paulinus, when the latter had been laid to rest in the church of St. Andrew, 'which king Ethelbert had built from its foundation in the city of Hrof[5].'

In 648, Kenwalch was enabled, mainly by the help of his nephew Cuthred, to return into Wessex. Once more a king, he did not fall back from the promises made at his East-Anglian baptism. He showed his gratitude to Cuthred by giving him three thousand hydes[6]—each hyde being, in

---

[1] Chronicle, and Florence a. 646.

[2] See Bede, ii. 15; iii. 20; Maskell, Mon. Rit. iii. 214.

[3] Ultimately transferred to Ramsey; Malm. G. Pontif. iii. 74.

[4] 'But,' says Bede, 'equal to his predecessors in conduct and learning;' iii. 14. This is paraphrased by Malmesbury, Gest. Pontif. i. 72, 'in quo nihil perfectæ sanctitatis . . . nihil *elegantiæ* Romanæ . . . . minus desiderares.'

[5] Bede, iii. 14. 'Secretarium' usually means a room or building used for ecclesiastical business; here, and in ii. 1, iii. 26, it has the sense of 'sacristy.' Paulinus had been a bishop rather more than nineteen years. According to the Glastonbury traditions, he had visited that sacred place, and it was he who covered the church of wreathed osiers (above, p. 11) with wood and lead; Malmesb. de Antiq. Glaston. in Gale, i. 300. But this is probably a legend. Churches are dedicated to his memory at Crayford and Paul's Cray in Kent. Compare p. 127. Rochester Cathedral contains his grave.

[6] Chron. a. 648. See Kemble, i. 92, 487 ff., Stubbs, Const. Hist. i. 83 (or 74, ed. 1) on 'the vexed question of its extent.' Bede uses 'familia' to express it; e.g. Thanet is of 600 familiæ, i. 25; Hilda's land at Whitby is of 10 familiæ,

idea, an amount of land sufficient for one family—about chap. v.
Ashdown in Berkshire, east of ' Cwichelm's-law,' the scene
of the defeat of the Danes by Ethelred and Alfred in
871. He showed his religious thankfulness by forthwith
ordering the erection of a church in the royal city of
Winchester[1]: it was hallowed, says the Chronicler, by
Birinus, in honour of St. Peter. This event, setting
aside the legendary notices[2] of a British church at Winchester, profaned by the West-Saxons under Cerdic, is
the opening of the history of one of the most venerable of
English cathedrals. Birinus lived two years longer, and died
peacefully at Dorchester[3], on the 3rd of December, 650 ; and
his body lay in his own church until it was removed to
Winchester by his fourth successor Heddi. His first successor
was a Frank named Agilbert, who had been consecrated,
apparently, in Gaul[4], ' but had lived some time in Ireland for

iii. 24 ; her former property on the Wear had been of one, iv. 23 ; Sussex
contains 7000, iv. 13 ; Selsey, 87, ib. ; the Isle of Wight, 1200, iv. 16 ;
Wilfrid's land at Stamford, 10, v. 19 ; at Ripon, 30, ib. ; the abbey-land at
Wearmouth, 70, Hist. Abb. 4 ; at Jarrow, 40, ib. 6. Another Latin equivalent
is ' cassatus,' a ' housed ' or married man ; Kemble, i. 92.

[1] According to a Winchester story of later date, this foundation had been
designed by Kenwalch.) See Rudborne, Hist. Maj. Wint. c. 1 (Angl.
Sac. i. 189). In Annal. Winton. (Ann. Monast. ii. 5) Kynegils is said to
have made Kenwalch swear by his soul, before St. Birinus, that he would build
a church for the bishopric in Winchester. The oldest property of the church
of Winchester is the estate at Chilcombe, which it has held from the sixth
century ; the gift is *ascribed* to Kynegils. But these traditions are more
than questionable. Malmesbury says quaintly that Kenwalch was ' primus
antecessorum suorum ' to build a ' temple ' to God at Winchester ; Gest. Reg.
i. 19. Cp. Ch. Quart. Review, xx. 377.

[2] See Rudborne (a Winchester monk of the fifteenth century) : he begins
with king Lucius, as founder of the church : tells how, after the Diocletian
persecution, a second but smaller church was built in honour of ' St. Amphibalus,' and took the name of the Vetus Cœnobium ; how Cerdic turned it
into a temple of Dagon ; how Kynegils destroyed the temple, and assigned
lands for a third church. So Geoffrey speaks of the British church of Amphibalus ' intra Gayntoniam,' ii. 5.

[3] Bede, iii. 7 : ' Ubi . . . migravit ad Dominum.' His name is retained in
' a spur of the Chilterns, in Ipsden parish, called Berin's Hill ' (Short Acc. of
Dorch., by Rev. W. C. Macfarlane, p. 17).

[4] He was probably a ' vacant ' bishop (σχολάζων). Three such signed the
acts of the Council of Macon in 585 (Mansi, ix. 959). Those Irish bishops
who never had sees were not properly ' vacant,' though Todd so regards them
(St. Patrick, p. 45). See Bingham, b. iv. 2. 14.

the sake of studying the Scriptures [1].' Ireland was then pre-eminently a land of contrasts: amid a series of 'battles, burnings, slaughters [2],' which darken year after year in its native records, there flourished a passionate love of learning [3], and a generous eagerness to impart its benefits, 'without money and without price,' to foreigners who came in search of them. What Bede says of English-born students in Ireland at a slightly later time [4] is probably true of all who, during this period, resorted to Irish teachers; 'they went the round of the cells of different masters, and the Irish readily gave them daily food without charge, books to read, and free instruction.' Camin of Iniskeltra was at work with numerous pupils in his monastery on an island of Loughderg: he 'wrote a commentary on the Psalms collated with the Hebrew text [5].' The great school which Carthagh had founded at Lismore was in its glory [6]. Patristic learning had been brought to bear on the Easter question by Cummian, in his letter to Seghine of Hy and others [7], who disapproved of his departure from the Scotic system, and of his successful advocacy of the 'Catholic' Easter in South Ireland [8]. At Clonard a theological college flourished, in which Aileran the Wise, whose tract on the names of Christ's ancestors is still extant, was chief professor [9].

---

[1] Bede, iii. 7.

[2] See Tighernach (in O'Conor's Rer. Hibern. Script. vol. ii.) for recurring entries of 'prœlium,' 'cædes,' 'jugulatio,' 'combustio,' between, e. g., A.D. 618 and 650. Compare also the Chronicon Scotorum. There had also been much religious declension early in the century; Todd, p. 109.

[3] On the educational work ascribed to St. Patrick, see Todd, p. 506 ff.

[4] Bede, iii. 27; cp. i. 1; v. 9. See Goldwin Smith, Irish Hist. and Irish Character, p. 28: 'The Irish Church . . . received with eager hospitality all who desired to be instructed in the Word of life.' Among the Englishmen who studied in Ireland during the century were Egbert, Ethelhun, Chad, Willibrord, Aldfrid (afterwards king), and Witbert.

[5] Lanigan, iii. 11. For Irish students cp. Adamn. i. 2. cp. Reeves, p. 196.

[6] Lanigan, ii. 353, says that after Carthagh died in 637, his 'school, or university, was for a very long time equal at least to any other in Ireland.'

[7] See above, p. 102; cp. Lanigan, ii. 395; King, Ch. Hist. Irel. i. 154 ff. The date is about 634. Cummian was also, 'in all appearance, author of . . . a very learned abridgment of the ancient penitential canons.'

[8] At the Councils of Maghlene and of White-field, 630 and 634.

[9] Lanigan, iii. 54. Zeal for the Catholic doctrine of grace was stirred up in Ireland by some revival of Pelagianising ideas, which were denounced in the letter of John IV, pope-elect, and two other Roman officials, to some Irish

After making use of such opportunities, Agilbert came over into Wessex, and offered his aid, as a bishop, to the West-Saxon king, who 'seeing him to be learned and energetic,' was glad enough to establish him at Dorchester.

We must now return to the North. While Kenwalch was passing through the phases of headstrong pride and salutary humiliation, the Christians of Deira had before them a royal example of singular loveliness. The character of King Oswin is one of Bede's best portraits. In personal appearance tall and handsome, kindly in address, open-handed to gentle and simple [1], and withal eminent for piety, he won the love of all by 'the royal dignity of his mind, his countenance, his conduct,' so that from almost every province men of noblest birth flocked together to be 'thanes' in the hall of Oswin of Deira. Among all the graces of character which marked him out as under 'a special benediction,' Bede selects his humility as the chief, and illustrates it by one sufficient example. The bishop of Lindisfarne, while visiting the southern part of his huge diocese, became naturally intimate with a prince who would recall to him his beloved Oswald. As we have seen, he had been accustomed to make his circuits on foot; but Oswin, thinking of the rough paths and streams that had to be encountered [2], gave him a horse 'fit for a king.' But soon afterwards, a poor man begged alms of Aidan, who, under a compassionate impulse, at once dismounted, and gave him the horse with all its goodly trappings. Oswin heard of this; and the next time they were going in to dinner, he said to Aidan, 'What did you mean, lord bishop, by giving away the horse that was to be all your own? Had not I many other horses

bishops, priests, and abbots, or doctors; Bede, ii. 19. See Lanigan, ii. 409. The school of Clonard, according to a hymn quoted in Todd's Life of St. Patrick, p. 98, 'produced 3000 disciples'—probably an exaggeration. The founder was St. Finnian; see Reeves's Adamnan, p. lxxii. St. Columba is said to have studied there; on this see Lanigan, ii. 117. The point is of some interest, because St. Finnian (probably before Columba's birth) had studied in Wales; ib. i. 464. Compare Maclear's Ap. of Mediæv. Eur. p. 58, on the ancient school of Cluaininis; and for other monastic schools, Lanigan, i. 402.

[1] Nobilibus simul atque ignobilibus,' Bede, iii. 14; i.e. eorl-kin and ceorl-kin, Freeman, i. 82.

[2] On the wild parts of Yorkshire, see Bede, iii. 23; and cp. Ep. ad Egb. 4, 'montibus inaccessis et saltibus dumosis.'

CHAP. V.

of less value, or other things that would have served as alms-gifts?' Aidan answered with something of Irish promptness: 'What say you, O king? Is that son of a mare worth more in your eyes than that son of God[1]?' They entered the hall: Aidan took his usual seat, attended, as usual, by a presbyter: the king, who was fresh from the chase, stood with his thanes by the fire, thinking: suddenly he took off his sword, gave it to a thane, and threw himself at Aidan's feet, entreating him not to be angry: 'Never again will I say a word about this, or judge as to what or how much of our money you bestow on sons of God.' Aidan was astonished, even awe-struck: he rose, and lifted up the sensitive prince, assuring him that he was not at all angry, that all would be right if he would but sit down to his meal and cease to distress himself. Oswin's face brightened, and he obeyed[2]: but then it was Aidan's turn to be sad, and his tears began to flow. The priest who sat by him, a 'Scot' like himself, asked him in Irish, so that no one else understood, what was the matter. 'The matter is,' replied Aidan, 'that I am sure the king will not live long. I never till now saw a king humble[3],' or perhaps, 'so humble. It is in my mind that he will soon be hurried out of this life; for this people does not deserve to have such a ruler.'

Murder of Oswin.

The foreboding was soon verified: Deira did lose Oswin. Occasions of jealousy between two princes, situated as he and Oswy were[4], could not be wanting; at last, under what circumstances we know not, the smouldering fires blazed out into war. But before the two hosts had met, Oswin ascertained that the Bernician king, who was by this time growing into greatness, had more 'auxiliaries' than he could muster. He therefore resolved 'to give up his intention of fighting, and to reserve himself for better times. He broke

---

[1] Higden, misunderstanding this 'filius Dei,' turns it into 'Filius Mariæ;' Polychronicon, b. 5 (vol. vi. p. 71).

[2] The story, which appears quite genuine, shows a want of good sense on the one side, and an excess of docility on the other. Oswin's objection to the disproportionateness of the gift was not really met by a rejoinder which would make a virtue of indiscriminate generosity.

[3] 'Nunquam enim ante hæc vidi humilem regem,' or, 'tam humilem.'

[4] Bede, iii. 14: 'Sed nec cum eo,' &c.

up his army' at Wilfaresdun, a hill about twelve miles north-
west of Catterick, and, accompanied by one faithful thane [1]
named Tondhere, 'turned aside' to seek refuge in the house
of a 'count[2] named Hunwald,' whom he believed to be most
friendly to him : 'but, alas! it was far otherwise.' Hunwald
betrayed the fugitives to Oswy, who sent his 'reeve[3]' Ethelwin
to put Oswin and his companion to death, at Gilling, on the
20th of August, 651. This was the one crime of Oswy's life ;
he gave some token of speedy repentance by granting the
request[4] of his wife Eanfled, the daughter of Edwin and
'kinswoman' of Oswin, that he would give to Trumhere, a
Northumbrian priest akin to Oswin in blood, but of Scotic
training and ordination, land for a convent on the spot of
the murder, where 'prayers[5] might be offered for the souls
both of the slain man and of him who ordered him to be
slain.' The corpse of the former was buried at Tynemouth,
where a chapel of St. Mary had already been built, and where,
soon afterwards, one monastery, if not two, arose[6]. In later
days, after the desolation caused by the Northmen had been
repaired, and the bones of the 'humble king' had been oppor-

---

[1] 'Cum uno tantum milite :' Alfred renders, 'thegn.' Cp. Bede, ii. 9, 'alium
de militibus,' used as equivalent to 'ministris ;' also iii. 1, Eanfrid's twelve
chosen 'milites ;' and iv. 22, 'timuit se militem . . . confiteri ;' v. 13, 'in
officio militari ;' and iv. 13, H. Abb. 1, Ep. Egb. 6. Above, p. 118.

[2] 'Comitis,' a 'gesith ;' so Alfred renders. Cp. Bede, i. 25, Ethelbert with
his comites ; iii. 22, the two comites who slew Sigebert ; iv. 22, 'comitem
Ædilredi ;' v. 4, 5, the comites Puch and Addi. Above, p. 48.

[3] 'Præfectum suum ;' probably the manager of the royal property, the
officer who was to do justice between the king's tenants : see Kemble, ii. 169,
on the king's reeve. The legend of St. Oswin calls Ethelwin the steward of
Oswy's household. Cp. Ep. Egb. 7 ; Vit. Cuthb. 15.

[4] Bede, iii. 24 : 'Nam regina,' &c.

[5] Bede, l. c., 'orationes . . . pro . . . salute ;' and iii. 14, 'pro . . . animæ
redemptione.' Cp. Bede, Vit. Cuthb. 7, and the charter of Ethelward, Kemble's
Cod. Diplom. i. 64 ; of Forthere, ib. i. 73 ; of Ethelbald, ib. i. 82 ; and Wilfrid
in Eddi's Life, c. 62. Cp. 'pro remedio animæ.' After Trumhere the house
of Gilling seems to have had for superiors Kynefrid and Tunbert ; Anon. Hist.
of Abbots of Jarrow, in Bede's Works, vi. 416 (Giles).

[6] Cp. Bede, v. 6, for Herebald, abbot of the monastery near the mouth of the
Tyne when Bede wrote. See Vit. Cuthb. 3, 35, for the house first of monks,
then of nuns, 'non longe ab ostio Tini,' but.' ad meridiem,' and distinct from
Herebald's. Smith places it on the Scottish Tyne. For legends as to the first
foundation at Tynemouth, see Monast. Angl. iii. 302 ; Gibson, Monast. of
Tynemouth, i. 12.

tunely discovered [1], a Norman monastery rose up on the cliff, where the ruins of a later church, in the delicate grace of 'First-Pointed' architecture, overlook the ocean, and witness to the days when 'the Peace of St. Oswin' gave security to fugitives who came within a mile of his tomb [2].

This tragedy had some effect in shortening the days of Aidan. He had continued to be on good terms with Oswy: he had held communications with Utta, the head of a monastery at Gateshead, who was charged to ask in Oswy's name for the hand of Edwin's daughter, then in Kent [3]; and he had invited Edwin's grand-niece Hilda from East-Anglia [4] into Northumbria, where, after 'dwelling for a year, with a very few companions, on the north bank of the Wear, she became in 649 the superior of a nunnery near Hartlepool [5], from whence the abbess Heiu, the first of all Northumbrian women to receive the monastic habit from Aidan's own hand, had retired to another 'abode' at Tadcaster [6]. Hilda's rule at Hartlepool was formed by the best lessons that she could gain from 'learned men;' and it was one of Aidan's special pleasures to visit her, and to give instructions that met with full response from a mind naturally thoughtful, and a will devoted to the service of God [7]. But earthly sorrows and earthly solaces were soon to be over for the holy bishop. It was about twelve days from the murder of Oswin [8] that he was staying at a royal 'vill' near Bamborough, from whence he had often made preaching circuits [9]. An attack of illness, it seems, came on so suddenly that he could not be taken into

Death of St. Aidan.

---

[1] The discovery took place in 1065 (Florence), and a monastery was founded soon afterwards. The bones were for a time kept at Jarrow.

[2] Gibson, i. 34. See above, p. 93.

[3] See Bede, iii. 15, 25. Gateshead, 'Ad capræ caput,' is Goatshead.

[4] Bede, iv. 23. See p. 157.

[5] 'Heruteu, id est, Insula Cervi,' Bede, iii. 24 (as if 'Hart-ey'). The cemetery of the nunnery was discovered in 1833, under a field; see Murray's Durh. and Northumb. p. 115.

[6] Bede, iv. 23: 'Deinde ab Aidano,' &c. 'Calcaria,' a Roman station on the Wharfe, called by the English 'Kælcaceaster' (Tadcaster). Heiu's nunnery was probably at Healaugh (Heiu's læg, or territory), three miles north of Calcaria.

[7] Bede, iv. 23: 'Prælata autem . . . nam et episcopus Aidan,' &c.

[8] Bede, iii. 14: 'Sed et ipse antistes,' &c.

[9] Bede, iii. 17: 'Hunc cum dies mortis,' &c.

his bedroom, but was laid on the ground, screened by an awning, and supported by a wooden buttress that propped the church's western end [1]. In this position, significant of his habitual detachment from worldly interests [2], he breathed his last on the 31st of August, 651. The little village which now represents 'the burgh of queen Bebba' is less really ennobled by its grand castle, and its associations with Northumbrian royalty and with a modern prince-bishop's munificence, than by the fact that, in visiting its interesting church [3], we stand upon the ground where Aidan died.

[1] This buttress escaped unhurt in two fires, although the holes by which it was fixed to the church were burnt through; Bede, iii. 17. The church itself was evidently of wood.

[2] See Kingsley's Hermits, p. 291. The touching phrase of the Irish annals is very appropriate in this case: '*Quies* Adani episcopi Saxonum;' Tighernach. See too the story of Cuthbert's vision in Bede, Vit. Cuthb. 4.

[3] It is dedicated in honour of St. Aidan.

CHAPTER VI.

Prepara-
tions for
organisa-
tion.

As yet we have not been able to speak of one organised
Church for Saxons and Angles. The period now immediately
before us exhibits a threefold process of preparation for such
an unity. We shall see missions extending over a wider
extent of country : we shall see the resisting force of Paganism
gathering itself up, and sinking back paralysed : we shall
see the removal of the difference which practically kept
Christians of one class from coalescing with Christians of the
other.

Let us begin by looking at the several bishoprics, as they
were occupied at the close of 651. Honorius was still at
Canterbury, connecting the Kentish Church in his own person
with the generation that had sat at Gregory's feet. He had
seen much more than he had taken part in : he had had little
to do, personally, in the extension of the Church, beyond the
consecration of Ithamar for Rochester and of Thomas for
Dunwich. The East-Anglian mission might, in one sense, be
traced to his suggestion of that sphere for the activities of
Felix : with the work in Wessex he had had nothing to do,
although Kent lay near to the eastern line of that kingdom.
Agilbert was carrying on the work of Birinus in entire independence of Canterbury. The archbishop could not regard
him as a suffragan ; the only two bishops with whom Hono-

Finan at
Lindis-
farne.

rius had any close relations were Ithamar and Thomas. As
we have seen, he had heartily respected Aidan ; but they did
not come near each other in any effective sense. And now,
in Aidan's place, there was come from Hy[1] a bishop named

---

[1] Bede, iii. 17, 'et ipse . . . ab Hii . . . . destinatus ;' ib. iii. 25, 'a Scottis
ordinatus ac missus.' The consecration of Finan must have been performed by
a Scotic bishop, or bishops, at Hy, as Aidan's had been. Tighernach calls him

Finan, who was destined to be in one respect more closely
connected with 'South-country' Church life than Aidan had
ever been, but who, although a good man, did not possess
those rare qualities which made all men acknowledge in Aidan
a living saint. We gain some notion of the extremely humble
aspect of Aidan's own church at Lindisfarne by observing that
when Finan arrived, he found it desirable to build a church
'suitable to the episcopal see[1], and constructed it, in the
Scotic fashion, not of stone, but entirely of hewn oak, with a
covering of reeds,' for which a later bishop, named Eadbert,
substituted sheets of lead. Soon after Finan's arrival, the
Paschal question was again revived, by the anti-Scotic zeal
of some who came from Gaul or from Kent. Among these
was one whose Irish birth must have rendered him very
obnoxious to the Scotic clergy, 'a very ardent upholder of the
true Easter,' named Ronan[2], who had studied in Gaul or
Italy, and would appear to his own countrymen as little better
than an apostate. He hesitated not to enter into controversy
with Finan. The debate, says Bede, 'brought many to
right views, or impelled them to a more diligent inquiry as to
the truth. But Ronan could by no means convert Finan: on
the contrary, as he was a man of rough temper[3], by sharp
language he embittered him further, and made him an open
adversary of the truth.' If Finan had such a temper, it must
be allowed that he was somewhat severely tried by such
objurgations on the part of an inferior, especially when he
found that James the Deacon, now venerable from years as
well as from self-devotion, had made proselytes to the foreign

son of Rimed (a. 660). We meet with an Irish monk named Finan in Adamn.
i. 49 ; and see above, p. 167, for Finnian of Clonard. Another Finnian was of
Maghbile or Moville ; Lanigan, ii. 25 ; Reeves, p. 103.

[1] Bede, iii. 25 : 'Qui in insula Lindisfarnensi fecit ecclesiam,' &c. See
Lingard, A.-S. Ch. ii. 369 ; and Reeves's Adamnan, p. 177, 'The walls were
made of wooden sheeting, which was protected from the weather outside by
a coat of rush thatch.' See above, p. 150.

[2] Bede, iii. 25 : 'Erat in his acerrimus veri Paschæ defensor,' &c.

[3] 'Quod esset ferocis animi.' Lanigan, from the use of 'acerrimus' and 'casti-
gando,' inclines to refer 'ferocis animi' to Ronan, although he admits that the
context seems to favour an allusion to Finan ; ii. 427. See Grub, Eccl. Hist.
Sc. i. 83 : 'Finan was deficient in the gentle and winning temper' which Aidan
had shown, but ' in other respects was an admirable prelate.'

CHAP. VI. system, and that the queen Eanfled and her Kentish chaplain Romanus were using influence on the same side. Was it come to this, Finan might ask, that Ronan was to be in Northumbria what Cummian had been in Munster, the means of discrediting the usages of his native Church? As yet, Oswy was faithful to his own training among the Scots; but how long would he resist domestic pressure, and an array of Gallic or Roman authorities? The inconvenience of the discordant reckonings came practically to the front when, on one occasion, Oswy was keeping his Easter-day with Finan, while Eanfled and her attendants were observing their 'day of Palms[1].' It was a visible discrepancy such as had occurred when some Gallic churches in 577 differed from the rest by a whole month as to the reckoning of Easter[2], or when some Irish visitors to Rome found that their fellow-lodgers, a Jew, a Greek, a 'Scythian,' and an Egyptian, went to St. Peter's for the Easter service while they were keeping a Lenten Sunday at home[3]. In effect, this curious duplication of Easters in one royal household might illustrate the unseemliness of such a want of Paschal uniformity as was deprecated, after the Nicene Council, in a letter professing to be from Constantine himself[4]. Doubtless, it prepared the way for a decisive contest between the Scotic and 'Catholic' parties; but Finan succeeded in preventing any open breach, as long as he occupied the see.

Conversion of Peada.

There was, indeed, matter of interest far worthier to engage the attention of Northumbrian Churchmen. The Mid-Angles[5], as Bede calls them, who dwelt between the Trent and the Bedford district, had been placed by the Mercian king under the government of his son Peada, 'an excellent youth,' says Bede, 'most worthy of the title and

---

[1] Bede, iii. 25: 'Et cum rex Pascha Dominicum solutis jejuniis faceret,' &c.

[2] See above, p. 81. Later, in 633, the fourth Toledan Council refers, c. 5 (Mansi, x. 618), to the mistakes caused in Spain, as to Easter, by 'diversa observantia laterculorum.'

[3] Cummian's Ep. to Segenius, &c. in Usher, Sylloge, p. 23; King's Hist. Ch. Ireland, i. 162.

[4] Eus. Vit. Con. iii. 18; Soc. i. 9.

[5] Bede, iii. 21; iv. 12. See Green, Making of Engl. p. 298: 'The Middle English or Leicester-men.'

character of a king[1].' His father allowed him to visit chap. vi.
Northumbria on a peaceful errand, during some cessation of
his own frequent inroads on its border[2]. Peada requested
the hand of Alchfled, the daughter of Oswy and Eanfled.
Oswy replied as Eadbald had replied to Edwin's suit for her
grandmother Ethelburga : 'I cannot give my child to a
Heathen. If you would wed her, you must accept the faith
of Christ, and baptism,—you and the people under your rule.'
Peada was disposed to listen to Christian teaching: he had
been impressed by the conversation of Alchfrid son of Oswy,
a prince who had a strong love of learning, and who had
married Peada's sister Kyniburga, one of those five children
of the fierce old Heathen conqueror who were afterwards
canonised as saints[3]. The promise of 'a resurrection, of a
heavenly kingdom, of future immortality,' spoke to the heart
of the young Mercian[4]. 'I *will* be a Christian,' he said
emphatically, 'whether I obtain the maiden or not.' Once
more, as in the case of Oswald the son of Ethelfrid, 'out of
the strong came forth sweetness;' and the heir of Penda's
realm was baptized by Finan in the well-known royal town
called 'At the Wall,' which has been identified variously
with Walton, Walbottle, and, more probably, with Pandon,
now included within Newcastle, and somewhat to the north
of the 'Black Gate' of that city[5]. Finan then commissioned four priests, three of whom, Cedd, Adda[6], and Betti,
were Northumbrians, and the fourth, Diuma, was an Irish-

[1] Bede, iii. 21 : 'Qui cum esset juvenis optimus,' &c. Malmesbury calls
him Weda ; G. R. i. 75.

[2] Bede, iii. 24 : 'Acerbas atque intolerabiles .... irruptiones .... regis
Merciorum.' Cp. iii. 16, 17.

[3] Ethelred, Merewald (himself the father of four saints), Mercelin, Kyniburga,
Kineswith. Kyniburga, in her widowhood, ruled a religious house at Caistor
(Kyniburgacaster) ; see Alb. Butler, March 6. 'Nearly all Penda's children
and grandchildren died in the odour of sanctity ;' Stubbs on Foundation of
Peterborough, p. 7. Cp. Florence, App. and a. 675.

[4] 'At ille audita,' &c. ; Bede, iii. 21. Compare the speech of the thane in
Bede, ii. 13, and 'promissis eorum suavissimis,' i. 26 ; and 'cælestia sperare,'
iv. 13 : see too St. Boniface's fifteenth sermon, 'Ibi est vita cum Deo sine
morte, lux sine tenebris,' &c.

[5] Bede says it was 'twelve miles from the eastern sea ;' iii. 22.

[6] He was the brother of Utta (see p. 170), who, acting on Aidan's advice,
poured oil on waves in a storm, with a success which Bede thought supernatural ; iii. 15.

man, to accompany Peada home, and to evangelize his Mid-Angles. Thus was formed the first mission to the Midlands, in 653. The priests, 'being well qualified for their work by learning and by character, were willingly heard; and day by day many of the nobles and of the lowest people renounced the filth[1] of idolatry, and were washed in the fountain of faith[2].' But they also ventured into Mercia proper; and its old king, while for himself he held fast to his old gods, was yet so far softened by age as to offer no opposition to their preaching, and also shrewd enough to note some cases of Christian profession discredited by inconsistent practice, and honest enough to fling at them a few words of contemptuous disgust[3]. 'The mean wretches, who have put their faith in this new God, and then will not trouble themselves to obey him!' This speech, the only one recorded of Penda, betokens a healthy vein of thoroughness, which would incline him to respect Christian belief when represented by men who lived up to their creed.

Second Mission to the East-Saxons.

Another very important step taken by the Northumbrian Church at this time was the second mission to the East-Saxons. It was thirty-seven years after the expulsion of Mellitus when Sigebert the Good[4], as he is called, successor of that Sigebert the Little who had succeeded his father and uncles in 617, paid one of his 'frequent' visits to his friend king Oswy, and profited by his host's exhortations as Sabert had done by those of Ethelbert, as Eorpwald by those of Edwin. The passage in which Bede summarises the Northumbrian king's pleading against idolatry is one of the finest in his book: it reads like a combination of some well-known arguments of Isaiah with those grand words into which Tacitus compresses the case for Monotheism[5]. Surely, said Oswy, Sigebert would understand that a God could not be made out of wood and stone, the remnants of which were

---

[1] Cp. Bede, iii. 1; and iii. 30, 'in perfidiæ sordibus.'

[2] Bede, iii. 21; cp. iv. 16, 'fonte Salvatoris ablutos.' Above, p. 105.

[3] Bede, iii. 21: 'Quin potius odio habebat,' &c.

[4] Bede, iii. 22: 'Erat enim rex,' &c. Florence surely inserts too many generations between him and Sabert's brother (tom. i. p. 250).

[5] Isa. xliv. 10 ff.; Tac. Hist. v. 5, 'Judæi mente sola unumque numen intelligunt, profanos qui deûm imagines . . . effingant,' &c.

burned, or fashioned into household vessels, or even thrown away, trodden under foot, and turned into earth. Surely 'He alone could be thought of as God, who was incomprehensible in majesty, invisible to human eyes, almighty, eternal, the Creator and Ruler and righteous Judge of the universe, whose eternal abode was not in poor perishable metal, but in heaven, where eternal rewards were in store for all those who would learn and do their Maker's will.' Such ideas, 'frequently inculcated with the earnestness of a friend or even a brother,' told fully upon Sigebert: he consulted with the 'friends' who had accompanied him to the north, took his own resolution, advised them to join with him; and after they had all 'assented to the faith,' he and they were baptized at the same place and by the same hands as Peada, and apparently in the autumn of the same year 653. Like Peada, Sigebert asked for a supply of Christian teachers, to convert and baptize his people: and Oswy summoned [1] Cedd from his work among the Mid-Angles, and sent him to preach to the East-Saxons, in company with another priest. They traversed that kingdom, and 'gathered together a large Church:' and ere long, probably in 654, Cedd 'happened to return home and visit Lindisfarne to converse with bishop Finan, who, on learning how the work of the Gospel had prospered with him, made him bishop for the race of the East-Saxons, having called in two other bishops to assist him in the ordination.' These two prelates must have been Scoto-Celtic,—a fact which gives special significance to Bede's next words: 'Cedd, having received the degree of the episcopate, returned to his province, and, fulfilling with greater authority the work which he had begun, made churches in different places.' It would have been impossible for Bede to write thus, had he suspected that there was the slightest real flaw in the episcopal character of Finan or of the two other Scotic consecrators, although he knew the two latter to be subject to the authority of the abbot of Hy, as primate of the Scottish Church; and from this one passage [2]

Cedd, Bishop of the East-Saxons.

[1] 'Clamavit ad se;' Bede, iii. 22; so in iii. 23, iv. 14, and v. 3.

[2] Bishop Russell uses it 'to expose the absurdity of those writers who imagine that the monks of Iona were hostile to episcopacy,' and to warrant

N

CHAP. VI. we might confidently infer that actual bishops had been employed, in Scotland, to confer the episcopate on Aidan and Finan. Let us now follow Cedd in his mission-circuits amongst the East-Saxons. ' He built churches, and ordained presbyters and deacons to assist him in preaching and in baptizing, especially in that city which in the Saxon tongue is called Ythancæstir, but also in that which is called Tilaburg; the former of these places is on the bank of the river Pent, the latter on that of the Thames.' In this sentence of Bede's we observe, first, a foreshadowing of the parochial system,—which, however, grew up very gradually in England, and was by no means thoroughly established in Northumbria in the last years of Bede's own life [1]: and secondly, the absence of the name of London, which is probably to be explained by the fact that the great city was 'fluctuating between the condition of an independent commonwealth and that of a dependency of the Mercian kings [2].' Strictly speaking, therefore, Cedd seems not to have been bishop of London [3]: and of the two places named by Bede as centres of his mission work, 'Ythancæstir' appears to have a precedence over Tilbury. It has been placed near Bradwell-on-the-sea, at the mouth of the Blackwater, formerly called the Pent, and has also been identified with the Roman station of Othona [4]. Tilbury, which is familiarly associated with the Spanish Armada, would have the advantage of being near the mouth of the Thames. At each of these two places Cedd established not only a body of clergy, but also a 'swarm of servants of Christ [5],' or monks: whom he

'the conclusion that Aidan, Finan, and Colman were consecrated by bishops;' Hist. Ch. Sc. i. 34. So Grub, Eccl. Hist. Sc. i. 155. Observe also the presence of *three* consecrators. See above, p. 141.

[1] Bede, Ep. ad Egb. 3: 'Necessarium satis est, ut plures tibi sacri operis adjutores adsciscas, presbyteros videlicet ordinando ... qui in singulis viculis prædicando ... adsistant.' That the system had no founder, but grew up naturally out of the relation of the priests to townships, see Stubbs, Const. Hist. i. 260 (or 227). See Add. Notes, F.

[2] Freeman, i. 24. Palgrave, E. C. p. 414: 'Strictly speaking, we have no proof that London ever formed part of the early Anglo-Saxon kingdoms.'

[3] Florence, indeed, calls him so, a. 621.

[4] Camden, Britannia, i. 411; Horsley, Brit. Rom. p. 487.

[5] Bede, iii. 22: 'famulorum Christi,' used technically. So iv. 23.

taught to observe 'the discipline of the regular life,'—that
is, the monastic system of the Scotic Church,—'as far as
their untrained minds could receive it,'—a phrase which is
suggestive of some such austerity as we know to have
characterised the rule of Columban. Yet, stern as this discipline may have been, the East-Saxon monks heartily loved
their bishop: witness the touching story [1] of thirty brethren
of 'his monastery,'—probably that of Ythancester,—who, on
hearing of his death and burial in Northumbria, came all the
way to his Yorkshire monastery in order to live or die beside
his grave, and in fact did all die there of the then raging
pestilence, save one little boy, long afterwards 'useful' as
a priest. Thus, for some years, all went well in Essex:
Christianity regained its hold on the people, or, as Bede
phrases it, 'the teaching of the heavenly life received a daily
increase, to the joy of the king and amid the sympathy of his
subjects [2].' But Cedd could not be satisfied without periodical
visits to his native North-country, in order to preach to his
own folk [3]: and one of his three brothers, a priest named
Cælin, comes before us as chaplain to Ethelwald [4] the son of
Oswald, whom his uncle Oswy permitted to act as sub-king
in Deira. This prince exhibits a strange combination of his
father's devout habits with a mean jealousy which impelled
him into a shameful treason [5]; but the religious side of his
nature comes out in his relations with Cedd, who was introduced to him by Cælin, and to whom, 'seeing him to be a
holy and wise man, and approved in conduct,' he offered a
piece of land for the building of a monastery, whither he
himself might come 'to pray and to hear the Word, and
where he might eventually be buried. For,' says Bede [6], 'he

---

[1] Bede, iii. 23 : 'Cum ergo episcopum defunctum,' &c.

[2] Bede, iii. 22 : 'Cumque tempore non pauco,' &c.

[3] Bede, iii. 23 : 'Solebat autem idem vir Domini,' &c.

[4] Bede gives the name its rough North-country form, Oidilwald. Cælin
'used to minister the Word and the "sacramenta fidei"' to him and to his
household (familiæ). 'Sacramenta fidei' means the sacraments as connected
with, and involving, the faith; see above, p. 115.

[5] This union of a certain kind or amount of piety with an utter want of
nobleness of character reminds us, in some measure, of Henry III.

[6] 'Nam et seipsum,' &c. Cp. iii. 24, 'supplicandum pro pace gentis.'

sincerely believed that he would be greatly helped by the daily prayers of those who would serve the Lord in that place.' The site being left to Cedd's choice, he fixed upon a wild spot under the Pickering hills [1], where, says Bede, ' there seemed to have been haunts of robbers and lairs of wild beasts rather than dwellings of men.' This place was Lastingham, where Cedd, after the custom of Lindisfarne, began by hallowing the ground on which the building was to be erected [2]: he asked leave of Ethelwald to spend a whole Lent there, ' fasting on all week days until evening, when he took an egg, a morsel of bread, and a little milk and water. For he said that this was the usage of those from whom he had learned the rule of regular discipline.' When ten days of this Lent still remained, he was summoned to the king; but his brother Kynibil, who was also ' his presbyter [3],' completed the series of prayers and fasts, and a monastery after the Scotic type was founded at Lastingham,—the first church being built of wood.

Such was the tenor of Cedd's episcopal life. It began when the see of Canterbury was vacant by the death of Honorius, which is dated by Bede on the 30th of September, 653 [4]: and the vacancy continued until the 26th of March, 655, when a signal testimony was borne by king Erconbert and his advisers, and by the clergy and monks of Canterbury, to the reality of that Church-work of Birinus with which Canterbury had had no concern whatever. A Wessex man called Frithona, the first ' Saxon' successor of Augustine, was consecrated [5] by Ithamar of Rochester alone, without the assistance of Bertgils, or Boniface as he called himself, who had succeeded Thomas at Dunwich in 652, and who, as a born Kentishman, would feel a special interest in the consecration

---

[1] ' In montibus arduis ac remotis;' Bede, iii. 23. He applies the words of Isaiah xxxv. 7, 'In the habitation of dragons ... shall be grass with reeds and rushes,'—' that is, the fruit of good works should spring up in the place where formerly beasts had their haunts, or men lived like beasts.' Comp. Bede, iv. 3, and Præf.

[2] See above. p. 151.

[3] Compare 'presbyter suus' in iii. 14. Above, p. 168.

[4] Bede, iii. 20: ' Et ipse quoque Honorius,' &c.

[5] Bede, iii. 20: 'Electus est ... Deusdedit, de gente Occidentalium Saxonum.' Elmham gives his original Saxon name; H. Mon. S. Aug. p. 192.

of an archbishop[1]; but perhaps the journey from the distant sea-port in Suffolk was too inconvenient at that time. Frithona imitated Bertgils by adopting the name of Deusdedit[2], which had been borne by a Pope from 615 to 618[3], and which, while intended as an equivalent for 'Theodore,' somewhat reminds us, by its very awkwardness, of that singular anticipation of Puritanic names which we find in the ancient African Church[4]. Under Deusdedit, as under Honorius, the archbishopric continued to be little else than a high dignity shut up within a narrow area: except for its hold upon East-Anglia, it had no practical effect on the general life and work of the Church: it was like a great force lying dormant until the epoch that was to wake it into energy.

The year of Cedd's consecration, also distinguished by the vacancy of Canterbury, was tragically marked by another, and the last, of Penda's fatal victories. Anna had mortally offended him by sheltering Kenwalch: and he now fell on the East-Anglians 'like a wolf on timorous sheep, so that Anna and his host were devoured by his sword in a moment, and scarcely a man of them survived.' Such is the vivid account of Henry of Huntingdon[5]. The conqueror allowed Ethelhere, Anna's brother, to reign as his vassal, and employed him, in some way unexplained, to give occasion for another Mercian invasion of Northumbria in the following year, 655[6]. Oswy had done his utmost to propitiate Penda: beside the double alliance between their houses[7], 'he

Death of Anna.

---

[1] Bede, iii. 20, 'de provincia Cantuariorum.' Cp. iv. 5.

[2] An Irish missionary in Picardy, named Fricor, 'changed his name into Adrian, as more pleasing to his auditors;' Lanigan, ii. 442. So Willibrord became 'Clement,' and Winfrid 'Boniface.'

[3] Also by an archbishop of Milan in Gregory's time; Greg. Ep. xiii. 30.

[4] Adeodatus, son of St. Augustine; Quodvultdeus, in the conference of Carthage; Deogratias, bishop of Carthage. We also meet with a deacon Donadeus in Numidia in the time of Gregory the Great; Ep. xii. 8.

[5] Hen. Hunt. ii. 33. See Bede, iii. 18: 'Anna . . . qui et ipse,' &c.

[6] Bede, iii. 24: 'In quibus Ædilheri, . . . auctor ipse belli,' &c.

[7] Thus—

had placed another son, Egfrid, as a hostage in the hands of the Mercian queen Kynwise[1];' he now offered to purchase peace with a gift of royal ornaments, 'greater than can be believed[2].' All was in vain: Penda was resolved, this time, to make sure work: having again crossed the Northumbrian border, he would not turn back, as in 633 or 642, until he had annihilated Northumbria as a kingdom, or, as Bede says,

Battle of Winwid-field.

had 'exterminated the whole people, small and great.' His host is described in terms which remind us of the Syrian Benhadad's: thirty chiefs of princely rank[3], including, it seems, the East-Anglian king, were serving under his banner; and Oswy's much smaller force was diminished by the desertion of Ethelwald, who, through some personal grudge, was alienated from 'his uncle and his country,' and stained his father's memory by 'acting as guide to the invaders,' although, at the last moment, either compunction or cowardice restrained him from giving them his aid[4]. Thus the odds which Oswy had to face appeared indeed desperate. He had recourse to his religion: 'If the Pagan will not accept our gifts, let us offer them to Him who will—the Lord our God[5]:' and vowed that if he should be victorious, he would dedicate his daughter Elfled, a babe of a year old, to the monastic life[6], and give twelve pieces of land for building

---

[1] Bede, iii. 24: 'Nam alius filius ejus Ecgfrid,' &c.

[2] 'Innumera et majora quam credi potest ornamenta regia,' &c.

[3] 'Triginta legiones ducibus nobilissimis instructam . . . Duces regii triginta qui ad auxilium venerunt,' Bede. 'Cynebearna,' Chron. See Stubbs, Const. Hist. i. 186, 198 ; Green, Making of Engl. p. 301.

[4] See Lingard, H. E. i. 96. Bede takes the unfavourable view, 'eventum . . . tuto in loco exspectabat.'

[5] 'Si Paganus, inquit, nescit accipere nostra donaria, offeramus ei qui novit, Domino Deo nostro.'

[6] The special case of Samuel's dedication had come to be deemed a precedent. The second Council of Toledo in 531 had so far guarded the free agency of persons devoted in childhood to 'clerical service,' as to excuse them from proceeding to holy orders if at eighteen they expressed a desire to marry. But the Benedictine movement encouraged parents to offer their young children for monastic life, wrapping their little hands 'in palla altaris' (Reg. Bened. 59) ; and a feeling grew up which gained expression in c. 49 of the fourth Council of Toledo, A.D. 633, 'Monachum aut paterna devotio aut propria professio facit : quidquid horum fuerit, alligatum tenebit,' no regard being had to the impossibility of ascertaining in childhood any real aptitudes for an avowedly

as many religious houses. 'Relying on Christ as their Leader[1],' he and his son Alchfrid awaited the great crisis at a place described by Bede as 'in the region of Loidis, near the river Winwæd,' by Florence of Worcester as Winwidfield, and by 'Nennius'[2] as the Field of Gai. This last transfers the scene to Scotland, and represents Oswy as taking refuge in 'Judeu' or Inchkeith, and giving up his treasures there to Penda, before he resolves to risk a battle. Hence it has been supposed[3] that Bede's 'Loidis' means Lothian, as if Penda had pursued Oswy to the northern extremity of the Northumbrian realm: and that the 'Winwæd' means the Avon in Linlithgowshire. It is difficult to reconcile this with Bede's account; we can hardly doubt that by 'Loidis,' here as elsewhere[4], he means the Leeds district: and, as in regard to Edwin's baptism, we have to choose between the great Northumbrian historian and a Welsh writer of the next century and of far inferior authority, with a strong turn for patriotic romance[5]. Whatever was the spot, the armies met on the 15th of November; and the many were scattered before the few. The terrible old man, who had slain so many, was himself smitten down at last: and the same fate befell nearly all his auxiliaries[6], including Ethelhere the East-Anglian[7]. Again we recall the story of Hebrew warfare: the Winwæd, swollen by autumnal rains, was to Penda's host what the Kishon of old was to Sisera's; it

---

exceptional life. Thus Æsica, a boy of three, was bred up in the religious house of Barking (Bede, iv. 8); Bede was 'given to abbot Benedict' at seven (v. 24); and Odelirius so dedicated his son Ordericus Vitalis at ten (Ord. Vital. xiii. 45).

[1] 'Perparvum . . . habens exercitum, sed Christo duce confisus.'

[2] C. 64 (ed. Stev.); also the Annales Cambriæ.

[3] Skene, Celtic Scotland, i. 254. Cp. Florence, 'in Berniciam.'

[4] Bede, ii. 14. See above, p. 112. The Winwæd has been supposed to be the Aire, or the Went. See Whitaker, Loidis and Elmete, p. 3.

[5] See Whitley Stokes, Tripart. Life, i. p. cxvii, on Nennius. What we are told of Ethelwald and of Ethelhere suits better with a battle-field in Yorkshire; so does Bede's expression that Oswy 'met' the 'thirty legions of Penda's host.' The tale which transforms their thirty commanders into British kings, and makes them share in Oswy's surrendered treasures, may well have grown out of Welsh 'nationalism.'

[6] Nennius says that *one* of the British kings, Catgabail, escaped, and so got the discreditable name of Catguommed, or 'Would-not-fight.'

[7] He was succeeded by his brother Ethelwald (Florence).

CHAP. VI. swept away 'many more in their flight than the sword had destroyed while fighting.' Hence came the saying which handed down the names of the five kings whom Penda had slain, in connection with his own final overthrow: 'In Winwed stream was avenged the slaughter of Anna, the slaughter of the kings Sigebert and Egric, the slaughter of the kings Oswald and Edwin[1].' It was a great day: it saved the independence of Northumbria, although it only arrested for some four years the advance of Mercia to primacy among the kingdoms; but it was far more eventful in regard to higher interests, for 'with Penda fell Paganism[2].' Since the battle of Winwidfield, no English ruling power has formally disowned the faith of Christ.

Diuma bishop of Mercia.

Oswy lost no time in advancing the cause of that faith, not only by the punctual fulfilment of his vow as to the twelve monasteries, and the consignment of the infant Elfled to the care of Hilda at Hartlepool[3], but by effectually promoting the extension of Christianity throughout Mercia. He retained in his own hands the government of Mercia proper[4]: but the South Mercians, whom Bede describes as separated by the Trent from the North Mercians, and who were the same as those elsewhere called the Mid-Angles[5], were placed as before under the viceroyalty of Peada[6], who obtained a bishop for all the Mercians[7] in the 'Scot' Diuma, already mentioned as

[1] Hen. Hunt. ii. 34.

[2] Milman, Lat. Chr. ii. 244. Compare Freeman, i. 37; and the somewhat less decided language of Kemble, i. 150.

[3] Bede, iii. 24: 'Tunc rex Osuiu, juxta quod Domino voverat,' &c. The monastic communities then founded were to 'practise the heavenly warfare instead of the earthly, and to pray for the eternal peace of that nation.'

[4] Bede, iii. 21: 'Ipso autem occiso,' &c., and iii. 24: 'Idem autem rex . . . Merciorum genti . . . præfuit.' This is implied in Bede's words, iii. 21, 'Cum Osuiu . . . regnum ejus acciperet,' &c., and iii. 24, 'Quo tempore donavit,' &c. The Chronicle says, Peada became king of the Mercians; but this must mean, of the South Mercians. See Palgrave, p. cclxxvii.

[5] See above, p. 174. Compare Bede, iii. 21, 'Mediterraneorum Anglorum,' and iii. 24, 'Australium Merciorum;' and Cod. Diplom. i. 96, Ethelbald 'king not only of the Mercians, but of all the provinces which are named generally South-Angles.' Green says that the old division of Mercians into Northern and Southern 'reappeared' after 'the great defeat;' p. 303.

[6] Bede, iii. 24: 'Quo tempore donavit præfato Peadæ,' &c. It was a grant from his father's conqueror.

[7] For, says Bede, iii. 21, the paucity of bishops rendered it necessary that

one of the four priests sent home with him by Finan in 653.
The consecration of Diuma must be dated at the beginning
of 656 ; and immediately afterwards, according to tradition,
Peada ' began to build a monastery to the glory of Christ
and St. Peter [1] ' at a place called Medeshamstede, ' the
dwelling-place in the meadows,' where in the tenth century
the town that had grown up around this ' first resting-place
of Christianity in central England' acquired the name of St.
Peter's Borough. But Peada, if, as is probable, he had a
' share in the act [2],' could do no more than plan this foundation, and select its first abbot in the person of a monk named
Saxulf, rich, high-born, devout, and widely esteemed, whom
Bede calls the builder of the monastery [3]. A mysterious Death of
crime soon blighted the hopes associated with the noble- Peada.
spirited Peada. He was murdered, ' as they say, by the
treachery of his own wife,' the Northumbrian princess Alchfled [4], in the Easter-tide of 656 [5], or, according to the Chronicle,
in 657. The event was one of the numerous tragedies which
had warned the Saxon and Anglian converts that neither the
adoption of Christianity as a creed, nor the most consistent
Christian goodness, were any security against misfortune and
violent death [6]. And one more warning of this sort was given Murder of
some time later in Essex. Bishop Cedd had excommuni- Sigebert
cated a retainer and kinsman of Sigebert for obstinately the Good.
adhering to an unlawful marriage. The king, disregarding

---

one prelate should be set over ' duobus populis.' Diuma probably fixed his
seat at Repton, an old seat of Mercian royalty.

[1] This is from a later addition to the Chronicle. A good deal of such matter
was inserted for the honour of the abbey of Peterborough. See Bede, iv. 6,
for ' Medeshamstedi in the country of the Gyrvians ' (Fen-men). See above, p.
164. See Smith's note in loc. and Monast. Angl. i. 344; Green, Making of
England,-p. 80.

[2] Stubbs on Foundation of Peterborough, p. 7 ; Haddan and Stubbs, iii. 100.

[3] ' Constructor et abbas,' &c. ; Bede, iv. 6. He became bishop of Lichfield
in 675.

[4] Bede, iii. 24: ' Sed idem Peada . . . proditione, ut dicunt, conjugis suæ.'
Bede was not likely to have a prejudice against Alchfled. Florence adopts
the story.

[5] So it is usually dated. It happened, says Bede, ' proximo vere ' after
Oswy had given Peada ' regnum australium Merciorum ;' which he did, it
seems, upon the death of Penda in November, 655.

[6] Compare Edwin, Oswald, Eorpwald, Sigebert the Learned, Oswin, Anna.

CHAP. VI. the sentence [1], accepted an invitation to the offender's house, but met with Cedd on his return. Trembling, he leapt from his horse, and knelt to the bishop for pardon : but Cedd exhibited all the austerity of Columban. Touching the king with a wand which he held, he predicted that Sigebert would die in the very house where he had been feasting with a reprobate man. And, in effect, this man and his brother murdered Sigebert, and when questioned, gave no other reason for the deed than that he had become too ready to pardon and spare his enemies [2]; a significant indication of the irreconcileable opposition between the Christian and the heathen-Saxon character. 'The new lore,' it would be said, 'has made the king womanish, too mild to rule over men.' Sigebert the Good was succeeded by his brother Swidhelm [3], who was baptized by Cedd himself at Rendlesham in Suffolk. This royal baptism exhibited the bishops of Essex and of East-Anglia as on brotherly terms ; and Ethelwold, the East-Anglian king, brother and successor of Ethelhere, acted as sponsor to the East-Saxon, and 'received him as he came up out of the holy font [4].' It was about two years since the East-Anglian Christians had heard with interest of the foundation of a monastery on the Gallic model among their neighbours the northern 'Gyrvians' of South Lincolnshire. The founder was Botulf; the place, Ikanho, is usually identified with 'Botulf's town' or Boston, or with the neighbouring village of St. Botulf. The foundation is dated in 654 [5], and king Anna's successor Ethelhere is said to have used influence in its favour with a certain 'South-Anglian' king, or rather sub-king, called Ethelmund, whose sisters Botulf had met in Gaul, and who had some of Botulf's kinsmen in his service. Botulf asked simply to have a piece of unoccupied land given to him : his request was granted, and he chose Ikanho because it was

---

[1] No one was to visit him or eat with him ; Bede, iii. 22.

[2] Bede, l. c. : ' Quod ille nimium suis parcere soleret inimicis, et factas ab eis injurias mox obsecrantibus placida mente demitteret.' They were 'comites.' See above, p. 48.

[3] After Swidhelm Essex became subject to Mercia.

[4] See above, p. 154.

[5] Chronicle, and Florence. See the Life of St. Botulf in Act. SS. Bened. sæc. iii. 1. 4, and Alb. Butler, June 17.

desolate. Monks gathered around him, to whom he gave a CHAP. VI.
Rule compiled from 'old and new' authorities: the fame of
his learning and piety was wide-spread when, about 670,
Ceolfrid, afterwards abbot of Jarrow, paid him a visit[1].

The death of Peada did not arrest the mission-work in
South Mercia: Diuma 'in a short time won not a few to the
Lord, and died among the Mid-Angles in the country called
Infeppingum,'—a district which cannot now be identified. He Cellach,
bishop of
the Mer-
cians.
was succeeded by another 'Scottish' or Irish priest, named
Cellach, who, like Diuma and like Cedd, was consecrated
by Finan. But 'when three years had elapsed from the Revolt of
Mercians:
Wulfhere
king.
slaughter of king Penda[2],' that is, at earliest, at the close
of 658, three Mercian chiefs revolted against the direct
government exercised by Oswy over their country. Observe
the irrepressible and manful sympathy which the Northumbrian Bede here indicates for a patriotic movement against
Northumbrian supremacy. 'They drove out the ealdormen
of a king who was none of theirs, and bravely regained at
once their boundaries and their freedom: they lifted up, as
king, Wulfhere, son of Penda, a young man whom they had
been guarding in concealment: and thus being free, with a
king of their own, they rejoiced to serve Christ the true
King[3].' This is one of the noblest sentences in Bede's
History, and is the more impressive, because we have no
evidence that Oswy had played the tyrant over Mercia; what
was done, and what Bede thus describes, was done purely for
the sake of national independence. Thus chosen as a national
monarch, Wulfhere reigned vigorously[4] for seventeen years:
he is described as 'the first king of the Mercians who re-

---

[1] Anon. Hist. of Abbots of Jarrow, in Bede's Works, vi. 417.

[2] 'Completis autem tribus annis,' &c.; Bede, iii. 24. But the Chronicle
dates Wulfhere's accession in 657, Florence in 659.

[3] Bede, iii. 24: 'Fines suos fortiter,' &c. Mark the word 'levato;' and see
Kemble, i. 154. Compare the lifting-up of Alaric on a shield, Gibbon, iv. 31.
So the Neustrians proclaimed Sigebert in 575, 'impositum super clypeo;'
Greg. Tur. iv. 52. So the Spanish Visi-Goths inaugurated the leader of their
host; Palgrave, Eng. Comm. p. 129.

[4] He 'inherited his father's courage' (virtutis); Hen. Hunt. ii. 34. His reign
finally put a stop to Northumbrian overlordship; Green's Making of Engl.
p. 306.

CHAP. VI. ceived the faith and the laver of holy regeneration [1],' Peada having been only under-king of part of Mercia. Wulfhere established his supremacy over the East-Saxons, and reconquered Lindsey from Northumbria. He married Ermenild, daughter of Erconbert of Kent ; their daughter Werburga became a directress of Mercian nunneries, and the minster of Chester grew up around her shrine [2]. One of Wulfhere's brothers, named Merewald, ruled Hecana or Herefordshire [3] as under-king, married Ermenburga the niece of Erconbert, and became the father of St. Mildred and two other daughters, and of Merewin, a boy of remarkable piety [4]. The king is

Medes-
hamstead.
credited with carrying out the intentions of his brother as to Medeshamstede ; though the details of the consecration of the minster and the speeches ascribed to Wulfhere [5] are hardly more trustworthy than the later and calumnious legend which represented him as killing his two sons for turning Christians, and then, in penitence, building the abbey of ' Burgh [6].' We do know that, in 659, he established Trumhere, abbot of Gilling, in the Mercian bishopric, when Cellach, probably in disgust at the separation of Mercia from Northumbria, had 'abandoned the episcopal office,' and re-

---

[1] Florence, a. 675.

[2] For St. Werburh, or Werburga, see Alb. Butler, Feb. 3. She died about 700. Seven of the churches dedicated to her are within the old Mercian realm : the other six have been supposed to record 'strategic movements' of the great Mercian king Ethelbald in the next century, one being as remote as Plymouth Sound (Kerslake, Vestiges of Supremacy of Mercia, reprinted from Transact. of Bristol and Gloucestershire Archæological Society).

[3] Kemble, i. 150 ; Stubbs, Const. Hist. i. 198. Florence identifies the Hecanas with the Magesetas, or Mægsetan (H. M. B. 621), whom Kemble treats as a portion of them, i. 80.

[4] Above, p. 158. Ermenburga, or Domneva, was daughter of the Kentish subking Ermenred, a son of Eadbald, and sister of the princes Ethelred and Ethelbert, slain by Thunor. Of her daughters, Mildred became abbess of Minster, Milburga of Wenlock : a third was Mildgith.

[5] See them as insertions in Chron. a. 657. Kemble, ii. 243, says that this forgery 'throws no well-grounded doubt upon the fact.'

[6] This myth was set forth in stained glass along the western cloister of Peterborough abbey ; Mon. Anglic. i. 377. See the strange descriptive verses, one couplet being,

'Wulfhere in *woodness* his sword out drew,
And both his sons anon he slew.'

turned to Hy, and thence to Ireland [1]. Trumhere, though
an Englishman, was of Scotic consecration like his predecessor [2]; and so apparently was Jaruman, who succeeded
him in 662.

Another abandonment of a bishopric took place in 660,
under circumstances which give it considerable importance.
Agilbert had been successful as bishop of the West-Saxons in
all respects but one. It was from him probably that Kenwalch
learned to be zealous for the 'Catholic Easter [3].' But Agilbert
had not acquired the Saxon tongue; and Kenwalch, who
knew no other, became 'weary of his foreign dialect [4]', and
clandestinely introduced into the province another bishop
who spoke Saxon, named Wini,—who himself also had been
ordained in Gaul: and dividing the province into two
dioceses'—here, as in other passages, Bede uses 'parochia' in
this its older sense [5]—'he assigned to Wini an episcopal seat
in the city of Winchester,' where a minster had been hallowed
twelve years before by Birinus. 'Whereupon Agilbert, being
highly offended that the king should do this without consulting him, returned into Gaul, and having accepted the
bishopric of the city of Paris, died there an old man and full
of days.' This sentence gives an inaccurate impression; for
we find Agilbert four years afterwards in Northumbria, and
Bede speaks of him on that occasion as bishop of the West-
Saxons [6]; and, moreover, the see of Paris in 660 and for some
time afterwards was filled by Chrodobert [7], and two bishops

---

[1] Bede, iii. 21: 'Reversus est ad insulam Hii, ubi plurimorum caput et
arcem Scotti habuere cœnobium;' and iii. 24, 'vivens ad Scottiam rediit.'

[2] Bede, iii. 24: 'de natione quidem Anglorum,' &c.

[3] See Eddi, Vit. Wilfr. 7.

[4] Bede, iii. 7: 'Tandem rex, qui Saxonum tantum linguam noverat, pertæsus
barbaræ loquelæ,' &c. Milner understands this of a mere foreign pronunciation,
Hist. Winch. i. 73; but Bede implies more.

[5] 'In duas parochias.' Comp. Bede, v. 18: 'in duas parochias . . . ad
civitatis Ventanæ parochiam.' See the second decree of the Council of Hertford,
Bede, iv. 5; and Bede, Vit. Cuthb. 29; Ep. Egb. 8. For παροικία as the
aggregate of Christians dwelling in one place or district under the care of a
single chief pastor, see Euseb. i. 1, ii. 24, iii. 14. &c.; Bingham, b. ix. 2. 1.

[6] Bede, iii. 25, v. 19. Eddi calls him at that time 'transmarinus episcopus,'
but this may mean only a bishop of foreign birth and consecration; c. 9.

[7] Mabillon, Ann. Bened. i. 470, on a document signed by him in 663: and
he had been bishop when Chlodwig II. died in 659; ib. i. 459.

CHAP. VI. intervened between him and Agilbert [1]; so that the latter's accession must be referred to a later period. The inconsiderate arbitrariness of Kenwalch, in this transaction, is what might be expected in a prince whose impatient temper had not been subdued by his sufferings or his conversion, and whose sense of royal power had been enhanced by his recent military success in driving the Britons beyond the river Parret [2]. It will appear that his choice of Wini was less fortunate than his former choice of Agilbert; and though Winchester may have been a more desirable seat for a West-Saxon bishopric than a little town so near the Mercian frontier as Dorchester then was, it cannot be said that the old home of West-Saxon royalty has reason to be proud of its first bishop. Kenwalch had soon enough on his hands to make him forget ecclesiastical complications; for in 661 [3] Wulfhere invaded Wessex, and laid waste the Berkshire country as far as Ashdown; and the death of Cuthred, the lord of that territory, which is assigned to the same year, probably took place in this Mercian border-war. Wulfhere also got possession of a Hampshire district occupied by the Meonwaras [4], and made the important

Conquest of Wight by Wulfhere.

conquest of the Isle of Wight [5], which had belonged to Wessex ever since Cerdic subdued it in 530. Both these acquisitions he handed over to Ethelwalch, king of the South-Saxons [6], who had been baptized in Mercia, 'by the persuasion and in

[1] Sigebrand and Importunus; Mabillon, i. 478. The former was murdered in 664. The latter witnessed a 'privilegium' for a nunnery at Soissons, June 26, 666; ib. 482. Dubois, therefore, must be wrong in dating Agilbert's accession to the see of Paris in 664, immediately on his return to Gaul after the conference of Whitby; Hist. Eccl. Paris. i. 204. We are told that, in 680, he and the bishop of Reims were employed by Ebroin to lure a rival into his power; Fredeg. Chron. continuat. 97. He is said to have died on Oct. 11 (on which day he was venerated), in 680.

[2] Chron. a. 658 on the battle of Pen. See Freeman, i. 385.

[3] See Chron. a. 661, and Florence. Henry of Huntingdon says that Wulfhere, 'traversed his enemy's land with a great host,' and conquered Wight; ii. 35. Ethelwerd, ii. 7, transfers the victory at Ashdown to Kenwalch.

[4] The Meonwaras' district ran from Southampton Water to the South Downs. See Camden, Britan. i. 146: 'Their country is now divided into three hundreds . . . Meansborow, Eastmean, Weastmean.' They were Jutes; Pearson, Hist. Engl. i. 106; Green, p. 385.

[5] Chron. l. c.; Lappenberg, i. 248.

[6] See Bede, iv. 13: 'Erat autem rex,' &c. 'His policy was to establish a counterpoise to the West-Saxon kingdom;' Milner, Hist. Winch. i. 74.

the presence of Wulfhere,' and had then become Wulfhere's godson. His wife Eaba was already a Christian : she came from the Hwiccian country, which consisted chiefly of Worcestershire and Gloucestershire [1] : and its rulers, Eanhere and his brother Eanfrid, Eaba's father, had become 'Christians with their people.' But the king and queen of the South-Saxons could produce no effect on the Paganism of their kingdom [2], which had never been evangelised from Kent or from Wessex, and was detained by marshes and by the 'Andred' forest in a peculiarly barbaric isolation [3]. One man of its race, named Damian, had indeed not only become a Christian, but had succeeded Ithamar as bishop of Rochester in 656 [4] : but, speaking generally of the realm of Sussex, its time, in a Christian sense, was yet to come ; and to come from that distant North-country to which our story now returns.

Finan died, after a ten years' episcopate, in this year 661 ; and was succeeded by Colman [5], also of Irish extraction and Scotic ordination [6], and also a man of simple and austere piety, and of an 'innate prudence' which won Oswy's regard [7]; but not destined to a peaceful and successful episcopate, such as Finan's on the whole had been. A change, in fact, was coming over the mind of the great ecclesiastical province which looked to Lindisfarne as its centre. Deliverance from the terrors and anxieties which Penda's name had aroused, and which passed away at his death, had given the Northumbrian Church a

Colman of Lindis-farne.

---

[1] See above, p. 77, and Freeman, i. 35 ; and comp. Stubbs, Const. Hist. i. 186, and Kemble, i. 149, on the long continuance of a special kingship of the Hwiccas. Cp. Bede, iv. 23.

[2] Bede, iv. 13 : ' Cæterum tota provincia Australium Saxonum divini nominis et fidei erat ignara.'

[3] Rocks and woods had made it 'inexpugnabilis ;' Eddi, Vit. Wilfr. 41 ; Lappenberg, i. 106. In the reign of Alfred, the 'Andread-weald' was more than a hundred miles long, and thirty broad ; Chron. a. 893. The name of Andred is significant ; ' the land without dwellings.' The Weald of Kent and Sussex is the remains of this forest ; Taylor's Words and Places, p. 360. It extended to the border of Romney Marsh. See Green, pp. 11, 40.

[4] Bede, iii. 20. Damian was consecrated by archbishop Deusdedit.

[5] Bede, iii. 25 : ' Defuncto autem Finano,' &c. The name was common among Irishmen of that period ; Lanigan, iii. 2. Several instances occur in Tighernach. A St. Colman was the first bishop of Cloyne.

[6] Bede says that Colman had been appointed (destinatus) from Hy ; iv. 4. But he also indicates that he had come originally from Ireland ; iii. 26.

[7] Bede, iii. 26 : ' Multum namque eumdem,' &c.

CHAP. VI. time of 'refreshing' and of spiritual revival. There was, all around, a stirring of ecclesiastical life, which, however, in its more vigorous growths, was not likely to be content with the somewhat narrow and homely type represented by the Scotic traditions of Lindisfarne. True, there was a strong attachment in many minds to those traditions; and many persons of high as well as of low birth actually went over to settle in Ireland, for the sake of monastic self-devotion, or of theological study[1]. Among these English students were two young men of 'eorl-kin,' Ethelhun and Egbert, the latter of whom, having edified the Irish by his teaching and his example, and persuaded the monks of Hy to adopt the Catholic Easter, died a few years before Bede wrote his work[2]. Colman might think that such an appreciation of Irish learning and sanctity promised well. Moreover, there were in Northumbria monasteries newly founded, in which the rules and practices of Aidan were held sacred and all-sufficient; the six in Bernicia and the six in Deira which commemorated the day of Winwidfield, the house at Gilling, a monument of royal penitence,—another at Tynemouth, where the monks had to contend with the doggedness of half-Christianised rustics who complained that 'old rites had been taken away, and that no one knew how to observe the new ones[3];' Heiu's religious house near Tadcaster, and her earlier foundation at Hartlepool[4]; and, more famous by far, that community which Hilda had planted in 657–8 on an estate of ten hydes or 'families'[5] at Streanæshalch, or, as the Chronicler writes it, 'Streoneshalh[6],' which we

Founda-
tion of
Whitby.

---

[1] See above, p. 166. Northumbrians would probably resort first to Bangor in Ulster, and to the sacred city of Armagh, a third part of which was occupied by 'Saxon' students; McGee, Hist. Irel. i. 49.

[2] Bede, iii. 4, 27; iv. 3; v. 9, 22.

[3] Bede, Vit. Cuthb. 3. See Stevenson's Chron. of Abingdon, vol. ii. p. xxxiv.

[4] See above, p. 170. The cemetery of this ancient monastery was discovered in a field called Cross Close in 1833; Hübner, Inscr. Brit. p. 69.

[5] Bede, iii. 24: 'Quæ post biennium comparata possessione,' &c. Ib. iv. 23: 'Cum ergo aliquot annos . . . contigit eam suscipere etiam construendum,' &c.

[6] Bede's interpretation, 'Sinus Fari,' 'bay of the lighthouse,' iii. 25, has been called 'unaccountable.' See a discussion in 'Notes and Queries' for 1886. A probable suggestion is, 'the stronghold' or 'stone house (halch or healh) of Stréon,' perhaps an abbreviation of some lost proper name.

had better designate by its familiar Danish name of Whitby. CHAP. VI.
In this house, as, according to some, at Kildare [1], and afterwards at Coldingham, Barking, Wimborne, and Repton, and in
some great houses on the Continent [2], the nuns and monks
formed a 'double foundation, a lady abbess being set over
both, the former always taking precedence [3] :' and Hilda,
whom all that knew her called 'Mother,' taught the inmates
'to practise thoroughly all virtues, but especially peace and
love ; so that after the pattern of the primitive Church, no
one there was rich and no one was poor, but all had all things
in common, for nothing seemed to be the property of any
individual [4].' Further north, a little nunnery was established
about this time, on the banks of the Derwent, at a place
which takes its name of Ebchester from the foundress, a half-
sister of Oswald and of Oswy [5], well known to us in Oxford
from the title of one of our churches,—that 'Ebbe' who afterwards founded a double convent at Coldingham, close to the
promontory still called St. Abb's Head. If we look beyond
the present Border into a country then strictly English [6], we
are attracted by a religious house organised on the Lindisfarne model, and situated in a valley which the genius of
Scott has made peerless throughout Britain. On the upper Melrose.
road from Dryburgh to Melrose there is a point where one
looks down on a wooded projection of land, almost encircled by
the Tweed [7]. This is Old Melrose, to the east of its younger
and world-renowned namesake ; but it is memorable as the
site of a humble monastery where, in 661, holy men prayed

---

[1] Haddan's Remains, p. 277 ; Todd's St. Patrick, p. 12. But see Lanigan, i.
410, 414. He thinks that the 'monks' of Kildare were clerics.

[2] At Autun, Brie, Rémiremont, Laudun, Fontevrault, &c. See Mabillon,
Ann. Bened. i. pp. 315, 382, &c. ; Lingard, A.-S. Ch. i. 214 ; Stubbs, Const.
Hist. i. 258. See Theodore's Penitential, b. ii. c. 6. s. 8, disapproving of
any extension of this 'custom.'

[3] Kitchin, Hist. Fr. i. 252.

[4] Bede, iv. 23 (the chapter on St. Hilda).

[5] Bede, iv. 19 ; Vit. Cuthb. 10.

[6] See Freeman, i. 36, 123, on Lothian.

[7] 'Quod Tuidi fluminis circumflexu maxima ex parte clauditur ;' Bede, v. 12.
Scott's description of the western site in ' The Eve of St. John,'
     ' Where fair Tweed flows round holy Melrose,'
might apply still better to the eastern.

CHAP. VI. and taught, and one young monk was unconsciously preparing for a life which made him the great popular saint of Northern England. Eata, of whom we shall hear much, was abbot : he had been one of those twelve boys whom Aidan, in the early days of his episcopate, had received from their parents to be 'instructed in Christ [1],' and through life he was true to his old training, being, as Bede describes him, 'the gentlest and simplest man in the world [2].' Under him, acting as 'præpositus' or prior, was Boisil, whom Bede calls 'a priest of great virtues and of a prophetic spirit,' and whose name is

Cuthbert. still perpetuated in the little town of St. Boswell's. About ten years before, in the beginning of the winter of 651 [3], there had come to Melrose a robust youth [4], with a servant who held his horse and spear [5] when he had dismounted in order to pray in the church. His name was Cuthbert. From his eighth year he had lived in the house of a widow named Kenspid, whom he used to call 'mother [6].' As a younger boy, he had been remarkable for high spirits, and had excelled in all bodily exercises [7] : the solitary hours spent in tending sheep, on the hills beside the Leader, had opened his mind to

---

[1] Bede, iii. 26. Above, p. 146.

[2] Bede, iv. 27.

[3] Bede, Vit. Cuthb. 5. This 'Life' was compiled with special care, and before publication submitted to friends of St. Cuthbert, and finally read and examined for two days by the Lindisfarne community, under bishop Eadfrid. The Anon. Vit. Cuthb. in Bede's Works, vi. 357 ff., was also written under Eadfrid. The legend of his Irish birth, as the son of an Irish king's daughter, is Irish, and is confuted by Bede's words in the prologue to his poem 'De miraculis S. Cuthberti' (Works, i. 3) describing him as born in Britain.

[4] 'Adolescens,' Bede, V. C. 4 ; 'robustus corpore,' 6 ; 'of full age,' Vit. An.

[5] Bede, V. C. 6. The Anon. Vit. says he had once served 'in castris.'

[6] She was alive when the Anon. Vit. was written.

[7] 'He took pleasure in jokes and noisiness . . . delighted to share in the sports of other boys . . . Sometimes, when the rest were tired out, he, unwearied, would ask in the joyous tone of a conqueror, whether any others had a mind to contend further with him.' He excelled his equals in age, and even some of his seniors, in leaping, running, wrestling, 'seu quolibet alio membrorum sinuamine.' Yet even in those days, a little boy of about three once burst out crying, and, calling Cuthbert 'bishop,' told him that he ought not to play among children. Cuthbert, as 'bonæ indolis puer,' was struck with this strange warning, and, caressing the child affectionately, went home, and became from that day 'steadier, animoque adolescentior.' Bede, V. C. 1. (The boys, according to the Anon. Vit., were playing at 'standing on their heads.') On his lameness and its cure, see Bede, V. C. 2.

serious thought; and a dream, which he took to be a vision, CHAP. VI, occurring on the night of Aidan's death, had determined him to enter a monastery[1]. The fame of Boisil drew him to Melrose : and Boisil, standing at the gate as he came near, said to others who were present, ' Behold a servant of the Lord[2] !' He soon surpassed all the brethren in studies, vigils, prayers, still more in manual work: only, we are told, he ' could not endure so much abstinence from food,' lest the strength required for labour should be diminished[3]. When Eata received from Alchfrid, who had succeeded the traitor Ethelwald as sub-king of Deira, an estate of thirty or forty hydes at Ripon, for the erection of a monastery, Cuthbert was among the brethren sent to form the new settlement, and appointed to act as hospitaller[4] ; but at the time of Colman's arrival the monks had just given up their abode, rather than accept, at Alchfrid's bidding, the continental Easter rule and other Roman usages[5] : and Cuthbert was again at Melrose, ' attending to the precepts and the example of Boisil[6].'

And this brings us to the name of him who concentrated Wilfrid. and intensified, by his energy and influence, the preference for ' Catholic' over ' Scotic' usages,—to the splendid name of Wilfrid. Born in 634[7],—that is, in the ' year of apostasy,' —the son of a Northumbrian thane, he began, at thirteen or fourteen[8], ' to think of forsaking his paternal fields, and to

---

[1] Bede, Vit. Cuthb. 4; Sim. Hist. Dun. Eccl. i. 3, and Auct. Hist. de S. Cuthb. 2. It was August 31, 651. He thought he saw angels carrying a holy soul into heaven ' as in a globe of fire ;' Anon. Vit. ' Next morning he gave over the sheep to their owners;' Sim. Dun. Eccl. i. 3.

[2] Bede, Vit. Cuthb. 6.

[3] Ib. : ' Non autem tantam escarum valebat subire continentiam.'

[4] Ib. 7. On monastic hospitality see Reeves's Adamnan, p. 345.

[5] Bede, iii. 25; and v. 19, ' optione data maluerunt loco cedere.' Vit. Cuthb. 8: ' Eata cum Cuthberto . . . domum repulsus est.' The Anon. Vit. says that Cuthbert received the Roman tonsure at Ripon.

[6] Vit. Cuthb. 8; comp. H. E. iv. 27, ' quod ipsum etiam Boisil,' &c.

[7] Florence, a. 634 : ' Sanctus Wilfridus nascitur.'

[8] Eddius, Vit. Wilfr. 2 : ' In his fourteenth year, in corde suo cogitabat,' &c. So Bede says, v. 19. Fridegod and Eadmer say he had passed his fourteenth year. Eddi, or Hædde, called Stephen, was his attendant in after years. Fridegod wrote a metrical Life of him by desire of arch-bishop Odo; Eadmer, a prose Life in St. Anselm's time. See Act. SS. Bened. sæc. iii. I. 169 ff. Fridegod's ' euphuism' of style is portentous, and

seek for heavenly gifts.' In spite of a stepmother's un-
kindness, he was well equipped with all that could enable
him to make a good appearance at the court of Oswy[1], and
his father bade him God-speed. He stood in the presence
of Queen Eanfled,—a handsome boy of quick intellect and
graceful bearing,—introduced to her by nobles on whom he
had waited at his father's table; and besought her to promote
his desire of 'serving God,'—the phrase then used, with an
unhappy restriction of meaning, for monastic life[2]. One of
the king's 'companions[3],' seized with paralysis, was preparing
to become a monk at Lindisfarne: and under his care, and as
his attendant, Wilfrid entered that monastery, where, although
he did not receive the Scotic tonsure[4], he acquired all that he
could learn of the Scotic discipline, learned by heart the
Psalter in Jerome's more correct or 'Gallican recension[5],' and
was 'loved by the other boys as a brother, by the seniors,' and
doubtless by Aidan, 'as a son[6].' Some three years afterwards,
having a strong desire to visit Rome, to gain the blessing
of the successor of St. Peter, and to study monastic rules
of a better type than the Scotic[7], Wilfrid, by his father's
advice, and with the frank assent of the bishop and monks of
Lindisfarne[8], obtained a letter of commendation from Eanfled

---

often unintelligible. Eadmer alludes to him, and mentions Bede, but does not
mention Eddi; see Historians of Ch. of York, i, 163.

[1] See Turner, Angl.-Sax. iii. 16.

[2] See above, p. 178, and comp. Bede, Hist. Abb. 1, 15, &c.

[3] A gesith, or comes, named Cudda. Eddius calls him Wilfrid's 'dominus.'

[4] 'Adhuc laicus capite,' Edd. 2.

[5] 'Citissime,' says Bede. 'Secundum Hieronymi emendationem,' Edd. 3.
This translation was made at Bethlehem, from the Septuagint Version according
to the 'Hexaplar' text, in 389. It became current in Gaul and elsewhere
before it was accepted in Italy. The 'Roman Psalter' was Jerome's earlier
and cursory revision of the old Italic version, made in 383. It was used at
Canterbury after the 'Gallic Psalter' was received in other English churches;
and is still in use in St. Peter's at Rome. See Waterland on Ath. Creed, c. 4;
Vallarsi, Vit. Hieron. c. 20. Jerome's version from the Hebrew was never in
public use, and has been very unfortunately neglected. Wilfrid afterwards,
at Canterbury, learned the 'Roman' Psalter by heart.

[6] Edd. 2.

[7] Bede says nothing of his desire for the Pope's blessing. Nor are we told
how, at Lindisfarne, he learned to think that there were better rules abroad.

[8] Bede, v. 19: 'Quod cum fratribus,' &c. This speaks well for Finan's
generosity, if the lad's somewhat premature discontent with Lindisfarne customs

to her cousin King Erconbert, who was just the man to
appreciate the brilliant gifts, the intent studiousness, and the
religious fervour of the young Northumbrian. After about
a year's delay, which Wilfrid employed in observing the
Church usages of Canterbury, Erconbert found a suitable Benedict
fellow-traveller for him in one whose name is as closely Biscop.
bound up as Wilfrid's with Northumbrian Church history,
and who was to make himself a name as an ecclesiastical
traveller[1], a founder of monasteries, and a promoter of religious
art. This was Benedict Biscop, also called, as a patronymic,
'Baducing[2],' a nobly-born Northumbrian of twenty-five, who
had given up his rank as a 'king's thane,' and the goodly
estate which he had received from Oswy, in order, says Bede,
'to take service under the true King.' The two companions
set out for Rome towards the end of 653, soon after the death
of archbishop Honorius: and Eddi gives us a brilliant picture
of the youth of nineteen, 'pleasant in address to all, sagacious
in mind, strong in body, swift of foot, ready for every good
work, with a face that in its unclouded cheerfulness betokened
a blessed mind[3].' Such was Wilfrid when he reached Lyons,
and was introduced to 'Dalfinus,' as both our writers call its
archbishop, confusing the prelate Aunemund with his brother
Dalfinus, count of Lyons[4]. Benedict, impatient to be at
Rome, left Wilfrid at Lyons, where he spent some little time
with the archbishop, who was 'charmed with his beautiful
countenance, his prudence in speech, his quickness in action,
his steadiness and maturity of thought[5],' loaded him with

were made known to him: and Wilfrid, at seventeen or eighteen, was not
likely to be too modest in such a matter.

[1] He made six visits to Rome,—five of them being directly from Britain,—
in 653, 665, 667, 671, 678, 684. See Dict. Chr. Biogr. i. 308.

[2] Edd. 3 ; Fridegod, 96. See Moberly's Bede, p. 370. For Benedict Biscop,
see Bede, iv. 18, v. 19 ; Hist. Abb. 1 (*the* passage). See Alb. Butler, Jan. 12.
We find ' Beda ' and ' Biscop ' ranking sixth and seventh from Woden in the
genealogy of the kings of the Lindisfari ; Mon. H. Brit. p. 431. Moberly
suggests that Beda is equivalent to Badoc ; Introd. p. xii.

[3] Edd. 3, 4 : ' . . tristia ora nunquam contraxit.' The archbishop saw ' in
facie serena quod benedicta mente gerebat ' (al. benedictam mentem).

[4] See Mabillon, Ann. Bened. i. 425, 443 : ' Nullus in vetustis Lugdunensium
antistitum indicibus Dalfino locus est.' Aunemund had signed a royal diploma
for the immunity of the abbey of St. Denis from episcopal control in 653.

[5] Bede, v. 19.

CHAP. VI. presents, and offered, if he would remain, to give him the government of a district and the hand of his niece[1], and to treat him always as an adopted son. Wilfrid appears to have accepted the adoption[2], but he gratefully declined the other proposals, urging the purpose for which he had left his native land. The prelate could not but acquiesce, and sent him on to Rome with a guide and all necessaries, only entreating that he would 'remember to travel home by way of Lyons.' Wilfrid reached Rome probably in the spring of 654, and spent several months in daily visits to the sacred places[3], and in study of the Gospels, and of the received Paschal calculations, and of other Church rules which he could not have learned in Britain, under the tuition of the archdeacon Boniface[4], who, before his departure, presented him to the newly-elected Pope Eugenius I. Wilfrid, in his later career, must often have remembered how the pontiff 'laid his hand on his head, and blessed him with a prayer[5].' Returning, with a store of relics, to Lyons, he stayed three years with his kind host the archbishop, studied under learned ecclesiastics, and received the crown-like Roman tonsure[6]. The prelate's wish to make him his heir was defeated in the September of 658 by his own tragical death[7], which Eddi, and Bede simply following him, lay at the door of Queen Bathildis, properly Baldechildis, the widow of

---

[1] That is, the daughter of Count Dalfinus.

[2] Eddi calls the archbishop 'his father,' 5; so Fridegod, 168. The kings Cadwalla and Osred afterwards became Wilfrid's adopted sons; Eddi, 42, 59.

[3] Eddi says that he entered an oratory of St. Andrew, and invoked the Apostle. So Eadmer, 6; and Rich. of Hexham, X Script. 290, says that he prayed to be set free 'de ingenii sui tarditate et linguae suae rusticitate.'

[4] For the discovery of a leaden 'bulla,' with Boniface's name on it, at Whitby, see Raine, Historians of Ch. of York, i. 8.

[5] Eddi, 5. Eugenius, whom Hefele calls intelligent and orthodox, was elected under imperial pressure, while Pope St. Martin was still alive in exile, Sept. 8, 654; but 'St. Martin consented' afterwards 'to this election' (L'Art de Vérifier, &c. iii. 284; Hefele, Hist. Councils, b. xvi. c. 1. s. 309). Eugenius survived Martin, dying in June, 657.

[6] 'Crines, summo de vertice passos . . . . recidit;' Frideg. 177.

[7] Mabillon, in Ann. Bened. i. 443, quotes a statement that Count Dalfinus was executed on a false charge of treason brought against him by the nobles, and Aunemund was afterwards arrested by three 'duces' sent from the palace, who refused him a hearing and put him to death. This he thinks not improbable. Aunemund was honoured by his church on Sept. 29.

Chlodwig or Clovis II. Here is a difficulty; for while Eddi
compares her to Jezebel[1], the Church has canonised her for
recorded acts of piety, charity and humility[2]: and her
character has suggested that the execution of the archbishop
on a charge of disaffection may have been ordered by Ebroin,
at the beginning of his career as Mayor of the Palace for her
infant son Chlotair III.[3] Wilfrid attended his benefactor
to the scene of death, and even stripped off his cloak in order
to suffer with him. 'Who is that fair youth?' asked the royal
officers charged with the execution. 'A foreigner,' they were
told, 'from the Angles in Britain:' whereupon they commanded their men to spare his life. Wilfrid then returned
to Northumbria, apparently at the end of 658. He soon
became intimate with Alchfrid, who had learned from his
friend Kenwalch of Wessex[4] 'to love and follow the Catholic
Church-rules[5].' He treated Wilfrid with profound respect[6],
and asked him, 'for God's sake and St. Peter's,' to stay with
him in Deira. They became, we are told, as closely united

[1] 'Malevola regina ... sicut ... Jezebel;' Edd. 6. He adds that nine
bishops were slaughtered. So Fridegod, who compares her to an infernal
caldron, 186.

[2] See the Paris Breviary, Jan. 30. During her husband's life, she 'commended to him the poor and the churches;' while regent, she 'annulled
simoniacal ordinations,' forbade the selling of Christians as slaves, ransomed
many at her own cost, restored monastic discipline; and, after she retired
to the nunnery which she had virtually refounded at Chelles, she there
exhibited great humility and tenderness. See Alb. Butler, Jan. 30; Mabillon,
i. 438. It is interesting to remember that she herself came to Gaul as a
'Saxon' slave-girl from Britain, probably from Wessex. She was said to
be nobly born.

[3] See Mabillon, Ann. Bened. i. 443. He traces the accusation made by
Eddi to his ignorance, as a 'foreigner' who was not then a companion of
Wilfrid. Chlodwig died, æt. 25, Sept. 5, 656. Mabillon, i. 438, infers from
certain documents that Ebroin became mayor of the palace immediately
afterwards, if not a little before. Others date his accession to office, on the
death of his predecessor Erchinoald, as late as 659 (L'Art de Vérifier, v. 411);
which would overthrow Mabillon's theory. But the Continuator of Fredegarius
makes the deaths of the king and Erchinoald take place 'eodem tempore;'
c. 92. Erchinoald himself was incapable of any cruelty to bishops; Fredegar.
84.

[4] Edd. 7.

[5] Bede, v. 19: 'At ille Brittaniam veniens,' &c.

[6] The enthusiastic Eddi says that he prostrated himself before Wilfrid
and asked a blessing from him, for he seemed to him to speak like an angel
of God; 7.

as David and Jonathan: and Alchfrid gave Wilfrid land for building a monastery at Stamford near York, and not long afterwards put him in possession of the house at Ripon[1], lately vacated by the monks of Melrose. This may be dated in the same year, 661, in which Colman succeeded Finan. Thus began Wilfrid's connection with a place which for so many years he loved better than any other, and within which at last he found a grave.

His life at Ripon was happy. His charities endeared him to the poor, whose needs, at all times, moved his generous heart. He won the respect and affection of all classes. Men spoke of the abbot of Ripon as humble and tranquil, occupied in devotion and in almsgiving, benignant, sober, modest, merciful. His discourses were 'clear and lucid[2].' Yet he was not yet a presbyter. He received priest's orders[3] at Alchfrid's request, from Agilbert the ex-bishop of Dorchester, who was then visiting Northumbria, and who scrupled not to ordain in the diocese of Lindisfarne without consulting Colman, because, although he had long studied under Irish Church-teachers, he practically regarded the Scotic hierarchy as contumacious, or even schismatical.

This, at least, was Wilfrid's view, as we may infer from his subsequent conduct. In fact, he looked down on the old Northumbrian Churchmanship, and on that Northumbrian episcopate which had fostered his boyish aspirations, and given him the best training that it could, as if the latter had no claim on his reverence, or even on his forbearance, and as if the former needed a thoroughgoing renovation. The Scotic error on the Paschal question did but represent, and did not exhaust, the defects of Scotic Christianity. It seemed to him generally a poor, coarse, unsightly plant, such as might be expected to grow up in a corner, apart from all genial and expansive influences. It was his mission to educate his native

---

[1] Eddi, 8 ; Bede, v. 19.   [2] Eddi, 9.

[3] Fridegod's phrase, 'ordinis ... in honore secundi,' 241, shows that the theory which made the presbyterate the highest order was not dominant in the English Church in the tenth century, although it appears in Ælfric's Canons. Egbert makes the episcopate the highest of the seven 'gradus,' omitting that of acolyths, Pontif. p. 11.

Church,—to refine, enrich, develope it, by contact with the CHAP. VI. culture and the stateliness of Canterbury, of Lyons,—above all, of majestic Rome. He was right on the general merits of that question which seems to have occupied so inordinate a share of his thoughts; and right also, beyond doubt, in thinking that Scotic ways were too rude and too narrow to be permanently *the* ways for an English Church, with its continental associations and its great prospects of future self-extension. He had a real work to do for his countrymen: but in his way of rushing into it, and of going through with it, he exhibited the two faults of imperiousness and egoism. It seems as if his stay in Rome had infected him with the Roman love of domination: and with all his high qualities and many virtues was blended a self-complacent consciousness not only of abilities and force of character, but of exertions and sacrifices made for religion or the Church.

So stood matters in Northumbria when the disputes between the Scotic and anti-Scotic parties came inevitably to a head, in the early weeks of 664. Colman had the advantage, as he would consider it, of the presence of Bishop Cedd, then on a visit to Lastingham: and Hilda, already looked up to as a wise woman who could give 'good rede' to princes as to common folk[1], would be but the most prominent of several heads of convents who were prepared to stand by the customs of Lindisfarne. King Oswy inclined to the same side: his queen, as we know, supported the other, which was represented by Alchfrid, Romanus, James the Deacon, Bishop Agilbert and his priest Agatho,—above all, by Abbot Wilfrid. Ronan, the vehement Irish opponent of Irish traditions in Finan's time, seems to have been absent; but Colman[2] must have grieved to see another Irishman of higher dignity and more impressive character included in the same ranks. This was Tuda, who had been consecrated a bishop in South Ireland, and 'according to the custom' which now obtained in those parts, conformed to the 'Catholic' usages. He had lately come into Northumbria, and had been helpful

---

[1] Bede, iv. 23: 'Tantæ autem erat ipsa prudentiæ,' &c.

[2] One specimen of Eddi's heedlessness is his calling Colman '*metropolitan* bishop of the city of *York*;' Vit. Wilf. 10.

CHAP. VI. in setting forth Christianity, as Bede says emphatically, 'both by word and work[1].' To end the strife, a regular conference was arranged,—Bede calls it a 'synod,' but it was a gathering of 'all the ranks in the Church system,' as Eddi phrases it[2].

Conference of Whitby. The place chosen was Hilda's new monastery, elevated on that proud sea-ward height which is now crowned by the ruined church of a monastery founded two centuries after her minster had been laid desolate. The time was in the first half of 664; most likely in Lent, for the promoters might wish to secure uniformity of observance in regard to the coming Easter, which, by Catholic rules, fell on April 21. Moreover, some time is required for events which happened between the conference and the autumn.

King Oswy opened the proceedings by urging the benefits of uniformity of custom among those who were united in faith, and stating tersely the question for discussion: Of the two different traditions, which was the truer? He called on Colman to describe his usage and its origin.

Paschal Question. Before Colman answers, let us remember that the Paschal question, as it then stood, was twofold. (1) How many years must elapse before the Paschal full moon, and Easter Day as the Sunday after it, will recur on the same day? How can we settle for any given year the day on which that moon should fall, and therefore the right day of Easter[3]? This question was answered by the adoption of 'cycles:' and the Scotic and British Churches retained an old cycle of eighty-four years which Rome had used, but which she had cast off[4], adopting, finally, that of Dionysius Exiguus[5], according to which the lunar cycle for nineteen years[6], multiplied by the

---

[1] Bede, iii. 26: 'Venerat autem,' &c.

[2] Eddi, 10. See the 'Synodus Pharensis' in Mansi, xi. 67. Kemble treats it as a Witenagemot, ii. 243. It was a *concilium mixtum.*

[3] See Moberly's Bede, p. 195; Hefele, Councils, E. Tr. i. p. 326.

[4] Prideaux, ii. 255, 256; Dict. Chr. Ant. i. 592, 594; above, p. 81.

[5] See Bede, v. 21.

[6] In the nineteen years' cycle, the number of any given year was called the Golden Number, because marked with letters of gold in ancient calendars. At the end of the nineteen years 'the various aspects of the moon are within an hour the same as they were on the same days of the month nineteen years before;' Nicolas, Chron. of Hist. p. 24.

solar cycle for twenty-eight years[1], showed on what day in each year, during successive periods of five hundred and thirty-two years, the Paschal full moon would fall, and therefore what day would be Easter Sunday. (2) On what day of the Paschal month, or as it was expressed, 'on which moon,' being a Sunday (for on that point all were agreed), may Easter be kept? That is, if the Sunday after the full moon should be 'the fourteenth moon,' may that be Easter Sunday, or must Easter in that case be on the Sunday following, the twenty-first, so that 'the fifteenth moon' must be treated as the first possible day for Easter? Here, as we have seen, lay the point which called out the strongest feeling. The Celtic Churches included 'the fourteenth moon' within the number of possible Easter Sundays: the other Churches insisted on including it, urging the authority of the Nicene Council on the duty of keeping clear of the Jewish day[2]. In other words, Easter Sunday among the Scots might fall on any 'moon' from the fourteenth to the twentieth inclusive: at Rome, or in Gallic Churches, or at Canterbury or Dunwich, it might fall on any moon from the fifteenth to the twenty-first but not earlier; and to keep this rule was to observe the 'Catholic Easter.'

Now let us hear Colman, to whom Eddi gives credit for intrepidity. 'My usage is that which I learned from the elders who sent me hither, and which, we read[3], is traced up to St. John. I dare not change it, and I have no mind to change it. We hold it as an inspired tradition that the

---

[1] At the expiration of the twenty-eight years 'the days of the months return again to the same days of the week .... and the same order of leap-years and of Dominical letters returns' (i.e. there being seven letters, A–G, used to mark the seven days of the week, the first day of the year being reckoned as A, —if the year begins on Sunday, then A is the Sunday letter,—if on Monday, G, &c.). 'The cycles of the sun and moon, multiplied together, form a third, which is called the Paschal Cycle;' Nicolas, l. c.

[2] Constantine's letter after the Council shows that the Council had decided that Easter should never be kept at the time at which the Jews were keeping their Passover: therefore, if the fourteenth should fall on a Sunday, Easter was not to be celebrated on that Sunday, but a week later; Hefele, Councils, i. 325, E. Tr.; above, p. 81.

[3] 'Legitur,' Bede. Fridegod (whose metrical version of the conference is incredibly abject in point of taste) makes Colman claim Polycarp, 256.

CHAP. VI. fourteenth moon, being Sunday, is to be kept as Easter Day. Let the other side state their opinion.' Cedd interpreted his speech into Saxon ; and Oswy then called on Agilbert, who desired that his 'disciple' Wilfrid might state their case on his behalf. 'He can better explain in the English tongue what we hold than I can by an interpreter,' meaning by Cedd, who acted 'as a very watchful interpreter for both parties[1].'

Thereupon Oswy ordered Wilfrid to speak ; and the young abbot desired nothing better. He rose, confident in his cause, and in his power to do it justice. He began by dilating on the wide prevalence of the Catholic Easter, which he had found in Gaul, in Italy, and at Rome, where Peter and Paul had taught and suffered ; and which he had ascertained to be observed in Africa, Asia, Egypt, Greece,—in fact throughout Christendom[2], 'save only'—and here flashed out his scornful intolerance for what, to him, was mere local perversity— 'save only among these persons'—pointing to the bishop of Lindisfarne and his clergy—'and their partners in obstinacy, the Picts and Britons ; who, belonging to some parts only of two remote islands[3], are making these foolish efforts to fight against the whole world.'

If Bede gives the sense of Wilfrid's speech, his last words had been rather insulting than conciliatory : and Colman is represented as answering with quiet dignity, though with very inaccurate knowledge, 'I wonder that you should call us foolish for following the rule of the Apostle who reclined on the Lord's breast[4].'

Wilfrid's answer was a combination of good sense, unhistoric assumptions, and a decisive home-thrust. 'Granting for a

---

[1] 'Interpres in eo concilio vigilantissimus ;' Bede, iii. 25.

[2] Cummian similarly argues, How can we say, 'Roma errat, Hierosolyma errat, Alexandria errat, Antiochia errat' (he refers to these again as 'Apostolic Sees,' and ignores Constantinople), 'totus mundus errat,—soli tantum Scoti et Britones rectum sapiunt ?' Usher, Sylloge, p. 21.

[3] 'Britonum Scotorumque particula, qui sunt pæne extremi,' &c. ; Cummian, l. c.

[4] Comp. the Pseudo-Anatolius, Can. Pasch. 10 (Galland. iii. 548): 'The bishops of Asia received their rule from a teacher not to be gainsaid, John . . . who lay on the Lord's breast.'

moment,' he said in effect, 'that your custom does come from <small>CHAP. VI.</small> St. John; it was far from being folly on his part to adhere to Mosaic observances, while St. Paul himself found it necessary to avoid giving scandal to Jewish Christians [1]. Thus it was that John began his Paschal celebration on the evening of the fourteenth of Nisan, whether that was a Saturday evening or no. Peter, however, acted differently. Taking the Lord's Day as his fixed point, on account of the Resurrection, he agreed with John in not celebrating the Lord's Pasch before the rising of the fourteenth moon at evening, and if that were on a Saturday, would then begin his Easter, as we do now [2]: but if the Lord's Day were to fall not on the morrow of the fourteenth moon, but on the sixteenth or seventeenth, or any other day up to the twenty-first, he waited for that day.' Wilfrid spoke, evidently with the Roman archdeacon's lessons full in his mind, and with a confidence as to St. Peter's Paschal practice which showed that he could be as credulous on one side as his opponents on the other;—but he was on stronger ground when he pointed out that the Scotic practice could appeal to neither Apostle for its authority. It differed from the old Ephesine or Quartodeciman tradition, because it restricted the Paschal festival to the Lord's Day [3]. It differed from the Petrine or Roman usage, and even in principle from the Mosaic rules, because it allowed the thirteenth moon to be Easter Eve, and the morning of the fourteenth to be Easter Sunday morning: whereas Easter Eve ought not to be earlier than the fourteenth evening [4], nor Easter Sunday morning than the

[1] Bede makes Wilfrid cite St. Paul's conduct in circumcising Timothy, sacrificing in the Temple, and shaving his head at Corinth. On this last point, Wilfrid departs from the Vulgate of Acts xviii. 18.

[2] Meaning that such a Saturday evening would correspond to Holy Saturday, as observed by the Church's commencement of Easter rites on that vigil.

[3] As Bede says of Aidan, the Scots and Britons had neither the right to claim St. John, nor the discredit of adhering to 'Quartodecimanism.' St. John, and the Quartodecimans after him, took no account of the first day of the week; but the Celtic Churches would not celebrate Pasch on any other day.

[4] 'Ita ut tertia decima luna ad vesperam sæpius Pascha incipiatis, cujus neque Lex ullam fecit mentionem, neque auctor et dator Evangelii Dominus in ea, sed in quarta decima *vel* vetus pascha manducavit ad vesperam, *vel* Novi Testamenti sacramenta . . . . tradidit.'

CHAP. VI. morning of the fifteenth. The Scots, he urged, began their reckoning too early, and ended it a day too early: they let in, at the outset, the thirteenth moon; they left out, at the close, the twenty-first [1]. They agreed,—said Wilfrid, in a pithy summary of his case,—neither with John nor Peter, neither with Law nor Gospel. Colman replied by appealing to 'Anatolius' Paschal canon [2],' in which it was ruled that the Paschal limits should be 'the fourteenth and twentieth moons:' so that a 'fourteenth moon,' if a Sunday, might be Easter Sunday, and a 'twenty-first moon' might not. He also asked whether it were credible that Columba and his successors, men eminent for sanctity and for miracles, had been allowed to go wrong in such a matter. To this Wilfrid replied, 'Anatolius was indeed a holy and learned man; but why quote him, if you do not really follow him? He framed the cycle of nineteen years: the whole Church keeps to it, except *you!* And as to the fourteenth and twentieth moons, you do not observe that he used the Egyptian reckoning, and treated the fourteenth moon at evening as really the fifteenth just begun [3]: and if he assigned the twentieth as an Easter

[1] 'Item lunam vicesimam primam, quam Lex maxime celebrandam commendavit, a celebratione vestri Paschæ funditus eliminatis,' &c. Cp. v. 21.

[2] See the canon, erroneously (Dict. Chr. Ant. art. 'Easter') said to be a Latin version of that of Anatolius, in Galland. Bibl. iii. 545 ff. It contains, says Bucherius, several 'paradoxes' or errors, e.g. 'Paschæ Dominicam luna xiv. nullo scrupulo indicit, in quo cum Quartadecimanis . . . facit, etsi id illi perpetuum non sit:' in its nineteen years, Easter falls thrice on the 'fourteenth moon,' on April 1, March 29, April 4. 'Præterea, eamdem Paschatis Dominicam a xiii. luna saltem exeunte in xx. *duntaxat* diffundit: tametsi Scriptura et cum ea Alexandrini . . . in xxi. aperte propagent,' &c.; ib. 551. As to the necessity of keeping Easter always on a Sunday, this canon is emphatic; 'Better to put off Easter, on account of the Lord's Day, until the twentieth moon, than to keep it before the Lord's Day on account of the fourteenth;' c. 11. It distinctly denies that Easter can be kept so late as the 'twenty-first moon,' c. 8, i.e. later than a day of which the evening only is assigned to the twenty-first. Petavius (Animadv. in Epiphan. p. 193) censures Ruffinus for so abbreviating a sentence of Anatolius' Greek (preserved by Euseb.) as to make him allow Easter to be kept in the 'beginning of the first month,' i.e. on the fourteenth moon; and traces the Celtic error to this mistranslation.

[3] 'Ille sic in Pascha Dominico,' &c. Wilfrid means, 'In principle Anatolius was with us; an evening which you would reckon as the fourteenth he would include in the first hours of the fifteenth, and so on.' In the 'Anatolian' canon, c. 8, we find, 'Omnis dies in lunæ computatione, non eodem numero quo mane initiatur, ad vesperam finitur: quia dies quæ mane in luna . . . xiii. annu-

Sunday, he did so as considering that its evening began the chap. vi. twenty-first. You do not apprehend this peculiarity of reckoning: that is the reason why you sometimes keep your Easter even on the thirteenth moon, before the full moon. As for Columba and his successors, and the signs which, according to you, attested their holiness—I will *not* quote the text, "Many shall say to Me in that day," &c., for I doubt not that they were beloved by Him whom they served with pious intention, although with rustic simplicity. If they kept Easter wrongly, it was because they knew no better; therefore they took little harm by it [1]. If a "Catholic reckoner" had shown them the right way, I feel sure that they would have taken it; for in other matters they lived up to their knowledge. But you have not the excuse of ignorance in your resistance to the decrees made, under Scriptural warrant [2], by the Apostolic See,—I might say by the Universal Church, whose authority must needs outweigh that of a few men, however holy, in a corner of a distant island. If your Columba—let me say *ours* too, if he was Christ's—was a saint and a wonder-worker, ought he to be preferred to the blessed chief of Apostles?'—and here, with what a look and in what a tone we can well imagine, Wilfrid thundered out the text, 'Thou art Peter,' and left its echoes undisturbed by further speech.

His argument had been, on the whole, well adapted to the audience. True, he had treated the bishop of the Northumbrian Church with a dictatorial roughness which must

---

meratur, eadem ad vesperum xiv. invenitur.' Petavius says that Wilfrid ascribes to Anatolius 'opinionem quam ne somniavit quidem unquam,' as if Anatolius would have called that day only 'the fourteenth' which had a full moon before its sunset,—otherwise he would call it the thirteenth; whereas the Irish called *that* the fourteenth and kept it as Paschal, which was followed by a full moon in the ensuing night. 'The spurious canon of Anatolius, given in Bucherius, was perhaps designed to support the cause of the British Christians;' Dict. Chr. Ant. art. 'Easter.'

[1] 'Our elders,' says Cummian, 'simply and faithfully observed quod optimum in diebus suis esse noverunt;' Usher, Sylloge, p. 19.

[2] 'Wilfrid here assumes grounds which he had no claim to. . . If the Paschal day were to be followed by what we read in the Gospel, it would follow that Easter could never be celebrated earlier than on the sixteenth day, as had been the case at Rome;' Lanigan, iii. 66. What a contrast between Wilfrid's dogmatism and the language of Socrates (v. 22)!

have been highly offensive, especially to those Lindisfarne ecclesiastics who remembered him as a precocious boy, and might think that, as such, he had been but too kindly treated. True also, he had spoken of the glorious saint of Hy with a superb indulgence which could hardly be less irritating [1]. True, again, that he had, in good faith, said far more than could be verified as to St. Peter's own observance, and had spoken as if Rome's existing Paschal system had been her tradition from the first,—which 'was a great mistake [2],' for she had altered her cycle, and had also altered her Paschal limits, which once began with the 'sixteenth' of the moon [3]. But there was no one present who could expose the weak points of his pleading: it had one strong point,—the utter inability of the Scotic Church to prove itself heir to the Ephesine tradition [4]; and the appeal to the majesty of the first Apostle was more impressive to King Oswy than any array of proofs and authorities. He asked Colman whether those words were really spoken by Christ to St. Peter? 'Certainly.' 'Did He ever give the like power to your Columba?' 'Never.' 'You both agree, then, that this was said principally to Peter, and that to him our Lord gave the keys of the kingdom of heaven?' 'Yes,' they both said, 'assuredly.' Then said the king, with a quiet smile [5], but with an underlying seriousness which it is somewhat difficult for us to appreciate, with our knowledge of the dimensions of the controversy, 'And I say to you both, that this is that doorkeeper whom I do not choose to gainsay; but as far as I know and am able, I desire in all things to obey his rulings, lest haply when I come to the doors of the kingdom, I may find none to unbar them, if *he* is adverse to me who is proved to hold the keys.'

Close of the conference. Such was the close of the Whitby conference. Bede intimates that 'there was also no small debate on the question

---

[1] 'Throughout his life he was far too careless of the opinions and feelings of others.' Raine, Historians of Ch. of York, i. p. xxviii.

[2] Lanigan, iii. 64.

[3] Ib. ii. 375, 384, 390.

[4] Ib. ii. 386 : 'On this point Wilfrid had greatly the advantage of Colman.'

[5] Eddi, 10. Oswy's question to Colman must be understood to mean, 'Do you admit that Wilfrid has quoted correctly?'

of the tonsure [1];' but he has spared us its details. Enough
that on the points of difference between the Scotic and non-
Scotic systems, the king and the majority of the assembly
pronounced against the former. Cedd himself, who had
listened to both sides with so much attention, abandoned the Colman's
usages of Lindisfarne. To Colman the mortification must needs departure.
have been intense. He himself had no thought of adopting
the foreign customs: he would be true to Hy and to North
Ireland. His Irish monks stood by him, and so did some
thirty Northumbrians who had become members of the same
community [2]. The bishop announced his intention of going
to consult with his own people in Ireland as to his future
course. This would be well understood to be an abdication.
But he made a parting request to Oswy [3], which touchingly
indicates the generosity and tenderness of his nature. There
were some brethren in his monastery who had no mind to
leave their homes for his sake, or for the sake of old customs.
Be it so,—let them remain ; but would the king set over
them, as abbot, a Lindisfarne man who had been among
bishop Aidan's first pupils, and was now abbot of Melrose,—
Eata ? He would be to the remnant of the Lindisfarne monks
a gentle and congenial superior. Oswy readily granted this
request: and Eata became abbot of Lindisfarne, without
resigning the charge of Melrose [4]. Colman quitted the Holy
Island with his little company, and took with him some of
the bones of Aidan, ordering the rest to be buried in the
sacristy [5]. He paid a visit to Hy, where the tale he had to
tell must have been sorely trying to the then abbot, Cumine
the White [6]: and thence he went to the island of Inisboffin [7],
off the coast of Mayo, where he built a monastery. But

---

[1] Bede, iii. 26 : ' Nam et de hoc quæstio non minima erat.'

[2] Bede, iv. 4. The 'Petrine' argument did not move them.

[3] Bede, iii. 26 : 'Quod aiunt Colmanum abiturum petiisse,' &c.

[4] Bede, Vit. Cuthb. 16. Richard of Hexham, de statu Hagust. Eccl. c. 9.
This ' pluralism' was irregular.

[5] Bede, iii. 26, 'in secretario ;' above, p. 164.

[6] He sat from 657 to 669 ; Lanigan, iii. 36. See Adamn. iii. 5.

[7] ' Inisboufinde, id est, insula vitulæ albæ ; ' Bede, iv. 4. Cf. Tighernach :
' Navigatio Colmani episcopi, cum reliquis Scotorum, ad insulam Vaccæ Albæ,
in qua fundavit ecclesiam.' See Lanigan, iii. 79.

after a while, as Bede tells us with a touch of sarcastic humour, 'the brethren could not agree, inasmuch as the Irishmen used to leave the monastery when harvest-work had to be done, and roam about in places well known to them, but would return with the winter, and propose to share with the Englishmen what the latter had gathered in [1].' So Colman removed his Northumbrian monks to a small property which he purchased in Mayo itself: and the house thus founded was in Bede's time a large monastery, exclusively occupied by Englishmen, who lived under 'canonical rules,' and observed those very usages against which their founder had vainly striven in 664. Colman himself spent the rest of his life on his distant isle, and died in 676 [2].

Review of the Scotic Mission.

His departure from Northumbria marks an epoch, which we may pause to take note of in its manifold significance. It was the end of the Scotic ascendancy, the triumph of the 'Catholic Easter' and of other Continental Church usages, the opening of a free communication with Latin Christianity properly so called. It brought new facilities and opportunities, made room for new precedents, held up new models of excellence. There was good in this, and also some evil. A Church moulded on the Celtic type could never have sufficed for the needs of England. The Irish Church was too intensely monastic, too closely bound up with the tribal divisions of its people, and too widely separated from the general area of ecclesiastical civilisation [3]. The Latinising process gave system and order, and organised and concentrated force, and a certain magnificence which could symbolise devotion, and teach great lessons through the imagination, and overawe rough natures as by the visible presence of a Kingdom supreme over lord and ceorl alike. In its train came all that in that age could educate, or soften, or form taste, or

---

[1] Bede, iv. 4. The 'nota sibi loca' would be in Connaught.

[2] Tighernach : 'Colmannus' (Columbanus, Ulster Ann.) 'episcopus insulæ Vaccæ Albæ .. obiit.' See Reeves's Adamnan, p. 376.

[3] See Skene, Celtic Scotland, ii. 63 ff., 366; Green, Making of England, pp. 284, 317, 324. Professor G. T. Stokes owns that, in the twelfth century, ' the Celtic Christian organization had utterly broken down,' had failed to 'rule and tame the wild Celt;' Ireland and Celtic Ch. p. 341. It thus actually contributed to the chaos which gave an opportunity to Strongbow.

train the sense of beauty: it founded schools as well as convents, enlisted painting and architecture, though still of a rude and stern type, in the service of religion, and in various ways acted as an elevating and civilising power. That the Latin tone and spirit also fostered superstition and spiritual despotism, and that the tightening of links to Rome had some ill effects on English Church freedom, are positions which mediæval history sets far above all doubt. But the reader of Bede can hardly look forward, at this point, without soon looking backward, under the spell of that noble and loving testimony which the Northumbrian historian records in honour of the first three bishops of Lindisfarne, and of the clergy or monks who imbibed their spirit of single-hearted goodness, of pure unworldliness, of devotion to sacred duty [1]. 'The very place which they governed' spoke of these virtues by its appearance: there were, beside the wooden church, only just so many buildings as were absolutely necessary for the community life. The monastery had no money, but only cattle. Gifts of money glided through the hands of Finan or Colman, as through Aidan's [2], straight into the hands of the poor. No need was there for guest-houses to entertain noble visitors: such persons, if they did visit Lindisfarne, came but for prayer and sermon, and were content with the brethren's simple and daily food [3]. This was the case with Oswy himself, as with Oswald: 'he would come with five or six thanes, and depart when prayer in the church was over.' The effect produced on the people of Northumbria might be seen in the glad welcome given to any cleric or monk: if he were on a journey, people ran up to him and 'bent their heads in joyful expectation of being "signed" by his hand or blessed by his lips,—and then listened earnestly to his words of exhortation. And on Sundays they vied with each other in hastening to church, or to monasteries, not for the sake of getting a meal, but to hear God's word: and if a priest happened to come into a township, the inhabitants

[1] 'Quantæ autem parsimoniæ,' Bede, iii. 26.
[2] See Bede, iii. 5 : 'Ea potius quæ sibi a divitibus,' &c.; and iii. 14.
[3] Bede, iii. 26 : 'Nam neque ad susceptionem potentium sæculi,' &c.

would speedily assemble, and beg to hear from him the word
of life.' For 'well they knew that he was come for the sake
of souls, to preach, to baptize, and visit the sick,'—that is, on
one of those mission circuits which supplied to some extent
the lack of parochial organisation. They knew that the thing
farthest from a priest's thoughts was, what he could get out
of them [1]. Indeed, the bishops and clergy of that generation
were so clear of all suspicion of self-seeking, so free from 'that
pest of avarice,' that except under compulsion they could not
be got to receive lands for building monasteries. 'But enough
of this,' Bede concludes: and we can 'read between the lines'
of his panegyric a mournful and indignant reflection on the
contrast presented by the monks or clergy of his own time.
Here lies the point of his emphasis [2], 'For *then* the whole
anxiety of those teachers was, not how to serve the world,
but how to serve God: their whole care was to provide,
not for the belly, but for the heart. That was the reason
why, at *that* time, the religious habit was held in such
veneration.' 'The custom of not willingly accepting endowments was preserved in Northumbrian churches for some
time afterwards [3].' He means to say, 'We are living in a
changed world: the fine gold is become dim: secularity has
tainted and enfeebled the Church.' It was the last effort of
Bede for his Church when he wrote the memorable letter to
Egbert, then a young bishop of York, afterwards its first
archbishop, entreating him to correct abuses which had crept
into monasteries, to raise the tone of the clergy, to restore
pious habits among the people [4].

[1] Compare the title of 'the three blessed visitors' given to St. David, St.
Padarn, St. Teilo, because they taught without accepting any reward, even in
food, Rees' Welsh Saints, p. 197; Williams, Eccl. Antiq. of Cymry, p. 133.

[2] 'Tota enim fuit *tunc* solicitudo . . . *tempore illo* . . . aliquanto post hæc
tempore;' Bede, iii. 26. Compare another passage, iii. 5, 'nostri temporis
segnitia;' iv. 27, 'Erat quippe moris *eo tempore*,' &c.; and iv. 3, 'Non enim
ad otium, *ut quidam*, sed ad laborem, se monasterium intrare signabat.'

[3] A like custom existed in the old Irish Church, and was traced up to St.
Patrick; see Haddan and Stubbs, ii. 310: 'but the munificence of tribes and
princes was not to be restrained;' McGee, Hist. Irel. i. 134.

[4] Ep. ad Egbert. 2, 3, 4, 5, 6, 7, 10, &c. There is a melancholy emphasis in
the concluding words of the letter. Bede has urged Egbert to contend against
the prevalence of avarice: 'Cæterum si de ebrietate, . . . et cæteris hujusmodi
contagionibus, pari ratione tractare voluerimus, epistolæ modus in immensum

And so we bid farewell to that old Scotic Church of North-umbria. It could not but pass away, for it could not provide what Northumbria then needed: it had but a temporary mission, but that mission it fulfilled with a rare simplicity of purpose. It brought religion straight home to men's hearts by sheer power of love and self-sacrifice: it held up before them, in the unconscious goodness and nobleness of its re-presentatives, the moral evidence for Christianity. It made them feel what it was to be taught and cared for, in the life spiritual, by pastors who before all things were the disciples and ministers of Christ,—whose chief and type was a St. Aidan.

extenderetur.' His was the bitter experience of one who, personally loyal to a high and pure standard, lives to see it ignored by a generation which has succumbed to degrading influences, by a Church that has fallen from its first love.

CHAPTER VII.

THE vacant see of Lindisfarne was filled up, probably in
the early summer of 664, by the appointment of Tuda[1]. It
was the obvious choice to make ; and Northumbrian churchmen might look forward hopefully, in the phrase used at the
accession of a new prelate, to 'many years[2]' under one who
had been virtually acting as coadjutor-bishop, who would be
welcome to many as of the same race with the three former
bishops, and also unexceptionable to the most fastidious
orthodoxy on the questions of 'Catholic Pasch' and 'crown-
like tonsure.' But, as often befell in the chequered history
of newly-planted Churches, these hopes were soon disappointed
by an event which justifies us in placing our survey of the
Celtic episcopate of Lindisfarne after the retirement of his
predecessor. The bishop, 'a good man and a religious,
The Yellow governed the Church but a very short time[3].' There swept
Pest. over the island, in this year, one of those fierce pestilences
which gave to the word 'mortality' so terrible a significance
in the records of that age. It was about a century since the
plague which we connect with Justinian's reign had slain its
thousands all over Europe, had raged in Britain and in
Ireland[4], and had repeatedly, in the days of the pious
Frankish king Gontran, been made an occasion for 'Roga-

---

[1] Bede, iii. 26 : 'Suscepit pro illo pontificatum,' &c.

[2] The custom was probably older than the office which embodies it in
Muratori, Lit. Rom. ii. 443.

[3] Bede, l. c. : 'Vir quidem bonus,' &c.

[4] Gibbon, v. 253. Comp. Ann. Camb. a. 537, 'Mortalitas in Brittannia et
in Hibernia fuit.' Ib. a. 547, 'Mortalitas magna.' Tighernach mentions three
pestilences in the sixth century. See Rees, Welsh Saints, p. 243. King
Maelgwyn died of this plague. It returned in Teilo's time, whereupon he
retired into Armorica : and it carried off a Cornish king, Geraint.

tions' and public fasts[1]. In our islands it was known as the CHAP. VII. 'Yellow Pest,' from the ghastly yellow hue of its victims' bodies[2]: and now, before reappearing in Ireland, it visited Britain soon after a solar eclipse in May[3]. Its coming was unexpected[4]: it smote down high and low, not sparing the king of the Kentishmen, nor the archbishop of Canterbury himself. Both died on the same day, July 14[5]. Erconbert was succeeded by his son Egbert: but the seat of Augustine remained vacant for four years. It seems that Damian bishop of Rochester succumbed at the same time to the epidemic: and his seat was long unfilled[6]. When in its onward sweep the pest entered the North-country, it 'hurried Tuda out of this world,' and he was buried in a monastery called Pægnalæch[7],—supposed to be Finchale,—or, in the Chronicle, Wagele,—perhaps Whalley. It seems also that we must refer to the October of this year the death of Bishop Cedd, who, after returning home from Whitby as a conformist to the 'Catholic Easter,' had revisited Lastingham 'in the time of the mortality[8],' and there died. He was buried outside the wooden church which he had raised on the ground that he

---

[1] Greg. Turon. H. Fr. ix. 21, 22; x. 30.

[2] 'Flavos et exsangues,' Lib. Landav. p. 101. It is there added, in legendary style, that the pest seemed to float along like a pillar of watery cloud, or like showers traversing a glen. Those who tried to cure patients died themselves. See Pryce's Anc. Brit. Ch. p. 163, that its worst symptoms were inflamed tumours.

[3] See Bede, iii. 27: 'Facta erat,' &c. He dates the eclipse on May 3: but it was on May 1; see Usher, Antiq. p. 491. So the Irish annalists. They also say that 'the mortality came to Ireland' on Aug. 1. Tighernach gives the right year, 664; see O'Conor, Rer. Hib. Scr. ii. 203–4; the Ulster Annals say 663 (ib. iv. 55); and the Chronicon Scotorum, 660,—but the latter is 'four years in arrear' at this period (Introd. p. xlv). The pest broke out in Fothairt, co. Wexford. It carried off Ethelhun, but spared his companion Egbert, for whose prayer and vow see Bede, iii. 27. 'Innumerabiles mortui sunt,' Ulster Ann. Adamnan ascribes the immunity of the 'plebs Pictorum et Scotorum Britanniæ' to St. Columba's intercession; Vit. Col. ii. 46.

[4] 'Subita,' Bede; see v. 24, 'Et pestilentia venit.'

[5] Beda, iv. 1: 'Eodem mense ac die.' Tighernach names five Irish kings, and several prelates, including four abbots of (Irish) Bangor, and its victims.

[6] Bede, iv. 2, end.

[7] Bede, iii. 27: 'Qua plaga,' &c. See Haddan and Stubbs, iii. 444.

[8] Bede, iii. 23: 'Qui cum annis multis,' &c., and Stubbs, Registrum, p. 2. See Bede's touching story of the thirty Essex monks who came to live or die beside his grave.

and his brother had hallowed : another brother, Chad, succeeded him as abbot. His East-Saxons were differently affected by the scourge of the Yellow Pest. Some who were ruled, under the over-lordship of Wulfhere, then extending over all Essex, by Sebbi, brother of Sigebert the Little, stood the trial of their faith and patience, and 'clung with great devotion to the creed which they had received[1].' In the other division of the small kingdom, where Sebbi's nephew Sighere reigned, the sudden affliction—as was often the case on those ages[2]—had the effect of throwing the people back on their old worship, as if they were smitten for having deserted it, or as if they had expected the Cross to be a safeguard against suffering. 'Sighere, and very many of the people or the earls, loving this life, and not seeking another, or even not believing it to exist, began to restore the Pagan temples which had been forsaken, and to worship images, as if by means of these they could be shielded from the mortality[3].' In the valley of the Tweed also, some, in whose minds 'the seed had no deepness of earth,' 'neglected the mysteries of faith which they had received,' and tried to obtain relief from the disease by heathenish 'spells or amulets[4].' At Melrose Cuthbert himself caught the infection : he recovered, although for the rest of his life he felt some effects of his illness : but Boisil, his beloved prior, died, after tranquilly spending the

---

[1] Bede, iii. 30. Sighere had a son and successor, Offa.

[2] See Robertson, Hist. Ch. iii. 477. Compare Adamnan, Vit. Col. ii. 32 ; the Pictish 'magi,' seeing a newly-baptized boy dying of sudden illness, began to mock at his parents, and ' Christianorum, tanquam infirmiori, Deo derogare.'

[3] Bede, iii. 30 : ' Nam et ipse rex,' &c. These relapses were common enough, especially among the Frisians : e.g. see the anonymous Life of St. Boniface, ii. 20, 'Olim . . conversos sed . . . iterum quosdam eorum ad pristinum gentilitatis errorem devolutos.' Councils take cognizance of such cases, e. g. second of Orleans, c. 20, 'qui ad idolorum cultum revertuntur ;' Mansi, viii. 838. See also Greg. Ep. viii. 1, as to Corsicans. Comp. Maclear, Ap. of Med. Europe, p. 146, on heathen reactions ; and Alb. Butler, Nov. 21.

[4] Bede, iv. 27, and Vit. Cuthb. 9, 'per incantationes vel alligaturas,' or ' fylacteria.' Comp. the prohibition of phylacteries and ligatures by a German Council in 745, Migne, Patr. Lat. lxxxix. 812 ; and on the rumour that they were used even in Rome, ib. 747, and St. Boniface's Ep. to Cuthbert, c. 2. Compare the Report of the Central African Mission for 1876, p. 10 : 'One old chief . . . could not bring himself at the last moment to abandon his amulets, in which, he said, his fathers had trusted from time immemorial ; and so, for a time, his admission was deferred.'

last week of his life in reading St. John's Gospel with Cuthbert[1], who succeeded to his office, and added to its duties,
after Boisil's example, the work of an evangelist throughout
the adjacent country. To sustain the rude people in their
faith, or reclaim them to it, he would go out, on foot or
on horseback[2], and sometimes be absent from the monastery
for weeks together, penetrating into the wildest valleys,
climbing steep hill-sides, and thus finding access to poor
hamlets which other teachers had shrunk from visiting,
through 'horror' of their dreary situation, or distaste for
their 'poverty and rusticity[3].' Not such was this 'true man
of God,' as Bede repeatedly calls him. He attracted those
'shepherdless sheep' by the fascination of his presence and
his words. 'So great was his skill in speaking, so intense
his eagerness to make his words persuasive, such a glow
lighted up his angelic face[4], that no one of those present
dared to hide from Cuthbert the secrets of his heart: all
revealed openly[5], by confession, what they had done, for in

[1] Bede, 'quo tempore,' Vit. Cuthb. 8, would strictly refer to 661, when
Eata and his monks returned from Ripon to Melrose. But the following
words clearly point to the great epidemic of 664, 'morbo . . . quo *tunc* plurimi
per Britanniam . . . deficiebant.' For Boisil's last days see the beautiful
account in Bede, l. c. 'As I have but seven days to live,' said Boisil, 'learn
all you can from me.' 'What can we get through in seven days?' 'St. John's
Gospel: I have a codex in seven quarto sheets: we can take one each day.'
They read it through in that time, 'quia solum in ea (lectione) fidei quæ per
dilectionem operatur simplicitatem, non autem quæstionum profunda, tracta-
bant.' (Bede's own death-bed was to exhibit a scene somewhat like this, and
quite as touching.) Simeon of Durham says (Hist. Dun. Eccl. i. 3, Op. i. 22)
that a 'codex' in which Cuthbert used to read under Boisil's teaching was
still extant in Durham monastery, 'prisca novitate ac decore mirabilis.' See
also Bede, V. C. 22.

[2] So Bede, iv. 27, Vit. Cuthb. 9 ; (identical passages on the whole). See the
story in Vit. Cuthb. 12 : 'Cum prædicaturus . . . de monasterio exiret, uno
comite puero.' See above, p. 211, on the serious interest with which the
people then listened to preaching.

[3] Bede, iv. 27 : 'In viculis qui in arduis asperisque montibus,' &c. Cp. Scott,
'Where . . . Eildon slopes to the plain.'

[4] 'Tale vultus angelici lumen,' Bede. 'Erat aspectu angelicus,' Anon. Vit.
The beauty was probably in the expression; for at the exhumation of his
skeleton in 1827 he was found to have had a prominent upper jaw, a
turned-up nose, and a deeply-indented chin (cp. Reginald, Libellus de S. C.
c. 41). The skeleton measured 5 ft. 8 in. ; Raine's St. Cuthbert, p. 213 ff. He
had black hair, Sim. Op. i. 204.

[5] 'Palam,' in the sense of hiding nothing from *him*.

CHAP. VII. truth they supposed that he must needs be aware of those very deeds of theirs; and after confession they wiped away their sins at his bidding, by worthy fruits of repentance [1],' finding the best enforcement of his exhortations in the generous charity which brought him among them rather than into more attractive places [2], in the untiring energy with which he 'devoted himself to this pious labour,' above all in his personal example,—in himself [3]. Such was his life at Melrose for several years [4].

Wilfrid chosen bishop of York.

But we must return from the work of a young saint to the ecclesiastical politics of a kingdom. Who was to be the bishop of Northumbria? It seems that the Witan were assembled to decide the point, which, as may be inferred from later instances [5], fell within the province of the national assembly, including, as it did, the leading ecclesiastics. Alchfrid, as sub-king of Deira, would contribute much to the decision arrived at in favour of Wilfrid. 'There is no one of our race better and worthier than Wilfrid the presbyter and abbot.' He was then about thirty years old: his biographer dwells fondly on his ability in preaching, his discriminating treatment of different characters, his 'marvellous memory,' his devotion, his beneficence to the afflicted [6]. Wilfrid, then, was to be bishop: but, probably at his desire, and certainly with good reason, it was resolved to replace the bishopric at York. He was to preside in the minster 'that Edwin and Oswald had erected [7].' But who was to consecrate him? Deusdedit, and probably Damian, were dead: Cedd was still alive at

---

[1] 'Et confessa dignis, ut imperabat, pœnitentiæ fructibus abstergerent.'

[2] 'Solebat autem ea maxime loca peragrare,' &c.

[3] 'Verbo prædicationis simul et opere virtutis.' Compare Bede, i. 26, iii. 5, &c. See also Bede, Ep. ad Egb. 1; above, p. 52.

[4] 'Multos annos,' Bede, iv. 27, Vit. Cuthb. 16; 'aliquot annos,' V. C. 9. Even if he had become prior in 661, this would hardly allow us to date his removal to Lindisfarne in 664, as Simeon does, Dun. Eccl. i. 6.

[5] See Kemble, ii. 221, referring to cases in the Chronicle and in Florence; e.g. Oskytel was made archbishop of York by the favour of king Eadred and all his Witan; Chron. a. 971. See Stubbs, Const. Hist. i, 157. Comp. Greg. Turon. H. Fr. ix. 21, 'Charimerem referendarium cum consensu civium regalis decrevit auctoritas fieri sacerdotem.'

[6] Eddi, c. 11.

[7] Raine, Fast. Ebor. i. 62.

the time, but he would have the disadvantage, in Wilfrid's eye, of Scotic consecration: and the same drawback existed in regard to Jaruman of Mercia. Wini would be objectionable as the supplanter, in effect, of Agilbert. There remained Boniface of Dunwich, who had been consecrated by archbishop Honorius[1]; but Wilfrid would wish to have the canonical 'three consecrators'; and his own strong predilection for the country where he had spent some years, and learned so much, would be an additional motive for requesting to be consecrated in Gaul. It was so arranged: he went over to that country, and was consecrated at Compiègne, in Neustria, probably in the beginning of 665[2]. The place was a royal 'villa,' where 'the wild Chlotair[3]' had died, and where the treasures of Dagobert I. had been kept: it now belonged to the young 'Faineant' king, Chlotair III. The ceremony was performed with un-Consecration of usual magnificence, as if the Frankish hierarchy wished to Wilfrid in do special honour to the disciple of Aunemund and the Gaul. champion of the Catholic Easter. Twelve prelates officiated, including Agilbert, who had returned to his native country after the conference[4]: and 'after their custom they lifted

[1] Eddi makes Wilfrid say to the kings, 'It is not my place to accuse any one; but there are many bishops in Britain who are either Quartodecimans, as the Britons and Scots, or have been ordained by them.' According to Bede, he had virtually urged, at Whitby, that the Britons and Scots were *not* really Quartodecimans. Eddi is simply using the term loosely, in the temper of a partisan, as in c. 14, 15. Malmesbury does the same, Gest. Pontif. iii. 100.

[2] So Mabillon, Ann. Benedict. i. 478. Bede says that he died *after* forty-five years of episcopate; v. 19. Eddi assigns him forty-six years, meaning, doubtless, that he died in the forty-sixth; 65. He died, we know, in 709: if the day was in October (see Raine, i. 76), the literal construction of the reckoning places the consecration in the early autumn of 664; but as this crowds a good deal into that season, and causes some difficulty in regard to after events, we may perhaps suppose Bede to reckon from Wilfrid's *election*. The fixed points are, that he cannot have been elected before the autumn of 664: that in some sense he had full forty-five years of episcopate: that he returned to Northumbria three years before the late summer of 669, and that Chad, during that period, held the see of York: comp. Bede, v. 19; Eddi, 14. If Wilfrid went into Gaul towards the close of 664, he must have stayed there until the spring of 666. The consecration would be deferred until a large number of bishops could assemble: and some other circumstances, now unknown, may have contributed to keep Wilfrid in Gaul for more than a year.

[3] Carlyle, Fr. Rev. i. 28; see Greg. Turon. H. Fr. iv. 21.

[4] He was not yet, as Bede thought (iii. 28; v. 19), bishop of Paris. See above, p. 189.

CHAP. VII. Wilfrid up in a golden seat, and carried him with their own hands, assisted by no one else,' in a choral procession to the altar where he was to be consecrated[1]. This singular custom was known to Gregory the Great, who presented to Gregory of Tours 'a golden chair' for use in his church[2]. Wilfrid was thoroughly at home amid such splendour and such observance; and he was tempted to protract his enjoyment of Frankish church life[3], or otherwise detained by circumstances in Gaul, long after the time at which he was expected to appear in Northumbria. At last, in the spring of 666, he sailed for Britain, with a hundred and twenty attendants. A wind drove them on the Sussex coast; and then came a scene of excitement and peril to be remembered for the sake of a later chapter in his history, perhaps the best chapter of all. The Sussex barbarians rushed down to seize on the distressed vessel, and to despoil and capture all on board. Wilfrid tried to buy them off: they answered, like true 'wreckers[4],' 'All is ours that the sea throws up!' A pagan priest, standing on a high mound, tried to 'bind the strangers' hands' by magic[5]: one of Wilfrid's company slew him with a stone from a sling[6]: in the fight that followed, the bishop and his clerks prayed, while their companions did valiantly, losing only five men: at last the tide floated the vessel off, and it made Sandwich in safety.

Wilfrid's return.

Wilfrid was soon again at home, but found that he had been far too long absent[7]. The defeated party, while conforming to the Catholic Easter, disliked his general line, and thought, perhaps, that his rule would be too high-handed.

---

[1] Eddi, 12. 'Gemmata vehitur archontum more curuli;' Frid. 351. Cp. Martene, de Ant. Eccl. Rit. ii. 332.

[2] Bened. Vit. Greg. M. iii. 3. 8. Compare the 'sella gestatoria' of the Popes.

[3] Malmesb. p. 211: 'Moras nectente.'

[4] On this barbarous 'right of wreck,' which on many a coast long survived the introduction of Christianity, see Freeman, Norm. Conq. iii. 223.

[5] Comp. Bede, iv. 22, for 'litteras *solutorias* de qualibus fabulæ ferunt.' The South-Saxons were still immersed in paganism.

[6] 'He fell back a corpse, like Goliath;' Eddi, 13.

[7] Bede excuses him, as if he 'tarried' no longer than the 'ordination' required, in iii. 28; in v. 19 he omits 'propter ordinationem.' It does not seem possible to reconcile the former statement with Bede's other marks of time.

While he lingered in Gaul, they rallied, and represented to
Oswy that the Church could not await the leisure of a bishop
who did not come home to begin his work[1]. They had
thought of one who would be fitter for the bishopric: 'a
holy man, grave in character, sufficiently instructed in Scripture, diligent in acting up to Scripture precepts[2]:' a man
of prayer, study, humility, purity, voluntary poverty[3]: who
had been one of Aidan's original 'twelve boys[4],' and then,
as a youth, had lived in Ireland under monastic discipline[5].
This was Chad, abbot of Lastingham, and brother of the
East-Saxon bishop. Was not such a man the fittest occupant
of Aidan's seat? Oswy assented to this view: Alchfrid
would doubtless have stood out against it on behalf of his
absent friend, but that just at this time he fell under his
father's displeasure, who compelled him to give up his intention of accompanying Benedict Biscop on his second journey
to Rome[6]; and it would seem that Bede's brief unexplained
statement, naming Alchfrid with Ethelwald and the Mercians
among the various enemies of Oswy[7], refers to some rebellious
movement of Alchfrid after this time, which led to his being
disinherited and 'disappearing from history[8].' So it was
that Chad was elected bishop, and went into the south for
consecration, attended by the king's chaplain, Eadhed, afterwards bishop of Lindsey, and ultimately of Ripon[9]. They
had expected to find a successor appointed to Deusdedit[10], but
were disappointed. Whatever may have been the case with
Wilfrid, Chad seems to have forgotten that Boniface of

Chad con-
secrated
for York.

---

[1] See Raine, i. 48: 'They commented . . . upon the injury that Northumbria was sustaining by Wilfrid's prolonged and unaccountable absence.'

[2] Bede, iii. 28: 'Virum sanctum, modestum moribus,' &c.

[3] Bede, iv. 3: 'Namque inter plura continentiæ,' &c.

[4] Bede, iii. 28: 'Erat enim de discipulis,' &c. above, p. 146.

[5] Bede, iv. 3. Chad and Egbert had been 'adolescentes' in Ireland together.
Now Egbert was born in 639; see Bede, iii. 27. If Chad was about his age, he
would be only twenty-six at this time,—below the age for a bishop. Probably
he was some years older than Egbert.

[6] Bede, Hist. Abb. 2: 'Quem cum pater ejus,' &c.

[7] Bede, iii. 14: 'Et a filio quoque suo Alchfrido.'

[8] See Stubbs on Cathedral of Worcester, p. 2.

[9] Comp. Bede, iii. 28; iv. 12.

[10] Bede does not imply that they were unaware of Deusdedit's death simply;
'invenerunt iam migrasse . . . *et* necdum alium,' &c.

CHAP. VII.

Dunwich was available[1], for he repaired to Wini of Winchester, who thereupon took the first step towards effecting a union of the Welsh and English Churches[2], while at the same time he showed himself careful to observe the requirement of the 'three' consecrators, by obtaining the co-operation[3] of 'two bishops of British race,' most probably from Cornwall[4], who, it need not be said, were maintainers of the Celtic Easter,—and who therefore, by laying their hands on the head of the new Northumbrian bishop, unintentionally supplied the party which resented his appointment with an argument against the 'regularity' of his consecration[5]. In other respects, the combination of agents in the scene then witnessed by the Church-people of Winchester was specially interesting and appropriate. A prelate consecrated in Gaul joins with himself two prelates of a different rite, representing the old Church of Alban and Restitutus, of Dubricius and David, in the consecration of one who had sat as a boy at Aidan's feet, and had but very lately, it would seem, given up the British and Scotic observances,—and who was to shine forth, in a brief but beautiful episcopate, as one of the truest and purest saints of ancient England.

Chad
bishop of
York.

The date of this event must be ~~dated~~ *placed* in the latter part of 665, or the beginning of 666[6]. Chad returned to North-

---

[1] And so does Bede himself, when he says, iv. 28, that there was then no canonically ordained bishop in Britain except Wini: yet Boniface sat from 652 to 669; iii. 20; iv. 5.

[2] Churton, E. Engl. Ch. p. 82.

[3] 'Adsumptis in societatem ordinationis;' Bede, iii. 28. Bede knew nothing of the artificial theory which would make the presiding bishop the *sole* agent in the conveyance of the episcopal character: against it see Lee on English Ordinations, p. 230. Comp. Hincmar, Op. ii. 408, Ep. to Hincmar of Laon: 'Tuum est autem cum aliis mecum ordinare episcopum, et litteris canonicis, quas ordinatus ab ordinatoribus suis jubetur accipere, post me in tuo loco subscribere.' See also Vit. S. Anskar. 12, 'pariter consecrantibus;' and Goar's Euchologion Græcorum, p. 303, τῶν συγχειροτονούντων ἀρχιερέων, although the presiding prelate is called specifically ὁ χειροτονήσας.

[4] Haddan and Stubbs, i. 124.

[5] 'Ceaddam . . . inordinate ordinavit;' Eadmer, Vit. Wilf. c. 12.

[6] Bede allows Chad only three years of episcopate at York; which, taken by itself, would date his consecration in 666, for his rule at York certainly ended about August, 669. Bede may have misapprehended Eddi, who reckons the three years from Wilfrid's return to Northumbria; c. 14.

umbria, and was installed as bishop of York[1]. 'He began at once[2] to devote himself to the maintenance of ecclesiastical truth and purity; to practice humility and continence ; to give attention to reading; to go about among towns, country districts, cottages, townships, "fortified places", in order to preach the Gospel, not on horseback, but, after the manner of the Apostles, on foot. For he was one of the pupils of Aidan, and took pains to train his hearers to the same conduct and character, after Aidan's example and that of his own brother Cedd[3].' Meantime Wilfrid bore the trial of finding the see thus filled with a moderation which could hardly have been expected even from a less high-spirited man. It was his best policy to accept facts, and to bide his time[4]. He did so, and resumed his place as abbot of Ripon[5], where among his monks was Ceolfrid, whose name was to be so closely linked to those of Benedict Biscop and of Bede.

If Wilfrid could not fully appreciate the work which bishops of Scotic consecration had done for Christianity in South Britain, he must at least have rejoiced to hear, in the course of this year 665, that a bishop of that class had once more been the instrument in a reconversion of East-Saxons. It was doubtless Sebbi, faithful himself, with his own subjects, to Christianity, who induced his over-lord Wulfhere to send Jaruman to preach to Sighere and his people. This was the third mission to Essex. Jaruman, attended by priests, one of

Third mission to East-Saxons.

---

[1] Bede, v. 19 : 'Quo adhuc in transmarinis partibus,' &c.

[2] Bede, iii. 28 : 'Consecratus ergo,' &c. In this chapter, as in one sentence of i. 29, in ii. 8, 16, iii. 7, &c., we have 'consecrari.' Bede's more usual phrase is the general term 'ordinari;' i. 27, 29 ; ii. 3, 9 ; iii. 5, 20, 21, &c.

[3] Comp. Bede, iii. 5 : 'Discurrere . . . . pedum incessu vectus,' &c.

[4] Fridegod expresses this in a better-sounding line than usual :
'Spe meliore manet latebris contectus in illis.'
See Richard of Hexham, 'placido vultu et hilari pectore,' De statu Hagust. Eccl. 6 ; Eddi and Malmesbury, 'humiliter.'

[5] There is no sort of authority for saying that he might and ought to have 'entered on the duties of his bishopric at Lindisfarne,' leaving Chad to be bishop of York (Dict. Chr. Biogr. i. 429). He was himself consecrated for York (see above, p. 218 ; and Dict. Chr. B. i. 427, 'Wilfrid was thereupon raised to the see of York '); there was then no thought of dividing the diocese of Northumbria. Chad was placed in the see to which Wilfrid had been elected, and had all Northumbria under his jurisdiction.

CHAP. VII. whom lived to tell the story to Bede[1], 'went about the whole
district,' and brought back the wanderers into the right way :
'so that they abandoned or destroyed their fanes and altars[2],
reopened the churches, and gladly acknowledged that Name
of Christ which they had disowned, desiring rather to die with
the assurance of rising again in Him than to live amid idols
in the filth of disbelief;' words which intimate that the deadly
sickness which had scared them back to idolatry was still
raging, and therefore that Jaruman and his priests had faced
its perils while winning back souls to Christ with equal prudence[3] and energy. London is not mentioned in this account,
but its citizens had either retained their faith—which may
have been acquired through Cedd's work, even if he did not
establish himself among them—or were among those who now
regained it : and we hear of the see of London as associated,
in 666 or thereabouts, with a grave scandal. Kenwalch of
Wessex, with all his sincerity and zeal, his admiration for
men of learning, his orthodoxy on the Paschal question, and
his helpful kindness to such a man as Benedict Biscop[4],
was not, apparently, an easy prince for bishops to deal with.
He had quarrelled with Agilbert about dialect; he now, for
what cause we know not, constrained Wini to leave his
kingdom. The bishop took refuge in Mercia, and, as Bede
says, with stern laconic plainness, 'bought with a price the
see of the city of London from King Wulfhere[5].' Simony
had long been a sore and a disgrace in the Gallic Church[6],

[1] Bede, iii. 30: 'Juxta quod mihi presbyter, qui comes itineris illi et co-
operator verbi exstiterat, referebat; erat enim religiosus et bonus vir.'

[2] 'Arisque :' comp. 'arulam,' contrasted with the Christian 'altare,' in Bede,
ii. 15.

[3] 'Multa agens sollertia,' Bede.

[4] Bede, Hist. Abb. 4, says that Benedict 'had more than once enjoyed his
friendship and been assisted by his kindnesses.'

[5] 'Emit pretio,' Bede, iii. 7. 'Simoniacal sale of the dignities of the Church
existed to the most deplorable extent among the Anglo-Saxons;' Palgrave,
Engl. Comm, p. 174, referring to this case.

[6] Gregory of Tours says of the first part of the sixth century, 'Jam tunc
germen illud iniquum cœperat fructificare, ut sacerdotium aut venderetur a
regibus, aut compararetur a clericis;' Vit. Patr. 6. 3. See second Council of
Orleans, a. 533, c. 3. And, very late in his own life, in 591, he tells us that
one Eusebius procured the see of Paris 'datis multis muneribus;' H. Fr. x. 26.
Compare Gregory the Great, Ep. v. 53, 55; ix. 106, 109; xi. 55, 59. Much

within whose limits Wini had been consecrated; but we know no more than what Bede thus tells us of the circumstances under which Wini got possession of the see of Mellitus.

If Jaruman was, as doubtless he was, like-minded to the bishops of Lindisfarne, any such unhallowed trafficking between the king and Wini must have grieved him to the heart. He survived his good work in Essex for about two years, dying in 667. Wulfhere did not appoint a successor, but requested Wilfrid from time to time to discharge episcopal functions in Mercia[1], and gave him several pieces of land for the foundation of monasteries,—one of which, that at Oundle, happened to be long afterwards the scene of its founder's death. Wulfhere ultimately gave him a 'place' at Lichfield, where he might establish himself as bishop; but Wilfrid's heart clung to Northumbria, and he would not permanently bind himself to a Midland diocese. He would only administer it during the vacancy. Another such sphere of duty provided for him during these years was Kent. Invited by Egbert, he ordained in that kingdom many priests and not a few deacons[2]. It is interesting to combine the facts, that one of these priests was Putta, a man who had a special skill in chanting, acquired from 'disciples of Pope Gregory[3];' and that in Kent Wilfrid found, and closely attached to himself, Hædde, or Eddi, ecclesiastically named Stephen, who afterwards became a noted choir-master in Northumbria, and the enthusiastic follower and biographer of Wilfrid[4],—with another well-trained chanter, called Æona[5]. His brilliant attractiveness and lively versatile intelligence drew round him men of all classes, including 'masons, and

later, in 650, the Council of Chalons had had to forbid taking money for ordinations; Mansi, x. 1192.

[1] Eddi, 14, 15. Bede does not seem to be aware of this; see iv. 3.

[2] Eddi, 14; Bede, iv. 2, 'Ipse etiam in Cantia,' &c. 'Ekbertus vero ... poscit, Ordinet ut sacros ... ministros,' &c.; Frideg. 418.

[3] Bede, iv. 2, end. Compare the phrase as used in v. 20; Maban the chanter 'had been taught in Kent by successors of the disciples of Pope Gregory,'

[4] Bede, iv. 2 : 'Sed et sonos cantandi,' &c. Raine thinks the 'Life' was written soon after 710. 'Like so many biographers, he is an enthusiastic partisan;' Hist. Ch. York, i. pp. xxxii–xxxv.

[5] Eddi says simply, 'Cum cantoribus Ædde et Eonan;' 14.

CHAP. VII. artificers of nearly every sort[1],' who afterwards accompanied him into Northumbria. He made use of all opportunities: he could throw himself into various interests, and, in a sense, be 'all things to all men.' Within the precincts of the cathedral monastery at Canterbury, or at SS. Peter and Paul's, which lost its abbot Nathanael by death in 667, he studied minutely the Benedictine rule, which he was afterwards the first to propagate throughout the North-country[2].

It might have been expected that the Kentish king would think him the very man for the vacant archbishopric. But policy, perhaps, prevented such a step, which might have been distasteful to some in Kent, and also to some in

Wighard elected to Canterbury.

Northumbria. Egbert consulted with Oswy the 'Bretwalda,' and in some way or other the opinion of 'the Church of the English race' in general was ascertained. The result was the election of Wighard, 'one of Deusdedit's clergy,'— 'a good man and fit for the episcopate, very well instructed in ecclesiastical discipline and learning by Roman disciples of Pope Gregory[3],' still surviving in Kent. It was resolved that he should go to Rome, and be consecrated at that fountain-head, 'that he might be able to ordain Catholic prelates for the Churches of the English throughout all Britain.' Wighard set forth in 667, and arrived safely in Rome, with royal letters, and gifts, and gold and silver

His death at Rome.

vessels not a few[4]. But after his interview with Pope Vitalian, he and nearly all of his companions were cut off by an outbreak of pestilence.

Vitalian's letter.

Thereupon Vitalian wrote to Oswy a letter[5], which Bede for the most part transcribes, and which has led to some different opinions as to his relations with the English kings and Churches. He returned thanks for the gifts sent, as for offerings to St. Peter, and repaid them, in the Roman fashion,

[1] Eddi, 14: 'Cæmentariis, omnisque pæne artis institoribus.'

[2] Eddi's words are, 'In regionem suam revertens cum regula Sancti Benedicti;' 14. So in 47, Wilfrid says that '*nullus prior ibi* (in Northumbria) *invexit*' the Benedictine rule; Lingard, A.-S. Ch. i. 205.

[3] Comp. Bede, iii. 29, iv. 1; Hist. Abb. 3. Above, p. 128.

[4] Bede, iv. 1: 'Missis pariter apostolico papae donariis,' &c. Oswy understood, says Bede, that the Roman Church was Catholic and Apostolic; iii. 29. The Chronicle gives the date.

[5] Bede, iii. 29. He uses 'Saxonum' as equivalent to 'Anglorum.'

by relics[1]. He exhorted Oswy to follow the rule of St. Peter
as to Easter and all other matters[2]. He expressed his great
sorrow for the removal of Wighard from 'the light of this
world,' and intimated that he had been honourably buried ' at
the threshold of the Apostles.' He informed Oswy that he
had not as yet been able to find a fit man for the archbishopric 'according to the tenor of your letter,' owing to the
great distance of Canterbury from Rome, which, it seems,
deterred some from accepting the office: but when he could
find such a person, he would send him with due instructions,
in order that by his oral teaching and by the Divine oracles
he 'might eradicate all tares from the whole of the island;'
alluding, of course, to the Celtic Easter. What is meant by
'the tenor of Oswy's letter'? Vitalian's phrase would imply
that it had contained, first, a request to consecrate Wighard,
the recognised archbishop elect, and then a distinct commission to find some other person, if anything should happen to
Wighard[3]. But such further provision is not likely to have
been made by Oswy or by Egbert[4]: Bede, in his two references to the royal letter[5], does not say that it was actually
made: he says that the pope described Theodore as 'the
teacher' whom Benedict Biscop's 'native land had earnestly
sought for[6];' and when the archbishop who was at last sent
was passing through Gaul, his messengers described him to
Egbert as the bishop who had been 'asked for[7].' It has
accordingly been suspected that, in the first instance, a Pope

---

[1] Including relics of St. Pancras, with a cross, and a golden key made out
of the chains of SS. Peter and Paul, for Queen Eanfled.

[2] He combines St. Paul with St. Peter. A passage belonging to this
letter, omitted by Bede, but discovered by Usher, insists on the duty of
keeping Easter according to the apostolical rule of the 318 fathers (of Nicæa)
and the reckoning of the holy Cyril and Dionysius: and adds that the Apostolic see has not received the 'rule of Victor,' i.e. Victorius of Aquitaine;
Haddan and Stubbs, iii. 112. See above, p. 78. Gregory of Tours calls
Victorius 'Victor' in H. Fr. x. 23.

[3] Lingard, A.-S. Ch. i. 75, treats this as 'certain.'

[4] Kemble, ii. 366.

[5] Bede, iii. 29, iv. 1.

[6] 'Quem sedula quaesierat;' Hist. Abb. 3, i. e. *such* a teacher.

[7] 'Quem petierant; iv. 1. Bede describes Vitalian as taking counsel, 'ne,
legatariis obeuntibus, legatio religiosa fidelium fructu competente careret;'
Hist. Abb. 3.

CHAP. VII. who had had ten years' experience [1] would know how to infer the commission from the request, with no other warrant than the pretensions of his see. The subsequent words of the messengers just referred to might be simply an echo of this papal inference [2].

Hadrian.

It must be owned that Vitalian took great pains, and ultimately made a very wise choice [3]. At first he thought of Hadrian, an African by race, and abbot of a monastery not far from Naples, a man equally 'active and prudent, conversant with Scripture and all ecclesiastical rules,' and, which was then a rare attainment, 'a Greek as well as a Latin scholar [4].' 'Vitalian sent for him, and bade him accept the appointment and go to Britain.' 'I am unworthy of it,' said Hadrian [5]; 'but I can point out another better qualified by age and by learning.' He named Andrew, a monk from a neighbouring nunnery, where he apparently acted as chaplain. But Andrew, though 'deemed by all his friends to be worthy of the episcopate, was weighed down by feeble health:' and Vitalian again pressed Hadrian to consent, but he 'begged a respite,' saying, 'If I had time, I might find a suitable person.'

Theodore.

'There was at that time in Rome a monk, whom Hadrian knew, and whose name was Theodore.' Hadrian might be called a fellow-countryman of St. Cyprian and St. Augustine. Theodore was, in the same sense, a fellow-townsman of St. Paul, 'born at Tarsus, a city in Cilicia,' 'well trained alike in secular and in sacred learning, familiar both with Latin and Greek literature [6], of high character and of venerable age,

---

[1] Vitalian became Pope July 30, 657.

[2] Kemble, ii. 366, and Martineau, Ch. Hist. p. 85, suggest that Oswy and Egbert may have written again, leaving the case absolutely in the Pope's hands. Churton, E. E. Ch. p. 75, assumes it. But for this, according to the Chronicle, there would hardly be time. See Haddan and Stubbs, iii. 112.

[3] Haddan's Remains, p. 319. 'Habito de his consilio, quæsivit sedulus,' Bede, v. 1. 'Inito consilio,' Hist. Abb. 3.

[4] 'Græcæ pariter et Latinæ linguæ peritissimus;' Bede, iv. 1. Comp. iv. 2, 'Latinam Graecamque linguam,' &c.; v. 23, on Tobias as a pupil of Hadrian, 'Unde . . . ita Græcam quoque cum Latina didicit linguam,' &c.; and Hist. Abb. 3: 'strenuissimo et prudentissimo Adriano.'

[5] 'How edifying,' says Alban Butler (Life of Theodore, Sept. 19), 'was this contention, not to obtain, but to shun such a dignity!'

[6] Bede, iv. 1. So Hist. Abb. 3, &c. So Pope Zacharias called him 'xe Græco Latinus, ante philosophus et Athenis eruditus,' Ep. 11.

being sixty-six years old.' It was in the November of 667 that Hadrian presented him to Vitalian, as one able and willing, despite his years, to undertake the momentous charge of the see of Canterbury. Vitalian consented to send him to Britain, but on condition that Hadrian should accompany him—partly because he had already for several causes visited Gaul, and therefore knew most of the journey which Theodore would have to take, and had 'men of his own' sufficient to form an escort; partly 'in order that, by acting as his fellow-labourer in teaching, he might keep careful watch to prevent Theodore from introducing anything contrary to faith, after the manner of the Greeks, into the Church over which he was to preside.' This somewhat mysterious allusion is cleared up when we remember that the Monothelite controversy, which Archbishop Trench has described as often underrated by modern students, but as really a contest 'for life and death' to the Church [1], because it involved the reality of our Lord's willing self-sacrifice, had been troubling Christendom for more than thirty years : that Pope Martin I., nearly twenty years before, had affirmed the doctrine of Two Wills in the One Christ, corresponding to His Two Natures [2], and four or five years later had suffered, in that cause, the most brutal injustice, ending in exile and death [3], at the hands of a heretical Eastern Emperor, who had quite recently inflicted his presence upon Rome, constrained Vitalian to do him all outward honour, and 'plundered the churches of their precious ornaments [4].' Vitalian had no mind to be a confessor or martyr ; but he wished to bar out the imperial heresy wherever he could do so without personal risk. He had no reason, however, to be apprehensive of such tendencies in Hadrian's

---

[1] Trench's Huls. Lect. p. 214. For an account of Monothelitism, see Robertson, Hist. Ch. ii. 421. 'Although,' says Hardwick, M. Ages, p. 69, 'the human element in Christ was not verbally denied, it was reduced to a mere *passive* organ of His Godhead.' See Wilberforce on the Incarnation, p. 141 ; Bp. Forbes on the Nicene Creed, p. 204 ; Liddon, Bamp. Lect. p. 265.

[2] First Lateran Council, October, 649. Hefele, Councils, s. 307.

[3] See the account in Mansi, x. 860, and Alb. Butler for Nov. 12.

[4] See Robertson, ii. 433. Constans II. was a fratricide. Hefele says that Pope and Emperor took part in 'a double system of dissimulation;' Councils, s. 311.

nominee [1].　Learned and aged as he was, Theodore had never taken holy orders, which, according to Roman reckoning, included the subdiaconate.　To this office, then, he was promoted: but as his head was shaven quite bald, after the fashion styled St. Paul's tonsure [2], he had, as Bede gravely tells us, to 'wait four months, until his hair should be grown again, and be fit to receive the coronal tonsure [3].'　The four months came to an end about the middle of March, 668, and Theodore's head could then assume the aspect to which the zealots for Roman ceremonial,—Bede himself, we must say,

Consecration of Theodore for Canterbury.

included,—attached such importance: he was presented, at last, to Vitalian, who consecrated him with his own hands, praying, in the Roman form [4], that 'whatever of excellence had of old time been symbolised by the gold and gems and varied colours of the Aaronic vestments might shine forth,' in this new member of the Christian high priesthood, 'through brightness of character and of action:' that in him 'might abound constancy of faith, purity of love, sincerity in following after peace:' that the Most High 'Author of all dignities might give him the episcopal chair to rule His church and people,' and 'might be Himself his authority, his firmness, and his power.'　This memorable consecration, which was apparently the ultimate stock of the episcopate of the Church of England [5], took place on the 26th of March, the fifth Sunday in Lent, 668.

Yet two months more were spent by Theodore in Rome. At length, on the 27th of May, he set forth with Hadrian,

---

[1] Theodore's Orientalism was shown, not on dogmatic points, but in the 'Draconian' severity of his penitential rules; see Stevenson's Chron. of Abingdon, ii. p. lviii.

[2] 'The Greek monks,' says Mabillon, Ann. Bened. i. 493, 'were at that time entirely shaven, in imitation, as they thought, of St. James, the Lord's brother, and of the apostle Paul.'　See Smith's Bede, pp. 705, 715, on Germanus, patriarch of Constantinople at a later date, who had the whole of his head shaven.

[3] Bede, iv. 1: 'Donec ei coma cresceret, quo in coronam tonderi posset.'

[4] Greg. Sacram., Muratori, Lit. Rom. Vet. ii. 357.　The preceding words are very remarkable: 'Illius namque sacerdotii anterioris habitus nostræ *mentis* ornatus est; et pontificalem gloriam non jam nobis honor commendat vestium, sed splendor animarum.'　This had been the Gelasian form a hundred years before Gregory; Murat. i. 625.

[5] This point will be considered further on.

and with an Englishman signally fitted to assist him on CHAP. VII.
his journey. This was Benedict Biscop, who, having made
his second visit to Rome in 665, and after a few months
retired to the isle of Lerins, and taken the tonsure and vows
of a monk, had revisited Rome in 667, and was now requested
by Vitalian, who appreciated his religious earnestness and
energy, 'to lay aside the pilgrimage which he had undertaken
for Christ's sake' to the tombs of the Apostles, and, 'with an
eye to a yet higher advantage,' return homewards as guide
and interpreter to his country's long-desired archbishop[1].
'Benedict did as he was commanded.' But further delays had
to be endured when the party arrived at Arles. Ebroin, 'the
last great mayor of the palace of Neustria and Burgundy[2],'
to whom, as we have seen, has been attributed the execution
of archbishop Aunemund[3], and who scrupled at no extremities in support of Merovingian royalty as against 'the wild
anarchy of the chiefs[4],' imagined apparently that the travellers
were politically dangerous, and obliged archbishop John of
Arles to detain[5] them until his pleasure should be known.
When in the autumn they were allowed to depart, Theodore
proceeded to Paris, where Agilbert, now settled there as bishop,
entertained him 'kindly and for a considerable time.' Meanwhile Hadrian paid visits to old friends, Emmo archbishop of
Sens, and Faro the aged bishop of Meaux: as monk and
abbot, he would be specially attracted towards prelates one of
whom had given charters to monasteries[6], and the other
had built a 'suburban monastery' where any foreigners were
welcome guests[7]. These long visits were not causeless loiter-
ings; 'winter was at hand, and obliged them to remain quiet
wherever they could[8].' But when King Egbert was informed
by trusty messengers that his archbishop was now in the

[1] Bede, Hist. Abb. 3.
[2] Guizot, Hist. Fr. c. 9.
[3] See his after-proceedings in regard to bishop Leodegar or St. Leger,
October, 678. We shall see further on how he acted in regard to Wilfrid.
[4] Kitchin, Hist. Fr. i. 95.
[5] Bede, iv. 1.
[6] Mabillon, Ann. Bened. i. 448, 450.
[7] Mabillon, i. 343. Faro, or Burgundofaro, died about 672; ib. 509.
[8] Bede iv. 1: 'Coegerat enim eos imminens hiems,' &c.

CHAP. VII. realm of the Franks, he sent his reeve [1] Redfrid to bring him home. Ebroin gave his licence in regard to Theodore, but detained Hadrian for some time longer, suspecting that he was an envoy from the new Emperor Constantine IV. to 'the kings of Britain,' hostile to the dynasty which he both served and ruled [2]. When Theodore, escorted by Redfrid, arrived at Quentavic, or Etaples, in Ponthieu, a further brief delay was caused by an illness which attacked him: 'but as soon as he had begun to get better,' he crossed the Channel, and so 'arrived at his church,' as Bede says with reference to these long trials of English patience, 'in the second year of his consecration.'

Arrival of Theodore.

That was a great day in Canterbury, the second Sunday after Pentecost, May 27, 669 [3], when Theodore took his seat on the throne of Augustine, at the western end of the 'basilica of the Holy Saviour Christ.' It was seventy-two years after the arrival of the first archbishop: and now the seventh, though far on in life, had twenty-one years reserved for his wonderful energies as a ruler and organiser, which brought, says Bede, 'such an amount of spiritual benefit to the Churches of the English as they had never before received [4].' One of his first acts was to commit the vacant abbacy of SS. Peter and Paul to Benedict Biscop [5], who held it for two years, until Hadrian, who had arrived in Britain soon after Theodore, was made abbot, and so provided, according to the special directions of 'the apostolic lord [6]' at Theodore's departure, 'with a place in the diocese of

[1] 'Præfectum.' Comp. iii. 14, 'præfectum suum Ediluinum,' the slayer of St. Oswin; and Ep. Egb. 7; Vit. Cuthb. 15.

[2] Bede, iv. 1: 'Legationem aliquam imperatoris,' &c. 'When he had ascertained that Hadrian did not hold, and never had held, any such commission he let him go free,' &c. Constantine IV., 'the Bearded' (see Gibbon, vi. 76), had succeeded his father Constans in September, 668.

[3] Bede, iv. 2: 'Pervenit autem Theodorus,' &c. See Hook, Archbishops, i. 151.

[4] Bede, v. 8: 'Ut enim breviter dicam,' &c.

[5] Bede, Hist. Abb. 3. Elmham ignores this passage, when he says that Benedict Biscop was not abbot of St. Augustine's: p. 204. He adds that Hadrian received the abbacy from Theodore, not as archbishop, but as legate of the Pope; a very 'Augustinian' touch.

[6] Bede, iv. 1. 'Domnus apostolicus,' i. e. 'my lord the successor of the apostle,' was a common title for the Pope. See the Roman Litany.

Canterbury where he could live conveniently with his own CHAP. VII. attendants,' and we must add, keep watch over the 'Greek' archbishop's orthodoxy.

As soon as Hadrian arrived, Theodore took him as his Visitation companion and 'fellow-labourer' in a general visitation of by Theodore. what was now to be deemed his province, in order 'to consecrate bishops in fitting places,' and 'disseminate the rule of right living and the Catholic mode of celebrating Easter[1].' The archbishop was thoroughly bent on doing his work, and, for that end, putting in force his authority. He had, it must be owned, something of the autocrat about him[2]: but he had been specially appointed to a task which would require the energies of a resolute and commanding will. He had to make himself felt as the rightful chief pastor of the several English Churches, and to mould and compress them into unity under a more than merely nominal head. He probably felt that, at his years, he must work hard at his task, during what might remain to him of the 'twelve hours' of his day: he had less time than a younger man for gently feeling his way, and gradually developing his plans. He was conscious of the gifts of a born ruler: one does not think of him as of a saint, or a man who, *because* he 'loved,' in St. Augustine's exquisite phrase, could 'do whatever he liked[3],'—whose administrative success was the fruit of a genial nature, that gained obedience by the mere fact of evoking sympathy. *This* man of Tarsus was not like him whose heart was so tenderly 'enlarged[4]' towards all who were under his authority: and the idea of discipline and obedience had received in the continental Church-system so ample a development, the hierarchy was so much regarded as an organ of governmental action, and so little comparatively, as a presentation to mankind of a Divine Pastor in His various operations of love,— that one expects to find in the character of a bishop brought up in it a certain hard authoritativeness, which reminds one of

[1] Bede, iv. 2 : 'Ritum paschæ . . . disseminabat . . . ordinabat locis opportunis episcopos,' &c.

[2] See Bede, iv. 6, 28.

[3] 'Dilige, et quod vis fac ;' In Epist. Joan. Tract. 7. 8.

[4] 2 Cor. vi. 11.

the old Roman magistracy rather than of St. Chrysostom or St. Paul. But whatever Theodore was, whether we think him deficient or not in some characteristics of a shepherd of souls, we must recognise in him a man of vast practical ability, and sincere determination to do his best for the Church. And not only can we appreciate what he did for England during an unexpectedly long episcopate, but we can understand how at its commencement he ' was received as a public blessing by the kings and people, and was the first archbishop, Bede says, to whom all England submitted[1].' Great stress was naturally laid on his having been sent directly from Rome, and consecrated by the Pope's own hands and voice[2]: but this advantage was enhanced by the force of his own personality, so that, on all accounts, his arrival forms an epoch[3].

---

[1] Johnson, Engl. Can. i. 86; comp. Bede, iv. 2: 'Isque primus erat in archiepiscopis cui omnis Anglorum ecclesia *manus dare* consentiret.'

[2] See Conc. Herutf., in Bede, iv. 5: 'Ab apostolica sede destinatus.' So Eddi, 15, 'Unde emissus venerat;' ib. 29, 'illuc ab apostolica sede olim directi;' ib. 30, 'ab hac apostolica sede directus est;' ib. 4, 'a quam issus erat;' ib. 4, 'ex hac apostolica sede mandato.'

[3] Lingard, A.-S. Ch. i. 77. Bede says of his first years, ' Never were there happier times since the Angles came to Britain;' and cp. Bede, v. 8.

CHAPTER VIII.

When Theodore began his visitation, probably about mid-summer in 669, there were but three English bishoprics not vacant; and of these, one, that of Dunwich, was vacated by the death of Boniface in that same year [1]. In his place Theodore consecrated Bisi, 'a man,' says Bede, 'of much holiness and piety.' The see of Rochester was filled by Putta, whom Wilfrid had ordained priest: but this appointment was not altogether successful, for Putta, though a skilful Church musician, had no aptitude for 'mundane' affairs, and could not stand up against exceptional difficulties [2]. Proceeding Theodore and Chad. to the North-country, he found that 'for three years' Chad had been 'ruling the church of York' in a manner which Bede calls 'sublime [3].' But nothing escaped the keen eye of the archbishop [4] : from his rigidly Roman point of view, he noted a flaw in Chad's episcopal position. 'You have not been consecrated in a regular manner [5];'—he referred, apparently, to what might be represented as the intrusion of Chad into a see for which provision had been already made by Wilfrid's Frankish consecration, and also to the fact that two of Chad's consecrators were Britons, observers of the non-Catholic Easter, and as such condemned by 'the statutes of the Apostolic see,' which Theodore carried with him. Wilfrid's biographer cannot but admire Chad as 'an admirable teacher,' and more as 'a true servant of God, and a very meek man [6],' although he probably exaggerates his

[1] For Boniface became bishop in 652, and sat seventeen years; Bede, iv. 5.

[2] Bede, iv. 2, 12.

[3] Bede, v. 19, in sense of 'excellent;' so v. 19.

[4] 'Perlustrans omnia,' Bede, iv. 2.

[5] 'Non fuisse rite ordinatum,' ib.

[6] Eddi, 14, 15. A writer in Dict. Chr. Biogr. (art. 'Ceadda') thinks that

self-humiliation. According to Bede's simple account, Chad answered in a very humble voice[1], 'If you are persuaded that I received the episcopate in an irregular manner, I willingly retire from the office; for I never thought myself worthy of it[2]: indeed, it was only for obedience' sake, when commanded to undertake it, that I consented, though unworthy.' The command that he referred to must have been that of Oswy and the other authorities concerned. It is to be observed that according to this representation of his words, he did not confess, as a matter of personal conviction, that he had done wrong[3], or allowed himself to be wrongly consecrated; he simply announced that if Theodore felt sure of this, he would not defend his position. Theodore was touched and softened[4] by this utter want of self-assertion. 'No,' he said; 'you are not bound to resign the bishopric.' But Chad, it seems, insisted on retiring to his monastery at Lastingham[5], and left York accordingly, whereupon Wilfrid naturally took possession of the see. But very shortly afterwards an arrangement suggested itself, which might secure for the Church the episcopal services of Chad as well as of Wilfrid. The Mercian king desired Theodore to supply him and his people with a bishop[6]. Theodore instantly saw his way. 'He refused to consecrate a new bishop for the Mercians,

the objection was a mere 'pretext,' devised to get rid of Chad and make room for Wilfrid. This is not at all required by the facts.

[1] 'Voce humillima,' Bede, iv. 2.

[2] This partly reminds us of the famous speech ascribed by a 'legend' to St. Wulstan of Worcester, which was possibly modelled upon it. See Freeman, iv. 376.

[3] As Eddi would represent it, 'Peccatum, . . . pœnitentia humili secundum judicium episcoporum confessus emendavit. There were no other bishops in the North, at the time, beside Theodore, and, doubtless, Wilfrid, who would have returned from Kent to Northumbria.

[4] Malmesbury wrongly ascribes this feeling, not to Theodore, but to Wilfrid.

[5] Bede, iv. 3, v. 19. I follow Raine's order of events: it seems most likely that the 'consummating' of Chad's consecration took place, not, as Eadmer says, before his retirement to Lastingham, but when he was summoned back to be bishop of the Mercians. See Fast. Ebor. i. 51. All happened, evidently, within a few weeks. Richard of Hexham says that 'Chad was deposed, and returned to Lastingham;' X Script. 293.

[6] Bede, iv. 3. Eddi says that Wulfhere had previously given Wilfrid a sort of commission to find another bishop for Mercia; 15. This does not agree with Bede; and we cannot rely on Eddi's accuracy.

but asked King Oswy to give them Chad:'—an expression CHAP. VIII. which implies that the Northumbrian king's consent was necessary for the settlement of one of his subjects as bishop of a 'South-humbrian' Church. Chad had so many associations with former Church-work in Mercia, as the brother of Cedd, and as connected with Lindisfarne, that he would be specially fitted to succeed Jaruman: and any irregularities in his consecration might be corrected by Theodore himself. This was done: 'Theodore completed his consecration afresh, in the Catholic manner.' What does this imply? Eddi tells us that the bishops 'fully ordained Chad through all the ecclesiastical grades[1].' If the latter statement were literally accepted, it would imply that not only Chad's consecration, but his previous ordination, must have been regarded as null on the ground of the 'schismatic' character of the prelates who performed them. Undoubtedly great authorities had pronounced such consecration or ordination to be void[2]. But this was not universally ruled[3], and Wini at least was no schismatic[4]; so that a real reiteration of Chad's orders, including the episcopate, would have constituted one of those peremptory judgments which ignored the distinction, so obvious to all modern churchmen, between what is irregular and what is invalid[5]. If, however, we simply follow Bede's account, and illustrate it by an extant decision ascribed to Theodore[6], we

---

[1] Eddi, 15. Eadmer (c. 17) follows Bede, Malmesbury follows Eddi.

[2] As to schismatics, the natural sense of the Nicene Council's decisions respecting Novatians (can. 8) and Meletians (Ep. Synod. in Soc. i. 9) points in this direction. See Morinus, De Sacr. Ordin. par. 3. p. 120; Routh, Scr. Op. i. 416. Bingham, indeed, interprets the two decisions diversely, b. iv. c. 7. s.7, and s. 8; and Tillemont, vi. 678, 814, understands both as referring, not to reordination, but to a reconciliatory and confirmatory benediction.

[3] See Bingham, iv. 7. 7, 8, that there was no uniform rule in the ancient Church as to this question; e.g. the Donatist bishops were not reconsecrated, nor were those who had been consecrated by the heretical Bonosus, nor who came over from Macedonianism. He suggests that the 'benedictio impositæ manus,' ordered by the first Council of Orleans in 511 (Mansi, viii. 353) in case of converted Arian clerics, 'perhaps does not mean a new ordination, but only a reconciliatory imposition of hands.' But see Hefele on the other side, Councils, b. 13, s. 224. See Bede, v. 6, where 'St. John of Beverley' rebaptizes a youth who had been baptized by a priest too dull to learn the form of baptism.

[4] Consecration by one bishop was not deemed invalid.

[5] See a case in Milman, Lat. Chr. iii. 242. Cp. Hefele, s. 98 (ii. 359, E. T.)

[6] Theodore's Penitential, ii. 9. 1 (Haddan and Stubbs, iii. 197): 'Those

CHAP. VIII. may suppose that the archbishop intended simply to add whatever forms might have been omitted, to supply canonical defects, and then to rehabilitate Chad for all purposes of episcopal jurisdiction. If Theodore was over-punctilious in this matter, his next act exhibits him in a very pleasing and kindly light. He had evidently taken a strong liking to Chad; and hearing that it had been the latter's habit[1] to go about his diocese on foot, 'he ordered him to ride whenever he had a longer circuit than usual before him.' Chad objected, out of 'zealous love of pious labour,' and probably with remembrances of his old master Aidan. But the archbishop, in this as in graver matters, was masterful when he met with any resistance; and he saw that Chad's notions of humility and mortification were imperilling his practical efficiency. 'You *shall* ride,' he said; and with his own aged hands he lifted Chad bodily on horseback, 'because,' says Bede with charming simplicity, 'he had ascertained him to be a holy man.'

Chad, bishop of Lichfield.

It must have been in the September of 669[2] that Chad thus resumed episcopal work, and settled himself in that same Lichfield where Wulfhere had once desired to establish Wilfrid, but where no Mercian bishop, as yet, had 'held his see.' There he found, or built, a church of St. Mary, to the east of the site now occupied by 'the fair cathedral[3];' and also, near it, erected a house to be his dwelling 'when he was not at work in the ministry of the Word[4].' Seven or eight brethren used to share at such times his studies and devotions; but outside the walls was to be seen, engaged in manual labour, a man who had a remarkable

who have been ordained by bishops of Scots or Britons, who are not Catholic in the matter of Pasch or tonsure, have not been united to the Church, sed iterum a catholico episcopo manus impositione confirmentur.' Now these words describe a case beyond Chad's. Bede evidently regards Chad as having been a real bishop during his government of the church of York. Compare the Roman legend about Kentigern, that the Pope supplied 'quæ deerant consecrationi ejus,' Vit. Kent. c. 27, cp. c. 11. See Hook, i. 155; Warren, Lit. Rit. Celt. Ch. p. 68.

[1] Bede, iv. 2; compare iii. 28, 'non equitando,' &c.

[2] For Chad held the Mercian see two and a half years; and he died in March, 672.   [3] Marmion, vi. 36.

[4] At 'Chadstowe,' now Stowe, at the end of 'the Pool.'

history of his own. This was Ouini, or Owin, who had been CHAP. VIII.
born and bred in East-Anglia, and had come thence to
Northumbria, in 660, as steward of the household to the
princess Etheldred, when she married Egfrid son of Oswy [1].
The enthusiastic devotion of the East-Anglian court had taken
hold of its trusted servant. One day he had appeared in a
rustic dress, with axe and hatchet, like a common woodman,
at the door of Lastingham. He had quitted his high office,
'left all that he had [2],' and begged for admission into the
monastery. Study was not in his line, but he offered to
devote himself to field-work: and he ultimately followed his
abbot and bishop to Lichfield. Wulfhere also endowed the
bishopric with fifty 'hydes' of land for a monastery 'in a
place called Ad Barvæ, that is, At the Grove, in the province
of Lindsey,' supposed to be Barrow in Lincolnshire, where
'traces' of Chad's discipline existed when Bede wrote [3]. The
work of so large a diocese, even with the aid of a horse, must
have tasked all his energies. Bede tells us much of his profound
religious awe, on the authority of Trumbert, a monk 'who
had been brought up in his monastery and under his rule,'
and who was 'one of those who instructed' the future
historian 'in the Scriptures [4].' According to his account,
Chad represented, very markedly, that type of piety which
distinguished the great ascetics and the most earnest of
the early Teutonic Christians, and fixed their thoughts with
such intensity on the awful side of their religion. ' He was
ever subject to the fear of the Lord, and in all his
actions mindful of his end [5].' Everything which seemed to

---

[1] The date is given by Florence, and agrees with Thomas of Ely's account
of St. Etheldred. ' Owin' may possibly have had the administration of the Isle
of Ely; Vit. Etheldr. c. 8, in Act. SS. Benedict. ii. 745. Thomas calls Owin
a worthy 'custos et provisor' to Etheldred. He is said to have lived at
Winford, near Hadenham; Bentham, Hist. of Ely, p. 51. The monumental
inscription upon the tomb, '✠ Lucem tuam Ovino da, Deus, et requiem,
Amen,' is ' perhaps one of the most venerable monuments of Saxon antiquity ; '
Palgrave, p. cciii. ' It long served as a horse-block,' but is now in the south
aisle of Ely Cathedral.

[2] 'Pura intentione supernæ retributionis,' says Bede, iv. 3.

[3] Bede, l. c. He was thus bishop 'Merciorum simul et Lindisfarorum.'

[4] Bede, l. c. : ' Namque inter plura,' &c.

[5] 'Novissimorum suorum.' Ecclus. vii. 36 (40, Vulg.).

him a voice from God was taken as a loud call to self-scrutiny and contrition, a warning to prepare for the stroke that was still withheld[1]. If a high wind swept across the moors at Lastingham,—or, we may add, around the little cathedral at Lichfield,—he at once gave up his reading, and implored the Divine mercy for mankind. If it increased, he would shut his book, and prostrate himself in prayer. If it rose to a storm, with rain or thunder and lightning, he would repair to the church, and give himself 'with a fixed mind' to prayer and the recitation of psalms, until the weather cleared up. If questioned about this, he would quote the Psalmist's words, 'The Lord thundered out of heaven,' and urge the duty of preparing by a serious repentance for 'that tremendous time when the heavens and earth should be on fire[2], and the Lord would come in the clouds with great power and majesty, to judge the quick and the dead.' Yet with all this dread of Divine judgments, Chad, in his own words, had 'a continual love and desire of the heavenly rewards[3]:' and 'it was no wonder,' says Bede, 'if he rejoiced to behold the day of death, or rather the day of the Lord, seeing he had so anxiously prepared for it until it actually came[4].' It came by an access of the often-recurring pestilence, which had proved fatal to many members of the church of Lichfield before it attacked the bishop himself[5]. It was said that Owin[6], at his work in the fields near the 'mansion,' heard a sweet sound, as of angelic melody, come from the south-east and gradually reach and fill the oratory where Chad was, until after half an hour it rose again heavenward. While pondering

---

[1] 'Discussis penetralibus cordis nostri . . . . solliciti ne unquam percuti mereamur.'

[2] 'Cœlis ac terris ardentibus,' alluding to 2 Peter iii. 12.

[3] To him, as to Bede, there was no difficulty in harmonising such texts as Heb. x. 31 and 1 John iv. 8. Compare the account of Bede's own death: 'He sang the sentence, "Horrendum est incidere in manus Dei viventis," but also quoted St. Ambrose, "Nec mori timeo, quia bonum Deum habemus."'

[4] Bede, iv. 3 : 'Non autem mirum si diem mortis, vel potius diem Domini,' &c. Comp. Bede, iv. 24, on Cædmon.

[5] Bede, iv. 3 : 'Supervenit namque clades,' &c.

[6] Bede does not say through whom this came to him. He considers Owin to have been 'dignus cui Dominus specialiter sua revelaret arcana, dignus cui fidem narranti audientes accommodarent.'

what it might mean, he saw Chad open the window of CHAP. VIII.
the oratory, and clap his hands, as he was wont to do by
way of summoning any one who was outside. He entered:
the bishop bade him call 'the seven,' his special companions,
and come with them. All came: he bade them 'cherish love
and peace among each other, and towards all the faithful,' and
adhere to all 'the rules of discipline which they had learned of
him or seen him observe, or found in the acts or sayings of
the fathers who preceded him.' 'My time is very near: that
loveable guest [1] who used to visit our brethren has come to
me to-day. Go back to the church, and bid the brethren
commend to the Lord my departure, and also remember to
prepare for their own,—the hour of which they know not.'
And then, the story proceeds, after they had received his
blessing and departed in great sorrow, he told Owin privately
that the voices which he had heard were those of 'angels come
to summon him to those heavenly rewards which he had ever
loved and longed for, and that they would return in seven
days and take him thither with them.' He was speedily taken
ill, and on the seventh day, Tuesday the 2nd of March, 672,
after receiving his last Communion, he closed an episcopate
which, alike in Northumbria and in Mercia, deserved the
epithet of 'most glorious [2],' and procured for the name of
St. Chad of Lichfield a high place among the saints of his
country. He was buried in St. Mary's church, but afterwards removed to the later church of St. Peter [3]: and he was
succeeded by one who had long served him as deacon, a
'good and modest man' named Winfrid [4].

The desirableness of treating his Mercian life as a unity
has led us to anticipate the order of events. Changes had
taken place in Northumbria, in Wessex, and in Kent, while
Chad was at work in Mercia and in Lindsey. Oswy's reign, Death of
which Bede significantly characterises as 'most laborious [5],' Oswy.
was drawing near its end when he 'gave' Chad to Wulfhere.

---

[1] Meaning, the angel of death. Cp. a story in Bede, iv. 9.

[2] 'Gloriosissime,' applied to his Mercian episcopate; Bede, iv. 3.

[3] Bede describes his shrine as 'a wooden structure in the form of a small
house, with a hole through which part of his "dust" could be taken out.'

[4] Bede, l. c. : 'In cujus locum,' &c.

[5] Bede, iii. 14.

CHAP. VIII. He was then in his fifty-eighth year, 'weighed down,' says Bede, 'by illness,' but not thinking it fatal, and making plans, in case he should get better, for gratifying his late-grown admiration for Roman usages by going to Rome, and ending his days among its 'sacred places:' he even begged Wilfrid to be ready to act as his guide, and promised him 'no small gift of money [1].' This was not to be. He died on the 15th of February, 670, and was buried in the minster of Whitby, where also the bones of Edwin were deposited [2]. His crown passed to his son Egfrid, who was now twenty-five [3], and whom Bede in one passage describes as 'most pious [4]' on account of his friendship for Benedict Biscop, while Eddi dilates on his religious excellence, his gentleness among his own people, his bravery and success in war,—for instance, in his campaign against the Pictish leader Bernhaeth, when he 'filled two rivers with the corpses of the dead [5];' and, we may add, in another campaign with Wulfhere, by which he recovered Lindsey [6]. At the beginning of his reign he lived on friendly terms with Wilfrid, who was then at the height of his prosperity and popularity. We seem to see him going about his diocese with the energy of one born to 'repair the breaches' and 'build the old waste places [7]:' at York he 'shuddered [8]' to see his cathedral fallen into a miserable

Wilfrid bishop of York.

[1] Bede, iv. 5.

[2] Elmham, Hist. Mon. Ang. p. 188.

[3] See Bede, iv. 26, that in 685 he was in his fortieth year.

[4] Hist. Abb. 1.

[5] Eddi, 19; adding that the pursuers thus actually crossed the river 'siccis pedibus.' The rivers were probably the Forth and Teith, or the Tay and Earn ; Skene, Celt. Scotl. i. 261.

[6] Eddi, 20; Bede, iv. 12 : 'Superato . . . et fugato Wulfhere.' Malmesbury, 'Partem provinciarum Northanimbrorum regi cesserit ;' G. P. iii. 100. See above, pp. 159, 188.

[7] This was a duty prescribed to bishops ; e.g. 4th of Toledo, c. 36 (A.D. 633) ; 'Episcopum per cunctas diœceses parochiasque suas per singulos annos ire oportet, ut exquirat quo una quæque basilica in reparatione sui indigeat ;' Mansi, x. 629. On this use of 'diœceses,' cf. Greg. Turon. H. Fr. v. 5.

[8] 'Horruit spiritus ejus,' Eddi, 15. The windows, says Malmesbury, had been covered with thin linen or trellis-work ; G. P. l. c. Fridegod says,

'Humida contrito stillabant assere tecta ;
. . . . . . pluviæ quacunque vagantur,
Pendula discissis fluitant laquearia tignis.'

See Lingard, A.-S. Ch. i. 263; Freeman, v. 609.

dilapidation, which implies some negligence on the part of CHAP. VIII. Chad ; for otherwise Wilfrid would not have found the roofs decaying, the windows devoid of glass, and the inner walls blotched with rain and haunted by birds. He repaired the roofs, covered them with lead, glazed the windows, cleaned the walls with lime, decked the altar with new furniture [1], and obtained new property for the church. At his beloved Ripon he reared 'a basilica of polished stone, towering to a great height, with pillars of varied form, and arched vaults, and winding cloisters [2] ; ' and invited the king, his brother Alfwin, and a number of sub-kings, reeves, and abbots to attend the dedication ' in honour of the Prince of the Apostles.' On such a day he was truly in his element ; and we may imagine the interest with which the function of which he was the centre would be watched by a little boy then being trained up in the monastery, afterwards the great missionary arch- bishop Willibrord [3]. The altar, vested in purple and cloth of gold, was elaborately blessed, the paten and chalice hallowed, the Eucharist celebrated : then Wilfrid, in front of the altar, with his face towards the people [4], recited a list of the lands recently or previously bestowed upon him, and also of the sanctuaries once held by the British Church [5]. Then came a public feast, kept up with barbaric extravagance for three days and nights,—a strange concession, we may think, to the coarse tastes of the Yorkshiremen. Wilfrid added to his other ' gifts for the adornment of God's house ' a large golden

---

[1]   'Lymphis perfunditur absis,
       Albanturque suis lustrata altaria peplis.' Frideg. 451.

[2] Eddi, 16; and Malmesbury, G. Pontif. l. c., 'porticuum inflexu.' This church stood some 200 yards from the site of the present cathedral; and the crypt under the latter must belong to another church, built either by Wilfrid or by Eadhed, bishop in 679. Part of it is called ' St. Wilfrid's Needle.'

[3] Act. SS. Bened. sæc. iii. 1. 603.

[4] 'Stans . . . ante altare, conversus ad populum,' Eddi.

[5] 'Quas reges . . . illi dederunt.' Eddi names four districts, one being near the Ribble. Raine suggests that the other three are Gilling, the vale of the Duddon, and Cartmel. An extract from Peter of Blois' lost Life of Wilfrid, in Mon. Anglic. ii. 133, names three districts, all in Lancashire. For the claim on old British Church-property, see Raine in Dict. Ch. Biogr. iv. 1180.

CHAP. VIII. cross [1], and a copy of the Gospels in four volumes, written in letters of gold on richly coloured parchment, all contained in a case [2] wrought with gold and jewels,—a treasure long preserved in Ripon minster. At Hexham, also, on land given by the pious Queen Etheldred [3], he built, in honour of St. Andrew, a church of great length and height, with 'manifold columns and porches, a complication of ascending and descending passages [4].' And at this day, the visitor who looks round the exquisite minster of Hexham will find nothing worthier of his attention than the small crypt of Roman masonry, with two Roman inscriptions built up in its walls, on the western side of the transept: descending into it, he enters the only remaining part of Wilfrid's church, 'the building deep under ground formed of admirably carved stone,' which Eddi includes in his description of a structure that, as far as he knew, had no equal 'on this side of the Alps.' The bishop also exerted himself for the improvement of Divine service: he set Eddi and Æona to carry on the special work of teaching Church-song, or, as Eddi makes him express it [5], of 'training choirs to sing responsively, according to the custom of the primitive Church.' But if Wilfrid was munificent as a church-builder, and active as a promoter of choral worship, he was also indefatigable as a chief pastor: he is depicted as riding about

---

[1] Wilfrid's epitaph at Ripon, Bede, v. 19: 'Sublime crucis radiante metallo . . . trophæum.'

[2] 'Bibliothecam,' Eddi. So the epitaph, Bede, l. c., 'Ac thecam,' &c.

[3] The property had come to Etheldred as a marriage gift; Rich. Hexh. de statu Hagust. Eccl. c. 7, X Script. 294.

[4] Eddi, 22. Richard of Hexham expands this description: 'Parietes . . . columnis suffultus, et tribus tabulatis distinctos, . . . erexit. Ipsos . . . et capitella columnarum . . . et arcum sanctuarii, historiis et imaginibus, et variis cælaturarum figuris ex lapide prominentibus, et picturarum et colorum grata varietate . . . . decoravit. Ipsum quoque corpus ecclesiæ appenticiis et porticibus undique circumcinxit.' In the stone staircases and 'deambulatoria' and winding passages up and down, many men could stand without being seen by any one in the church. The cloisters had oratories and altars of their own. The minster was enriched with splendid 'ornaments,' vestments, and books: and the 'court' (atrium) was surrounded by a strong thick wall. Altogether, this minster 'surpassed all the nine monasteries' of which Wilfrid was 'father and patron,' and 'all others in England;' X Script. 290.

[5] Eddi, 47. See Benedict. Greg. Op. iii. 650. Comp. Joan. Diac. Vit. Greg. ii. 6, on Gregory's compilation of antiphons and his 'schola cantorum.'

incessantly to baptize and confirm [1], holding ordinations [2], CHAP. VIII.
forming new church settlements, and amid all this whirl of
activities retaining his habits of ascetic devotion. Of these
we are told that neither in summer nor in winter did he
drink more at his meal than the contents of one small cup,
and that he persisted in washing his whole body in cold
water before going to bed, until, when he was quite an old
man, the Pope directed him to abstain from so severe a discipline [3]. At the same time, no austerity of manner was
discernible in him : he made himself ' dear and loveable ' to
people of all races [4], and his gracious geniality, the outcome
of a genuinely kind heart, was like sunshine to all who felt
its presence. ' Abstinence,' in him, did *not* generate ' pride,'—
so says his biographer with much significance. He was the
typical man of Church and realm ; the king admired and
relied on him ; the queen confided to him her longings for a
monastic life, which her husband at last reluctantly permitted
her to gratify by taking the veil from Wilfrid's hands in
Ebba's convent at Coldingham ; abbots and abbesses made him
their heir or their trustee, and nobles committed their sons
to the great prelate who had been a thane's firstborn, that
under his eye they might be prepared for ' God's service, if
they chose it,' or if, when grown up, they preferred a secular
life, might be ' presented as soldiers to the king [5].' He played
an important part in Frankish politics by inviting Dagobert,
the young heir of Austrasia, from his place of exile in Ireland,
and sending him over in princely state, to ascend the throne of
his father [6]. This is the picture of Wilfrid in the splendours
of a well-deserved ascendancy [7] : we shall see ere long how the

---

[1] Eddi, 18. See the story of the Ripon monk surnamed ' Bishop's son,' whom
he had baptized and claimed for ' God's service.'

[2] 'In omnibus locis presbyteros et diacones sibi adjuvantes ordinabat ;'
Eddi, 21. Here we see the germ of a parochial system : so in Bede iii. 22,
we find bishop Cedd ordaining clergy ' per loca.' Yet in 734 Bede had
to exhort bishop Egbert to ordain priests for the several villages; Ep. to
Egb. 3.

[3] Eddi, 21.

[4] Eddi, l. c. 'Inflatur nullo, Jesu moderamine, typho ;' Frideg. 476.

[5] They were his gesiths or retainers ; Stubbs, Const. Hist. i. 176.

[6] Eddi, 28. Dagobert II. was son of Sigebert II.

[7] See Raine, Historians of Church of York, i. p. xxvii.

unique brilliancy of his position contributed to provoke a great vicissitude, which did but bring into fuller light the real nobleness of a princely and Christian soul.

Benedict Biscop.

The companion of his first journey in Gaul had, as we have seen, made three visits to Rome, before the year 671, when he resigned the abbacy of Canterbury, again repairing to the 'threshold of the Apostles,' and 'brought back not a few books of sacred learning of all kinds, which he had either bought or received as gifts from friends [1].' Returning by Vienne, he there took possession of other books which friends in that district had at his request procured for him. When he was again in Northumbria, he conversed with the king, went through the whole story of his life, 'did not conceal' his monastic fervour, explained all that he had learned at Rome or elsewhere on matters monastic or ecclesiastical, and exhibited his store of manuscripts and of relics; altogether impressing Egfrid so strongly that he received a royal grant of seventy hydes, in order to found a monastery in honour of 'the first pastor of the Church,'—a design executed, some time later, at Wearmouth.

School at Canterbury.

Such a zeal for ecclesiastical literature as Benedict Biscop had was united in his successor Hadrian, and in Theodore himself, who was popularly called 'the Philosopher,' with a love of learning much wider in its range, and kindred to that spirit which had made the great Alexandrian teachers employ the existing curriculum of secular studies as distinctly capable of serving the cause of Divine truth [2]. Hadrian, with the archbishop's hearty approval, founded at Canterbury a school in which religious training was combined with all other learning accessible at the time. As we have seen, Canterbury had a school in the early days of the archbishopric, which served as a model for that of Felix at Dunwich [3]: but now 'a crowd of pupils was assembled [4],' and 'streams of sound learning' of all sorts, sacred and secular, 'flowed daily for the watering of their minds;' so that Hadrian, and even

---

[1] Bede, Hist. Abb. 4.

[2] Euseb. vi. 18; Greg. Thaumat. Panegyr. in Origenem. Comp. S. Aug. de Doctr. Chr. ii. 40; Socrates, H. E. iii. 16.

[3] Bede, iii. 17; above, p. 131.   [4] Bede, iv. 2.

the archbishop in person,—so marvellous was the old man's versatility and energy,—'even delivered to their hearers the rules of ecclesiastical arithmetic' (i.e. for the calculation of Church seasons), of astronomy, of music, and even of medicine [1], side by side with 'the volumes of sacred letters [2].' Among these hearers were John, famous as 'St. John of Beverley,' bishop successively of Hexham and York; Aldhelm, afterwards abbot of Malmesbury and bishop of Sherborne; Oftfor, bishop of Worcester [3], Tobias of Rochester [4], Albinus, the successor of Hadrian, who understood Greek fairly, and Latin thoroughly, and to whom we mainly owe it that Bede undertook his great work [5]: and, when Bede wrote, there were others living who had studied under Hadrian, and who 'knew Greek and Latin as well as they knew their own tongue wherein they were born [6].' This great school became the prototype of the yet more famous school of York in the next century, which, when presided over by Albert, afterwards archbishop, dealt with grammar, rhetoric, metre, astronomy, physics,—and out of which arose the illustrious Alcuin [7].

Monasticism, also, received some impulse in Kent at this time. Egbert, in the year of Theodore's arrival, had given the royal abode at Reculver, whither Ethelbert had retired when he settled Augustine at Canterbury, 'to Bass, the mass-priest, to build a minster,'—so says the Chronicle. And in or about the next year, a tragedy of royal jealousy and suspicion produced a remarkable penitential foundation: Egbert, we are told [8], was so far swayed by a thane bearing the ominous name of Thunor as not effectively to forbid the murder of his young cousins Ethelred and Ethelbert, sons of his uncle Ermenred, and brothers of Ermenburga or Domneva, the pious wife of the pious Merewald, son of Penda and sub-king of the West-

Monasticism in Kent.

---

[1] See Bede, v. 3, for Theodore's opinion on bleeding.

[2] 'Apicum.' Cp. Bede, Ep. ad Egb. 1, and iii. 8.

[3] Bede, iv. 23, 'De medio nunc dicamus.'

[4] Bede, v. 23.

[5] Bede, v. 20; and Præf., 'Auctor ante omnes,' &c.

[6] Bede, iv. 2; Green, Making of Engl. p. 335.

[7] See Alcuin, de Pontif. Ebor. 1431 ff.; Raine, Fast. Ebor. i. 101.

[8] For the legend, ' to which,' says Lappenberg, i. 246, ' history will not refuse a space,' see Simeon of Durham, Hist. Reg. 2–5; Elmham, p. 192.

CHAP. VIII. Mercians. Legend was diffuse on the circumstances which struck Egbert with compunction: the result was visible in the erection of the nunnery of Minster, in Thanet, on land [1] given by the king to Ermenburga as a 'wer-gild' or satisfaction for her brothers' innocent blood. Theodore consecrated her as abbess [2], and she was succeeded by her daughter Mildred, who became conspicuous among the female saints of the Old-English calendar [3].

Lothere, bishop of Winchester.

It was in the same year 670 that Theodore went, for a much more important function, to the West-Saxon capital. There had been no bishop of Winchester or Dorchester since the departure of Wini in 666; and Kenwalch, regretting his breach with Agilbert, sent messengers to request him to return. But Agilbert, now bishop of Paris, naturally answered that he was bound to his present charge [4]. 'However,' said he, 'there is my nephew Lothere, a presbyter, whom I think very well fitted to be a bishop: if the king will receive him to my old place, I am willing that he should go.' The proposal was accepted: a West-Saxon 'gemot,' which Bede, with a lax use of the term, refers to as a 'synod [5],' received Lothere with all honour; and the archbishop consecrated him in his own church [6], which five years before had been the scene of Chad's very different consecration. Kenwalch closed his chequered, but on the whole very honourable life, two years afterwards; and his widow Sexburga, a woman of remarkable talents, succeeded in maintaining herself as queen regnant for a year [7], until in 674, Escwin, according to the Chronicle, became king of Wessex, or, properly speaking,

---

[1] As much land, said the story, as 'cerva quam nutrierat una die peragraret' (Sim.). The king followed the hind; Thunor sneered, and the earth swallowed him! The spot was called 'Thunor's law' or 'Thunor's mound.' Bede alludes to wer-gilds in iv. 21.

[2] Thorn says that Mildred was the first abbess; X Script. 1907.

[3] Every one, for instance, who passes up 'Brasenose-lane' traverses ground belonging of old to a church named after the canonised granddaughter of Penda. For St. Mildred see Alban Butler, Feb. 20. Her father Merewald founded a convent at Leominster; her sister Milburga became abbess of Wenlock.

[4] Bede, iii. 7.

[5] 'Ex synodica sanctione.' Cp. Murat. Lit. Rom. ii. 189.

[6] According to canons, e.g. fourth Council of Orleans, c. 5.

[7] Chron a. 672; Malmesbury, G. Reg. i. 32.

became chief among those petty kings whom Bede represents CHAP. VIII.
as dividing Wessex between them for 'about ten years' after
the death of Kenwalch [1].

Another change of rulers took place in Kent, when Egbert Death of
died in the July of 673 [2], and was succeeded by his brother Egbert.
Lothere, the third month of whose reign was distinguished
by an event which forms a landmark; for Theodore, already
secure in his majestic supremacy, and practically independent Council of
of royal support, held the first English provincial Council, on Hertford.
the 24th of September, at 'Herutford' or Hertford [3], a place
probably chosen as fairly accessible, being on the border of
South-east Mercia and of Essex.

The synod of a province, according to Nicene rules [4], ex- Provincial
pressing, as they did, the mind of the whole Church upon Synods.
the subject, was a necessary part of its organisation. It was
to meet twice a year, and to settle all disputes, and generally
all matters, which affected the province as a unity. A similar
provision was made by one of the 'Apostolical' canons, which
referred to the synods thus held 'the doctrines of religion,
and the ecclesiastical disputes which may arise [5];' and 'the
Council of the Dedication' at Antioch, in 341 repeatedly
enforces the supreme judicial authority of a provincial synod,
when fully constituted under the presidency of the metropolitan [6]. The Council of Chalcedon [7] found that the holding
of 'the provincial synods prescribed by rules' had been
neglected, and ordered that they should be duly held twice

---

[1] Bede, iv. 12 : 'Acceperunt sub-reguli regnum gentis,' &c. See Stubbs, Const.
Hist. i. 171. The Chronicler, Florence, and Ethelwerd call Escwin king of
the West-Saxons. He was of another branch of the house of Cerdic. On
the extension of West-Saxon territory through Kenwalch's victories, see
Freeman, Engl. Towns and Distr. pp. 83, 137.

[2] Bede, iv. 5.

[3] In Alfred's version, 'Heortford.'

[4] Nicene can. 5. Compare Euseb. Vit. Const. i. 51, as to Licinius' suppression of synods : Ἄλλως γὰρ οὐ δυνατὸν τὰ μεγάλα τῶν σκεμμάτων ἢ
διὰ συνόδων κατορθώσασθαι. Compare Bingham, b. ii. c. 16. s. 16, 17.
These assemblies began to be held in the latter part of the second century.

[5] Apost. can. 38 ; but this is supposed to be more recent than the Nicene and
Antiochene synods (see Hefele, Hist. of Councils, i. 474, E. T.).

[6] Antioch. can. 20, ordering it to meet twice a year ; cp. can. 3, 4, 6, 12.

[7] Chalced. 19.

CHAP. VIII. a year, for the purpose of setting right whatever needed correction.   Since the date of that Council, Western synods had frequently upheld the institution : a bishop duly cited, said the second Council of Arles, must attend the synod, or if too ill to come, must send a deputy [1] : the last canon of Agde in 506 ordered that synods should be duly held according to the constitutions of the fathers [2] : the second Council of Lyons ordered that bishops of the same province should settle their differences before their metropolitan and comprovincials [3]. The British Church, as we have seen, had kept up its synods even when driven within the Welsh border [4] : the Frankish bishops were duly convened according to precedent [5] : the Church of Spain was equally observant of the rule [6].   It was simply necessary that the new English Church, as soon as it could be organised and consolidated, should have its provincial synods : Gregory had, long before this time, taken for granted that, as soon as possible, there would be this system at work, in the southern parts of Teutonic Britain, and also, in due time, in the northern.   He had spoken of a 'synod' of the province of London [7], and virtually of a synod of the province of York.   As yet there was but one province, which included north and south under Canterbury.   And Wini did not appear at the Council : one would fain accept the story that he resigned his see in penitence in 672 [8].   At any rate, Theodore had only four suffragans present in person, with delegates sent to represent Wilfrid.   One does not see why Wilfrid did not make the journey [9] : but there is also

---

[1] C. 18 ; Mansi, vii. 880.   Compare Council of Tarragona, a. 516, c. 6, ib. viii. 542; Council of Epaon, in Burgundy, c. 1, ib. viii. 559 ; second of Tours, c. i, ib. ix. 792 ; second of Macon, c. 20, ib. ix. 957.   One Spanish Council (Emerita) in 666 recognises 'the king's order' to hold a synod.

[2] c. 71 ; Mansi, viii. 336.

[3] Mansi, ix. 787.

[4] Above, p. 32.

[5] See fifth C. of Paris, c. 11 ; Mansi, x. 542.

[6] See fourth C. of Toledo, c. 3 ; Mansi, x. 617.

[7] Bede, i. 29 : 'Quatenus Lundoniensis civitatis episcopus semper in posterum a synodo propria debeat consecrari.'   See above, p. 69.

[8] Rudborne, Hist. Maj. Wint. (Angl. Sac. i. 192).   Erkenwald, the next bishop of London, was consecrated in 675.

[9] Is it possible that Wilfrid did not wish to appear simply as one of Theodore's suffragans ?

something not easy to explain in the order in which the
prelates are named,—Bisi, Wilfrid by his own delegates,
Putta [1], Lothere (called Leutherius), and Winfrid. Wilfrid was
considerably senior in consecration to all, Theodore included ;
but Bisi may have been older than his fellow-suffragans [2].
Bede makes it clear that the prelates alone formed the synod :
it was a ' Council of bishops,' and no other persons were
constituent members of it : this was the ancient Catholic
constitution of synods [3]. But it was quite in accordance with
that constitution that ' many Church-teachers,' who were not
bishops, but who ' both loved and understood the canonical
statutes of the fathers,' should be present,—as Malchion had
been present at the first Council of Antioch [4], and Athanasius,
as a deacon, at the Council of Nicæa.

Theodore would be sure to observe whatever solemn forms
were in use on the Continent at the opening of a synod [5]. We
may presume that the bishops and ' teachers' prayed silently
for a while, and that then one bishop prayed aloud. The
members then sat down, two on each side the archbishop,
together with the representatives of Wilfrid. Our account
of the proceedings was drawn up by Theodore, and written
out, as in his name, by ' Titillus the notary' or scribe. The
solemn commencement, ' In the Name of our Lord God and
Saviour Jesus Christ,' was a usual one [6], and we find bishops
sometimes appending ' in the name of Christ' to their own
signatures [7]. The next words, ' The same our Lord Jesus

---

[1] He is the only one of the suffragans who is named after his see, which is
called ' the Castle of the Kentish-men which is named Hrofescæstir.' The rest
take national titles, such as ' of the East-Angles, of the Northumbrians.' See,
on this, Freeman, ii. 605 ff.

[2] See Bede, iv. 5, fin., on his incapacitating ' infirmity.' And Wilfrid
ranked, it is supposed, as bishop *de facto* of York from 669. But Putta was
apparently a little senior in consecration to Bisi ; see Stubbs, Registrum, p. 3.

[3] Potter on Ch. Government, p. 225 ; Pusey on Councils, pp. 34, 51.

[4] Euseb. vii. 29.

[5] See fourth C. of Toledo, c. 4, for an account of the forms prescribed by
that Council in 633 ; Mansi, x. 617. ' None of the laity attended the Council
of Herudford ;' Palgrave, Engl. Comm. p. 171.

[6] Council of Osca or Huesca, 598, begins, ' In nomine D. n. J. C. ;' Mansi,
x. 481. Comp. Council of Barcelona, ib., ' Cum duce D. J. C. ;' second of
Seville, 619, ' In nomine Domini et Salvatoris nostri J. C.,' ib. 557.

[7] E.g. Mansi, viii. 622, at Valencia, and x. 478, at Toledo.

CHAP. VIII. Christ reigning for ever and governing His Church,' were an amplification of a form used in the third Council of Braga in 572 [1], and contrast strikingly with the date from a regnal year found in canons of King Reccared's reign and in others of the Spanish synods [2]. Theodore began, as he himself says, by requesting his beloved brethren, for the fear and love of the common Redeemer, to join him in taking counsel together [3] on behalf of their faith, that 'whatever had been decreed and defined by holy and approved fathers [4] might be inviolably observed by all.' One might have expected that here, as in the case of other Councils [5], would have followed some dogmatic statement of faith : but Theodore goes on to say that he added ' other observations tending to the preservation of charity and of the unity of the Church.' After this prefatory address, he asked each of the members of the synod, in order, whether he agreed to keep the ancient and canonical decrees of the fathers. They all answered in the affirmative ; they would do so 'by all means,' 'most willingly,' 'with all their hearts.' Thereupon Theodore at once produced the book of canons referred to ; it was the collection of ancient canons made by Dionysius Exiguus in the opening of the sixth century [6], beginning with the 'Apostolic canons,' and then exhibiting those of Nicæa, Ancyra, Neocæsarea, Gangra, Antioch, Laodicea, Constantinople, Chalcedon, Sardica, and the African code. In this series Theodore 'had marked' ten points, occurring 'in different places,' as specially necessary to be observed by the English Church. These were taken up and considered, in the following form : Theodore calls them ' capitula,' heads, or as it is sometimes rendered, articles.

[1] Mansi, ix. 836. Compare Council of Clovesho in 747, ' Regnante in perpetuum Domino nostro J. C.' and Kemble, Cod. Dipl. i. 146, &c.

[2] Mansi, x. 471, 477, 481, 531, 614, 661.

[3] 'Tractemus,' i.e. treat of, consider. See Mansi, iii. 892 : 'Quoniam igitur universa fuisse arbitror tractata,' &c.

[4] 'Probabilibus.' So in Lateran I. c. 18 : ' Probabiles ecclesiæ patres.'

[5] E.g. Toledo IV. c. 1, Mansi, x. 615 ; Toledo VI. c. 1, ib. 661.

[6] See the Ballerini, de Antiq. Collect. Can. part 3. c. 1. s. 2. 9. This collection, they say, ib. s. 2. 6, excels in the translation of the Greek canons, in its order, in its titles, ' necnon ipsa omnium documentorum sinceritate.' Theodore would naturally bring it with him from Rome. See also Smith's Bede, p. 148.

(1) 'That we all keep the holy day of Easter together, on CHAP. VIII.
the Sunday after the <u>fourteenth moon of the first month</u>' (i.e.
so as to exclude the fourteenth moon from the list of possible
Easter Sundays). This was the Antiochene Council's rule,
can. 1, referring to the Nicene resolution[1].

(2) 'That no bishop shall invade the "parish[2]" (or diocese)
of another, but shall be content with governing the people
entrusted to himself.' This was from the fourteenth and
thirty-sixth 'Apostolic' canons, the thirteenth of Antioch, the
second of Constantinople, the forty-eighth of the African
code[3]. (The fifteenth Nicene, adduced by Johnson, refers to
the removal of a bishop from one see to another.)

(3) 'That whatever monasteries have been consecrated to
God, it shall not be lawful for any bishop to disturb them
in any matter, nor to take away by force any part of their
property.' This is an amplification of the twenty-fourth of
Chalcedon, which does not expressly refer to such encroachments on the part of a bishop, but only places under censure
those who permit the secularisation of monasteries once
dedicated by the consent of the bishop. That Council indeed
strongly asserted the jurisdiction of bishops over monasteries[4],
which during the last two centuries, through the growth of
the monastic system, had been restrained by canons[5] on the

---

[1] See above, pp. 82, 149, 203.

[2] The ancient or 'Eusebian' sense of παροικία, 'the body of Christians
dwelling within a certain area under one bishop' (see above, p. 189), naturally
passed into that of 'the area within which they dwelt,' i.e. what we call
a diocese; see Suicer in v. and Sclater's Orig. Draught of Prim. Church, p. 32.
Compare Bede, iii. 7, iv. 13, v. 18; Vit. Cuthb. 29, 33; Ep. to Egb. 8. We find
this use also in Wihtred's Privilege to Kentish churches, Haddan and Stubbs,
iii, 239; in can. 25 of Council of Clovesho, ib. 371; in the Legatine Synod
of 787, ib. 449; in king Kenulf's letter to Leo III., ib. 522; in Gregory III.'s
Ep. 10, to St. Boniface, Mansi, xii. 285; in Boniface's to Archbishop Cuthbert, c. 1; frequently in Hincmar; in a grant of King Ethelred, in 1012,
to 'Hrofenis parrochiæ episcopus,' Palgrave, Engl. Com. p. ccxxiv., &c.
Yet 'parochia' is used for our 'parish' by Council of Agde, c. 21; of
Epaon, c. 25; Vaison, III. or II. 1; Orleans III. c. 5; Toledo IV. c. 74; Chalons,
c. 5.

[3] So in inferior Councils, as Orleans III. a. 538, c. 15.

[4] Can. 4. See the writer's 'Notes on Canons of first four General Councils,'
p. 141.

[5] See Toledo IV. c. 51, Mansi, x. 631, rebuking bishops who set monks
to work for them like slaves, and almost turn the monasteries into pos-

Continent, and often ceded by 'exemptions' or charters of privilege.

(4) 'That the monks themselves[1] do not roam from place to place, that is, from monastery to monastery, except by the permission of their own abbot, but remain in that obedience which at the time of their conversion they promised.' This is based on the fourth and twenty-third canons of Chalcedon, which were framed to guard against disorderly interference in public affairs, ecclesiastical and civil, on the part of monks, such as those violent Eutychian partizans who had behaved like a 'gang of robbers' at the second Council of Ephesus. 'Conversion' here means forsaking of the secular life for the monastic[2].

(5) 'That no cleric shall leave his own bishop and roam about anywhere at his pleasure, nor, if he comes anywhere, be received without the commendatory letters of his prelate. And if, when once received, he refuses to return when summoned, both the receiver and the person who has been received shall incur excommunication.' This is made up from the fifteenth and thirty-fourth Apostolic canons, the third and seventh Antiochene, the forty-first and forty-second Laodicene, twenty-third of Chalcedon, and hundred-and-fifth African[3].

---

sessions of their own. The Council limits a bishop's right in a monastery to (1) exhorting monks to holy living, (2) instituting abbots, &c., (3) correcting breaches of the rule. See, too, Gregory the Great's Roman Council forbidding episcopal encroachments; e.g. no bishop shall take away any of the revenue, property, or documents of a monastery or of the cells and 'vills' which belong to it; Mansi, x. 486. Cp. Guizot, Civil. in Fr. lect. 15. The Council of Rouen distinctly recognises the bishop's duty of inquiring into the internal state of monasteries and nunneries; ib. x. 1201.

[1] 'Ipsi.' The other reading is 'episcopi.' This is defended by Todd, Life of St. Patrick, p. 49. But see Haddan and Stubbs, iii. 121.

[2] Cp. Reg. S. Bened. 1. So Gregory the Great used the term, ep. iii. 65. In Council of Gerona, c. 6, it is used for the entrance into clerical life; Mansi, viii. 549. So in Arles IV. c. 1, 2; ib. viii. 626, Compare Greg. Turon. de Mirac. S. Mart. iii. 15: 'converti decrevit, scilicet, ut humiliatis capillis . . . deserviret antistiti.'

[3] Compare Council of Reims, a. 625, c. 12: 'Quod si sine epistolis (sui pontificis) profectus fuerit manifestis, nullo modo recipiatur;' Mansi, x. 596. So Council of Agde, c. 38, ib. viii. 331; and of Epaon, c. 6. ib. viii. 560. Theodulf, a deacon of Paris, was often excommunicated by his bishop, because he delayed to return 'ad ecclesiam suam in qua . . . ordinatus fuerat;' Greg. Turon. H. Fr. x. 14.

Commendatory letters of this sort, called 'systaticæ,' were CHAP. VIII. natural and befitting guarantees of the cleric's character [1].

(6) 'That foreign bishops and clergy be content with the hospitality freely offered them, and that no one of them be allowed to perform any sacerdotal office without permission of the bishop in whose diocese (*parochia*) he is known to be.' This is based on the thirteenth Antiochene, and eleventh Sardican.

(7) 'That the synod be assembled twice in the year.' This was altered in discussion, on account of 'divers hindrances' to two meetings, exactly as the Nicene provision for two such meetings, before Lent and in the autumn, or the Antiochene specifying the third week after Easter and October, had been altered for Africa by the Council of Hippo into a yearly meeting [2]. The resolution stood thus, 'That we meet once a year on the 1st of August, in the place which is called Clofeshoch,'—a place most probably to be identified with Cliff-at-Hoe near Rochester,—the peninsula of Hoe or Hoo being a convenient basis for the Mercian supremacy in Kent [3], and also near at hand for Theodore. Councils did meet there in 716, 742, and—the most important—in 747.

(8) 'That no bishop shall set himself above another out of ambition, but all shall acknowledge the time and the order of their consecration.' This is based on the eighty-sixth of the African code [4].

(9) This was one of Theodore's favourite points, 'That as

---

[1] See Bingham, b. ii. c. 4. s. 5 (vol. i. p. 100). He distinguishes the 'commendatoriæ' given to clergy when about to travel (among others) from the 'dimissoriæ' given to clergy who wished to settle in another diocese. See 'Notes on Canons of first four General Councils,' p. 163.

[2] Mansi, iii. 919 : comp. another form of it, Cod. Afr. 18, ib. 719. So the second of Orleans in 533, and three others following it, prescribe *one* meeting ; the third of Toledo allows one to suffice because of distance and poverty ; Mansi, ix. 997. The fourth of Toledo names May 18 as the day.

[3] See T. Kerslake's 'Vestiges of the Supremacy of Mercia,' (reprinted from Transact. of Bristol and Gloucestershire Archæological Society), p. 27 ff. He observes with much force that this Kentish peninsula would be very accessible from Tilbury on the other side of the Thames. He identifies the Cealchythe of six later councils with Chalk in the same district, S. W. of Cliff, Hatfield with Cliff itself, and would even place Herutford in the neighbourhood.

[4] See Mansi, iii. 789.

CHAP. VIII. the number of the faithful increases, the bishops be increased in number.' Theodore did not extract this literally from his book: he inferred from certain African canons [1], restraining an irregular multiplication of bishoprics, and also from the sixth Sardican canon of like purport, that an increase, made regularly and for good reasons, was desirable [2]. In his native Cilicia, there were seventeen dioceses, mostly large [3]; and his provincial visitation had convinced him of the necessity of dividing the too large diocese of Lichfield and the enormous diocese of York. But although his proposition seems to us undeniably right, and Bede in his later years urged the same idea on Bishop Egbert [4] long after the Northumbrian diocese of 673 had been divided, Theodore could not carry his suffragans with him [5]; it may be that Wilfrid's deputies spoke out what they knew that their master would feel; and this opposition, successful at the time, though overborne afterwards, accounts for much of the difficulties that followed. The Council-record intimates a purpose only deferred, not abandoned: ' On this point, for the time, we said nothing.'

(10) ' As to marriages, that no one be allowed to have any but a lawful marriage. Let no one commit incest [6]; let no one leave his own wife, except, as the holy Gospel teaches, because of fornication. But if any one shall have expelled his own wife who has been united to him in lawful matrimony, if he is minded to be rightly a Christian, let him not join himself to any other, but remain in that state, or else be reconciled to his own wife.' Now, in Theodore's Peni-

---

[1] Afric. 53, 56, 98; Mansi, iii. 744, 749, 803.

[2] It is suggested with great probability by Haddan and Stubbs, iii. 122, that this plan for dividing the ' parochiæ' or dioceses was mistaken for an introduction of the 'parochial system,' such as Elmham attributes to Theodore. See also Lord Selborne's Ancient Facts and Fictions, p. 116 ff.

[3] Bingham, b. ix. c. 3. s. 16 (vol. iii. p. 112).

[4] ' Quis non videat quanto sit melius tam enorme pondus ecclesiastici regiminis in plures . . . dividi, quam unum sub fasce quem portare non possit opprimi?' Ep. to Egb. 5. He cites Gregory's programme as to twelve bishops for the North, under a metropolitan of York. Above, p. 69.

[5] Lingard, A.-S. Ch. i. 86.

[6] For canons of that period against incest, see Council of Reims, 8. a. 624, Mansi, x. 595; and Paris, V. c. 14. a. 615, ib. x. 542 (which forbids, *inter alia*, marriage of first cousins).

tential [1] severe penance is imposed on a husband who having CHAP. VIII. found his wife to be unfaithful, continues to live with her, as if the exception constituted an obligation to put her away. Far severer penance is assigned to one who marries another woman after putting away his wife; but this refers to the case of divorce *not* justified by that exception. There is a passage in the Penitential which allows [2] the husband of a faithless wife not only to put her away, but to marry another, as if the exception covered both a divorce and a re-marriage. This illustrates the sense of the Hertford 'capitulum,' which makes it, apparently, a Christian duty for the injured husband to abandon the faithless wife, and seems in the next words to contemplate a different case, that of one who, without such cause, has dismissed his lawful wife, and who is reminded that, as a Christian, he is bound to remain single or to be reconciled to her.

Nine resolutions, then, were passed,—one having been for the time withdrawn. Theodore was a thorough man of business: he would not go by understandings and vaguely expressed agreements: he would have everything set down definitely, and accepted formally: there should be no mistake as to what was or was not passed,—no loophole left whereby, in after days, any 'occasion of contention' should be caused by any one who had sat in the synod. There stood the record, fairly written out by the secretary: according to the orderly

[1] Pœnit. i. 14, 4; Haddan and Stubbs, iii. 188. The Penitential professes to represent Theodore's answers to questions about penance and other points of discipline, as they came to the knowledge of a 'disciple of the Humbrians' (Northumbrians?) mainly through the medium of a priest named Eoda.

[2] Pœnit. ii. 12. 5; Haddan and Stubbs, iii. 199. In this answer the divorced adulteress herself, if penitent, is allowed after five years to marry another man. The question of re-marrying in the excepted case of the wife's adultery was undecided in the ancient Church. St. Augustine personally held it wrong for an injured husband, who had put away his faithless wife, to marry again; but did not think the act expressly forbidden by Scripture, nor punishable by the Church. It was *tolerated*, though the Church (first Council of Arles, 10), dissuaded from it. On the one side were laws of the empire, and ecclesiastical practice, permitting such re-marriage; on the other side, the opinions of some great Church writers more or less strongly given against it. See Bingham, b. xxii. c. 2. s. 12 (vol. vii. p. 300). There can be no doubt that our Lord's questioners would understand the permission to divorce, in this one case, as involving permission to contract a new marriage.

S

CHAP. VIII. continental usage, each member must sign it with his own hand. They did so, probably in such words as, 'I, —, bishop of the church of —, have subscribed [1]:' and Wilfrid's delegates would each sign as 'in the place of my lord Wilfrid [2].' And, as a final guarantee of the stability of the resolutions, it was enacted, as was often the case in continental synods [3], that any bishop who should ever 'attempt to contravene or infringe' the decrees then subscribed, should incur 'separation from all sacerdotal office, and from the fellowship of his brethren.' 'May the grace of God,' Theodore concluded, 'keep us in safety, living in the unity of His holy Church.'

So ended the Council of Hertford, a memorable assembly in the annals of the English Church,—hardly less so in those of the English people. For while it gave expression and consolidation to the idea of ecclesiastical unity, it was also 'the first of all national gatherings [4]' for such legislation as should affect the whole land of the English, the precursor of the Witenagemots and the Parliaments of the one indivisible imperial realm. Theodore may thus far take no mean place among the men who helped to make England.

---

[1] E. g. Toledo IV. Mansi, x. 641. Sometimes the form was, 'Hæc statuta definiens subscripsi;' Toledo VII. ib. x. 770. We find the form, 'Relegi et subcripsi,' in Council of Epaon, ib. viii. 564; or 'Consensi et subscripsi,' Orleans IV., ib. ix. 120.

[2] E. g. in the third Council of Toledo, a. 589: 'Gaianus . . agens vicem domini mei Fructuosi episcopi subscripsi;' Mansi, ix. 1002. So Toledo V. ib. x. 657, &c. Or 'presbyter' or 'diaconus episcopi,' Toledo VIII. ib. x. 1223.

[3] E. g. Orleans III. c. 33, denounces any (bishops) who *neglect* to observe the decrees; Mansi, ix. 20: Orleans IV., 'Si quis . . . transgredi tentaverit;' ib. ix. 119: Braga III., ' transgressus;' ib. ix. 841.

[4] Green, Hist. Engl. People, p. 30, and Making of England, pp. 333, 382. Comp. Stubbs, Const. Hist. i. 190 (or 163). It has been truly said that 'under the masterly hand of Theodore the unity of the English Church afforded a model of unity for the nascent English State.'.

CHAPTER IX.

It might well seem that in the case of Archbishop Theodore, East-Anglian diocese divided. even a temporary check was to be followed by an advance, with hardly sufficient interval to allow of a sense of disappointment. As we have seen, he had not carried his point about the partition of dioceses, when he proposed it to the Council: it was considered, but the decision was deferred. Yet Bisi of Dunwich, on his return home, began to feel the pressure of infirmities[1], increased by the exertion of a double journey, and determined to resign his office. Theodore seized the opportunity; and, doubtless with the consent of the East-Anglian king Aldwulf, the son of Ethelhere and the nephew of Anna[2], he divided the diocese by forming a new see at Elmham, about the centre of our present Norfolk[3]. Badwin became its first prelate, while Acci was placed in the chair of St. Felix. It was the terrible irruption of the Northmen, two centuries later, which in its results annulled this partition; so that after Dunwich had been permanently abandoned, and the line of bishops of Elmham had continued until after the Conquest[4], the single East-Anglian bishopric was transferred to Thetford in 1075, and fixed at Norwich in 1094.

[1] Bede, iv. 5: 'Quo adhuc superstite,' &c.

[2] Not his son, as Thomas of Ely thought, Vit. Etheldr. c. 7, Act. SS. Bened. ii. 744. Aldwulf's mother was Hereswid, Bede, iv. 23; so that on her side he was the nephew of Hilda. He succeeded his uncle Ethelwold in 663, and reigned until 713. For his personal recollection of king Redwald's 'fanum,' see Bede, ii. 15. His daughter Redburge, or Edburge (or Egburge, Act. SS. Bened. iii. 279), became abbess of Repton; Tho. Eli. l. c. Two others, Ethelburga and Hwætburga, became abbesses of Hackness.

[3] He was adhering to 'tribal demarcations' within the kingdom; Green, Making of Engl. p. 343.

[4] See Jessopp's Diocesan History of Norwich. pp. 28, 29.

But the attention of East-Anglian Churchmen was probably attracted, in this year 673, with at least equal liveliness of interest, by an event which had all the charm of ecclesiastical romance, while it inaugurated an important monastic undertaking, and had the effect, early in the twelfth century, of restoring another episcopate to the eastern part of England.

Etheldred at Ely.
We must remember that Etheldred[1], the daughter of the devout king Anna, and the sister and aunt of several royal nuns, had become the reluctant wife, first of Tonbert the chief of the Southern Gyrvians or 'fen-land men,' who inhabited South Cambridgeshire, and afterwards of Egfrid of Northumbria. The jointure or 'morning-gift[2]' which she had received from her first husband was no other than the isle of Ely, which Bede describes as a district of 'six hundred hydes[3], like an island, surrounded either by marshes or waters, whence it took its name from the abundance of eels which are caught in those marshes:' which the historian of the Conquest describes as 'strictly an island' in the ages before those drainage works 'which have changed the course of the rivers and altered the face of the country[4].' Etheldred led a de-

---

[1] See Bede, iv. 19, and Thomas of Ely's Life of St. Etheldred in Act. SS. Bened. ii. 740, and epitomised in Angl. Sac. i. 597. Etheldred was born about 630 at Ermynge, now Ixning, in Suffolk, and married to Tonbert in 652, two years before her father's death. Tonbert died in 655: and she married Egfrid in 660. Bishop Stubbs has observed that the connection of the Gyrvii with East Anglia accounts for the fact that they were Christianised much earlier than their Mercian neighbours: for Thomas, a Gyrvian, was consecrated bishop of Dunwich six years before the mission to the Mid-Angles.

[2] Lappenberg, ii. 338; Turner, iii. 71. Hexham, as we have seen, was her jointure from Egfrid.

[3] As usual, he calls them 'familiæ.' See above, p. 164. Kemble, Cod. Dipl. iii. p. xxx, connects it with the root of 'higan, familia.' Bede, iv. 19: 'Est autem Elge,' &c. He had previously described the isle as 'undique aquis ac paludibus circumdata.' See Bentham's Hist. of Ch. of Ely, pp. 47, 79. Thomas of Ely describes it as 'locus difficultate adeundi et arboribus hinc inde circumdatus, habens aquas de supercilio collis tenues, sed irriguas;' Vit. S. Etheldr. c. 8, in Act. SS. Ben. ii. 745: and in his prefatory account of Ely, quoted by Wharton, Angl. Sac. i. xli, this twelfth-century chronicler celebrates the quietness and security of the 'famous isle,' its rich soil, its pleasant gardens and woods, its facilities for sport ('ferarum venatione'), its abundance of cattle and fish: 'Sunt in gremio insulæ duodecim ecclesiæ cum villis campestribus et modicis insulanis.' Malmesbury says (G. P. iv. 183) that the surprise of visitors at the abundance of fish was an amusement to the natives.

[4] Freeman, iv. 462: see his map there.

vout life during the five years of her widowhood : and after her second marriage, she lived twelve years in Egfrid's house, before she succeeded in extorting his consent to her retirement to the monastery of his aunt Ebba at Coldingham. At last, in 672, she was permitted to take the veil there from the hands of Wilfrid, to whom this unhealthy aversion for her wedded life as such,—for against Egfrid personally she had no complaint,—appeared a token of high sanctity[1]. After she had spent about a year in the house which reared its lofty buildings near the promontory which still bears the name of its foundress[2], her husband's longing to regain her, stimulated by the advice of his thanes, who doubtless regarded his previous concession as a weakness, brought him within a short distance of Coldingham. Etheldred had but just time to fly southwards : and legends grew up as to the marvels which had secured her escape and waited on her journey[3]. At last she found herself safe amid the fens and streams of her own domain ; and there, after some deliberation as to the choice of a site, she fixed upon 'an elevation which in that part of Britain passes for a considerable hill[4],' and there founded a double monastery after the model of Whitby and Coldingham[5], the precursor of the great abbey which has left

[1] Bede, iv. 19, quite agrees with Wilfrid. See too Thomas of Ely, c. 9. Contrast St. Columba forbidding a wife to think of going into a nunnery, and citing Rom. vii. 2, Matt. xix. 6; Adamnan, ii. 41. Gregory himself declared that 'the dissolution of marriage religionis causa, though allowed by human law, was forbidden by Divine,' quoting Matt. xix. 6; Ep. xi. 45.

[2] 'Ædificia sublimiter erecta,' Bede, iv. 25.

[3] See Thomas of Ely, c. 11. Etheldred appears in these tales as sheltered for a week by waters miraculously rising up around a hill called Coldbert's Head; and as halting near the Humber, where her staff, fixed in the ground while she slept, grew into the largest ash-tree in the neighbourhood of 'Etheldredstowe.' See Bentham, Ch. of Ely, p. 52 ; Handbook to Eastern Cathedrals, pp. 195, 229, on the sculptures representing the life of Etheldred, in the octagon of Ely Cathedral.

[4] Freeman, i. 275. She at first thought of a place called Cratunden, where, according to an Ely legend, a church had been built by St. Augustine and destroyed by Penda; comp. Thomas's preface in Angl. Sac. i. p. xlii, and his 'Vita,' c. 15, in Act. SS. Bened. ii. 754.

[5] 'Viros et mulieres in eodem simul monasterio . . . et in ecclesia diutius servatum;' Tho. Eli. 15. The whole isle was devoted to the purposes of the community ; ib. See above, p. 193.

us 'the most stately and varied[1]' of our cathedral churches. At last she was happy, in the life which represented her ideal, and she enjoyed the support of her cousin King Aldwulf, and the council and spiritual aid of her chaplain Huna[2],—and, ere long, the companionship of her elder sister Sexburga, the ex-queen of Kent[3]. 'It is said' that during her six years' abbacy 'she never wore linen, but always wool:' that she seldom used a warm bath except on the eves of the three great festivals, among which it is curious to find the Epiphany taking the place of Christmas[4]: and that on those occasions she would first wash, or cause her attendants to wash, the feet of the nuns. Moreover, it was reported that she seldom took more than one meal a day, except on the greater solemnities, or under some pressing necessity: and that she never failed, when in fair health, to stay in the church, intent on prayer, from the matin service[5], which was then said soon after midnight, until dawn. One vivid little touch in Bede's picture[6] combines the early habits of the young East-Anglian princess with the last illness of the abbess-queen, which was

[1] Freeman, i. 276.

[2] Tho. Eli. c. 15. After her death Huna became a hermit on an islet afterwards called Hun-ey. According to Thomas, Wilfrid alone exercised episcopal authority in Ely, and hallowed Etheldred as abbess. See Bentham, p. 56, that Ely was exempted from the jurisdiction of the East-Anglian bishop.

[3] Tho. Eli. c. 18 : 'Sed et sanctorum genetrix Sexburga,' &c.

[4] ' Paschæ, Pentecostes, Epiphaniæ ;' Bede, iv. 19. In Bede's Ep. to Egbert, c. 9, the chief days are named as the Nativity, the Epiphany, and Easter, Pentecost being omitted. The Epiphany occurs as a pre-eminent holy-day in his Life of Cuthbert, c. 11.

[5] 'Synaxeos.' This word, originally used for (1) a Church meeting for worship, and specifically (2) for the Eucharistic celebration, had come to mean (3) the Divine Office for the canonical hours; see Ducange in v. ; Bede, Vit. Cuthb. 10. Cp. Columban, Reg. Cœn. 7 ; Bonif. Ep. 29. 'Septem igitur sinaxes sancti patres canendas constituerunt,' Thorpe's Anc. Laws, p. 328. For references to the matin office, see Bede, iii. 12 ; iv. 7 ; v. 9. Thomas of Ely says that all the inmates of the monastery were taught ' to love Divine worship, et decorem domus Dei tota observantia custodire ;' Vit. Etheldr. 15.

[6] Bede, iv. 19 : 'Ferunt autem quia cum præfato tumore,' &c. He tells the story of the operation performed by her physician Kynifrid : she died with the incision still 'gaping.' Thomas of Ely says that she used to tell the postulants for admssion, 'illam esse veram vitam quæ præsentis vitæ emeretur incommodo ;' c. 15. See Alcuin, de Pontif. Ebor. p. 770 ff.

caused by the recurring pestilence, but was also accompanied CHAP. IX. by a huge and painful tumour under the jaw. ' This ailment pleases me well,' she would say : ' in my young days, I wore heavy necklaces of gold and pearls ;—now, in their place, I have to carry this hot red swelling : fit penance for my former vanity, if it may but avail !' She died in 679[1], and was succeeded as abbess by Sexburga.

Her stay at Coldingham had probably been subsequent Colding-
ham. to that visit which Cuthbert, we are told, paid to Ebba, when, ' staying there some days, he exhibited, both in action and in word, that way of righteousness which he preached[2]:' and it was, to all appearance, prior to that grave moral deterioration of this community, which by degrees infected all the officials except the abbess ; beginning with mere frivolity and a passion for ' fine garments,'—a frequent infirmity among the inmates of Saxon cloisters[3],—but proceeding, as Bede intimates, in other cases, to ' wickedness ' sufficient to discredit the system of double convents[4]. It is the first instance of monastic corruption which Bede has to record : in his later life he knew of much deflection from the received conventual

---

[1] See Alb. Butler, June 23. Florence gives the same date, ' 9 Cal. July.' There is apparently a mistake in the text of Tho. Eli. '9 Cal. *Junii*' (May 24). Sexburga in 695 caused her sister's remains to be re-interred in a white marble coffin brought from the desolate little city of Grantchester or Cambridge ; Bede, iv. 19. The abbacy was held in succession, after Etheldred, by Sexburga, her daughter Ermenild, late queen of Mercia, and her granddaughter Werburga. It was in Edgar's time that the whole jurisdiction within the bounds of the isle of Ely was granted to ' St. Etheldred,' that is, to her church ; Palgrave, p. 165. Comp. Hist. Eli. i. 4 (Gale, Script. i. 465). Her name became popularised as ' Audrey ' (whence ' tawdry,' used of cheap lace mementoes of Ely), and a place near Ely was called Aldreth ; see Freeman, iv. 463.

[2] Bede, Vit. Cuthb. 10. It was during this visit that he went down one night to the sea, went into it up to his neck, and continued singing psalms till daybreak, then came out, knelt down, and said his prayers, whereupon ' two quadrupeds which are commonly called otters' came up out of the water, fawned upon him, warmed his feet with their breath, and dried them with their hair,—then, when he had blessed them, ' patrias relapsa sunt sub undas.' A monk, watching the scene from a cliff, was so awed that he could scarcely totter home, and implored Cuthbert's pardon. ' Did you then act the spy on me ? Well, I forgive you, if you will tell no one of it while I live.'

[3] Haddan and Stubbs, iii. 450, 473, 509 ; Lingard, A.-S. Ch. i. 230 ; also ib. iii. 265, for St. Edith's defence of her splendid clothing ; Turner, iii. 47. See Aldhelm, de Laud. Virginitatis, 55-58, and Boniface's Ep. to Cuthbert, c. 9.

[4] Bede, iv. 25, ' a malitia inhabitantium,' referring to Vulg. Ps. cvi. 34.

CHAP. IX. standard[1], but he mentions none which can match the degeneracy at Coldingham. A priest named Ædgils[2], then a monk of the house, lived to tell him how an Irish-born inmate[3], devoted to penitential asceticism, was one day returning to Coldingham, after an excursion, with a brother-monk, when, looking at the monastery from afar, he predicted that a fire would consume it, and on being afterwards questioned by the abbess, reluctantly told her that he had learned this from a vision[4], but that the doom would not be accomplished in her days; how, after the community was informed of this strange prophecy, some amendment was observable, which, when Ebba was gone, gave place to the old sins, and worse. And so, Bede tells us, with his habitual awe-struck recognition of Divine judgments[5], 'while they said, "Peace and safety," the convent was burnt to the ground through some person's carelessness, but,' as 'all who knew the case could well perceive,' by 'a heavy vengeance from heaven[6].'

---

[1] Bede, Ep. to Egbert, 6.

[2] Bede, iv. 25 : 'Quæ mihi cuncta,' &c.

[3] His name was Adamnan. He had committed 'sceleris aliquid' in his youth, and when he came to himself had consulted a priest of his own race, asking for penance: 'he was strong, and could even fast a whole week.' 'Do so for three days,' said the adviser, 'and then I will return and tell you what more to do.' He never returned, being called away into Ireland. Adamnan, left to himself, took to fasting on all but two days in the week, Sunday and Thursday; Bede, iv. 25. So, it was afterwards believed, did St. Adamnan of Hy; Reeves's Adamn. p. lvii. Bede mentions a priest named Hæmgils, who, when he wrote, was an old man living on bread and water, as a hermit in Ireland; v. 12. In the Life of St. Guthlac by Felix, c. 32, an English attendant on bishop Heddi says 'inter Scottorum se populos habitasse et illic pseudo-anachoretas ... vidisse,' together with truly devout men; Act. SS. Bened. iii. 278. On Irish penances, see above, p. 152.

[4] An unknown person, he said, stood by him during his nightly devotions, and told him that he alone in the whole community was in earnest about his soul. 'The cells made for prayer or study were turned into places for revelry, conversation, or other allurements.'

[5] 'Lest, while we are yielding to the allurements of the flesh, repentina Ejus ira nos corripiat.' Comp. Bede, v. 13, 14, and Epist. 15, Bed. Op. i. 214.

[6] It is said that on account of these scandals at Coldingham, Cuthbert, when bishop of Lindisfarne, with full 'consent of men and women,' excluded all women 'from the threshold' of his monastic cathedral (see Lingard. A.-S. Ch. i. 215), and that a separate church was built on the island 'in campi viventis planitie,' thence called the Green Kirk. De Dun. Eccl. ii. 7; cp. Ann. SS. Ben. ii. 878 ; Lingard, A.-S. Ch. i. 215.

And now let us turn southward, and place ourselves, in chap. ix.
imagination, among the Churchmen of Kent attached more or Mercia.
less closely to the archbishop, and thus informed as to ecclesiastical affairs in the southern and central kingdoms. They
would hear a good deal about the state of the Church in
Mercia. King Wulfhere, after losing Lindsey in his war
with Egfrid[1], and gaining some dearly-bought advantage
over Escwin, then king of a part of Wessex, in the battle
of Beadanhead or Bedwin[2], ended his noble life in 675[3],
leaving the Church firmly settled in the Midlands: and his
son Kenred, being a boy, was passed over in favour of his
father's brother Ethelred[4], another of those sons of the great
Pagan whom Christianity had made so effectually its own.
The vacancy of the Mercian throne was contemporaneous with
the vacancy of the Mercian bishopric: Winfrid was deposed
by Theodore for some 'disobedience[5],' which is not explained
by Bede, but has been supposed to mean resistance to a partition of the great diocese of Lichfield. Gentle as Winfrid
was by nature, he may perhaps have thought himself bound
by reverence for Chad's memory to retain Chad's diocese as
he had received it. Whether Theodore went through the
form of a synodical trial and sentence, we know not; he

---

[1] Bede, iv. 12 ; see above, p. 242   Lindsey was a 'debateable land' between
Mercia and Northumbria.

[2] Chron. 675.   For Escwin, see above, p. 248.   On the result of the battle,
cp. Hen. Hunt. ii. 37.

[3] On his reign see Smith's Bede, p. 746 ; Lappenberg, i. 178. His chief fault
was the unworthy transaction with bishop Wini ; but against this are to be set
his exertions for Christianity, not only within his own realm, but in regard to
the South-Saxon king. 'Christi nomen ubique locorum regni sui prædicare
jussit;' Florence, a. 675. 'Christianitatem vix in regno suo palpitantem . . .
enixissime juvit;' Malmesb. G. Reg. i. 76. He was buried at Lichfield.
After his death his wife Ermenild took the veil at Sheppey, and his daughter
Werburga (above, p. 184) at Ely.

[4] See above, p. 163. So among the Picts, 'the law of primogeniture
was only partially recognised;' Robertson, Scotland under Early Kings,
i. 34.

[5] Bede, iv. 6 : 'Per meritum cujusdam inobedientiæ.' Malmesbury says
that he was expelled from Lichfield by king Ethelred, 'quia Egfridi partium
fuerat' (G. Pont. iii. 100) ; but this would place the expulsion in 679, whereas
Saxulf succeeded to Lichfield 'not long after' the Council of Hertford (Bede,
iv. 6), and probably in 675 (Stubbs, Registr. p. 3). 'He was unbuxum (disobedient) in som poynt ;' Trevisa's transl. of Polychron. b. 1. c. 55.

CHAP. IX. would be somewhat too likely to disregard such restrictions on his authority[1]: but Winfrid made no resistance, uttered no appeal. He retired to the monastery of Barrow, which seems to have been under his own personal jurisdiction : and after some experiences on the continent, which, as we shall see, were almost grotesquely unfortunate, he ended his life, under the peaceful roof of his own convent, ' in all holy conversation[2].' He was succeeded by Saxulf, the abbot, and, in a sense, the founder of Medeshamstede[3], who, after having, as the monastic chronicler, Hugh the White, assures us, ' given birth to several dependent monasteries,' left the parent house in the care of a monk named Cuthbald[4].

Erkenwald, bishop of London.

'At that time also,' writes Bede, ' Theodore appointed Erkenwald to be bishop, in the city of London, for the East-Saxons[5].' In after days, when this prelate was honoured as a saint, it was said that, when a little boy, he had heard Mellitus preach in London[6]. Bede has much to tell us of the ' two noble monasteries' that he founded, before his episcopate, for himself and for his sister Ethelburga[7],—one at Chertsey in Surrey, the other at Barking in Essex. The former was raised by the help of Frithwold, a Mercian sub-king[8]: the latter, like Whitby and others, was a double

[1] He acted ' pro placito ;' Malmesb. Gest. Pontif. i. 1. See Collier, i. 239. Bingham says that even if a metropolitan could depose a suffragan by his sole authority, the act was subject to revision by the synod ; b. ii. c. 16. s. 16. 'Occasionally he (Theodore) ventured to transgress the strict letter of the canons ;' Lingard, A.-S. Ch. i. 78.

[2] Bede, iv. 6 : ' Depositus vero Vynfrid,' &c.

[3] ' Constructor et abbas,' Bede, l. c.

[4] He had founded a monastery ' cum heremiticis cellulis' at a place called Ancarig, afterwards Thorney, in Cambridgeshire. See Hugo Cand. in Sparke, Scr. Varii, pp. 6–8 ; Sprott's Chron. ed. Hearne, p. 172.

[5] Bede, l. c. (he writes ' Erconvald.') Alb. Butler, April 30. Cp. Milman, Ann. St. Paul's, p. 11 ; Simpson, Chapters in Hist. of Old St. Paul's, p. 13.

[6] Dugdale, Hist. St. Paul's, p. 289.

[7] For ' Ædilburge,' as Bede writes her name, see Alb. Butler, Oct. 11.

[8] Malmesb. G. Pontif. ii. 73. See Monast. Angl. i. 426 ; Frithwald is called ' Surrianorum subregulus Regis Wlfarii.' A description of the boundaries of Chertsey abbey-land traces them from ' the mouth of the Way to the eels' ditch, to the old military way, to the great willow, . . . to the sweet well, the old spinney, the holm-oak, the three hills, . . . the march-brook, the three trees,' &c. Ethelburga was succeeded by Hildilith, a friend of Aldhelm ; comp.

foundation, having a separate area for the monks apart from CHAP. IX. the nuns' building, and even a separate chapel, or oratory, for each order [1]. Of Barking Bede tells us, on the authority of a memoir of contemporary date, some eight remarkable stories, several of which refer to the ravages of the Yellow Pest, and some belong to the class of instances of mysterious consciousness, or prevision, shortly preceding death [2]. When Bede wrote, men believed that the horse-litter [3] in which, when infirm, Erkenwald used to go about his diocese, was invested with wonder-working efficacy; a belief which could not have grown up unless the bishop had endeared himself to his people by true pastoral and self-sacrificing activity, such as would go far to consolidate the fabric of Church-life on ground that had once seemed to offer no sure foundation.

Another event of 675 would call forth eager interest in Aldhelm. the precincts of the ecclesiastical school in Canterbury. One of the students, Aldhelm [4], a youth of princely West-Saxon blood [5], who had shown a pre-eminent faculty for acquiring all the lore of the time,—Greek as well as Latin, and even Hebrew,—together with music and metrical rules [6], and had

Bede, iv. 10; Aldh. de Laud. Virgin. 1. Tanner, in 'Notitia Monastica,' dates the foundation of Chertsey, from its register, in 666.

[1] Bede, iv. 7: 'Cujus radius lucis,' &c. Comp. Mabillon, Ann. Benedict. i. 397.

[2] One story is of a vision, at dawn, of a radiant human body wrapt in linen, and borne up by cords brighter than gold out of the 'house' reserved for dying sisters,—shortly before the death of Ethelburga; Bede, iv. 9. In this passage we find the word 'pausare,' 'to go to rest' in death; comp. Bede, v. 8. In Adamn. Vit. Col. iii. 23 the word is applied to the remains of the dead, 'in quo . . . sancti pausant ossa.' Comp. Reeves's Adamnan, p. 378, 'Adomnanus . . . pausat.' Bede mentions the 'cottage' of the sick and dying at Whitby, iv. 24.

[3] Bede, iv. 6: 'Etenim usque hodie,' &c. Cp. Malmesb. G. P. ii. 73.

[4] Alb. Butler, May 25; Turner, Angl.-Sax. iii. 400.

[5] Faricius, abbot of Abingdon (1100), who wrote his Life (Migne, Patr. Lat. lxxxix. 65), makes him the nephew of king Ine; a manifest anachronism, as Malmesbury observes,—who adds that Aldhelm's father Kenten was a kinsman, not a brother, of Ine; Gest. Pontif. v. 88. See Elmham, p. 267, 'Aldhelm needs not to have his lineage supported by falsehoods.' Kemble (ii. 373) describes him as 'closely connected with the royal family of Wessex.'

[6] Bede calls him a man most learned 'all round, . . . a wonder of erudition in liberal as well as in sacred literature;' v. 18. See his Epist. 4, to bishop Heddi, on the study of metre and of calculations; his work 'De Septenario, et de Metris,' &c.; his frequent quotations from Latin poets. Faricius says that

astonished even such a teacher as Hadrian by his aptitudes and attainments [1], had returned into Wessex, and become a member of a small community under the teaching and government of an Irish monk named Mailduf [2],—probably Moeldubh,—'in erudition a philosopher,' who had been attracted by the woodland beauty of a peninsular hill named Ingelborne, had obtained leave to build a hut beneath the walls of its old castle [3], and had there lived by monastic rule, and taken pupils for his subsistence. He brought with him all the culture for which Irish scholars were then famous : a little society grew up around him; and his name has been thought to survive in ' Malmesbury [4].' Aldhelm had returned to Canterbury, but his second sojourn there was broken off by bad health, as we learn from his own letter to Hadrian, ' the revered preceptor of his childhood [5].' He returned to his studies under Mailduf, was ordained priest by Bishop Lothere [6], and in 675 was regularly appointed abbot. Better days now dawned on the poor and hard-working community. They had hardly been able to secure daily bread: but ' the renown of their new superior put an end to these straits [7],' and a crowd of new brethren bore witness to his attractive-

he could speak and write Greek; Vit. Aldh. c. 1. See Milner, Hist. Winch. i. 82. His reading, in fact, exceeded his literary discretion and good taste. We must not wonder at his believing that St. Clement of Rome wrote the ' Itinerarium Petri,' that Pope Sylvester bound a pestilent serpent, or that Constantine was healed of leprosy by being baptized; De Laud. Virg. c. 25.

[1] Malmesb. l. c. Aldhelm refers to Theodore as having personally given instructions; Ep. 3.

[2] Bede, v. 18; Malmesb. v. 189; Lanigan, iii. 100. An Irishman ' ignoti nominis' reminded Aldhelm, ' You were bred up under a certain holy man of our race;' Ep. 5. See Newman on University Education, p. 31 : ' Blessed days of peace and confidence, when Mailduf penetrated to Malmesbury,' &c.

[3] ' Nemoris amœnitate . . . captus;' Malm. l. c.; Mon. Angl. i. 253, 257.

[4] Bede, v. 18: ' Maildufi urbem.' Mr. James Parker, referring to ' Meldunensburg' in Ine's charter of 701 (Cod. Dipl. i. 56), suggests ' Mæl-dun,' hill of the cross (properly, mark), as ' Cristes mæle,' Chron. Abingd. i. 65, 338 (in lists of boundaries).

[5] Aldh. Ep. 7 : ' corporeæ fragilitatis,' &c. In Ep. 3 he alludes to Hadrian as ' urbanitate enucleata ineffabiliter prædito.'

[6] Faricius, c. 1. The grant of land at Malmesbury by Lothere is a manifest forgery; Cod. Dipl. i. 14.

[7] Malmesb. G. P. v. 197 : ' Correxit nobilitas Aldelmi victualium inopiam.'

ness as an instructor and a spiritual guide. It is probable chap. ix.
enough that one or another great landowner came forward
to assist the brotherhood[1]. The lowly chapel of Mailduf was
superseded by 'a more august church in honour of the Lord
and Saviour, and of the first apostles Peter and Paul[2].' One
incident of his earlier days at Malmesbury brings him more
lovingly before us than all the panegyrics on his sanctity
or his manifold acquirements, or on that style which to us
appears so full of turgid affectations[3], although to William of
Malmesbury it seems to combine the several excellences of
English, Greek, and Latin[4]. The anecdote was derived
from no less an authority than Alfred the Great[5]. It seems
that the rude West-Saxons of the district were wont to
hasten home after hearing mass, without waiting for the
sermon,—sometimes, perhaps, to neglect church altogether[6].
Aldhelm, who had learned to sing, and to compose ballads,
while a student at Canterbury, saw his way to making use
of that talent. He took his station on the bridge which
crossed the Avon southwards, and confronted the passers-

[1] Malmesb. G. P. v. 200. The charter ascribed to Kenfrith is very grandiloquent, and bespeaks a later time. That of King Ethelred is much simpler
(Cod. Dipl. i. 27). But both may be spurious, and yet the tradition of some
such grants may be trustworthy. One in which Baldred, in August 688, gives
'some land to abbot Aldhelm,' is referred by Kemble to Cadwalla's reign ;
Cod. Dipl. i. 32.

[2] Malmesb. G. P. v. 197. He afterwards built two other churches within
the precinct, St. Mary's and St. Michael's ; ib. v. 216. He adds that 'tota majoris ecclesiæ fabrica' subsisted to his own time, surpassing all other ancient
English churches in size and beauty. He was writing in 1125.

[3] E.g. Ep. 3, or the De Laudibus Virginitatis, c. 2, 12, 32. Of that work
Malmesbury says, 'Nihil dulcius, nihil splendidius ;' G. Reg. i. 3. His pedantry
frequently takes a classical form : he talks, e.g. of the 'dura Parcarum quies,'
and calls St. Athanasius a 'sacred flamen.' He is fond of Greek words, as
doxa, sophia, kata,—and of alliteration ; Ep. 3. 'Language that rivals Armado,
or Holofernes, or Euphues ;' Haddan's Remains, p. 267. See Turner, Angl.-
Sax. iii. 403, 'a series of bombastic amplifications ;' and Lingard, A.-S. Ch.
ii. 152. A similar 'Grecising' affectation characterises many of the Chartæ
Anglo-Saxonicæ in Kemble, e.g. 'Kyrius, archons, taumate, agie, catascopus,'
&c. See also the pomposities of Odo's preface to Fridegod's Life of Wilfrid.

[4] Malmesb. G. P. v. 196 ; and Gest. Reg. i. s. 31. Bede calls Aldhelm
'sermone nitidus,' v. 18 ; praise to which he himself is far better entitled.
See Lingard, ii. 153.

[5] Malmesbury, v. 190, referring to Alfred's Handbook, ib. 188. Comp.
Faricius, c. 1 : he gives it with some variations.

[6] So Faricius: 'ecclesiam non frequentabat.'

by [1], who were intent on their marketings, but, like all Saxons, were fascinated by music [2], and stopped when he began a lively song [3]. 'Having done this more than once, and gathered a crowd of listeners,' he glided from such minstrelsy into a strain that brought in sacred words, and brought home serious thoughts. This 'blameless guile [4]' proved effective, where ecclesiastical censures 'would have done no good whatever [5];' and his Pauline versatility was rewarded by a manifest increase of religious earnestness in his congregations.

Wessex.   His bishop Lothere died in the year following his own appointment to the abbacy [6]; and Theodore, in London, and doubtless with Erkenwald's assistance, consecrated Heddi, who, says Bede, was qualified for episcopal duties rather by an innate love of goodness than by any book-learning [7], but who evidently appreciated the abilities and the character of the scholar-abbot, for we find Aldhelm writing to him as to his 'peculiar patron,' and dilating on the difficulties of

---

[1] According to Faricius, he met them as they were flocking into the town; according to Malmesbury (or rather, Alfred), when they were hastening home 'statim cantatis missis.' See above, p. 105.

[2] See the story of Cædmon, below. Cp. Lingard, A.-S. Ch. ii. 155.

[3] This song was long afterwards popularly current; Malmesb. l. c.

[4] Christian Year, Fifth Sunday after Trinity.

[5] 'Profecto profecisset nihil,' Malmesb. l. c.

[6] See Kemble, Cod. Dipl. i. 16, for a charter dated on Nov. 6 in this year 676, and ascribed to 'Osric, king,' i. e. sub-king, of the Hwiccas. He is made to say that when first the Gospel doctrines were brought home to him after his baptism, he had confined himself to the erection of a 'pontifical chair:' but that he has 'now' resolved to found 'cœnobialia loca' for men and for women, and grants to abbess Bertana land near the city called Hât Bathu (i.e. Bath, called Hata-Bathum in Chron. a. 972). But the document exhibits the signatures of both Lothere and his successor Heddi, whereas Heddi was not consecrated in Lothere's lifetime; Bede, iv. 12. Osric might be sub-king as early as 676: he was so, apparently, in 681, when he is said to have founded the monastery of Gloucester; and see Bede, iv. 23. The difficulty caused by Florence's mention of Oshere as sub-king in 679 might be got over: he probably antedated Oshere. But the matter of the document would seem to show that, if genuine, it must be ascribed to a later year. Bishop Stubbs (On Worcester in the Eighth Century, p. 5) supposes Oshere to have been the son of Oswald who was the brother of Osric.

[7] Bede, v. 18: 'Bonus quippe erat,' &c. On this Malmesbury says, 'Non parvo moveor scrupulo, quippe qui legerim ejus formales epistolas non nimis indocte compositas;' G. P. ii. 75. See the lines addressed to him, and ascribed to Theodore, 'Te nunc, sancte speculator,' &c., in Haddan and Stubbs, iii. 203.

Roman law, of prosody, arithmetical calculations, astronomy, CHAP. IX. and astrology [1]. The West-Saxon realm was just now in a 'somewhat' chaotic state: there seem to have been several sub-kings,—one of them, Escwin [2], more potent than the rest, but no one acknowledged by all, until by degrees Kentwin [3], a brother of Kenwalch, established his sovereignty, and, although an elderly man, displayed on one occasion the warlike energy of his house by 'driving the Britons to the sea [4].' His name is of some interest to us in this Thames valley, in connection with the original foundation of the great abbey of St. Mary of Abingdon. For it was in the first year of his reign that Hean [5], the nephew of the sub-king Cissa, obtained from his uncle a grant of land for a monastery amid the 'Bagley-wood' of that period, on a spot called Abba's hill [6], a name transferred some twenty years later to Seukesham [7], when, after many delays [8], the design was

[1] Aldh. Ep. 4. On the study of Roman law at this period, see Kemble, Cod. Dipl. i. p. viii. Cp. Eddi, 43, on Wilfrid's proficiency in it.

[2] 'Nearest to the royal stock,' says Malmesbury, G. Reg. i. 2.

[3] Comp. Bede, iv. 12, with Chron. 676, which makes Kentwin succeed to Escwin. Some verses wrongly ascribed to Aldhelm describe a church founded by Bugge, daughter of Kentwin (prob. lect.) during the reign of Ine.

[4] Chron. 682. 'Victoriosus et vehemens,' Hen. Hunt. Hist. ii. 38.

[5] Chron. Abingd. vol. ii. pp. vii. 269. Hean is said to have been stirred by a sermon on 'the camel and the needle's eye.' This seems an imitation of the story about St. Antony. The land granted by Cissa was a piece of the public 'folcland;' ib. pp. xii. 497. Hean's sister Ceolswith, or Cilla, actually founded a nunnery in honour of St. Helen at a place called Helenstow: it was afterwards removed to Wytham; vol. i. 8, ii. 269.

[6] 'A little beyond the vill called Sunningwell, between two very lovely streams which enclose the spot quasi quemdam sinum;' Chron. Ab. vol. i. p. 3. In other words, 'near Bayworth;' ib. ii. 268. See Tanner, Not. Mon. p. 10, 'two miles nearer Oxford than the present' Abingdon, 'near Bayworth, or Chilswell,' where Chilswell farm now stands, on old property of the abbey, below Hen-wood (qu. Hean's?). The tale of an Irish (or British) monk 'Abben,' who dwelt on the 'mount' as an abbot, is a mere legend: 'Abingdon' is derived from Abba, an early settler in Berkshire; Chron. Ab. ii. p. v. The story mentions 'a hermit who dwelt in Cumnor wood;' ib. p. 270.

[7] Or 'Sheovesham.' The Chronicle describes Seuekesham as 'civitas famosa, .. divitiis plena,' surrounded by broad green meadows, where were found traces of British Christianity, and among them a black cross, which no one could profane by perjury 'sine periculo vitæ,' &c.; i. 6, 7; and which became the palladium of the abbey. A more modest account, tracing it to Cilla, is in ii. 269.

[8] See Stevenson's Chron. Abingd. i. 9, for the alleged charter of king Ine,

CHAP. IX. carried out on that ground near the river where we still see some scanty remains of the once stately monastery which made the new 'Abbendun,' our Abingdon, ecclesiastically and historically important. Heddi must have come into the valley,—at what time, we know not, but probably soon after his consecration,—when he removed the bones of St. Birinus from Dorchester to Winchester [1], in token that the West-Saxon capital was now the one seat of the West-Saxon prelacy,—and withal deprived Dorchester of cathedral rank.

Ethelred ravages Kent.

Kent itself was now to feel the sharp edge of an invader's sword. King Lothere had given some offence to Ethelred [2]; or, perhaps, Penda's son was fired with the passion of a conqueror. He came down on the weaker kingdom at the head of a hostile force, and laid waste not only towns or villages, but 'churches and monasteries, without respect to piety or the fear of God [3].' Even in Canterbury some alarm well may have been felt for the archiepiscopal church, and for the monastery of St. Peter, which had recently obtained a 'privilege' from Pope Adeodatus, denouncing spiritual censures against all who should disturb it [4]. But Rochester was actually destroyed. Its bishop, Putta, was just then absent; but on hearing of the disaster, he lost

---

dated 699, marked as spurious by Kemble, Cod. Dipl. i. 53, but supposed by Stevenson to be reducible into component parts, which, taken separately, present no difficulties; Chr. Ab. ii. 496. The transactions, in his view, were as follows: Cissa grants some lands to Hean for monastic purposes; Cadwalla, when king of Wessex, grants some twenty 'hydes' (including 'Cumnor wood'), which, according to the fragment of his charter (ib. i. 8), he had measured 'partim equitando, partim navigando:' Ine finds that Hean has not complied with the conditions of Cissa's grant, revokes it, and 'restores the land to the commonwealth:' Hean then promises that there shall be no further delay, takes the vows of a monk, and appoints an unnamed person as his abbot: thereupon Ine renews the grant. But within five years, Hean, with his abbot's consent, cancels this arrangement, and is absolved from his vows, A.D. 699. The actual establishment of the monastery took place some years later, during Aldhelm's episcopate. The Abingdon Chronicler did injustice to Ine's motives, vol. i. p. 9; see ii. p. xi.

[1] Bede, iii. 7.

[2] See Malmesb. G. P. i. 35, 'Nam Ethelredus,' &c.

[3] Bede, iv. 12. He dates this in 676. Compare Hen. Hunt. ii. 38.

[4] Elmham, p. 245. Another privilege, professing to come from Pope Agatho, May 15, 675, is 'of questionable authenticity;' Haddan and Stubbs, iii. 124. See above, p. 95.

all heart. 'His church had been stripped of all its property, and laid desolate.' The simple-minded, inactive man had no spirit or energy for such a crisis. He withdrew into Mercia,—into the very country whence the ravagers had come, — attracted, perhaps, by the known kindness and munificence of Bishop Saxulf, who gave him a church, and a small piece of land[1], where he dwelt, exercising his ministry in quietness, and, according to Bede, going about, when invited, to give lessons in his own art of choir - music. This does not point to the regular formation of a bishopric; yet Putta's name heads the list of bishops of Hereford[2]. From the first, of course, he would not refuse to perform episcopal functions in the surrounding district of Hecana, as a deputy for Saxulf[3]; and he might easily pass from this position into that of a recognised chief pastor of the country. In that tranquil home beside the Wye, perhaps where now the venerable cathedral and its dependent buildings give a special charm to the Hereford 'precinct,' Putta spent the rest of his life, 'never thinking at all' of a return to Rochester, where his successor Cwichelm found it impossible, for lack of means, to maintain himself, and resigned in 678, when Theodore consecrated Gebmund[4].

Once more let us look northwards. The year of Ethelred's raid in Kent, and Putta's settlement at Hereford, was marked in Northumbria by an event of importance in the life of one who was gradually becoming the typical saint of that realm. Cuthbert had been removed by his abbot Eata from Melrose to Lindisfarne, 'that he might there also teach the rule of monastic perfection with the authority of a prior, and set it forth by a virtuous example[5].' He improved the

Cuthbert, prior of Lindisfarne.

---

[1] 'Agelli non grandis,' Bede, iv. 12.

[2] Florence, append. See above, p. 180. The name of Hereford, 'the ford of the army,' records the passing of Saxon forces over the river 'to harry the Welsh borders;' Taylor's Words and Places, p. 268.

[3] See Haddan and Stubbs, iii. 130.

[4] Bede, iv. 12.

[5] Bede, iv. 27; Vit. Cuthb. 16; De Mirac. S. Cuthb. 14; Vit. Anon. l. 3 (Bede, vol. vi. p. 368). This cannot have been as early as 664, as Raine supposes (St. Cuthbert, p. 17 ff.), following Simeon. See above, p. 217.

CHAP. IX. discipline of the monastery by a compilation of new rules[1], drawn up at Eata's desire: and it was now his task to overcome the repugnance with which the monks regarded what they deemed an additional burden. Thus he had to face an opposition, on the part of daily and hourly associates, which, as Bede hints, extended to some bodily ill-treatment[2]; which would have certainly worn out one less firm, or exasperated one less loving, but which could not even ruffle his brow or sharpen his tones, and gradually yielded to the sweet power of his 'modest patience.' 'When, in discussions, he was harassed by insulting language, he would suddenly rise, break up the meeting, and go out with a calm face[3] and a quiet mind: on the very next day, as if he had met with no gainsaying whatever, he would repeat again the same exhortations, until, by degrees, he brought them round to what he desired.' His daily conduct was a lesson of devotion: sometimes he spent three or four nights together in vigil and prayer, without ever lying down: he was either alone in some retired place, or making something with his hands[4], while he recited psalms[5], by way of keeping

---

[1] The author of the Anonymous Life says, 'Et nobis regularem vitam primum componens constituit, quam usque hodie cum regula Benedicti observamus.' Bed. Op. vi. 369. See Lingard, A.-S. Ch. i. 217.

[2] 'Quæ vel animo vel corpori adversa ingerebantur;' Bede, V. C. 16.

[3] 'Placido vultu.' Further on, 'inter tristia . . . faciem prætendens hilarem.' 'His gentleness and firmness . . . proved too much for the malcontents . . . A difficult antagonist: he would not dispute; he would not quarrel; but he would be obeyed;' Christ. Remembr. No. 75. p. 69. On his personal appearance see above, p. 217.

[4] His hands were 'large and b oad;' Bede, iv. 31. Compare the ancient monks' habit of 'twisting ropes' (Coteler. Eccl. Gr. Mon. i. 340) or weaving palm-leaves into baskets; Sozomen, vi. 29.

[5] References to the devotional use of the Psalter are frequent in Bede. Thus, the monks of Hexham used to keep vigil with 'plurima psalmorum laude,' at 'Heavenfield,' on the night before the anniversary of St. Oswald's death; Bede, iii. 2. Psalms were said for the soul of Hilda; iv. 23: cp. v. 14. The Hewalds were constantly occup'ed in psalms and prayers; v. 10. For Cuthbert's psalmody see Vit. Cuthb. 5, 34. Psalms were sung in Benedict Biscop's cell during his last illness; Hist. Abb. 9. Bede spent a large part of his last days 'in psalmorum cantu;' see Cuthbert's letter to Cuthwin. The custom was carried to excess when, e.g. Ceolfrid and his companions recited the whole Psalter twice a day, beside the psalms of the hours, on their Romeward journey; Hist. Abb. 16: or when the English-born Willehad almost

off sleepiness, or going about the island to see that all was
well. If any of the monks complained of being disturbed
in their nightly or noonday slumber, he would say pleasantly,
'*I* am never annoyed by being aroused to do or think of
something useful[1].' When he celebrated, 'it was rather his
heart than his voice that was uplifted' at the 'Sursum corda :'
nor could he ever complete the service without tears[2]. As
an administrator of discipline, his zeal for what was right
became sternness towards all who were doing wrong : but
honest confession awakened all his sympathy, and the penitent
would be drawn into better ways by a renewed experience of
such tenderness united to such sanctity[3]. He used garments
neither over-neat nor slovenly ; and his proscription of rich
colours became a tradition among the Lindisfarne monks[4].
As at Melrose, he found work to do among the country people,
and by his frequent visits, as his custom was, he stirred up
many to seek after a heavenly reward. Stories were told, as
in his earlier life, about wonderful effects from his prayers[5].
Altogether, he seemed to be eminently the man for the place :
yet after several years thus spent, he took a step which must
seem strange to us, though to the men of his time it appeared
to be the very crown of contemplative and ascetic perfection.
In 676[6], when he was about forty-five, he gave up his duties Cuthbert,
as prior of Lindisfarne, in order to live as a 'recluse' on Farne.

hermit on

---

always sang 'one psalter' a day, sometimes even two or three ; Vit. S. Will. 9.
Compare Bede, iii. 27, on the amount of Egbert's psalmody.

[1] Bede, Vit. Cuthb. 16 : 'Nemo . . . mihi molestiam facit me excitando de
somno,' &c. It was usual for monks to sleep for awhile before or after
the matin service ; comp. Bede, v. 9. St. Liudger used to sleep, after the
'psalmody' of nocturns, in a 'solar' of the church of Utrecht ; Vit. Liudg. 16.
See too Benedict's Reg. Mon. c. 22, 48.

[2] Bede, V. C. 16. The celebration was still, as in Aidan's time, confined
to Sundays ; ib. 44. See above, p. 151.

[3] Bede, l. c. : 'Erat zelo justitiæ fervidus,' &c.

[4] Bede, l. c. : 'Vestimentis utebatur communibus,' &c.

[5] Bede, V. C. 15.

[6] Simeon, de Dun. Eccl. i. 7, gives this date. It appears, indeed, that
Simeon antedates his coming to Lindisfarne by some years ; but he may be
right as to the time of his resignation, as having taken place in 676, and in
the third year before the consecration of Eata, which was late in 678. Bede
assigns to him, vaguely, 'many' years of priorship both at Melrose and at
Lindisfarne ; V. C. 16, 17.

CHAP. IX. the neighbouring islet of Farne, which Aidan had used for his periodical retreats[1]. His biographers regarded him as 'having thus chosen the better part[2];'—as if he had not proved his own signal capacities for that union of service and of devotion which he had enjoyed while dwelling in a community. The unhealthy extravagance into which the ecclesiastical mind of that age was led, on such subjects, by the accumulating influences of its hagiology, mingles with the good sense which such a writer as Bede exhibits on other matters. No one, apparently, remonstrated with Cuthbert: every one thought he was doing the very thing which would make him still more pleasing to God. He himself, however, was accustomed after his retirement to warn his friends against an exaggerated estimate of his hermit-life, and to extol as truly admirable the life of obedient monks in a community[3]. It was for his own special profit, as he viewed it, that he determined to live in solitude: and accordingly, he took up his abode in an island which had never before been regularly inhabited[4], and constructed for himself a round hut roofed with logs and straw: its wall, made of huge stones and turf, rose

---

[1] See above, p. 146.

[2] So Sim. Dunelm.: 'O pater dulcissime . . . sedebas cum Maria secus pedes Domini, optimam partem eligens.' (Comp. Life of St. Deicolus, 16, Act. SS. Ben. ii. 108, much to the same purport.) Bede (Vit. Cuth. 17) considers that he was thereby advancing 'de virtute in virtutem.' Before retiring to Farne he spent some time in 'a secluded place in the outskirts of the monastery ('cellæ') of Lindisfarne; Bede, l. c.; evidently this, his first essay at hermit-life was made in a cave bearing his name near Howburn; Raine's St. Cuthbert, p. 20. Probably it was in some remote part of Holy Island, such as that to which his successor retired for Lenten devotions; Bede, V. C. 42: Skene says, in the S. W. corner, Celt. Sc. ii. 211. Irish monasteries sometimes had 'diserts' or places for solitary devotion: there was one such, near the shore, in Hy; Reeves's Adamnan, p. 366. Fiacc is said to have spent the time from 'Shrove Saturday' 'to Easter Saturday' (i.e. Easter Eve) in a cave; Tripartite Life of St. Patrick, i. 243.

[3] 'Ne conversationem ejus quasi singulariter excelsam mirarentur . . . . "Sed jure," inquit, "est cœnobitarum vita mirabilis . . . quorum plurimos novi meam parvitatem longe . . . anteire;"' Bede, V. C. 22.

[4] See Raine's St. Cuthbert, p. 20 ff.; Murray's Durham and Northumberland, p. 212. It is 'a little island of basaltic rock;' Green, Making of Engl. p. 378; see Bede, iv. 28. It is referred to in several passages of Reginald of Durham's 'Libellus de S. Cuthberto.' (Surtees Soc.)

externally above a man's height, but internally was sunk
much deeper, 'so that the pious inhabitant might see nothing
but the sky[1].' The cottage, as Bede once calls it[2], had
two compartments, one of which served as an oratory[3]:
and one window, which looked to the west. In the centre,
with the help of Lindisfarne monks, he dug a pit, which
next morning appeared like a well full of water,—of water,
it was thought, miraculously produced from the hard rock[4].
A larger hut, for visitors[5], was built at the landing-place,
looking towards Lindisfarne, with a spring of water near
at hand. Cuthbert, at first, used to leave his cell in order
to greet his brethren, and wash their feet with warm water[6],
a service which they sedulously returned. They used to
supply him with bread, until, in order not to burden the
monastery, he made them bring him some instruments of
husbandry, and some grain:—wheat, when sown, did not
come up, but in the next year barley answered better[7].
To his brethren these visits must have been landmarks in
their life[8]: but other friends came to see him, as Herbert

---

[1] Bede, V. C. 16: 'Quatenus . . . pius incola nil . . . præter cœlum posset
intueri.' Or, as in iv. 28, 'cœlum tantum . . . cujus introitum sitiebat,' &c.

[2] 'Casula,' Bede, Vit. Cuth. 27. In c. 18, 'tuguriunculum,' 'mansio,'
or 'monasterium;' cp. iv. 28, 'mansionem angustam.' On this cell, see Anderson, Scotland in Early Christian Times, p. 125.

[3] In Vit. Cuthb. 46 Bede speaks of its walls as '*tabulis* minus diligenter
coaptatis compositi.' It looked southwards: he afterwards erected a cross
outside it, and placed under the turf, to the north of it, a sarcophagus given
him by the abbot Cudda, ib. 37. On the site stands a chapel of St. Cuthbert, probably 700 years old, fitted up for service, which is performed 'about
twice a year;' Murray's Durham and Northumberland, p. 213.

[4] The water never failed, and never 'flooded the pavement;' Vit. Cuthb.
18; cp. iv. 28.

[5] 'Major domus,' Vit. Cuthb. 17. He had himself been hospitaller at
Ripon. There was such an office at Lindisfarne; Bede, iv. 31; cp. Vit. Cuthb.
44. There were 'guest-houses' in Irish monasteries, as at Armagh; see
Reeves's Adamnan, pp. 157, 361.

[6] Cp. Adamnan, Vit. Col. i. 4. He very seldom took off his leather buskins.
Bede says that he kept them one year, from Easter to Easter, save for the
solemn feet-washing on Maunday Thursday; Vit. Cuthb. 18.

[7] 'Adferte, rogo, hordeum, si forte vel illud fructum facere possit.' Vit.
Cuthb. 19. He had promised them that if he could not grow corn for his
own food, he would return to Lindisfarne: Bede, iv. 28, 'Si mihi Divina
gratia,' &c.

[8] According to Bede, Vit. Cuthb. 8, he used to tell them that if he were on a

CHAP. IX. the hermit of the isle on Derwentwater, who paid him a yearly visit to enjoy his 'salutary instructions[1].' And beside these, from distant parts of Britain came strangers to tell him of their private troubles, 'and no man took home with him the sorrow that he brought.' Cuthbert knew well how to cheer the afflicted with thoughts of heaven, or of the fleetingness of earthly evil or good: he could 'describe to the tempted the various lures which might ensnare a soul destitute of love for God or for the brethren, but which a soul strong in perfect faith could pass through like a spider's web[2]:' 'his speech, seasoned with salt, was wont to instruct the ignorant, reconcile those who were at variance, and make all feel that nothing was to be preferred to the love of Christ[3].' True it is, that the account of those nine years in Farne cannot stop here: solitude acted on Cuthbert's nerves and imagination as it had done on those of other hermits[4], and conjured up phantoms of visible fiendish

---

rock in the midst of the ocean, hidden from all men's view, he should still not think himself free from the snares of the world and the love of money. And Bede (Vit. Cuthb. 27) tells a striking story, which Cuthbert himself told in a sermon at Carlisle. One Christmas day, some Lindisfarne monks came over to Farne, and begged him to leave his cell, and spend the 'solemn and joyful day' with them in the guest-house. He consented; and they all sat down to their Christmas dinner, in the midst of which, as if stirred by an inward impulse, he began to talk of watchfulness against trials. The monks thought there was a time for all things. 'Do let us spend this day in gladness: it is our Lord's birthday.' 'Well,' said he, 'we will do so.' Presently, while they were enjoying themselves 'epulis et fabulis,' he was again moved to speak of preparing for trials. The poor monks became a little impatient; they thought the advice good, but inopportune. 'We have more than enough days for fast and vigil: to-day let us rejoice in the Lord, in memory of the great joy for all people.' 'Very well,' he said. But when, once more, the irrepressible warning broke from his lips, they felt that it meant something, and said, 'Let us do as you say.' He declared afterwards that he knew no more than they did of any approaching trouble; but when they returned home, they found one of their brethren dead of the pestilence, which raged for nearly a year afterwards, carrying off the majority of that 'noble society.' 'And now, brethren,' Cuthbert concluded, 'do *you* also be watchful in prayer, that if any tribulation should come upon you, it may find you ready to meet it.'

[1] Bede, V. C. 28; cp. Bede, iv. 29.

[2] Bede, V. C. 22.

[3] Anon. Vit. Bed. Op. vi. 372.

[4] See the Life of Antony, ascribed to St. Athanasius, c. 9: ἦν ὁ τόπος εὐθὺς πεπληρωμένος φαντασίας λεόντων ἄρκτων . . . , and for St. Guthlac, below, c. xii.

assault; and as time went on in that wild and grim retreat[1], the morbid element in his devotion became stronger; he would not come forth on the arrival of visitors, he would but look at them through the window; at last he even kept this closed, save when his blessing was expressly besought[2]. Enough of this: yet let us remember, in order to do justice to a phenomenon which to us may bear a fanatical aspect, that the hermit-life of Cuthbert was to the rude minds around him an impressive representation of spiritual power[3], and was largely overruled for the comfort of many a sore heart which would not otherwise have come under his ministry. Nor did it impair his gentleness, his lowliness, his habitual brightness of countenance and temper[4]. Still, when all this is said, we must still think that he was less truly a saint while dwelling in Farne than when, at Lindisfarne or at Melrose, he 'lived according to Holy Scripture, leading the contemplative *within* the active life[5].'

Passing on, in imagination, further south, we reach that Wearmouth. domain, situated on the north bank of the Wear[6], which King Egfrid had granted to Benedict Biscop on his return from his fourth visit to Rome. As the grant was made out of the king's private property, there was no need of any legal process to convert a piece of the national 'folkland' into 'bookland' to be held under charter[7]: the land

---

[1] Compare Bede, v. 1, for the sounds which a dweller on Farne would often hear, 'fragore procellarum ac ferventis oceani;' and Reginald Libell. 31.

[2] Bede, V. C. 18, end.

[3] See Kingsley, The Roman and the Teuton, p. 180.

[4] Anon. Vit. C.: 'Omni hora hilaris et lætus;' Bed. Op. vi. 372. See Reginald on Cuthbert's taming the eider-ducks, which ever since 'se palpantes contrectare permittunt . . . in gremio tui . . . se componendos præbent,' Libell. 27. Raine describes the dalmatic in which his bones were found wrapt as having eider-ducks embroidered on it; St. Cuthbert, p. 194. On his fondness for these animals see Kingsley, Hermits, p. 295; and compare Columba fondling his old white horse. Adamn. iii. 23.

[5] Anon. Vit. C.

[6] See Surtees, Hist. and Antiq. of Durham, ii. 2.

[7] 'De suo largitus;' Bede, Hist. Abb. 4. See Lingard, A.-S. Ch. i. 240; if a royal founder did not thus 'give a parcel out of his own bocland,' he had 'to convert, with consent of the witan,' a part 'of the national folcland into an estate of perpetual inheritance.' Cp. Stubbs, Const. Hist. i. 85. 'Bookland' was land thus held by 'book' or charter.

CHAP. IX. was simply transferred as bookland from Egfrid to Benedict, with the injunction to raise on it a monastery in honour of St. Peter. The foundation is dated in 674[1]: a year later, Benedict made a special journey to Gaul in order to obtain skilled masons, such as he could not find nearer home, for the erection of the abbey church. In this he was aided by a friend, an abbot named Torthelm[2]: the church, 'built of stone after the Roman fashion, which the founder always loved[3],' rose with great rapidity: when it was nearly finished, he sent for Frankish glaziers, who not only glazed the windows of the church[4], cloisters, and refectory, and made lamps and vessels for the church, but taught their craft to the Northumbrians[5], and so far contributed to English civilisation. All the furniture and vestments 'which Benedict could not procure at home, he took care to purchase abroad[6].' It must have been a stirring time at Wearmouth while the works were in progress, and new products of foreign art were continually coming in. So energetic, and so well served, was Benedict, that he found it possible to roof in the church, and to use it for mass within one year from the foundation[7]. The rule for the brethren was framed by Benedict, probably from that of Lerins, but certainly with reference to whatever seemed best in the customs of all those seventeen 'very ancient' monasteries which he had visited during his travels[8]. The system of his great name-sake, as we infer from words of his own, was highly esteemed by him, but was not adopted indiscriminately or in the lump.

---

[1] Bede, Hist. Abb. 4.

[2] Anon. Hist. Abb.; Bed. Op. vi. 418.

[3] 'Lapideam . . . juxta Romanorum quem semper amabat morem;' Bede, Hist. Abb. 5. Cp. Bede, iii. 4; v. 21. See Reeves's Adamnan, p. 177; and above, p. 14.

[4] Above, p. 243; cp. Greg. Tur. de Glor. Mart. i. 59.

[5] Bede, Hist. Abb. 5. See Malmesb. G. Pontif. iv. 186.

[6] 'De transmarinis regionibus advectare,' &c. Bede, l. c.

[7] Bede, l. c. Freeman considers the porch of Monkwearmouth church to be 'plainly a piece of the work of the seventh century,' v. 899.

[8] Anon. Hist. Abb., Bed. Op. vi. 418; Bede, Hist. Abb. 9; Lingard, A.-S. Ch. i. 208. So St. Boniface sent Sturmi to visit the great monasteries of Italy, in order to study their rules and 'traditions,' with a view to the new foundation of Fulda; Vit. S. Sturmi, 14; Pertz, Mon. Germ. Hist. ii. 371.

In these and all his labours he had a 'most active coadjutor' CHAP. IX.
in Ceolfrid[1], whose history was only less interesting than his Ceolfrid.
own. It was in some sense like his own: for Ceolfrid also
was nobly born, and had been piously trained[2], and at
eighteen had entered the monastery of Gilling[3], then
ruled by his kinsman Tunbert, afterwards for a short time
bishop of Hexham. With him Ceolfrid afterwards went to
Ripon, and entered the monastery of Wilfrid, who ordained
him priest, at the age of twenty-seven, in 669. He then
travelled into Kent, in order to study the monastic discipline
of the great Gregorian houses: and also visited the abbot
Botulf at Ikanho, by way of enlarging and varying his
experience of such institutions. Yet, when he returned to
Ripon, he undertook the homely office of baker to the
monastery[4]; and, while heating the oven and preparing the
loaves, used mentally to go over, and perfect himself in,
'the ceremonial acts of the priesthood.' He was soon, however, elevated to the priorship, and Benedict obtained Wilfrid's leave to transfer him to the same office at Wearmouth.
At first he had some trouble with high-born monks, who
had been attracted to the new house by the secular rank
once belonging to its founder, or by the royal patronage
lavished on his undertaking, but who 'could not endure
regular discipline[5].' So vexatious was their bearing, that

[1] Anon. Hist. Abb., Bed. Op. vi. 416; Bede, Hist. Abb. 6. See Lingard,
A.-S. Ch. ii. 392; Alb. Butler, Sept. 25; Church Quart. Rev. xxv. 437.

[2] His father, a 'comes,' had one day prepared a rich banquet for Oswy: a
call to arms prevented the royal visit, and then 'ille, gratias divinæ dispensa-
tioni referens,' assembled all the poor, sick, and wanderers within reach, set
them down to the meal which had awaited 'the earthly king,' and with his
wife waited on 'the heavenly King in His lowly ones;' Anon. Hist. Abb.

[3] Above, p. 169. The former superior, Kynefrid, went to Ireland 'for the
purpose of studying the Scriptures and seeing the Lord more freely in tears
and prayers;' Anon. Hist. l. c.; see above, pp. 166, 192.

[4] Anon. Hist.: 'Siquidem tempore non pauco pistoris officium tenens,' &c.
Different handicrafts were practised by the monks; see Bede, v. 14, on the
wicked monk who was skilful as a carpenter. St. Columba had a Saxon as
baker at Hy, Adamn. Vit. Col. iii. 10; and see ib. iii. 12, on 'diversa opera.'
Cp. St. Boniface, Ep. 69: 'Stirme in coquina sit, Bernardus ... ædificet do-
munculas vestras.' St. Sturmi, remembering the rule that 'artes diversæ'
should be practised in a monastery, set some of his monks to make a new
channel for the river Fulda; Vit. Sturm. 20. Cp. Benedict, Reg. c. 57.

[5] Anon. Hist.: 'Nam et invidias quorumdam nobilium,' &c. Cp. Bede, Hist.

Ceolfrid even threw up a task which they seemed to render hopeless, and went back to Ripon as to a home. But he was induced by Benedict to return, and thenceforward his character developed a stedfast energy and soundness of judgment which through a long period of monastic rule were united with a simplicity and affectionateness, a ready sympathy, and a fervour of devotion, which commanded the love of the whole society[1]. Another of the first inmates of Wearmouth stands out in Bede's pages as a very attractive figure: we see a young man of twenty-four, strong and handsome, with 'a sweet voice and a cheerful temper,' taking pleasure in sharing the commonest labours with his fellow-monks, at work in kitchen or garden or bakehouse, threshing or winnowing, or milking the cattle[2],—who yet, like his cousin the founder-abbot, had been a 'king's thane[3]:' his name was Easterwine. A third brother, who, like these two, attained to the highest dignity in the house, was a deacon named Sigfrid, who is described as 'preeminently intent on Scriptural studies,' but amid them had to bear the burden of weak health, so that, as Bede quaintly expresses it, 'his efforts to keep innocency of heart were carried on under pressure of an incurable affection of the lungs[4].'

Easterwine.

Sigfrid.

Hilda at Whitby.

Let us go southward again, and observe the condition of that already famous convent which had been the scene of the Conference, and which looked down in its pride of place over the German Ocean. In Hilda, the royal grand-niece of the great Edwin, we see the old Teutonic type of a woman of

Abb. 9, where Benedict warns his monks against choosing an abbot for the sake of his noble blood. Comp. Green, Making of Engl. p. 346.

[1] Bede, Hist. Abb. 12, 13 : 'Industrius per omnia . . . acutus ingenio, actu impiger, maturus animo, religionis zelo fervens . . . Incomparabilem orandi psallendique sollertiam . . . mirabilem et coercendi improbos fervorem, et modestiam consolandi infirmos' (here 'modestiam' seems to mean gentleness), &c.; and ib. 14, 'nutritoris tutorisque . . . spiritualis . . . libertatis et pacis.' The Anon. Hist. Abb. speaks of him as 'acer ingenio, strenuus actu . . . flagrans amore simul et timore divino,' &c. (Bed. Op. vi. 422.)

[2] Bede, Hist. Abb. 7 : ' Ventilare cum eis et triturare, oves vitulasque mulgere, in pistrino, in coquino, in cunctis monasterii operibus, jocundus et obediens gauderet exerceri,' &c. Cp. Benedict, Reg. c. 46.

[3] 'Minister.' See above, p. 118.

[4] Hist. Abb. 8 : ' Irremediabili pulmonum vitio.' Cp. Anon. Hist. Abb.

wise 'rede' and mighty influence, a Veleda [1] or an Alioruna, softened and transfigured into 'the Mother' whose advice was sought by princes, and who 'held out to many' at a distance 'an example of the works of light [2].' Hers had been a career signally conspicuous and widely effective. Born three years before the fall of Ethelfrid,—baptized at York by Paulinus, at thirteen,—bent on joining her sister, Queen Hereswid, in a Frankish convent, and only recalled, by Aidan's express summons, to Northumbria,—for one year a nun in a small cell on the north of the Wear,—then abbess of Hartlepool [3] in succession to Heiu,—then foundress and abbess of Whitby in 657, she was sixty years old when, in 674, she began to suffer from recurring attacks of fever, and 'for six years ceased not to labour under the same disease, but in all that time never omitted to give thanks in her own person to her Maker, and publicly as well as privately to teach the flock committed to her charge to serve the Lord obediently while they had health, and under adversity or bodily infirmity to be faithful in rendering thanks to Him [4].' A noble woman, we may well say,—strong and wise, true-hearted and firm of purpose, with warm affections and clear discernment, using her great capacities for rule and guidance in the true spirit of ' a mother in Israel,'—in some sense a mediæval Mère Angélique : one sees how she had largely succeeded where Ebba had ultimately failed, impressing her own mind on the double community

[1] Tacitus, Germ. 6. 'The name of Hild was that of a Saxon war-goddess; also nearly synonymous with Fate ;' Stevenson, Chron. of Abingdon, ii. p. xxxviii. Cp. Merivale, Conversion of Northern Nations, p. 150. So Wilson, Prehistoric Ann. of Scotl. ii. 387 : ' In an ancient poem in the Icelandic Saga, Hilda, the Scandinavian goddess of war and victory, is introduced with her weird sisters, the Valkyries,' &c.

[2] Bede, iv. 23 : ' Tantæ autem erat ipsa prudentiæ,' &c. For Hilda's career see above, pp. 123, 170, 192.

[3] Bede mentions several Northumbrian religious houses of lower rank, as Abercorn, Carlisle, Tynemouth, Hartlepool, Gilling, Hackness, Coquet Island, Watton, Derawood or Beverley, a place near the Dacre, and one in Elmete.

[4] Bede, iv. 23 : ' Percussa etenim febribus,' &c. The discipline of bodily affliction is a favourite theme with Bede : cp. ii. 17; iv. 9, 19, 31 ; Vit. Cuthb. 28, 37 ; Hist. Abb. 9; where also he says that Benedict Biscop during a long illness took care 'in dolore semper Auctori gratias referre,' &c. He repeatedly refers to medical treatment, e. g. iv. 19; v. 3 ; V. C. 23, 30, 37, 45. He mentions various kinds of ordinary disease, as fever, paralysis, tumour, affection of lungs, pleurisy, dysentery, diarrhœa.

CHAP. IX. which bowed to her as its head, establishing a tradition of
unanimity and unselfishness[1], and, as Bede says, 'making
her monks give so much time to the study of Scripture, and
so much heed to the practice of good works[2],' that bishops
came to think of her house as the best place for supplying
competent 'ordinands,' and five of the brethren[3], whom
Bede enumerates, 'all of them persons of signal worth and

Cædmon. holiness,' attained the episcopal dignity. But there was one
inhabitant of the monastery whom his brethren venerated for
a gift which they ascribed to special inspiration; although
they could not have imagined the unique place which he was
to hold, through all generations of their race, as the father of
English poetry. Rude warlike ballads were doubtless current
among the Angles who came with Ida, and the Saxons who
came with Cerdic,—songs of the great deeds of ancestors,
such as might form, when mingled with lays of lighter mood,
'the salt of the feast[4]' alike to eorl and ceorl: but something
greater announced its presence, perhaps before Oswy's death,
certainly during Hilda's abbacy, under circumstances as
unpromising as ever attended a literary epoch. To know
what it was, we must take a glimpse of the life of common
herdsmen[5] in a Northumbrian farm-stead, which stood on
part of the abbey property. One of these rustic labourers, a
man well on in years, bore the name of Cædmon. He was
behindhand with his fellows through inability to sing[6]: and

---

[1] Bede, iv. 23: 'Maxime pacis et caritatis custodiam docuit, ita ut, in exemplum primitivæ ecclesiæ, nullus ibi dives, nullus esset egens, omnibus essent
omnia communia,' &c.

[2] Bede, l. c.: 'Tantum lectioni divinarum Scripturarum,' &c. Higden,
Polychron. b. 5. c. 19, calls her 'sancta, prudens, litterata.'

[3] Bosa bishop of York, Ætla of Dorchester, Oftfor of Worcester, John of
Hexham and York, Wilfrid II. of York.

[4] Lord Lytton's 'Harold,' p. 29. See Turner, iii. 58; Palgrave, Engl.
Comm. p. 390; and Freeman, v. 587, who more than once remarks (i. 392,
iii. 733) that there are fragments of old ballads in Henry of Huntingdon:
see the sayings recorded by him as to great battles, (above, pp. 112, 138,
159, 184). Compare the story of the Frisian Bernlef, who was much loved
because . . . 'antiquorum actus regumque certamina bene noverat psallendo
promere;' Vit. S. Liudg. ii. 1.

[5] For an Old-English description of their duties, see Turner, ii. 546.

[6] See Lingard, A.-S. Ch. ii. 154: 'To chant the songs of gleemen to the harp
was an acquirement common even to the lowest classes.'

whenever he made one of a 'beer-party[1],' at which it was expected that 'for mirth-sake' each in turn should play the 'gleeman,' he could not see the harp being passed round towards him without starting up from the unfinished meal, and going home shamefast[2]. One evening he had thus left his mates, and gone, not to his own dwelling, but to the cattle-shed which for that night was under his charge. There he lay down and slept, and in his dream some person stood by him, and greeted him by name. 'Cædmon, sing me something.' He thought that he answered, 'I cannot sing: that is why I came away from the party.' 'However, you have got to sing to me[3]!' 'What must I sing?' 'Sing of the creation.' And so, in his sleep, these verses came to him: 'he sang, in praise of God the Maker[4],'—

> 'Now should we praise the Guardian of the heaven-realm,
> The Maker's might and His mind-thought,
> Works of the glorious Father, as He of each wonder,
> Eternal Lord, created the beginning[5].
> He erst shaped for children of men
> Heaven as a roof,—the holy Creator:
> Then the middle world did mankind's Guardian,
> Eternal Lord, afterwards create,
> Earth for men, Lord Almighty.'

On waking, he retained in memory what he had seemed to sing in his dream, and presently added other words to the same purport. He then told his bailiff, or 'tun-reeve[6],' what had happened, or, as Bede says, 'what a gift he had received:' and was by him straightway conducted to the abbess, who, 'in the presence of many learned men,' heard his story. All

---

[1] So King Alfred translates 'convivium.' Cp. Turner, iii. 31.

[2] Bede, iv. 24: 'Surgebat a media cœna, et egressus ad suam domum repedabat.'

[3] 'Attamen mihi cantare habes.' Cp. Bede, iii. 22, 'in ipsa domo mori habes;' and also iv. 14, 'exspectare habes;' iv. 24, 'neque enim mori adhuc habes.'

[4] See the original Northumbrian text in Sweet's Anglo-Saxon Reader, p. 195. Bede's Latin professedly gives the sense, rather than the exact order of the words. See Lingard's version of Alfred's text, ii. 408; and Turner, iii. 266. Compare the verses on death, repeated by Bede when dying.

[5] Bede renders, 'cum sit æternus Deus, omnium miraculorum auctor exstitit.'

[6] Kemble, ii. 176. A 'tún, enclosure, farm, vill, or manor.' See Green, Making of England, p. 180, Stubbs, Const. Hist. i. 93, for the wider sense.

agreed that it was a Divine boon bestowed on the herdsman : they then read to him a portion of Scripture, and bade him turn it into poetry if he could. He went off with his task, and ' next morning produced the passage excellently versified :' whereupon ' the Mother [1] ' persuaded him to become a monk, solemnly received him into the community, and ordered that he should be instructed in the whole course of sacred history. He listened attentively to all that he was thus taught, and ' ruminating it over, like a clean animal, turned it into most sweet verse :' and then his teachers were his hearers while ' he sang to them of the creation of the world, the origin of mankind, the whole history of Genesis, the Exodus, the entrance into Canaan, other events of Scripture history, the Incarnation, Passion, Resurrection, the coming of the Holy Spirit, the preaching of the Apostles [2]. Many a poem also did he make about the awful future judgment, the terrible punishment in hell, the sweetness of the heavenly kingdom, the judgments and the benefits of God ; in all which, his aim was to draw men away from the love of wickedness, and to stir them up to the love and diligent practice of well-doing. For he was a man very religious, and humbly obedient to the discipline of the rules, but kindled with fervent and zealous indignation against those who chose to be disobedient.' As to ' frivolous ' songs, we are assured that Cædmon *could not*

[1] Bede, iv. 24 : ' Unde mox abbatissa,' &c.

[2] On the ' Metrical Paraphrase,' now extant under the name of Cædmon, see Dict. of Chr. Biography, i. 370 ; Green, Making of Engl. p. 370. Thorpe, in his edition of it (1832), inclined to regard it as generally authentic. It has, however, characteristics which do not suit a Whitby cowherd. Evidently it is a compilation from several writers, one of whom must have really known war, when ' the fowls sang amid the dark-shafts,' and ' men saw the grim war-*mote*, the hard hand-play.' There are very noble passages in the poem ; in Adam and Eve, while unfallen, ' was burning love of the Lord ;' ' Mickle wonder that God eternal would ever bear that so many a "thane" were misled by the lies' of Satan ; ' Let us turn thither where He sits . . . the Saviour Lord, in that dear home,' &c. The poem begins with words in the same tone as the undoubted fragment, but not identical with it : and ends with the fiends' words to Satan, ' Thus be now in evil : good erst thou wouldest not.' It is curious that Satan is described as sending an inferior fiend to beguile Adam and Eve : this tempter twines himself, in form of a worm, round the tree of knowledge, and announces himself as God's angel, &c. The harrowing of hell takes place on the dawn of Easter-day ; Eve and Adam plead with Christ, and are released.

compose any such. All his works were the outflow of a CHAP. IX. pious mind, and were often found effective as stimulants to piety, to 'contempt for the world, and craving for heavenly life.'

How long he lived as a monk in Whitby, we know not. But it is natural to connect this account of the outburst of his poetic powers with the exquisite narrative of his happy death, which probably happened not long afterwards. With all his own vividness and pathos, Bede makes us see the old man in the fortnight of his last illness, which does not confine him to his bed. One evening he asks the attendant to prepare for his reception in the out-building assigned to the sick and dying[1] : the man wonders, but takes Cædmon thither before midnight. After some pleasant talk to the other patients, he asks, ' Have you the Housel[2] within?' meaning the Holy Eucharist, reserved (in one kind only) for the sick. They answer, 'What need have you of the Housel? you have not got to die just yet[3],—you talk too cheerily for that.' ' However,' he rejoins, 'bring me the Housel.' He takes it into his hand[4], and asks whether they all feel kindly towards him[5]. They reply, 'Surely, and we pray you to feel so towards us.' ' Dear children,' such is the sweet answer, ' I feel kindly towards *all* God's servants[6].' He then ' fortifies himself with the heavenly viaticum[7],' and asks how soon the brethren would be ' awakened for nocturnal lauds[8].'

---

[1] Cp. Bede, iv. 9.

[2] Alfred's rendering of Bede's 'eucharistiam,' *husle* from ' hostia.' The chalice was not in this case reserved. Compare the story of Serapion in Euseb. vi. 44 ; and Bede, iv. 14, ' oblationis particulam.'

[3] ' Neque enim mori adhuc *habes*.'

[4] The ancient practice of receiving the Eucharist into the hands (e. g. Cyril Hier., Cat. Myst. 5. 21 ; and see Bingham, b. xv. c. 5. s. 6) was still retained in the case of *men*. Cp. Greg. Turon. H. Fr. x. 8.

[5] ' Had they all a *mild mood* towards him?' ' Yes, they were all blithe of mood,' &c. Cp. Hist. Abb. 13, on Ceolfrid's farewell.

[6] ' God's *men*,' Alfred. On the Old-English custom of choosing a lord, or becoming the ' man ' of a superior or lord who was to give protection in return for fealty, see Freeman, i. 119 ; Stubbs, Const. Hist. i. 90.

[7] Cp. Bede, iv. 14 : ' viatico Dominici Corporis et Sanguinis ;' iv. 23, ' viatico sacrosanctæ communionis ;' and v. 14, ' sine viatico salutis.'

[8] Alfred inserts, ' to teach God's folk.' ' Nocturn lauds ' mean matins : cp. Vit. Cuthb. 40, ' nocturnæ psalmodiæ ;' and Hist. Trans. Cuthb., Bed. Op. vi.

' It will not be long,' they say.   ' Good ; then let us wait for that hour.'   He signs himself with the cross, lies back on the pillow, falls asleep, and so ' in stillness' passes away : his last words harmonising with all that he had uttered ' in praise of his Creator.'   Such was the death of the poet-monk of Whitby : read the account of Bede's own last moments, written by an eye-witness and prefixed to his History, and you will find the two scenes very similar in form, and altogether identical in spirit.   Of Bede also it might be said, as he has said in express words of Cædmon, and also implicitly of Aidan, Hilda, Chad, and others, that ' he closed his life with a beautiful and tranquil end [1].'

414.   Bede refers to the time 'matutinæ laudis,' iii. 12 ; and to the ' psalmody matutinæ laudis,' iv. 7, in a way which shows that at this period lauds were the last part of matins.   So Hist. Abb. 7.   See Benedict, Reg. Mon. 10.   So in the ' Excerptions' ascribed to Egbert, but of later date (Haddan and Stubbs, iii. 415,) no service intervenes between the nocturnal synaxis (matins or matin lauds) and prime (No. 28, Johnson, Engl. Can. i. 189).   Compare, on the antiquity of this close union between the nocturns and the day-break ' praises,' Archdeacon Freeman, Principles of Div. Service, i. 10.

[1] Bede, iv. 24 : ' Unde et pulchro vitam suam fine conclusit . . . tranquilla morte mundum relinquens.'

CHAPTER X.

To pass from the convent-life of Wearmouth or of Wilfrid's troubles. Whitby to the personal troubles and public dissensions which constitute the great 'cause of Bishop Wilfrid,' is as if one were suddenly transported from the margin of a land-locked harbour to a rough coast lashed by a rising sea. That the sea, so to speak, would rise,—that, sooner or later, Wilfrid's splendid prosperity would be interrupted, must have been evident to him, one would think, ever since he placed the veil on the head of Queen Etheldred. Her husband knew well, and could not be expected to forget, who it was that had Alienation of Egfrid. upheld her, with the whole force of his spiritual influence, in a resolution the reverse of wife-like [1], and at whose feet she had sealed it by pronouncing those new vows which were to nullify the old in her estimation. To that step, indeed, a consent had been wrung from him by what he would regard as her impracticable and unnatural obstinacy [2]: the marriage

[1] Thomas of Ely unintentionally makes the case worse for Wilfrid, saying that he 'dissimulavit, provide atque prudenter,' as if agreeing with the king, and promised to persuade the queen to abandon her purpose; 'veritus ne, sicut contigit, ob rem hujuscemodi offensum illum haberet. Et dum circa talia, ut æstimabatur, sanctus pontifex reginam alioqui intenderet . . . egit vir beatus sua industria, ut potius divortium quæreret,' &c.; Vit. Etheldr. 9; Act. SS. Bened. ii. 747. Neither Bede (iv. 19) nor Eadmer Vit. Wilf. (25) knows of any such insincere promise.

[2] Thomas represents him as objecting strongly to a separation from a beloved wife, but at last yielding to her importunities, 'licet invitus, tamen eam dimisit invincibilem;' Act. SS. Ben. ii. 749. A maiden espoused to Sigebert II. of Austrasia, on arriving at his court, 'concealed her purpose' for a week, and then took the veil 'within closed doors:' the king (afterwards canonised, but a 'Fainéant') 'gave her over to the Lord.' She had acted, we are expressly told, 'by the advice' of St. Gall; Vit. S. Galli, i. (Pertz, Mon. Germ. Hist. ii. 12). Trickeries devised for a monastic interest were not then deemed unworthy of religion.

had, under the peculiar circumstances, been declared void, and Egfrid had been allowed to contract another; but he was not the less alienated from the prelate who had so systematically thwarted him in regard to his domestic comfort. He would utter that complaint, often enough heard afterwards, and in his case at any rate not unjust, that the Church had come between wife and husband: and his new queen, Ermenburga, from a personal dislike[1] to her predecessor's confidential guide, appears to have stimulated the irritation of Egfrid by appealing to his susceptibilities as a prince. Wilfrid's magnificent position, his 'secular glory and riches,' the number of monasteries under his obedience[2], the stately buildings which he had reared, the 'host' of attendants, nobly born and nurtured, who appeared in his halls, arrayed like the king's thanes in the palace[3],—these things were easily represented as unbefitting any one ecclesiastic, and as proving that he ought not to hold a bishopric coextensive with the kingdom.

Scheme of diocesan partition.

We seem to hear the first mutterings of a storm that afterwards assailed the proud elevation of a mitred chancellor or a prince-bishop: and it so happened that these royal jealousies were excited just when Theodore was bent on carrying out his scheme of diocesan partition. That scheme he pursued from motives of a public character; in regard to Northumbria,

---

[1] Eddi compares her to Jezebel, c. 24. See Fridegod, 'ceu garrula perdix Culpabat justum collatis rebus abuti,' 606 : and Eadmer, 26, 'Per hanc igitur diabolus,' &c. : and Richard of Hexham, 'in cujus corde Sathanas contra . . . episcopum odiorum et invidiæ fomenta conflans;' De stat. Hagust. Eccl. c. 7, X Script. 294.

[2] Richard of Hexham, ib. c. 5, calls him 'the father of nine monasteries,' and says that many abbots and abbesses 'commended their houses to his keeping, others named him their successor.'

[3] Eddi, 24 : 'Enumerans ei . . . Wilfridi . . . omnem gloriam sæcularem et divitias, necnon cœnobiorum multitudinem et ædificiorum magnitudinem . . . exercitum sodalium regalibus vestimentis et armis ornatum.' Eadmer, 26, makes her say to Egfrid, 'Your whole kingdom is his bishopric. What if,' in time of war, 'he should keep back his men from fighting on your side?' Malmesb. G. P. iii. 100, p. 219 : 'Conflavit ergo pontifici regina invidiam, quod tot abbates, tot abbatias, haberet, quod aureis et argenteis vasis sibi ministrari faceret, quod "clientum turba," nitore vestium superbiens, illius latus obambularet.' He had just before intimated that some jealousy of this sort had existed earlier, and had been allayed by Etheldred, 'sanitate consilii.' See Stubbs, Const. Hist. i. 176.

it involved the abatement of Wilfrid's ecclesiastical great-ness [1]: but Theodore's misfortune and fault consisted not simply in aiming at this as a step necessary for the general good of the Church, but in associating himself with the animosities of a court as instrumental towards his object, and in neglecting such considerations of order and justice as would have checked the march of his own high-handed [2] absolutism. We are in some difficulty as to the facts, between the open partisanship of the biographer and the disappointing reticence of the historian : Bede had evidently a strong reluctance to go into the subject [3], and it is one of the very few cases in which he has laid himself open to the charge of keeping back what he must have known. He says so little in the way of explanation, that he does not help us to know whether or when Eddi says too much,—although we may be sure that he does say too much when he imputes to Theodore the coarse guilt of taking a bribe from Egfrid [4]. However, as far as we can make out anything, it seems that in 678 Egfrid invited Theodore to revisit Northumbria ; that they discussed the division of the Northumbrian diocese, and Theodore allowed himself to be persuaded that Wilfrid's cooperation or assent was not to be hoped for, and must be dispensed with ; and that, acting on this assumption, he

Theodore in Northumbria.

[1] Lappenberg suggests that he may have feared that Wilfrid was laying the foundations of an independent archbishopric (such as St. Gregory had contemplated); i. 182. Malmesbury says, the queen prejudiced him.

[2] 'He carried it with a high hand towards the bishops;' Johnson, Engl. Can. i. 87. See Ornsby, Dioc. Hist. of York, p. 62.

[3] See Raine, Fast. Ebor. i. 81. In his last work, Bede lets fall words which might suggest that he supposed selfish motives to have prompted Wilfrid. 'Cum antistes, dictante amore pecuniæ, majorem populi partem . . . in nomen sui præsulatus assumpserit;' Ep. to Egb. 4. He had also strong personal ties to one of the bishops who were more or less opposed to Wilfrid, 'St. John of Beverley;' a fervent admiration for others, as Bosa, Eata, and St. Cuthbert; and a high esteem for the scholarly king Aldfrid. That he knew Wilfrid personally appears from iv. 19. In Ep. 3 he shows respect for him.

[4] Eddi refers to Balak and Balaam, 24. Malmesbury, G. Pontif. p. 220, follows him in this imputation, 'xeniorum obtentu;' which naturally excites Elmham's wrath, Mon. S. Aug. p. 276. Malmesbury, however, elsewhere ranks Theodore and Wilfrid together as 'those two eyes of Britain;' G. Pontif. i. 1. Fridegod says that the king and queen deceived Theodore, 'veri doctorem, justi quoque pæne sequacem;' 614.

summoned more than one bishop [1] to support him in the proceedings which he meditated, but did *not* communicate with
the bishop most directly concerned. An assembly, partly
secular and partly ecclesiastical, was convened; and in Wilfrid's absence it was resolved to form, out of his over-large
diocese, two other bishoprics for Bernicia and Deira, and
another for the district of Lindsey, lately recovered from
Mercia. But this plan would have left Wilfrid in possession
of the see of York, and the charge of part, probably the larger
part, of Deira [2]. According to the combined statements of
Wilfrid and Eddi, the suffragan bishops did not concur in the
consecration [3], and Theodore, without their assistance, consecrated Bosa, a monk of Whitby, a man, says Bede, 'of great
holiness and humility [4],' Eata, the devout and gentle-hearted
abbot of Lindisfarne; and Eadhed, who had accompanied Chad
on his journey to the south for consecration [5]. The elevation
of these three to the episcopate took place in Wilfrid's own
cathedral at York [6]: he could not but receive tidings of such
an event, and could not but repair to the court [7], and ask why
his diocese was to be thus cut up against his will. The
answer of the king and the archbishop was, ' We find no fault
in you, but we have thought good to do this, and we shall
abide by it [8].' Theodore, not to say Egfrid, had committed
himself by thus acting without Wilfrid's knowledge. It

[1] Wilfrid says, 'in conventu Theodori . . . aliorumque tunc temporis cum
eo convenientium antistitum;' in Eddi, 30. Who these prelates were we
know not.

[2] So Malmesbury says that Theodore maintained 'sufficere tantos sumptus
tantæque diœcesis circuitum *quattuor* episcopis;' G. P. p. 220.

[3] Wilfrid says, 'absque consensu cujuslibet episcopi . . . ordinaret;' in Eddi,
30: and Eddi, 'inordinate solus ordinavit;' 24. Can it be that the suffragans,
whoever they were, declined, when it came to the point, to follow Theodore?
Or did they merely abstain from taking part in the new consecrations?

[4] Bede, v. 3; iv. 23.

[5] He had been Oswy's chaplain; Bede, iv. 28. Eddi permits himself to
describe these three Northumbrian ecclesiastics as 'non de subjectis illius
parochiæ;' 24.

[6] Bede, iv. 21, 'Eboraci.' Wilfrid was absent; Eddi, 24.

[7] Eddi, 24: 'Regem et archiepiscopum . . . cum omni populo.' Eadmer
says he came to the palace 'hilari corde, alacri vultu;' 27. Fridegod makes
him ask, ' Cur lædor, pater?'

[8] Malmesbury quotes Juvenal's 'Sic volo, sic jubeo,' &c.

could not be said that the division of the diocese had been proposed to Wilfrid, and he had deliberately set himself against it. Theodore had taken for granted that he would do so ; and by this premature judgment had damaged his own case, and exhibited that fatal indifference to equity which so often besets a rigid disciplinarian invested with hierarchical supremacy, and resolute to ignore the rights of subordinates, and even the requirements of fair dealing, for the sake of a policy beneficial to the Church [1].

Thus hardly used,—we must needs say, thus unjustly treated,—Wilfrid took a step which, in Britain, was new, and which also was such as Chad would never have taken. He had too high a spirit to succumb, and had no hope of obtaining better terms, or a reconsideration of the case, by appealing to a provincial synod under the presidency of Theodore [2]. He looked, as if by instinct, to that great Church for which from early years he had entertained so profound a reverence : he recalled his own visit to Rome, which had been crowned by the special blessing of the then Pope ; it occurred to him that wrongs done at home could be set right by means of an appeal to that 'Apostolic See,' from which Theodore himself had derived his mission : and 'after taking counsel,' says Eddi, 'with his fellow-bishops,' he declared in their presence that he did thus make appeal [3]. The announcement which he

[1] The partition, says Martineau, though ' desirable, could only be lawfully and canonically effected with the consent of Wilfrid ; and it is a serious charge against Theodore . . . that, under the pretence of effecting what was unquestionably a good thing for the Church, he stooped to gratify the enmity of Egfrid and Ermenburga against Wilfrid by assisting in the persecution of that prelate;' Ch. Hist. Engl. p. 93. So Malmesbury says, ' Et hæc quidem recte dicta possent videri, si eum . . . vel non omnino spoliatum dejiceret, vel saltem cum consensu ejus ageret ; ' G. P. iii. 100, p. 220.

[2] Raine, i. 78 : 'I cannot blame him,' &c. Cp. Dict. Chr. Biog. iv. 1181. Hook's judgment is biassed and inequitable.

[3] Eddi, 24 : 'Cum consilio coepiscoporum suorum.' Wilfrid, in Eddi, 30 : ' Consacerdotes meos . . . episcopos tantummodo protestatus.' According to Eddi,—who compares the appeal to St. Paul's appeal from the Jews to Cæsar (!) —it was then that Wilfrid, 'turning away from the royal tribunal, said to the flatterers who were laughing merrily, "On the anniversary of this day on which you are now spitefully laughing at my condemnation, you will be weeping bitterly amid your own confusion,"' which was fulfilled at the burial of prince Alfwin in 679. It is probable that Eddi, an enthusiastic partisan, wrongly inferred, from the fact of the protestation in presence of the suffragan bishops,

CHAP. X.

His entire exclusion from Northumbria.

had made required his instant departure for Italy, and seems to have been treated, at once, as involving the forfeiture of all his rights in the see of York. The design of setting up three prelates to work in Northumbria along with him, and of reserving to him the first place and the church of the royal city, was now altered into a plan for superseding him altogether. Thus Bosa was appointed to preside over the whole of Deira, as bishop of York: Eata was to superintend all Bernicia from his own church of Lindisfarne, or from Wilfrid's minster of Hexham: while Eadhed[1] became the first bishop of Lindsey as such, then once more attached to Northumbria[2]. It was at this time that Theodore hallowed Finan's church at Lindisfarne in honour of St. Peter[3], with a view, no doubt, to the exhibition of his metropolitical authority within the former stronghold of 'schismatic' Celticism, as well as to the due performance of such dedication-ceremonies as would probably have been omitted by a Celtic bishop[4].

Aspects of his appeal.

Such were the circumstances under which took place the first appeal to Rome against the action of English Church authority. What are we to say of this appeal? No doubt, it contrasts very pointedly with the action taken by the African hierarchy in the latter years of the great Augustine's life, when, ignoring the 'Sardican Council's' resolutions[5] which

that they had encouraged Wilfrid to appeal. If they did encourage it, they seem to have repented of having done so; for we do not find that any bishop supported Wilfrid's cause between his expulsion and his restoration.

[1] Bede, iv. 12: 'Et hunc primum eadem provincia proprium accepit præsulem.' Chad had held it with Mercia.

[2] Lindsey was Northumbrian under Edwin and Oswald, was conquered by Penda (p. 156), regained by Oswy, re-conquered by Wulfhere, again recovered by Egfrid before 675, and again conquered by Ethelred in 679. Thus Lincolnshire was finally separated from Northumbria; but even in 1092 the archbishop of York claimed Lincoln as belonging to his own 'parochia' or diocese: Florence, Chron. vol. ii. p. 30. He was obliged to give up the claim for a supposed equivalent; see Raine, Fast. Ebor. i. 151.

[3] Bede, iii. 25: see Lingard, A.-S. Ch. ii. 385.

[4] Walafrid Strabo, in his Life of St. Gall, speaks of Columban as dedicating a church, with holy water and chrism and processional psalmody; Act. SS. Bened. ii. 233. The older 'Life' omits the chrism. See above, p. 83.

[5] Sardic. can. 3–5; Mansi, iii. 7. The bishop of Rome was to order a fresh hearing before (1) the bishops of the next province to that in which the case had arisen, and then, if the complainant should be still dissatisfied, (2) before those bishops with presbyters delegated from Rome. These provisions were

empowered the Roman bishop in certain cases to appoint a new trial, and relying on the genuine Nicene canon [1] which ordered ecclesiastical causes to be terminated in the respective provincial synods, they declined to acknowledge a 'transmarine' sentence pronounced by Rome, in regard to cases which had arisen in Africa [2]. At the same time, it must be remembered, first, that the principle of appeal from a provincial episcopate to a patriarch or quasi-patriarch had been admitted, as to the East, by the Œcumenical Council of Chalcedon [3]: and next, that the relations in which the African Church stood towards Rome in 426 were not those in which the English Church stood towards Rome in 678. During that interval, the first see in Christendom, the one 'Apostolic see' in the West, had grown mightily in all the elements of command: and even if Wilfrid had admitted the principle of the African Council, he would have pleaded that a Church so recently founded as the English, and so recently consolidated by a metropolitan sent from Rome direct, the successor of that first English archbishop whom Rome, in the person of the sainted Gregory, had sent to plant the faith among English heathens, might naturally and rightly look to Rome for guidance, and that guidance implied supervision, to be exercised on appeal; and further, that whereas causes were decided in Africa with all due ecclesiastical forms, the very rudiments of ecclesiastical justice were ignored by the recent partition of a diocese in the bishop's absence, and without his consent [4], and his actual

quoted by the agents of Rome as Nicene. The African bishops ascertained that they were not in the genuine text of the Nicene canons; and the 'Council of Sardica,' as such, they did not recognise, confounding it with its Arian rival at Philippopolis; Fleury, b. 24. c. 6. It must be admitted that the whole affair throws grave doubt on the genuineness of these canons, even *as Sardican.*

[1] Nic. can. 5.

[2] See their final letter, Mansi, iv. 515; Fleury, b. 24. c. 35; Robertson, Hist. Ch. ii. 237, and Growth of Papal Power, p. 90; Hussey on Rise of Papal Power, p. 47. I may refer to my 'History of the Church,' &c., p. 301.

[3] Chalc. can. 9, directing a bishop or cleric who had a complaint against his metropolitan to appeal to the exarch of the 'diocese' (aggregate of provinces), or to the see of Constantinople.

[4] Theodore might have remembered Cod. Afric. c. 56, 98, which expressly forbade this. Mansi, iii. 747, 803.

deprivation after he had spoken of applying to Rome for remedy. But Wilfrid would *not* have admitted the African principle. He stood at a marked distance from the old Patristic position, strictly so called, in regard to the 'See of Peter.' Whatever respect he may have felt for the great names of the Gallican Church, he would have disapproved of the conduct of Hilary of Arles in reference to the appeal of Celidonius from a Gallic Council[1], and would have regarded the conduct of Leo the Great as simply a just assertion of authority; and the law obtained by Leo from Valentinian III., commanding all Western Churches to obey the 'Pope of the eternal city[2],' would to his mind express the legitimate subjection of the hierarchy to its divinely appointed chief.

But not so thought the great body of English clergy and laity at this time. They stood, indeed, in different degrees of obligation to the Roman Church. She was directly a mother-Church to Kent, and also to Wessex[3], and indirectly to East-Anglia[4]; in a limited sense, considering the retreat of Paulinus, to Northumbria; in a technical but ineffective sense, considering the failure of Mellitus, to Essex, including London; not at all, Lindsey excepted, to Mercia. In so far as the several dioceses had been welded together in subordination to Canterbury, they were debtors through Canterbury to its spiritual parent; and they had all concurred in accepting Theodore as a special gift from the hands of Rome. They all, though probably not all with equal definiteness of conception, acknowledged in Rome a peculiar pre-eminence, a special heritage of apostolic grace; to all of them 'the See of Peter' was a title of august and sacred import, and they were too simple to analyse its significance, or to test its grounds. But, with all this, they had not, as a body, in 678, any clear notion that gratitude or reverence could bind them to recognise a systematic interference on Rome's part in their domestic Church matters[5], by virtue of

---

[1] See Robertson, ii. 239.

[2] Hussey, p. 63; Robertson, ii. 241.

[3] Above, p. 152.

[4] Above, p. 130.

[5] See Freeman, i. 32: 'The English Church, reverencing Rome, but not slavishly bowing down to her,' &c. Comp. Stubbs, Const. Hist. i. 246, 280.

which any national Church decision might at any time be nullified by a court of appeal sitting far beyond the Alps. The aversion to 'outlandish' authority, keen and strong in the insular mind even through the later Middle Ages, was now, in Northumbria, even scornfully incredulous as to any practical exercise of such authority; and, as far as we know, Benedict Biscop, with all that enthusiasm for Roman sanctities which repeated visits to Rome had fostered, never thought, on his return from the fifth of those visits, or afterwards, of taking Wilfrid's part in this quarrel. As for Theodore himself, he was duly conscious of the value of his Papal appointment, but he was not minded to be a mere Roman legate, nor willing to let his administration be overruled by Papal intervention on appeal. The increased stringency of his acts after that appeal is one of the most significant facts in this portion of the story[1].

And now let us follow the dauntless and indefatigable Ebroin. appellant. His biographer assures us[2] that his foes, in their eagerness to arrest his course, had requested Ebroin, as mayor of the palace for the Frankish king of Neustria and Burgundy,— the feeble Theodoric III.,— to seize on Wilfrid if he passed through that kingdom, and either send him into exile, or kill his attendants and strip him of his property. It is curious that the same formidable minister should have checked Theodore's journey through Gaul, and set men in wait to fall upon Wilfrid. But, in fact, Ebroin had his own reasons, quite independent of English disputes, for hostility towards the man who, in the days of his splendour and wealth at York, had materially contributed to the elevation of the young king of Austrasia, Dagobert II., lately at war with Theodoric about frontiers. And Ebroin's hatred was deadly: it was in the October of this very year 678 that he put to death his old rival Leodegar, or 'St. Leger,' bishop of Autun[3]. But on this occasion he missed his blow:

---

[1] Nor did he, as we shall see, take any steps towards conforming to the Papal judgment in favour of Wilfrid until six years after it was made known to him.

[2] Eddi, 25 : 'Præmiserunt nuntios . . . ad Eadefyrwine impium ducem.'

[3] See Alb. Butler, Oct. 2 ; Fredegar. Contin. 96 ; Kitchin, Hist. Fr. i. 94.

his emissaries did catch and despoil an English bishop,
whose name was identical with Wilfrid's except in a single
letter,—Winfrid, the deposed prelate of Lichfield, then
travelling, for his misfortune, in Neustria. He was cruelly
maltreated, and some of his attendants were actually slain [1].

Wilfrid had not landed in Gaul: he had proceeded to
Friesland, the land beyond the Zuyder Zee, the inhabitants
of which dwelt nearer to Britain than Saxons or Angles
or Jutes had dwelt while still on the mainland, and are
named by Bede as first among six nations akin to the English,
and 'corruptly called Garmans' by the Britons [2]. Adalgis,
the Frisian king, received the English prelate with all
honour [3], and was rewarded by hearing the Gospel from
his lips. And here, more brightly than at any earlier
period of his life, shone out the true Christian greatness of
'St. Wilfrid.' He was far too earnest in the cause of religion
not to make every other purpose give way to a good opportunity of missionary work, such as he found among the
Frisians. He preached, with the king's license, every day [4],
expounding the main doctrines of Christianity,—the Holy
Trinity, 'the one baptism for remission of sins, and eternal
life, after death, in resurrection [5].' As the year's fishing was
unusually successful, and the autumn brought an abundant
harvest, the simple-hearted people ascribed these blessings to
the God whom Wilfrid served; and before winter set in he
had, after due instruction, baptized many of the commonalty,
and most of their chiefs. Then a striking scene followed.

---

[1] Cp. Eddi, 25 on his misfortune: 'Omni pecunia spoliatus, multisque ex
sociis suis occisis, misere ad extremum sanctum episcopum nudum reliquerunt ...
errore *bono* unius syllabæ seducti.' So Malmesbury: 'Luit ergo ille ambi-
guitatem vocabuli;' G. P. p. 221. Fridegod, 'tantum monogrammate lusus.'

[2] Bede, v. 9. See Freeman, i. 22. 'In mythical genealogies, Saxo and
Friso are brothers;' Pearson, Hist. Engl. i. 105. We read of a young Northumbrian being sold as a slave to a Frisian in London, Bede, iv. 22.

[3] Malmesb. l. c.: 'Ejectus a patria, dilectus in Frisia.'

[4] Eddi, 26. On the great historical importance, to a large portion of the
Continent, of this sojourn of Wilfrid in Friesland, see Lappenberg, i. 181.

[5] Eddi, l. c. A definite instruction in Christian doctrine, a systematic 'de-
livery of the Creed,' was in ancient times held essential to all Christian pro-
selytism. Compare St. Augustine, de Catechizandis Rudibus, s. 52; and
Alcuin, Ep. 28 (A.D. 796), on such orderly teaching before baptism. See
Neale's Essays on Liturgiology, p. 146. See above, p. 125.

Ebroin sent to Adalgis, promising with an oath, in written CHAP. X. words, to give him 'a bushel full of golden *solidi*' for Wilfrid's person or for Wilfrid's head[1]. The letter was read to the king at a feast, probably the great midwinter feast, in the presence of Wilfrid and his companions. He heard it read through, took the scroll into his hands, tore it deliberately to pieces, and flung them into the fire burning before him. Then, turning to the startled messengers of the powerful Frank, he spoke out his indignation[2]. 'Tell your lord what I now say: So may the Maker of all things tear in pieces and utterly consume the life and kingdom of one who is forsworn to his God, and keeps not the covenant into which he has entered!' 'It was thus decreed' to Wilfrid to be the first of the long line of English missionaries[3]. He 'spent the winter happily,' as Bede expresses it, 'with the new people of God[4];' but the impression then made on the Frisian mind must have been to a great extent superficial, for about ten years later we find that a devoted missionary 'preached for two years to the same nation without seeing any fruit of all his toil among his barbarian hearers[5];' when, shortly afterwards, Willibrord and Wulframn began to work among them, they found a great ignorance of the first principles of Christianity; and to the close of the century, Pagan reaction was periodical in Frisia[6]. As was often the case in

---

[1] Eddi, 27. A golden 'solidus' was then = forty silver denarii; in the next century it was lowered to the value of twelve. See Ducange.

[2] See the words in Eddi, 27: 'Sic rerum Creator regnum et vitam in Deo suo perjurantis, pactumque initum non custodientis, scindens destruat, et consumens in favillam divellat.'

[3] Lappenberg, i. 181. Among the English missionaries of the succeeding period were Willibrord, the Hewalds, Boniface, Lull, Albert, Lebwin, Marchelm, Willehad.

[4] Bede, v. 19: 'Cum nova Dei plebe feliciter exigens.' Comp. Eddi, 26: 'Populum multum Domino lucratus.' So Fridegod, 665.

[5] See the touching account of Wictbert in Bede, v. 9.

[6] Alcuin, Vit. S. Willibr. i. 6; Vit. S. Wulfr. 3; Vit. S. Liudgeri, i. 3: 'In diebus Radbodi ... gens illa ... in errore infidelitatis erat excæcata.' Alb. Butler says (Nov. 7) that 'the seeds sown by Wilfrid must have been almost rooted out before St. Willibrord's arrival in 690 or 691.' St. Boniface worked under him for three years, and long afterwards met his death in 'the still Pagan portion of Friesland' (Maclear), where he had to 'drive away Pagan rites,' and baptized 'multa millia hominum' before he was martyred; Willibald, Vit. S. Bonif. c. 11. Comp. Bonif. Ep. 90. Yet

CHAP. X. these wholesale conversions, the seed had at first sprung up rapidly, '*because* it had no depth of earth.'

In the spring of 679 Wilfrid resumed his journey, and was warmly welcomed in Austrasia by his former client Dagobert, who in gratitude urged him to accept the see of Strasburg [1], and, failing in this, did his best for his benefactor by loading him with presents, and sending him on southwards under the guidance of a Frankish bishop named

Wilfrid in Lombardy, Deodatus. Crossing the Alps, he descended into Lombardy, and was kindly received at Pavia by King Pertharit [2], a prince who, like his father, professed the Catholic faith, and was altogether a very different personage from the Lombards who had kept St. Gregory in such alarm. He had had many troublous experiences, extending from his exile in 662 to his restoration in 671. He told Wilfrid that he had received overtures from Britain to the effect that if he would detain 'the runaway bishop' on his journey, he should receive 'very great gifts;' and had answered by referring to those early days when he, too, was a fugitive from the usurper Grimoald, and found shelter in Pannonia with the Khan of the Avars. 'He, a Pagan, swore by his idol to befriend me, and answered Grimoald's offers of a bushel of golden solidi by saying, "May the gods cut my life asunder, if I thus forswear myself to them." How much more am I, who know the true God, bound not to ruin my soul, were it to gain

and at Rome. the whole world [3]!' The good king sent Wilfrid on, with honour and due guidance, to Rome, where he arrived about

later, in 772, Willehad the Northumbrian (Vit. Will. c. 1) heard that the Frisians, 'hactenus pagani,' began to desire baptism; and on arriving in Frisia, was well received by St. Boniface's converts, but narrowly escaped with life from their Pagan countrymen. Again, Liudger had to destroy 'various idolatries' in Frisia; Vit. Liudg. i. 14: but his work had to stand the test of two Pagan persecutions.

[1] 'The greatest see in his realm,' at 'Streithbyrg;' Eddi, 28.

[2] Or Bertarid. Eddi calls him 'Berhther king of Campania,' by a mistake. When he died in 686, he 'carried with him the regrets of his subjects, whose hearts he had won by his gentle and wise rule.' See l'Art de vérifier, &c., iv. 385. 'Justitiæ tenax, mitis per omnia et suavis;' Paul. Diac. Gest. Lang. v. 33, 37. In 673, he built a monastery on the scene of a former escape. Fridegod, 719, makes him talk to Wilfrid 'post epulas, et post grati carchesia Bacchi!'

[3] Eddi, 28. He had been once on the point of taking shelter in Britain. The wife of his son Cunibert was an Englishwoman.

the middle of 679. Twenty-five years had passed since he
visited the 'Eternal City' in the buoyancy of his enthusiastic
youth, studied its ecclesiastical rules under Boniface, prayed
habitually in its sanctuaries, and bowed his head for the
benediction of Eugenius I. The present Pope was Agatho,
who had come to the see in the summer of 678: a prelate
much loved for his kind-heartedness and geniality[1]. To him
Theodore had sent a monk named Kenwald, with documents
stating his view of Wilfrid's case: so that 'the dissension,'
as Eddi says, 'was not unknown to Agatho.' Wilfrid had Council
an audience of the Pope, and placed a written statement of of fifty
the case in his hands: and some time afterwards, a Council bishops.
of fifty bishops, with presbyters in attendance, was held by
Agatho for the formal consideration of the matter[2]. The
scene was that illustrious 'basilica of Our Saviour in the
Lateran,' the true cathedral church of Rome, the 'mother
and head,' in its own proud though inaccurate estimation, 'of all churches,' the prototype of the metropolitan
church of Canterbury. It was distinguished among Roman
churches by the name of 'the Constantinian,' and had been
originally erected by the great imperial convert in the
latter years of his reign[3]. Like his other and grander
basilica of St. Peter, it had five aisles: but the baptistery
of St. John, from which it gradually acquired the name
that has popularly superseded its august dedication, was

[1] Anastas. Vit. Pontif. i. 135; Mansi, xi. 165. He was a Sicilian. He
died Jan. 10, 682. By one account, he came to the see, not in 678, but in 679.
Capgrave says of him, 'He kissed a misel' (leper) 'and mad him hool;'
Chronicle, p. 97.

[2] In Mansi, xi. 179, is an account of a Roman Council of sixteen bishops,
held in October, 679, on episcopal dissensions in Britain, but without express
reference to Wilfrid,—on the number of the bishoprics, which were to be twelve
with the archbishopric,—on the conduct of the clergy,—and for a Council of
bishops, kings, princes, &c. in 'all Saxony,' to be held by Theodore. But
'Eddius, Bede, and William of Malmesbury, all know nothing of this Council'
(Haddan and Stubbs, iii. 135), which professes to have sent John the Precentor
to Britain, with the canons of the Council of 649. It rests on one MS. of
Spelman's; it suits neither the time before nor after Wilfrid's arrival; and it
reads as if concocted in the interest of Canterbury.

[3] Fergusson, Hist. Archit. i. 369; cp. 362. Martin I. describes the Constantinian church as 'juxta episcopium,' Ep. 15, Mansi, x. 851. See Alb.
Butler, Nov. 9, 'Dedication of the Church of Our Saviour.'

a work of the fifth century[1]. The church, for all its unique
dignity, had associations which to a thoughtful prelate
would speak as forcibly of ecclesiastical troubles as of ecclesiastical majesty and strength. For the chapel of St.
John the Evangelist was a memorial of Pope Hilary's
narrow escape from the 'Robbers' Council' at Ephesus[2]:
and only twenty-six years had elapsed since Pope Martin had
been dragged from the basilica by the imperial 'exarch,' and
carried away from Rome for maintaining, at a Council held
on that same spot, the doctrine which the Byzantine court
had proscribed[3]. The present Council, like the former, met
in the 'secretarium' of the church, the chamber which served
as the place for meetings of the bishop and clergy, and the
transaction of ecclesiastical business[4]. Wilfrid, at first, was
kept waiting outside the doors, as was usual in regard to
petitioners or appellants. Agatho began by stating the
business: they were met to consider a dissension which had
arisen in the Churches of Britain. The bishops of Ostia
and of Portus Romanus then said[5] that they had read the
memorials presented on both sides,—those which had come

[1] Hemans, Hist. and Monum. Rome, p. 658.

[2] Hemans, l. c.

[3] Mansi, x. 849; Hefele, Hist. Councils, b. 16. c. 1. s. 309; Milman,
ii. 325; Dict. Chr. Biogr. iii. 854.

[4] 'Secretarium' was a Roman law-term for the justice-room of a magistrate
(compare the 'secretum' which Paul of Samosata made for himself, Euseb. vii.
30), as in Act. Scill. Mart., 'in secretario Carthaginis;' comp. Act. Procons.
S. Cypr., 'Carthagine in secretario.' Ecclesiastically, the word has two senses:
(1) a room where bishops received the greetings of their people ('salutatorium,'
Greg. Ep. v. 56), transacted business, held meetings of clergy, or sat in synod:
the second Council of Arles forbade deacons to *sit* in the secretarium with the
priests. So the Council of Hippo in 393 met 'in secretario basilicæ Pacis,'
Mansi, iii. 732; other Councils, at Carthage, in the secretarium of the basilica
Restituta, ib.; or of that of Faustus, ib. 699; the second of Seville, in that of the
Holy Jerusalem Church, ib. x. 557: compare the Council of Constantinople,
A.D. 448, ib. vi. 651. Hence, the sittings of the first Lateran Council are called
'secretarii;' and see Pope Zacharias, 'præterito secretario,' Migne, Patr. Lat.
lxxxix. 833. Compare Greg. Ep. i. 19, and Benedict. note there, and Ep. iii.
56. The 'lesser secretarium' was (2) a vestry or sacristy, 'which the Greeks
call Diaconicon;' Council of Agde, c. 66, Mansi, viii. 336: so in Bede, ii. 1.
Gregory is buried 'ante secretarium;' and iii. 14, 26 on the 'secretaria'
of Rochester and Lindisfarne. Above, p. 164.

[5] Malmesbury, G. P. p. 226, abbreviates their speech, as given by
Eddi, 29. It begins with an assertion of Papal supremacy.

from Theodore and others[1] 'against a certain bishop who,
as they assert, has fled privily away, and, as they suppose, has
come hither,' and the counter-memorial embodying the appeal
of the 'bishop of the holy church of York:' and that they
found Wilfrid to have committed no offence which would
canonically require his degradation, and to have 'observed
moderation by not mixing himself up in any factious strife[2].'
Agatho then ordered that Wilfrid should be admitted into
the 'secretarium,' with the petition which he was said to have
brought. He entered accordingly, and desired that his
petition should be read. 'John, the Notary, read it to the
Council.' Its purport was as follows. Wilfrid, a humble
and unworthy bishop of Saxony[3], had by Divine guidance
come to this 'apostolical summit,' as to a fortified place and
tower of strength, from whence the rule of the canons was
communicated to all the Churches. The Pope would know,
from his private interview with Wilfrid, and from the
memorial already presented[4], that 'certain invaders of his
bishopric, not one only, but three,' had, 'at a meeting of
Archbishop Theodore and other prelates,' presumed to take
away the see which he had held for more than ten years,
and uncanonically to promote themselves to be bishops 'in
his own church' during his lifetime; and that Theodore had
consecrated them without his assent, and even 'without the
assent of any bishop.' It was not for him to ask why this
was done: he would refrain from accusing one who had been
sent[5] from that apostolical see. It would appear that he
had been expelled without having been convicted of any

---

[1] Including, apparently, Hilda; Eddi, 54. Malmesbury reckons her among
the bitter enemies of Wilfrid; G. Pontif. iii. 107.

[2] 'Neque secundum sanctorum canonum subtilitatem convictum cum de
aliquibus facinoribus, et ideo non canonice dejectum, reperimus . . . potius
autem et modestiam hunc tenuisse perpendimus,' &c., Eddi, 29.

[3] 'Saxonia' was sometimes used for what we should call England. So
Adamnan, Vit. Col. i. 1, 9, ii. 46: cp. Reeves's Adamnan, p. xlv, and 'Four
Masters,' a. 684. So Huætbert of Wearmouth, writing to Gregory II.; Bede's
Hist. Abb. 14. Boniface speaks of 'Saxony-beyond-Sea;' Ep. 49: cp. S. Greg.
Ep. xi. 64. Kenulf of Mercia says that Augustine 'ecclesiis præfuit Saxoniæ;'
Haddan and Stubbs, iii. 522.

[4] 'Quæ viva voce præsentialiter intimavi, et per satisfactionem petitionis
scriptis narrantibus obtuli,' Eddi, 30.

[5] 'Directus.' So in Andrew's speech. See above, p. 234.

CHAP. X.   canonical fault: yet, after such treatment, he had raised no
seditious contention, but had invoked the assistance of Rome,
and 'simply called the comprovincial bishops to bear witness'
to the proceeding.   He would accept any decision from the
Council.   If he were placed in his old see, let the invaders be synodically ejected[1].   If, again, it was resolved
to have more bishops in Northumbria, let them at least
be chosen from the clergy of his church by a provincial
synod[2], so that he, Wilfrid, might 'serve God with them
in peaceful unity.'   We must pause a moment to observe
that this statement suppresses what, no doubt, was prominent in Theodore's,—the fact that the subject of a
division of dioceses had been mooted years before at the
synod of Hertford, and had been acted upon in East-
Anglia.   It might also be inferred from Wilfrid's paper that
Theodore's first notion had been to take from him even York
itself; and, certainly, that Bosa, Eata, and Eadhed were
strangers to the Northumbrian diocese,—which was the reverse of the fact.   After a few eulogistic words from Agatho
on the moderation of the appellant's conduct, the Council
pronounced its decision.   Let us carefully observe what
this came to.   Wilfrid was to be reinstated in his original
diocese, that is, the diocese as it stood before the division[3].
The bishops who had been irregularly promoted were, 'as
a matter of course,' to be expelled.   But, *when* this was done,
he was, with consent of a council to be assembled at York,
'to choose bishops as assistants[4], with whom he could live
peaceably,' and who were to be consecrated by Theodore.
The advantages of diocesan subdivision were thus to be
secured, but without the sacrifice of due order: Theodore's
work was to be undone, that it might be done over again in

*Decision
in favour
of Wilfrid.*

---

[1] 'De pristinis parochiis ecclesiæ.'   Here 'parochiæ' is used somewhat
laxly, as if to mean, 'from those newly-erected bishoprics which originally and
properly formed parts of the diocese of York.'

[2] 'Et si rursus in eadem parochia, cui præfui, præsules adhibere providerit,
saltem tales jubeat prævidere promovendos . . . .'   Again, 'Si ita placuerit
archiepiscopo et coepiscopis meis ut augeatur numerus episcoporum,' &c.

[3] 'Decernimus ut episcopatum, quem nuper habuerat, recipiat,' Eddi, 32.

[4] 'Adjutores.'   This is not to be understood of mere coadjutors or assistant
bishops in an *un*divided diocese.   Compare Bede, Ep. to Egb. 5.

a better way. The usual penalties were then denounced CHAP. X. against all who should 'attempt to resist this sentence, or not receive it obediently, or, after a time, attempt to infringe it in whole or part.' Such a person, if bishop, priest, or deacon, was to be deprived and put under anathema: if clerk (i. e. in any order below the diaconate) or monk, or layman of any rank, *or king*, he was to be excluded from the Holy Communion. On the other hand, whosoever should sincerely accept and help to carry out the decision, might well hope to 'be Divinely rewarded for that obedience which God prefers to all sacrifices.'

Such was the issue of the Roman Council. Wilfrid indulged himself by staying in Rome until the spring of 680. To him it was doubtless a time of intense refreshment; and on the following Easter Tuesday, March 27, 680, the Pope gave him a token of support which must have yet further inspirited so devoted a client of Rome. A large Council of Council a hundred and twenty-five prelates met on that day to pro- of 125 bishops. vide materials for the expected Council at Constantinople on the question of Monothelitism[1]. Wilfrid 'having been acquitted,' as the Council-record says, 'on matters certain and uncertain,' i. e. on charges definite and indefinite, sat in this assembly as bishop of York, and professed the orthodox doctrine of the 'two wills and activities' of the one Christ in behalf of 'all the northern part of Britain and Ireland, and the islands, which were inhabited by the nations of the Angles and Britons, and also of the Scots and Picts[2]:' and was even described in the catalogue as representative of the 'synod' or episcopal college of Britain[3]: the secretary of the Council having mistakenly imagined that his testimony to the orthodoxy of the insular Churches was given in the character of their accredited 'delegate.' He signed the synodal letter addressed to the Emperor Constantine IV. and

---

[1] Mansi, xi. 185; Hefele, b. 16. s. 313. Compare the Council of Milan held in 679 against Monothelitism; Mansi, xi. 173. See above, p. 229.

[2] Eddi, 53; Bede, v. 19; as Haddan and Stubbs read (iii. 140), omitting the comma placed after 'parte' by Smith and Hussey, and inserting 'que' after 'insulis.'

[3] Mansi, xi. 306. What Wilfrid really meant to say was, 'I can assure you that in those countries there is no heresy on this point.'

his two brothers[1], and containing a long dogmatic statement: and he thus committed himself to the assertion, that the Council had 'expected that Theodore, archbishop of the great island of Britain, and philosopher, would attend, with others who still tarried in Britain[2].' But they came not.

At last Wilfrid tore himself away from the holy places of Rome. He had spent many days in farewell visits to churches, and had obtained many relics, with an exact register of the saints to whom they were ascribed,—together with many *Wilfrid in Gaul.* other things 'for the adornment of the house of God[3].' His passage through Italy was like a triumph: but on entering the Frankish territory he experienced a painful shock. Dagobert of Austrasia had been murdered at the preceding Christmas by a conspiracy of 'dukes,' and of some prelates whom Ebroin had intruded into sees, and whose position was menaced by the young king[4]. Eddi tells us that one of these bishops endeavoured to intercept Wilfrid, and represented the slain prince as having played the part of Rehoboam, by despising the bishops and laying burdens on his people. Wilfrid appears to have given a softer answer than the case merited[5], but one which had the effect of shaming the Frankish prelate by its very gentleness. 'Woe to me, a sinner!' he rejoined: 'thou art more righteous than I.'

Return to Northumbria. Wilfrid pursued his journey until he once more found himself at home. And then came the shock of a supreme disappointment. He had, in fact, been too much elated by his success at the Roman Council to estimate the situation as it would present itself in Northumbria. To begin with, it is

---

[1] Mansi, xi. 285. See Finlay, Hist. Gr. i. 381.

[2] Mansi, xi. 294 ; Hefele, s. 314. This expectation shows that Wilfrid was not formally regarded by the Council as delegate for his own Church ; Haddan and Stubbs, iii. 141. Did he wait at Rome to meet Theodore?

[3] 'More suo,' says Eddi, 33. Thomas of Ely says that he brought a privilegium for the monastery of Ely, according to Etheldred's request ; Vit. S. Eth. 19. He bought one for Ripon and Hexham ; Eddi, 51.

[4] Mabillon, Ann. SS. Bened. iv. præf. p. cxlv. This prince is identified with the 'St. Dagobert, king and martyr,' who was venerated at Stenay.

[5] It was for your good, not your harm, that I exalted him;' Eddi, 33. Fridegod and Eadmer amplify this, as if the chief of the regicides had drawn his sword against Wilfrid and menaced him with death.

not easy for brilliant and fervid natures to understand the CHAP. X.
resisting force inherent in those who are strangers to their
enthusiasm. Wilfrid fancied, it seems, that 'the Apostolic
See' would be practically as potent a name to his countrymen as it had been through long years to himself. Again,
he forgot, or did not sufficiently consider, that the settlement
against which he could now use that name with all distinct-
ness and authority was one in which many interests were now
bound up, to which the king of the Northumbrians and the
archbishop of 'all Britain' were alike committed, and which,
if now assailed, would call out national feeling, both civil
and ecclesiastical, in its defence. The Roman decree, duly
drawn up, with its leaden 'bullæ' and its 'apostolic' seal, was
in his eyes 'a banner of victory:' he never reflected that to
others it might be a provocation and an insult. The first
step which he took was to show himself to his monks who
had been wearying for his return, and, as Eddi expresses it,
'crying out to the Lord with tears;' the next was to visit
King Egfrid, offer him a greeting of peace, and exhibit his
treasured document, which he afterwards showed to the assembled Witan[1]. It is not difficult to imagine his amaze-
ment when the reading of the decree was interrupted by
angry dissent on the part of 'some persons present,' and
then by an anticipation of that bitter complaint which recurred so often in later days: 'The writings have been
bought,—the "doom" was corruptly obtained[2]!' The line
taken by Egfrid 'and his counsellors,' if we may believe Eddi,
—and we have no other informant,—was signally unworthy,
yet not impolitic as an expedient for the time. They did not
touch the broad question of Rome's right to receive the appeal: they assumed that Wilfrid had got a verdict by bribing
the tribunal, and dealt with him accordingly,—but never
took any measures for ascertaining at Rome what would be
its decision apart from such influence as he, by hypothesis,
had used. Eddi affirms that the prelates 'who held posses-

---

[1] Eddi, 34: 'Omnibus principibus . . . necnon servis Dei.'
[2] Eddi, 'Diffamaverunt . . . ut pretio redempta essent scripta;' Hook's
suppression of the reason given for non-compliance is strangely disingenuous;
Archbishops, i. 161.

sion of his bishopric' acquiesced in the resolution to 'imprison him for nine months without any token of respect[1].' Accordingly, everything was taken from him save the clothes which he wore. Ermenburga, firmly believing in the virtue of his reliquary[2], appropriated it to herself, hung it up beside her in her carriage when she drove out, and kept it in her bedroom like a talisman. Egfrid swore 'by his own salvation' that none of Wilfrid's friends should visit him in his captivity: they were allowed one parting interview, in which the undaunted bishop reminded them of Israel's thraldom in Egypt, of the trials of Moses and the prophets, of the sufferings of the Divine Chief Shepherd, of the great 'teacher's' exhortations in Heb. xii. 1, 5[3]. He then passed into the custody of Osfrid, the reeve[4] or governor of a place which Eddi calls Bromnis, and which may, perhaps, be identified with Broomridge in Northumberland[5]. There, at the setting in of the winter, the bishop was immured in a cell which was seldom lighted by sunshine, and never by a lamp. Darkness, however, had no terrors for Wilfrid: he sang his psalms as regularly as if he had been in one of his own minsters, and the guards are said to have been awestruck by an appearance of light within the dungeon[6]. The imprisonment was meant as a menace: Egfrid offered to give him back part of his old bishopric, and some other gifts, if he would submit to royal

---

[1] Eddi, 34.

[2] 'Chrismarium,' properly a vessel containing the hallowed chrism, had come to be used for a 'theca reliquiarum;' see Ducange. He cites Greg. Turon. de Mirac. S. Mart. iv. 32, where the name is applied to a small case or box containing dust from St. Martin's tomb. Gregory's parents carried relics about their persons; de Gl. Mart. i. 84. St. Gall carried with him a 'little case' of relics, and made his prayers before it; Vit. S. Gall. When a pagan attempted to behead St. Willehad, the blow swerved aside on the leather band of the case of relics which 'in collo suspensam habebat;' Vit. S. Will. 4. The fashion became very general. William the Conqueror wore a reliquary round his neck on the day of his great victory; Freeman, iii. 464.

[3] Eddi, 35. The speech begins, 'Be mindful, and tell my brethren, of the days of old, how we read,' &c.

[4] Above, p. 127. The burghreeve or burhgerefa 'was essentially a royal officer, charged with the maintenance and defence of a fortress.' (Kemble.)

[5] See Raine, Historians of Ch. of York, i. 51.

[6] Eddi, 36. 'Absentem diem lux agebat æmula,' Malmesb. G. P. iii. 101.

authority, and disclaim the genuineness of the document chap. x. brought from Rome. 'I would rather lose my head,' was the answer. But Osfrid, believing that his wife's recovery from a death-like stupor was due to some holy water dropped by Wilfrid into her mouth [1], entreated Egfrid, with adjurations, 'not to compel him any longer to afflict the holy and innocent bishop to his own perdition:' and the king transferred Wilfrid to Dunbar, where the reeve Tidlin was a man of 'sterner stuff [2].' But while the king and queen were visiting Coldingham, Ermenburga fell ill one night, and in the morning seemed to be dying of convulsions [3]. The abbess Ebba [4], remembering how Wilfrid had officiated in her church at Etheldred's profession, took advantage of her nephew's anxiety to reprove him for his injustice. If he wished his wife to recover, he must either restore Wilfrid to his bishopric,—which would be best,—or let him go whither he would. Egfrid yielded to his aunt's exhortations, released Wilfrid, gave him back his reliquary, allowed him to depart with his friends, when they had been re-assembled: 'and the queen was healed.'

This is the tale as told by Eddi. We know him well enough by this time to be mistrustful of his details, even when they do not assume a miraculous form. If he persuaded himself, also, that Egfrid repented of what he had done, the facts hardly bear out such a view. But his diffuseness is only the exaggeration of facts which Bede astonishes us by all but passing over; he ignores altogether this visit of Wilfrid to Northumbria, in his professed account of Wilfrid's life [5]; while

---

[1] Eddi, 37. Fridegod, 861: 'conjunx ... Præsidis infaustas, ha! ha! procurantis habenas.' (Fridegod's 'quantities' are erratic.)

[2] Eddi has another marvel to tell: Tidlin caused iron chains to be made; they were tried on Wilfrid's hands, but proved to be either too tight or too loose; 38.

[3] Eddi, 39: 'Contractis membris simul in unum stricte alligatam.' Malmesbury says, 'Cœpit aliena facere, insana dicere.'

[4] She is said to have died August 25, 683 (Alb. Butler). The Chronicle's date of 679 for the burning of Coldingham is too early; for it was burnt after her death (Bede, iv. 25), and this account of Eddi represents her as alive in 681,—let alone the received date of her death. Eadmer carelessly calls her the king's mother, c. 37, from a mistake as to 'mater' in Eddi.

[5] Bede, v. 19: 'Post hæc reversus Brittaniam, provinciam Australium

CHAP. X. in the course of his History he just says that 'on account of the king's enmity he could not be received in his country or diocese [1].' Nor does he say anything about the next event in Wilfrid's story,—his second sojourn in Mercia, which apparently began in the spring of 681. Berthwald, the nephew of King Ethelred, an ealdorman or sub-king, whom Eddi calls a prefect, asked Wilfrid to accept some of his own land for the building of a monastery. 'Abide with me, for the Lord's sake!' Wilfrid was only too glad to comply: a sojourn in Mercia was for him a renewal of pleasant memories, centering in the kindly beneficence of Wulfhere [2]: he 'thanked God, who had given him some solace of rest;' and set to work to build 'a little monastery, which monks of his still held' when Eddi wrote [3]. But again his troubles returned. There had been a fierce feud between Mercian and Northumbrian royalties. Egfrid had crossed the Mercian border, and been defeated by Ethelred, in 679, near the Trent; and Alfwin, Egfrid's brother, a youth of eighteen, apparently subking of Deira, and much loved in both kingdoms, had fallen [4]. It was exactly a year after Wilfrid's expulsion when the corpse of Alfwin was brought into York amid the wild wailings of the people, who 'wept bitterly, and tore their garments and their hair [5].' This victory of Ethelred had reunited Lindsey to

---

Saxonum . . . convertit.' 'There was but little sympathy between Wilfrid and the great scholar;' Raine, Historians of Ch. of York, p. xxxiv. See above, p. 291.

[1] Bede, iv. 13: 'in patria sive parochia.'

[2] Eddi, 14.

[3] Eddi, 40.

[4] Bede, iv. 21. Malmesbury says quaintly, that Ethelred attacked Egfrid in battle, 'and admonished him to return home;' G. Reg. i. 77. The scene of the battle is said to have been at Elford on the Trent, in Staffordshire; Coxe's Wendover, i. 170. Tighernach calls Alfwin 'Almuine.' See above, p. 293.

[5] Eddi, 24. He adds that Egfrid thenceforward 'usque ad mortem sine victoria regnabat. For the adventures of a young noble named Imma, who had been in Alfwin's following, see Bede, iv. 22. He was taken prisoner, but his brother Tunna, an abbot, deeming him to be dead, took care to say mass often for his soul. Bede was told by some who heard it,—so he tells us,—from Imma himself, that his chains repeatedly fell of,—most frequently (as he ascertained by subsequent conversation with Tunna) at the time when the masses were said. The chapter indicates, moreover, the current belief in purgatory; compare Bede, v. 12: Hom. 49.

Mercia[1]; and bishop Eadhed had been fain to flee into CHAP. X.
Deira, where he 'became bishop of the church of Ripon,'
that is, if we take the words literally, had a diocese made
for him out of York, with Ripon, as at present, for its see[2].
Peace had been made, when a protracted war seemed inevitable, by the 'salutary exhortations of Theodore, which
wholly quenched the fire of a great peril[3],' and induced the
Northumbrian king to be content with a wer-gild, or pecuniary satisfaction[4], for his brother's blood. But one of the
fruits of this peace[5] was Wilfrid's compulsory removal from
Mercia: Ethelred, and his wife Osthryd[6], Egfrid's sister,
commanded Berthwald to send him away at a day's notice.
Leaving his monks behind him, and taking with him several
priests, as Eappa, Padda, Burghelm, and Oiddi, together with
other attendants who were in his service[7], Wilfrid travelled
across the border into Wessex: but ere long the vindictive
hatred of Ermenburga dispossessed him, for her sister, being
Kentwin's wife, persuaded the king to banish him from the
realm[8]. And then, as Bede says, tranquilly resuming his
story, 'Wilfrid turned aside to the province of the South-
Saxons[9],' whose king Ethelwalch gave him a solemn assurance
of protection[10].

[1] 'Integritate regni recepta,' says Malmesbury of the Mercian king; G. P.
p. 220; Bede, iv. 12, 'recepisset.' See above, p. 294, and Freeman, Engl.
Towns and Districts, p. 202.

[2] Bede, iii. 28 : 'Hrypensis ecclesiæ præsul factus est.' More express than
iv. 12 : 'Hrypensi ecclesiæ præfecit.' So Florence, App. in M. H. B. p. 625.
'The possible see of Ripon,' Haddan and Stubbs, ii. 6.

[3] Bede, iv. 21. Compare Gregory of Tours, Hist. Fr. ix. 20.

[4] 'Multa.' See Stubbs, Const. Hist. i. 188 (or 161, ed. 1); Thorpe's Anc.
Laws, p. 79, Glossary, in v. Compare, on the principle of such compensation,
Tacitus, Germ. 21. See Gibbon, iv. 367; and Robertson, Scotl. under Early
Kings, ii. 286. He refers to this intervention of Theodore, and gives various
scales of 'wer-gilds,' English and foreign. See above, p. 248.

[5] It lasted a long time, says Bede; in fact, fifty-eight years. See Chronicle,
a. 737.

[6] See Bede, iii. 11; iv. 21. She was, long afterwards, murdered by Mercian
nobles; Bede, v. 24; Chronicle, a. 697.

[7] Bede, iv. 13. The Chronicler erroneously says that 'Eoppa' was sent by
Wilfrid *and* Wulfhere to preach in the Isle of Wight in 661.

[8] Eddi, 40.

[9] Bede, iv. 13 : 'Siquidem divertens ad provinciam,' &c.

[10] Eddi, 41 : 'That none of his enemies should terrify him by the threat of
the sword, nor make void the promise by greatness of gifts.'

And now we come to the most beautiful chapter in his life : that which furnishes the best example of the remark, that his character was ever noblest in adversity [1],—the strongest title which it can show to the aureole of pure saintship.

That little South-Saxon realm, traditionally one of the oldest of the kingdoms, was by far the most insignificant. It is simply omitted in Florence of Worcester's dynastic tables, as if, after the great things which Ella and his three sons had done from their landing at Kynor in 477 [2] to the destruction of Anderida in 491, a spell had stiffened the South-Saxons into the utter negation of all stirring national life. Fenced in by the huge dim forest of the Andred-weald, which extended its arms into Kent and Hampshire [3], and into which the first Saxon invaders drove ' some of the Welsh [4],' or by Romney Marsh eastward, the people seemed to be inaccessible to the influences which were swaying their neighbours hither and thither, and, in particular, were unconscious of the great spiritual movement which had formed Kent and Wessex into districts of Christendom. Twenty years before, their king Ethelwalch, who, as we have seen, had become a Christian and married the Hwiccian Eaba, increased his dominion by receiving the Isle of Wight, and a strip of Hampshire called Meon, as a grant from his godfather Wulfhere [5]. He seems to have invited into his realm some six Irish monks, Dicul being their abbot [6], who built themselves a very small monastery at Bosham [7], near ' Cissa's-caster,' the Saxon town, called after one of Ella's sons, on the site of the Roman Regnum. They dwelt there, unregarded by the

---

[1] Raine, i. 61. But Churton is not warranted in suggesting that his ' prosperity had gone near to quench ' his ' zeal for the cause of God ;' E. E. Ch. p. 91.

[2] Cymenes-ora (Chronicle, a. 477) is Kynor on Bracklesham Bay, near Wittering.

[3] See Pearson, Hist. Maps, p. 5 ; Camden, i. 195. Above, p. 191.

[4] Chronicle, a. 477.

[5] See above, p. 192.

[6] Bede, iv. 13. See Murray's Handbook for Kent and Sussex, p. 339 ; and Stephens's Memorials of See of Chichester, p. 7. But Dicul's little monastery was not ' one of the waifs and strays of the early *British* Church.' We meet with a Dicul, an Irish priest, in Bede, iii. 19.

[7] See Freeman, iii. 222.

heathens around them, holding their 'little Christian fortress,' but gaining no ground whatever. 'Not one of the country people cared to imitate their humble and poor life' of devout service, 'nor so much as to listen to their preaching[1].' It seemed a hopeless case ; Irish zeal had done wonderful things in other mission-fields, on the Continent[2] and in Britain,—it fell flat and dead on the as yet unimpressible barbarians of Sussex. Dicul and his brethren had to live on amid the woods, bearing the burden of apparent failure, and keeping up by their presence and their devotions what seemed a fruit-less testimony for God. Theirs was the position assigned in various ages to faithful labourers[3], who have worked and waited, not really in vain, just before the time appointed for other men's success. This was the condition of Sussex, 'wholly ignorant of the name of God, and of the faith,' when Wilfrid found refuge within its frontier in 681.

With what thoughts must he have entered its woodlands, or looked forth on the sea from its coast! Fifteen years before, he had narrowly escaped with his life, and the lives of nearly all his companions, from the ferocity of Sussex wreckers, urged on by their Pagan priest[4]. He now came once more among the people, shielded from actual peril by their king's patronage, but otherwise devoid of adventitious claims on their respect. Some of them may have heard that he was an exile, under the ban of his own king and Witan. If he was to do them any good, to bring any light into their darkness, he must do so by his own missionary capacities ; and we have seen how he put off the prosecution of his appeal in order to be a missionary among the Frisians. As Bede well says, although he was shut out from his own diocese, 'he could not be restrained from the ministry of evangelising[5].' He

---

[1] Bede, iv. 13 : 'Sed provincialium nullus,' &c.

[2] See Haddan's Remains, p. 268 ; Goldwin Smith, Irish Hist. p. 27. Bishop Forbes says that 'all the west of Europe, from Iceland to Tarentum, felt the power' of the Irish Church ; Kalendars, p. 341. See above, p. 100.

[3] Palladius in Ireland ; Wictbert in Frisia, Bede, v. 9 ; the predecessors of the Moravians in Greenland ; Henry Martyn.

[4] Above, p. 211.

[5] Bede, iv. 13 : 'Non tamen ab evangelizandi potuit ministerio cohiberi.' In this part of Wilfrid's life, Bede far exceeds Eddi in vividness and fulness.

CHAP. X. began in a fashion which may be called Pauline: he seized a temporal emergency as a spiritual opportunity. A long drought had produced sore famine: so great was the despair produced by exhaustion, that men would go by forties and fifties to some cliff or beach, and with joined hands leap or rush into the sea [1]. The people were so truly barbaric that they were ignorant of fishing except for eels, although the sea and rivers abounded with fish. Wilfrid's versatility was equal to the occasion. He had always, it seems, taken interest in handicrafts: he bade his attendants collect nets used in eel-fishing, and cast them into the sea [2]: presently they hauled in three hundred fish of different sorts, which they divided into three parts,—for the poor, for the lenders of the nets, and for themselves. 'By which good service,' writes Bede, 'the prelate turned their hearts powerfully to love him,—and they were the readier to listen hopefully to his preaching about heavenly benefits, after they had through his agency received temporal good [3].' 'The hour' was indeed 'come, and the man.' 'The dull hard stone' of their hearts was melted: they gathered round the stranger who had lifted them out of their physical misery, and gratitude and confidence towards Wilfrid became faith—however rudimentary— in his Lord. He spent some months in a regular course of instruction [4]; and with such effect that ealdormen and thanes set the example of receiving baptism from his hand, and his four priests, then or afterwards, baptized the rest of the people. No doubt, as in other multitudinous conversions, there were some which were conversions only in name; and if we can rely on Eddi, the delight with which the king surveyed the good work led him to use direct pressure on those who would otherwise have held aloof [5]. On the day

[1] This Bede tells as a report,—'ferunt.'

[2] St. Gall, on the Lake of Constance, was wont 'squamigero gregi insidias componere:' see the legend about the water-spirit who tried to damage his nets, Vit. S. Galli; Pertz, Mon. Germ. Hist. ii. 7.

[3] 'Quo beneficio multum antistes cor omnium in suum convertit amorem,' &c. Bede, iv. 13. 'To supply bodily needs πολλάκις εἰς ψυχὴν φέρει, δι' εὐνοίας δουλούμενον,' St. Greg. Naz. Orat. 43, c. 34, on St. Basil.

[4] Above, p. 298. Cp. Bede, ii. 14; iii. 7; iv. 16; v. 6.

[5] Eddi, 41 : 'Alii vero coacti regis imperio.' Milman, ii. 265, exaggerates this.

of the great general baptism, we are told that the long-delayed rain 'fell gently and copiously, the parched earth began to recover its freshness and verdure, the year came round again glad and fruitful[1].' 'And so, having cast off their old superstition and renounced their idolatry[2], the heart and the flesh of the people rejoiced in turning to the living God, understanding that He who is the true God had enriched them by His heavenly grace with both inward and outward blessings[3].'

Thus, at last, the dew came upon that 'fleece' which had been dry in the midst of the watered ground. It came with the beginnings of civilisation[4], to accompany and recommend it: some 'promise of the life that now is,' some initiation into the arts which improve its condition, assisted the announcement of 'that which was to come.' Wilfrid was now 'the Apostle of the South-Saxons:' and he became their first resident bishop. Ethelwalch made over to him a royal 'vill,' his own place of abode[5], and added to it a domain of eighty-seven hydes consisting of Selsey, 'the Isle of the Sea-calf,' as Bede calls the seal: it was, in fact, a peninsula joined on the west to the mainland by a strip of ground about a sling's throw

[1] Bede becomes poetical : 'Rediit viridantibus arvis annus lætus et frugifer.' Alcuin imitates him in de Pont. Eccl. Ebor. 595.

[2] 'Exsufflata ;' alluding to the old custom of spitting as if in abhorrence of the Evil One, at the time of renouncing him and his works. See Bingham, b. xi. c. 7. s. 5 ; Palmer, Orig. Lit. ii. 177. In the Eastern Church this custom still continues ; in the Office for making a Catechumen we find, 'Hast thou renounced Satan ?' 'I have renounced him.' 'Breathe out then ($\dot{\epsilon}\mu$-$\phi\acute{\upsilon}\sigma\eta\sigma\sigma\nu$) and spit at him.' Goar, Euchologion, p. 358. In Bede, v. 6, is a reference to the similar custom of breathing on the catechumen's face at the first exorcism : 'Exsufflante illo in faciem meam.' So the Gelasian Sacramentary, Murat. Lit. Rom. i. 593 : 'Exsufflas in faciem ejus.'

[3] Bede, iv. 12 : 'Sicque abjecta,' &c. Cp. Ps. lxxxiv. 2. Alcuin, de Pont. Eccl. Ebor. 601, refers to the same text, and adds,

'Certius æternis inhiantes pectore donis,
Quo sumpsere prius sibimet terrena per illum.'

[4] See Raine, i. 70. Meinhard won over some Lieflanders by teaching them to build a fortress for defence of their trade ; Maclear, Conv. of Slavs, p. 158. John Eliot 'found it absolutely necessary to do what he called carrying on *civility* with religion ;' Miss Yonge, Pioneers and Founders, p. 16. Price 'wisely qualified himself to act as a physician' before going to Rangoon ; ib. 142. Comp. Memoir of Bp. Steere, pp. 154, 168.

[5] Eddi, 41. Compare Ethelbert at Canterbury ; above, p. 55.

CHAP. X. across[1]. Here the bishop was to establish a home for him-self and his fellow-exiles, and a centre for missionary and episcopal work. The minster arose—doubtless, amid many pensive recollections of Ripon and Hexham—on a spot which has since then been submerged by the encroachments of the Channel, and is supposed to have been about a mile eastward of the present church[2]. He began his episcopate with a characteristic act of Christian kindness. The king had given him two hundred and fifty persons, living on the estate, 'as bondsmen and bondswomen: he saved them all, by baptizing them, from slavery to the devil, and by granting them their liberty, set them free from the yoke of slavery to man[3].' He set his faithful priest Eappa over the monastery; and Bede tells us how the pestilence made its way into the Selsey pen-insula[4], and carried away many of Wilfrid's attendants, and also of his new converts; one of these being a boy who, on the 5th of August, had a dream which shortly preceded his death, and in consequence of which that day was observed by masses in memory of King Oswald in 'all the oratories' of this Northumbrian colony at Selsey,—no other member of which, beside the boy, was at that time 'hurried out of the world,'—' and also in many other places[5].'

[1] See Bede, iv. 13 : 'Quo tempore,' &c. 'Such a place is called, by the Latins, a peninsula; by the Greeks, a cherronesos.' See Stephens's Memorials of See of Chichester, p. 15.

[2] In Camden's time it was visible at low water; Britann. i. 199. See Murray's Kent and Sussex, p. 327.

[3] Bede, iv. 13 : 'Et quoniam illi rex,' &c. Kemble, Sax. Engl. i. 211. On such manumission of slaves, see Lecky, Europ. Morals, ii. 74, and above, p. 36. Cp. Council of Celchyth (Chalk ?) in 816, c. 10; Haddan and Stubbs, iii. 583.

[4] It wrought great havoc in monasteries, as at Lastingham, Bede, iii. 23; Lichfield, ib. iv. 3; Barking, ib. iv. 7, 8; Ely, ib. iv. 19; Wearmouth, Hist. Abb. 8; Lindisfarne and Carlisle, Vit. Cuthb. 27.

[5] Bede, iv. 14. This 'puerulus,' an inmate of the monastery, and a boy of great simplicity, gentleness, piety, was taken ill of the plague, and was lying in bed alone, at 7 a.m. on the second of three days which had been appointed for a 'triduanum jejunium,' when he seemed to see 'the blessed *princes* of the Apostles,' Peter and Paul, who, as Bede heard the story, told him that he would die in grace on that very day, but 'had to wait' until mass (missæ) had been celebrated, that he might receive the viaticum : and that all the other patients would recover. This had been granted to the prayers of the king Oswald, beloved of God, who, in dying, prayed for all his nation, and therefore for them. The boy described the two appearances as having faces 'most pleasant and fair;' one was shorn like a cleric, one had a long beard. Eoppa

And here let us leave Wilfrid among his South-Saxons.
The strange restraint which had checked Bede's hand in that
part of his narrative which should have described Wilfrid's
sufferings is removed when he has to write, not of the magnificent prelate who seemed rather the first than the second
man in Northumbria, but of the exile who knew so well how
to make his own misfortunes ' turn out for the furtherance
of the Gospel.' ' For five years he exercised in those parts
the office of the episcopate, both by words and by deeds, deservedly honoured by all[1] ; ' with the little cathedral of Selsey
instead of York, with the poor simple neophytes of Sussex
instead of the Northumbrian Church in its stately organisation, with Ethelwalch and Eaba—a happy exchange—instead of Egfrid and Ermenburga ; his troubles settling down
into the quietness of an ' apostleship,' which might for a while
seclude the man whose name had been heard through Europe,
but which, in the general estimate of his life, may be truly
said to constitute its crown.

looked in his ' annale,' and found that it was the anniversary of Oswald's death.
He ordered ' missas fieri,' and all to communicate, and a particle of the oblation
to be carried to the sick boy ; after which all the monks went to their morning
meal (prandium). The boy died that day. It is easy to see how the story
grew from this detailed form. The hour assigned to the vision falls in with the
fact that 9 a.m. was the usual hour for the celebration ; Bede, iv. 22 ; Orleans
III. c. 14, Mansi, ix. 16 ; Greg. Turon. Vit. Patr. viii. 11. See Scudamore,
Notit. Euch. p. 34. Bede's informant, bishop Acca, had heard the story from
monks of Selsey. See above, p. 287.

[1] Bede, iv. 13 : ' Nam ipse illis in partibus,' &c.

CHAPTER XI.

It has been natural to treat the first series of Wilfrid's troubles as one subject, and to pursue it without interruption: it is time now to look at the progress of the Church in various kingdoms since the division of his diocese in 678.

We meet, in the first instance, with a statement by Florence of Worcester [1], which assigns to 679 a five-fold partition of the Mercian diocese, the effect of which was to establish Bosel as bishop of Worcester, Cuthwin of Lichfield, Saxulf of Leicester, Ethelwin of 'Siddenacester,' and Ætla of Dorchester. This, it is said, was done by Theodore at the request of Ethelred, who was himself prompted by Oshere, 'king' of the Hwiccas. But the statement requires 'analysis and criticism [2].' Let us see what can be made good. As to Worcester, Bede tells us [3] that several years after this, when

---

[1] In the appendix to his Chronicle; 'Cui Hwicciorum,' &c. Oshere, the alleged promoter of the partition, is referred to in a charter of 734–737 as having induced Ethelred to give lands to two nuns; Cod. Dipl. i. 98. If Florence is correct, Osric must be dated after Oshere, for Osric was in office about 690; Bede, iv. 23. On the other hand, the evidence preponderates in favour of assigning the earlier date to Osric (see above, p. 270), and placing the accession of Oshere shortly before 693, when he granted land at 'Penitanham' to abbess Cutswid; Kemble, Cod. Dipl. i. 41. Bp. Stubbs supposes him to have been succeeded by his three sons, as 'comites,' about 704. Cath. of Worc. p. 5.

[2] Haddan and Stubbs, iii. 128. Florence, says Sir T. D. Hardy, 'is very good original authority as far as the see of Worcester is concerned;' Mon. H. Brit. p. 122. Still, the date of his death is 1118.

[3] Bede, iv. 23 : 'De medio nunc dicamus.' He implies, by 'paulo ante' further on, that Bosel had not a long episcopate. Florence dates its termination (when, as Bede says, he resigned on account of illness) in 691. Probably, while bishop, he lived with monks around him, even if his cathedral 'family' was not composed entirely of monks; Stubbs, Cath. of Worc. p. 7. His

Osric was 'king,' or sub-king, of the Hwiccian district, of CHAP. XI.
which Worcester was the capital, Bosel was the bishop of
that province, having been appointed when Tatfrid, once a
monk of Whitby, had been elected, and then had died before
he could receive consecration [1],—a circumstance which appears
in the narrative of Florence. This enables us to believe that
the bishopric of Worcester—a city which had a British name
as Cair Guilagor [2], and which, says Florence, 'exceeded many
other cities in the height and stateliness of its walls'—
may be traced back to a time somewhat near 679. Leicester
was also made a bishopric for the Mid-Angles ; but Cuthwin [3],
not Saxulf, was its first prelate, as Florence himself intimates
in his catalogue of bishops : Saxulf retained his seat at Lichfield. We have heard how Eadhed was sent from Northumbria to preside over Lindsey: when Lindsey became again
Mercian, Ethelwin, who had spent some time in Ireland as a
student of theology [4], was established as bishop of Sidnacester,
commonly identified with Stow, a village between Gains-
borough and Lincoln [5]. Florence does not mention Hereford :
Putta had probably settled there, and his presence, as that
of a bishop who had been obliged to quit Rochester, would
prepare for the erection of a regular bishopric. The chief

church was called St. Peter's ; Kemble, Cod. Dipl. i. 35 ; Green, Hist. Worc.
p. 16.

[1] Bede, iv. 23.

[2] Nennius, p. 62. Also written 'Guoeirangon.' Ethelred's charter of 691–2
speaks of 'Weogorna ;' Ethelbald's charter of 716 of 'Uigranceastre ;' another
of his, of 'Wigorna ;' bishop Milred's, in 774, of 'Weogernacestre' (Kemble,
Cod. Dipl. i. 35, 80, 108, 152) ; the Chronicle of 992, of 'Wigernaceastre.'
'The chieftain of "Hwiccas" had as much authority in his good city of
Worcester as the king of Essex had in London ;' Palgrave, Angl-Sax. p. 46.
The Mercian capital was Tamworth.

[3] 'Virum religiosum ac modestum,' Flor. There was no regular succession
at Leicester until 737 ; Stubbs, Registr. 162.

[4] Bede, iii. 27 : 'Erant inter hos,' &c. Ethelwin was of noble 'Anglian'
blood, and had come home from Ireland 'bene instructus ;' his brother Ethelhun
had died there of the pestilence. Ethelwin ruled the church of Lindsey 'multo
tempore nobilissime,' and was succeeded by Edgar ; Bede, iv. 12.

[5] 'Stow, the ancient Sidnacester ;' Freeman, ii. 49. See Camden, Britan. i.
572 : he observes that Eadnoth II., bishop of Dorchester, Leicester, and
Sidnacester, in the eleventh century, built 'the church of Our Lady in Stow ;'
and that it was commonly believed 'in those parts that Stow was the mother
church to Lincoln.' See, however, Haddan and Stubbs, iii. 129, 547.

difficulty is about Dorchester. Florence evidently got his account of Ætla from a brief statement of Bede[1], that Ætla, a monk of Whitby, became bishop of Dorchester,—to which statement he added one of his own, that Dorchester was treated, in 679, as a Mercian bishopric for 'South Anglia[2].' Now, in no other passage does Bede tell us of a see of Dorchester, distinct from that of Winchester, while Heddi presided over the latter church; and, beside this, we do not know that the district ecclesiastically dependent on Dorchester, was then in any sense Mercian[3], if it ever did become so before the battle of Bensington in 777[4]. It has been suggested that the statement of Florence is incorrect, and that Bede's is to be explained by identifying Ætla with Heddi[5]. Against this latter suggestion it is to be urged that Bede could not have confounded one of the scholarly disciples of Hilda with a prelate whom he repeatedly names Heddi, and expressly describes as *not* learned[6]. On the whole it seems not unlikely that, in the weakened and distracted condition of Wessex, Ethelred might have repeated the policy of Wulfhere by invading Wessex on the north, annexing Oxfordshire for the time to Mercia, and installing Ætla in the church of St. Birinus[7]. Very likely Florence erred in assigning all these arrangements to one time, and to Oshere what was rather due to a predecessor in the Hwiccian sub-kingship[8], Osric, the nephew of Ethelred,

---

[1] Bede, iv. 23: 'De secundo (Ætla) breviter intimandum,' &c.

[2] Kemble, i. 80. The term 'South-Anglian' had, however, a wider application. Thus in Kemble, Cod. Dipl. i. 96, 100: 'Ethelbald, king not only of the Mercians, but of all the provinces which are called by the general name of South-Angles;' where the lands referred to are in Staffordshire, Warwickshire, Gloucestershire; Pearson, Hist. Maps, p. 40.

[3] It was certainly West Saxon under Kynegils in 635. See above, p. 153. Wulfhere's invasion of Wessex might be merely a raid.

[4] When Offa defeated Kynewulf; Chronicle, a. 777. See Freeman, Old-Engl. Hist. p. 82; Haddan and Stubbs, iii. 130; Green, Making of Engl. p. 419.

[5] Mabillon, Ann. Bened. i. 595, distinguishes them.

[6] Bede, iii. 7; iv. 12; v. 18.

[7] Dorchester reappears as a Mercian bishopric in 869: so that the see of Lincoln, as transferred from Dorchester by Remigius, is thus akin rather to Lichfield than to Winchester.

[8] See above, p. 270.

and apparently the son of Alchfrid of Northumbria. But it is probable that Theodore, encouraged by his success in Northumbria, would be eager to carry out his scheme in the Midlands. It was contemporaneously with these movements of Church extension in Mercia that the monastery of St. Peter at Gloucester[1], apparently, like Whitby, a community including monks and nuns, was founded, or completed, under the patronage of Ethelred, and by the munificence of Osric, the sub-king.

A more illustrious place than any of those now mentioned, in a purely ecclesiastical sense, received a new endowment which formed an era in its history. From 658, when Kenwalch drove the Britons beyond the Parret, their oldest sanctuary, 'the Isle of Avalon,' had come into Saxon hands. 'The one famous holy place of the conquered Briton which had lived through the storm of English conquest[2],' the famous 'Old Church[3],' originally of woven rods, then covered with wood and lead, was inevitably abandoned by the one race, and reverentially occupied by the other. Saxon ecclesiastics walked at will over the time-hallowed ground, ascended the 'Tor of the Archangel' on the east, looked northward towards the Mendips, southward towards the fen

---

[1] See Monast. Angl. i. 531; Hist. Mon. Glouc. i. pp. xiii. lxxii. 3 ff. (ed. Hart); where the date in the so-called charter of Ethelred, 671, is corrected to 681. Osric is said to have been Ethelred's nephew, although in this charter he and his brother Oswald, the reputed founder of the monastery of Pershore, are described only as 'ministri of noble race;' a description fatal to the genuineness of the charter. He is also usually identified with the Osric who reigned over Northumbria from 718 to 729, for whom see Bede, v. 23. Now, this king Osric, according to Simeon of Durham (Dun. Eccl. i. 13), was son of Aldfrid the Wise, the successor of Egfrid; but if the identification is correct, he was really the son of Alchfrid their brother, who might be distinguished as 'the Disinherited;' for Alchfrid's wife was Kyniburga, sister of Ethelred; Bede, iii. 21. See Stubbs, on Hist. of Worc. Cathedral, p. 3. The first abbess of Gloucester, according to the local documents, was Kyniburga, the sister of Osric, apparently named after her mother, Alchfrid's wife, afterwards abbess of Caistor. She was consecrated, we are told, by bishop Bosel, and died in 710. See above, pp. 175, 270.

[2] Freeman, i. 436; cp. his Engl. Towns and Districts, p. 82 ff.

[3] Malmesb. de Antiq. Glaston. Eccl. and Gest. Reg. i. 20. The English learned to call it 'Ealdcyrc:' 'St. Joseph's Chapel' afterwards rose on its site, west of the great church. Compare the 'virgæ' used for making a 'hospitium' in Hy, Adamn. Vit. Col. ii. 3, and Reeves's note, that Irish churches were sometimes so constructed, e.g. one at Glendalough. See above, p. 11.

called Allermoor [1], and all around on similar marshes with fair green islands rising out of them, as Bekerey or Little Ireland, and meadowy Ferramere, and Andredesey 'more beautiful than all the rest [2].' A Saxon community of monks took possession of 'the wooden basilica' of the Virgin, consecrated by the memory of so many real and legendary saints [3]: the Ynys-vitryn of Celtic speech, afterwards called Avalon, settled down into its Saxon name of Glastonbury [4]: and Bishop Heddi, on July 6, 680, granted lands in the district, at Lantocal and in the isle of Ferramere, to Hemgils the abbot [5], by a deed which in its business-like brevity puts to shame not a few pompous pseudo-charters, while its solemn opening formula has a special emphasis as contrasting the 'change' of 'the old order' with the changeless 'reign of our Lord Jesus Christ [6].' We must also apparently assign to this period the foundation of a West-Saxon monastery within the limits of the British kingdom of Damnonia at Exeter [7], the

---

[1] See the plan in Monast. Angl. vol. i.

[2] Monast. Angl. i. 22. Yet Malmesbury (Gest. Pont. ii. 91) describes 'Glastonia' as 'in quodam recessu palustri posita . . . nec situ nec amœnitate delectabilis.'

[3] Cp. Malmesb. Gest. Reg. i. 20.

[4] Malmesbury's account is, that one Glasting from North Wales followed his lost sow until he found her under an apple-tree, near the Old Church in 'Yniswytrin,' whence he called the isle Avallon (Apples' Isle),—unless it was so called from one Avalloc who dwelt there for seclusion; Gale, i. 295. Glastonbury is in fact 'the burgh of the Glæstings,' a Saxon patronymic; Freeman, i. 573. See 'Glestingaburg' in Bonif. Ep. 70. Above, p. 11.

[5] Haddan and Stubbs, iii. 164; Kemble, Cod. Dipl. i. 24; Churton, E. E. Church, p. 113. Afterwards a charter was forged ascribing the grant of Ferramere, together with 'two small islands,' to Kenwalch in 670. Cod. Dipl. i. 10.

[6] 'Regnante et gubernante nos D. n. J. C. . . . Nihil intulimus in hunc mundum,' &c. These are common formulas: as to the latter, cp. charters of Ethelbald, Cod. Dipl. i. 107, 122. For the former, see p. 252.

[7] I. e. if 'Adestancastre' in Willibald's Life of St. Boniface, or 'Adescancastre' in Othlon's, is equivalent to 'at Eaxancester' or Exeter, as is usually said: see Pertz, Mon. Germ. Hist. ii. 355. Cp. Mabillon, Act. SS. Ben. xix. iii c. 30; Alb. Butler, June 5; Maclear, Ap. Med. Eur. p. 110. On the early history of Exeter, see Freeman's 'Exeter,' p. 5 ff. Winfrid was born about 680, for he was about seventy-five when martyred in 755. Tradition names Crediton as his birthplace; Camden, Britan. i. 39. Freeman suggests that West-Saxons may have advanced into this part of Damnonia through Dorset, while North Devon was still British. When the boy prevailed on his father to let him enter a monastery, he was, according to Mabillon (Ann. Ord. Ben. ii. 15), about seven years old.

ancient Caer Wisc. For we find that about seven years after chap. xi. 680, this house, then ruled by an abbot named Wulfard, opened its doors to receive a boy from the neighbouring Crediton, whose name of Winfrid was to be lost in the glory of 'St. Boniface,' Apostle of Germany and martyr.

To return to Northumbrian affairs. The fifth Romeward journey of Benedict Biscop—the fourth, as Bede prefers to reckon it, taken directly from Britain[1]—was probably made five years after the foundation of Wearmouth, and in the year of Wilfrid's arrival at Rome. He was accompanied by 'his fellow-worker' Ceolfrid, who wished, as Bede expresses it, 'to learn what was needful' as to Roman rules of discipline[2], and to offer up his prayers in Roman sanctuaries[3] : and Agatho received the pilgrim-abbot with all honour, and granted him a letter of 'privilege' for Wearmouth[4]. Another boon was craved by Benedict, which in its results affected the whole Church of England. Would the Pope send back with him the abbot of St. Martin's, who was also 'arch-chanter' or precentor of St. Peter's, that he might teach the Wearmouth monks 'the system of chanting and reading' established in the Apostle's basilica ? Benedict's whole heart was absorbed in the welfare of his new foundation ; but Agatho saw that a much wider purpose might be served by compliance with this rather bold request. It was, no doubt, a good thing to establish the Roman 'course' in a North-English monastery ; but it was more important to secure the English Church, even by superabundant precautions, against the heresy of the Monothelites, which, after long troubling the East, was soon, as he hoped, to receive its death-blow at Constantinople[5]. Now, if John the Precentor were to go to Britain, he might carry a copy of the decrees

---

[1] Bede, Hist. Abb. 5 ; see too iv. 18. Cp. Haddan and Stubbs, iii. 126.

[2] In Anon. H. Abb. ' desiring to learn the duty of his degree more fully at Rome than he could in Britain.'

[3] Bede, Hist. Abb. 6. 'Adorandi' seems to have the sense of ' visiting with religious reverence;' so ib. 2, 14.

[4] Bede, iv. 18: 'In munimentum libertatis monasterii, . . . juxta quod Ecgfridum,' &c.; Hist. Abb. 5, 12. See above, p. 103.

[5] See Constantine Pogonatus' overtures to Pope Donus I. (676-678), and Pope Agatho ; Hefele, b. 16. c. 2. s. 312.

of Pope Martin's Lateran synod, and communicate them formally to the English bishops, so as to be able to report on their theological position, and thus promote the triumph of orthodoxy[1]. So it was that, in 680, Benedict and Ceolfrid escorted John to Gaul, and halted at Tours, where the monks of St. Martin's own church received them with kindly hospitality, entreated the abbot of the Roman ' St. Martin's ' to visit them on his return-journey, and furnished him with ' assistants for the work' which he had undertaken. It is easy to picture the joyous welcome with which the party were received at Wearmouth ; the solemn reading of the ' privilege' which, as the brethren would be reminded, had been granted by the Pope at the express desire of king Egfrid : the delight with which the untravelled monks would turn over a goodly store of books of all kinds, brought from Rome to enrich their library[2], and, still more, the fair paintings which were to beautify their church,—here, those of the Virgin Mother and the Apostles, which were to be fixed to a board running across from wall to wall,—there, scenes from Gospel history to be hung along the southern wall of the minster, and there, again, representations of Apocalyptic visions to confront them on the north[3]. ' So that,' as Bede says, in a passage truly ' Gregorian ' in tone, 'all who came into the church, however ignorant of letters, might be able, whichever way they looked, to contemplate, albeit only in painting, the ever-loveable countenances of Christ and His saints, or to dwell with quickened intelligence on the grace of His Incarnation, or by having as if before their eyes the trial of the Last Judgment, might remember to be stricter in examining themselves[4].' The monks, too, would highly value

---

[1] Bede, iv. 18: ' Unde volens Agatho,' &c. If Agatho had hoped, up to Easter of 680, to see Theodore in Rome (see above, p. 306), he would hardly have made these arrangements at an earlier date.

[2] One of the books was a ' Pandectes ' or complete Bible ' of the old translation ;' Bede, Hist. Abb. 12. Cp. Alcuin, Ep. 13, to the monks of Wearmouth and Jarrow : ' Videte librorum thesauros.'

[3] Bede, l. c.: ' Quintum, picturas imaginum sanctarum,' &c. See Lingard, A.-S. Ch. ii. 107; Green, Making of Engl., p. 373.

[4] Bede, l. c. : ' Quatenus intrantes ecclesiam,' &c. Observe Bede's ever-recurring thought of the Last Judgment. See Bede, iv. 24; v. 12, 13, 14; Vit. Cuthb. 14; Ep. to Egb. 1 ; and the account of his last hours.

the privilege of learning the orthodox mode of chanting and chap. xi. reading, under their own roof, from the most eminent of all choir-masters [1], who, beside his oral lessons, took the pains to write out for them the whole Roman scheme of yearly festivals, which was long preserved at Wearmouth, and copied out for neighbouring monasteries from time to time [2]. Nor did the kindly Roman limit his good offices to Benedict's monks: from 'almost all' the religious houses in Northumbria those who had studied chanting,—probably the elder of them under James the Chanter, the younger under Eddi Stephen,—came to listen to John, and many besought him to come and give lessons in different places in the neighbourhood [3]. He also permitted the copyist of the monastery of Wearmouth to transcribe the Lateran Council's decrees, before he was called away, in the autumn, to attend the second provincial synod of the English Church [4].

This assembly was called by Theodore in order to certify the Pope as to the orthodoxy of the Church under his rule [5], and so to add to the testimony of the Western Churches, now to be brought to bear on the East. It was hardly likely that the subtle variety of Eutychianism which had so long disturbed the East should have found supporters in distant Britain [6]: but Agatho wished to make assurance doubly sure.

---

[1] The monk who wrote the Anonymous History of the Abbots records this gratefully: 'Qui nos abundanter ordinem cantandi per ordinem et viva voce simul et litteris edocuit.' See Bed. Hom. 25. Probably the youngest of all those who heard John chant in the choir of Wearmouth was Bede himself.

[2] Bede, iv. 18: 'Ordinem ... ritumque canendi et legendi,' &c. See Lingard, A.-S. Ch. ii. 197, on the Roman course of services as observed at Wearmouth and Jarrow.

[3] John the Deacon says (Vit. Greg. ii. 7, 8) that the Germans or Gauls, partly from 'levity of mind,' partly from natural roughness of voice, could not retain 'the sweetness of the Gregorian melody,' and that to remedy this defect, John the Roman chanter was sent by Vitalian through Gaul into Britain, 'qui circumquaque positarum ecclesiarum filios ad pristinam cantilenæ dulcedinem revocans, tam per se quam per suos discipulos multis annis Romanæ doctrinæ regulam conservavit.'

[4] Bede, iv. 18: 'Nam et synodum ... in præfato ... monasterio transcribendam commodavit.'

[5] Bede, l. c.: 'Unde volens Agatho,' &c.

[6] It had, indeed, been brought into Gaul, and promptly condemned, forty years before; Hefele, Councils, b. 16. s. 302; Mansi, x. 759.

The place of the Council was Heathfield or Hatfield[1],
which may perhaps be identified with Cliff-at-Hoe, the
'Cloveshoch' selected in 673. The day was the 17th of
September, in a year described by the record of the Council
as the tenth of Egfrid, the sixth of Ethelred, the seventeenth
of Aldwulf of East-Anglia, the seventh of Lothere of Kent,
and the eighth indiction[2]. There is a slight error in these
regnal reckonings, for the September of 680 was in Lothere's
eighth year and Egfrid's eleventh[3]. The other dates
point to Sept. 17, 680. Precise as the record is on other
points, it omits the names of the bishops who attended;
but beside them, as at Hertford, other 'teachers' appear to
have been present, although not as constituent members of
the synod[4]. According to the symbolic precedent of other
and grander Councils[5], the book of the Gospels was displayed,
apparently on a raised seat or desk, in the centre of the
assembly. John the Precentor attended as commissary from
the Pope, and produced the Lateran dogmatic decrees, which
were read. They began by a statement of the Incarnation,
adopted from the Chalcedonian exposition of faith, but
enlarged by an assertion of 'two natural wills' and 'two
natural energies' or activities[6], Divine and human, existing
harmoniously in the one Christ, who, being both God and
Man, must have spheres of will and action corresponding to
His two Natures, without prejudice to the indivisible unity of
His Person. Then followed sixteen anathematisms whereby

[1] For this Council, see Bede, iv. 17; Mansi, xi. 175; Wilkins, i. 51; Haddan
and Stubbs, iii. 141. Collier calls it 'the council at Hatfield or Clyff near
Rochester,' i. 249. Above, p. 255.

[2] See l'Art de vérifier, i. 142; Haddan and Stubbs, iii. 144; above,
p. 44.

[3] The latter came to the throne in February, 670; the former in
July, 673.

[4] Toled. IV. c. 4. See Smith's Bede, p. 744: 'Non ideo ... ut sua
auctoritate decreta vel facerent vel firmarent,' &c.

[5] As the Council of Ephesus (Cyril, Apolog.), and that of Chalcedon (Mansi,
vi. 580). Also Martin I.'s Lateran Council; Mansi, x. 866.

[6] The controversy arose out of an attempt by Sergius, patriarch of Constantinople, to reconcile the Monophysites to the Church by the formula of
'one energy,' i.e. one mode of acting, in the God-Man (Hefele, Councils, b. 16.
c. 1. s. 291). This began about A.D. 619. See above, p. 229.

Pope Martin had endeavoured to guard this faith in detail[1] : CHAP. XI. and four others explicitly enforcing the theology of the Five Œcumenical Councils which had then been holden, and condemning by name twenty-six 'heretics,' among whom Origen was included[2], but the authors of the Monothelite theory, Theodore of Pharan, Cyrus of Alexandria, Sergius[3] and Pyrrhus and Paul of Constantinople, together with the 'impious' Ecthesis of Heraclius and the 'wicked' Type of Constans[4], were branded with specially emphatic condemnation. The record of the Council of Hatfield tells us that its members, firmly adhering to the teaching delivered by Christ to His original disciples, to 'the Creed of the holy (Nicene) fathers,' to 'all the holy and universal synods,' and to 'the whole

---

[1] E.g. Nestorianism was excluded by a repeated description of the Blessed Virgin as 'Dei genitrix,' and by the assertion that God the Word, one of the Holy Trinity, had come down from heaven and been incarnate. The Cyrilline phrase, 'One nature incarnate of God the Word,' though it might seem *prima facie* to favour Monophysitism, was adopted with an explanation which did not, however, bring out its true 'Cyrilline' sense, as equivalent, in effect, to 'One Person,' &c. The two wills were affirmed, because Christ willed in both His natures to save us; and similarly the two 'activities.' Martin meant to say, 'If He did not, in His human sphere of being, really desire to work out our salvation, and really give Himself up for that purpose,—if such willing and acting took place *merely* in the sphere of His Godhead, then He is not our Saviour as God *and Man*.' He also guards the sense of 'Theandric energy:' it must be acknowledged to be 'twofold,' not single : see Robertson, H. Ch. ii. 423.

[2] He had been anathematised in a Council at Constantinople (in 543 ?). See Robertson, ii. 298 ; Hefele, b. 13. s. 257.

[3] Pope Honorius' letters to him were passed over.

[4] The 'Ecthesis' was promulgated, at the urgency of Sergius, who himself composed it, in the latter part of 638 : it acknowledges the two natures in the one Person of Christ ; but it condemns the phrase 'two energies,' as if inconsistent with the truth that the Energiser was One, and as appearing to many to imply two wills *acting against each other :* and on this account it affirms 'one will.' It also prohibits the phrase 'one energy,' as appearing to some to deny 'the two natures personally united in Christ our God.' The 'Type' was promulgated ten years later, in 648, by the advice of the Monothelite patriarch Paul. It endeavoured to quench the whole controversy, without reflecting on the orthodoxy of either side : it proscribed, for peace' sake, the phrases 'two wills,' 'one will,' 'two energies,' 'one energy,' and all explanations of received language in the sense of any of these formulas. 'This pretended impartiality,' says Hefele, s. 306, 'is what distinguishes the Type from the Ecthesis.' See them in Mansi, x. 992, 1029. Next year, Martin held his synod. His sufferings, and those of Maximus, which, like his, amounted to martyrdom, followed in 653–662.

CHAP. XI. choir of approved doctors of the Catholic Church,' confessed
the Holy Trinity, that is, 'the One God in three consubstantial Subsistences[1] or Persons, of equal glory and honour'
(words taken from the Lateran document[2]); and after some
similar affirmations omitted by Bede, the statement of faith
went on to acknowledge the Five Councils, and the Lateran
Council held 'in the time of the blessed Pope Martin[3].' 'And
we glorify our Lord Jesus, even as they glorified Him, neither
adding nor taking away anything. And we anathematise,
with heart and mouth, those whom they anathematised, and
receive those whom they received; glorifying God the Father
without an origin[4], and His only-begotten Son, begotten
of the Father before the ages, and the Holy Spirit proceeding ineffably from the Father *and the Son*[5]; even as the
above-mentioned holy apostles, prophets, and doctors have
proclaimed. And we all subscribe, who with Theodore the
archbishop have expounded the Catholic faith.'

These words suggest an important question. Theodore
and his brethren here include in their 'exposition' a plain
assertion of the Double Procession of the Holy Spirit. To
refer the words, 'and the Son,' to the mission of the Holy
Spirit as Paraclete, would be to ignore the phrase 'ineffably[6],'
which clearly points to an eternal relation within the life of
the Godhead. Now, the Council of a hundred and twenty-five

---

[1] 'Subsistentiis,' for the Greek ὑποστάσεσι, 'vel Personis.' The Roman
Council of 680 also used Subsistentia for Hypostasis or Person; Mansi,
xi. 290.

[2] See it in Haddan and Stubbs, iii. 146: 'Omnes sanctæ . . . synodi, et omnis
probabilium catholicæ ecclesiæ doctorum chorus.' 'Tribus subsistentiis,' &c.

[3] It is added, 'imperante Constantino piissimo,' a mistake for 'Constante.'
So the Lateran Synod, c. 18, called him 'serenissimo . . . Constantino.'

[4] 'Sine initio:' alluding to the distinction of the Father as the Unbegotten,
as 'a nullo.' In the formulas of the third, sixth, and eleventh Councils of
Toledo, the phrase is applied to the Son, meaning 'without beginning,' 'existing from eternity,' as in Rufinus in Symb. 6. See Treatises of St. Athanasius,
Lib. Fath., ii. 513, on ἀρχή.

[5] 'Procedentem ex Patre *et Filio* inenarrabiliter.'

[6] On this confessed inadequacy of human language to the full expression of
Divine truth, compare S. Aug. de Trin. v. s. 10; vii. s. 7, 9, 11; and C. Toled.
XI. præf.: 'Pater . . . qui de ineffabili substantia Filium ineffabiliter genuit;'
Mansi, xi. 133. Compare 'the ineffable union,' in seventh anath. of fifth Œcum.
Council, Mansi, ix. 381.

bishops, held by Agatho in the spring of this same year, had
omitted all reference to the Double Procession, in its solemn
exposition of the 'limits' of the Catholic Faith [1].   How came
the English Council to act differently ?   It has been suggested
that the adoption of ' et Filio,' by a 'philosophical' archbishop
of Eastern birth and Eastern Church training, tends to show
that the Eastern Church of his time was not averse to this
addition to that 'Constantinopolitan' recension of the Creed,
which had been solemnly accepted, together with its original
Nicene form, by the Council of Chalcedon.   But a much more
probable explanation lies ready at hand [2].   Abbot Hadrian
was, as we have seen, sent to Britain with Theodore in the
capacity of his theological adviser ; and he, as an African,
would have a natural predilection for the theological language
of St. Augustine, which contains explicit assertions to the
same effect [3] ; and would desire the English Council to follow
the precedent of Spanish Councils, as the great Council
called the third of Toledo in 589 [4], the fourth in 633 [5], the
sixth in 638 [6], the eighth in 653 [7], the eleventh in 675 [8]
—a precedent largely due to the ignorance of Spanish
prelates as to the true text of the Creed, and to the 'firm

---

[1] Mansi, xi. 290.

[2] Swete, Doctrine of Procession, p. 190.   As he observes, it does not
follow that the Council received the 'interpolation' as part of the Creed.

[3] S. Aug. de Trin. xv. s. 29 : 'Ideo enim addidi' (as to the Spirit's proceeding from the Father) '*principaliter,* quia et de Filio Spiritus Sanctus
procedere reperitur . . . Sic ergo eum genuit, ut etiam de illo Donum com-
mune procederet, et Spiritus Sanctus Spiritus esset amborum.'   Compare ib.
xv. s. 47 ; and ib. iv. s. 29, 'Nec possumus dicere quod Spiritus Sanctus
et a Filio non procedat, neque enim frustra idem Spiritus et Patris et
Filii Spiritus dicitur.'   This is in a passage in which the Father is owned
to be the 'principium' of the Godhead.   So ib. v. s. 15 : 'Patrem et Filium
principium esse Spiritus Sancti.'   So, a century later, Ferrandus of Carthage, Ep. 4 (Galland. Bibl. xi. 355), 'Catholici . . . de Patre et Filio Spiritum
Sanctum procedere sentiunt ;' and Ep. 7, 'Proprium Spiritûs Sancti de utroque
procedere.'   Cp. Greg. Tur. H. E. Fr. prol.

[4] Mansi, ix. 978, 'et a Filio,' in the 'Tome ;' ib. 982, in the text of the
Creed ib. 985, 'et Filio,' in the 3rd canon.

[5] Ib. x. 615, 'et Filio ;' in a dogmatic statement,

[6] Ib. x. 662, 'Filioque ;' in a dogmatic statement.

[7] Ib. x. 1210, 'et Filio ;' in the text of the creed.

[8] Ib. xi. 133, 'ab utrisque,' in a dogmatic statement ; but a later sentence
appears to explain 'processisse' by 'missus.'

CHAP. XI. footing [1] ' already obtained in that Church for what was originally a gloss intended to strike at Visigothic Arianism by emphasising the doctrine of a coequal and consubstantial Son.

So ended the Council of Hatfield, without any reference to the case of the great prelate who a few months before had answered at Rome for the orthodoxy of the English bishops, and who in this very autumn was experiencing in Northumbria the full bitterness of an aggravated wrong. At Hatfield, every one seems to have ignored his name, though no one can have forgotten it [2]. The Roman Precentor must have heard of the story; one would think that he must have been at Rome when judgment was given on the appeal. But it did not lie in his commission to enter on such matters; and if any suffragan bishop had been minded to pronounce the name of Wilfrid, he would have been summarily put down by the autocratic president. Shortly after the Council, John set forth on his return, duly provided with an authenticated copy of the proceedings [3]. But he never again saw his abbey of St. Martin; he never again 'ruled the choir' above the grave of the chief Apostle. He fell sick in Gaul, and died; and his promise to the good monks of Tours that he would stay with them on his homeward journey was fulfilled in strangely mournful fashion by their solemn reception and interment of his corpse [4]. The document in his charge was forwarded to Rome, and gave much content to the Pope and 'to all who heard it read,' as a proof of 'the Catholic belief of the English people [5].' Agatho was at this time engaged in watching, by correspondence, the proceedings of the great Council, reckoned as the Sixth Œcumenical [6], which

[1] Swete, p. 170.

[2] The Peterborough forger, whose account of the proceedings occurs in the Chronicle for 675, makes the Witan assemble at Hatfield to receive from Wilfrid a privilege sent by Agatho in favour of the abbey of Medeshamstede, whereupon king Ethelred ratifies and enlarges all former grants, and the act is attested by Theodore, and by Wilfrid, 'archbishop of York.'

[3] Bede, iv. 18: 'Datumque illi exemplar.'

[4] Bede, l. c.: 'Verum ille patriam revertens,' &c.

[5] Bede, l. c.: 'Exemplum catholicæ fidei Anglorum ... gratantissime exceptum.'

[6] See Mansi, xi. 207.

had assembled under the personal presidency of the Emperor CHAP. XI. on the 7th of November, and continued its sessions until the September of 681.

During those November days a life was ebbing out, Death of Hilda. which had for years represented in Northumbria the unity of the Church of Egfrid and Wilfrid with the Church of Edwin and Paulinus. A long and weary illness had broken down the strength of the great abbess of Whitby; yet she persisted in doing what work she could[1] until, in the seventh year of her infirmity, in the night of the 17th of November, 680, 'when her pain had struck inward,' as Bede expresses it, she felt that her hour was at last come. It was 'about the cock-crowing' when she sent for 'the viaticum of the most Holy Communion,' received it with the 'handmaids of Christ' belonging to the monastery, uttered her last admonitions to 'live in evangelical peace with each other, and indeed with all, and while uttering them looked cheerfully on death, or rather, if I may use the Lord's words, passed from death unto life[2].' Bede then describes a 'beautiful harmony of events, whereby, while some were beholding her departure from this life[3], others were being made cognizant of her entrance into the perpetual life of souls.' Thirteen miles from Whitby, and three miles to the west of Scarborough, lies Hackness, where in that very year Hilda had founded a dependent house, under the government of Frigyd. Among its inmates was Begu[4], a nun of more than thirty years' standing, who in her dream that night saw Hilda's soul 'guided by angels to the threshold of eternal light,' and thereupon aroused the prioress, who assembled the other nuns in the church, and bade them

---

[1] Bede, iv. 23 : 'In quo toto tempore nunquam ... gregem ... docere prætermittebat,' &c.

[2] Ib. 'Septimo ergo,' &c. St. John v. 24. Cp. Bede, Hist. Abb. 11.

[3] Ib. 'Pulchraque rerum concordia,' &c.

[4] This may be the Bega who came from Ireland, and founded a religious house on the coast of Cumberland, and whose name clings to the noble church, the little adjacent town, the theological college, and the 'towering headlands' of St. Bees. She may have become a member of Hilda's community. The identification of her with Heiu (above, p. 170), in a twelfth century 'Life,' is legendary.

CHAP. XI. 'say prayers and psalms[1] for the soul of the Mother.' In the morning arrived some monks from Whitby to announce the great bereavement. 'We know it already,' said the inmates of Hackness: and they then, on inquiry, ascertained that the hour of Begu's dream had been the hour of Hilda's death[2]. Hilda was succeeded in the abbacy by the princess-nun Elfled, who had been given into her charge as a mere infant before the foundation of Whitby, and just after the victory of Winwidfield[3].

We do not find in the account of the synod of Hatfield any mention of the subject which was adjourned from that of Hertford, but had been to a considerable extent presented during the interval in the form of an accomplished fact. In the year after the Council, however, a fresh opportunity for diocesan subdivision presented itself to Theodore. Eata gave up Hexham to Tunbert,—whom we have met with as the kinsman, and for a time the monastic superior, of Ceolfrid, —and retained for himself his own Lindisfarne[4]. And a new see was established on the northern frontier of the realm, in a monastery at Abercorn on the Firth of Forth, west of the present Queensferry. The place is described by Bede, in his first book, as 'about two miles' to the east of 'a spot called in the Pictish language Peanfahel,' whence the last wall built by the Britons 'took its course westwards[5];' in the fourth book, as within the territory of the English, but near the arm of the sea which divides their lands from

Bishopric
of Aber-
corn.

---

[1] Compare Bede, iii. 2, on the psalms said at Heavenfield for the soul of St. Oswald. And so in the Life of St. Amatus, 19 : 'Canite psalmos, quoniam jam mater nostra nos relinquit ;' Ann. SS. Ben. ii. 133. Above, p. 274.

[2] Bede adds that at Whitby one of the younger sisters, who loved the Mother 'with intense affection,' being in a distant part of the convent reserved for novices, had a similar dream at the same hour, and told it to her companions before the rest of the community knew of the death. But this seems inconsistent with Bede's account of Hilda's last Communion.

[3] Bede, iii. 24. See a letter of hers, Bonifac. Ep. 112.

[4] Bede, iv. 12 : 'Qui etiam post tres abscessionis Vilfridi annos,' &c.

[5] Bede, i. 12 : 'Incipit autem duorum ferme millium spatio a monasterio Aebbercurnig,' &c. On 'Peanfahel' see Robertson, Scotl. under Early Kings, ii. 380, and Skene, Celtic Scotl. i. 219. They consider the Picts to have been Gaelic Celts, akin to the Irish Picts or Cruithnech, on whom see Skene, i. 131. See above, p. 14.

those of the Picts[1]. Egfrid's previous successes over the CHAP. XI. Picts had seemed to confirm the Northumbrian supremacy; and it was natural to employ a religious house within a short distance of their own territory[2] as a base of missionary operations among them, and perhaps as a centre of episcopal supervision for part of Lothian[3]; and Trumwine was consecrated for this outpost of the English Church.

And while that Church was thus 'lengthening her cords' northwards, the great monastic work of Benedict Biscop was developing itself into a new foundation on the south bank of the Tyne. There lay a domain of forty hydes, situate on the 'Gyrwy,' literally a marsh (as we see in the name of the Gyrvians of Cambridgeshire[4]), but here denoting the 'Slake' or smooth[5] bay, where the king's ships were wont to ride at anchor. The old word lives in that name of Jarrow which is for ever illustrious from its association with Bede. This estate was given to Benedict by Egfrid, very soon after his return home with John the Precentor, that is, apparently, in the autumn of 680[6]. The king 'saw

Founda-tion of Jarrow.

[1] Bede, iv. 26: cp. 12. In the App. to Florence, Trumwine is named as bishop of Candida Casa. This is a strange error. That see was not revived until shortly before 731. Bede, v. 23.

[2] The proper 'Pictland' included at least the whole of Eastern Scotland from the Firth of Forth northwards, and certainly a considerable portion of the north Highlands, bordering westward on the territory of the Dalriads or Scots from Ireland; Burton, i. 183: cp. Robertson, ii. 371, Skene, i. 230. But the name 'Picts' was applied to tribes settled south of the Forth; Skene, i. 131, 238. The great Northumbrian kings deprived them of independence: they regained it in 685. Robertson explains the 'terram Pictorum qui Niduari vocantur' in Bede's Vit. Cuthb. 11, as the neighbourhood of Abernethy, ii. 383, where a Pictish king Nechtan, probably he of Bede, v. 21, dedicated a church; but Skene understands it of the district of the river Nith, i. 133.

[3] It seems probable that advantage would be taken of this new foundation to relieve Lindisfarne of part of its charge in Lothian. The 'Historia de S. Cuthberto,' after narrating the appointment of Cuthbert to the see of Lindisfarne, marks the northern boundary of the diocese as a line from Lammermoor to Eskmouth; Sim. Op. i, 199.

[4] See above, p. 260.

[5] I. e. the 'sleek' bay. 'Wira ... qui ... naves serena invectas aura placidi ostii excipit gremio;' Malmesb. G. Reg. i. 3.

[6] 'Eight years,' says the Anon. Hist. (Bed. Op. vi. 419), 'after they had begun to found' Wearmouth; this reckoning begins from Benedict's return home in 672.

CHAP. XI.   that his former grants had been well and profitably bestowed[1]:'
he could reasonably hope that the new endowment would be
equally satisfactory, but could never have foreseen the glory
which was to rest upon it.   Visit the place as it is, and
on your way to the ancient church[2] (now excellently cared
for), you see only a crowd of mean cottages occupied by
pitmen, and enveloped in a murky atmosphere: strange
contrast to the appearance which it must have presented
when, 'a year after[3]' the land had been obtained, that is,
in the autumn of 681, the buildings actually necessary for
conventual life[4] were so far completed that twenty-two
inmates of Wearmouth, 'ten of them being already tonsured,
and twelve still awaiting the privilege of the tonsure[5],' were
conducted by Ceolfrid as their abbot to take possession of
their new home at Jarrow. This house 'of St. Paul' was
to be united with St. Peter's at Wearmouth in 'the brotherly
fellowship of the first Apostles,' so that the two should be
virtually 'one monastery[6] of SS. Peter and Paul situated
in two places,' the inmates of both being bound together
by 'a common and perpetual affection and intimacy,' and
rendered as inseparable as the body and the head of a living
man.   The building of the abbey church was not taken
in hand immediately[7], as in the case of Wearmouth, but

[1] Bede, Hist. Abb. 6: 'Quia bene se ac fructuose donasse conspexit.'

[2] Its chancel contains some portions of the original structure; but on
this point J. H. Parker (Introd. Goth. Archit. p. 36) speaks less unre-
servedly than Freeman (N. Conq. v. 899). 'Bede's chair,' in the sanctuary,
is not authentic.

[3] So Bede, l. c. In Anon. Hist. Abb., 'locum primis autumni abscessum'
may be corrected to 'locum priore autumno concessum.'

[4] Anon. Hist. Abb.

[5] 'Tonsuræ adhuc gratiam exspectantibus;' Anon. Hist. Abb. Bede is less
exact: 'Monks in number about seventeen.' 'By no means all of them were
able to chant, still less to read in church, or to recite antiphons or responsories;
but they made rapid progress, through their monastic zeal, and the example of
their ruler's assiduity;' Anon. Hist.

[6] Bede, Hist. Abb. 12: 'Sicut rectius dicere possumus, in duobus locis
posito uni monasterio beatorum . . . Petri et Pauli.' See ib. 6, 'ut sicut
corpus a capite,' &c.; and v. 24, 'monasterii . . . Petri et Pauli quod est ad
Viuræmuda et Ingyruum.' Alcuin, in 793, writes 'fratribus Wirensis ecclesiæ
et Gyrvensis,' as forming one 'congregatio;' Ep. 13.

[7] See Anon. Hist. Abb. The work began at the spot 'where Egfrid himself
had fixed on the site for the altar.'

in the third year from the foundation of the monastery;
yet, in spite of the small number of workmen employed, it
was finished in the second year from the commencement ;
so that, according to an ancient inscription once visible on
the wall of Jarrow church, on the 24th of April in the
fifteenth year of Egfrid's reign, and the fourth of Ceolfrid's
abbacy,—that is, in 684[1],—the 'dedication of the basilica
of St. Paul was solemnized.' Among the twelve unton-
sured monastic colonists was a little boy of about eight,
who had been born, in 673[2], on the lands which very shortly
afterwards were granted to Benedict Biscop for the foundation
of Wearmouth abbey. The child Bæda (a namesake of an
ancient prince of Lindsey [3], and also of a priest accustomed to
attend upon Cuthbert[4], was ' given[5] by the care of his kinsfolk
to abbot Benedict,' when he was 'seven years old, to be
educated.' From that day forward he lived under monastic
rule as a member of the community, being taken by Ceolfrid
to Jarrow about a year after he had been received at Wearmouth. There lay before him, at that date, some fifty-four
years[6], which were to be almost eventless in regard to his
personal history, and unmarked by anything which could
associate him with what may be called the political history
of his Church. We seem to be looking, not on a landscape
of grand and varied outline, but on some rich level land

[1] Egfrid's fourteenth year ended in the February of 684. A copy of the
inscription is in the north porch of the church.

[2] Bede was in his fifty-ninth year (so he tells us) when he wrote the precious
little autobiography which follows the epitome of events in v. 24. Now that
epitome, like the History proper (see v. 23, end), ends in A.D. 731. And there
is no reason to think that the autobiography was written a year later. If, then,
he had completed fifty-eight years in 731, he was born in 673. So Mabillon
in his ' Elogium,' in Smith's Bede, p. 799. So Lingard, A.-S. Ch. ii. 189. See
too Moberly's Bede, p. xiii. The 'anonymous presbyter's' Life of Bede wrongly
assigns the year 677. So Simeon, Dun. Eccl. i. 8.

[3] Florence, App. See Moberly, p. xii, on this 'Beda,' father of ' Biscop,'
and on Benedict Biscop as called ' Baducing' by Eddi.

[4] ' Major Beda :' Bede, Vit. Cuthb. 37.

[5] ' Datus sum ;' Bede, v. 24. See above, p. 182. For the routine of a boy's
life in a monastery, see Turner, iii. 18.

[6] He died on the afternoon of Wednesday, the eve of the Ascension, May 25,
735. See Lingard, A.-S. Ch. ii. 196.

watered by soft streams and reposing in broad sunlight. There is monotony, but it is the monotony of tranquil, regular, and nobly fruitful work. Ever since the lad began his Scriptural studies under the care of Trumbert, a monk who had been trained by Chad[1], and other such instructors, he showed the true spirit of a Christian scholar. He studied with unremitting industry, and with the dutiful single-heartedness of one who knew that he had to form himself into a teacher,—that this was the path in which he was appointed to walk, the sphere in which he was to work for the glory of God and the good of his fellow-men. He has no literary ambition, although he enjoys his work as keenly as a poet or an original thinker might rejoice in the out-pouring of verse or the construction of theory : 'I ever found it sweet,' he says, looking back upon those years of happy labour, 'to learn, or to teach, or to write[2].' In one sense, it is true, he 'is original in nothing[3];' but looking at him as a literary phenomenon rising up all at once in a remote corner of the England of his time, he is one of the most original personages in history. And he is more,—he is one of the most admirable and loveable. Our first truly national scholar and author, the father of our history, the man in whom our 'literature strikes its roots, in whom,' although he never saw foreign countries, 'the whole learning of his age seemed to be summed up[4],' the 'adapter of the sacred

---

[1] Bede, iv. 3 : 'Sicut mihi frater quidam de eis qui me in Scripturis erudiebant,' &c. During these boyish studies, he fell in with the work of a 'chronographus hæresiarches' of the fourth century ; Ep. 3, to Plegwin, Op. i. 151.

[2] Bede, v. 24 : 'Amid' monastic duties, 'semper aut discere, aut docere, aut scribere, dulce habui.' See Alcuin, Ep. 13 : 'Recogitate nobilissimum nostri temporis magistrum Bedam . . . . quale habuit in juventute discendi studium.'

[3] Chr. Remembrancer, No. 52, p. 344 (April, 1846).

[4] See Turner, iii. 408, and the worthy estimate in Green's Making of Engl. pp. 399-404. Aldhelm, of course, preceded him as a scholar, but he has no permanent connection with English literature. See the minute references to classical writers in Bede's 'De Orthographia,' where also it appears that he had studied Greek. Compare the 'De Retract. Act.,' and the 'De Arte Metrica,' 3, and 'De Tropis.' Chronological points had a great attraction for him, especially as bearing on the question of Easter. His erudition did not, indeed, preserve him from some errors then current. His

lore of the' ancient 'Church to the peculiar wants of his CHAP. XI.
nation[1],' conspicuous, as a narrator, for honest carefulness[2],
and by the vivid sympathy which makes incident or story
so luminous under his touch, Bede is throughout the man
of patriotic feeling, who loves old English songs[3], and hates
whatever enfeebles his country or degrades the national
life[4];—the man of warm heart, whose affections go out to
friends and pupils, who is spoken of as a 'dear father' and
a 'most beloved master[5],'—and the man of thoroughly pious
soul, who 'shudders' when ignorantly charged with heresy[6],
calls sin by its right name in monks or prelates[7], and lives in
the thought of Divine judgment and Divine mercy[8]; who describes himself through life as 'rejoicing to serve the Supreme
Loving-kindness[9],' and, student as he is, comes regularly to
the daily offices[10], and is supposed to have said in his sweet
way that the angels must not find him absent[11]; who closes

erudition did not, indeed, preserve him from some errors then current. His style
is remarkably free from the pedantic affectations which disfigure that of Aldhelm.

[1] Chr. Remembr. l. c.

[2] 'An extremely honest narrator, with a strong sagacity for finding
historical truth;' Burton, Hist. Scotl. i. 68. Cp. Dict. Chr. Biogr., i. 301;
Geeen, p. 402; Skene, ii. 44. For his honesty as to Biblical difficulties, e. g.
that of the 'second Cainan,' see his comment on Luke iii. 36, Prolog. in
Exp. Act., Præf. de Retract. Act., and Ep. to Plegwin.

[3] 'Erat doctus in nostris carminibus;' Cuthbert's account of his death, Bed.
Op. i. p. clxiv. He wrote Latin hymns, and knew the Ambrosian hymns;
De Art. Metr. 24. His own hymns are poor. One is in iv. 20.

[4] Ep. to Egbert, 6, 7.

[5] See Cuthbert, as above. Cp. the end of Bede's De Arte Metrica : 'Hæc
tibi, dulcissime fili . . . Cuthberte,' &c. Cp. Ep. 13, 15.

[6] Ep. 3, to Plegwin (A.D. 707). This charge meant that he had denied the
Incarnation to have taken place in the sixth age of the world. Cp. Ep. 14.

[7] Bede, iv. 25 ; v. 14. Ep. to Egb. 2, 3, &c.

[8] See above, p. 324. Afflictions, in Bede's eyes, were often 'grace-tokens.'
See Hist. Abb. 9, ' Divina utrumque pietas temporali ægritudine prostravit in
lectum ;' cp. iv. 9, 23 (quoting 2 Cor. xii. 9), 29, 31, and Ep. 6.

[9] 'Supernæ pietati deservire gaudeo,' v. 24. Among his last words
were, 'Bene mihi pius Judex vitam meam prævidit.' ' I never saw or
heard of any one who was so diligent in rendering thanks to the living
God ;' Cuthbert.

[10] 'Quotidianam cantandi in ecclesia curam ;' Bede, v. 24. See above,
p. 262. Cp. Bede, iv. 19 ; Hom. 8 fin., and 40 fin. ; Hist. Abb. 13.

[11] See Alcuin, Ep. 219 (Op. ed. Froben. i. 282): 'Fertur dixisse Bedam,
"Scio angelos visitare canonicas horas . . . quid si ibi me non inveniunt inter
fratres? Nonne dicere habent, Ubi est Beda?"' Quoted in Haddan and
Stubbs, iii. 471. See above, p. 287.

his History with a thanksgiving to the 'good Jesus' for the 'sweet draught' of Divine knowledge, and a prayer to be brought safe to the Divine Fountain of all wisdom[1]; who in his last hours combines a loving trust in God and a 'desire to be with Christ' with a sense of the awfulness of the 'need-fare' and the Doom[2]; who spends his last minutes of working power in dictating an English version of St. John's Gospel[3], calls his work 'finished' when the last sentence has been written, and passes away with his head resting on a pupil's hands, with his eyes fixed on his wonted place of devotion, with the 'Gloria' to the Trinity as the last utterance of his lips[4]. 'A truly blessed man,' we may well say with the eye-witness to whom we owe this record; a man 'venerable' and dear to all generations of English Christianity, a 'candle,' in the words of the great St. Boniface[5], 'which the Lord lighted up' in Northumbria, and which has burned with a calm lustre through the centuries that have canonised his name.

Invasion of Ireland.

The year of the completion of the minster of Jarrow was marked by trouble and anxiety among Northumbrian Churchmen. Their king, excited by dreams of conquest, resolved to make an expedition against Ireland[6], a country, says Bede, which had ever been 'friendly to the English[7],' and

---

[1] 'Teque deprecor, bone Jesu,' &c.; Bede, v. 24. Cp. the verses in De Loc. Sanct. 19, and Vit. Cuthb. 42; Hom. 34 and 42, fin. Even when treating of the changes of the moon, he cannot help alluding to 'illam vitam . . . beatissimam, quando erit lux lunæ sicut lux solis' (Isa. xxx. 26); De Temp. Rat. 43.

[2] Cuthbert, as above. 'The *need-fare*, Death's stern "must-go;"' Green, p. 403. He repeated both Heb. x. 31 and Phil. i. 23. Cp. Bede, v. 13, 14.

[3] Cp. Ep. to Egb. 3, on his English versions of the Creed and the Lord's Prayer given to 'many unlearned priests.' On one occasion he says he has been his own 'secretary, scribe, and copyist;' Ep. 9.

[4] 'Cum Spiritum Sanctum nominasset, spiritum e corpore exhalavit ultimum;' Cuthbert. Cp. Anon. Vit. Bed. fin.

[5] Ep. 38 to Archb. Egbert. He is speaking of Bede's 'treatises.'

[6] Bede, iv. 26, calling it both 'Hiberniam' and 'Scottiam;' cp. ii. 4, and iii. 19, on Fursey's life 'in Scottia.' So Adamnan, Vit. Col. i. 2, 'Columba . . . de Scotia ad Britanniam . . . enavigavit,' and in many other passages. See Burton, Hist. Scotl. i. 201, and Skene, Celt. Sc. i. 2, that until the tenth century 'Scotia' meant simply Ireland.

[7] Bede, l. c.: 'Gentem innoxiam et nationi Anglorum semper amicissimam.' Lanigan (iii. 90) thinks that Egfrid might have been jealous of 'the shelter

had furnished homes of study and devotion to many of all
ranks among the Northumbrian people[1]. The most eminent
of these English residents was Egbert, whom Bede describes
with such admiration as a 'priest beloved of God' and 'to
be named with all honour[2],' one who lived in great humility,
gentleness, continence, simplicity, righteousness, and did
much good both by his persuasive teaching and the consistency of his life[3]. This eminent man earnestly dissuaded
Egfrid from his unrighteous design of 'attacking Ireland, which was doing him no hurt:' but ambition silenced
Egfrid's conscience, and he sent his ealdorman Bert[4], at
the head of a strong force, into Ireland, in June, 684.
'Miserably,' says Bede, was the land wasted; 'not even
churches nor monasteries' were spared. The scene of these
unprovoked and sacrilegious ravages is laid by the Irish
chronicles in the rich 'plain of Bregh[5],' the present East
Meath. The natives, failing to repel the invasion, had
recourse to a weapon which suited the wilder side of Celtic
religion: they 'called down vengeance from Heaven' on
the invaders 'by long-continued imprecations[6].' 'And

granted by the Irish to his brother Aldfrid;' see below. It was probably
part of a scheme for extending his sovereignty (Raine, Hist. Ch. of York,
i. p. xxx) or maintaining it over the Scots in Argyll (Skene, i. 265). Bede, we
see, has no feeling against Celts as such—only against Welsh men.

[1] Bede, iii. 27 : 'Erant ibidem eo tempore multi,' &c. See above, pp. 166,
192, 268 : and Bede, i. 1, on 'codices' from Ireland. Cp. Aldhelm, Ep. 3,
that English students flocked to Ireland like swarms of bees gathering honey.

[2] Bede, v. 9, 'Eo tempore venerabilis,' &c., and v. 22. See also iii. 4, 'At
tunc veniente,' &c., and iv. 3, 'Convenit autem.' On this 'favourite of Bede,'
see Burton, Hist. Sc. i. 275.

[3] Cp. Bede, iii. 27 : 'Duxit autem vitam in magna humilitate,' &c., and v. 22,
'Qui quoniam et doctor suavissimus,' &c.

[4] Bede, iv. 26; in v. 24, Berctred (or Brectrid, Ulster Ann.). Cp. Chron.
a. 684, 'and Briht his ealdorman.' This 'dux' was slain by the Picts in 698.

[5] Chron. Scotorum, p. 107; but the date, 681, is wrong. The Ulster
Annals give the right year (Chron. Scots and Picts, p. 351). Tighernach
(giving a wrong date, 685) says, 'The Saxons wasted the field of Bregh and
many churches, in mense Junii.' The Four Masters say, 'And they took
away many captives and much spoil;' (O'Conor, Rer. Hib. Scr. iv. 63).
For this 'plain,' see Adamnan, Vit. Col. i. 38, ii. 39, and Reeves, p. xlv.

[6] Imprecation was freely employed against enemies by Irish saints, as by
Columba himself; Adamnan, Vit. Col. ii. 22. See Reeves's remarks, App. to
Pref. p. lxxvii. It was freely attributed by legend to St Patrick (in
the Tripartite Life, i. 109, 111, &c.), and it appears in the story of St.

CHAP. XI. although,' continues Bede, 'those who curse cannot possess the kingdom of God, yet it has been believed that those who were thus cursed in requital of their impiety did quickly pay the penalty of their guilt under the avenging hand of the Lord.' We shall presently understand this allusion.

In the early part of the year, Theodore, for some reason unexplained, had thought fit to depose Tunbert from the see of Hexham [1]. Who was to succeed him? The question was speedily answered by Egfrid: he thought of Cuthbert, still an anchorite on Farne. After this intention had become notorious, Cuthbert met the royal abbess of Whitby, by appointment, on an island at the mouth of the river Coquet, which was occupied by a large monastic community [2]. During their conversation, he was said to have predicted to Elfled [3] that her brother would have but one more year of life [4], and that his successor would be found amid the isles of the sea; alluding, as it was thought, to 'Aldfrid, who was said to be a son of her father, and was then dwelling far from home, in the isles of the Irish, for the sake of learning.' Cuthbert then returned to Farne; and in the autumn a numerous assembly, or, as Bede calls it, a synod,—clearly Synod of Twyford. a mixed body of ecclesiastics and laics,—met at 'Twyford,' —perhaps where the Aln is crossed by two fords near Whittingham,—under the presidency of the archbishop [5], as representing the Church, and of Egfrid as the head of the nation. Cuthbert was unanimously chosen bishop: many envoys were sent to Farne to announce the election, but the hermit sat secure and inaccessible in his cell. 'At last the king himself [6],' with bishop Trumwine of Abercorn, and a

Ruadan cursing the royal hill of Tara for the crime of the arch-king Dermid; McGee, Hist. Irel. i. 30. Cp. Reeves, p. liv. on 'fasting against enemies.'

[1] Bede only mentions this incidentally; iv. 28.

[2] Bede, Vit. Cuthb. 24. Elfled believed that she had been cured of an infirmity in the limbs by putting on a linen girdle sent by Cuthbert; ib. 23.

[3] Believing in his prophetic powers, she adjured him, says Bede, 'by that awful and adorable name of the Heavenly King and His angels.'

[4] He quoted Eccles. xi. 8, and Ps. xc. 9, in proof of the short duration of even a long life.

[5] Bede, iv. 28; Vit. Cuthb. 24; Haddan and Stubbs, iii. 165.

[6] Bede, iv. 28. The Anon. Vit. calls the bishop 'Tumma.'

numberof monks and 'powerful men,' proceeded to Bamborough,
crossed the ' Fairway ' strait, and landed on Farne, where they
were met by many of the Lindisfarne brethren.   Cuthbert
could no longer keep himself in seclusion.   His visitors, we
are told, even knelt at his feet, ' adjuring him by the Lord,
with tears,' to accept the election.   At last, with tears in
his own eyes, he yielded, went with them to Twyford, and,
although very reluctantly, 'bowed his neck to the yoke of
the episcopate [1].'   The consecration was deferred until the
spring ; but during the interval Cuthbert spent some time
with Eata at Melrose, and on his return visited a thane of
Egfrid, and was believed to have cured the deathlike illness
of his servant [2].

So it was, that on Easter-day, March 26, 685, Theodore, Cuthbert,
with six other bishops, consecrated Cuthbert in St. Peter's bishop of
minster at York [3].   He had been elected for Hexham : but farne.
out of deference to his love for Lindisfarne, the gentle Eata,
his old superior, returned to Hexham, and Cuthbert was now
not only, as Boisil had predicted [4], a bishop, but bishop of
that revered church in which he had been so active a prior.
Before he quitted York, the king, in Theodore's presence,
gave to Cuthbert the land 'from the wall of St. Peter's to the
great gate westwards, and to the city wall southwards,'
together with the village of Crayke as a halting-place in his
journeys to and from York [5], and the far more valuable
possession—one which seemed to herald the future princedom
of his successors in lordly Durham—of the old Roman city of
' Lugubalia ' or Carlisle [6], which had been conquered from the

[1] 'Ad suscipiendum . . . officium collum submittere compellitur;' Bede,
iv. 28; Vit. Cuthb. 24; De Mirac. Cuthb. c. 21.

[2] Bede, Vit. Cuthb. 25; Anon. Vit. calls the thane ' Sibba.'

[3] Bede, iv. 28: ' In ipsa solemnitate paschali,' &c.   Cp. Rich. of Hexh.,
Hagulst. Eccl. 10; X Script. 295.

[4] Bede, Vit. Cuthb. 8.

[5] Sim. Hist. Dun. Eccl. i. 9.   Crayke would be a convenient halting-place
to one travelling from the north, before entering the Forest of Galtres, which
lay between it and York, and covered nearly 100,000 acres.   Cuthbert is said
to have established an abbot and monks at Crayke, which within this century
continued to be part of the diocese of Durham.   St. Cuthbert's remains, in their
' wanderings,' halted for four months ' in sua quondam villa . . . Creca;' Bed.
Op. vi. 392.   Cp. De Mirac. et Transl. in Sim. Op. i. 237.

[6] Sim. l. c.   A charter as to these grants (Wilkins, i. 55 ; Smith's Bede,

Britons of Cumbria, together with a territory of fifteen miles around,—and afterwards the district of Cartmel in Lancashire, with the Britons belonging to it as serfs [1]. And so the shepherd youth of Lammermoor, the scholar of Boisil, the evangelist of Tweedside, the prior of Melrose and Lindisfarne, the hermit of Farne, began his short career as a bishop.

The first weeks of his episcopate were clouded by a public anxiety, which was soon to be justified by a national disaster. Egfrid, remembering how, fifteen years before, he had crushed the Picts' revolt, determined to invade their country, then governed by a king named Bruide [2]. His 'friends,' and Cuthbert with them, urgently remonstrated [3], but in vain. As when the Irish expedition was in question, so in this more perilous venture, in which he was personally to take the chief part, he was deaf to the best counsels. He would go, and he went [4]. Then fell on many a thoughtful Northumbrian the shadow of a great dread. Was the king blinded as by a doom? Were the curses of the wronged Irish working their effect by leading him to his destruction? It was just then that the bishop of Lindisfarne made a journey to his new domain of Carlisle, whither Ermenburga had repaired to pass the time in suspense in a nunnery governed by her sister [5]. The day after Cuthbert's arrival was Saturday, the

Cuthbert
at Carlisle.

---

p. 782) is clearly spurious; it exhibits the names of Cedd and Chad. Lugubalia (Bede, iv. 29) was also called Caer Ligualid or Lualid (Nennius, 76 or 67), and afterwards 'Luel,' and in the ninth century 'Lulchester;' Freeman, Engl. Towns and Districts, p. 427. See Haddan and Stubbs, ii. 6, 8.

[1] The Hist. de S. Cuthb. 6 (Sim. Op. i. 200) says that Cuthbert entrusted this property to abbot Kineferth. Carham was also said to have been given to him, Hist. de S. Cuthb. 7.

[2] This was Bruide, or Bruidi, Mac Bili, who had become king in 672, and died in 693 (Skene, i. 262). Nennius, 57, calls him Birdei, the cousin of Egfrid: see above, p. 134. He had established himself as king of ' Fortreun,' in a stronghold east of Loch Earn. The name was common among Pictish kings. Another Bruide had died in 641; the more famous Bruide Mac Malcon, St. Columba's convert (Bede, iii. 4; Adamn. Vit. Col. i. 37, ii. 35, 42), had reigned (one of his strongholds being probably near Inverness) from 554 to 584 (Reeves's Adamnan, p. 151).

[3] Bede, iv. 26: 'Siquidem anno post hunc proximo.'

[4] 'Bellum Ecfridi,' Adamn. Vit. Col. ii. 46.

[5] Bede, Vit. Cuthb. 27; Anon. Vit. Cuthb., Bed. Op. vi. 377. When Bede

20th of May: at 3 p.m. the townsfolk, headed by Paga[1] their
reeve, and delighted to receive the saintly bishop as their
lord, were showing him their walls, on which, just then,
'the sun shone fair[2],' and conducting him to a fountain
within the city, 'the wondrous work of Roman hands[3].'
Cuthbert was attended by several of his clergy. Suddenly,
while leaning on his staff, he seemed to go through strong
mental agitation. His face, usually so bright and sweet, became
sad and downcast; after a while he looked up, gazed on
the sky, which had rapidly darkened, groaned deeply, and
muttered as to himself, 'Perhaps even now the contest is
decided[4]!' A presbyter, standing close beside him, asked what
he meant[5]. He answered evasively by a general reference
to the changing weather, and then to the inscrutable judgments of God. But he straightway returned to the convent,
saw the queen in private, and said to her, 'Set off early on
Monday for York[6], lest haply the king may have fallen:—
it is not lawful to drive on the Lord's day[7]. I have to

wrote, there was a monastery near the little river Dacre, near Penrith; Bede,
iv. 32.

[1] The anonymous biographer gives this name, and the hour.

[2] Lay of the Last Minstrel, vi. 11.

[3] Comp. Malmesb. G. Pontif. p. 208, on the Roman 'triclinium lapideis
fornicibus concameratum,' existing in his time at Carlisle. See Freeman,
Engl. Towns and Districts, p. 439.

[4] So Bede. The anonymous Life, less probably, makes him refer explicitly
to the war. 'O, o, o! existimo enim perpetratum esse bellum.'

[5] Anon. Vit., 'Quid factum esset;' Bede, 'Unde scis?'

[6] 'The royal city,' Bede.

[7] 'Dominicorum die a labore terreno cessandum est;' Greg. Ep. xiii. 1. Various
Frankish canons of the sixth century forbade all Sunday labour: e.g. Council
of Auxerre, c. 16, 'Non licet die Dominico boves jungere;' Mansi, ix. 913: so
Council of Chalons as to rural work; ib. x. 1193. The Council of Narbonne
allowed for cases of necessity; c. 4. The third Council of Orleans condemned
Sabbatarian notions as to the unlawfulness of Sunday travelling, but forbade
rural work on Sundays as detaining men from church; Mansi, ix. 19. Gregory
of Tours tells us that some men at Limoges were killed by lightning for doing
'public work' on Sunday; H. Fr. x. 30. For a story about St. Patrick warning
some heathens not to built a 'rath' on the Lord's day, see Stokes's Tripartite
Life, ii. 289. Theodore's Penitential says, 'Greeks and Romans do not go "in
curru" on the Lord's day, except to church;' ii. 8. 1; Haddan and Stubbs,
iii. 196; cp. ib. 226 (Willibrord?), 332 (Bede). The Council of Clovesho
forbade Sunday travelling save in necessity, c. 14; ib. 367: and the Laws of
Northumbrian Priests, no. 55, forbid it whether in a wain, or on a horse, or
with a burden; Thorpe, Anc. Laws, p. 420; Johnson, Engl. Can. i. 380.

go tomorrow to a neighbouring monastery, in order to dedicate its church; and will follow you after the service is completed.' His Sunday sermon was on the necessity of being prepared for any tribulation, and was understood to refer to a return of the pestilence [1]. On the Monday there arrived a man 'who had escaped from the war,' and brought tidings such as filled Edinburgh with terror and anguish after the day of Flodden. Egfrid and his host had crossed the Firth, had even crossed the Tay, and destroyed two forts, one of which probably stood at the mouth of the Almond [2]: the native forces, by feigned retreats [3], had lured them into a defile at Dunnechtan [4], or Nechtansmere [5], identified as Dunnichen near Forfar. There the king had fallen, with nearly all his men, on the very day, and at the very hour, when Cuthbert was standing by the Carlisle fountain like one who saw what he durst not reveal [6].

Battle
of Dun-
nechtan.

This battle of Dunnechtan may well rank in our memories with such decisive conflicts as those of the Idle, of Heaven-field, and of Winwidfield [7]. It marks an epoch, it closes a period,—the period of the great Northumbrian kings. It was long ere the crown of Edwin and Oswald resumed the majesty of their wide over-lordship. From that fatal after-noon in the May of 685, 'the hope and force of the Anglian kingdom'—so Bede says, recurring to his favourite poet—

[1] He told the story of the monks visiting him on Christmas Day,—of his forebodings,—of the outbreak of the pest. Above, p. 278.

[2] Robertson, Scotl. under Early Kings, i. 12.

[3] Bede, iv. 26: 'Simulantibus fugam hostibus in angustias inaccessorum montium.' The Chronicle says the place was near 'the North Sea.'

[4] Tighernach. He gives the day of week and month, but a wrong year, 686. The Ulster Annals are again right as to the date.

[5] Reeves's Adamnan, p. 186. Sim. Dunelm. calls it 'Nechtansmere, quod est Stagnum Nechtani;' de Dun. Eccl. i. 9: Nennius, Lin-garan, 'the lake of the heron;' Mon. H. Brit. 74. 'This lake formerly occupied the place of Dunnichen Moss;' Reeves, p. 187. More than one Pictish king had been called Nechtan: one had died in 621; Reeves, p. 373. For the adoption of the Catholic usages by a later king Nechtan, see Bede, v. 21.

[6] Eadmer exhibits monastic bitterness of an extreme type in his story of the vision of Egfrid's perdition seen by Wilfrid while saying mass at this same hour; Vit. S. Wilfr. 43.

[7] See Wilson, Prehistoric Ann. of Scotl. ii. 180; Burton, Hist. Scotl. i. 282; Robertson, Scotl. under Early Kings, i. 12. Nennius says, the English never again took tribute from the Picts.

' began to retreat like an ebbing tide[1].' The Picts not only shook off the Northumbrian supremacy, but regained some hold upon Lothian[2]: the Dalriad Scots, and ' some of the Britons, recovered their independence,' which they still enjoyed when Bede wrote thus, about 731. The old Northumbrian glory returned for a while after his death, when Eadbert made himself lord of Picts and Scots, and was attended by his Pictish vassal-king, Unnust or Angus, when he received the submission of the capital of Strathclyde[3]. This was seventy-one years after the over-throw of Egfrid's host. Many of his followers were made captives, or had to flee for their lives: and fight was the only course for a small band of nuns whom Cuthbert after-wards settled in an English township[4], and for bishop Trum-wine and his monks, who abandoned Abercorn, and with it their hopes of mission-work in ' Pictland.' ' He com-mended them to his friends in different monasteries, wherever he best could ; and he chose his own abode' in the great house of Whitby, where, ' with a few of his companions, he spent many years in monastic strictness, leading a life useful not to himself only, but to many others[5].' The corpse of the self-willed king received honourable burial in Hy[6] at the hands of abbot Adamnan, the biographer of St. Columba[7], who would remember how Egfrid's saintly

e/

---

[1] Bede, iv. 26 : ' Ex quo tempore spes cœpit et virtus regni Anglorum fluere, ac retro sublapsa referri' (Æn. ii. 169). Cp. Bede, ii. 12 (Æn. iv. 2), ii. 13 (Æn. ii. 502). See above, p. 336.

[2] We may infer as much from the break-up of the establishment at Abercorn, and the peril and confusion which spread south of the Firth. Bede's sentence, ' Nam et Picti terram,' &c., clearly means that ' the Picts regained their land which the English had held, and the Scots in Britain and some of the British regained freedom, i. e. independence, the ' Britons' being those of Strathclyde. See Haddan and Stubbs, ii. 3, 5, and above, p. 27.

[3] I. e. of Alcluid or Dunbarton ; Sim. Dunelm. de Gest. Reg. 42. See Palgrave, pp. 437, 470; Robertson, i. 18. Before this, the Northumbrians had been strong enough to re-establish, in an English form, St. Ninian's see of Whithern ; Bede, v. 23 ; cp. Haddan and Stubbs, ii. 7, Skene, i. 271, ii. 224.

[4] Bede, Vit. Cuthb. 30.

[5] Bede, iv. 26 : ' Eosque ubicunque poterat,' &c.

[6] Sim. Dunelm., Dun. Eccl. i. 9. See Reeves's Adamnan, p. 232.

[7] Adamnan was born about 624, became abbot in 679, and died in 704 or 705. See Reeves, pp. xl, xliv, lvii ; Haddan and Stubbs, ii. 135, iii. 229.

CHAP. XI. uncle had sent to the island community for a bishop. Egfrid's widow was driven by the shock of her bereavement into monastic life, and Eddi accordingly describes her as having been changed from a ' Jezebel into a perfect abbess, from a she-wolf into a lamb[1].'

Aldfrid the Wise, king of Northumbria.

The anticipations of Cuthbert were fulfilled. Egfrid's natural brother[2], Aldfrid,—who must, of course, be carefully distinguished[3] from his legitimate elder brother Alchfrid, the friend and pupil of Wilfrid, and the sub-king of Deira,—was called to the vacant throne. He had been living as a recluse student in the ' islands ' or ' regions of the Scots,'—as Bede expresses it[4]; a phrase which would include, with Ireland itself, some of the smaller isles occupied by men of Irish race, and known as seats of learning and piety[5]. Bede calls him a man ' most learned in the Scriptures and in knowledge of all sorts[6]:' and tells us that he bargained with Benedict Biscop to give him eight hydes of land for the monastery of Jarrow, in exchange for a splendid manuscript of ' The Cosmosgraphers,' which Benedict had bought at Rome[7]. We know that Adamnan himself calls him his ' friend,' and visited him in 686 in order to regain the sixty Irish captives

[1] Eddi, 24.

[2] Bede, iv. 26: 'Qui frater ejus, et filius Osuiu regis, esse dicebatur.' De Mirac. S. Cuthb. 21:

' Et nothus in regni frater successit honorem.'

And so, Vit. Cuthb. 24: ' Frater ejus nothus.'

[3] Lappenberg, i. 187. Turner confounds them, i. 388.

[4] Bede, Vit. Cuthb. 24; De Mirac. S. Cuthb. 21. The Irish said that Aldfrid's mother was Fina, or Fiona, a princess of Meath, and called him Flann Fina; Tighernach, a. 704; Inisfallen Ann. Bede says that a love of sacred learning was the cause of his sojourn among the Irish. Malmesbury, Gest. Reg. i. 3, says confidently that a party of nobles having deemed Aldfrid, though the elder son, unworthy to reign, he retired to Ireland.

[5] So Lanigan, iii. 96. Among these island-sanctuaries were Arranmore, Inisboffin, Iniscattery in the mouth of the Shannon, &c. But the Anon. Vit. Cuthb. says that Aldfrid was then at Hy, b. 3.

[6] Bede, iv. 26; v. 12. He was, in effect, called ' The Wise.' Aldhelm inscribes one of his works to him under the name of Acircius, after a friendship of twenty years (Lib. de Septenario). See Green, Making of Engl. p. 397.

[7] Bede, Hist. Abb. 12. Aldfrid's grant of land was ' near the river Fresh.' Benedict had ' settled the terms ' of this purchase, but he died before it could be carried out : it was Ceolfrid who placed the coveted manuscript in the hands of the scholar-king.

carried away by Bert,—all of whom were given up by Aldfrid[1] :
and that, two years later, he received a second visit from
Adamnan, accepted from him the work 'On the Holy Places,'
which he had compiled from the accounts of the pilgrim-
bishop Arculf, and with royal munificence distributed copies
of it to men of lower degree [2]. He repeatedly listened to
Drythelm's account of his ' visions ' of the unseen world, and
procured his admission into the monastery of Melrose [3].
Aldfrid seems also to have had a taste for rich attire ; for we
find him, 'in conjunction with his counsellors,' buying of
Benedict Biscop ' two cloaks, all of silk, and of exquisite
workmanship,' for an estate of three hydes on the south bank of
the Wear,—a purchase effected soon after his accession [4]. This
prince, the first of our literary kings, was a man of practical
vigour, and well able to ' restore, though within narrower
limits, the humbled state of the realm [5].'

The northern part of that realm, on which the blow fell Cuthbert
heaviest, might well seem to have received in its necessity an as bishop.
opportune gift in the ministry of a bishop such as Cuthbert,
' great in his humility, glorious in the reality of his faith and
the ardour of his charity [6].' His personal habits of asceticism
were unaltered : he ' continued steadfastly,' says his anonymous
biographer, ' to be the same man that he had been before [7],'
with the same lowliness of heart, the same intensity of devotion. His voice while celebrating was still low, still broken
by tears ; the grace of ' compunction,' as Bede calls it, ' kept
his mind fixed on things heavenly ; above all things there
glowed within him the fire of Divine love [8].' His tenacious

[1] See Vit. Col. ii. 46, and Reeves, pp. xlv, 187 ; Lanigan, iii. 96 ; Haddan and
Stubbs, ii. 109. Tighernach dates this (captivos reduxit) in 687 ; Ulster Ann.
rightly, in 686. See Skene, ii. 171.

[2] On this 'legatio' see Bede, v. 15. One of these copies was used by Bede.
His own ' De Locis Sanctis' is an epitome. It was during this second visit
that Adamnan became a convert to ' Catholic' usages, Bede, v. 15, 21.

[3] Bede, v. 12 : ' Narrabat autem,' &c. Drythelm was supposed to have
actually died and returned to life.

[4] Bede, Hist. Abb. 8 : ' duo pallia holoserica.'

[5] Bede, iv. 26: ' destructumque regni statum,' &c.

[6] Chr. Remembr., Jan. 1852, p. 78.

[7] ' Idem etiam constantissime perseverat, qui prius fuerat ;' Anon. Vit. b. 4.
See above, p. 274. He still retained his ordinary plain dress.

[8] Bede, iv. 28. ' The holy corpor*ax* cloth, wherewith he covered the chalice

memory 'supplied the place of books[1];' the canons of the Church, the lives of the Saints, were habitually present to his mind. As a preacher he was 'clear and plain, full of dignity and of gentleness; he used to dwell on the providential office of the law[2],' the doctrines of the Gospel, the obligations of the Christian life; 'addressing to different minds the exhortations which they severally needed[3], as knowing beforehand what to say, and to whom, and when, and how to say it.' He had, says Bede with characteristic emphasis, 'that qualification which is above all others helpful to a teacher, for whenever he bade any person to do a thing, he showed the way by doing it himself[4].' Always genial and friendlike to all who came to pour out to him their troubles, as he had been during his hermit-life, he 'deemed'—the words are very memorable— 'that to advise and comfort the weak was equivalent to an act of prayer[5],' for he had in full measure 'that most excellent gift of charity, without which,' says the anonymous writer in words which anticipate our Quinquagesima Collect, 'all virtue is nothing[6].' But in these private interviews he was strict in 'recalling to godly sorrow all who indulged in any unholy joy[7].' It need not be said that he exhibited all active beneficence, giving food to the hungry and clothes to those who were shivering with cold; welcoming strangers, ransoming captives—doubtless out of the hands of the Picts,—protecting widows and orphans, rescuing the poor from the oppressor[8],

when he used to say mass,' was preserved, and long afterwards inserted into the banner which hung over his shrine. This corporal was actually displayed on the top of a spear, at the battle of Neville's Cross, in 1346. Etheldred was said to have given Cuthbert some vestments.

[1] Anon. Vit. [2] 'Ministerio legis,' ib.

[3] 'Unumquemque diversa admonens exhortatione,' ib. Bede's 'Life' tells us how on one occasion, while prior of Melrose, he urged his hearers to be 'attentive and watchful while the mysteries of the heavenly kingdom were being preached;' c. 13.

[4] Bede, Vit. Cuthb. 26; iv. 28, 'Et quod maxime doctores juvare solet,' &c. See above, p. 52. Comp. Vit. S. Sturmi, 14: 'In omni disciplina . . . . prius semetipsum exercere curavit.'

[5] Bede, iv. 28: 'Hoc ipsum quoque orationis loco ducens,' &c.

[6] Anon. Vit.: 'Et illam supereminentem caritatem, sine qua omnis virtus nihil est.' Comp. Eddi, 11, copying this, and applying it (somewhat boldly) to Wilfrid.

[7] 'Male gaudentes,' Bede, Vit. Cuthb. 26.

[8] Comp. Bede, Vit. Cuthb. iv. 26; Anon. Vit.

and showing how little his habits as a recluse had unfitted him for the work of a bishop in the face of the world. He went about his diocese with the energy of a younger man, reviving, doubtless, many of his old remembrances while he traversed the wild moor or penetrated the outlying glen. In one woodland place the inhabitants of neighbouring hamlets had assembled to receive confirmation at his hands, had spread tents [1], in default of a church, for the bishop and his clergy, and cut down boughs of trees for their own shelter. For two days they all remained on the spot, until Cuthbert had finished his ministrations [2]. It was told afterwards that on this very occasion some women carried [3] a youth wasted with fever, on a rude pallet, to the entrance of the wood, and Cuthbert, being asked to give him a blessing, caused him to be brought near, prayed over him, and blessed him,—whereupon the lad arose, took food, thanked God, and returned to the women who were waiting for him. The pestilence had nearly depopulated some parts of the country; Cuthbert did his best to console the survivors, and in one place on asking whether there were any one else whom he could visit, had his attention directed to a poor woman who was weeping bitterly; she had lost one son, and held in her arms another who seemed to be dying. Cuthbert went up to her, kissed and blessed the boy, and assured the mother that he would recover, and that no one else of her household would die of the plague. He did recover, and bore witness long afterwards to the fulfilment of the prediction [4]. Cuthbert made another journey to Carlisle, partly to ordain priests, and partly to give the monastic habit to Ermenburga and to other women,—and also, as we infer from a later writer, to

[1] Comp. Willib. Vit. S. Bonifac. s. 36: 'Suorum tantum stipatus clientum numero, erexit tentoria.'

[2] Bede, Vit. Cuthb. 32. The Anon. Vit. says that this was while he was going from Hexham to 'Vel.' But he had no episcopal relations to Hexham. Perhaps he had been on a visit to Eata.

[3] 'In grabato;' Bede, l. c.; Anon. Vit.

[4] Bede, Vit. Cuthb. 33. The author of the Anon. Vit. says that this story was told him by Tidi, the presbyter to whom Cuthbert put the question, and that the place was 'Medilpong.' The plague-struck boy was 'swollen all over.' Cp. Adamn. ii. 46.

establish schools [1]. It was then that his dear friend Herbert, the hermit-priest of Derwentwater, came to meet him, and asked him to pray that they might both die at the same time, which, we are told, came to pass [2]. This visit took place in 686, when Cuthbert was looking forward to his end, which, he felt sure, could not be far off [3]: it is probable that his excessive austerities had prematurely worn out his once robust frame, and entailed a proportionate loss upon his

Cuthbert retires to Farne.

Church. In order to prepare for the last hour by an interval of undisturbed devotion [4], he resolved to return to Farne, to 'devote himself, undisturbed, to prayer and psalmody,' and to 'burn away the thorns of worldly care [5].' He made one farewell circuit of the diocese, visiting the dwellings of the faithful, and giving them needful exhortations. He also went to see Elfled at one of the dependencies of her convent, and, although it was not in his diocese, consecrated a newly-finished church. It is specially said of him, on this occasion, that he was physically wearied by his functions,—and also that he retained his playful humour [6]. We also find him at 'the mouth of the Tyne,' where the abbess Verca entertained him 'magnificently [7].' It was almost immediately

---

[1] Bede, Vit. Cuthb. 28; Hist. S. Cuthb., X Script. 69.

[2] Bede, Vit. Cuthb. 28, iv. 29; see Wordsworth's 'Inscriptions,' No. xv, 'for the spot where the hermitage stood on St. Herbert's Island, Derwentwater :'

'. . . Though here the hermit numbered his last day
Far from St. Cuthbert his beloved friend,
Those holy men died both at the same hour.'

[3] 'Divino admonitus oraculo;' Bede, iv. 28; so Vit. Cuthb. 35.

[4] A sample of the morbid pietism fostered by the monastic spirit is in the Anonymous Life, where Cuthbert's retirement from episcopal work is described as a 'forsaking of *secular honour*' (Op. vi. 379 ; comp. Alcuin, de Pontif. Ebor. 673). Yet Cuthbert's object, apart from the means which he took to attain it, was the same which bishop Zachary Pearce of Rochester had in view, when he vainly sought permission to resign his see in 1763. Some pious bishops before Cuthbert's time, as Dubricius, Magloire of Dol, and Arnulf of Metz, had resigned their sees in advanced life for the sake of religious retirement, and Licinius of Angers had been restrained by his colleagues from doing so: but Cuthbert, to the last, was regarded as bishop of Lindisfarne.

[5] Bede, Vit. Cuthb. 34, 36. The allusion, of course, is to Matt. xiii. 22.

[6] Ib. 34. He is at table, a good deal tired : his face changes colour, his knife drops on the board. Elfled asks him what he had seen. He tries to turn it off : 'Did you think I could go on eating all day?' Then comes an instance of a vision coincident with a death.

[7] Ib. 35. After rising from his noonday repose, he said he was thirsty, and

after the Christmas of 686 that he returned to his solitary CHAP. XI. islet; and at the end of February his last illness came on. Herefrid, abbot of Lindisfarne[1],—who was probably appointed to the office when Cuthbert ceased to reside there,—had been visiting the bishop for three days[2]; on a Thursday morning he gave the usual signal of his presence near the cell, and Cuthbert came to the window, received his greeting in silence with 'a sigh,' and on being asked whether his indisposition—an old familiar ailment—had come upon him in the night, replied quietly, 'Yes, I have been ill[3].' 'Give us your blessing,' said Herefrid; 'it is time to put to sea.' Cuthbert bade him go, but added precise instructions as to his own burial[4]. Herefrid asked whether some of the monks who had accompanied him from Lindisfarne might not stay behind to take care of the bishop[5]. Cuthbert refused to allow it: they departed, and the wild winds of the first week of March prevented them for five days from revisiting Farne. When they could do so, they saw a sad sight. In the guest-house, instead of in his cell, they found Cuthbert sitting on a couch, his face ghastly with exhaustion. Herefrid warmed some wine which he had brought, induced him to taste it, applied warm water to his foot, which had a bad ulcer of long standing; and then sat down beside him, and uttered some words of sympathy. 'Why did you forbid any one to attend upon you?' 'It was God's will,' said Cuthbert simply, 'that

asked for drink. They asked whether he would have wine or beer. He chose water. Then comes a story of the water being afterwards tasted by the attendant, 'et visa est ei aqua quasi in saporem vini conversa.' In Raine's St. Cuthbert, p. 16, her monastery is placed at Tiningham, on the Scottish 'Tine,' north of Dunbar. But the 'Tina' of Bede, v. 21, is the 'Tyne.' See p. 169.

[1] See Vit. Cuthb. præf. and c. 8, 23.

[2] Ib. 37. Other monks were with him.

[3] 'Etiam, languor me tetigit nocte hac.' Cp. 'Etiam' in Bede, v. 6.

[4] His body was to be wrapt in linen, which had been sent by abbess Verca: he would not wear it while alive, but had kept it for his shroud. A 'sarcophagus' given by abbot Cudda would be found under the turf, north of the oratory: he was to be buried in it, &c. On the use of the 'sindon' or linen shroud, compare Bede, iv. 9, and the account of Wilfrid's burial, Eddi, 65, and of Columba's, Adamn. iii. 23. St. Boniface gave special directions about the 'linteum' which was to be his shroud; Willib. Vit. Bonif. s. 33.

[5] Several of the Lindisfarne monks were 'skilful physicians;' Bede, Vit. Cuthb. 45, cp. 37; so Anon. Vit. in Bed. Op. vi. 381. Cp. Bede, iv. 19.

CHAP. XI. I should suffer some distress without human help at hand. I became worse as soon as you had departed ; and so I left my cell in order that any of you, when coming to see me, might find me here ; and here for five days and nights I have continued without moving.' Turning up his couch, he showed five onions, one of them nearly half eaten : he had had nothing else [1]. He dropped some mysterious allusions to persecutions on the part of enemies [2]. Herefrid durst not say more than ' Will you not *now* have some attendants ? ' He consented ; some of the monks who had had occasion to go over to Bamborough, and had returned, were appointed to nurse him ; among them were ' Bede the elder,' who had always attended on his person, and Walstod, who, though himself suffering from ailment, was deemed specially fit to hear his last words. Herefrid came and went ; and, after consulting with the community, reported to Cuthbert their earnest wish to bury him in Lindisfarne. He answered, with a strange disparagement of his 'active life,' that he had wished to rest on the islet 'where he had fought his poor fight for the Lord ; ' and he feared that if he were to be buried in Lindisfarne, the monastery would be troubled by fugitives, or criminals seeking sanctuary beside his grave [3]. At last, however, he yielded, on condition that he might be interred in ' the inmost part of the church.' They ' thanked him on bended knees for this permission and counsel,' and then went home, but paid him other visits. At last, on the morning of Tuesday the 19th of March, Herefrid and others carried him—for he was now too feeble to walk—back to his cell. Walstod went in with him [4] ; no one else for years had done so. Six hours passed away : at three in the afternoon Herefrid found him lying down in a corner of the oratory, opposite to the altar ; and sitting down beside him, begged

---

[1] As often as my mouth became very dry and parched, 'hæc gustando me refrigerare ac recreare curavi.'

[2] He had never, he said, been so much ' persecuted ' as in those five days.

[3] On the privilege of sanctuary, see above, p. 92.

[4] They asked him to let one of them go in to wait on him. He gazed round on all, and fixed his eyes on the invalid brother, saying, ' Let Walstod come in with me ; ' Bede, Vit. Cuthb. 38. It is added that, from that moment, Walstod (Pallistod, Anon. Vit.) was free of his infirmity.

for his farewell message as a 'legacy' to the brethren [1]. Very faintly, and 'at intervals,' the voice which had held such sway over its hearers uttered a few sentences inculcating 'Divine charity,' unanimity, agreement with 'other servants of Christ,' hospitality to strangers, avoidance of self-righteousness, strictness in abstaining from communion with those who 'swerved from Catholic unity, either by observing Easter out of its time, or by living perversely.' 'Remember that I had rather you took up my bones, and left your home to dwell wherever God may provide, than put a yoke on your own necks by consenting to schismatics in their iniquity [2]!' They were to study and observe the rules of the monastic fathers, and those which they had received through his ministry: 'for I know that although in my lifetime some have despised me [3], after my death it will be seen that my teaching is not to be despised.' So, according to Bede, the abbot reported these last words of Cuthbert: but doubtless he received them with some amplification of the original [4]. Cuthbert passed the evening in 'tranquil expectation of future bliss,' and continued his prayers until past midnight. Then, 'when the usual time of nocturn-prayer was come,' he received from Herefrid 'the communion of the Lord's Body and Blood, to strengthen him for his departure [5],' and 'with eyes gazing heavenward, and hands lifted high above his head [6], he breathed his last in a sitting posture, and passed away,

Death of Cuthbert.

---

[1] 'Quem hæreditarium sermonem, quod ultimum "Vale," fratribus relinqueret;' V. C. 39.

[2] Bede, Vit. Cuthb. 39. It would seem from this that there was some remnant of a Scotic party still existing in Northumbria. The words, it is said, were remembered by bishop Eardulf when he resolved on removing the body; Hist. Transl. S. Cuthb. c. 2 (Bed. Op. vi. 37); Sim. Dun. de Dun. Eccl. ii. 6.

[3] Could this be an allusion to those in Northumbria whose ideal of ecclesiastical excellence was Wilfrid?   [4] 'Hæc et his similia.'

[5] It is certain that he received Communion in both kinds, and clearly not during mass. So Bede, de Mirac. S. Cuthb. c. 36:

> 'Residens antistes ad altar'
> Pocula degustat vitæ, Christique supinum
> Sanguine munit iter.'

So Guthlac 'munivit se Communione Corporis et Sanguinis Christi,' both kinds being kept ready on the altar; Act. SS. Bened. iii. 281. Not so Cædmon.

[6] Bede, Vit. Cuthb. 39; Anon. Vit. Cp. Bede, iv. 28: 'mortis, vel vitæ magis,' &c.

without a groan, into the life of the fathers [1],' in the first hours of Wednesday, the 20th of March, 687. The corpse was carried to Lindisfarne, duly washed [2], and arrayed in priestly vestments and shoes; the head was wrapt in a handkerchief; 'oblates,' or bread, as if prepared for the Eucharist [3], were placed upon the breast, and a linen sheet [4], rubbed with wax, was folded round the body, which was then laid in a stone coffin on the right hand of the altar in St. Peter's church,—there to remain until the terror of the Northmen's invasion impelled the monks of Lindisfarne, in 875, to begin that series of 'the wanderings of St. Cuthbert' which ended, in 999, with his final interment

> 'Where his cathedral, huge and vast,
> Looks down upon the Wear [5].'

So lived, so died, the great popular saint of the North-country [6]. It is next to impossible to abridge the story of his death; and as in the case of St. Chad, it has seemed desirable to preserve unbroken the continuity of his last two years. But we must now again take up the thread of events preceding the year 687.

---

[1] Anon. Vit. He was probably about fifty-six, for he was just grown up when he came to Melrose in 651. See above, p. 194.

[2] Anon. Vit.: 'Toto corpore lavato, capite sudario circumdato,' &c.

[3] 'Offletes;' see Lingard, A.-S. Ch. i. 292.

[4] When the coffin of Cuthbert was opened at Durham in 1104, he was found wrapped in a 'sindon subtilissima,' with face-cloth, 'sudarium,' vestments, 'pallia,' and three sheets (Reginald Libellus, c. 40).

[5] 'Marmion,' ii. 14. See Hist. Transl. S. Cuthb. c. 2, in Bed. Op. vi. 387; Handbook of Northern Cathedrals, ii. 231.

[6] Bede's Life of Cuthbert was written after very careful investigation and 'accurate examination' of surviving eye-witnesses. When finished, it was submitted to the criticism of Herefrid and others; and, thus amended, was presented to the bishops and monks of Lindisfarne, and read during two days by the elders of the community, who found nothing to correct, but mentioned to Bede 'alia multa, nec minora his quæ scripsimus.' These incidents, however, he refrained from inserting in his book; Præf. V. C. The anonymous Life, written earlier, during Aldfrid's reign, has very little about Cuthbert's death. Bede devotes a chapter, v. 1, to his successor in the hermit life, Ethelwald, a priest bred up at Ripon, who dwelt on Farne for twelve years, and died in 699. The third occupant of Farne was Felgeld, who lived there many years; Vit. Cuthb. 46. Tokens of the widespread reverence for Cuthbert's memory are found in dedication of churches, not only throughout his own Northumbria, and at Carlisle, or in Scottish towns like Kirkcudbright and Edinburgh, but at Wells, and at Cubert in Cornwall.

Benedict Biscop had made a sixth and last journey to CHAP. XI.
Rome in 684[1]. The kindly and single-hearted Easterwine Easterwine
had been appointed by him coadjutor-abbot of Wearmouth in mouth.
the ninth year from its foundation — i.e. in 682[2]. 'When
thus made a ruler,' according to the advice of 'the Wise
Man[3],' he 'did not lift himself up:' he still shared the
common meals, and slept in the common dormitory: he was
as ready as ever to take part in manual work with the monks,
to handle plough or hammer or winnowing-fan. If he had
to rebuke, he did not shrink from his duty: but 'from his
inborn affectionateness he preferred to admonish his brethren
not to do wrong,'—an admonition the more telling because
it was felt that to break rule was to sadden the bright face
of the good abbot[4]. His death, caused by the pestilence,
partook of his life's serenity. He was ill for just a week, but
did not remove into a private sleeping room until the third
day: on the seventh he came out, sat down in the open air,
sent for all the monks, and 'in his loving fashion[5]' gave to
each the kiss of peace, while they were weeping and mourning
for the loss of 'such a father.' He died in the course of the
next night, March 7, 686, aged only thirty-six, and having
spent twelve years in the monastery.

Benedict had not yet returned. When he arrived at Wear- Ceolfrid
mouth, he found[6] that Sigfrid had been elected, according and Bede.
to the right of choice secured to the community[7], to succeed
Easterwine. At Jarrow the deadly epidemic swept away
'all who could read, or preach, or chant antiphons and responsories, except the abbot Ceolfrid and one little boy, who
had been bred up and taught by him[8].' In his distress, the
abbot told his young companion that they would now go

[1] See above, p. 197.

[2] Bede, Hist. Abb. 6, 7.

[3] Ecclus. xxxii. 1. Bede adds that he was 'mitis, affabilis, benignus omnibus.'

[4] 'Ne qui peccare vellet, et limpidissimam vultus ejus lucem nubilo sibi suæ
inquietudinis abscondere;' Hist. Abb. 7.

[5] 'More naturæ misericordis.'

[6] Hist. Abb. 8: 'Verum inter læta,' &c. Sigfrid seems never to have been
ordained priest. Anon. Hist. Abb., 'abbas et diaconus.'

[7] Hist. Abb. 9. See Lingard, A.-S. Ch. i. 208.

[8] Hist. Anon. Abb., Bed. Op. vi. 421.

CHAP. XI. through the psalmody without antiphons [1], at all the hours except vespers and matins. They did so for a week, and then Ceolfrid, whose tears had often interrupted the 'maimed rite,' resumed the use of antiphons; and the services were thenceforward recited in full by the two voices, 'until Ceolfrid could train up or procure competent associates in the Divine work.' The boy here referred to, and described as having grown up to be a priest in the house, and written an account of Ceolfrid's administration, could be no other than Bede himself, then about thirteen years old [2]. He would take a keen interest in Benedict's new store of gifts from Rome, especially a series of paintings for Jarrow, representing types and antitypes, which were ranged on opposite sides of the church [3], so that the scenes of the journey to Moriah and of the Brazen Serpent confronted those of the Way of Sorrows and the Crucifixion, and 'the harmony of the Old and New Testaments' was vividly represented to those who entered the church. Other paintings from the Gospel history were hung round the chapel of the Virgin in 'the greater monastery' at Wearmouth [4].

We cannot but remark that not only Benedict, but Cuthbert also, a typical saint, was content to ignore the claims of Wilfrid. The consecration and the episcopate of Cuthbert were totally inconsistent with the expressed will of Rome; yet Cuthbert never seems to have given a thought to that part Wilfrid of the question. Perhaps he assumed what Northumbrian ignored by authorities had thought fit to assert, that the decree pro-Church of Northumbria. duced by Wilfrid was unfairly obtained [5]. But, anyhow, the

[1] See the Benedictine rule, as to prime, terce, &c.: 'Si major congregatio fuerit, cum antiphonis; si vero minor, in directum psallantur,' c. 57. Bede, in his last illness, 'cantabat antiphonas,' as, 'O Rex gloriæ.' 'An antiphon, in the original sense of the word, was the intercalation of some fragment or verse between the verses of the Psalms which were being then sung;' cp. Neale, Comm. on Psalms, i. 35 ff. A 'double' feast, as is well known, means one in which the antiphons are said entire both before and after the psalms. Also above, p. 334, and cp. Greg. Tur. viii. 31, and the Breviary of Quiñones, ed. Legg, p. xxi, '*omissis* antiphonis,' &c.

[2] See Lingard, A.-S. Ch. ii. 190.

[3] Bede, Hist. Abb. 8: 'Proxima super invicem regione.'

[4] Bede, l. c.

[5] Above, p. 307.

Northumbrian Church went on its way, doing its work, as CHAP. XI.
if Wilfrid had never appealed, or as if his appeal was a
nullity[1]. Cuthbert was installed at Lindisfarne ; Eata resumed
his throne in Wilfrid's own Hexham ; Eadhed appeared as
bishop in his still dearer church of Ripon. And no one said
a word for him who had once had all Northumbria at his feet,
and who was now completing in Sussex the conversion of the
kingdoms. He did not neglect his own cause; he obtained
from Pope Benedict II., who held the see for ten months
from the June of 684, a recognition of his innocence and his
rights[2] ; and he procured for himself the friendship of a
princely exile who might well seem destined to become a
power, and whose story reads like a startling romance. This Cadwalla
was Cadwalla, the descendant of a younger branch of the in Sussex.
West-Saxon dynasty[3], but apparently connected by blood
with the British race[4], and at this period leading a wild
outlaw life amid the forests of Sussex, in consequence of the
jealousy of the West-Saxon king Kentwin. Wilfrid be-
friended him by gifts, and gained a certain hold on his
affections. The connection thus formed was probably less
confidential and intimate than Eddi would represent it[5] ; but
Wilfrid thought he saw in the young untamed barbarian the

---

[1] Above, p. 297.

[2] Eddi, 51, ' et electo Benedicto ; ' ib. 52, 53, ' electus Benedictus.' Probably
he wrote while still ' elect,' as in a letter in Mansi, xi. 1085.

[3] He was the son of Kenbert, great-grandson of the warlike West-Saxon
king Ceawlin; see Sax. Chron., and Florence, a. 685. Malmesbury says
he was ' expelled from Wessex by a faction of the chief men ; ' G. Pontif.
iii. 102.

[4] His name, clearly British, led the Welsh writers to claim him as a British
king, and identify him with Cadwalader ' the Blessed,' son of that Cadwallon
who was slain at Heavenfield. See Brut y Tywysogion, or Chronicle of Princes
of Wales, Mon. Brit. Hist. p. 841. So Geoffrey says (b. 9) that ' Cadwalader,' in consequence of famine and pestilence, went over to Armorica,
was miraculously forbidden to return, went to Rome, and there died (the link
between this myth and the real history of Cadwalla), having sent his son Ivor
and nephew *Ini* to attack the English in Britain, &c. And see Angl. Sac.
ii. p. xxxi ; and Elmham, p. 254. See Rees, Welsh Saints, p. 300, on this
confusion. In fact, Cadwalader, whom the Welsh regarded as a saint, died of
the plague of 664. Above, p. 138.

[5] He says that they became to each other as father and son ; Eddi, 42. See
above, p. 199. Malmesbury says that Wilfrid gave him both horses and
money ; Gest. Pontif. l. c.

rough material of future nobleness,—a force that might be guided, and a heart that might be won. He hoped to train, soften, and Christianise this strong ardent nature [1]; but one would think he must have felt a shock when Cadwalla, 'beginning to contend for the realm' of Wessex [2], not only gathered around him a band of 'broken men' resembling in some sort the garrison of Adullam, but attacked and slew the bishop's own royal patron Ethelwalch, as an ally of Kentwin, and therefore an obstacle in his path. He then wasted Sussex 'with cruel ravages,' until the two earls whom Wilfrid had converted, Berchtun and Andhun, combined to drive him out [3]. In 685 [4], the death of Kentwin was immediately followed by Cadwalla's accession to the throne: he used his new power to avenge himself on Sussex, which he conquered [5], slaying Berchtun: and one cannot but ask whether the apostle of Sussex was passive in such a crisis, or whether his influence was used in vain. Cadwalla sent his brother, who was called Mul, 'the half-breed,' and who is described as a brave and spirited youth [6], to make a raid on Kent, which was in an unsettled condition, owing to the recent death of king Lothere [7] while under treatment for wounds received in battle with South-Saxon auxiliaries of his revolted nephew

---

[1] To 'the new nations the ministry of Christianity was' mainly 'to lay hold on fresh and impetuous natures . . . to train and educate and apply to high ends the force of powerful wills and masculine characters;' Dean Church, Gifts of Civilization, &c. p. 317.

[2] Chronicle, a. 685.

[3] Bede, iv. 15 : 'Sæva cæde . . . mox expulsus est a ducibus regis,' &c.

[4] So Florence. It has been said that Kentwin resigned the crown and became a monk (see a poem, not by Alcuin, in Alcuin. Op. ii. 549), and that he named Cadwalla his heir (Malm. G. P. v. 205). The poem referred to, 'On the basilica built by Bugge, daughter of a king of England' (Kentwin), is ascribed to Aldhelm. It was written in Ine's days. It describes the 'sacellum' which Bugge erected, its dedication-day, its rich altar-cloths, &c. The 'Bugge' who was also called 'Heaburg' was perhaps the same person.

[5] Bede, l. c. Hence, in Thorn (X Script. 1770), he is called king of Sussex.

[6] Hen. Hunt. iv. 5, calls him 'fortissimus,' and says that the invasion was by his own request. Bromton calls him 'Wolf,' X Script. 741. See Lappenberg, i. 260.

[7] Bede, iv. 26 : 'Quo videlicet anno,' &c. Lothere died Feb. 6, 685. Among the 'Dooms' ascribed to him and to Eadric is a reference to the practice of giving evidence at the altar; Thorpe, Anc. Laws, p. 15.

Eadric, who then reigned a year and a half, and on dying[1] left
the realm in confusion. But the third campaign of Cadwalla
had more important results. He resolved to recover the
Isle of Wight, which, as we have seen, had been conquered
by Wulfhere and given to Ethelwalch[2]. He would again
people it with West-Saxons; and, although he was not yet
baptized[3], and must therefore have been a cause of anxiety
to the West-Saxon clergy who looked back to the days of
Kenwalch, he vowed that if he were victorious, he would devote a fourth part of the isle and of the spoils to the God of
his friend Wilfrid[4]. The conquest was marked by a pathetic
tragedy: two young brothers of the island sub-king Arwald
had fled to the mainland, hidden themselves at Stoneham[5]
on the Itchen, and had there been betrayed to Cadwalla, who
doomed them, as a matter of course, to death. A West-Saxon
abbot, Kynibert, living in a monastery at the neighbouring
Reedford or Redbridge[6], took courage to 'repair to his king,
who was then being cured of wounds inflicted on him while
fighting in the island,' and begged that if the youths must
die, they might first be instructed in Christianity and
baptized[7]. Cadwalla made no objection to this request;
and the abbot, 'after teaching them the word of truth, and
washing them in the font of salvation, assured them of being
received into the heavenly kingdom; so that when the

CHAP. XI.

Conquest
of Isle of
Wight.

The
brothers
of Arwald.

[1] Elmham says, he fell in battle with Cadwalla and Mul; Hist. Mon. Aug.
p. 252. He had long harassed his uncle by 'civil war,' Malmesb. G.
Reg. i. 1. He reigned 'without the love and respect of the Kentishmen;'
Bromton, X Script. 741 : but in 686 he gave some land to SS. Peter and Paul's
in Canterbury, 'adjoining that which king Lotharius of holy memory is known
to have given to blessed Peter;' Cod. Dipl. i. 31.

[2] See above, p. 190.

[3] 'Necdum regeneratus, ut ferunt, in Christo;' Bede, iv. 16.

[4] Bede, iv. 16. On this see Malmesb. G. Reg. i. s. 34: 'Etsi approbamus
affectum, improbamus exemplum;' and Elmham, p. 253: both quote Ecclus.
xxxiv. 24, Vulg. The Chronicle says that he gave to Medeshamstede 'Hoge,
which is in an island called Heabur-eahg,' in the times of abbot Egbald. But
he was not abbot until about 709; Monast. Angl. i. 346. Cadwalla appears
to have witnessed a grant of land to Malmesbury, made in 688; Cod. Dipl. i.
32. And see above, p. 269.

[5] 'Ad Lapidem,' Bede, l. c.

[6] See Lappenberg, i. 260; Freeman, Engl. Towns and Distr. p. 174.

[7] 'Fidei sacramentis imbui,' Bede, l. c. In this phrase (see it also in Bede,
ii. 15, iii. 1, iv. 27) 'sacramenta' means sacred truths.

slaughterer came, they gladly underwent temporal death, as a passage to life eternal[1].' These 'martyred brothers of king Arwald, crowned by the special grace of God,' and long commemorated on the 21st of August[2], on which day in 686 they were put to death, should be remembered as 'the first fruits of all people of that isle who were saved through faith.' Christianity made its way into the Isle by means of Cadwalla's promise: Wilfrid received three hundred hydes of its land, and assigned them to Bernwin, his nephew and one of his clergy, giving him also a priest named Hiddila, 'who might administer the word and the laver of life to all who wished to be saved[3].' So passed away the old Teutonic idolatry, so came in the new faith of the world's 'Healer,' as the professed religion of the last English district that had remained in the darkness which had begun to retreat before Augustine, and which was now expelled from its insular haunts by Wilfrid[4].

And when this work of his had been done in the far south, his severance from the north came to an end. Theodore was too great and good a man to be untouched by admiration for the mission-work which Wilfrid had done in exile; and as he was now a very old man, his rigorous and imperious nature had naturally been softened by years. Nor could he, we may well think, be wholly free from compunction when he recalled the events of 678[5]. He made overtures for a reconciliation; and Wilfrid met him by appointment in London, in the house of bishop Erkenwald. Eddi puts into the archbishop's mouth[6]

---

[1] Bede, iv. 16: 'Ubi silentio prætereundum,' &c.

[2] Lappenberg, i. 260. The term 'martyr' was thus laxly applied to Kenelm of Mercia, Ethelbert of East-Anglia, and 'Edward the Martyr,' all cruelly slain.

[3] Tradition names Brading as Hiddila's abode.

[4] Thus, says Henry of Huntingdon, 'universæ regionum partes Christi lumine et gratia fruebantur;' ii. 39.

[5] See Smith's Bede, p. 754: also Raine, i. 71; and by him correct Hook's characteristic dogmatism, to the effect that Theodore 'had nothing to regret,' and therefore *did* regret nothing, but thought that Wilfrid had been punished enough, &c.; i. 175.

[6] Eddi, 43. 'O holy bishop, I have sinned against thee, by consenting to the act of the kings who, without any sin on thy part, despoiled thee of thine own property . . . I confess to the Lord and to St. Peter the Apostle.' It is curious to see how Eddi speaks of the spoliation, when we should expect him rather to speak of the uncanonical encroachment and deprivation. Fridegod

words of self-humiliation which cannot be literally accepted;
but it is clear that he said what was equivalent to regret for
Wilfrid's sufferings, and to a desire to promote his restoration.
We are even told that he proposed to recommend him for the
succession to his own see [1], which in the course of nature
would soon be vacant; and that Wilfrid, naturally enough,
preferred to return, if possible, to Northumbria. Theodore
then wrote to King Aldfrid, referring, says Eddi, to the
decision of Pope Agatho, and the later declaration of Pope
Benedict in Wilfrid's behalf, and exhorting him, 'for the
redemption of his brother Egfrid's soul,' to come to terms
with Wilfrid. He wrote similarly to the abbess Elfled, who
probably inherited Hilda's feelings against Wilfrid [2]: and
Eddi preserves for us a letter in which the aged archbishop,
in a tone of pathetic pleading, entreated Ethelred of Mercia
to be the 'patron' of an oppressed bishop who, 'deprived for
a long time of his own property, had laboured much in the
Lord among the heathen [3].' ' Do therefore, my son, my son,
in regard to that holy man, as I have besought thee; and if
thou wilt obey thy father, who is not long for this world, it
will greatly avail for thy salvation.' The letter contained
also a request that, although such a journey might seem too
long, Ethelred would visit Theodore; 'let mine eyes see thy
pleasant face, and my soul bless thee before I die [4].' Ethelred,
we are then assured, 'received Wilfrid willingly' into his
kingdom, while he was on his way homewards, and restored
to him the monasteries and lands which he had possessed in

puts into Theodore's mouth three lines of regret and sympathy : ' Poenitet,
en, fili,' &c. 1005. Malmesbury says, G. Pontif. iii. 103, that Theodore confessed all his sins to the two bishops (!).

[1] As Eddi words it, ' ut in sedem meam . . . superstitem et hæredem vivens
te constituam.' Malmesbury, ' Rogo te . . . ut . . . sedem archiepiscopatus
mei subeas,' &c. (G. Pontif. p. 233). Eadmer puts into Wilfrid's mouth a
grotesquely insincere compliment: ' I think you treated me in that way with
the intention that I should be exercised in patience . . . and thus reach perfection;' Vit. Wilf. 44.

[2] This seems to be implied in Eddi's words, ' Nam ad Ælfledam,' &c. Later,
we find Elfled taking part with Wilfrid; Eddi, 60.

[3] Theodore was sure to appreciate Wilfrid's work among Frisians and South
Saxons.

[4] Eddi, 43.

CHAP. XI. Mercia; and Aldfrid himself 'invited Wilfrid to his court, according to the archbishop's injunction [1].'

Wilfrid returns to Northumbria.

Once more, therefore, Wilfrid returned to his native country, probably in the autumn of 686 [2]. But on what terms did he return? Let us remember that, according to the Roman decree, the subdivision of the original diocese of York was to be annulled, and Wilfrid was to be reinstated in that diocese, as it had existed before 678: that done, a new Council was to be held in Northumbria, with the assent of which he was to choose new bishops, who were thereupon to be consecrated by Theodore. What was actually done appears to be this:—Wilfrid, on arriving in the North-country, found the new see of Hexham vacant by the recent death of Eata [3]. He was thereupon put in possession of that church; and after a certain interval, Bosa being compelled or induced to retire from York, and Eadhed to give up Ripon, Wilfrid regained both the cathedral church for which he had been consecrated, and the minster which he had ruled as abbot [4]. Thus, as Bede says, in his curt reference to these events, 'he recovered his own see [5]:' but was it the centre, as before, of a diocese coextensive with the kingdom? It was not, for the diocese of Lindisfarne retained its distinct existence: Cuthbert was regarded as legitimate bishop of Lindisfarne, in flat disregard

Regains part of his former bishopric.

---

[1] Eddi, 44.

[2] Haddan and Stubbs, iii. 172.

[3] Eata died, says Bede, v. 2, in the beginning of the reign of Aldfrid. He had been (1) abbot of Melrose, (2) of Melrose and Lindisfarne, (3) bishop of Hexham and Lindisfarne, (4) of Lindisfarne only when Tunbert became bishop of Hexham in 681, (5) again of Hexham only in 685.

[4] Eddi, 44, says that Aldfrid (1) bestowed on Wilfrid the monastery of Hexham, and (2) 'post intervallum temporis,' according to the decree of Pope Agatho and his synod, 'his own see in York, and the monastery at Ripon, expulsis de eo alienis episcopis.' ' Pelluntur *mœchi*,' says Fridegod.

[5] Bede, v. 19: 'Et secundo anno Aldfridi (i. e. between May, 686, and May, 687) . . . sedem suam . . . recepit.' The Chronicler and Florence appear to confound Wilfrid's first restoration in 686 with his second in 705: that is, they ignore the latter, and thus are led to say that he received the see of Hexham in 686. There is inconsistency in their statements as to the length of John's episcopate, which they make to begin in 685 (see below). Florence says that Bosa died in 686, and John succeeded him at York. This ante-dating of Bosa's death arose from a misapprehension of Bede's words in v. 3, which refer in fact to A.D. 705. Bosa was alive in 704; Eddi, 54; Smith's Bede, p. 759; Stubbs, Registr. Sacr. Angl. p. 4.

of the Roman decree, until his death in the March of 687, some months after the return of Wilfrid, who then took charge, as we should say, of that diocese, and 'kept' it until, a year afterwards, Eadbert was consecrated, as Bede expressly says, 'in place of Cuthbert[1].' This occupancy or administration of the most northern of the bishoprics appears to have had a parallel in Wilfrid's relation to Hexham until the consecration of John for that bishopric; an event which, if the Chronicler's reckoning of the duration of his episcopate be accepted, together with the date of his death[2], must be placed on the 25th of August, 687, about five months after the death of Cuthbert. Certainly, during that interval, Wilfrid must be regarded as the one chief pastor of Northumbria; but while he was undoubtedly bishop of York, and, as such, 'ordinary' of the Church in Deira, it appears that he was only the 'administrator' of Hexham and Lindisfarne, probably with the understanding that he should approve of the selection of prelates for those two churches, but without any prospect of a provincial Council to be held for their appointment. Lindsey was treated as out of the question, being no longer within the Northumbrian realm[3]. Thus, on the whole, we see that Wilfrid was content to accept an arrangement which fell short of the strict requirements of Rome.

Those months during which he discharged episcopal func-

[1] Bede, iv. 29: 'Episcopatum . . . uno anno servabat . . . Vilfrid, donec eligeretur qui *pro Cudbercto* antistes ordinari deberet.' This one phrase shows clearly that the Roman decree was *not* really obeyed.

[2] Bede himself says, v. 6, that he 'continued in episcopatu' thirty-three years, and that he died in 721. This might be understood to mean that he retired to his monastery after thirty-three years of active episcopal work. But the Chronicle is more precise: 'In 721 the holy bishop John died; he was bishop thirty-three years, eight months, thirteen days.' Florence says that he died on the 7th of May, 721. Therefore he was consecrated on August 25, 687 (see Stubbs, Registr. p. 4; Raine, i. 86), and not in 685. In other words, John was *not* bishop of Hexham when Wilfrid returned, and did not retire to make room for him, as Richard of Hexham (X Script. 296) and Elmham (Hist. Mon. Aug. p. 280) say, and as Smith supposed, p. 754, and Lingard, A.-S. Ch. i. 140. Smith adds the suggestion that Cuthbert retired to make room for Wilfrid; Bede's account of the matter disposes of this entirely, iv. 28. See Haddan and Stubbs, iii. 171.

[3] On the principle here involved, that the ecclesiastical divisions should be conformed to the political, see the writer's 'Notes on Canons of First Four Councils,' p. 176.

tions in the diocese of Aidan and of Cuthbert were marked by some distress or peril to the Lindisfarne community, which, in Bede's prose Life of Cuthbert, is described mysteriously as a 'breeze of trial' under which many of the brethren were minded to 'leave their home rather than dwell there at such risk of expulsion[1]:'—in his metrical work on the Miracles of St. Cuthbert he gives a little more information, or at least helps us to infer that what he there refers to as a 'north wind shaking the roofs of Lindisfarne[2]' may have been some threatened descent of the Picts, now free to harry the Border.

Wilfrid, as we have seen, parted with the charge of Hexham in the late summer of the year after his return. On Sunday the 25th of August, 687, a bishop was consecrated for that 'goodliest of Transalpine churches,' who was to become the object of greater reverence than any northern saint except Cuthbert[3], and to be invoked as a patron by 'the glorious Athelstane' on his way to the field of Brunanburgh[4]. This was John, famous as 'St. John of Beverley' from 'the monastery which he founded in Deira-wood[5],' and to which he at last retired to die. He was sent, while a youth, to the ecclesiastical school of Canterbury, where he received from Theodore himself instructions in theology[6], and also some maxims in medicine, which, when a bishop, he remembered and applied[7]. He afterwards entered the monastery of Whitby[8]: and Bede

---

[1] Bede, Vit. Cuthb. 40 : 'Tentationis aura,' &c., and 'repellendi ac destruendi essent.' It was, he says, foreshown by the circumstance, that at the moment of Cuthbert's death the monks then in Farne, and also the Lindisfarne community, were singing in their nocturns the Psalm, 'Deus, repulisti nos.'

[2] De Mirac. Cuthb. s. 37 : 'aquilo niveis confisus in armis.'

[3] See Raine, i. 90, and Scott's 'Gray Brother.'

[4] Ailred, in X Script. 357 : 'Audiens . . . hæc . . . rex, "Magnus est," inquit, "iste Johannes."' He prayed at the shrine, and gave the privilege of sanctuary to the minster of Beverley. See above, p. 93.

[5] Bede, v. 2 : 'Monasterii quod vocatur Inderauuda, id est, In Silva Derorum.' The present name is derived from 'a colony of beavers in the Hull river.'

[6] Bromton, in X Scriptores, 794.

[7] Bede, v. 3 : 'I remember that archbishop Theodore used to say that it was very dangerous to bleed a person when both the moon is waxing and the tide is rising.' Cp. Bede, 'de Minutione Sanguinis.'

[8] Bede, iv. 23.

reckons him among the five monks of that house whose merits raised them to the episcopate. Some traits of character which Bede mentions give us a very pleasing impression of his genial kindness towards young men under his authority [1]; while, as bishop of Hexham, he showed his love for devotional retirement after the fashion of Aidan and Cuthbert, by providing himself with a house, surrounded by a belt of wood and an earthwork, and adjoining a cemetery of St. Michael, a mile and a half from Hexham, and on the north bank of the Tyne [2]. Here he used to spend such time, especially in Lent, as he could secure for prayer and study, and would 'keep with him, for charity, some poor man afflicted by special sickness or need.' The fervent affection which Bede shows for his memory is explained by the fact that he received deacon's and priest's orders from his hands, in the years 691–2 and 702–3 [3].

And the successor of Cuthbert was a man of the same pious simplicity. Eadbert, says Bede, was consecrated a year after Cuthbert's death, i. e. about Easter in 688 [4]; 'a man remarkable for his knowledge of Scripture and his observance of Divine precepts, and particularly for almsgiving; insomuch that, according to the law (i.e. of Moses), he gave to the poor a tenth part not only of animals, but of all fruits of the earth, and even of his clothes [5].' He restored tranquillity to the

---

[1] See the beautiful story of Herebald in Bede, v. 6. The young cleric is riding with some young laymen in attendance on the bishop, but persists, against the latter's wish, to join them in a gallop; he overhears the bishop say, 'What pain you are giving me!'; he is thrown, and fractures his skull: the bishop spends the night alone in prayer for him, visits him in the morning, and asks, 'Do you know who is speaking to you?' 'Yes, you are my beloved bishop.' John calls a physician to attend to him. Herebald quickly recovered, and lived to become abbot of Tynemouth.

[2] Bede, v. 2: 'Est mansio quædam secretior,' &c. Richard of Hexham calls the place Erneshow (Eagles' hill), and believes the 'oratory' of St. Michael to have been begun by Wilfrid; X Script. 291. Bede got his information from Berctun, abbot of Inderawood. For Aidan, see above, p. 146.

[3] Bede, v. 24. He was ordained deacon at the early age of nineteen.

[4] Bede, iv. 29: 'Ordinatus est autem.'

[5] The 'tithe' thus set apart was not 'tithe in its modern sense,' in that it went to the poor; Stubbs, Const. Hist. i. 261. In Theodore's Penitential we find, 'Presbitero (for this, rather than 'presbiter,' must surely be the reading) decimas dare non cogitur,' b. ii. c. 2. s. 8; and 'Decimas non est legitimum

CHAP. XI. agitated community of his island[1]; and improved the cathedral church of thatched oak which Finan had reared, and Theodore had dedicated to St. Peter, by removing the reeds from the roof, and covering both it and the walls with lead[2]. He too, like John, was wont to retire for devotion to a secluded projection of land ' enclosed by the waves of the sea[3],' and there pass Lent, and the forty days before Christmas. We seem to get a glimpse of his inward life when we read that he used to pray against a sudden death, and desired to pass away after a long illness;—and such an end, says Bede, was granted to him[4].

End of Benedict Biscop.

Such an end too was appointed, in the first year of his episcopate, first to the acting abbot of Wearmouth, and then to its venerable founder. Sigfrid was a chronic invalid; and Benedict, the indefatigable traveller, was for three years affected by what we should call a creeping palsy[5]. Yet while his lower limbs were motionless, he ceased not to 'praise God and exhort the brethren.' He bade them observe the rule which he had compiled with such care and after such varied experience; urged them to keep entire the library which he had brought from Rome; but above all things insisted on the duty of choosing an abbot not for the sake of high birth, but purely for personal merits. 'I tell you of a truth,' he said, 'that of two evils I should much prefer that this monastery should become a wilderness for ever, than that my brother by blood, who, we know, does not walk in the way of truth[6], should succeed me here as abbot.' He exhorted them

---

dare, nisi pauperibus et peregrinis, sive laici suas ad ecclesias,' b. ii. c. 14. s. 10. See Lord Selborne, Anc. Facts and Fictions, p. 107, on the purport of this, as placing the payment of tithes on ' the footing of customs,' &c. Haddan and Stubbs, iii. 191, 203. Later, Bede speaks of a ' tribute' to the bishop as generally enforced; Ep. to Egb. 4. See Lingard, A.-S. Ch. i. 183.

[1] Bede, Vit. Cuthb. 40. To this relief from perils, Herefrid (quoted by Bede) applies the words of Ps. cxlvii. 2, 3.

[2] Bede, iii. 25 : 'Sed episcopus loci ipsius Eadberct,' &c.

[3] Bede, Vit. Cuthb. 42. It has been so used by Cuthbert.

[4] Bede, V. C. 43 : ' Ut non repentina morte, sed longa excoctus ægritudine, transiret e corpore.' Cp. Bede, Hist. Abb. 11.

[5] Bede, Hist. Abb. 9.

[6] 'Fratrem . . . inopia cordis a se longissime distantem ;' Anon. Hist. Abb. Benedict was thus strongly opposed to the notion of treating abbacies as

always to choose out the fittest man from their own community, according to the rule of 'the great abbot Benedict,' and according to the provisions of the letter of privilege belonging to their house; and to 'present the person so chosen to the bishop for benediction[1].' Very touching is Bede's account of this long decline of Benedict Biscop. His nights were often wearisome from sleeplessness; he would then 'call to him a reader, and desire to hear the account of Job's patience, or some other passage of Scripture, which might alleviate his depression;' and at each canonical hour he summoned some monks, and joined his voice to theirs in the antiphonal psalmody. He and Sigfrid had a farewell meeting, the latter being carried on a couch into Benedict's cell: the old friends were assisted to take a tender embrace of each other[2]; Sigfrid was laid down beside Benedict with his head on the same pillow, and their attendants had to bring their faces together for the last kiss. 'After taking counsel with Sigfrid and the whole brotherhood,' Benedict sent for Ceolfrid the abbot of Jarrow, and, with the approval of all, made him head of both houses, on the 12th of May, 688[3]. Sigfrid died on the 22nd of August: Benedict lived on into the next year, and passed away early in the morning of the 12th of January, 689, while the monks assembled in church were singing 'Deus, quis similis[4]?' and those who kept watch in his chamber, after hearing the

'family benefices;' see Stubbs, Const. Hist. i. 257. In the old Scotic monasteries 'the abbatial succession came to be confined to members of the clan of the founder;' Stuart, Pref. to 'Book of Deer,' p. cviii; Reeves, Adamn. p. 335; Skene, ii. 68, 338.

[1] Comp. Faricius, Vita S. Aldhelmi, c. 2, speaking of Aldhelm's care to secure free and worthy elections: 'Jam tunc enim ambitio monachorum inoleverat: jam non ut pastor per ostium, sed ut fur aliunde, volebat mercenarius intrare,' &c. Cp. Theodore's Penit. b. 2. c. 6. s. 1–5.

[2] 'Nec tantum habuere virium ut propius posita ora ad osculandum se alterutrum conjungere possent, sed et hoc fraterno compleverunt officio.' Bede calls it 'a lamentable sight;' Hist. Abb. 10.

[3] The Anon. Hist. gives this date, 'the third year of king Aldfrid, the eighth from the foundation of St. Paul's monastery.' The third year of Aldfrid began May 20, 687,—reckoning from Egfrid's death.

[4] Bede dwells on the leading idea of this Psalm (our 83rd), that 'the foes of the Christian name' will be baffled and routed in their attempts to destroy the Church and every faithful soul; Hist. Abb. 11.

CHAP. XI.

Cadwalla
goes to
Rome.

Gospels read by a priest throughout the long wintry night, looked at his face for the last time in life, shortly after his last Communion. He was not more than sixty years old.

That year of Ceolfrid's accession to the abbacy of both houses, or of the one twofold house, was marked in Wessex by the strange end of a brief reign, which had blazed 'like a meteor' in 'the troubled air' of the south. Cadwalla's brother Mul, in the course of a fierce raid in Kent, had fallen with twelve adherents into the hands of foes whom he despised as womanish[1]. They suddenly beset the house wherein he was, and burned it with all whom it contained[2]. Cadwalla avenged him by another irruption into Kent[3]; but this was the last of his wars. He had now, at last, resolved to be baptized; and the intensity of his nature, combined with that extreme form of local religiousness which he may well have imbibed from Wilfrid, made him resolve on going a long way for the cleansing 'laver,' even to the shrine of the chief Apostle. According to Bede's conjecture, he had a hope that he should die soon after his baptism, and so secure his salvation[4]. So it was that Pope Sergius I., who had come to the see on December 15, 687, saw in the following year this remarkable catechumen at his feet[5]. He who, for all his admiration of a missionary bishop, had in his own person, and beyond all other English princes of his time, represented the wild Teutonic thirst for slaughter and conquest, who had

[1] 'Nam cum hostes effœminatos duceret,' &c. ; Hen. Hunt. iv. 5.

[2] Chronicle, a. 687; Florence, a. 687; Bromton, X Script. 741. Elmham says that Mul has been erroneously ranked by 'some persons' in the list of Kentish kings, and that his ashes were buried in St. Augustine's, 'juxta reges Cantiæ præcedentes.' According to Henry of Huntingdon he had 'deserved and brought down on himself the curses' of Kentish monks.

[3] Chronicle, l. c.

[4] Bede, v. 7 : 'Simul etiam sperans,' &c. Elmham imagined that both 'Cadwalader king of the Britons' and Cadwalla king of the West-Saxons went to Rome, and died there, on the same day! p. 270. The Abingdon Chronicler (i. 4) puts into Cadwalla's mouth a penitential confession, 'Creator creaturarum Deus, miserere mei super omnes homines miseri,' &c., and adds that he resolved to be baptized 'cum majori solemnitate, although the sacrament has not the less efficacy in itself propter personas baptizantium.'

[5] The Chronicle dates Cadwalla's journey in 688: compare Bede's date, 'the third year of Aldfrid.' Cadwalla, then, staid at Rome some months, for he died there in the spring of 689. He probably went through a course of instruction; see above, p. 298.

borne the banner of Wessex through so many battles against
the defenders of their own soil, who had dipped his hands in
the blood of a Christian king and earl, of crowds of Christians
in Kent and Sussex, and of the two royal boys whom he
allowed to be christened before he slew them,—who, himself
as yet unpledged to Christ, had thought to secure His favour
for invasion by promising to give part of its spoils to Wilfrid,—this prince got the benefit of a corrupt tone of thought
among contemporary Christians, and bought, far too cheaply,
even at such hands as Bede's[1], the honours of Christian
piety by receiving baptism under the name of Peter, and from
the hands and under the sponsorship of ' Peter's successor[2],'
on Easter Eve, April 10, 689. His own anticipation was
fulfilled : he was taken ill during Easter-week, while he still
wore his white baptismal garment[3], and died on the 20th of
April. A convert of such rank and renown was naturally
honoured with a burial in St. Peter's : and Bede preserves the
tumid verses in which the writer of his epitaph celebrated
his abandonment of his kingdom, his 'wondrous faith,' his
reverence 'for Peter and for Peter's see,' and his speedy removal
to a heavenly kingdom, and to the fellowship of 'the sheep
of Christ,' after the 'cleansing grace' had renewed his soul,
and he had partaken of light at the source of its world-wide
diffusion[4]. According to the few words in prose which the
visitor to St. Peter's would read immediately below this
intensely Roman panegyric, Cadwalla was about thirty years
of age. He was succeeded on his abdication—for his journey

[1] Bede, v. 7 : ' Devotionis ipsius .... studium religionis.' It never occurred
to Bede (and that it did not, is a fact of painful significance) that Cadwalla's
manifest duty was to receive baptism from his own West-Saxon bishop, and
then to remain at home and govern his people like a just man and a Christian.

[2] The epitaph calls Sergius 'ipse pater Fonte renascentis.' We may assume
that the Chronicle is right in saying, 'He received baptism from the pope.'
So St. Birinus was both the baptizer and the godfather of Cuthred ; see above,
p. 155.

[3] ' In albis adhuc positus.' Although the metrical epitaph says, ' quem .. gratia
... Protinus albatum vexit in arce poli,' and again, ' candidus,' he cannot have
strictly retained the ' whites ' until the day of his death, which was outside the
Paschal octave. The poem, ' de Templo Buggæ,' says he was taken ill ' *post*
albas.' See above, p. 124.

[4] ' Splendificumque jubar ... carperet ... Ex quo vivificus fulgor ubique
fluit.'

to Rome, as Bede says, was equivalent to an abdication—by Ini, or Ine, often called Ina, descended from a younger son of Cadwalla's ancestor Ceawlin [1]: whose accession suggests to Bede the mention, not of his 'laws' or of his ecclesiastical benefactions, but of his own abdication and departure to 'the Apostles' threshold,' in the hope, as a dominant superstition taught even Bede to say, that the saints might give him all the friendlier welcome in heaven. But, in 688, according to Bede's reckoning [2], thirty-seven years lay between the accession of Ine and that journey which he undertook when his wife, by a strange symbolic lesson, had taught him that this world's glory would pass away [3].

His first act, it seems [4], was to renew the war against Kent; it lasted until the people, weakened by previous invasions and intestine divisions, were glad to make terms with him by a 'wer-gild' for the death of Mul. There is a difference of reckoning as to the accession of their next king Wihtred, the legitimate representative of the 'Æscingas' or descendants of Æsc son of Hengist [5]. He was the brother of the slain Eadric; but he did not for some few years succeed in making good his claim to the whole realm of Kent [6]. And while the

---

[1] See the Genealogies in App. to Florence. Ine there appears as son of Kenred the 'sub-regulus,' and great-grandson of Cutha, who was son of Cuth-wine, the younger brother of Cadwalla's great-grandfather Cutha. He had a brother Ingels, and two sisters reputed as saints, Cuthburga, the foundress of the Abbey of Wimborne, and Cwenburga. The fiction that he was Cad-walla's nephew is connected with the Welsh tale about 'Cadwalader' and his nephew 'Ini.' See above, p. 357.

[2] Bede dates Ine's abdication in 725: the Chronicle dates it in 728.

[3] Malm. G. Reg. i. 35.

[4] According to some MSS. of Malm. l. c.: see Elmham, p. 264. Bromton dates this later, X Script. 758; as the Chronicle dates the peace in 694. The wer-gild in this case is variously described; see Palgrave, p. 408.

[5] He was son of Egbert, and great-grandson of Eadbald.

[6] According to the Chronicle, a. 694, he succeeded in 694, and reigned thirty-three winters, having been joint king with Webheard (Swebhard) in 692. But his death is dated in 725, as if he had only reigned thirty-one years. Bede says, iv. 26, that after Lothere's death, Eadric reigned for a year and a half, i. e. until August, 686: 'quo defuncto, reges *dubii* vel externi' ravaged Kent for some time, ' donec legitimus rex Victred, id est filius Ecgberti, being estab-lished in the kingdom, delivered his people, by his piety and his activity, from external invasion.' Bede says that Wihtred and Swebhard were reigning in Kent in 692 (v. 8): and that in 725 Wihtred died after a reign of thirty-four and a half years (v. 23)—reckoned, of course, so as to begin before his

secular affairs of the ancient realm were in this confusion, it CHAP. XI.
was bereft of its great ecclesiastical head. Theodore was Death of Theodore.
eighty-eight years old in the year after Cadwalla's baptism.
He had already, it seems, approved of the publication, by
some South-English cleric, of certain answers given by himself, mostly to a presbyter called Eoda, to questions on points
of penitential discipline[1]. Hence the collection of these
answers is called Theodore's Penitential. But it contains
some statements of opinion which cannot well have come
from Theodore[2]. On the whole, and with some exceptions,
it is characterised by austerity, and a disposition to provide
by express and detailed rule for all varieties of cases. It
exhibits that knowledge of Greek customs as differing more
or less from Roman, which we should expect from a native
of Tarsus[3]. It also shows, here and there, a certain loftiness
and insight which well become the character of the great
primate[4]. And it points to something like a settled system
of district church life[5], as if Theodore had endeavoured to

sole kingship. Hen. Hunt. says, ' he held the kingdom of Kent thirty-two
years, nobiliter et pacifice. He went to meet Ine with pacific entreaty, and
persuaded him to accept a fine for Mul's death.' Later, he assigns to Wihtred
nearly thirty-four years ; Hist. Angl. iv. 619. Malmesbury celebrates the
king's piety and prosperity, Gest. Reg. i. 35.

[1] Above, p. 257. Cp. Haddan and Stubbs, iii. 173 ff. The compiler describes
himself as a ' discipulus Umbrensium,' and says that Eoda is ' reported '
to have obtained the greater number of these rules, or statements of opinion,
from Theodore himself, in answer to his inquiries. From the ' Dialogue of
Egbert ' we learn that Theodore established the observance of a fast during
the twelve days before Christmas ; Haddan and Stubbs, iii. 413.

[2] E.g. b. 1. c. 5. s. 6,—the opinion that a person baptized by a heretic who
did not believe rightly in the Trinity ought to be baptized again. The compiler
says, ' Hoc Theodorum dixisse non credimus contra Nicenæ concilium,' a
mistake for the Council of Arles. See too b. 1. c. 9. s. 12 as to one ordained
while unbaptized. In b. 2. c. 12. s. 5 the husband of a faithless wife is allowed
to divorce her and take another. See above, p. 257.

[3] See b. 1. c. 11. s. 1 ; c. 12. s. 1, 3 ; b. 2. c. 2. s. 14 ; c. 3. s. 2, 7, 8 ; c. 4. s. 4 ;
c. 8 ; c. 12. s. 6, 8.

[4] E.g. ' True conversion can take place at the last hour, quia Dominus non
solum temporis, sed et cordis inspector est ;' b. 1. c. 8. s. 5. ' Confessio autem
soli Deo agatur licebit, si necesse est. (Et hoc *necessarium* in quibusdam
codicibus non est') ; b. 1. c. 12. s. 7. ' Foolish and impracticable vows are to
be broken ;' b. 1. c. 14. s. 6. ' De mortuo autem Dei solius est notitia ;' b. 2.
c. 14. s. 2. ' The sick may take food and drink at any hour ;' b. 2. c. 14. s. 13.

[5] E.g. b. 1. c. 9. s. 7, ' presbiter in propria provincia ;' b. 2. c. 1. s. 1,
' ecclesiam licet ponere in alium locum ;' c. 2. s. 7, ' presbitero licet . . . popu-

establish such a system in the Kentish church, and had largely succeeded.

Theodore died on the 19th of September, 690 [1]. It was said that he had long before foretold the age at which he would die, as having had it impressed on him in a dream. He was buried in the monastery of SS. Peter and Paul, and within the church itself, because the northern ' porch,' the burial-place of his predecessors, was now full [2]. On his tomb was engraven an epitaph of thirty-four verses [3], of which Bede gives us, as sufficient specimens, the first four and the last four, and surpasses all that they may have said by the simple testimony, ' In his episcopate the English Churches received more spiritual benefit than they could ever gain before his time.'

lum benedicere in Parasceue ; ' and on laics paying tithe ' suas ad ecclesias,' c. 14. s. 10. Cp. Bede, v. 4, 12. Willibrord planted this system in Frisia ; Alcuin, Vit. Willibr. i. 11. See above, pp. 178, 245, and Lord Selborne, Anc. Facts and Fictions, p. 118.

[1] Bede, v. 8.

[2] Bede, ii. 3. Elmham, p. 286.

[3] For ' pausare ' as used in the first line see above, p. 267.

CHAPTER XII.

THE burial-day of such a prelate as Theodore must always be an epoch in the history of a Church. It is not hard to enter into the thoughts of the high ecclesiastics who preceded the corpse, as it was borne, for the first time at the interment of any archbishop, through the northern porch, now full of sacred remains, into the actual church of St. Peter;—who looked down, at the close of the rite, into that open grave, dug where the inner wall of the nave just ran between it and the sepulchre of Augustine. There stood the venerable Hadrian, in his place as abbot of the minster which thus asserted its high privilege; he who had escaped the burden of the archbishopric by recommending the stronger man who had just laid it down; he who, as companion, adviser, and fellow-teacher, had not a little aided him to bear it. And near the grave there would be a few prelates who had been suffragans to the first effective metropolitan: Gebmund of Rochester, we may be sure, attended, and probably Erkenwald of London, infirm as he was, and Heddi of the great West-Saxon diocese, unless the war between Kent and Wessex had prevented his coming. Since Wilfrid had returned to York, there had been no bishop in Sussex. By one account, Tyrhtel was now bishop of Hereford [1]; Cuthwin of Leicester was apparently dead: Saxulf was probably failing: Bosel of Worcester was doubtless detained at home by infirmities which disabled him for his work. Acci and Badwin would

[1] Mon. H. Brit. p. 538.

hardly travel from Dunwich and Elmham, nor Ethelwin from Sidnacester, nor Wilfrid, John, and Eadbert from the North. The bishops actually present at these memorable obsequies would feel that 'a prince and a great man' was indeed gone from them: they might occasionally have fretted under his absolutism, but they could not fail to appreciate the blank caused by his departure. All would have a sense of a void which could not be filled; the Church was inevitably the weaker and poorer for the loss of that majestic character, with its dominating will and its rare faculties for government. Whenever any difficulty or emergency might arise, it would be the harder to confront without Archbishop Theodore.

For the present, the bark of the Church appeared to be in smooth waters. The kings were friendly, on the whole, to the episcopate: if uncertainty still hung over the future of the throne of Ethelbert, Sebbi of Essex was a man of exceptional piety, of whom it was even said that he would have been fitter for a bishopric than for a kingdom[1]: Aldwulf of East-Anglia was he who had aided in the foundation of Ely: Ethelred of Mercia possessed a large measure of that personal religiousness which distinguished so remarkably the offspring of the 'strenuous' Pagan Penda: and Wessex and Sussex had exchanged Cadwalla, with his fierce passions and inconsistent impulses, for a king who deserves the name Ine's Laws. of great[2], and who in one of the early years of his reign[3] convened a West-Saxon Witenagemot which enacted what are

----

[1] Bede, iv. 11 : 'Unde multis visum et sæpe dictum est, quia talis animi virum, episcopum magis quam regem ordinari deceret.'

[2] Freeman, Old-Engl. Hist. p. 69. 'As a warrior Ina was equal, as a legislator he was superior, to the most celebrated of his predecessors;' Lingard, H. E. i. 135. ' Whether he came to the throne by Cadwalla's adoption or by election of the great men, .. is unknown to us;' Schmid, Die Gesetze der Angelsachsen, p. xxxvi. ' From the time when he first appears on the stage of history until in the fulness of his prosperity he put on the pilgrim's dress, and died in obscurity and poverty at Rome, his conduct is everywhere pure, noble, disinterested ;' Stevenson, Pref. to Abingd. Chron. ii. p. xi.

[3] See Johnson, Engl. Canons, i. 129. He would date these laws in 693: see too his editor's note. Lingard, H. E. i. 135, adopts this date. Haddan and Stubbs, iii. 214, say, 'probably A.D. 690.' Erkenwald seems to have died in 693 (ib. 218): and it is hardly probable that he would be able, from his

called the 'Dooms' or Laws 'of Ine[1].' At this assembly not
only Heddi of Winchester, but Erkenwald of London was
present; both are spoken of similarly as Ine's bishops, and
this would suggest that Ine had succeeded, for the time, in
establishing his supremacy over London, which was generally
connected by some such ties with Mercia rather than with
Wessex[2]. 'A great number of' monastic 'servants of God'
were present at this gathering: among them, we may be
tolerably sure, Aldhelm of Malmesbury had his place. The
'right laws' there enacted had reference to 'the health of
souls' as well as to the stability of the realm, and thus
illustrate the peculiarly close union of 'Church and State' in
the Old-English Christian kingdoms[3], in which it was natural
to describe the Witenagemot as a 'Synod,' and its secular
decrees were sometimes blended with ordinances of a directly
religious character[4]. This interpenetration of the spiritual and
temporal societies was exhibited on an inferior stage when
bishop and ealdorman appeared, sitting side by side, at the
shire-mote, 'to expound God's law and the world's law[5].' Of
the seventy-nine laws of Ine, those which relate to the
Church deal with various points of Church-life and Church-
rights. Thus, they enforce, under penalty of 'bôt[6]' or pecu-

infirmities, to come into Wessex for a laborious session of the Witan, in the
last year or two of his life. On the other hand, a year or two at least must
have elapsed between Ine's accession and this assembly.

[1] Johnson, i. 131; Thorpe, Anc. Laws, p. 45; Haddan and Stubbs, iii.
214. One remarkable point in these laws is that Ine legislates in the lifetime and 'with the counsel and teaching of his father Kenred,' who never
reigned.

[2] Lingard, H. E. i. 136; Haddan and Stubbs, iii. 218.

[3] Freeman, i. 369, 'The nation was deeply religious; the Church was deeply
national;' and Stubbs, Const. Hist. i. 268, 'The relation of the Church to the
State was thus close, although there was not the least confusion as to the
organisation of functions, or uncertainty as to the limits of the powers of each.'

[4] See the laws of Cnut, made in a Gemot at Winchester. They begin by
ordaining 'that men above all other things should ever love and worship one
God.' Alfred's 'Dooms' begin with the Decalogue, and include the decree of
the Council of Jerusalem. For a lax use of 'synodus' see Bede, iii. 25;
iv. 28; v. 19; Muratori, Lit. Rom. ii. 190.

[5] Lingard, A.-S. Ch. i. 101; Kemble, ii. 385; Robertson, Hist. Ch. iii. 187.
The Roman legates who held a synod in 787 forbade bishops 'in conciliis suis
sæcularia judicare;' Haddan and Stubbs, iii. 452.

[6] See Thorpe, Anc. Laws, p. 393, for a list of ecclesiastical 'bôts.'

CHAP. XII. niary satisfaction, the baptism of infants within thirty nights from birth[1],—the abstinence from work on Sunday[2],—the observance of 'right rule' by all God's 'theowes' or bond-servants, i.e. the monastic bodies[3],—the due payment of 'Church-scot[4]' every Martinmas for the roof and hearth owned at the preceding mid-winter. They recognise the position of a communicant, or one who 'goes to Housel[5],' as making his oath of higher value. They refer to the institution of sponsorship, and define the 'bôt' for the slaughter of a 'bishopson,' or godson in confirmation[6], as half that for a godson properly so called. They presuppose the special solemnity of an oath taken before a bishop. They guard the privilege of sanctuary[7], as sheltering even capital offenders. They order that he who buys a slave or freeman of his own race, and sends him over sea, shall pay his wer-gild, and 'make deep satisfaction to God,' i.e. submit to severe penance inflicted by the bishop[8].

It would have been difficult under any circumstances to find a successor to Theodore; and the election was apparently yet further delayed by the troubles of the kingdom of Kent. And during this interval, the question between Wilfrid and his adversaries was again stirred in Northumbria. For some time after his return in 686, we learn from his biographer that 'peace and quietness abounded between him and the most wise king, with the enjoyment of nearly every form of good.' But, by degrees, disagreement began to alternate

---

[1] See canons under king Edgar, no. 15, Thorpe, p. 396, that every child is to be baptized within thirty-seven nights. Laws of North. Priests, no. 10, ib. 417, say, within nine nights.

[2] See above, p. 343.

[3] 'Servus,' 'famulus,' 'famula,' or 'ancilla Dei,' being used in a specific sense; e.g. Bede, Præf., i. 23; iii. 8; iv. 8, 23.

[4] On Church-scot, a Church-due consisting principally of corn, see Lingard, A.-S. Ch. i. 190; Kemble, ii. 559; Stevenson's Chron. of Abingdon, ii. 437; Thorpe's Glossary to Ancient Laws.

[5] 'Husl-gengea,' Laws, 15, 19. Bede lamented the infrequency of Communion among Northumbrian Churchmen, Ep. to Egb. 9. See Council of Clovesho, 747, c. 23, urging more frequent Communion.

[6] 'To be bishopped' was an old phrase for being confirmed; see Donne's Poems, p. 173.

[7] See above, p. 93.

[8] Johnson, i. 134.

with concord: and Eddi tells us, with a rapid variation of CHAP. XII. metaphors, that those who had caused the former enmity succeeded in rekindling the torch of dissension, and stirring the sea until they wrecked the bark [1]. Three grounds of difference, we are told, came definitely to the front 'after five years' had elapsed from Wilfrid's restoration—that is, in the latter part of 691.

The first was a grievance of long standing: certain property belonging to the church of York was unjustly detained in other hands [2].

The second matter was of broader significance: it seems that ever since Eadhed had returned from Lindsey and established himself as bishop at Ripon, there had been a desire on the part of the Northumbrian government to make that church a permanent see. The prospect was specially galling to Wilfrid. To take from him Ripon, the home of his presbyterate and of his first years in the episcopate, was to touch him in the tenderest point: this minster was dearer to him than Hexham, dearer in one sense than York itself [3]. There was doubtless no day in his past life to which he looked back with greater pleasure than to the day on which, in the presence of all the magnates of Northumbria, he had solemnly dedicated the basilica, and, standing before its altar, with his face to the assembly, had recited a list of all the lands secured to him by royal grant, and of all the sacred places which the British clergy had held and forsaken [4]. When he resumed the see of York, he had also recovered Ripon, Eadhed having made way for him. But now it seemed that he was himself to make way for the return of Eadhed, and the minster of St. Peter was to be changed for good into a cathedral church. Never again, if this plan were carried out, would he be able to call Ripon his own: the church with its stately columns and cloisters, the special treasure which it boasted in a superbly jewelled and richly coloured Gospel-book, the very ground associated with early plans and hopes, and with not

---

[1] Eddi, 45.

[2] Eddi, 'Territoriis et possessionibus suis injuste privatur.'

[3] See Lingard, A.-S. Ch. i. 139.

[4] Above, p. 243.

CHAP. XII. a little of self-restraining patience, would pass into other keeping [1].

But, thirdly, this requirement, to him personally so grievous, was but part of a wider demand. He must accept, it was said, 'the decrees of Archbishop Theodore [2].' What decrees? Not the canons of the Council of Hertford, to which he had, by his deputies assented at the time. Nor, again, those arrangements which Theodore had made 'in his last days, when he invited all the Churches to canonical peace and unanimity:' that is, apparently, the arrangements by virtue of which Wilfrid had returned to York in 686. The decrees now pressed upon his acceptance were 'those which Theodore ordained in the middle part of his time, when discord had arisen' in Northumbria [3]: in other words, the partition of the old Northumbrian diocese, without Wilfrid's consent, into several dioceses, according to the original plan of Egfrid and Theodore, which would not have ousted Wilfrid from the church of York, but would have made him one of four bishops of the Northumbrian kingdom, then including Lindsey; against which partition he had signified his intention to appeal, and had been thereupon deprived of York itself. He was now, in effect, called upon to acknowledge that this mode of increasing the episcopate in Northumbria had not been matter for protest, still less for appeal; and to give up, once for all, those safeguards under which, according to the Pope's synodical judgment, such an increase might be canonically

---

[1] About forty-three years later, Bede complained that owing to the 'very foolish grants of preceding kings' to monastic communities, 'it was not easy to find a place where a new episcopal see might be erected;' i.e. the most desirable places were monopolised by monasteries. He advised that some monastic church should, by proper authority, be turned into a cathedral, and the community be permitted to choose the bishop, one of themselves, if possible,—at any rate from within the diocese; Ep. to Egb. 5.

[2] See Eddi, 45.

[3] Malmesbury calls them 'decrees which, when pronounced in the middle period, are known to have stirred up discord;' C. P. iii. 104. Eadmer, ever loyal to Canterbury, says that whereas no English bishop could safely gainsay, 'vel leviter,' the decrees of the primate, those decrees which Wilfrid resisted were 'ea quæ . . . ut fertur, pro libitu, non pro ratione statuerat;' c. 46. See Smith's Bede, p. 754, 'of which decrees, however, they were not ignorant that Theodore had repented.'

secured. After his return in 686, he had accepted what he
could get, the full possession of the diminished diocese of
York, including his minster at Ripon, and also the temporary
government of Hexham and of Lindisfarne, considered as
existing dioceses. He had not been recognised, in the first
instance, as the one legitimate bishop of all Northumbria,
nor enabled to meet his brethren in provincial synod in
order to choose bishops for new dioceses, to be then formed
out of his own. And now, most probably in consequence
of something that he had done or said, the king required him
to surrender definitely his claims asserted in 678, and affirmed
and guarded by Rome in 679, to a control over the diocesan
subdivision of Northumbria. The question was immediately
connected with the proposed severance of Ripon from York :
but it really brought out the entire difference between the
Northumbrian authorities and the Roman Council. Wilfrid
held himself free, when Aldfrid proffered a reconciliation,
to waive for the time a part of his full rights; but not
to abandon them wholly and in perpetuity. Reverence for
Rome, as he would say, of itself forbade such a surrender :
and he said so in plain words, which became an occasion
for depriving him once more of York. Bosa, no doubt,
returned to York as bishop; and Eadhed, perhaps, resumed
possession of Ripon. It is not to be supposed that Wilfrid
on this occasion, any more than when he stood before the
Roman Council[1], denied the expediency of a plurality of
bishops for the North : he had, on the contrary, admitted
that it might be desirable to appoint more bishops, and
the dispute was as to the terms of their appointment, and
the questions of order and justice involved in Theodore's
decrees.

If we had only Bede's narrative, we should indeed know
little of many events in Wilfrid's story. He says nothing
of the exiled bishop's attempts, after his release from imprisonment at Dunbar, to find a home in Mercia or in Wessex.
He says nothing of that imprisonment itself[2]. So on this
occasion, it is but incidentally, in the course of chapters on

[1] Above, p. 304.
[2] Bede, iv. 13; v. 19. See above, p. 308.

CHAP. XII. the monastery of Whitby and on missions [1], that he alludes
to the sojourn of Wilfrid in Mercia after his second 'expulsion' from York.   That sojourn is briefly described by Eddi
as following immediately on his refusal to accept the terms
proposed by Aldfrid. 'He went to his faithful friend, Ethelred
king of the Mercians, who, out of reverence for the Apostolic
See, received him with all honour:' it was not now as in 681,
when Ethelred compelled Berthwald, for political reasons,
to send Wilfrid out of his district.   Every piece of property
—and there were many such—which Wilfrid held in the
Midlands, had, as we have seen, been restored to him at
Theodore's request: and now, when he entered the Mercian
realm, episcopal work was at once found for him.   While
Saxulf of Lichfield [2] was succeeded by Hedda, the see of
Leicester [3], formerly held by Cuthwin, was placed in Wilfrid's
keeping; and he ranks, accordingly, in Florence's catalogue,
as the second of twenty-three bishops of 'Mid-Anglia [4].'
One of his first episcopal acts must have been specially
interesting to him as a Northumbrian.   Bosel, bishop of
Worcester, was no longer able to discharge his duties [5]: age
or illness had broken him down.   It was arranged, therefore,
that he should resign, and that another bishop should take
his place.   By an unanimous resolution, a priest named Oftfor
was elected: he had been a monk of Whitby under Hilda,
and, in his desire of some 'more perfect' system of discipline, as Bede expresses it, had gone to study at Canterbury
under Theodore.   After some time thus spent, he had visited
Rome, and on his return had settled among the Hwiccians
in Gloucestershire and Worcestershire, still governed by the
Consecration of Oftfor. sub-king Osric.   In that district Oftfor preached, and, as
Bede is careful to add, lived in consistency with his preaching:

[1] See Bede, iv. 23, 'per Vilfridum beatæ memoriæ antistitem,' &c.; and
v. 11, 'Vilfrid qui tunc ... in Merciorum regionibus exulabat.'

[2] Eddi makes Saxulf's death precede Wilfrid's Mercian episcopate. The
Chronicle is wrong in dating it A.D. 705. The true date is 691.

[3] Not that he was regularly settled there as bishop of the place; see Smith's
Bede, p. 755, who, however, thinks that it was Lichfield which was entrusted
to him, between Saxulf's death and Hedda's consecration.

[4] Saxulf had for a time held both sees.

[5] See Bede, iv. 23.

and after he had for some time commended himself to the _{CHAP. XII.} estimation of the Hwiccian Church, he was, at Ethelred's bidding, consecrated by Wilfrid in 692, 'because no one as yet was ordained bishop in place of Theodore [1].'

Wilfrid's troubles again bring us into the circle of missionary activities. We must go back a little, and observe that the priest Egbert, whom we last heard of as remonstrating against Egfrid's invasion of Ireland, had soon afterwards conceived the idea of going as a missionary [2] to some of the German tribes 'from which the Angles and Saxons of Britain were known to be sprung [3].' Mysterious intimations, however, were said to have warned him that he was not to go to the Continent, but to 'the monasteries of Columba, because their ploughs did not go straight, and it was his duty to recall them to the straight path [4]:' he at first neglected the alleged oracle, and had actually prepared to embark, when a storm destroyed no small part of the ship's cargo. Egbert then abandoned his hopes: a friend of his named Wictbert, who had been a hermit for many years in Ireland, attempted to make some impression on the Frisians to whom Wilfrid had preached with such success about ten years before. In this good work he laboured, but in vain. The Frisian chief [5]

Missions to Frisia.

Wictbert.

---

[1] See Ethelred's grant of lands 'to my venerable bishop Oftfor' for the church of St. Peter in Worcester, Kemble, Cod. Dipl. i. 35.

[2] 'Well-descended men' among the English of this period 'cannot rest till they have wandered forth to carry the tidings of redemption into distant and barbarous lands; a life of abstinence and hardship, to be crowned by a martyr's death, seems to have been hungered and thirsted after by the wealthy and noble;' Kemble, ii. 363. See above, p. 299.

[3] Bede, v. 9: 'a quibus Angli,' &c.

[4] 'Aratra eorum non recte incedunt.' The story is remarkable. A brother who had formerly attended on Boisil of Melrose told Egbert that Boisil, 'once his most loving teacher and nourisher,' had appeared to him in a dream, and given him this message. Egbert bade the monk say nothing about it, 'ne forte illusoria esset visio;' an indication that stories of this kind were scrutinised. 'But while silently pondering the matter, he feared it was true: yet still he would not abandon his purpose of going to teach the heathen.' The 'brother' again came, and said that Boisil had rebuked him for having given the message negligently. Again Egbert replied as before; and 'though thus assured of the vision, he nevertheless attempted to begin journey.'

[5] Bede calls him a king; v. 9. So Alcuin, Vit. Willibr. i. 6. Alcuin says that he received Willibrord kindly, but was hardened against his preaching,

CHAP. XII. Radbod was not like Adalgis : he did not, indeed, prohibit the preaching of Christianity, and in after-days he yielded so far to the exhortations of bishop Wulframn of Sens as to come to the very edge of the baptismal font, and only drew back when, in reply to his sudden question, the bishop told him that his ancestors were undoubtedly among the lost [1] :—but still he did not hearken to Wictbert, who had to accept disappointment, return to Ireland, and confine himself to the work of 'edifying his neighbours by his example, since he had failed to win strangers to the faith [2].' Two years having been spent in the effort thus abandoned, Egbert looked about

Willi-
brord.

for other instruments, and found a mighty one in Willibrord, a pupil of his own, and like him of Northumbrian birth [3], who had spent some time as a boy in Wilfrid's abbey at Ripon, and had gone to Ireland at the age of twenty, partly from desire of 'a still stricter life,' and partly in order to profit by Irish learning. He now, in his thirty-third year [4], accepted the call to go to Frisia, and set forth with twelve companions in 690 [5]. One seems to see him, tall and dignified in person, with signal attractions in the grave beauty of his face, and the cheerful kindness of his speech and manner [6]. The party landed at the mouth of the

until, after a bold warning from the bishop, he said frankly, 'I see that you do not fear my threats, and you speak as you act;' Vit. Will. i. 9, 10. (Op. ii. 188.)

[1] Vit. S. Wulfr.: 'Certum est damnationis accepisse sententiam.' Whereupon Radbod 'pedem a fonte retraxit,' saying, 'he could not go without the company of his predecessors, and sit down with a few poor folk in *that* heavenly kingdom;' see Maclear, Apostles of Med. Eur. p. 106.

[2] Bede, v. 9: 'Tunc reversus,' &c. See above, p. 303, on Dicul. For other cases of missionary failure, see Hardwick, Ch. Hist. M. Ages, p. 118, Friedrich in Iceland; p. 129, Gottschalk king of the Wends, who after twenty years of labour was murdered by his subjects; p. 229, Meinhard in Livonia. Olga failed with her son, but succeeded with her grandson; p. 130. See above, p. 117.

[3] His father Wilgis became a hermit on a promontory in the Humber. While yet an infant, Willibrord was given over by his pious mother to the brethren at Ripon. See Alcuin, Vit. Willibr. i. 1, 3. See above, pp. 160, 182.

[4] Alcuin, Vit. Will. i. 5. See Frobenius on Vit. i. 23. Bede, v. 10.

[5] Frobenius (Alcuin, ii. 185) and Lingard (A.-S. Ch. ii. 330) give this date. On the fondness shown by saints for the apostolic number of twelve, see Reeves's Adamnan, p. 299. See above, p. 146.

[6] Alcuin, Vit. Will. i. 23 : 'statura decens,' &c. His courage was of the

Rhine, in the harbour of Catwic[1], visited the old Roman
town of Trajectum, ‘the Passage,’ Trecht or Utrecht, where
six years later Willibrord was to fix his archbishopric, and then
finding Radbod and his Frisians, as Wictbert had left them,
in the ‘foulness of Pagan customs[2],’ ‘turned aside to Pippin
duke of the Franks,’ called Pippin of Heristal, the great
Austrasian who, four years previously, had virtually put an
end to the Merwing period of ‘chaos,’ and was ‘ruling
unquestioned over the whole Frankish race[3].’ He, the true
founder of the new sovereignty which became imperial in the
person of his great-grandson, anticipated Charles himself in
his readiness to promote Christian and ecclesiastical activity.
Even as Boniface, many years later, found ‘the patronage’ of
another ‘prince of the Franks’ indispensable for his episcopal
success[4], Willibrord received a glad welcome from Pippin,
who ‘sent him to preach to the heathen people of
Hither Frisia[5],’ the land of the Meuse, and supported his
work ‘with sovereign authority, conferring great favours
on those who were willing to receive the faith, insomuch that
by aid of Divine grace, the missionaries in a short space
converted many from idolatry[6].’ Willibrord lost no time in
repairing to Rome, to obtain the ‘license and blessing’ of
Pope Sergius for his missionary enterprise; and during his
absence ‘the brethren who were in Frisia chose one of their
own number to be ordained for them as bishop[7].’ His name Swidbert.
was Swidbert[8], ‘a man of virtuous life and humble in heart;’
and at the request of the missionaries, there being still no arch-

heroic type; see the story of the Fositeland well, and that of his assault on
the idol; ib. i. 10, 13. See Maclear, p. 101. But he gently restrained his
attendants from punishing an insult offered to him (ib. i. 14), and ‘ut erat
mitissimus,’ gave wine from his flask to poor men asking alms (16).

[1] Alb. Butler, Nov. 7.

[2] Alcuin, Vit. Will. i. 6, 9. Radbod’s ‘heart’ proved ‘stony.’

[3] Kitchin, Hist. Fr. i. 95, 99. The victory of Pippin over the Neustrians,
at Testry, was in 687.

[4] Bonif. Ep. 12.

[5] He had recently won this land from Radbod; Bede, v. 10.

[6] Bede, v. 10.

[7] Bede, v. 11 : ‘Quo tempore fratres,’ &c.

[8] Ann. SS. Bened. iii. 239; Haddan and Stubbs, iii. 225; Lingard, A.-S.
Ch. ii. 334. Alcuin (de Pontif. Ebor. 1073) associates a priest called Vira
with Swidbert.

CHAP. XII. bishop at Canterbury, Wilfrid performed the consecration in 693. The new bishop returned to the Continent, and laboured with much success among the Boructuarians or Bructerians in Rhenish Prussia : but after that people had been expelled by the Saxons, he took refuge with Pippin, who, at his wife's request, gave Swidbert land for a monastery on the isle of Kaiserwerth, then called 'On-the-shore [1],' where he led a very

Martyr-
dom of
the two
Hewalds.

ascetic life, and died in 713. Bede also dwells on the touching story [2] of two Anglian priests, called respectively the Black and the Fair Hewald. They had spent years of study and devotion in Ireland [3], when the examples of Willibrord and his companions led them, with some others [4], into Saxony. They were admitted into the house of a village headman [5], who promised to send them on to the ealdorman [6] of the district ;— in the meantime they 'devoted themselves to prayer and psalmody, and daily offered to God the sacrifice of the salutary Victim, having with them sacred vessels, and a hallowed table to serve as an altar [7].' These strange rites aroused suspicion [8] : if the Angles were allowed to have speech with the ealdorman, 'they might draw him away from the gods to their newfangled Christian religion, and so the whole province might ere long, perforce, be turned from the old ways to the new.' So they suddenly 'fell upon' the two

[1] Bede, v. 11.   His 'heirs' owned the monastery in 731.

[2] Bede, v. 10 : 'Horum secuti exempla.'   Neither Bede nor Alcuin (Pont. Ebor. 1043) hints that they were brothers, as Lingard infers.

[3] Of the two, he of the black hair was the more scholarly.

[4] One of their 'socii' was Tilmon, a man of noble English birth, who had been a thane ('miles'), and had become a monk; Bede, v. 10.

[5] Villicus, the 'town-reeve,' or governor, of a 'vicus.'   See Stubbs, Const. Hist. i. 47, 93.   See above, p. 285.

[6] Bede says that these 'Old Saxons' had no king, but a number of 'satraps' (or governors of districts) who, in war time, cast lots which should lead the army.   These were 'dukes or ealdormen ;' Freeman, Growth of Engl. Constit. p. 34.   See Stubbs, l. c.   The biographer of St. Lebuin says (Pertz, Mon. Germ. Hist. ii. 361) that every Saxon 'pagus' (or 'hundred,' Stubbs, i. 96) had its 'princeps' (see ib. 29).   We find 'satraps' mentioned after 'dukes' in Wihtred's Privilege; Haddan and Stubbs, iii. 242.

[7] Bede, v. 10 : 'Victimæ salutaris.'   See above, pp. 106, 151.

[8] Probably they seemed parts of a 'magicalis scena :' see Vit. S. Lebuini, where the Saxons are made to ask, 'Quidnam est illud phantasma vagabundum, quod suis præstigiis alienat mentes ?' &c. ; and forthwith burn Lebuin's 'little oratory.'

priests, 'and slew Fair Hewald with a rapid sword-stroke, but chap. xii.
Black Hewald with long tortures and horrible dismember-
ment;' and cast the martyrs' corpses into the Rhine. Their
blood was promptly avenged by the ealdorman, who put to
death all the inhabitants of the township, and burned their
houses to the ground. The bodies were recovered, and buried
by Pippin's orders at Cologne. The day of their martyrdom
was the 3rd of October; the year, probably, 695 [1]. It may
be added here that Willibrord was consecrated archbishop of
the Frisians by the hands of Pope Sergius, in St. Cecilia's [2]
at Rome, on the festival of that saint, Nov. 22, 696 : his name
being changed by the Pope to Clement [3]. He staid only a
fortnight in Rome, and then returned to his mission-field,
where he received from Pippin 'a place for his episcopal chair'
at Utrecht, which Bede, here referring to it, calls Wiltaburg [4].
Near this royal fortress he built a cathedral church and
monastery, called that of Our Saviour [5], in imitation of the
Lateran basilica. His episcopate, which included among its
energetic onslaughts on heathenism a desecration of the
fountain and cattle belonging to the idol Fosite in Heligo-
land [6], had lasted thirty-five years when Bede wrote [7], and was
closed by his death in his eighty-second year [8], A.D. 739.
It was a grand career of 'manifold contests in the heavenly

[1] Lingard, A.-S. Ch. ii. 334. So Alb. Butler, 'most probably.' He adds,
'They are honoured through all Westphalia;' Lives of Saints, Oct. 3.

[2] So Bede, v. 11 : 'Ordinatus est autem,' &c. Alcuin says, at St. Peter's
(Vit. i. 7); a not unnatural mistake.

[3] For other such cases, see p. 181.

[4] Cp. Vit. S. Lebuini, Pertz, Mon. Germ. Hist. ii. 361: 'Castrum Wilten-
burg antiquitus dictum, modo vero Trajectum.' Afterwards the monastery at
Utrecht, under its abbot Gregory, included a flourishing 'school,' whence
missionaries went forth. See Vit. S. Liudgeri, i. 9; Pertz, ii. 407.

[5] Boniface, Ep. 90: 'In honore Sancti Salvatoris.' Above, p. 56.

[6] Alcuin, Vit. Will. i. 10. No one might touch the cattle, nor, save in
silence, drink of the well. Willibrord bade his companions kill some of the
cattle for food, and baptized three men in the well 'cum invocatione Sanctæ
Trinitatis.' He thus drew down on his party the fury of the heathen islanders :
one of his band was marked by lot for slaughter, and killed. Cp. Vit. S. Liudg.
19. See above, p. 72.

[7] Bede, v. 11, says, 'he is still sighing after his heavenly reward.' In Vit.
Cuthb. 44, he speaks of a 'clericus Wilbrordi' who paid a visit to Lindisfarne.

[8] Alcuin, Vit. Will. ii. 24. St. Boniface says that he preached fifty years
(a round number) in Frisia; Ep. 90.

CHAP. XII. warfare [1],' during the whole of which, says his illustrious biographer, 'so long as he lived with us, he ceased not to labour in the love of Christ [2].'

Bertwald, archbishop of Canterbury.

Such was the missionary spirit in these typical English Christians towards the close of the first century of the English Church. It is now time to see how the chief seat in that Church was filled, after the vacancy which had caused the application to Wilfrid on behalf of Swidbert. As we have seen, Wihtred, 'the legitimate king of Kent [3],' was obliged for a while to share the kingdom with Swebhard [4]: and these two princes are mentioned by Bede [5] as concurring in the election, on the 1st of July, 692, of Bertwald, otherwise Briht-wald, abbot of the monastery in that old Roman town of Reculver whither Ethelbert had retired from Canterbury in 597, and where Egbert had enabled 'Bass the mass-priest' to build a minster in 669 [6]. Bertwald was 'learned in the Scriptures, and thoroughly conversant with ecclesiastical and monastic rules, although,' as Bede adds, 'he could not be compared to his predecessor.' What we first hear of as to his conduct is not much in his favour. It seems that he declined to be consecrated by any of his future suffragans [7]; and this

---

[1] Bede, v. 11.

[2] Alcuin, Vit. Will. i. 23. See the Judicium Clementis, a series of twenty rules, in Haddan and Stubbs, iii. 226. It has some remarkable points: it forbids any one to fast and take another man's sins on him, for hire. Offerings 'de præda' cannot be received. He who, by negligence, works or shaves himself, &c. on Sunday, and he who communicates after eating, must do penance for a week. He who 'denies God without compulsion' must do penance ten years. Prayer may be made for the soul of a demoniac suicide. But, strange to say, a man who cannot recover his wife from the enemy may, after a year, marry another.

[3] So Hen. Hunt. calls him; Hist. iv. 6. See above, p. 370.

[4] Elmham says that Swebhard was the son of 'Sebba' king of East-Saxons (p. 235), made himself king of Kent by violence (p. 231), and gave a charter to Minster (ib.). But the charter is dubious.

[5] Bede, v. 8.

[6] Chron. a. 669. See Kemble, Cod. Dipl. i. 21; king Lothere grants land in Thanet, called 'Westaney,' 'to thee, Bercuald, and to thy monastery,' with consent of Theodore and Edric, at Reculver, in May, 679. Bertwald was sometimes confounded with Beorwald abbot of Glastonbury, as by Malmesbury in his De Antiq. Glaston. Eccl. (Gale, Script. i. 308): 'Iste Beorwald, transactis decem annis in regimine Glastoniæ, Cantuariensis archiepiscopus fuit.' But Beorwald was abbot while Bertwald was archbishop; Bonif. Ep. 104.

[7] On this, see Haddan and Stubbs, iii. 229.

led to a year's further delay. It was not until St. Peter's
festival in the following year, 693, that he received consecration from Godwin, archbishop of Lyons, whom Bede calls
'metropolitan bishop of Gaul;' and in fact, although it was
not until the eleventh century that the church of Lyons
'obtained the primacy' over three other metropolitan
churches[1], we find its bishop signing before those of Vienne,
Rouen, and Sens, at the Council of Chalons, about 650[2]. It
is interesting to observe that our episcopal succession, inaugurated at Arles, and renewed at Rome, was now reinforced
from the illustrious see of St. Irenæus[3]. On Sunday the
31st of August, the throne which had been nearly three years
vacant in the basilica of Canterbury received its new occupant[4]. Work for him was not wanting, and we find him
joining with King Ethelred and several bishops, including
those of Worcester, Lichfield, Hereford, Elmham, Rochester,
and—which is observable—Wilfrid, now of Leicester, together
with Alric, probably of Dunwich, and another whose name is
lost, in witnessing a grant of land for a nunnery by Oshere,
the new Hwiccian under-king, the date of which is 693[5].
This proves that Oftfor's short episcopate extended at least

---

[1] Neale, Essays on Liturgiology, p. 296. Gregory of Tours calls Nicetius of Lyons a patriarch; H. Fr. v. 21. For Godwin, cp. Gall. Christ.
iv. 50.

[2] Mansi, x. 1193.

[3] When Bertwald arrived, he found at least three bishops in office who had
been consecrated by Theodore,—Heddi, Bosa, and John : and Heddi, as bishop
of Winchester, must surely have taken part in the consecration of Tobias of
Rochester, who would naturally be associated with the archbishop in the
consecration of Daniel, from whom the line descends to archbishop Jaenbert
in 766. Cp. Stubbs, Registr. Angl. pp. 4–11. Elsewhere he suggests that
John may have assisted in Daniel's consecration: Apost. Succ. in Ch. Engl.
p. 21. See above, p. 230.

[4] The 'letters of Sergius' to kings Ethelred, Aldfrid, and Aldwulf, and to
'the bishops throughout Britain,' exhorting them to receive Bertwald, are,
like others given by Malmesbury, very questionable. The tone of this series
of letters suggests that they were written at Canterbury in order to magnify
the archbishopric in connection with Rome. The letter to the king is suspicious even in its address: it omits the West-Saxon king and names the East-
Anglian.

[5] Cod. Dipl. i. 41; Haddan and Stubbs, iii. 232. Oshere's son Ethelward, 'subregulus,' with king Kenred's consent, granted land at Ombersley
to bishop Egwin for Evesham in 706. See Cod. Dipl. i. 64; above, p. 318.

CHAP. XII.

to the latter part of this year : and Gebmund, whose death is referred to the same year by the Chronicle, appears from better evidence to have survived until 696 [1].

Death of
St. Erken-
wald.

It is not quite certain, but it is probable, that the year of Bertwald's arrival was the year of the death of the saintly bishop Erkenwald. He had held the see of London from 675 : he is commonly supposed to have died on the 30th of April, 693 [2]. 'He was regarded in London as an eminent saint,'—so says Malmesbury, who adds that his successors for several generations 'lie under the cloud of obscurity, so that even their tombs are not known :' it is thought a great thing, he adds, among the inhabitants to know even their names [3]. The first of these undistinguished prelates was Waldhere, who received in 694 no less a postulant for the monastic habit

Death of
King
Sebbi.

than his own East-Saxon king, Sebbi. This prince, the son of Seward [4], one of the Pagan sons of King Sabert, must have been far advanced in life when, after thirty years of kingship, he was attacked by an illness which seemed the signal of approaching death. He had been through all those years a devout Christian : at the beginning of his reign, he and those East-Saxons who were under him, in contrast with

[1] See Haddan and Stubbs, iii. 241. Gebmund appears at the Witenagemot of Berghamstede in 696.

[2] Stubbs, Registr. p. 3. Another account would give him only eleven years ; Alb. Butler, April 30. Another prolongs his life to 697 ; see Dugdale, Hist. St. Paul's, p. 215. It was said that the clergy of St. Paul's and the monks of Chertsey contended as to the place of his burial. The mediæval account (Dugdale, Hist. St. Paul's, p. 290) which commits the blunder of calling London a 'metropolitan' church, gives a lively picture of the quarrel : the Londoners forcibly carry off the corpse from Barking, despite the cry of the Chertsey monks, 'He was our abbot !' The rain having swollen the river which they must pass, the monks interpret it as a Divine warning. The Londoners doggedly answer, 'We will go through an armed host, we will besiege strong cities, ere we lose our patron !' A disciple of Erkenwald preaches charity, and suggests prayer for a sign : the waters divide, the weather clears up, the corpse is borne in triumph to St. Paul's. He was buried at first in the nave of his church ; in the later cathedral his shrine was in the Lady chapel. See Dugdale, p. 74; and Dr. Simpson's Chapters in the History of Old St. Paul's, pp. 20, 89. The epitaph contained several fictions.

[3] Malmesb. G. Pontif. ii. 73.

[4] Florence, app. He was therefore the brother of Sigebert the Little, and a kinsman of Sigebert the Good. See a grant, by 'Hodilredus parens Sebbi,' to the abbess of ' Beddanhaam,' witnessed by Sebbi, Erkenwald, and Wilfrid, in Kemble, Cod. Dipl. i. 39.

his nephew and colleague Sighere, had held fast the faith
under the trial of pestilence [1] : ever since, he had been a man
of prayer and almsdeeds, and would even have followed the
perilous example of Sigebert the Learned, and given up his
crown in order to become a monk, had not his wife steadily
refused her consent to such a separation [2]. But now, at last,
when he said to her, 'Let us even at this close of our wedded
life devote ourselves to God's service [3], when we can no longer
enjoy, or rather serve, the world,' she yielded reluctantly to
his desire. He 'took the habit' accordingly before the bishop,
and brought with him a large sum to be spent on the poor,
reserving nothing for himself. His sickness increased, and
brought with it that dread of the last enemy which has often
been permitted to burden the spirit of a faithful servant of
God. But, as it was with Johnson, with the Mère Angélique,
with Maria Theresa, with Charles Wesley, so was it with
Sebbi when the supreme moment really drew near. He had
begged Waldhere to visit him at his palace in London. 'What
if he were to say, or even by gesture express, in the agony of
death, something unworthy of his character [4]? Would the
bishop promise to come, when the hour had arrived, and
assist him in his last struggle, allowing no one else, save
two of his attendant thanes, to be present?' Waldhere
willingly undertook to do so: soon afterwards, the old man
had a dream which persuaded him that he should have a quiet
departure [5]; and he died on the afternoon of the third day
afterwards, 'as if gently falling asleep.' He was buried in
the church of St. Paul, and succeeded by his two sons Sighard
and Swefred [6].

---

[1] See above, pp. 216, 223.

[2] Bede, iv. 11 : 'Erat enim religiosis actibus,' &c. In Ireland, Aodh king
of Leinster had died as abbot and bishop of Kildare in 638 : and Finnachta
the Festive, arch-king, 'became a cleric' for a year in 688 (Four Mast., Tighernach).

[3] Again we observe the unhealthy restriction of this phrase, see p. 376.

[4] 'Personæ,' meaning, of his character as a king.

[5] He seemed to see three men in bright clothing approach him. One sat
down before his bed, and said to the others who were still standing, and who
asked as to Sebbi's condition, that his soul 'would depart on the third day,
without any pain, and amid a great splendour of light.'

[6] Swefred, or, properly, Swebred, united with 'Pæogthath cum licentia

A few months, perhaps, before the death of the 'bishoplike king,' Oftfor of Worcester died about the end of 693 [1], and was succeeded by a prelate whom Bede, to the surprise of William of Malmesbury [2], passes by in silence, but who was afterwards venerated as St. Egwin. He was of princely birth [3], and, like Wilfrid and Benedict Biscop, had at an early age renounced all secular prospects, and in due time entered the priesthood. His biographer tells us that he had much work to do in reclaiming the people of his diocese from heathenish observances and heathenish license. They would retain some practices which were essentially idolatrous [4]; and they would not conform to Christian rules of purity. He 'spoke to them repeatedly,' and usually in tones of stern rebuke [5]. The obstinate natures which his admonitions could not bend were the more embittered against him: we are told that he was accused [6] before King Ethelred, and deprived of his bishopric, and also denounced to the Pope, and that he thereupon repaired to Rome [7], was received with special honour, acquitted of all blame, and sent home with the apostolic benediction; after which he was restored to his see, and became godfather

---

Ædelredi regis comis (comes)' in giving lands at Twickenham to bishop Waldhere, June 13, 704; Cod. Dipl. i. 59. The charter begins, 'Quamvis solus sermo sufficeret ad testimonium, attamen pro cautela futurorum temporum,' &c. It is witnessed by Kenred, the successor of Ethelred.

[1] Haddan and Stubbs, iii. 232.

[2] Malmesb. G. Pontif. iv. 160. He could not account for it.

[3] See his 'Life' in Ann. SS. Bened. iii. 331, and in Chron. Abbatiæ de Evesham (Rolls Series), p. 3 ff. Cp. Alb. Butler, Jan. 11.

[4] See above, pp. 74, 216.

[5] Usually, we infer from his 'Life,' c. 13, he was 'pleasant in speech.'

[6] The common people, 'eum paullatim conjecturis et adinventionibus et rumoribus malis diffamans . . . ab episcopatu eum expulit. Permisit potestas primatis, et admisit hoc excitatus contra eum livor regius;' Chron. Evesh. p. 5.

[7] Here comes in the wild legend of his having loaded his feet as in penitence ('because he did not deny that he was a sinner in God's sight') with chains, the key of which he flung into the Avon: when he reached Rome, his servants bought a large fish for food, and within it the key appeared. The pope heard of this, and, when he saw Egwin, asked absolution and blessing from him, instead of imparting them to him, &c. The pope is called Constantine; but Constantine was not pope until 708, when Egwin went to Rome with king Kenred. Of the story of the chains Malmesbury asks, 'Credendumne putatur quod tradit antiquitas?' G. Pontif. l. c.

to the king's children. This story seems to have grown out of his journey to Rome at a later period.

The war between Wessex and Kent was concluded, as we have seen, by an agreement on the part of the Kentish-men to make pecuniary satisfaction for the death of Mul[1]. This is dated in the year after Bertwald's arrival; and two years later, on the 6th of August[2], in 'the fifth year of King Wihtred, and the ninth indiction,' that is, in 696,—Wihtred's regnal year being reckoned from an earlier date than the death or fall of Swebhard,—a Kentish Witenagemot was held at a 'place called Berghamstyde,'—not the Berkhampstead in Hertfordshire, which would be Mercian, but Bearsted near Maidstone[3]. Bertwald, 'high bishop of Britain,' as he is loftily styled, was present, with Gebmund of Rochester, 'and every degree of the province spoke in accord with the obedient people.' Among the 'Dooms' then enacted were several affecting the Church. It was to be 'free of impost[4]:' but it is probable that already its lands were not excused from contributing to the repairs of roads and fortifications, and to the military service of the realm[5]. The

[1] See above, p. 368.

[2] So 'Rugern' in the record is explained, Johnson, Engl. Can. i. 141.

[3] Johnson, l. c.; Haddan and Stubbs, iii. 238. The vicar of Bearsted informs me that sessions were formerly held on a moated mound, which has tiers of seats above it, near this village.

[4] 'Impost' would here mean the land-tax, estimated in produce or stock; Churton, E. E. Ch. p. 122. Another reading, however, would mean 'freedom in jurisdiction and revenue;' Haddan and Stubbs, iii. 233.

[5] The 'trinoda necessitas,' or 'onus inevitabile,' consisted of the 'bryg-bot,' the 'burh-bot,' and the 'fyrd;' Lingard, H. E. i. 320, and A.-S. Ch. i. 241 ff.; Kemble, i. 301; Freeman, i. 93; Stubbs, Const. Hist. i. 86. It was imposed, apparently, on all church lands in Kent; and Offa of Mercia says of it expressly 'ab eo opere nullum excusatum esse;' cp. Cod. Dipl. i. 92, 204. At first, in Northumbria (and generally, Lingard thinks) lands devoted 'to pious purposes were most likely relieved from all burdens whatsoever;' Kemble, i. 302. Whitby was thus exempt from 'militia terrestris;' so some monastic lands in ancient Scotland were to be free till the day of judgment from tribute or custom, or even from maintenance of the national fabric; Stuart, Book of Deer, p. lxxxvii. It was immunity of this sort which led to the scandal of pseudo-monasteries held by laymen pretending to be abbots; Bede, Ep. to Egb. 7. His indignant censure of this abuse was written at a time when a reaction was setting in against over-indulgence to monasteries; not only was care taken not to free them from the 'necessitas,' but St. Boniface found reason to complain of the 'forced service in royal

CHAP. XII. clergy were to pray for the king, and to 'revere him without command, of their free will,' i.e. pray for him, as a matter of course, in the ordinary Church service[1]. The 'mundbyrd[2],' or penalty for violating the Church's protection, was to be the same as that for violating the king's. Unchastity was to be ecclesiastically punished. A priest who allowed of it, or 'neglected to baptize a sick person, or was so drunk that he could not do it'—a significant provision[3]—was to desist from his ministry until the bishop should judge his case. A tonsured man seeking for hospitality here or there was to have it once; not oftener, unless his rovings were licensed[4]. Emancipation of slaves[5] at the altar was recognised. Servile labour between sunset on Saturday and sunset on Sunday[6] was prohibited. 'Offerings to devils' were to be punished by forfeiture of goods, and such a fine as would have been required to save a man from the pillory[7], had it been in use, or, on another theory, to loosen the grasp of the avenger of blood[8]. To eat flesh on a fast-day, or to give it to dependents, was penal. A bishop, like the king, was excused from oath in giving evidence[9]. A priest, if accused, was to clear himself

building works,' required from English monks in his time; Ep. to Cuthb. c. 11. Such services or burdens, together with 'vectigalia,' were remitted by charters of the eighth century (Cod. Dipl. i. 119, 144, 151). See Lingard, A.-S. Ch. i. 241. The legates in 787 were content to provide against unjust or excessive exactions from 'God's churches;' Haddan and Stubbs, iii. 455.

[1] Stubbs, Const. Hist. i. 203 (or 175).

[2] Properly, the 'holding out of the hand,' as of a patron in defence of a client; see Robertson, Scotl. under Early Kings, ii. 452. Cp. Stubbs, Const. Hist. i. 210. Here it is used for the penalty of violating this protection. On the privilege of sanctuary, cp. Ine's Laws, 5, and see above, p. 93.

[3] Cp. Theodore's Penitential, i. 1; Boniface, Ep. to Cuthb. 10. Drunkenness was already a national vice. Cp. C. of Clovesho, c. 21.

[4] See fifth canon of Hertford, above, p. 254.

[5] See above, p. 316.

[6] Literally, Sunday eve and Monday eve. So Ine's Laws, 3. Comp. Malmesbury, G. Pontif. v. 276, for a story of a woman blamed by her neighbours for spinning after sunset on Saturday. See above, p. 376.

[7] Heals-fang: Johnson, i. 147; Thorpe, Glossary to Ancient Laws.

[8] Robertson, Scotl. under Early Kings, ii. 288.

[9] 'His word, or testimony, like that of the king, was conclusive in itself, and did not require to be supported by the oaths of compurgators;' Palgrave, p. 164. To be excused from oaths was a privilege.

by saying, in his sacred vestments, before the altar, ' I say CHAP. XII.
the truth in Christ, I lie not;' a deacon might do the same.
Inferior clerics, and laymen, were to clear themselves by oath
at the altar. The privileges of a 'housel-ganger' or communicant were recognised, as in the laws of Ine.

It would seem that soon after this assembly bishop Tobias,
Gebmund of Rochester died[1], and was succeeded by Tobias, bishop of
Rochester.
one of the many prelates[2] whom Bertwald consecrated, and
one of the scholarly ecclesiastics who had been trained in the
great school of Canterbury; 'a man,' says Bede, 'of multi-
farious learning, in the Latin, Greek, and Saxon tongues.'
He held the see of Rochester until 726. He was present at Privilege
another Kentish Witenagemot held at Baccanceld[3] or Bap- of Wihtred.
child, near Sittingbourne, when Wihtred forbade 'any layman
to usurp or appropriate what had been given to the Lord and
confirmed with the cross of Christ, and dedicated:' sacrilege
of this sort was described as a 'stripping of the Living God,
or rending of His coat and His heritage.' In the name of
God Almighty, and all Saints, the king commanded all his
successors and all laics of his realm not to take possession
of any monastery which he or his predecessors had given
over to Christ, the Holy Apostles, and the Virgin Mother.
Whenever an abbacy[4] should become vacant, it was for the
bishop of the diocese[5] to give 'counsel and consent' for a
good election, and to bless the person elected. In the archiepiscopal diocese, the archbishop's sanction was to be necessary for any abbatial appointment. All these matters were
to be exempt from secular authority, and subjected to the
metropolitan's control. For greater security, a list of the
monasteries was appended: St. Peter's or Upminster, i.e.

---

[1] See above, p. 388.

[2] Bede, v. 8. For Tobias, see also Bede, v. 23.

[3] Haddan and Stubbs, iii. 238.

[4] In this genuine form of the charter (see Haddan and Stubbs, iii. 241)
nothing is here said about the vacancy of a bishopric, as if that was also
to be filled up by free election. But this is found in the version given
by Wilkins, i. 57, 'Ut quando . . . defungitur, *episcopus*,' &c. Cp. Chron.
694. Lingard says, 'Under Theodore and his immediate successors the
appointment of bishops was generally made in the national synods;' Angl.-
Sax. Ch. i. 91.

[5] 'Parochiæ.' So in Bede, iii. 7: v. 18; Ep. to Egb. 8.

SS. Peter and Paul in Canterbury, Reculver, Southminster, Dover, Folkestone, Lyminge [1], Sheppey, and Hoe. By Southminster was meant Minster in Thanet, where the royal abbess Mildred was still presiding [2] : she signed the document first among five abbesses. 'A further liberty, so the king was made to say, was added [3],' by a grant of entire immunity from all burdens greater and lesser [4], and all exactions on the part of kings or earls, to Christ Church in Canterbury, and to the church of Rochester, and to 'the other above-named churches of God;' but with a salvo that such exemption should not be turned into a bad precedent. Any violator of this grant, whether king or bishop, or abbot, or thane, or any human power, was to be excommunicated, and to forfeit pardon in this world and the next, unless he should have made full satisfaction to the bishop [5] : and the charter itself was to be carefully preserved in the 'Church of the Saviour,' the metropolitan church of Canterbury, as a record and a safeguard for all churches 'in this Kent.' The date of this Privilege of Wihtred seems to fall within the last years of the seventh century.

Of these years there is not much more to be said. Wilfrid continued at Leicester; he did not neglect his own cause, for we find that he made application to Pope Sergius, and received from him a letter confirmatory of the previous Roman decrees [6]; but for any practical effect of such a document he could scarcely hope until some change had passed over the mind of King Aldfrid. He was safe and tranquil under the shadow of the throne of Ethelred; but he must have sorrowed

---

[1] See Wihtred's grants to the basilica of St. Mary at Lyminge, Cod. Dipl. i. 50, 54. On Dover and Folkestone see above, p. 115.

[2] See above, p. 248. She 'died towards the close of the seventh century;' Alban Butler, Feb. 20.

[3] 'Adhuc addimus majorem libertatem.'

[4] 'Ab omnibus difficultatibus sæcularium servitutum . . . ab operibus, majoribus minoribusve gravitatibus,' &c. See above, p. 391.

[5] Menaces of spiritual punishment were often—not always—added as sanctions to charters. Sometimes what is denounced is 'separation from communion of the Body and Blood of Christ,' e. g. Cod. Dipl. i. 30. Another form is, 'Let him know that he will answer for it to Christ,' ib. i. 25; cp. i. 82, 84, 90.

[6] Eddi, 46, 51.

deeply with that prince when the fierce Mercian nobles in chap. xii. 697 put to death his Northumbrian queen Osthryd[1]. In Guthlac of that same year there began that strange and intensely mediæval saintship which made the name of Guthlac of Crowland as fascinating to Mercian piety as Cuthbert's had been to Northumbrian. We hear[2] of the boy as born to a Mercian earl of royal descent, named Penwald, and his wife Tette, baptized after a 'tribe' called Guthlacings,—the original name, as borne by him, signifying Battle-sport[3]: he is described as growing out of childhood without any taint of childish perversity, gentle, sweet-tempered, dutiful, as if 'irradiated by spiritual light:' in early youth the warlike temper wakes up in him,—he is fired with emulation at the thought of 'ancient heroes,'—he becomes the captain of a fierce band, carrying fire and sword through the lands of his enemies, but even then restoring to the plundered a third part of the spoil. Nine years of this foraying life suffice him[4]: he begins to see what life and what death means: he thinks of 'the woeful ends' of mighty princes, estimates the vanity of earthly glory, trembles at the thought of 'the inevitable end.' These musings come into his mind by night[5], and in the morning he bids his comrades find another leader. Their remonstrances are vain: he enters the monastery of men and women,—ruled, like Whitby, by an abbess, named Elfrida,—which had for some time existed in the royal town of Repton[6]. This took place in 697, when he was only twenty-four years old. He at first offended his brother-monks by never tasting any strong

---

[1] Bede, v. 24; Chron. a. 697.

[2] Act. SS. Bened. iii. 265; Life of St. Guthlac by Felix of Jarrow, written in the middle of the eighth century, and evidently after the model of Aldhelm's grandiloquent periods, and with much of the conventionalism of hagiology.

[3] Kingsley's Hermits, p. 304. 'Laking' is an old North-country word for 'playing.'

[4] He spent some time 'in exile' among the Welsh; Felix, 20.

[5] Felix says, 'He remembered to have heard the words, Ne in hieme vel sabbato fuga vestra fiat;' c. 11.

[6] 'Ripadum,' Felix,—'Hreopandun, Repandune,' &c. It was the burial-place of Mercian royalty. Elfrida was succeeded by 'Egburga,' daughter of the East-Anglian king Aldwulf, who sent to Guthlac a leaden sarcophagus and a shroud, Ann. Ord. Ben. ii. 39; Angl. Sac. i. 595.

CHAP. XII. drink[1] 'save in time of Communion;' but his frank, modest, and affectionate disposition disarmed all animosity; and he on his part set himself to imitate the several excellences of the other inmates of the house, and, as his biographer touchingly says, 'the gentleness of all.' After two years spent at Repton[2], he resolved to adopt the hermit-life; and for that purpose, 'with the leave of his elders,' took his journey towards the vast fens which, 'beginning from the banks of the Granta[3]' or Cam, spread northwards in a dreary succession of ponds and marshes and 'black wandering streams[4],' amid which, here and there, islets uplifted their dark masses of wood, 'forests of fir and oak, ash and poplar, hazel and yew.' Arriving in this desolate region, Guthlac asked some of the inhabitants whether they knew of any islet which was uninhabited. One of them, Tatwin by name, said that he knew of one in the remoter parts of the fen, which many had endeavoured to occupy, but had been driven away by 'monsters of the wilderness, and awesome shapes of divers kinds.' Guthlac begged Tatwin to show him the spot, and thereupon was conducted in a fishing-boat to an islet in the marshlands crossed by the Welland and the Nen. This was Crowland[5],

[1] See above, p. 392. He took up this rule of 'total abstinence' from the day on which he received 'the apostolic (i. e. Roman) tonsure.'

[2] 'Psalmis, canticis, hymnis, orationibus, moribusque ecclesiasticis per biennium imbutus;' Felix, 13.

[3] Felix, 14: 'Est in mediterraneorum Anglorum Britanniæ partibus immensæ magnitudinis acerrima palus,' &c. See this copied by Orderic, iv. 16. Compare Malmesb. G. Pontif. iv. 182, that the fens were more than a hundred miles in length. See Turner, i. 322 ff.; Green, Making of Engl. p. 351.

[4] Kingsley's Hermits, p. 301; a very vivid description. Compare Felix: 'Nigris fusis vaporibus et laticibus,' 'umbrosa solitudinis nemora,' 'nubilosos ... eremi lucos,' 'loca spinosa,' 'stagnosa paludis ligustria,' 'densas arundinum compagines.' Henry of Huntingdon describes the fens more pleasantly: 'Palus illa latissima et visu decora, multis fluviis ... irrigata, multis lacubus ... depicta, multis etiam silvis et insulis florida et amœna;' Hist. v. 25, followed by Bromton, X Script. 868. This was 'after the industry and wisdom of the monks ... had been at work to ... cultivate the wilderness;' Kingsley, p. 302.

[5] Croyland is a corruption. It is properly Cruland ('Crudeland, cænosa terra,' Felix, 41), and hence Crowland. See Freeman, iv. 596. It is described in one spurious charter as enclosed within four, in another within five 'waters;' Rer. Angl. Script. i. 3, 9. 'In sanctuary of the four rivers;' Kingsley, p. 306. The stone church built there in 716 had to be supported on oak piles and a mass of hard soil from a distance.

a name which Guthlac has made famous, for he took it as his
abode, on a summer day when probably it wore its least repulsive aspect,—on the feast of St. Bartholomew[1] in 699. He
practised all the austerities which belonged, as of course, to
the life of an anchorite; and they combined with the wisp-
fires, and wild sounds of winter nights among the fens, and
probably with intermittent attacks of marsh fever[2], to call up
those hideous fancies of fiendish visitation and onslaught
which read in Guthlac's life like an exaggeration of the 'trials
of St. Antony[3].' Whatever were his illusions, he preserved
his faith, courage, and cheerfulness: the hagiologist indicates
that he could repel with promptness, perhaps with humour,
fantastic temptations to impossible feats of abstinence[4]: like
Cuthbert, he was 'in league' with the fowls of the air; the
wild birds, and even the fishes of the marsh, would eat from
his hand; swallows came to sit on his arms and his bosom,
and it was when his friend, an abbot named Wilfrid[5], who
often visited him, expressed surprise at this familiarity, that
Guthlac uttered the memorably beautiful answer, 'Have you
not read that he who is joined to God with a pure spirit finds
all things uniting themselves to him in God[6]?' We cannot

[1] After his first visit to the isle, he returned to Repton to say farewell to
his companions, for he had left them 'insalutatos.' He repaired to Crowland
after a short sojourn with them, taking two boys with him. Felix is not quite
distinct as to the St. Bartholomew's day in question, whether it was the
occasion of his first visit, or of his regular occupation of Crowland. His sister
Pega took up her abode 'as a recluse in another part of the fens, four leagues
off to the west;' Alb. Butler, April 11. Bishop Hedda (of Lichfield) visited
Crowland, and ordained Guthlac priest; Felix, 32.

[2] Kingsley, Hermits, p. 303. See Churton, E. E. Ch. p. 140.

[3] 'Erant enim adspectu truces, forma terribiles, ... dentibus equinis ....
trucibus oculis ... gutture flammivomo .... immensis vagitibus,' &c.; Felix,
19; comp. 22. The fiends, we are told, tossed him into the muddy streams,
dragged him through thorny thickets, &c. On one occasion, says Felix gravely
(c. 20), they came in the form and with the speech of Britons (Welshmen).
Palgrave quotes this (p. 462) in proof of the extent of the British element still
left in the population. See above, p. 27.

[4] The suggestion was to fast rigidly for six days. Guthlac rose and sang
out, 'Let mine enemies be turned backward!' and then quietly ate his daily
meal of barley-bread; Felix, 18.

[5] Felix, 16, 25.

[6] 'Nonne legisti quia qui Deo puro spiritu copulabitur, omnia sibi in Deo
conjunguntur?' Felix, 25. Comp. Bede, Vit. Cuthb. 21.

wonder that, as in Cuthbert's case, the solitude of the devout hermit was broken by crowds of visitors of all kinds [1], 'abbots, brethren, earls, the rich, the sick, the poor, not only from the neighbouring districts of Mercia, but from the remoter parts of Britain,'—who came to tell him of their troubles, and never came without finding relief [2]. So that, like Cuthbert on Farne, the inmate of Crowland was exercising a true ministry of consolation, and doing a work of wide effect, which showed that the superstitious form impressed by circumstances upon his devotion had not dulled his moral insight, nor chilled his discriminating sympathy. But it must be remembered that what we, perhaps, should look upon as the redeeming point in a grave mistake was to Guthlac a mere incident in a life which, in its physical conditions, was far more terrible than that of the old Egyptian solitaries [3], and which in fact could not be protracted beyond fifteen years [4]. But so to live, and so to die, appeared to the men of his time, under the influence of a false ideal, to be the summit of Christian attainment.

And while in that southernmost corner of Lincolnshire a Mercian hermit was thus attracting the homage which in after days expressed itself by the foundation of a great monastery, described by its inmates as 'the holy sanctuary of St. Guthlac' under the protection of St. Mary and St. Bar-

Foundation of Evesham.

---

[1] Felix, 31.

[2] E.g. 'Nullum tædium sine exhortatione, nulla mæstitia sine consolatione, nulla anximonia sine consilio ab illo reversa est.' Felix had evidently been reading Bede (Vit. Cuthb. 22), whose memory he naturally cherished. He tells us that Guthlac supported all that he said by authority of Scripture; 32: and calls him 'alacer, efficax, in discernendis causis.' 'Nothing staid in his mind but charity, peace, pity, forgiveness. No one ever saw him angry ... excited ... sorrowful,' &c.; 38. Cp. Athan. Vit. Ant. 14.

[3] See Kingsley's Hermits, pp. 130-134.

[4] See Kingsley, p. 306; and on 'the vast longevity of many of' the fathers of the desert, p. 134. Paul is said to have lived 113 years, Antony 105, Elias of Antinous 110 (Soz. vi. 28), &c. Guthlac died, aged forty-seven, on April 11, 714, and was succeeded in his solitude by Cissa, a convert from Paganism; Florence, a. 714. One of the strangest things in the story is that a cleric named Beccelin, having come to live as Guthlac's servant, and being about to shave him as usual, was sorely tempted to cut his throat, 'ut ... locum ipsius postea cum magna regum principumque venerantia habiturus foret.' Guthlac bade him 'spit out the venom' of this wicked thought; he fell on his knees and confessed all; Felix, 21.

tholomew [1], a Mercian bishop was designing and establishing
a religious house which became one of the greatest in the
Midlands, at a place which was to be associated with a crisis
in English secular history [2]. It was a wild and lonely spot
rising abruptly above the Avon, and covered with thorny
thickets, but marked by a small church of ancient, probably
of British, construction [3]. Here Eoves, one of Bishop Egwin's
herdsmen, professed to have seen an appearance of the Virgin [4];
and accordingly at 'Eoves-ham [5]' arose a minster in her
honour. Although its early history is marred by fiction and
forged documents, one interesting detail may probably be
received as authentic. Some eight miles from Evesham, at
Alcester, was a royal estate [6], inhabited by persons who disliked Egwin and his preaching, and devised an ingenious
expedient for ridding themselves of both [7]. In the neighbouring wood many 'blacksmiths' carried on their trade.
One day, while Egwin was pleading with his untoward
audience, there rose up such a din of hammers [8] and anvils

[1] See the alleged charter of Bertulf, in the false Ingulf, Rer. Angl. Script.
i. 14; Cod. Dipl. ii. 41. See Kingsley, Hermits, p. 307.

[2] The battle of Evesham was fought on August 4, 1265.

[3] Malmesbury, G. Pontif. iv. 160.

[4] Ann. SS. Bened. iii. 335; Chron. Evesh. p. 9; Monast. Angl. ii. 1. She was
said to have appeared to Eoves as brighter than the sun, holding a book and
singing heavenly songs with two other virgins; he told his master what he had
seen; and Egwin on a subsequent morning, attended by three companions, went
barefoot to the place and saw a similar vision. Egwin was said to have first
obtained an old monastery at Fladbury, and to have exchanged it for Stratford.
But the documents are marked as spurious; Cod. Dipl. i. 36.

[5] Originally 'Eoves-holm,' *holm* being any ground surrounded or washed by
a river. The British name was Hethbo. See Tindal's History of Evesham,
p. 2. The Mercians had called it Hethomme (Athamne, Mabillon) and Cro-
nuchomme: Egwin, according to the legend, had there flung the key of his
chains into the river, and afterwards obtained the place from the king, as
pasture-ground for monks. Florence dates the foundation a few years after
Egwin's consecration; Tanner dates it 701. See Cod. Dipl. i. 64.

[6] 'Regale mansum . . . nemoribus consitum, fluminibus . . . et rivulis circum-
datum, necnon muris et turribus vallatum.' A council had been held there,
'non multo prius,' which had confirmed the immunities of Evesham; Chron.
Evesh. p. 25. But the story of this council of 709 is very doubtful. See
Haddan and Stubbs, iii. 279–283: cp. Lingard, A.-S. Ch. i. 209.

[7] Ann. SS. Bened. iii. 336; Chron. Evesh. p. 25.

[8] 'Præ concussione, immo confusione, malleorum et incudum adhuc tin-
niebant ambæ aures ejus,' &c.; Chron. Evesh. p. 26. See Green, Making of
Engl. p. 351.

that he was 'fain to depart with tingling ears.' Passing over a story of the miraculous removal of this hindrance, we may see a not improbable intimation of the resistance which still, in outlying parts, was offered to Christianity by the adherents of the defeated Paganism.

And now we must resume consideration of the case of Wilfrid, the last stage of which commences with the second year of the eighth century.

CHAPTER XIII.

EVER since the second expulsion of Wilfrid, a monotonous tranquillity had reigned in the Church of Northumbria. Ecclesiastical interests were sedulously cared for by King Aldfrid: ecclesiastical life was surrounded with all that could give it security and honour. Bishop Eadbert of Lindisfarne had died, after some weeks' illness, on the 6th of May, 698 [1], having caused the tomb of Cuthbert to be opened on the 20th of March, when the saint's body was found 'entire as if he were still living, and his joints still flexible as if he were but asleep [2].' Part of the grave-clothes were brought to Eadbert, who 'kissed them as if they still covered the father's body,' and ordered others to be put in their place. He himself was ere long laid in the same grave, but under the saint's coffin [3]. He was succeeded by Eadfrid, the prelate to whom, along with his monks, Bede, many years later, inscribed his Life of St. Cuthbert [4]. The community to which Bede himself belonged flourished under the presidency of Ceolfrid, who,

Death of bishop Eadbert.

---

[1] Bede, Vit. Cuthb. 42, 43.

[2] Bede, Vit. Cuthb. 42 ; Vit. Anon., Bed. Op. vi. 380.

[3] 'Relics' of Eadbert and others, with the head of Oswald (see above, p. 159), were found beside Cuthbert's body in 1104.

[4] In the dedication preface Bede reminds Eadfrid that he had promised to enrol his name, after his death, among those of persons to be prayed for at Lindisfarne; and in pledge of such future enrolment had ordered Guthfrid, the 'mansionarius' or sacristan, to place his name, during his life, in the 'white book' of the community. This prelate had written out with his own hand, 'in honour of St. Cuthbert' (i.e. for Cuthbert's use), a copy of the Gospels, which was adorned by his successor's orders with gold and jewels, and ultimately preserved at Durham; Simeon, Dunelm. Eccl. ii. 12. Cp. Anderson, Scotl. in Early Ch. Times, p. 149. He also, early in his episcopate, repaired the time-worn oratory of Cuthbert in Farne; Bede, Vit. Cuthb. 46.

as we have seen, had united the abbacy of Wearmouth to
that of Jarrow: and we find him sending some monks to
Rome in the year 700 [1], with a gift or 'blessing' for Pope
Sergius, intended, no doubt, to recommend the petition
which they were to make for a new letter of privilege, like that
Pope Ser-
gius and
Ceolfrid. which had been received from Pope Agatho. Sergius complied
with the request of Ceolfrid: and also entrusted to one of the
messengers a letter [2], in which he informed the abbot that
certain questions of an ecclesiastical kind [3] had arisen, which
could not be settled without a long inquiry; that therefore
he must needs confer with men of literary acquirements;
and that he desired Ceolfrid to send to Rome, at once, 'the
religious servant of God,'—here, in a manuscript exhibiting
the letter, 'N.' occurs instead of a name,—'belonging to
his monastery,' in full confidence that, after the matters in
hand should have been settled, he would return home in
safety, by the Lord's favour and Ceolfrid's prayers. Malmesbury's version of this letter contains the name of Bede, and
adds the designation of 'presbyterum.' But Bede the
historian never did visit Rome,—never, indeed, went beyond
Northumbria [4]: nor was he ordained priest until 701–2 [5].
Yet he may, nevertheless, have been recommended to Sergius

---

[1] See Lingard, A.-S. Ch. ii. 412, referring to Bede, De Temp. Ratione, c. 47,
which shows that the monks, on Christmas day of 700, reckoned then as
the first day of 701, were in St. Mary Major's, and there saw a waxen tablet
recording, 'From the Passion of our Lord there are 668 years.'

[2] Haddan and Stubbs, iii. 248.

[3] 'Ecclesiasticarum causarum capitulis.'

[4] Comp. Bede, v. 24: 'Qui natus . . . . . . suscepi.' 'His Epitome
seems to show that he never left England;' see Smith's Bede, p. 799. He
adds that it might be rejoined that a very short stay in Rome would not
necessarily be inconsistent with the Epitome.

[5] The MS. Cotton in the British Museum, referred to the tenth century,
gives the passage thus: 'Religiosum famulum Dei N. venerabilis monasterii
tui . . . dirigere.' Bede's name 'is inserted in the margin' (Giles's Bede, i.
p. lxix.). 'N.,' for 'nomen,' shows that the copyist had before him an acci-
dental blank where the name should have been. Malmesbury, G. Regum, i. 58,
quotes the letter thus: 'Religiosum Dei famulum Bedam, venerabilis monasterii
tui presbyterum.' Giles suggests that this last word might have been 'inno-
cently' inserted by Malmesbury, since Bede afterwards became a priest; or it
might be 'a mistake on the part of the pope,' Dict. Chr. Biogr. i. 301.
Lingard's suggestion that 'the elder Bede,' not the historian, was meant,
seems very improbable; A.-S. Ch. ii. 413.

by the Wearmouth monks, as an eminently promising scholar:
the title of 'presbyter' may have been a mistake or a gloss:
the invitation was not improbably sent for him, and his
non-compliance may have been simply caused by the Pope's
speedy death. The privilege was duly exhibited before
the Northumbrian Witan, and confirmed by the signatures
of the king and the bishops. Whatever the questions were
to which the Pope's letter alludes, it is evident that about
the beginning of the eighth century an uneasy feeling was
stirring in the minds of Northumbrian Churchmen, and of
others in other districts, as to the position of Wilfrid;
accordingly, Aldfrid resolved to assemble a general 'synod' Council of
at which the whole English Church should be repre- Easterfield.
sented. It was held, in 702, at a place which Eddi calls
by the two names of 'Ouestraefelda' or Estrefeld, and 'Æts-
winapathe [1].' This 'Easterfield' must have been somewhere in
Yorkshire, perhaps at Austerfield near Bawtry [2], which would
be a convenient place for persons arriving from the south.
Among the latter was Archbishop Bertwald; and nearly all
his suffragans are said to have attended him. Wilfrid was
'respectfully' invited to appear, in order that 'according
to the canonical statutes' whatever had been wrong might
be set right. He came accordingly, attended by several
abbots of his monasteries. On his arrival, Eddi tells us,
there was 'much altercation,' mainly caused by prelates,
and by abbots who from 'avaricious motives' were opposed
to any scheme of agreement. The king himself, we are
assured, was practically on that side. Accusations were
brought up against Wilfrid, which Eddi declares to be false.
At last the point at issue was clearly raised. Would Wilfrid
comply with the regulations of Theodore? According to
such light as we have on the matter, this demand meant,
Would he submit to such a partition of the old diocese
of York as had been devised by Theodore in despite of
his remonstrances? To yield to this demand, absolutely,

---

[1] Eddi, 46, 60. Compare 'Edwinscliff' in Chronicle, a. 761; Raine, Hist. of
Ch. of York, i. 65. He suggests, however, that the second name may mean
only '*At the swine's path.*' Near Austerfield is 'Swine-car' (morass).

[2] Haddan and Stubbs, iii. 254.

CHAP. XIII. would have been to give up the position in which he had been placed by the Roman Council,—a position of manifest advantage from his point of view. He therefore answered with a qualification : 'Yes, I am willing to comply with those regulations—according to the rule of the canons;' meaning, virtually, so far as they could be brought into harmony with the decree of the Council[1]. This saving clause, like Thomas of Canterbury's 'Saving my order[2],' was clearly calculated to exasperate his opponents: they would regard it as nullifying any verbal concession. And Wilfrid further damaged his case by indulging in what his panegyrist acknowledges to have been an outburst of sharp reproaches ; 'Here you have been for two and twenty years contentiously standing out against the Apostolic authority. With what front can you still prefer any ordinances of Archbishop Theodore, framed in time of discord between prelates, to the salutary decrees of Pope Agatho, Pope Benedict, and Pope Sergius[3]?' The Council, apparently, adjourned at this point; and Wilfrid retired to take counsel with his friends. He then received two visitors in succession. One of the king's thanes, who when a boy had, like other 'earl-born' lads, been bred up in the house of the great bishop of York, and was warmly attached to him[4], emerged in disguise from the king's tent, and 'mingling like an unknown person with the soldiers who surrounded it,' found his way to his old patron, and said, 'They want to induce you to promise in writing that you will submit to whatever they shall determine. And what they determine will be this ; that you shall resign into the archbishop's hands

---

[1] Eadmer makes him say, 'You accuse me because I do not receive those decrees of Theodore, quas ipse non auctoritate canonica, sed discordia dictante composuit ;' c. 46.

[2] See Milman, Lat. Chr. v. 47.

[3] 'Wilfridus igitur non ideo sibi injuriam illatam existimabat, quod episcopatus suus in plures divideretur,' but that bishops had been exercising jurisdiction in it in virtue of Theodore's arbitrary decree. 'Pontifices enim Romani decernebant diœcesim illam tam longe lateque extensam in plures esse partiendam, non tamen mera apostolica auctoritate, sed concilio rite congregato, depositis iis qui in Vilfridi absentia in episcopos contra canones ordinarentur ;' Smith's Bede, p. 755.

[4] 'Unus ex ministris,' Eddi; 'juvenis quidam curialis,' Eadmer.

whatever you have held,—bishopric or monastery, in Northumbria or in Mercia,—to be disposed of at his will.' Having given this information, the friendly thane departed as secretly as he had come[1]. Presently afterwards a bishop entered, commissioned by Aldfrid and Bretwald to urge Wilfrid to promise, beforehand, that he would adhere to any decision of the archbishop. Wilfrid answered as any one in his position would have answered : 'I must first know what that decision will be like.' '*I* do not know, for my part,' said the envoy: 'nor will the archbishop give any information until he is assured under your hand that you will abide by what he says.' 'I never before heard,' said Wilfrid, 'of any attempt to bind a man to obey a judgment not yet given, before he knew what it would be. He might find that it ordered what was impossible.' But he came to the Council when it again assembled, and promised that he would heartily accept the archbishop's decision, *if* it were found to be agreeable to the canons and statutes of the Fathers, and not inconsistent with the judgments of the three Popes who had pronounced their decisions in the cause[2]. Again the qualification seems to have stirred up fresh bitterness: it was proposed by the king and the archbishop,—so, at least, Eddi informs us[3],—that Wilfrid should give up all his houses, so that he would not, in that case, have had 'even a little bit of a single dwelling' in Northumbria or in Mercia. But others, hearing this, were disgusted at such relentless severity ; it would be 'impious' to strip a person of such well-known eminence, 'famous through all the nations around,' of all his property, 'without convicting him of any capital crime.' At last his adversaries modified their proposal, but in terms which showed not only the jealousy, but the alarm which Wilfrid's manifold ability and energy had inspired : — Let him have his monastery of St. Peter at Ripon, with all that pertained to it,—but on

---

[1] This we learn from Eddi, 47.

[2] See Wilfrid's speech at Rome, Eddi, 53. Eadmer says that they caught up his words and said, 'One canonical rule of Theodore's is, that disobedient persons should be put down.'

[3] Eddi, 47.

CHAP. XIII. this condition, to which his written assent was required,
that he should not without the king's leave go beyond the
precincts of the monastery, nor perform any episcopal [1] act,—
a condition which, as Eddi expresses it, would amount to
a self-deprivation. The spirit of Wilfrid took fire at such
a suggestion. He broke forth into an indignant recital of
his services to religion in Northumbria [2]. 'Was it not I
who laboured, before any one else took the work in hand,
to root out the evil plant of Scotic usages? Was it not I
who converted all Northumbria to the true Easter and the
crown-shaped tonsure, who established antiphonal chanting,
who organised the monastic life according to the Rule of
the holy father Benedict, which no one before me had brought
in [3]? And now, after nearly forty years spent in the
episcopate [4], you ask me, in effect, to condemn myself, when
I know of no crime that can be charged against me; I am
to resign my office, on account of this question that has
Wilfrid's but lately come up. No, indeed! I appeal to the Apostolic
second see: whosoever would wish to depose me, let him meet
appeal. me, as I this day challenge him to meet me, at *that*
tribunal.' One seems to hear the raised tone [5], to see
the proud and wrathful look, with which the indomitable
man, at sixty-eight, confronted and defied his opponents,
secular and hierarchical. They were, however, neither abashed
nor overawed. The new appeal was a new offence: 'He is
all the more blameable,' said the king and the archbishop,
'in that he has chosen to be judged at Rome rather than
by us.' Aldfrid even added a proposal to have Wilfrid put

---

[1] 'Sacerdotalis officii' must have this sense. Eadmer says that he was
advised to accept these terms, and use the opportunity for a contemplative life.
But he well knew the source whence this counsel emanated, and answered that
the 'gift of counsel' had in it nothing of duplicity. All this is Eadmer's
invention; it is what he thought likely to have been said.

[2] Lingard, A.-S. Ch. i. 141 ; Milman, ii. 269 ; Raine, i. 73.

[3] 'Of his noble apostolic labours, his conversion of the heathen, his culti-
vation of arts and letters, his stately buildings, his monasteries, he said nothing;'
Milman, ii. 269. On the Benedictine rule see above, p. 226.

[4] If he was consecrated early in 665, he had been a bishop, by this time, for
thirty-seven years. Eddi, 47 ; Fridegod, 1096. See above, p. 219.

[5] 'Intrepida voce elevata;' Eddi. 'Fecit ille quod erat constantissimi
præsulis;' Smith's Bede, p. 756.

under arrest [1], that he might be effectually compelled to be CHAP. XIII.
content with home-authorities 'for one while.' But this was
too much for the other bishops: they agreed to the sentence
of deposition from episcopal dignity, but they would not
violate the safe-conduct without which, as they said, Wilfrid
would not have ventured to come to Easterfield. Let him
go without hindrance; 'and let us, too, go quietly to our own
homes.' 'After this conversation the fruitless Council [2] was
dissolved.'

Wilfrid returned into Mercia, and reported to Ethelred Wilfrid in
what the bishops had said at Easterfield, 'against Ethelred's Mercia.
own directions,' as Eddi tells us, alluding to some letter
which the Mercian king had apparently written on his
behalf. 'And what do you mean to do,' asked Wilfrid, 'as
to the lands which I hold in your kingdom [3]?' 'I mean,'
said Ethelred, 'to add no new trouble to your trouble. I
will keep those lands for you until I can send messengers,
or a letter, with you to Rome, to ask for instructions as
to my conduct.' Far different was the conduct of some who,
as Eddi says [4], 'usurped possession of Wilfrid's inheritance.'
One is loth to think that Bosa or John would personally
go to such extremities as are described; but we are told that
the usurpers treated Wilfrid and the members of his monastic
communities as excommunicate. If any of them, at the
request of a layman, were to bless food with the sign of the
cross, it was to be flung away as if it had been an offering to
idols: even the vessels used by them at meals [5] were to be
washed, before others might handle them without incurring
ceremonial pollution.

In this state of public opinion, when a deep and persistent
antipathy [6] was making itself felt against the exile and the

---

[1] 'Si præcipis, pater, opprimam eum per violentiam;' Malmesb. G. P.
iii. 104.

[2] 'Inutile concilium;' Eddi, 48.

[3] He said nothing, Smith observes, about any bishopric as belonging to him
in Mercia. He regarded himself as there a *locum tenens*.

[4] Eddi, 49.

[5] 'Vasa de quibus nostri vescebantur.'

[6] The existence of such a feeling is sufficient proof that, in Northumbria at
any rate, there was a powerful mass of opinion which, in a practical sense,
might be called anti-papal. In other districts the feeling was different.

CHAP. XIII. appellant, there was some reason to expect that the pressure might be too great for the fidelity of some of his monks or clerics,—that they might be scared into forsaking as hopeless the cause of 'a man forbid.' It was therefore an act of

Aldhelm. opportune generosity when the man who stood highest in ecclesiastical reputation throughout the English Churches, the unrivalled scholar,—the admired writer,—the popular and venerated abbot, Aldhelm of Malmesbury, interposed to inspirit and exhort the adherents of Wilfrid. We have already seen how Aldhelm had succeeded to the abbacy at Malmesbury; his administration was brilliantly successful; the community which had grown out of a little knot of scholars gathering round a foreign teacher beneath the walls of an old fortress had 'broken forth on the right hand and on the left,' for Aldhelm had been enabled to found another monastery at Frome, and another yet at Bradford-on-Avon [1], and the very ancient little church remaining at the latter place has been thought to be actually of his building. King Ine had given several lands for the augmentation of the parent monastery [2]: there had been 'a rush along all roads,' as William of Malmesbury expresses it, 'to Aldhelm [3]:' and among his disciples was Pecthelm, who afterwards held the restored bishopric of St. Ninian at Whithern or Candida Casa [4]. He was a friend and correspondent of the scholarly king of Northumbria; and Artwil, the scholarly son of an Irish king, submitted to Aldhelm all his literary compositions,

---

[1] Faricius, Vit. Aldh. c. 2; Malmesb. G. Pontif. v. 198. When he wrote the church of Frome was still standing, and so, he says, was the 'ecclesiola' of St. Laurence at Bradford; but the monasteries had perished. On the church at Bradford see Freeman, Engl. Towns and Distr., p. 140; Parker, Intr. Goth. Arch., p. 15. Aldhelm also (ib. v. 217) built a church near Wareham in Dorset, which in the twelfth century still existed, unroofed, save for a prominence just above the altar: within its precinct, it was said, rain never fell.

[2] Kemble admits this charter, which belongs to 701; Cod. Dipl. i. 55. The Mercian sub-king Berthwald, who had been so friendly to Wilfrid, gave a piece of land on the Teme to Aldhelm's monastery; and Ethelred attested the grant in a 'synod' held at Burford, July 30, 685; Cod. Dipl. i. 30.

[3] 'Currebatur ad Aldelmum totis semitis;' Malmesb. G. Pontif. v. 200.

[4] Malmesb. iii. 115. Haddan and Stubbs, ii. 7. Bede knew Pecthelm: see v. 13, 18, 23. He lived as 'deacon or monk' under Aldhelm as bishop.

which were not few in number[1]. The fame of the learned West-Saxon abbot had reached the ears of Pope Sergius, who invited him to Rome[2], allowed him to celebrate in the Lateran basilica[3], and sent him home with a letter of privilege for his monasteries[4], a store of relics, and a massive altar of white marble, which he gave to King Ine, who placed it in the royal 'vicus' of Bruton[5]. Traditions spoke of the rapturous joy with which Aldhelm's return was welcomed, when monks met him with cross and thurible and processional chant, and laymen expressed their delight by dancing or by other 'gestures of the body[6].' He was, we cannot doubt, the most popular of monks or priests: his scholars loved him passionately, as their 'most loving teacher of pure learning[7];' and he well deserved their affection by the tender thoughtful interest with which he watched over their progress[8], and after they had left him still exhorted them, in extant letters, to avoid youthful follies, such as daily drinking-bouts, protracted feastings, or any excess in amusements[9],—to prefer the study of Scripture to immoral specimens of heathen poetry,—to keep clear of all sensuality, and to be simple in dress and habits,—and in all secular studies to keep in view

[1] Malmesb. G. P. v. 191.

[2] So says Faricius : ' Huic . . . Sergius adserverat quia . . . de eo persæpe audierat ;' c. 2. Malmesbury says he went in order to get ' privileges ' for his monasteries, but before setting out, built a church at Wareham, the roofless walls of which still existed. Among Aldhelm's verses are some in honour of SS. Peter and Paul, composed while he ' was entering their church at Rome.' He invokes them both.

[3] Faricius has a tale of wonder about his chasuble being supported on a sunbeam. Then comes another, about his clearing the pope, by miracle, from a calumny. Comp. Malmesb. v. 218, that this red chasuble, preserved in the abbey, showed ' the saint to have been a tall man,' as did his relics.

[4] Faricius and Malm. v. 220.

[5] Malmesb. v. 222. He inclines to think that a camel bore this ' moles ' to the foot of the Alps ; but there the beast of burden, camel or not, ' stumbled ;' the altar was broken, but miraculously put together again, &c. It was extant ' ad hanc diem.'

[6] Malmesb. l. c.

[7] ' Mi amantissime puræ institutionis præceptor ;' Epist. 6, Ethelwald to Aldhelm.

[8] ' Ab ipsis tenerrimæ cunabulis infantiæ fovendo, amando,' &c. ; Ep. 6.

[9] Ep. 10, Aldh. to Ethelwald. He mentions ' equitandi vagatione culpabili ' (cp. Bede v. 6), with ' conviviis usu frequentiore ac prolixiore inhoneste superfluis,' the latter a coarse Saxon habit : see above, p. 243.

CHAP. XIII. sacred knowledge as the end to which all other lore should minister [1]. He himself had practised, in this matter, what he taught [2]: his literary activity never chilled or suspended his devotions: when he concludes his book on Metres with a pious aspiration 'that abundance of things perishable may not prove to be poverty in the world to come,' one seems to see into his mind [3], and to understand the moral and spiritual force exercised by one who is enthusiastically described in his capacity as a scholar, and as a teacher and controversialist, in the words of his Malmesbury biographer, —'wonderful in each of his qualities, and peerless in them all [4].'

Such was the man who now wrote 'to the clerks of Bishop Wilfrid [5],' entreating them not to be 'scandalised' by the raging storm that had broken over the Church, even if some of them had to share their prelate's lot in expulsion from home and compulsory wanderings abroad. Let them not be thankless to one who had lovingly trained them up from early childhood to opening manhood; let them cling to him, as bees cling to *their* monarch [6] through all weathers; let them remember the scorn and derision which would be poured out on laymen who forsook a kind lord in his adversity; 'and what, then,' he proceeds, 'will be said of you, if you leave a bishop who nourished and brought you up, alone in his exile?'

The persons addressed appear to have responded to the exhortation [7]. Solemn prayers and fasts, on the part of all Wilfrid's monastic communities, preceded his departure. Among those who accompanied him was a man in several respects like-minded to himself, and who lived to do good service to the Northumbrian Church, and, indirectly at least, to the ecclesiastical literature of England. This was Acca,

Acca.

---

[1] Ep. 13, to a Wilfrid, going to study in Ireland.

[2] So Malmesbury says generally of him, v. 213. Cp. Lingard, ii. 187.

[3] See too the pious little Epist. 2.

[4] Malmesb. v. 200. He says that Aldhelm was like lightning in confuting adversaries, but soft as nectar in his instructions to pupils.

[5] Epist. 11; Malmesb. v. 192; Haddan and Stubbs, iii. 254.

[6] A *king*-bee, according to Aldhelm: 'Rex earum spissis sodalium agminibus vallatus,' &c.

[7] Eddi, 50.

afterwards for some twenty-three years bishop of Hexham.
He had been 'trained up from boyhood among the clergy of
Bosa [1],' but attached himself to Wilfrid 'in the hope of a
better plan of life [2].' He was thoroughly imbued with Wilfrid's love of ecclesiastical magnificence; and when he had
the opportunity, he distinguished himself in the adornment
and enrichment of churches, in the collection of theological
books, in the organisation of a school of Church music,—'for
he himself was a very skilful chanter.' His own learning
was considerable, his orthodoxy exact, his observance of all
ecclesiastical rules punctilious. But our chief reason for
gratitude to his memory is his practical encouragement of
the labours of Bede. While he was yet an abbot, not a
bishop, he requested Bede to collect, as from 'a flowering
paradise,' the best thoughts of the Fathers on the beginning
of Genesis, for the sake of those who had not access to the
originals [3]. To him also Bede addressed a tract on the Temple
of Solomon, which seems to have been written when Acca
had some troubles to endure [4]; and an allegorical exposition
of the First Book of Samuel, which Acca had requested him
to undertake [5]. Some questions which Acca propounded as
to the 'stations' of the Israelites in their wanderings, and
as to the mysterious text, 'They shall be shut up in prison,
and after many days shall be visited,' diverted Bede for a
while from the work on the book of Samuel [6]. And Acca's
influence was effectual in regard to Bede's writings on the
New Testament: we find that Bede sent him, for transcrip-
tion, a work on the Apocalypse; and he then wrote to Bede,
exhorting him to compile a Patristic commentary on St. Luke.

[1] See Bede's account of him, v. 20: 'Strenuissimus, et coram Deo et
hominibus magnificus . . cantator peritissimus . . in litteris sanctis doctissimus,
in catholicæ fidei confessione castissimus, in ecclesiasticæ quoque institutionis
regulis sollertissimus.' 'Utpote qui a pueritia in clero . . . Bosa . . . nutritus
atque eruditus erat,' &c. Cp. Eddi, 22. He succeeded Wilfrid as bishop of
Hexham, but was expelled in 732, Sim. Dur. Hist. Reg. 31: and Skene conjectures that he may have brought 'St. Andrew's relics' from Hexham to
'Kilrymont,' or St. Andrews, Celtic Scotl. ii. 273.

[2] He *may* have accompanied Wilfrid into Sussex: but this is not proved by
the reference to him in iv. 14, and he is not mentioned in iv. 13.

[3] Bed. Op. i. 169 and vii. 1 (Giles).

[4] Ib. i. 171; viii. 263.　　[5] Ib. i. 195; vii. 369.　　[6] Ib. i. 198 ff.

CHAP. XIII. Bede sent him, by way of instalment, a work on the Acts[1]: after reading which, as we learn from a very interesting letter of Acca, prefixed to the 'Exposition of St. Luke's Gospel[2],' Acca, both in conversation and by letters, urged him to comment on that Gospel, and replied, not without playfulness[3], and with several allusions to great Fathers, to his excuses for not attempting such a task. The urgency, so affectionate and so delicate in its tone, was irresistible : and Bede at once set to work, 'dictating,' as he says, ' to himself, and writing from his own dictation[4].' Acca, with many other brethren, pressed him further to write on the Gospel of St. Mark,—a work not accomplished until after a long interval[5]. It is worth while to glance at these occasions on which Bede, as commentator on Scripture, introduces his readers to Acca as to ' the dearest and most loving of prelates that live on the earth,' his ' most beloved and truly blessed lord[6].'

Such a companion as this—so loyal, sympathetic, and intelligent—must have been indeed a solace to Wilfrid, on this his third journey to ' the Apostles' threshold.' Twenty-five[7] years had passed since his former appeal ; and now, after many disappointments and troubles, and after a period of tranquillity which had seemed likely to be permanent, the work had to be done all over again ;—although the precedent of Agatho's decision would be morally certain to sway the councils of Rome, yet the treatment of that decision by English authorities might easily be repeated in regard Wilfrid's to a new sentence. But Wilfrid's heart did not fail him : journey to Rome.

[1] Bede, Op. i. 184 ; xii. 1.

[2] Ib. x. 265. The bishop begins, ' Reverendissimo in Christo fratri et consacerdoti Bedæ presbytero.'

[3] Bede had quoted the proverb, ' Why put fish into the sea ?' Acca replies, ' Juxta comicum, Nihil sit dictum quod non sit dictum prius ;' and urges the claim of charity. He desires Bede to prefix his letter to the Exposition when completed, in order to show that he had written it ' non ob aliam quam condescensionis fraternæ gratiam.'

[4] Bede, Op. i. 179 ; x. 268 : ' Mox lectis tuæ dulcissimæ sanctitatis paginulis, injuncti me operis labori supposui, in quo . . . ipse mihi dictator simul notarius et librarius exsisterem.' ' Librarius '= copyist.

[5] Ib. i. 177 (Ep. 8) ; x. 2.

[6] Bede, vii. 369, Introd. to Samuel ; and i. 184, Ep. 10.

[7] He probably set forth late in 703, and wintered in Frisia.

he went forth, to all appearance, with the same cheerful CHAP. XIII.
courage as on the previous occasion : his journey across the
continent was made on foot[1], in spite of his seventy years,
and included a visit, which must have been full of interest,
to Archbishop Willibrord, in Frisia, when the conversation
often turned on the wonderful things which, according to
Willibrord, had been wrought in that province by contact
with relics of the holy king Oswald. The archbishop also
told a story of his own sojourn in Ireland, about the recovery of an Irish student from the pestilence, after drinking
water into which Willibrord had dipped a splinter of the
oaken stake on which Oswald's head had been fixed : the
sick man, he assured his hearers, not only regained health,
but passed from his former irreligiousness to a thoroughness
of Christian devotion[2].

In due time Wilfrid and his companions found themselves Pope John
once more at Rome, probably in the early part of 704. VI.
The existing Pope was John VI. who had been consecrated
in the October of 701[3]. He gave Wilfrid a speedy
audience. The bishop presented to him, as he had presented to Agatho, a written memorial; and said that he
had come to 'that most glorious see, as to a mother's bosom[4],'
and not for the purpose of accusing any one, but in order
to meet any charges that might be brought against him
in the presence of the Roman Council. If they were true,
he would confess them to be true; if they were false, he
was ready to refute them. The Pope received the petitioners kindly,—the account unites Wilfrid closely with his
attendant priests and deacons; and they enjoyed some days
of repose in a lodging freely provided for them. Meanwhile
certain envoys from the archbishop of Canterbury arrived
with written charges against Wilfrid. It is surprising to
find that only one of them was even in deacon's orders[5].

[1] 'Pedestri gressu ;' Eddi, 50.
[2] Bede, iii. 13. See above, p. 160.
[3] On the virtues of this pope, as a peace-maker and a ransomer of captives,
see Milman, ii. 336. He died Jan. 9, 705.
[4] Eddi, 50. Cp. Bede, v. 19, 'veniensque Romam,' &c.
[5] 'Unus diaconus, et alii omnes sine aliquo ecclesiasticæ dignitatis
gradu;' Eddi, 53. Compare ib. 50, 53, on these ' legati ' and ' nuntii.'

They, like Wilfrid, formally craved a hearing; and John assembled a synod of the neighbouring bishops together with their attendant clergy. Wilfrid's memorial was read. It addressed Pope John by that epithet of 'universal' which, a little more than a century before, had been rejected and reprobated by the greatest of his predecessors[1]. In substance it was to this effect: 'Once more, I invoke your see. I doubt not that you will adhere to the decisions of your predecessors; for myself, I accept whatever you may ordain. I come hither, because disturbances have arisen in Britain on the part of those who, contrary to the decree of Pope Agatho, took possession of my bishopric, my monasteries, my lands. I now ask that what was ordered by Agatho, by Benedict, and by Sergius, may be confirmed. But I am ready to meet any charges against me: let me have my accusers face to face. I also ask that Ethelred king of the Mercians may be commanded, for the comfort of my life[2], to protect my monasteries in his realm from disturbance,— as indeed he desires to do,—in accordance with the directions of former Popes. And I earnestly beg that King Aldfrid may be adjured[3] to comply with the decisions of Pope Agatho and his Council; or, if that should seem too much, let the see of York be disposed of as you will,—but at least let me have Ripon and Hexham. And I promise to show all brotherly charity, and all due reverence, to Archbishop Bertwald, if he will treat me according to the decrees of your predecessors[4].'

The memorial having been read, Wilfrid and his companions were allowed to return to their lodging. Bertwald's envoys were then admitted, and their paper of accusations was read. They also were bidden to retire, with the promise of a regular hearing at a future time. Pope John then told the Council that it was necessary to go through the documents on both sides. This was agreed to: a second sitting took place, in which the accused and the accusers met, and each charge

---

[1] See above, p. 65.

[2] ' De vitæ nostræ solatio imperare dignemini;' Eddi, 51.

[3] 'Obsecretis.'

[4] Malmesbury, G. P. iii. 104, abbreviates this.

was taken separately. The first was, 'Wilfrid contumaciously chap. xiii. refused to comply with the synodical decree of Bertwald, who was sent from this Apostolic see [1],' a clause in which one of Theodore's strong points was ingeniously transferred to Bertwald. Wilfrid then rose, and gave his account of what had passed at Easterfield: it was accepted by the Council. 'And then,' says Eddi, 'they began to talk in Greek among themselves [2], with subdued smiles, and keeping us in the dark;' 'and afterwards said to the accusers,'—one can imagine the smooth Italian politeness barely hiding a quiet sneer,—'You are well aware, dear brethren, that according to the canons, when the accusers of a cleric fail to prove the first point of their charge, they are not allowed to go on to the rest. However, out of respect to the archbishop sent from this Apostolic see, and to Bishop Wilfrid here present, we will go thoroughly into the whole case, spending days or months, if need be, in bringing it to a conclusion.' The Council again adjourned: and, strange as it seems, devoted no less than seventy sittings, during four months, to a full investigation. At last, the record of Wilfrid's presence and testimony at the Roman Council of Easter Tuesday in 680 on the subject of Monothelitism was publicly read, 'in the Roman fashion, before all the people' who were present at the last of the seventy sittings, and we are told that 'all the wise citizens of Rome were astonished when they heard it read.' When the reader's voice stopped, all began to ask each other, 'Who is this Bishop Wilfrid [3]?' And then Boniface, 'a counsellor of the Pope,' and Sisinnius [4], with others, who had seen Wilfrid at Rome in 679–680, declared that the appellant now present was the same Wilfrid whom [5] Agatho had acquitted and sent home, and

---

[1] Eddi, 53: 'Hoc est primum capitulum,' &c.

[2] 'Inter se Græcizantes,' &c.; Eddi. He probably means that they spoke in low tones, so as not to be understood.

[3] Bede, v. 19: 'Quod ubi lectum est,' &c.

[4] They are named in that account of a smaller council which does not mention Wilfrid, and is probably an invention. See above, p. 301.

[5] Eddi. As Bede puts it, 'who after a thorough investigation and hearing of both sides was found by pope Agatho to have been unrighteously expelled from his see, and was held by him in such esteem that he ordered him to take

CHAP. XIII. who now, unhappily, had been again compelled to leave his own see after an episcopate of about forty years; what was to be said of the men who had dared to present false documents, as containing accusations against him, in that venerable presence? Did not they deserve to wear out their lives in a dungeon? 'And the Romans affirmed, "You say the truth."' Here, perhaps, we may suppose Eddi to have indulged in amplification: but the next words, in which Pope John declared Wilfrid to be innocent, must be

Decision of the Synod.

substantially genuine. 'We find[1] after full inquiry, that no crime is proved against Bishop Wilfrid. Let him be acquitted by authority of the Prince of the Apostles, who has power to bind and loose from hidden offences. What Agatho, Benedict, and Sergius decreed concerning him, our humility, with consent of the synod, has resolved to affirm, by writings sent to the kings and the archbishop.' Accordingly John wrote a letter to Ethelred and Aldfrid. Pope Agatho, he said, had considered the charges against Wilfrid, and had rejected them. His successors had followed his judgment: Theodore himself had not, to all appearance, resisted,—had sent no new accusation,—had rather, according to his own statements, rendered obedience. So much for the past. As to the present, the accusers had not proved their case against Wilfrid: rather, he had refuted them.

How modified by Pope John.

The Council had gone minutely into the question. But the Archbishop of Canterbury and Bishop Wilfrid ought to meet face to face: the former therefore was now ordered to assemble a synod together with Wilfrid, and then to summon the Bishops Bosa and John, and hear both sides. If the result should be a synodical settlement, that would be best for both sides; failing this[2],

his seat in a Council of bishops . . . as a man of pure faith and upright character.' Bede corrects Eddi's 'forty years and more' to 'nearly forty years.'

[1] Eddi, 53. 'They all said, together with the pontiff, that a man of such high position . . . ought by no means to be condemned, but to return home with honour, entirely acquitted of all charges;' Bede.

[2] Here Eddi's text, as given in Raine, is not clear; as in Haddan and Stubbs, it is unintelligible. Smith reads, 'moneat ut commonitionibus suis quæque [quæ?] prodesse suis partibus possunt unaquæque (sc. pars) consideret, et ad hanc sedem,' &c. Smith's Bede, p. 758.

let the parties be admonished to repair together to Rome, CHAP. XIII. that the case might be finally settled in a larger Council. Whosoever should delay to come, or ('which is to be abhorred') refuse to come, would incur deprivation. The kings were then exhorted to promote peace, and to remember the decision which several Popes had given as with one mouth; and so they were commended to the Divine keeping.

Truly a characteristic document, one is disposed to say, was this letter of Pope John. He felt himself to be in a difficulty. On the one hand, he and his Council had come to the same conclusion with former Popes, and that was a conclusion in favour of Wilfrid. On the other hand, experience had shown that a Roman decree was by no means sure to be all-powerful with English kings and their ecclesiastical advisers. It would not be wise to issue too stringent a mandate; yet it would be scandalous to sacrifice Wilfrid, or compromise Papal consistency and authority. Therefore, while the kings' attention is solemnly called to the Papal judgments, and Theodore's tardy reconciliation with Wilfrid is magnified into a dutiful acceptance of those judgments, the Pope's letter does not imperatively demand the carrying-out of the decree by a reinstatement of Wilfrid. The dignity of Rome is saved, yet a loophole is provided for something short of simple obedience. That policy of delay, in which the Roman court became afterwards so skilful, is resorted to : on the pretext that Bertwald and Wilfrid ought personally to confront each other, the matter is referred to a synod in England, and Bertwald is soothed by the commission to hold such a synod. It is hoped that by this means the quarrel may be made up: if not, another and 'a larger Council' at Rome can be summoned to effect that settlement which, by hypothesis, a four months' inquiry at Rome and a national Council in Britain would have failed to effect : thus time is gained, and the English authorities are not alienated by severity.

By this time, not only had John VI. found it desirable to write cautiously to Aldfrid, but Wilfrid himself had become weary, and perhaps for the first time despondent.

CHAP. XIII. He wished to give up the cause, and to end his days beside the throne of St. Peter[1]. But its occupant, and the other bishops, urged him to return home and finish the business, which could not be left in its present condition. He set forth accordingly, taking a last farewell of the sacred city, and carrying with him, 'as his custom was,' a store of relics duly catalogued, and vestments of silk and purple for churches,—together with the letters for the kings and the metropolitan; and also, probably, a letter, still extant[2], in which Pope John informed the English clergy that those of their body who had lately visited Rome had, after due deliberation, on the vigil of St. Gregory, laid aside the 'flowing laic garb,' and adopted close cassocks[3] after the Roman fashion,—an example which they were exhorted, 'by apostolic authority,' to imitate.

Wilfrid at Meaux.   The homeward journey was very trying to the aged bishop[4]. He became very ill, and after travelling on horseback as long as he could, was carried on a litter into Meaux, amid the wailing prayers[5] of his attendants, who thought that they were about to lose him while yet in a strange land. For four days and nights he lay as in a stupor, never tasting food or drink, and giving no token of life save by a faint breathing and by the animal warmth in his worn-out frame[6]. At last, on the fifth morning, while the watchers around his bed were weeping and reciting psalms, he raised himself up like one waking from sleep, and asked, ' Where is Acca the presbyter?' Acca came in, found him better and able to sit up, thanked God, and afterwards[7], when the rest were gone out, heard from Wilfrid that he had in his trance seen St. Michael, who had told him that he should live four years longer[8]. The

---

[1] Eddi, 55.

[2] Haddan and Stubbs, iii. 264.

[3] 'Talares tunicas.'   See above, p. 6.

[4] Eddi, 56.

[5] ' Mærentium, ad Dominumque clamantium;' Eddi.

[6] Eddi; Bede, v. 19 says, ' halitu pertenui.'

[7] Bede characteristically adds, 'They sat down together for a space, ac *de supernis judiciis trepidi*, began to talk a little,' &c.

[8] Bede reckons these ' four years' from his restoration.

story of the apparition is one of those imaginations which
degrade the sacred names introduced; the prolongation of
Wilfrid's life is not only ascribed to the intercession of the
Blessed Virgin, but the Archangel is made to remind the
great church-builder that he had 'never reared any house for
St. Mary,' and that 'he had to amend this' defect[1]. That
some such dream was described by Wilfrid to Acca, who told
it to Eddi, is not to be doubted: it would fall in with Wilfrid's
conceptions on such a subject. The bishop, Eddi then adds,
washed his face and hands in the sight of his delighted
followers, and, 'like Jonathan, felt his eyes to be enlightened
after taking some food;' after a few days he resumed his
journey, landed in Kent, and sent some of his clerks to confer
with Bertwald. We are informed that the archbishop was
overawed by the Pope's letter to him[2], which is not extant;
and that he 'promised to mitigate the harsh decrees formerly
passed in the synod.' Attended by a number of 'his abbots,'
Wilfrid passed by London, and entered Mercia, meaning to
present himself to King Ethelred. But Ethelred was king
no longer. He was the abbot of Bardney; he had resigned Ethelred
his crown after reigning twenty-nine years[3], and had retired abbot of
to the monastery in Lindsey which he and his murdered Bardney.
Northumbrian wife had 'greatly loved, reverenced, and
adorned[4].' One thinks of the ex-king, the son of Penda,
gazing at the tomb of his father's sainted victim, where the
banner of gold and purple, or the shreds that might remain
of it, still bore witness to Oswald's majesty[5]. And here, under
the roof of this royal abbey, Wilfrid was fain to meet Ethelred.
The old men embraced, and wept for joy: Ethelred, on seeing
the papal letter,—a duplicate, of course, of the one addressed
to Aldfrid conjointly with himself,—looked on its 'bulls' and

[1] Eddi, 56. Bede omits this.

[2] Eddi says, 57, 'per nuntios scriptis directis,' as if the pope's letter had
been entrusted to Bertwald's envoys; while it appears from Eddi, 53, 55,
that it was entrusted to Wilfrid. But from c. 60 we learn that the envoys had
one copy, and Wilfrid brought another.

[3] See Chronicle, a. 704; Florence, a. 716. Ethelred had resigned before
June 13, 704; Cod. Dipl. i. 60.

[4] Bede, iii. 11: 'Ut monasterium nobile,' &c. See above, p. 159.

[5] Above, p. 160.

seals very differently from Egfrid on a former occasion. He bowed to the very ground after hearing the letter read, and promised that he would do his best to procure compliance

Kenred king of Mercia.

with its directions. He kept his word by summoning his nephew Kenred [1], who had succeeded him on his abdication, and who assured him that he also would 'obey the precepts of the Apostolic see.' During a short stay in the Mercian realm, Wilfrid probably met Edgar, then bishop of Lindsey [2], and would hear that in the neighbouring realm of East-Anglia the see of Elmham was held by Nothbert [3], and that of Dunwich perhaps by Aldbert [4], while the foundation of his friend Queen Etheldred was under the care of Ermenild, the widow of Wulfhere, or possibly of her daughter Werburga, who had been active during her uncle Ethelred's reign in founding nunneries at Trentham, Hanbury, and Weedon [5]. Before leaving Lindsey, Wilfrid, by Ethelred's advice, sent an abbot named Badwin and a 'teacher [6]' called Alfrid to apprise the Northumbrian king of his return, and to ask leave for Wilfrid to come to him with the Apostolic letter of greeting, and with the Apostolic decisions in the cause. Aldfrid gave them a courteous reception, and appointed a

Obstinacy of Aldfrid.

day for his definite answer. But when, on that day, they again appeared before him, he, by advice of his counsellors, spoke thus : 'Venerable brothers both, ask of me whatever you want for yourselves, and I will give it you. But, from this day forth, never ask of me anything for Wilfrid

---

[1] He was son of Wulfhere, and brother of St. Werbura. He confirmed a grant of land at Twickenham to bishop Waldhere; Kemble, Cod. Dipl. i. 60. Bede tells a terrible story (v. 13, told him by bishop Pecthelm) respecting a thane in Kenred's service whom the young king often admonished to amend his conduct, but who always answered that he had time enough before him. He died in despair, and Malmesbury sees in this a main cause of Kenred's resolution to go to Rome and turn monk; G. Reg. i. 4.

[2] See Bede, iv. 12. He signs, as bishop, a charter of Ethelward, 'sub-regulus' of the Hwiccas, in favour of Egwin's new monastery, in 706; Cod. Dipl. i. 65.

[3] Florence, App., Mon. H. Brit. p. 618. He signs the same charter.

[4] He was bishop when Bede wrote; v. 23: the date of his accession is unknown. Florence calls him Æsculf.

[5] Cp. Alb. Butler, Feb. 3. See above, p. 188.

[6] Comp. Bede, iv. 5 : 'Magistris ecclesiæ pluribus.'

your lord. For what my predecessors[1], and the archbishop, with their advisers, determined, and what I myself with the archbishop[2] and nearly all the bishops of the nation have decided upon, this I am resolved never, while I live, to alter for any alleged writings from the Apostolic see[3].'

It was afterwards said that Aldfrid, on his death-bed, regretted his treatment of Wilfrid, and exhorted his future successor to obey the Pope's decree. His sister Elfled is cited by Eddi[4] as an authority, among other 'eye-witnesses,' for the king's 'repentance,' and for this speech, which included a promise on his own part, if his life should be spared. Eddi presumes that Aldfrid 'the Wise' knew his illness to be 'a stroke of the Apostle's power.' He did not recover: for some days he was speechless, and on the 14th of December, 705[5], he died at Driffield, 'the field of Deira,' an ancient town in the East Riding. For eight weeks the kingdom was in the hands of Eadwulf, who is ignored by the Chronicle: and his usurpation was the first specimen of several feeble and ignoble kingships, which caused men to look upon the close of Aldfrid's nineteen years as a disastrous epoch for Northumbria[6]. Wilfrid had ventured to return to Ripon[7] before

---

[1] So Eddi, 58, by a slip for 'predecessor.'

[2] Again, as in Eddi, 53, the phrase, ' ab apostolica sede emisso,' is applied without propriety to Bertwald.

[3] 'Propter apostolicæ sedis, *ut dicitis,* scripta.' Hook's mistranslation, ' from the apostolic see, *as you call it,*' i. 191, is a serious misrepresentation.

[4] Together with ' Ethelburga, abbess ;' Eddi, 59.

[5] Bede and the Chronicle give the year; the Chronicle gives the day and place.

[6] Bede, Ep. to Egbert, 7. Boniface, Ep. 62, tells king Ethelbald of Mercia that the privileges of Northumbrian churches remained inviolate until the time of king Osred.

[7] Eddi says, ' cum filio suo proprio veniens de Hrypis ;' 59. On this it has been asked, Was Wilfrid ever married? Kemble supposes that he had been; ii. 444. But this would be inconsistent with Eddi's account of his early life, and with his own affirmation, Eddi, 21. Raine thinks that the relationship was a spiritual one, Hist. Ch. York, i. 89 ; and although the word ' proprio' is remarkable, as followed by the statement, that Osred became his ' filius adoptivus,' it may be used to indicate a ' sonship' more sacred and intimate than would be constituted by simple ' adoption.' See Eddi, 18, for the story of the boy (Eodbald), surnamed ' Bishop's son.' Above, p. 247.

CHAP. XIII. he sent messengers to Eadwulf, who repelled them with an 'austere' reply, swearing by his salvation that unless Wilfrid left his realm within six days, any of his companions found

Osred king of Northumbria. in it should be put to death. But in February, a successful conspiracy overthrew Eadwulf and enthroned Osred, son of Aldfrid, a boy of eight, in the first year of whose reign [1] another Council was called to settle the 'cause of Wilfrid' in the manner suggested by Pope John. The place of this assembly was somewhere on the river Nidd [2], which flows from the north-west by Knaresborough, and is invested with remarkable associations of later date.

Council of the Nidd. This Council of the Nidd was not, like that of Easterfield, a representation of all the English Churches. Bertwald was the only Southern prelate present : he and Wilfrid arrived on the same day. The boy-king and his earls appeared with the three Northumbrian bishops, Bosa, John, and Eadfrid, and certain abbots, and the abbess Elfled, 'ever the comforter and best counsellor of the whole province [3].' The archbishop was in a different mood from that in which he had seconded Aldfrid's rigorous line of conduct towards Wilfrid. He rose, and at once took the line of a peacemaker : 'Let us pray to our Lord, that He would by His Holy Spirit infuse into our hearts the spirit of concord.' Then, speaking as Theodore would never have condescended to speak, in the deferential style of one who was not certain of his own authority in Northumbria, Bertwald said that he and Bishop Wilfrid had certain letters directed to him from the Apostolic see, which they wished the Council to hear ; and the document, of which, it appears, there were two copies, was read accordingly. Bertfrid, the chief ealdorman, said to the archbishop, 'We should like to hear it translated into our own language.' Bertwald answered by remarking—a true remark for many an age—on the periphrastic lengthiness of the Papal style [4], and added

---

[1] It was a bad reign ; see Boniface, Ep. 62. He was a profligate youth, and was killed in battle, when only nineteen, Chron. a. 716 ; Hen. Hunt. iv. 8 ; cp. Malm. G. R. i. 53. Bede records his violent death, v. 22.

[2] Bede, v. 19, 'juxta fluvium Nidd.' Eddi adds, 'ab oriente,' 60.

[3] 'Consolatrix optimaque consiliatrix.'

[4] 'Longo circuitu et ambagibus verborum ;' Eddi.

that he could give the sense of the letter in few words. The Apostolic see, which had power to bind and to loose, had ordered that in his presence the bishops of Northumbria should be reconciled to Bishop Wilfrid. They must choose one of two courses. Either let them make peace with Wilfrid, and restore, as the Witan should decide together with the archbishop, 'those parts of the churches which Wilfrid himself once ruled;' or else let all the parties concerned meet at Rome, to have the affair settled by a greater Council. To refuse both these courses would be to incur deposition: a layman so offending would incur excommunication 'from the Body and Blood of Christ.' The three bishops, who evidently deemed their chief a weak deserter, boldly asked, 'How can any one have power to change what our predecessors, and Theodore, and King Egfrid, ordained, and what afterwards, in the field called Easterfield, we and nearly all the bishops of Britain decreed, with King Aldfrid, and in your presence, O Archbishop?' The tide, however, had turned against them. Elfled declared that Aldfrid had in his last days expressed his intentions in favour of Wilfrid with the solemnity of a vow as to himself, of an injunction as to his heir; and Bertfrid, speaking for the king and the ealdormen, announced their mind to the same purpose. He told what had lately happened: when besieged in Bamborough[1] by Eadwulf, and shut up within the limits of a rocky fortress, he and his fellow-earls had vowed that if 'their royal boy' should gain his father's kingdom, they would adhere to the decisions of Rome about Wilfrid; straightway the besiegers had come over to their side, and sworn friendship towards them,—the gates of the city had been thrown open, they had been delivered from their distress,—their royal boy was king. The three bishops saw that it was a time for peaceful settlement, on such terms as could be accepted. They conferred with Bertwald, and then with Elfled; and the result—the end of the whole weary controversy—was another compromise. For all the big words about obedience to Papal mandates, the mandates of Agatho, of Benedict, and of Sergius were *not* obeyed: the

Final compromise.

---

[1] 'Bebbanburg.' See above, p. 25.

CHAP. XIII. liberty of decision conceded by John VI. to a Northumbrian synod was used in such a manner as Wilfrid himself had in some sense foreseen, when he intimated that his full claim might be more than Northumbrian authorities would grant. Bede says indeed, in one place, that he was 'received again to the prelacy of his own church[1];' but in another he explains that this church was Hexham, and that when Wilfrid 'after his long exile' was restored to this bishopric[2], John, on the death of Bosa[3], was placed in the see of York[4]. So that, in fact, the second compromise was less favourable than the first: Wilfrid, in 686, became bishop of York, though with a diminished diocese; in 706 he had to be content with the see of Hexham and the minster of Ripon,—clearly, in the first instance, with Ripon only, until Bosa's death, which soon followed, opened the way for an arrangement. Wilfrid had thus to abandon his claim on the ancient see of the royal city, the mother-church of Northumbria; he had to acquiesce in the translation of John from Hexham to York, and to take possession of Hexham as John's successor. He recovered, however, all his domains and monasteries, in Northumbria and in Mercia. The arrangements made in the Council were sealed by a solemn Eucharist, at which the four prelates of Northumbria exchanged the kiss of peace, and shared in the Bread of unity. And so, writes Eddi, 'they returned to their own homes in the peace of Christ;' and the once fiery and imperial spirit of Wilfrid, bent and chastened by age and troubles, was content with the prospect of quiet and peace in exchange for the hope of triumphant ascendency. But, from a purely Roman point of view, the settlement was somewhat

---

[1] Bede, v. 19. So Eadmer, who wishes to make it appear that Wilfrid simply triumphed, 51.

[2] Bede, v. 3. He plainly refers to the second exile.

[3] Bosa's death, as we have seen, was erroneously ante-dated by Florence. See Haddan and Stubbs, iii. 171; Stubbs, Registr. Angl. p. 4; and Smith's Bede, p. 759, 'Bosa ante annum 705 non obiit.'

[4] It was as bishop of York that John visited the nunnery of ' Wetadun,' and prayed over a sick nun, Bede, v. 3; and dedicated a church on the estate of an earl named Puch, two miles from Beverley (v. 4), and another church founded by earl Addi in the neighbourhood (v. 5)—indications of the growth of that parochial system which 'needed no foundation;' Stubbs, Const. Hist. i. 260: see above, p. 178, and below, Add. Note F.

of an impotent conclusion: an ardent supporter of Roman claims would be disappointed at such a result of reiterated Papal decisions, although he might console himself by the reflection that if Wilfrid had not, in effect, secured all that he had once hoped for, his protracted cause had at least familiarised his fellow-Churchmen with the thought of appeals to the 'Apostolic see.' His pertinacity had not led to any immediate and brilliant success; but it had formed a precedent which might, under favourable auspices, be productive of greater things hereafter [1].

---

[1] On the 'system of appeals to Rome,' as having begun with Anselm, see Dean Church's Life of St. Anselm, p. 223.

CHAPTER XIV.

WE must now, once more, turn back from the continuous story of Wilfrid's contests and troubles to the quiet development of Church life and work in the southern districts, and particularly among the West-Saxons. We have seen something of Aldhelm's unrivalled celebrity and influence; and the interest of ecclesiastical annals, as regards the ordinary progress of the English Church, centres at this point in him. Of him probably Bertwald thought, when he urged on the Wessex authorities the partition of their great diocese, —a step which Heddi seems to have regarded with disfavour, and to have hindered during his own lifetime. The difficulty was so serious that in 704, the year of Wilfrid's sojourn at Rome, a provincial Council in its yearly meeting threatened to suspend communion with Wessex, if there were further delay in the appointment of another bishop, at least, for that kingdom[1]. But in the following year, 705[2], we find a number of English bishops[3] taking part in a synod which was held, apparently, within the bounds of Wessex, and which resolved to remonstrate with the neighbouring British clergy and laity on their obnoxious Easter-rule. Who so fit as the

---

[1] Haddan and Stubbs, iii. 267, 275: the letter of bishop Waldhere. This throws a doubt on a quotation by Rudborne of a 'decree of Theodore,' to the effect that the diocese was not to be divided in Heddi's lifetime; Angl. Sac. i. 193; Haddan and Stubbs, iii. 126.

[2] Faricius says, indeed, in 706; but this would not suit the notes of time for the episcopate of Aldhelm. Probably he was misled by a record connecting this synod with the first year of the Northumbrian Osred, whose right to his father's crown would in some sense be traced to the end of 705. See Haddan and Stubbs, iii. 268.

[3] Aldhelm, Ep. 1: 'Ex tota pæne Britannia innumerabilis Dei sacerdotum caterva confluxit.' It was not, then, as Faricius says, a mere West-Saxon synod.

abbot of Malmesbury, the foremost scholar in all the English
Churches, to undertake such a task?   To him, accordingly, it
was committed[1]; and he wrote, at once, what is reckoned as
the first of his letters[2], and is addressed, in highly respectful
terms, to 'the most glorious lord, swaying the sceptre of the
Western realm, whom the writer embraces with brotherly
charity,—to King Geruntius, and at the same time to all
God's priests[3] dwelling in Domnonia.' This potentate was the
British king Geraint, who appears in the Chronicle for 710
as defeated by Ine: his realm was nearly the whole of
Dyfnaint[4], that is, of Devonshire and Cornwall, the 'West
Wales' of English speech, which still maintained its Celtic
independence, and only by degrees gave place to the advance
of the Saxon.   Geraint, indeed, held part of Somerset-
shire, until Ine built Taunton as a frontier-fortress[5].   To
this prince, then, Aldhelm wrote, in effect as follows.   'I
am commissioned by a large Council of bishops to call your
attention to four points which are faulty in regard to the
clergy of your nation.   First, your priests are said to be
contentious: they do not live in harmony with each other.
They ought to remember the sayings of Scripture in praise
of concord.   Secondly, there has been a rumour, widely spread,
to the effect that certain priests and clerics in your province
obstinately refuse the tonsure of St. Peter, on the ground of
adherence to the tradition of their predecessors.   As for the
tonsure which they use, it is, according to the opinion of
most persons[6], traceable to Simon, the inventor of art-magic;
and this I take to be the case, because the Clementine books
testify to his machinations, as a wizard, against St. Peter.

---

[1] 'Jubente synodo,' Bede, v. 18. Aldhelm refers, in 'De Laud. Virginit.' 2,
to a 'pontificale conciliabulum' which he had attended.

[2] See it in Migne, Patr. Lat. lxxxix. 87; Haddan and Stubbs, iii. 268.

[3] As we have seen (p. 222) two of Chad's consecrators were probably from
this part of the British Church. See Haddan and Stubbs, i. 150.

[4] Probably 'the dark valleys,' e.g. of Dartmoor. Strictly, Dyfnaint would be
distinguished from Cernau, or Cornwall. For this king Geraint, and for
an earlier who has left his name at 'St. Gerrans,' in Cornwall, see Dict. Chr.
Biogr. ii. 664, 666.

[5] Soon after his victory, Chron. 716. See above, p. 322. Wessex had
stretched to the Parret since 658.

[6] 'Secundum plurimorum opinionem.' See above, p. 81.

CHAP. XIV. We, bearing testimony, according to Scripture, concerning our tonsure, assert that St. Peter appointed it for several reasons [1];—but we see an indication of it in the ancient Nazarites, and it seems to be a symbol both of royalty and priesthood, so that the heads of clerics illustrate St. Peter's own saying, "Ye are . . . a royal priesthood [2]." But, thirdly, there is another and a more cruel mischief to souls, in that your priests do not follow the rule of the Nicene Council as to Easter. That rule prescribed the use of a cycle of nineteen years [3], and made the fifteenth moon the beginning of the Paschal "calculation," and the twenty-first moon the end of it,' (i. e. the possible Easter Sundays were those from the fifteenth to the twenty-first moon inclusive). 'But your priests, following the canon of Anatolius [4], or rather that of Sulpicius Severus, keep Easter with the Jews on the fourteenth moon: whereas the Roman pontiffs have not sanctioned either canon, nor that of Victorius, which embraces five hundred and thirty-two years. For there was an old sect of heretics called Tessareskaidecaditæ, who were excommunicated for keeping the fourteenth moon with the Jews as the time for the Paschal festival. Fourthly, the priests of the Demetians [5] (i. e. the people of our present

---

[1] Three are then given: (1) to represent the crown of thorns; (2) to distinguish the old from the new priesthood; (3) 'that Peter and his successors might bear ridiculosum gannaturæ ludibrium in populo Romano, quia et eorum barones et hostes exercitu superatos sub corona vendere solebant.'

[2] It would almost seem as if Aldhelm thought that 1 Pet. ii. 9 was addressed to the clergy as such.

[3] He adds, 'composed of an ogdoad and a hendecadas;' see Bede, De Temporibus, c. 11: 'Cyclum decennovenalem propter xiv. lunas paschales Nicæna synodus instituit, eo quod ad eundem anni solaris diem unaquæque luna per xix. annos . . . redeat . . ;' 'Octo enim anni lunares totidem annos solares duobus tantum diebus transcendunt, quorum alter ad explementum occurrit hendecadis,' &c.; and his verses 'De Ratione Temporum.' On the nineteen years' cycle, see also Ceolfrid (in effect, Bede) in Bede, v. 21.

[4] See Bede, iii. 3, 'æstimans, &c. . . . Anatolii scripta secutam;' and iii. 25, where Colman argues that Anatolius reckoned from 'the fourteenth,' and Wilfrid replies that *he* framed a cycle of nineteen years which Colman ignored, and that he regarded the fourteenth evening as the beginning of the fifteenth moon. See above, pp. 80, 206.

[5] Demetia is here used for Deheubarth or South Wales; Palgrave, p. 457; Pearson's Hist. Maps, p. 22; although in a stricter sense it meant the south-western part, Pembrokeshire and the parts next to it, otherwise called Dyfed;

South Wales), who dwell beyond the Severn, will not even CHAP. XIV.
pray with a Saxon in church, nor eat with him at table.
On the contrary, they throw to dogs and swine the remains
of his meal, and insist on cleansing with sand or ashes [1] the
dishes or bowls from which he has eaten and drunk. They
refuse us the kiss of peace ; they even refuse us an ordinary
greeting. If any of our people, that is, of Catholics, go to
dwell among them [2], they put them under penance for forty
days. This is like those heretics who called themselves
"the Pure [3]." Alas! it is like the Pharisees who incurred
the "woe" for cleansing the outside of cup and platter, and
for indulging in a spirit of self-righteous intolerance. I
entreat you, "do not superciliously and doggedly refuse to
obey the decrees of St. Peter, nor in tyrannous pertinacity
spurn the tradition of the Roman Church for the sake of the
statutes of your own forefathers." It was to Peter that the
keys were given: who then can hope to enter the gate of
paradise, if in this world he despises the statutes of Peter's
Church? But perhaps some one, proud of his knowledge
of Scripture, will say, "I sincerely believe both Testaments,
and will freely proclaim to the people the true faith as to
the Trinity, the Incarnation, the Passion, the Resurrection."
But "faith without works is dead;" faith, if it is Catholic,
is inseparable from charity, or else it profits nothing; good
works are profitless outside the Catholic Church, even if they
include strict observance of cœnobitic discipline, or even the
severest asceticism of the anchorite: in one word, it is idle to
boast of true belief, unless one follows the rule of St. Peter.'

It must be owned that this letter does not raise our opinion
of Aldhelm. It is superior to many of his remains in point
of style, that is, it is comparatively free from the extravagant

---

see Lappenberg, i. 120; Haddan and Stubbs, i. 144; Jones and Freeman's
Hist. St. David's, p. 237. Giraldus, in Descr. Kamb. i. 2, calls Demetia a
portion of Deheubarth containing seven ' cantrevs ' or hundreds.

[1] ' Aut harenosis sabulorum glareis, aut fulvis favillarum cineribus.' See
above, p. 102.

[2] The West-Saxons who gradually settled beyond our present Somerset,
amid a British population, called themselves Defnsætas, dwellers in Dyfnaint,
—whence ' men of Devon.'

[3] Novatians, the ' Cathari;' Nicene can. 8.

CHAP. XIV. and often ludicrous grandiloquence[1] which, being a characteristic of one so greatly admired and honoured, did much to pervert the taste of those who looked to him as a model, especially of the charter-writers of the ninth century[2]. We have more serious matter in this letter to King Geraint. The absurdity of Aldhelm's remarks on the tonsure is disappointing; but the unfairness (shown also by Eddi) of confounding the Britons with Quartodecimans, the virtual identification of faith like St. Peter's with conformity to all the decrees or observances of Rome[3], the conspicuous lack of a sense of proportion in matters ecclesiastical or religious,— these things awaken a stronger feeling than that of mere disappointment. If so good a man and so well-read a student could sink into such petty narrowness, what must have been the effect of Latin rigorism on the rank and file of Latinised clergy? The calm assumption that the British Church was not Catholic is in full accord with the apparent unconsciousness of any provocations of the 'Saxon' side which had stirred the resentful Celtic nature to such coarse demonstrations as are here denounced, or as, in the Irish bishop Dagan's case, had shocked the first successor of Augustine[4]. The intense antipathy of the British to the English Church, described by Bede as a virtual non-recognition of its Christianity[5], was of course connected with the bitter recollections of the English conquest, the humiliating experiences of English ascendency. After all such allowances, it was doubtless excessive and unchristian-like; it must have been fostered by the continuous neglect or refusal of all responsibility in regard to the evangelisation of the 'Saxons' while yet

---

[1] See above, p. 269.

[2] Lingard, A.-S. Ch. ii. 152, 404, says that Boniface showed traces of this bad habit, but that it hardly reappears afterwards until in the ninth century it was 'revived in all its extravagance' by charter-writers.

[3] Aldhelm undoubtedly treats Rome as the centre of unity and the standard of doctrine and discipline. He puts into sonorous form the argument with which Oswy closed the Whitby conference.

[4] Above, p. 101.

[5] Bede, ii. 20. See Lingard, A.-S. Ch. i. 61: 'In their estimation the Saxons were . . . the children of robbers . . possessing the fruit of their fathers' crimes, and therefore still lying under the maledictions formerly pronounced by the British bishops against the invaders.'

heathen; but we have Aldhelm's word for the existence, among these remoter Welsh, of the theological learning and the monastic self-devotion which had distinguished the Church of Padarn and Illtyd, of Dubricius and David. The effect of Aldhelm's exhortations was confined, says Bede, to those Britons who were 'subject to the West-Saxons[1],' that is, who dwelt in parts of Devon and Somerset which were no longer British. No inhabitants of Wales adopted the 'Catholic Easter' until 755–777, when 'their Easter was altered' first in North Wales, then, after much resistance, in South Wales, by the counsel 'of Elbod, a man of God,' who is also described as 'archbishop of Gwynedd[2],' and after whose death the contest was renewed; while, so far as 'West Wales' was concerned, there was no surrender of the national 'Pasc' until after the foundation of the Saxon bishopric of Crediton in the early part of the tenth century[3], although a Cornish bishop, some fifty years before, had submitted to Canterbury. However, it pleased Malmesbury to say, 'The Britons even to this day owe their correction to Aldhelm[4].' The Celtic persistency had given way in more than one quarter when Aldhelm was thus employed against its southwestern strongholds. The Northern Irish had followed, about 704, the example set by the Southern Irish after the Council of the White Field in 634: they had yielded to the influence of Adamnan[5], who had candidly examined the subject, and

---

[1] Bede, v. 18. Were these the 'nonnulla pars de Brettonibus' to whom Bede refers in v. 15? The reference to Adamnan there might seem to point to Britons of Strathclyde. The laws of Ine treat Britons as subjects, though of a lower class; s. 23, 24, 32, 46: see Freeman, i. 34, and Hist. Cath. Ch. of Wells, p. 18.

[2] See Ann. Camb., and Brut, in Mon. Hist. Br. pp. 834, 843, and another form in Haddan and Stubbs, i. 204, and Ann. Menev. in Angl. Sac. ii. 648. See Lingard, A.-S. Ch. i. 62. According to Rees, Welsh Saints, p. 66, North Wales adopted the Catholic Easter soon after Elbod became bishop of Bangor in 755. The South Welsh resisted until 777: and when Elbod died in 809 they returned for a time to their old rule. For Elbod or Elfod, as probably bishop of Bangor, and as not proved to be a metropolitan, although clearly not under a metropolitan, see Jones and Freeman, Hist. St. David's, p. 258.

[3] Haddan and Stubbs, i. 676. The Cornish bishop was Kenstec; the first bishop of Crediton was Eadulf: see Haddan and Stubbs, i. 674, 676.

[4] Malmesb. Gest. Pontif. v. 215. He adds, 'Although, in their ingrained wickedness, they ignore the man and set at nought the book.'

[5] See Bede, v. 15: 'Navigavit Hiberniam, et praedicans eis,' &c.

CHAP. XIV. come to the conclusion that the Roman system was correct, but, abbot of Hy as he was, had failed to carry his own monks along with him, and even in North Ireland those who were specially under the sway of Hy stood out against the arguments of its head [1]. But after several years, they were 'brought round' by his influence 'from their ancestral errors.' The Pictish Church was persuaded or constrained by its king Nechtan or Naiton (himself convinced by a missionary named Boniface) [2] to yield to the representations of Abbot Ceolfrid in a letter which Bede himself may well have penned [3], five years after the letter of Aldhelm to Geraint: and even the stubbornness of St. Columba's own monastery was broken down by the persuasions of the priest Egbert, six years later yet, in 716 [4].

The obstacle to the partition of the West-Saxon diocese was removed in 705, on the 7th of July [5], or more probably earlier, by the death of Heddi, after an episcopate of nearly thirty years. Then, at last, the partition took place; but it was not an equal one [6], for Winchester retained only Hampshire and Surrey, while the other parts

West-
Saxon
diocese
divided.

---

[1] Adamnan was in Ireland in 686; on his return to Hy, he vainly endeavoured to establish there the 'Catholic' Easter. He revisited Ireland in 692, and again in 697; then remained there seven years, and 'taught nearly all of those who were free from the dominion of the monks of Hy to observe the legitimate time of Easter;' Bede, v. 15. Whether the English-born St. Gerald of Mayo lived thus early, and was his host, is uncertain. He had the satisfaction of celebrating the 'true' Easter of 704 in Ireland, returned to Hy, and died on Sept. 23, 704; so that, as Bede expresses it, he was spared 'a more serious contest, at the return of Easter, with those who would not follow him to the truth.' See Lanigan, iii. 150; Reeves's Adamnan, p. lvi.; Haddan and Stubbs, ii. 110; Skene, Celt. Sc. ii. 174.

[2] He afterwards 'drove the non-conforming Columbian monks past his frontier;' so Reeves, p. 184 (i. e. monks dependent on Hy). Cp. Skene, i. 284.

[3] Bede, v. 21. The letter is a repository of the Roman topics of argument as to 'Pasch' and tonsure.

[4] Bede, v. 22. Haddan and Stubbs, ii. 114.

[5] See Alb. Butler. But this day is too late, if Aldhelm died in the fifth year of his episcopate; Malmesb. v. 231. It is probable that after the threat of suspension of communion at a synod of 704, there was an agreement that the division should take place as soon as the now aged bishop had passed away.

[6] See Malmesb. Gest. Pontif. v. 223. The Chronicle says that Aldhelm 'was bishop on the west of Selwood.'

of Wessex—Wiltshire, Dorsetshire, Berkshire, and part if not CHAP. XIV.
the whole of Somerset—were annexed to the new see, which
was established at Sherborne.   For Winchester a bishop was
found who is best known to us through his correspondence
with the great St. Boniface.   This was Daniel, who was still Daniel,
living when Bede wrote[1]: it was he who overcame the repug- bishop of Winches-
nance of the Isle of Wight to West-Saxon dominion sufficiently ter.
for the regular annexation of its church to his bishopric, and
who promoted the revival of the South-Saxon bishopric of
Selsey[2].   He gave most opportune encouragement to the
mission-schemes of Winfrid, afterwards known as Boniface,
who at the time of his consecration for Winchester was living
as a young monk of twenty-five in a Hampshire monastery
called Nutscelle[3], where under the abbot Winbert he studied
the 'tripartite' sense[4] of Scripture, together with grammar
and metres, and, while he attended diligently to his portion of
manual labour and to all the details of Benedictine observance, was making himself eminent as a teacher, kindling
enthusiasm for sacred knowledge in the minds of his auditors,
every day learning by heart something from the Scriptures,
or from the 'acts' of those martyrs whom he was one day
gloriously to join, and was uniformly cordial and helpful to all
who came under his influence, whether poor or rich, whether
thrall or free[5].   Daniel discerned in him a 'vessel for honour,' Boniface in
and gave him, on his second journey into Frisia, a letter of Frieseland.
commendation to any kings, dukes, bishops, abbots, presbyters, and 'spiritual sons,' asking them to show hospitality,
after the manner of the patriarchs, to the religious presbyter
Winfrid[6].   A letter written long afterwards by Boniface to
Daniel informs us that the latter in old age became blind[7];

[1] Bede, v. 18.   He supplied Bede with some documents, and survived him
ten years.
[2] Bede, iv. 16; v. 18.   Stephens, Memor. See of Chich. p. 22.
[3] Willibald, Vit. S. Bonifac. c. 2.   See above, p. 323, and Maclear, Apostles
of Med. Eur. p. 110.   Winbert 'left behind him' a MS. of the Prophets in
'clear and distinct letters;' Bonif. Ep. 12.
[4] The threefold spiritual sense, moral, allegorical, and 'anagogical.'
[5] Willibald, c. 3.
[6] Bonif. Ep. 1.   This was in 718.
[7] Bonif. Ep. 12.   He retired to Malmesbury (his old home?) in 744.

CHAP. XIV. and two letters from Daniel [1] give us an insight into his mind and character, showing how he could advise and comfort. He urged Boniface not to be disheartened by his difficulties, not to attempt an impracticable separation of all the bad from all the good, a complete avoidance of all contact with false teachers; but here he carries his principle to toleration to the point of sanctioning, or imagining Scripture to sanction, a temporary simulation [2]. More interesting,—indeed, specially interesting,—is the other letter, in which Daniel suggests topics for missionary argument against polytheism, intended to draw the polytheist by a Socratic process into difficulties [3], and at the same time insists that these points are to be advanced with all gentleness, and to be followed up by indirect contrasts between Christianity and Pagan 'superstition.' But, it must be owned, Daniel again provokes criticism by recommending Boniface not only to insist on the argument, as we now call it, from *Christendom*,—from the world-wide spread of the Gospel,—but to point out that Christians enjoy the temporal blessing of 'lands fruitful in corn, wine, and oil,' while Heathenism is confined to climates of 'perpetual winter [4],'—a perilous exaggeration of 'the promise of the life that now is.'

This was the prelate, then, who in the autumn of 705 succeeded Heddi at Winchester. For Sherborne there could be but one choice; all orders, including a multitude of the people [5], turned at once to Aldhelm, 'who was specially re-

Aldhelm,
bishop of
Sherborne.

---

[1] Bonif. Ep. 13, 14. Of these letters, Ep. 13 was written several years after Ep. 14, i.e. when Boniface was archbishop.

[2] Following Jerome, and thereby forsaking St. Augustine, he treats St. Peter's conduct in Gal. ii. 12 as right, and compares it to the conduct of St. Paul in Acts xxi. 26, &c. He seems not to see the difference between any kind of 'simulation,' or even of pretending (fingendi), and such an 'economy' as is free of insincerity.

[3] E.g. 'Since the gods had a beginning, what of the world? If it had a beginning, who made it? Not the gods, who were confessedly not eternal. If it was eternal, who ruled it before the gods? How was the first god produced? Will any more come into being? How do they know what god is the mightiest? Valde cavendum est ne in potiorem quis offendat. Do they expect temporal or eternal happiness? Do the gods *need* their sacrifices?' &c.

[4] 'Frigore semper rigentes terras.' See above, p. 127.

[5] Faricius, c. 3. 'Omnis aetatis et ordinis conflatur sententia;' Malmesb. G. P. v. 223. The 'people' or laity were active in this election.

commended by the very fact that he showed reluctance to accept the promotion [1].' He was, of course, present at the Witenagemot; we picture him according to a pupil's description, as a tall man with white hair and sparkling eyes [2]. He endeavoured to decline the great office. 'I am too old, I need rest.' Instantly, and by acclamation, came the reply: 'The older, the wiser and the fitter [3]!' He still held out as long as he could without unseemliness; but 'as he had not been drawn on by ambition, so neither did he draw back in disobedience: in each respect he observed the mean [4].' He yielded, and was conducted to Canterbury for consecration. With what recollections must he have trod the precinct of Christ Church, and visited his old master Hadrian, still living and officiating as abbot in St. Peter's! After his consecration, the archbishop detained him for some time in order to get the benefit of his counsels [5]. When he took possession of his new bishopric, he built a church at Sherborne, which Malmesbury tells us that he himself had seen [6]. The little town, he says elsewhere, was 'not an agreeable place; it had neither a good situation nor a large population; it was surprising, it was almost disgraceful, that it should have retained an episcopal see for so many ages [7],'—in fact, through twenty-seven episcopates, of which the most noteworthy was that of Asser, the Welsh counsellor and biographer of Alfred, and the last was Herman's, who after uniting Sherborne to the younger bishopric of Ramsbury [8], removed his see

---

[1] Faricius, c. 3. See above, p. 268.

[2] See Ethelwald's 'carmen' in Migne, lxxxix. 308.

[3] Malmesbury, v. 223.

[4] 'Servavit modum,' Faricius.

[5] Malmesbury; who brings in here a story of Aldhelm's visiting Dover, and finding some sailors at work in landing a store of books. Attracted by one, which includes both Testaments, he turns over the leaves and begins to bargain for it: they abuse him for trying to beat down the price of their property. He only smiles; they row off, are caught in a storm, and cry out to him for pardon; he signs the cross and rows to their vessel; they make the shore safely, and offer to give him the book: he insists on paying for it,—and it is preserved at Malmesbury as a specimen of antiquity; v. 224. Faricius tells this tale rather differently, and dates it earlier.

[6] 'Ecclesiam quam ego quoque vidi mirifice construxit.'

[7] Malmesb. G. P. ii. 79. Cp. Stubbs, Registr. Sacr. Anglic. p. 165.

[8] Founded for Wiltshire, to relieve Sherborne, in 909.

to Old Sarum, in obedience to the Council of 1075. Aldhelm wished to resign the headship of Malmesbury and its dependent monasteries; but his monks could not brook such a loss[1]. They rejected the notion of having any other

'president[2]' in his lifetime. His object had been to secure desirable appointments; and when he yielded to his monks' affectionate resistance, he took care to guard their right of free election by a document which is said to have been duly signed and attested at Wimborne in the presence of Ine and Daniel, and afterwards confirmed by a Council on the Nodder. But this deed is at least of doubtful authenticity[3]. That he possessed a great influence, in things ecclesiastical, over Ine, may be taken for granted. It was probably through his influence that the foundation of the monastery of Abingdon, long interrupted by the delays and inconsistencies of Hean, was finally accomplished[4], by the renewed co-operation between him and his sovereign. And although the document which represents Ine as granting endowments to abbot Hemgils and his monks, in 'the old city which is called Glastingea,' and which professes to have been executed in the ancient 'wooden church' of that sacred isle, has been condemned as spurious,—being dated in 704, yet referring to the counsel of Aldhelm as bishop[5],—and although the Glastonbury tradition cannot convince us that Ine gave splendid gifts to that church, such as a chapel enriched with gold and silver[6], yet we may believe that he bestowed upon it some gifts which were afterwards exaggerated, and raised to the east of it a new minster, the

[1] Faricius, c. 3; Malmesbury, G. P. v. 225.   [2] 'Patronum.'

[3] Kemble rejects it, Cod. Dipl. i. 61. See Haddan and Stubbs, iii. 276. Another 'charter of Ine,' exempting West-Saxon monasteries from taxation, is dated in 704, and therefore is inconsistent with the date of Aldhelm's episcopate, while it refers to him as a prelate; Cod. Dipl. i. 57.

[4] See Stevenson, Chron. Abingd. ii. p. xiii. He adds, 'Aldhelm must have been conscious that, in promoting this object, he was promoting the interests of civilisation as well as those of Christianity,' &c. Above, p. 272.

[5] See this Parvum Privilegium Regis Inæ in Malmesb. de Antiq. Glast. Eccl. (XV Script. p. 309) and Cod. Dipl. i. 58. The Magnum Privilegium, which is clearly spurious, is in Malmesb. (Gest. Reg. i. s. 36) and Cod. Dipl. i. 85: it is dated in 725. A grant of lands at Brent (Cod. Dipl. i. 83) is at least very questionable (Haddan and Stubbs, iii. 307).

[6] XV Script. p. 310.

predecessor of the mighty abbey church [1].   Whether he did
anything in the way of founding a church at Wells must be,
at least, extremely uncertain : that he planted a bishopric at
Congresbury, afterwards removed to Wells, is a story without
real groundwork [2].

Aldhelm's ascetic habits had probably made him prematurely old.   But he abated none of them, while he discharged
his new duties indefatigably, visiting every part of his diocese, and preaching by night as well as by day [3].   This labour
wore him out in four years: the spring of 709 was the last
of his life.   He was at Dulting in Somerset, when his last
hour drew nigh.   He assembled a number of clergy, monks,
and laics, enforced on them the observance of the bond of
charity, and after commending his flock to the Divine care,
desired to be carried into the little wooden church [4] of the
village, and there, seated on a stone, breathed his last, on
the 25th of May, 709 [5].   He was buried, by his own desire,
in St. Michael's church at Malmesbury [6], and succeeded by
Forthere, a man of much theological learning, who was still
living when Bede wrote [7].

We draw towards the end : this year is the last of the great
period which we are reviewing.   Wilfrid had passed some
quiet years—between three and four—in the bishopric of
Hexham, with leisure for looking back, as from a well-loved
home and refuge, on the storms and the splendours of the past.
It was during this interval, in 707 [8], that some monks of the

---

[1] Freeman, Engl. Towns and Districts, p. 98.

[2] See Freeman, Hist. Cath. Ch. Wells, p. 13.

[3] Malmesb. G. P. v. 227 : he uses 'diœceses' for parts of the diocese.

[4] Afterwards rebuilt of stone by a monk of Glastonbury.   Comp. p. 50.

[5] See Faricius, c. 3 ; Malmesb. v. 228.

[6] The distance was fifty miles : a great crowd attended the corpse, each
thinking himself 'beatiorem qui propior esset,' and glad to see, if not to touch,
the bier on which the form and face, undefaced by decay, were visible.   Stone
crosses were afterwards set up at every seven miles of the road, which long
stood uninjured, and were called 'Bishopstones;' Malmesb. v. 230.   He
tells us that bishop Egwin came to Dulting to conduct the funeral.

[7] Bede, v. 18 : 'Quo defuncto,' &c.   See a grant of his in Cod. Dipl. i. 73.

[8] Bede, Ep. 3, to Plegwin; cp. Giles's Bede, i. p. cxxxv, for this date.
In the letter Bede refers to his Opusculum de Temporibus, as published five
years before.   This tract ends in the fifth year of Tiberius III., i. e. 701-2.
Hence we infer that the Wilfrid referred to in the letter was 'St. Wilfrid,' not

countryside [1], in his presence and over their cups, spoke of
Bede as 'a heretic.' Plegwin, one of the monks of Hexham,
hearing this, sent a messenger to inform Bede, who at first
'turned pale with horror,' then, on inquiring, found that
the reason was 'that he had denied that the Saviour had
come in the sixth age of the world.' On reflection, he concluded [2] that this was a misapprehension of what he had said,
five years before, in his tract 'On Times,' wherein he had
preferred the shorter or Hebrew chronology of Genesis,
according to which Christ must have come when five thousand
years were not completed [3]. He desired Plegwin to cause
this letter to be read [4] before their 'most reverend father and
lord Wilfrid, that as he was present when I was senselessly
assailed, he may hear, and judge for himself, how little I
deserved it.' The incident is curious, as a proof of the extent
of interest in questions of Scriptural chronology which was
felt at this time even by the 'rustic' monks of the North.
Often, no doubt, with Acca by his side, the bishop would
'walk about' the precinct of that basilica which Eddi has
called superior to all churches north of Wilfrid's beloved
Italy. Once, when going out of Hexham on some occasion,
he was struck with an illness of the same kind as that which
had prostrated him on his approach to Meaux. The tidings
brought a number of his abbots, and of the hermits dependent on his monasteries, to pray with his monks as he lay
unconscious; the aim of their prayers being that he might
at least have a return of consciousness, which would enable
him to dispose of his monasteries and his property [5]. He did
recover, not only consciousness, but a measure of health, and

---

Wilfrid II. (bishop of York, 718–732), as Smith (App. to Bede, p. 802) and
Raine (i. 93) assert.

[1] 'Rusticis.' See his Life of St. Felix, c. 8: 'Rusticus, non rustice, sed
docte ac fideliter agens.'

[2] 'Cogitare sedulus cœpi, unde hæc in me calumnia devolveretur.'

[3] Nor, indeed, four thousand; De Tempor. 22. Bede solemnly professes his
belief that Christ came in the sixth age, but says that an age has not a fixed
number of years. He cites Jerome in behalf of the Hebrew text; Ep. 3.

[4] By a certain David, who on the occasion referred to, when some other
'brother' vilified Bede, spoke in his favour, but could not explain what he had
meant.

[5] Eddi, 61: 'Ne nos quasi orbatos sine abbatibus relinqueret.'

lived a year and a half longer,—the illness having happened,
it would appear, in the spring of 708. In the following year,
when at Ripon, he caused his 'hoard' to be opened in the
presence of two abbots and six monks of proved fidelity [1].
They gazed on the shining store of gold and silver and jewels:
he bade his treasurer divide it into four parts. Then said the
bishop, 'Dearest brothers, you know that I have long thought
of making yet another visit to the see of St. Peter, where
I have so often been delivered from troubles, and there, if
God so willed, to end my life. I meant to offer gifts, from
the best part of this treasure, at the churches of St. Mary
and St. Paul at Rome. But should God provide for me otherwise,—as often happens to old men,—and my last day should
come sooner, then I charge you to send my gifts to those
churches. Of the three other parts, give one to the poor of
my flock, 'for the redemption of my soul [2];' let the abbots of
Hexham and Ripon share another between them, so that they
may purchase the favour of kings and bishops [3]. But as to
the last part,'—one may imagine the old man's eyes be-
dimmed as he proceeded,—'distribute it, according to each
man's proportion, among those who have suffered long exiles
with me, and to whom I have given no lands; let it go to
maintaining them when I am gone.' The tender and noble
heart, unchilled by age, felt warmly for the possible needs of
adherents so loyal and loving as those who had stood by him
through all troubles: he could not bear to think that they
should want when they had no longer the comfort of his
presence and protection. Soon afterwards he announced that
he had appointed one of these true companions, his own kinsman Tatbert, to preside over the minster of Ripon after his
death. This was spoken to his confidants: he then ordered

---

[1] Eddi, 62. See Lingard, A.-S. Ch. i. 270.

[2] A common phrase in ancient charters; see Kemble, Cod. Dipl. i. 73,
82, 90, 108. Bede, in his preface to his Life of Cuthbert, asks that
prayers may be made for him at Lindisfarne after his death, 'for the redemption of his soul.' 'Redemption,' in such phrases, was not used in its
strict sense; the phrase is equivalent to 'pro remedio animæ;' Cod. Dipl.
i. 1, 16, 26, 41, 55, &c. See above, p. 169.

[3] Contrast Aidan in Bede, iii. 5: 'Nullam potentibus sæculi pecuniam . . .
unquam dare solebat.' But 'old times were changed.' Above, p. 212.

CHAP. XIV. the bell[1] to be rung, and 'the whole family[2] of Ripon' obeyed
its summons.   He entered the chapter-house, sat down, and
said : ' Our brother Celin, sometime prior, wishes to adopt
the hermit-life ; and I will not detain him.   Do you all keep
to your rule, until, if God wills, I return to you.   But these
two abbots of ours, Tibba and Ebba, have come hither from
the Mercian king Ceolred, with an invitation for me to speak
to him on the affairs of our houses in Mercia, and have persuaded me to go.   When I return, I will bring with me the
person fittest for the presidency of this house ; but if anything
else should happen to me through my infirmities, then I bid
you all to accept as abbot whomsoever these who sit by me,
Tibba and Ebba, Tatbert, Hadufrid, and Aluhfrid, shall present
to you,'—meaning, of course, that Tatbert himself should be
so presented.   All the monks bowed to the ground, promised
obedience, received his benison, 'and, as a body, saw his face

Wilfrid in
Mercia.

no more.'   He proceeded into Mercia : King Kenred had, in
the spring of that same year, imitated, in part, the example of
Cadwalla by resigning his crown and going to Rome, accompanied by Offa, the young, handsome, and popular East-Saxon
king, son of Sighere[3],—and, according to an inferior authority,
by Egwin of Worcester, who wished to procure from Pope

---

[1] On the use of bells in ancient monasteries, see Wilson's Prehistoric Ann.
of Scotl. ii. 162.   Comp. Adamn. Vit. Col. i. 8, 'Cloccam pulsa ;' and iii. 23,
'media nocte pulsata personante clocca.'   So Vit. Sturm. 24 : Sturmi, dying,
orders ' omnes *gloggas* pariter moveri.'   Eddi calls it ' signum.'

[2] Eddi, 63.   So again, 65, 'familia tota ;' and 23, on the 'familia' of
Hexham.   So Bede, v. 2, on the 'familia' of bishop John.   So the community
of Hy was regarded as a ' familia ;' Reeves's Adamnan, p. 342 : comp. ib. 304 :
the term was also applied to all the Columbian communities as forming one
body ; ib. 162.   It meant a society of ' God's servants.'

[3] Chronicle, a. 709 ; Lappenberg, i. 223.   Bede, v. 19, calls Offa 'juvenis
amantissimæ ætatis et venustatis, totæque suæ genti ad tenenda servandaque
regni sceptra exoptatissimus . . . Qui . . reliquit uxorem . . . et patriam propter
Christum,' &c.   Even Bede could not see that Offa, in the prime of strength,
would have more truly acted ' propter Christum ' by doing the royal duty laid
upon him.   (Above, p. 369.)   See the striking anecdote of the Emperor
Henry II. being received by an abbot at Verdun into his community, and then
commanded, in virtue of monastic obedience, to return to the government confided to him by God ; Dunham's Germ. Empire, ii. 138.   Hen. Hunt. is enthusiastic : ' O Deus bone, quæ et qualia diademata eis reddes !'   Elmham, p. 236,
says that Offa acted by advice of Ethelred's sister Kineswith, or Kyneswide,
a nun at Caistor.   He was succeeded by Selred, son of Sigebert the Good.

Constantine a 'privilege' for Evesham [1]. Kenred had been CHAP. XIV.
succeeded by Ceolred, son of Ethelred, a prince who appears
in history as warring with Ine [2], in the legend of St. Guthlac
as persecuting the future King Ethelbald [3], and in the wild
and hideous 'vision' of a Wenlock recluse as a lost reprobate [4].
In his realm Wilfrid found all honourable reception : the
monasteries which he was anxious to visit were all in good
order : he went about among them, 'increasing their livelihood
by domains, or gladdening their hearts with money [5].' Once,
while riding along with Tatbert, he recounted from memory
all the events of his past life. Nothing was forgotten : every
bit of property which he had given, or now willed to give,
to his abbots, was duly specified : he named his beloved Acca
as the future abbot of Hexham. That ride must have been
a memorable one to the future abbot of Ripon : he must have
listened to an autobiography of almost matchless interest,—
the whole splendid exciting story, beginning with the boy's
presentation to Queen Eanfled, and passing through scenes so
varied and so eventful as no other prelate of that age could
have claimed as portions of his experience. At last Wilfrid
reached his minster of St. Andrew at Oundle, where another
illness ere long warned him that the hour was at last come ; Death of
he uttered a few parting admonitions, 'leaned back his head Wilfrid.
upon the pillow, and went to his rest without groan or
murmur,' just at the moment when the monks in choir, who
were keeping up on his behalf a ceaseless round of psalmody,

[1] Ann. SS. Bened. iii. 334; Chron. Evesh. p. 10. The extant 'privilege of
Constantine' is called by Haddan and Stubbs, iii. 281, 'spurious.' Egwin
could not have set off before June if he buried Aldhelm.

[2] Chronicle, a. 715. He is mentioned as a benefactor to the church of St.
Mary at Evesham; Chron. Evesh. p. 72.

[3] Ann. SS. Bened. iii. 279.

[4] Boniface, Ep. 20. In Ep. 62 Boniface denounces him and king Osred for
'adulterium nonnarum,' and adds, with a terrible positiveness, that he died at
a feast, mad, and impenitent. See Lappenberg, i. 224. Henry of Huntingdon
calls him 'patriæ et avitæ virtutis hæres,' iv. 7.

[5] Eddi, 64. The legend of St. Egwin (Chron. Evesh. p. 11) makes Wilfrid
take part in the dedication of the minster of Evesham in this very year, after
the return of Egwin, and by order of a synod; but this is incredible. He
may have become acquainted, then or in 704–5, with the Mercian ealdorman
Friodored, 'a man full of the missionary spirit' (Stubbs, on Found. of Peterborough, p. 10), the founder of a church at Bredon.

had reached the sublime inspiriting verse, 'Thou shalt send forth Thy Spirit, and they shall be created, and Thou shalt renew the face of the earth.' It was probably on a Thursday [1], in October,—the year being doubtless 709.

He was buried in his best-loved church, the minster of Ripon, after an elaborate and solemn preparation of the corpse [2], and a processional funeral-journey. Hardly any one refrained from weeping while, amid the loud chant of the monastic choir, the great bishop was borne to his grave on the south side of the altar. He was 'in his seventy-sixth year, and had been forty-five years a bishop [3],' reckoning, probably, from his election in the early autumn of 664.

Close of a great period.

So passed away the 'St. Wilfrid' of our forefathers [4]; a man by no means free from faults or weaknesses,—a man whose public conduct had some results prejudicial to his native Church, and who does not rise entirely superior to the influences of power and high state,—but after all one who worthily concludes the most 'brilliant period [5]' of our ancient ecclesiastical history. After his death, a generation of lesser men succeeds: there is hardly any striking or impressive character among those who appear in the public life of the

[1] Tatbert used to keep all Thursdays, in memorial of his death, as if they were Sundays, with a feast, 'in epulis;' Eddi, 64. October 12 was the day always kept in his honour; but it could hardly be the day of his death, for in 709 it fell on a Saturday. Probably the true day was October 3 (a Thursday in 709), for 'the obituary of the church of Durham fixes' his 'depositio' on that day; see Raine, i. 81. To date his death earlier than the autumn of that year would disturb our notes of time, for he could not be said to have completed forty-five years of episcopate in April of 709, nor would this give time for Ceolred's message after his accession and for the Mercian sojourn: and yet the Martyrologium Poeticum of Bede dates his death April 24, and so Smith's Bede, p. 759, and Alb. Butler on Oct. 12. The abbot of Oundle at this time was Cuthbald.

[2] An abbot named Bacula spread a linen cloth (sindonem suam) on the ground, and upon it the corpse was washed and arrayed. Comp. Lingard, A.-S. Ch. ii. 48. On the question whether his bones (all but a small portion) were translated to Canterbury, see Raine's preface to Hist. Ch. York, i. p. xliii. His shrine stood in the north choir aisle of Ripon.

[3] Eddi, 63, says forty-six. Bede, v. 19, 'post quadraginta et quinque annos accepti episcopatus.' Eadmer says, c. 61, in the seventy-fifth year of his life and forty-fifth of his episcopate. Eadmer begins by dating his birth in 634; c. 1. See above, p. 219.

[4] 'In many respects the star of the Anglo-Saxon Church;' Raine, i. 77.

[5] See Freeman, i. 30.

Church [1], until Egbert of York establishes and adorns the
Northern archbishopric, and his successor Albert carries on
the glory of its theological school. Corruptions of various
kinds become rife in monasteries : the vivid intensity of religious faith, the fresh enthusiasm of devotion, which marked
the earlier time, die out piteously among clerks and laics :
a lofty and holy soul like Bede's finds itself left to look on a
deteriorated clergy, and a people practically relapsing towards
indifference [2] : one can conceive of him as taking refuge from
contemporary decadence amid the noble forms which he per-
petuates in his History. A great age, in short, expires with
Wilfrid ; and it is but fitting that the death of the Apostle
of Sussex and of Wight should terminate the story of the
extension of 'the Vine' through the land, as, amid many
vicissitudes, 'room was made for it,'—the story of a work
more solidly and healthily accomplished [3] than in other lands
and by other agents, the work of our national conversion.
That conversion, it is obvious to remark, involves the formation of a new 'Church of the English,' not the development
or extension of the 'ancient British Church.' The English
Church did not grow out of the British ; the missionaries
who brought the Saxon or Anglian tribes into the fellowship
of Christ's Kingdom were men from the Continent, or men
of Irish race, or Englishmen like Cedd or Wilfrid ; they were
in no instance 'Britons' or 'Welshmen.' Long after the
conversion was completed, the 'British' Christians held aloof
from the 'Saxon' Christians [4] ; it was but by degrees during

---

[1] For St. Boniface does not count as one of the great churchmen living and
working in England ; and Bede hardly ever left his cloister.

[2] See his Ep. to Egbert ; and on the general apathy as to learning, his
Explan. Apocal. præf. 'Anglorum gentis inertiæ . . . ad lectionem.'

[3] 'In no part of the world did Christianity make its way in a more honourable manner ;' Freeman, i. 29. 'Nowhere else did Christianity make a deeper
or more lasting impression ;' Kemble, ii. 363,—and see the whole striking
passage. 'In a single century England became known to Christendom as a
fountain of light . . . Scarcely was Christianity presented to the Anglo-
Saxons . . . when they embraced it with singular fidelity and singleness of heart.'
Bp. Stubbs, Const. Hist. i. 251. Compare also Dean Church's summary in
his 'Beginnings of the Middle Ages,' p. 67.

[4] See Bp. Stubbs, Const. Hist. i. 252, on this 'attitude of the Britons ;'
but compare Lingard, quoted above, p. 430. Of course it is likely enough that,

CHAP. XIV. the next centuries that they conformed to the 'Catholic Easter,' and entered into fellowship with the younger and stronger Church. It is necessary to state this in plain words, because of the inaccurate language which has often obscured the facts under the influence, perhaps, of a strong preconception, controversial or 'patriotic.' And these facts, for history's sake, must be kept distinctly in view.

Conclusion. But whatever else we remember or forget as to this great religious movement to which our own debt is so incalculable, let us bear in mind two things that shine out in those who responded most readily to its touch, whose lives were the best monuments of its power. One is, the simple loyal thoroughness, the unreserved 'perfectness of heart,' with which, having accepted the Faith as the explanation of man's destiny, they accepted withal the practical obligations which were proposed to them as arising out of it, or even seemed to think only of how they could do most in order to attain holiness and salvation. The other is that passion for 'winning souls,' for spreading the new-found light among their heathen countrymen or their Teutonic kinsmen abroad, which passed on through those first generations of English Christians the 'fiery torch' of missionary ardour. It is the typical laymen of the several kingdoms who most conspicuously illustrate these true conditions of Church life. We think not only of the noble earnestness of Ethelbert, of the heroic sanctity of Oswald, of the sweet humility of Oswin, but of the genuine conversions of Eadbald and Kenwalch, of the thoughtful co-operation of Edwin and Sigebert the Learned with Paulinus and with Felix, of the family piety of the court of Anna, of Edwin 'persuading' Eorpwald, of Oswy discoursing to Sigebert the Good, of the wonderful outburst of Christian enthusiasm among the children and grandchildren of Penda, of Sebbi sustaining his people's faith under 'a great trial of affliction.' Nor can we forget how impressive and attractive was the manifest consistency of the preachers' conduct with

here and there, Britons, 'living on, as useful theows' (Freeman, Four Lectures, p. 109), under Saxons or Angles, used influence in favour of the faith to which they clung. But of such 'witnessing for Christ,' however effective, history can know nothing.

their Gospel [1]; nor how effectively the representatives of re- ligion in Kent and East Anglia, in Northumbria and in Wessex, maintained its alliance with the learning and education of their time. To say this is not to idealise, to ignore any tokens of superstition or of 'zeal not according to knowledge,' or to think lightly of some accretions on primitive Christianity which our fathers received along with it, and which grew in bulk and tenacity after their time. All these allowed for, the Conversion is among the *magnalia Dei.* Its records, moreover, abound in illustrations of a Divine discipline administered through reverses and disappointments, through seemingly premature deaths, and seemingly fruitless labours; and then, again, of an 'excellency of power' put forth in ways unexpected, when need was sorest and hearts were like to fail [2]. It is this which gives to the whole period so pathetic and solemn a charm for the Christian student. He feels that the years of the Conversion were emphatically 'years of the Right Hand.'

No words could be more appropriate for the close of such a survey than those in which one of the most gifted writers of our time concludes a lecture on 'Christianity and the Teutonic Races.' 'Those ancient and far distant ages ... we may, we ought to leave far behind, in what we hope to achieve. But, in our eagerness for improvement, it concerns us to be on our guard against the temptation of thinking that we can have the fruit or the flower, and yet destroy the root; that we may retain the high view of human nature which has grown with the growth of Christian nations, and discard that revelation of Divine love and human destiny of which that view forms a part or a consequence; that we may retain the moral energy, and yet make light of the faith that produced it. ... It concerns us that we do not despise our birthright, and cast away our heritage of gifts and of powers, which we may lose, but not recover [3].'

---

[1] See above, p. 52. [2] See above, p. 54.

[3] Dean Church, Gifts of Civilisation, &c. p. 343. See also his Beginnings of the Middle Ages, p. 67, that the main causes of the Conversion were 'the breadth and greatness of Christian ideas, and the purity, courage, enthusiasm, and indefatigable self-devotion, though not always innocent of superstition, of the Christian teachers,' &c. See the whole passage.

ADDITIONAL NOTES.

NOTE A.

CHRISTIAN ADOPTION OF PAGAN SITES.

To the illustrations of this subject in the text may be added the following passage in one of Mr. Tozer's notes to his edition of Dr. Finlay's 'History of Greece.' It occurs in vol. i. p. 424 :—

'The adaptation of Pagan beliefs and ceremonies to Christian use must not wholly be attributed to superstition and priestcraft. Even in the Catacombs we find numerous Pagan emblems used as a means of symbolizing Christian truth. Nor was it unjustifiable at a later period to facilitate in this manner the transition from an old to a new religion—for instance, in building Christian churches on the sites of Pagan temples. The extent to which this took place is shown by M. Petit de Julleville in a paper entitled, *Sur l'emplacement et le vocable des Églises Chrétiennes en Grèce*, in the *Archives des Missions*, deuxième série, vol. v. According to this writer (p. 525) more than eighty churches in Attica were built on sites of ancient temples, and the names of their dedication usually recall the names of those temples. . . . Athena becomes Haghia Sophia,' &c.

NOTE B.

BEDE AND GREGORY OF TOURS.

A COMPARISON between the 'Ecclesiastical Histories' of Bede and Gregory of Tours would illustrate what has been said as to the first age of English Christianity. The books have naturally not a little in common. Gregory's 'faculty of story-telling' (see Freeman,

Four Lectures, p. 64) is not far inferior to Bede's: take, for instance, the escape of young Attalus and the faithful cook Leo (H. Fr. iii. 15), the adventures of a priest buried alive amid a 'fœtor letalis' (iv. 12), the murder of Chlodomir's two boys by their fierce uncle (iii. 18), and of bishop Prætextatus 'while he leaned upon a form' during the Easter service in Rouen cathedral, and none of his clergy durst answer his cry for aid (viii. 31). We seem almost to see the townsmen of beleaguered Orleans, alternately praying and looking out for relief (ii. 7); or to hear the terrible 'Vua!' of Chlotair in his death-agony (iv. 21). Some beautiful and solemn touches occur at intervals in the narrative: the description of Nicetius of Lyons as showing such love to all men 'ut in ejus pectore ipse Dominus, qui est vera caritas, cerneretur' (iv. 36), and the expansion of Ps. xlix. 17 in regard to the man of ill-gotten gains who died with an outside show of penitence, 'nihil exinde secum aliud portans nisi animæ detrimentum' (vi. 28), are just what might have come from Bede himself. When we read that bishop Salvius, if constrained to accept money, 'forthwith made it over to the poor' (vii. 1), we cannot but think of St. Aidan: when we hear of 'the common saying, "If a man has to pass between Pagan altars and God's church, there is no harm in his paying respect to both"' (v. 44), we are reminded of the compromise of Redwald of East-Anglia. Both writers give us much information about ecclesiastical usages, such as the clerical tonsure (Gregory even mentions the British tonsure, x. 9), the nocturnal or 'matin' service, the frequent psalmody, the 'reception' of the neophyte 'from the font' by his godfather; about the estates or other property of churches, the infliction of spiritual censures, the appointment of bishops, the holding of synods, the life of 'recluses,' the veneration of relics, and so on. Both narrate 'miracles' wrought at saintly shrines (compare, e.g. Greg. iv. 19 with his Vit. Patr. c. 2, where he tells us that he himself, when a youth, had been cured of a fever at the tomb of St. Illidius), and dreams which are accepted as visions (e.g. Greg. v. 14, vi. 29). The description of Heaven in the 'vision' of Greg. vii. 1 surpasses that of Paradise in the story of Drythelm (Bede, v. 12). Both writers seem prone to treat ordinary events as supernatural (cp. Greg. x. 25). The Paschal question, on which the later historian is so exuberant, is not unnoticed by the earlier (Greg. v. 17, x. 23). Each records a case of episcopal appeal to Rome; but that in Greg. v. 21 is made with royal permission. Other resemblances

might be mentioned; but, in spite of all, the moral difference
between the two books is even startling. The atmosphere, so to
speak, of Gregory's is as heavy and lurid as that of Bede's is
luminous and pure. The contrast lies not merely,—it may be said,
not mainly,—in the exceptional wickedness of Frankish royalty in
the sixth century, and the remarkable excellence of English royalty
in the seventh. It is the ecclesiastics of the two neighbour countries
who are so unlike each other. Bede has to tell us of one prelate
who 'purchased' a see (iii. 7); in Gregory's pages we meet
with two bishops who rush into wild orgies of crime (v. 21);
another who assaults his archdeacon, on suspicion of fraud, in
church on a Christmas morning (iv. 44); another who perse-
cutes, even to death, the friends of his holy predecessor (iv. 36);
another who asks, 'Because I have taken orders, am I therefore to
forego my revenge?' (viii. 39); another who drinks himself into
epilepsy, and orders a priest to be shut up in a tomb in order to
extract from him his own title-deeds (iv. 12); together with clerics
who plot against the reputation or the life of a bishop (v. 50, vi.
36), or are chosen by the worst of all queens to despatch a young
king with poisoned daggers, and are only afraid that the task
will be found 'difficult' (viii. 29). Allowing for inevitable exag-
gerations,—although we may believe Gregory's protest that he has
set down nothing in malice (iv. 13),—and bearing in mind the
multitude of office-bearers necessarily belonging to a long-settled
Church in a wide region, we must suppose that 'the Gallo-Roman
bishops who crowded round' the proselyte of St. Remigius
(Kitchin, Hist. Fr. i. 74), condoning his brutality for the sake of
his orthodoxy, and hoping to train him into Christian kingliness,
became gradually infected by the barbarism which made them
potentates, and bequeathed to their successors a tradition of violence or of laxity. And so we can understand how the pedantic
tyrant Chilperic, who shocked Gregory (v. 45) by Sabellianising,
and made episcopal faults the chief topics of his sarcasm, 'would
frequently say' that the churches had impoverished the 'fiscus,'
and that 'the bishops alone really reigned' (ib. vi. 46); and
this, although some of them could incur reproach for abandoning
a colleague to his enmity (ib. v. 19). A hierarchy thus secularised
might well be apathetic about missions, and indifferent to the disgrace of simony. Perhaps the saddest indication of its lowered
moral tone is given by Gregory himself, who, good man as he was,
hating the bloody feuds of princes, and ready to withstand a king

in the cause of justice (ib. v. prol. and 19), could pause in his recital of the crimes of Chlodwig to observe that 'God increased his dominion, because he walked before him with an upright heart' (ii. 40). Of course, the greater the corporate deterioration, the more honour is due to those individual prelates or clerics whose genuine piety was the salt of the Frankish Church, and who, doubtless, made a better use of such a memory as St. Martin's than by representing him as a formidable tutelary power, to be propitiated by savage warriors who did not, in any practical sense, know or fear God (cp. Greg. iii. 28, iv. 2, 16, &c. on the 'virtus consueta beati Martini'). It is matter of thankfulness that the English Church and nation have had no such period in their history. After the age of the Conversion, when missionary ardour had no more scope, religion in England—Bede himself being the witness—lost much of its fruitfulness and its power. But it never fell so low as in Gaul under the Merwings; and that, because, when addressing our fathers, it escaped the trial of a corrupting support, and relied, in the main, on its own Divine vitality.

NOTE C.

THEODORE AND CHAD.

THERE is a remarkable coincidence between Theodore's phrase 'confirmentur,' quoted on p. 238, and the language of the Nicene Council as to bishops and priests ordained by the schismatic bishop Meletius (Socrates, i. 9). 'Those who have been appointed by him are to be admitted to communion' (on their return to the Church) 'after having been confirmed ($\beta\epsilon\beta\alpha\iota\omega\theta\acute{\epsilon}\nu\tau\alpha\varsigma$) with a more sacred ordination ($\mu\upsilon\sigma\tau\iota\kappa\omega\tau\acute{\epsilon}\rho\alpha$ $\chi\epsilon\iota\rho\sigma\tau\sigma\nu\acute{\iota}\alpha$).' This sentence has been sometimes interpreted as Theodore's sentence is interpreted in the text; and the word $\beta\epsilon\beta\alpha\iota\omega\theta\acute{\epsilon}\nu\tau\alpha\varsigma$, of itself, might mean only an act of benediction, rehabilitating the recipients for the canonical exercise of their ministry. But, even if we take it as referring more naturally to an act *ejusdem generis* with their former schismatical 'appointment,' i.e. to an ordination 'more sacred' because performed by a Catholic bishop (as Valesius says, 'Cum præter consensum ipsius ordinati fuissent, vult synodus ut ante omnia ab episcopo Alexandrino ordinentur'), still it does not seem strictly necessary to impose this sense on Theodore's 'confirmentur;' the preceding clause, 'adunati ecclesiæ non sunt,' may be taken as referring it to an act which would 'establish' the persons in question as thenceforth legitimate ministers of the Church. And the next rule in the Penitential employs the same verb in a somewhat similar sense: churches hallowed by Scotic or British bishops are to be sprinkled with holy water, 'et aliqua collectione confirmentur:' words which point to a completion of what was lacking to their previous consecration (see above, p. 294), and do not imply that it was treated as simply null. (Compare the rule as to a removed church, in Theodore's Penitential, b. 2. 1. 1.) Theodore adds significantly, 'And if any one of their race . . . has doubts as to his own baptism, let him be baptized:' he does not say, 'conditionally,' as St. Boniface afterwards said (Concil. Liptin. c. 28). About a year after Theodore's death, the Council in Trullo, can. 84, ordered baptism to be administered in such doubtful cases, as it seems, unconditionally, according to Cod. Afric. 72. Compare the story of Herebald in Bede, v. 6.

NOTE D.

THE COUNCIL OF HERTFORD.

IT is interesting to compare the third canon of Hertford, as to monasteries, with canons of the Council of Clovesho in 747. In the interval there had grown up—in consequence of the privileges attached to monastic property—the gross abuse denounced in Bede's letter to Egbert, c. 7. A king's thane or reeve would procure lands chartered as for monastic uses, build on them a so-called monastery, fill it with worthless monks (of whom Bede says, 'Wasps can make combs, but not honey'), and preside over it as 'abbot,' without abandoning his secular habits: his wife would often do the like, and figure as 'abbess' of a mock nunnery. The Council of Clovesho did not venture absolutely to proscribe this flagrant perversion of the conventual idea, but ordered the bishops to mitigate its evils by visiting these houses and exhorting the inmates (can. 5). The same Council also deplores the decay of studiousness in real monasteries (c. 7); and intimates that some abbots were wont to treat their monks as slaves, not as sons (c. 4). Worldliness had evidently infected many convents: there had sprung up (as previously at Coldingham) a love of 'pompous' and 'parti-coloured' dress: gleemen and harpers were entertained within the precincts: monks would drink freely before Terce, and even constrain others 'intemperanter bibere.'

It may be observed that while Theodore was proposing that bishops should not 'disturb monasteries in any respect,' he forgot the danger of such disturbance on the part of kings: compare Haddan and Stubbs, iii. 394, on the seizure of three Northumbrian monasteries, one of them at Coxwold, by king Eadbert, in 757; and see Clovesh. c. 29.

The fourth canon of Hertford undoubtedly refers to monks: the reading 'episcopi' is, as Smith calls it, 'most absurd.' Compare Clovesh. c. 29, that no monks or nuns shall live in the houses of laymen, 'sed repetant monasteria,' &c.

The sixteenth Nicene canon is not named by Johnson, nor by Haddan and Stubbs, among the sources of the fifth canon of Hertford. But although it does not refer to cases of aimless wandering ('passim quolibet,' Hertf.) it may have been in Theodore's thoughts, as forbidding clerics to 'depart from their church in a random way, without regard to the fear of God or to ecclesiastical rule.'

There is no discrepancy, such as Johnson supposed (Engl. Canons, i. 94), between the tenth canon of Hertford and a passage in Theodore's Penitential, if we take 'Quod si,' &c., in the former, as relating not to divorce, but to the 'expulsion' of a wife who has *not* forfeited her rights by adultery.

One omission in these canons may surprise us. Provisions are made as to episcopal jurisdiction, precedency, and unity of action: a proposal is made, but deferred, as to increase of the episcopate: but nothing is said as to episcopal election. Yet Theodore could not be ignorant of the standing law of the Church on this matter; and it might have been thought desirable to take the first opportunity of formally incorporating it in the legislation of the English Church. The Cyprianic requirement of the 'suffragium plebis' or 'populi' (Cypr. Ep. 55. 7; 59. 7) and the Nicene sanction of 'the people's choice' (Soc. i. 9) had received in the Western Church a terse and pointed expression from Pope Celestine I. in his letter to the bishops of the provinces of Vienne and Narbonne. '*Nullus invitis detur episcopus:* cleri, plebis, et ordinis' (i. e. the magistracy) 'consensus et desiderium requiratur' (Celest. Ep. 2. 5; Mansi, iv. 466, A.D. 428). This maxim took hold of the ecclesiastical mind, and is cited by Gallic Councils, as Orleans V. A.D. 549, can. 11, which also guards against any forcing of the consent of 'the citizens or clerics' on the part of 'powerful persons,' and (can. 10) recognises three conditions of a legitimate accession to the episcopate: (1) the king's will, (2) election by clergy and people, according to 'ancient canons,' (3) consecration by the metropolitan, or his deputy, with the comprovincials (Mansi, ix. 131); and Paris III. circ. A. D. 557, can. 8, which amplifies the formula thus, 'Nullus *civibus* invitis ordinetur episcopus;' and after reciting the fact that in some respects the old custom has been neglected and the decrees of canons have been violated, orders that no 'command of the sovereign, nor any other condition,' shall 'bring in' a bishop without (1) an election by people and clergy, expressing their 'fullest will,' (2) the 'will' of the metropolitan and comprovincials: and further, that any one who 'shall have presumed to enter upon this high office in virtue of a royal appointment' shall be disowned by the comprovincials as a person 'unduly ordained' (Mansi, ix. 746). Cp. Greg. Tur. ix. 23. Bede does not give us very full information as to the several appointments of bishops. In some of the earlier cases, it is probable that the affair was left in the hands of the king and the archbishop, as when Honorius consecrated Thomas for Dunwich, or Deusdedit consecrated Damian for Rochester. Kenwalch was likely enough to dispense with canonical forms in regard to Agilbert, and he must have done so in regard to Wini (Bede, iii. 7). Bede attributes the appointment of Wilfrid to Alchfrid, and that of Chad to Oswy, whom he describes on that occasion as 'imitating the activity of his son;' yet we know from Eddi (Vit. Wilfr. 11) that Wilfrid was elected by the Northumbrian Witan, and may infer that this was also the case with Chad, as with the three prelates consecrated in 678 for parts of the diocese which Wilfrid had ruled, and, according to Bede's plain statement, with Cuthbert (iv. 28) and Oftfor (iv. 23). The same plan would be followed in other districts. Faricius, as we have seen, emphasises the point in regard to Aldhelm. In such elections the clerical voice was represented by that of the high ecclesiastics present among the 'Witan,' who acted together with those of the 'freemen' who attended that assembly (see Freeman, Norm. Conq. i. 102).

It need hardly be said that Bede's application of the term 'synodus' to a Witenagemot (iv. 28, v. 19; cp. iii. 7, end) proves nothing against the essentially episcopal character of the synods of Hertford and Hatfield. They were composed of bishops: the 'magistri' or 'doctores' who also attended them were simply

advisers, and their 'votum' was merely 'consultativum,' not 'decisi-
vum.' They were no more constituent members of the synod than
Athanasius was of the Nicene Council, or than Thomas Aquinas
would have been of the Council of Lyons, had he lived to attend it.
(See Hefele, Councils, Introd. 4. 11.) No laymen appear to have
had anything to do with the synods of Hertford and Hatfield:
although we find king Ethelbald of Mercia 'presiding,' like a Constantine Pogonatus, at the Council of Clovesho in 742, and present
with his ealdormen and 'duces' at the greater Council of Clovesho
in 747, at which many clerics were present, and were consulted.
It should be remembered that laymen might even be asked to
sign the doctrinal canons of a Council, in token of their assent,
without being at all regarded as members of the Council, or authors
of its decrees;—as at the second Council of Orange, A. D. 529
(Mansi, viii. 718). The 'synod' of Whitby was rather a conference
than a regular ecclesiastical council; but the persons named by
Bede as present were all clerical, except Oswy, Alchfrid, and the
abbess Hilda (iii. 25).

It may be observed, that the African rule as to one yearly synod
referred, not to a provincial synod, but to the 'general council for
Africa.'

NOTE E.

THE AGE OF ST. ALDHELM.

IN p. 268, I have given the received date of 675 for Aldhelm's
appointment as abbot of Malmesbury. It may not improbably
rest on some better basis than the forged charter of bishop Lothere:
there may have been an old tradition in the monastery that Aldhelm
had ruled it thirty-three years when he died in 709 (Malmesb. Gest.
Pont. v. 231). William of Malmesbury cannot have been unaware
of the difficulties attaching to this date: for he cites Aldhelm's
letter, describing Hadrian as the preceptor of his 'simple childhood' ('*rudis infantiæ*'). Now Hadrian became abbot of Canterbury in 671 (Bede, Hist. Abb. 3). On Malmesbury's showing,
therefore, 'infantiæ' must have been used very laxly, and with a
sort of exaggerative modesty, by Aldhelm: and if he was, in fact,
a youth of sixteen or seventeen in 671, he must have been ordained
priest by Lothere, according to Malmesbury's date, when he was
much below the canonical age, although Malmesbury rejects that

supposition. The bishop might think the case exceptional. The difficulty, in fact, is one which reappears on a comparison of Aldhelm's language about his 'infantia' with Ethelwald's allusion to his 'white hair,' in verses written before he became a bishop: for these verses (see Lingard, A-S. Ch. ii. 164, 188) were appended to a letter addressed 'sacrosancto abbati Aldhelmo :' and although Aldhelm retained the abbacy until his death, he would have been addressed, after 705, as bishop. That his ordination to the presbyterate preceded his appointment to the abbacy, is affirmed both by Faricius (c. 1) and Malmesbury (v. 198).

NOTE F.

GROWTH OF A PAROCHIAL SYSTEM.

BEDE tells us that Paulinus built no church in Bernicia, and in Deira only those of York and Campodonum; but that he built one at Lincoln, doubtless through the munificence of Blæcca. (Cp. Bede, ii. 14, 16; iii. 2.) Under Aidan 'churches were reared in different places' (iii. 3): some of these were adjacent to the royal 'villæ,' as at Bamborough (iii. 17). Birinus 'built and dedicated' churches in Wessex (iii. 7): Cedd 'made churches in different parts' of Essex (iii. 22). This latter passage is the first which associates church-building with anything like a settled local ministry, for Bede adds, 'presbyteros et diaconos ordinavit.' But Aidan and Birinus had probably done the like. It has, indeed, been supposed that Cedd's churches were of the class called 'baptismal' or central (see Lord Selborne, Ancient Facts and Fictions, p. 55 ff.). The lack of district churches was largely supplied by the missionary activity of monks, as we learn from the early life of St. Cuthbert (iv. 27). We are not told whether Chad left any churches behind him as the result of his evangelical journeys through towns, country-sides, townships, and 'castles[1]' in Yorkshire (Bede, iii. 28), but Wilfrid 'ordained presbyters and deacons in *all* places to assist him in his work' (Eddi, 21), and doubtless supplied them with churches for their ministrations. His energy as a founder of basilicas would not exhaust itself in great works, like that at Hexham or Ripon. The sites of his smaller churches would usually be the central points of the several 'vici' or townships (Stubbs, Const. Hist. i. 260).

[1] Fortified towns.

Bede expressly observes that 'among the mountains' no church could
be found to receive Cuthbert when he was making his rounds of
visitation (Vit. Cuthb. 32). In two instances 'comites' build
churches, and ask bishop John to consecrate them (Bede v. 4, 5; at
'South Burton and North Burton;' Lingard, A.-S. Ch. i. 157): and
in such cases a rule would be observed like that which was laid
down in 541 by the fourth Council of Orleans, c. 33: 'Si quis in
agro suo aut habet aut postulat habere diœcesim' (here 'diœcesis'
means a district church,—comp. Council of Epaon, c. 8, 'presbyter
qui diœcesim tenet') 'primum et terras ei deputet sufficienter, et
clericos qui ibidem sua officia impleant' (Mansi, ix. 119). In other
words, something like an endowment was necessary. Once more,
when Drythelm awakes out of his trance (or, as Bede would say,
returns to life), he goes at once 'ad villulæ oratorium' (Bede, v. 12).
Gallican synods indicate a disposition to watch with some jealousy the use made of these outlying hamlet churches; we find
them forbidding any citizen to keep the great festivals in a 'villa'
unless he is known to be in bad health (Orleans I. c. 25, a. 512),
and ordering every cleric who officiates in the 'oratorium' of a
'villula' to keep the great feasts with his bishop in the city
(Auvergne I. c. 15). Compare Council of Agde, c. 21, which also
distinguishes these 'oratoria' as external both to 'civitates' and to
'parochiæ.' In Bede's last days, as we learn from an often-quoted
passage, Ep. to Egb. 3, many of the smaller townships of Yorkshire were still without any resident clergy. But, as has been
already observed, Theodore's Penitential, irrespectively of any
'capitula' wrongly ascribed to him, supposes such a ministry to be
at work. Compare St. Boniface's activity in providing each of his
churches 'in Hessis et Thuringia' with 'custodes;' Willibald, Vit.
Bonif. c. 9.

Since the above was written, Lord Selborne has discussed the
question minutely in his 'Ancient Facts and Fictions concerning
Churches and Tithes.' I venture to think that he has somewhat
understated the extent to which the elements of a parochial
system, as distinct from that system in full-formed development,
were present in England in the latter part of the seventh and in
the eighth centuries. Bede's words about Cedd, naturally taken,
imply a certain amount of localised pastoral care, and need not be
restricted to two central or baptismal churches. The use of 'propria
provincia' in Theodore's Penitential points in the same direction, for
the 'provincia,' though not called a 'parish,' is clearly a defined

sphere of clerical duty. What Bede says of the remoter districts in Northumbria suggests that there were stationary pastors where population was less sparse. Ine's laws (56) distinguish a 'church' from a 'minster'; Wihtred's also contemplate some public 'church-altars': the canons of Clovesho distinguish 'monasteries' from 'ecclesiæ,' and after providing for Sunday observance in the former, proceed ('sed et hoc quoque') to order that 'the priests of God shall invite the people to frequent the church.' If this synod contemplated no non-monastic clergy, the establishment of rural churches or oratories on estates, which Lord Selborne, p. 293, takes as the type of modern parish churches, must have come to an end, which is inconceivable.

NOTE G.

Miscellaneous.

1. The tradition about a great number of Roman-British martyrs during the 'great persecution' has had a legendary connection with Lichfield, being represented in the sixteenth-century seal and modern arms of that city, and supported by the popular derivation of its name from 'lic' in the sense of a corpse (compare 'lich-gate,' 'lyke-wake'). But the 'Licetfelda' of the Chronicle (A.D. 716, 731), the 'Licitfelda' of a marginal statement in the 'Gospels of St. Chad,' an Irish MS. preserved in the cathedral library, is much more naturally explained to mean the 'watered field' (from 'leccian,' to irrigate), in allusion to the streams which feed its twin 'pools.'

2. The general character and position of the original stone 'basilica' which Edwin began to build 'per quadrum,' so as to enclose the wooden 'oratory' in which he had been catechized and baptized, and which was completed by Oswald, have been described, and illustrated by plans, in Browne's 'History of the Metropolitan Church of York.' I have also had the advantage of visiting the present crypt under the guidance of the Dean. On descending from the north aisle of the choir, one reaches a platform with steps on the left leading into the newer portion of the crypt, and, on the right, a well, which is exactly under the ancient site of the high altar. This platform appears to represent the site of the 'oratory.' Browne (p. 7) understands

'per quadrum' in the general sense of 'rectangular,' and considers that the seventh-century cathedral, the church of Paulinus and Wilfrid, had quasi-transepts very near the east end, and that its internal length, as extended westward, was about 106 feet. Several 'black broad lines' in his Plate 3 represent 'hewn oaks which have been imbedded in the concrete foundation of the structure.' Figures in the same Plate represent 'moulded stones of arches of small dimensions, probably belonging to the church of Paulinus;' and stones supposed to have 'formed the face of' its walls, and still remaining in the south side of the crypt, are represented in Plate 5.

3. The 'ancient British Church' has been credited with 'a considerable indirect share' in the conversion of Northumbrians and of Mercians, because it had contributed, in the preceding century, to a revival of Irish piety and learning. But although this revival would stimulate religious activities in a missionary direction as well as in others, we can hardly trace Columba's great enterprise in any special way to a Welsh impulse. His birth in 521 was probably subsequent to the return of one of his future teachers, Finnian of Clonard, from Wales. Between 546 and 562 he was founding monasteries in Ireland. He went to Hy two years before the visit of Gildas to Ireland which is mentioned by Haddan and Stubbs (i. 45, 115); and he died 38 years before the mission of St. Aidan, who seems never to have looked to 'Britons' for assistance in his own work. The traditions of the Isle of Man appear to indicate Ireland, rather than Wales, as the country of its first evangelists, the 'Coindri and Romuel' of the 'Tripartite Life,' who may possibly have been in connection with St. Patrick. (See Lanigan, i. 306, 465.)

4. It is a somewhat ungracious task to note errors in Dean Hook's 'Lives of the Archbishops.' But not only does he antedate by nearly a thousand years the erection of the *arch*bishopric of Paris (vol. i. p. 141), and repeat the old mistake about the formation of the parochial system by Theodore, but his *animus* against what is Roman appears in the extraordinary statement, that whereas both Augustine and Theodore 'had to confer with bishops jealous of any encroachment upon their rights, when Augustine laid down the law, Theodorus invited discussion' (i. 157), as if Augustine had not held two discussions with the

British bishops, and used, according to Bede, 'entreaties' as well as 'fraternal admonition,' 'exhortations,' and 'rebukes.' Elsewhere he claims Eddi as saying that 'Wilfrid refused to receive consecration from Deusdedit' *because* the latter had 'put himself into communication with the Celtic party :' whereas Eddi, in the passage referred to, does not name Deusdedit, who had died before Wilfrid's election. In 'eos qui schismaticis consentiunt,' Eddi clearly alludes to Cedd and Jaruman. The remark in one of Hook's notes, 'that Theodorus had so far condescended as to employ an agent at Rome to explain to the Roman court the real state of affairs,' indicates the same bias. The mistranslation in his report of Aldfrid's 'refusal of all concession' has been noticed in the text.

5. When Irish ecclesiastics uttered imprecations against those whom they regarded as the enemies of religion or of the Church, they probably forgot that the language held by some of the Psalmists was not to be literally reproduced by Christians. But something is to be attributed to the vehemence of the Celtic *perfervidum ingenium.* A similar habit appears to have existed among the Cymry, and sometimes in separation from all pretence of religious zeal, as when the well of St. Elian in Denbighshire was believed (in comparatively recent times) to be potent for cursing purposes. For a Breton superstition see Dean Church's Miscellaneous Essays, p. 124 : 'it is a fearful thing, yet nothing new, that faith can coexist . . . with violence and hatred,' &c.

6. A curious pictorial representation of the popular stories about St. Cuthbert will be found behind the northern stalls of Carlisle Cathedral. One scene exhibits him as forbidden 'layks and plays, As S. Bede i' hys story says.' 'Her saw he Aydn' sowl up go To hevyn blysse w^t angels two.' 'Her bosile teld hym y^t he must de, And after y^t he (prior) suld be.' In the death-scene, Cuthbert rests, with hands clasped, in the arms of an attendant (Herefrid), while another monk kneels in front of him : 'When bishop two yerys he had beyn, On Farne he died both holy and clene.'

7. An interesting paper on 'St. Wilfrith in Sussex,' by Mr. F. E. Sawyer, has been reprinted from the ' Sussex Archæological Collections.' The author thinks it not improbable that the king

of the South-Saxon heathen, mentioned by Eddi in his account
of Wilfrid's peril in 666, was Ethelwalch, as yet unconverted.
He suggests that the grant of Pagham to Wilfrid, set forth in
a charter of Cadwalla, which Kemble marks as spurious, and of
which the date is earlier than Wilfrid's arrival, may have been
made 'shortly before he came into the country;' but this is surely
very improbable. He quotes the eloquent tribute to Wilfrid's
memory rendered by the late Archdeacon Hannah in a sermon
at St. Wilfrid's church, Hayward's Heath, in 1881 : 'The happy
work of first preaching the Gospel to the heathen worshipper
of Woden in Sussex is the fairest passage in that troubled life,
the purest of the rays of glory that have gathered round that
great historic name. . . . Great as an administrator, as a ruler,
as a founder of churches and monasteries, as a zealous promoter
both of art and learning, he was greater by far in our regard as
a missionary,' &c. Mr. Sawyer follows Preb. Stephens (Dioc.
Hist. Chich. p. 13) in accepting the story of St. Lewinna as a
convert of Wilfrid, martyred by a heathen Saxon before 690.

8. In regard to Ine's connection with Glastonbury, it may be
well to refer to Mr. James Parker's published lecture on
'Glastonbury Abbey,' together with Mr. Freeman's 'English
Towns and Districts,' p. 98. Ine may be regarded as 'the first
founder,' and Dunstan as the restorer, of the church of SS. Peter
and Paul, built eastward of the 'lignea' or 'vetusta ecclesia' of
St. Mary, now represented by the so-called 'chapel of St. Joseph.'
'There is no saying what Ine's church was like :' it 'may well
. . . have been raised and enlarged some 200 years after.' It
is now represented by the ruined abbey church.

9. It should have been observed that the opinion which places
Ausgustine's Oak at Aust or Austcliff is supported by a charter
of Ethelred of Mercia, which ~~mostly~~ closely connects Henbury (near Bristol)
with a place called 'Æt Austin' (Cod. Dipl. i. 35). But if Augustine's Oak was in that district, Bede's information would seem
to be inaccurate; for he understood the spot to be between the
Hwiccian and West Saxon territories : and, in his view, all
Gloucestershire would be Hwiccian.

TABLE OF PRINCIPAL EVENTS.

TABLE OF ROYAL AND EPISCOPAL SUCCESSION.

A.D. 597–709.

I.

	A. D.
1. Kent :—	
Ethelbert . . .	[560?]
Eadbald . . .	616
Erconbert . . .	640
Egbert . . .	664
Lothere . . .	673
Eadric . . .	685
Wihtred . . .	690–1
2. Sussex :—	
Ethelwalch	
3. Wessex :—	
Ceolwulf . . .	597
Kynegils . . .	611
Kenwalch . . .	643
Sexburga . . .	672
Escwin (part of Wessex)	674
Kentwin . . .	676
Cadwalla . . .	685
Ine	688

	A. D.
4. Essex :—	
Sabert	
Sæward, Sexred, Sigebert	616
Sigebert the Little	about 617
Sigebert the Good .	before 653
Swidhelm . .	about 657
Sebbi and Sighere . .	664
Sighard and Swefred .	694
Offa . . .	before 709
5. Northumbria :—	
Ethelfrid . . .	[593]
Edwin . . .	617
[Eanfrid in Bernicia; Osric in Deira . .	633]
Oswald	634
Oswy in Bernicia; Oswin in Deira . .	642
Oswy sole king . .	651
Egfrid	670
Aldfrid	685
[Eadwulf . . .	705]
Osred . . .	706

A.D.

A.D.

6. East-Anglia :—

	A.D.
Redwald	
Eorpwald	617
Sigebert the Learned	631
Egric	634
Anna	636
Ethelhere	654
Ethelwold	655
Aldwulf	663

7. Mercia :—

	A.D.
Cearl	
Penda	626
[Mercia under Oswy	655]
Wulfhere	658–9
Ethelred	675
Kenred	704
Ceolred	709

II.
[Sees in order of foundation as English bishoprics.]

1. Canterbury :—

Augustine	597
Laurence	605
Mellitus	619
Justus	624
Honorius	627
Deusdedit	655
Theodore	668
Bertwald	693

2. London :—

Mellitus	604
[Cedd, in Essex	654]
Wini	666
Erkenwald	675
Waldhere	693
Ingwald	704 ?

3. Rochester :—

Justus	604
Romanus	624
Paulinus	633
Ithamar	644
Damian	655
Putta	669
Cwichelm	676
Gebmund	678
Tobias	693

4. York :—

Paulinus	625
Chad	665–6
Wilfrid, consecrated 665, in possession	669
Bosa	678
Wilfrid again	686
Bosa again	691
John	706

5. Dunwich :—

Felix	631
Thomas	647

Boniface	652
Bisi	669
Acci	673
Aldbert	675 + 731 [1]

6. Lindisfarne :—

Aidan	635
Finan	651
Colman	661
Tuda	664
Eata	678
Cuthbert	685
Eadbert	688
Eadfrid	698

7. Dorchester or Winchester :—

Birinus (Dorchester)	635
Agilbert (Dorchester)	650 [2]
Wini (Winchester)	662
Lothere (Dorchester)	670
Heddi (Winchester)	676
Ætla (Dorchester)	about 679 ?
Daniel (Winchester)	705

8. Lichfield [the seat of the first four Mercian bishops not ascertained] :—

Diuma	656
Cellach	658
Trumhere	659
Jaruman	662
Chad	669
Winfrid	672
Saxulf	675
Hedda	691

9. Elmham :—

Badwin	673
Nothbert	693 + 706

10. Hereford :—

Putta	676
Tyrhtel	688

[1] The date of his accession is unknown. He may have been bishop in 709. See Stubbs, Registr. Sac. p. 5; ('Astwulf).   [2] Birinus died in Dec., 650.

	A. D.
11. **Hexham :—**	
Eata (also holding Lindisfarne)	678
Trumbert	681
Eata again	685
John	687
Wilfrid	706
12. **Sidnacester** (for Lindsey) :—	
Eadhed	678
Ethelwin	680
Edgar . . before	706
13. **Worcester :—**	
Bosel	680

	A. D.
Worcester (continued)—	
Oftfor	692
Egwin	693–4
14. **Leicester :—**	
Cuthwin	680
[See administered by Wilfrid	691]
15. **Selsey :—**	
Wilfrid	681–2
16. **Sherborne :—**	
Aldhelm	705
Forthere	709

This list includes two bishoprics whose existence at Wilfrid's death might be regarded as temporarily suspended, Leicester and Selsey, but excludes the ephemeral and extinct see of Abercorn, and—if it can be regarded as constituted in 679 for Eadhed—that of Ripon, and also passes over the brief administration, by Wilfrid, of Hexham in 686, and of Lindisfarne in 687.

GENEALOGICAL TABLES.

I.

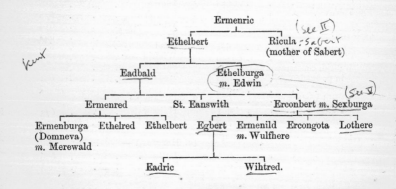

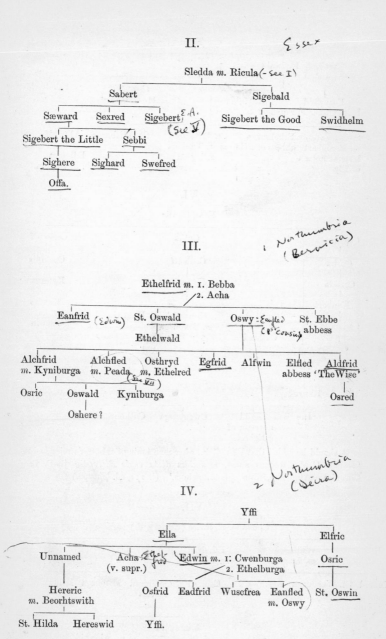

II.

Essex

Sledda *m.* Ricula (- See I)

Sabert — Sigebald

Sæward — Sexred — Sigebert; E.A. (See V) — Sigebert the Good — Swidhelm

Sigebert the Little — Sebbi

Sighere — Sighard — Swefred

Offa.

III.

1 Northumbria (Bernicia)

Ethelfrid *m.* 1. Bebba
2. Acha

Eanfrid (Edwin) — St. Oswald — Oswy: Eanfled 1st cousins — St. Ebbe abbess

Ethelwald

Alchfrid *m.* Kyniburga — Alchfled *m.* Peada (See VII) — Osthryd *m.* Ethelred — Egfrid — Alfwin — Elfled abbess — Aldfrid 'The Wise'

Osric — Oswald — Kyniburga — Osred

Oshere ?

IV.

2 Northumbria (Deira)

Yffi

Ella — Elfric

Unnamed — Acha (v. supr.) — Edwin *m.* 1: Cwenburga 2. Ethelburga — Osric

Hereric *m.* Beorhtswith — Osfrid — Eadfrid — Wuscfrea — Eanfled *m.* Oswy — St. Oswin

St. Hilda — Hereswid — Yffi.

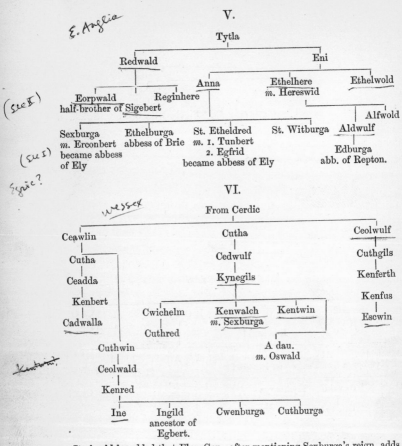

V.

E. Anglia (handwritten)

```
                              Tytla
            ┌───────────────────┴──────────────────┐
          Redwald                                 Eni
   (see X)  │              ┌──────────┬────────────┬──────────┐
   Eorpwald   Reginhere   Anna    Ethelhere    Ethelwold
   half-brother of Sigebert               m. Hereswid
                                                          │ Alfwold
   ┌────────┬──────────┬────────────┬───────────┬────────┘
 Sexburga  Ethelburga  St. Etheldred  St. Witburga  Aldwulf
 m. Erconbert abbess of Brie  m. 1. Tunbert
 became abbess            2. Egfrid          Edburga
 of Ely          became abbess of Ely     abb. of Repton.
```

(see X) *(see I)* *Egric?* (handwritten marginal notes)

VI.

wessex (handwritten)

```
                         From Cerdic
      ┌──────────────────────┼──────────────────────┐
   Ceawlin                  Cutha                 Ceolwulf
      │                       │                      │
   Cutha                  Cedwulf                Cuthgils
      │                       │                      │
   Ceadda                 Kynegils               Kenferth
      │               ┌───────┼───────┐              │
   Kenbert        Cwichelm  Kenwalch  Kentwin     Kenfus
      │               │      m. Sexburga             │
   Cadwalla       Cuthred                         Escwin
                            A dau.
   Cuthwin              m. Oswald
      │
   Ceolwald
      │
   Kenred
   ┌────┬──────────┬─────────────┬──────────┐
  Ine  Ingild   Cwenburga   Cuthburga
       ancestor of
       Egbert.
```

Kentwin (handwritten marginal note)

It should be added that Flor. Gen., after mentioning Sexburga's reign, adds, 'Deinde Cenfus duobus annis, *secundum dicta regis Ælfredi;* juxta vero Chronicam Anglicam, filius ejus Æscwinus.' (i. 272, ed. Thorpe.)

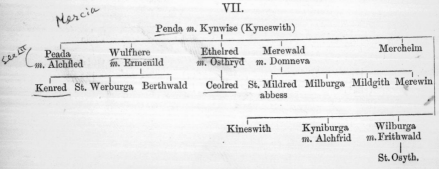

VII.

Mercia (handwritten)

```
                    Penda m. Kynwise (Kyneswith)
  (see IX)  ┌──────────┬──────────┬────────────┬─────────────────┐
   Peada   Wulfhere   Ethelred   Merewald                  Merchelm
 m. Alchfled m. Ermenild m. Osthryd m. Domneva
   ┌──────┬──────────┬────────┬───────┬─────────┬─────────┬────────┐
 Kenred St. Werburga Berthwald Ceolred St. Mildred Milburga Mildgith Merewin
                                        abbess
                 ┌──────────┬────────────┬──────────┐
             Kineswith   Kyniburga    Wilburga
                         m. Alchfrid  m. Frithwald
                                        │
                                     St. Osyth.
```

Insignificant names have been omitted.

INDEX.

THE END.